AGING
A CHANGING
SOCIETY
Second Edition

James A. Thorson
University of Nebraska at Omaha

Brunner-Routledge
New York   Hove

Published by
Brunner-Routledge
29 West 35th Street
New York, NY 10001
www.brunner-routledge.com

Published in Great Britain by
Brunner-Routledge
27 Church Road
Hove, East Sussex
BN3 2FA
www.brunner-routledge.co.uk

Brunner-Routledge is an imprint of the Taylor & Francis Group.
Printed in the United States of America on acid-free paper.

10 9 8 7 6 5 4 3 2

A CIP catalog record for this book is available from the British Library.

Cataloging-in-Publication Data is available from the Library of Congress.
ISBN 1-58391-009-3 (pbk.)

For Judy Thorson—Grow old with me.

Contents

Preface

The twentieth century is now behind us. Five hundred years from now, what will people remember about it? The moon landing in 1969, certainly, will be remembered then much as Columbus' voyage in 1492 is remembered now. Personalities, however, even ones that now loom large in our consciousness, will be all but forgotten. Churchill, Hitler, Stalin, Roosevelt, and others will no doubt have faded into the collective consciousness by the year 2500. People then will recall these men much as we now remember Isabella and Ferdinand V—perhaps with a vague sense of recollection, but not in any great detail. There is one thing, though, that people of the future will definitely know about the twentieth century, and that is the topic of this book. It was a revolution.

The demographic revolution of the twentieth century was this: for the first time in human history, most people born lived to see old age. Infant mortality and diseases that formerly carried off young people now affect only a very small proportion of the population, and this is true in most of the parts of the world, not just in Western countries. Consequently, a populace with a significant number of older members is a new thing in the history of the world. The three biggest killers in the American Civil War of 1861–1865 were tuberculosis, measles, and mumps, diseases that simply do not kill significant numbers of people any longer. Children of the twentieth century for the most part survived the things that had killed children in all previous centuries. They lived long enough to become old people.

At the beginning of the twentieth century in the United States and Canada, fewer than one person in twenty was an older person; now, as the twenty-first century begins, it is more like one in seven. This demographic revolution is world-wide: in less than twenty-five years, China will have the same percentage of older people that the United States has now.

As more people survive to live into later life, there is a corresponding increase among those who are very old. We are starting to see parent care as an important issue among retirees: there are many people in their 60s who provide care for one or more parents who are in their 80s or 90s.

Social changes related to this demographic revolution have emerged as important issues on the national agenda. Social Security and Medicare are at the forefront of the political debate in the United States. Generational equity is an emergent political theme concerned with a supposed inequality of benefits received by the elderly at the expense of children and young adults. Services to help keep people independent and out of institutional care are now a national priority. Financing medical care continues to be in the headlines. Early retirement and corporate downsizing at the expense of older workers are vital concerns in the world of business. At the basic science level, the possibility of extension of life itself raises important practical and ethical issues.

Thus, the field of gerontology, the study of aging, has emerged as area of inquiry of increasing importance. It has only been a recognized field of study for about fifty years. For many years, gerontology was such a small field that virtually all important publications relating to aging could be included in a running bibliography published in *The Journal of Gerontology*. This effort, first begun in April of 1950, was abandoned 30 years later; the job had become too overwhelming (Shock, 1980). A similar effort to catalog Internet resources on aging in *The Gerontologist* was given up in 1996; there were simply too many of them, and any directory was obsolete before it returned from the printer.

Similarly, the study of gerontology in higher education has mushroomed. A generation ago there were only a handful of academic gerontology programs at universities in the United States and Canada. Gerontology programs at colleges and universities now number over five hundred, with over a thousand campuses offering some type of credit instruction in aging-related courses.

So, gerontology as a field of study has started to reach a certain level of maturity. At the campus where I teach, students are now taking a course or two in gerontology because they recognize it as an important area of inquiry. Gerontology is no longer a just sub-specialty for sociology or psychology students; gerontology coursework is now taken among general education electives by people majoring in all sorts of departments. Outside of our own majors, the largest group taking at least one course in gerontology on our campus comes from the College of Business. Out of approximately 650 student registrants each semester, about 300 are taking the introductory course. For most of them, this will be their first and only exposure to study in the field of aging. This is not a unique situation on just our campus—it is the trend nationally as well.

This represents a dramatic shift in gerontology instruction at colleges and universities. Academic units in gerontology were at one time focused mainly on providing specialized instruction only for a comparatively few students who were planning to go to work with the elderly. This mission continues, but the change in recent years is that gerontology is increasingly seen as a legitimate area of study for the non-specialist. The majority of our students in Introduction to Gerontology in fact do not go on to specialize or major in the field; they take the course as a part of their liberal education, just as they take coursework in English, math, history, and the sciences.

Given this situation—not all gerontology students come with a ready social science background, and not all introductory gerontology students will go on to major in the field—a unique problem has developed. One wants the introductory course in the field to serve as a foundation and prepare those who specialize in it for further study, and one also wants a course that is comprehensive enough to expose those who will only be taking one course in gerontology to the critical issues in the field.

Hopefully, this book helps to achieve these goals. In a way I've not seen in too many other texts, this book is self-revelatory: the first boxed-off commentary is a memory of my own grandparents. I've put a lot of my own observations and experiences in this book; the reader of it will get to know me in a certain way. I've been teaching gerontology at the university level for 30 years, and this book includes many of the personal illustrations I've found to be useful in communicating with my own students. I hope the writing style is more engaging than that found in some books.

In addition to the goal set out for me by the publishers, I had a few of my own. First and foremost, the writing of a text that is to provide a comprehensive foundation in the field has to be well-documented, and I've tried to do this throughout the text. In order that the documentation not be a barrier to the reader, though, the References have been placed at the back of the text. They're there if one wants to track down a particular source.

Another goal was that this book had to be consistent with a solid theoretical background in the field of gerontology, yet it had to have practical value as well. I've attempted to describe theory in the disciplines of sociology, psychology, biology, economics, and political science as it applies to gerontology in terms that are understandable to the lay reader. And, especially in the boxed-off marginal notes, I've made a serious attempt to give the reader practical implications of research findings in the field. And, this text is consistent with the curriculum goals set out in the *Core Principles and Outcomes* document issued by the Association for Gerontology in Higher Education (Wendt, Peterson, & Douglass, 1993).

Definitions of key terms and a glossary are also included to assist the reader. These definitions were not take from a standard dictionary, but are provided to highlight specific examples in the text.

I wish to acknowledge with thanks Phillip L. Berman, editor of *The Courage to Grow Old* (Berman, 1989); quotations from older people at the beginning of chapters are taken, with permission, from that book.

New content in this second edition includes a complete updating of all statistical information, an expanded section on Medicare, consolidation of the book as a whole into fewer chapters, more data on the feminization of poverty in later life, more information giving international perspectives, and more content dealing with intergenerational programs.

Come grow old along with me.

PART

Social Aspects of Gerontology

The world is experiencing a massive population shift, a revolution unprecedented in human history. Up until the twentieth century, the worldwide pattern showed women bearing many children, only a minority of whom lived into adulthood. An even smaller number of them survived until *old age*.

The demographic revolution of the 20th century is this: children have stopped dying. By 1900, in most Western countries, the infant *mortality rate* had gone down from over 50% to about 16%. By the end of the twentieth century, that childhood death rate had dropped to about seven-tenths of one percent.

Accompanying the decline in infant deaths has been a decline in the deaths of children, adolescents, and young adults. The result of this is that the great majority of people who are born will now live into old age. The great swelling of the world's older population is a result of the conquest of communicable disease at younger ages. More people are living long enough to get old.

Not only have the numbers of older people been changing, but the ways in which different *generations* see the world have been changing as well. In this section, these changing numbers and changing values will be examined.

An Aging Population

Chapter Outline

"Life was more difficult back then. It is hard for people today, who enjoy lengthened life expectancy, to realize the primitive state of medicine, surgery, immunology, and the paucity of resources for treating illness, which was commonplace in my youth. If my people considered the possibility of living to ripe old age, I think they would have been more likely to approach it with joy than courage."

—Margaret Cousins, born 1905
The Courage to Grow Old

Introduction

No group in North America is changing as quickly as older people. Their numbers are growing more rapidly than any other group in the population, and the percentage of the population made up of older adults is growing faster than any other. What older people represent as a part of the population is dynamic and rapidly changing.

young old — People
65 to 74 years of age.

old old — Those
persons 75 years and
older.

oldest old — Those
persons aged 85 and
older.

And older persons not only are a part of a changing population, but are also themselves changing. People in their 60s and 70s no longer seem to be "old." We no longer have a "rocking chair" image of old people. Grandparents today are not expected to sit on the front porch and rock; they're often expected to keep going, to enjoy leisure time, enjoy their families, and enjoy a wide variety of interests in life.

This creates some confusion, because we can in fact speak of two categories of older people: people in later middle life who are for the most part active and enjoying life, and others who are older who are slowing down, have more aches and pains, and who have a harder time living up to an image of active aging. We need to be careful not to stereotype old people as all being in the second group. The majority of people 65 years of age and older are doing quite well, leading satisfying, active lives.

The issues that concern the *"young old"* (those aged 65 to 74) and the *"old old"* (those 75 and older) are different. In fact, one of the emerging problems we often see among today's grandparents is the necessity to provide care for one of their own surviving parents. Many people who now reach retirement age and are looking forward to leisure and travel may have the responsibility of caring for a father or mother who is 85 or 90 years of age and in failing health. Gerontologists now speak of a third group, the *"oldest old,"* those aged 85 and above. This is the fastest-growing segment of North American society. Providing for their care will represent a major social issue in the twenty-first century.

One practical implication of the changes we now see among the elderly is the increasing problem among the young old that is represented by care of the next older generation. People who are now in their 60s or 70s may well have responsibility for the care of parents who are in their 90s.

This phenomenon had never been much of a problem in prior generations in human history. Certainly, some people in previous centuries attained great age; historians have documented the problems families had to confront, even hundreds of years ago, when faced with care of a frail elder (Hanawalt, 1986). However, this happened in only a small number of families. It is much more common today.

Now, when the majority of people survive into old age (and a good many of them continue on into very old age), the society as a whole is confronted with a host of new issues. Two examples are caring for a larger number of frail people and providing income support for a larger group of people who no longer work.

The problems confronted by families responsible for care of a person of great age who is no longer independent are not new. What is new is that many more people—a much larger segment of society—are confronted with them. As a result, the society as a whole now has to grapple with issues like medical care for the elderly, pension and social security issues, and providing home care or nursing home care for greater numbers of people nearing the end of life. These issues had to be dealt with by only a small proportion of those in earlier times when fewer people lived into later life; now that these issues have emerged as more universal problems, the entire society must deal with them.

The changes taking place in contemporary society that relate to an aging population make up the substance of this book. In addition to the issues we have examined in this introduction, we will focus on some practical implications: what do these changes mean and what we might be able to do about them?

While this text takes a problem-solving approach, however, all of the issues related to aging are not "problem" issues. An increasing number of surviving grandparents, for example, is usually thought of as a blessing rather than a problem. And, not all problems relating to aging have readily available solutions. We will look at the changing population of the elderly in practical terms, and we will look at the benefits as well as problems these changes represent.

Changing Visions and Values

Many of today's older people are different in a number of ways from prior generations of elders. This is most striking not in terms of their numbers—which are not often all that visible—but in their values: the ways they see the world and react to it. Today's *"baby boomers"* are adults now in midlife who were born after World War II during the high birthrate years from 1945 to 1960. They remember their grandparents—people who were themselves born, for the most part, between 1880 and 1910—as old people nearing the end of life, people slowing down, full of aches and pains, often with lives dominated by chronic illness.

It could be said that the baby boomers represent an *age cohort*. A cohort is any category that can be defined in a particular way: we could say that very old people, those 85 and above, represent a cohort. In this instance, the oldest cohort represents a generation. Or, we could say that all children in kindergarten this year are a cohort. These children do not make up a whole generation, just people who are five or six years old at the moment. So, it's important to specify a definition when we speak of a cohort of people. Do we mean a whole generation, or just a group born during a particular year or years?

Let's speak for the moment of the grandparents of the baby boomers, the cohort that represents the oldest generation now living (those who are now between the ages of 90 and 110). As an example of changing values and changing visions of the aged, it can be said that the values of many of these people in the oldest generation were shaped in part during the nineteenth century, during the reign of England's Queen Victoria. This Victorian outlook may seem awfully constricted by today's standards. Victorian values, for one thing, dictated that women were not allowed to work outside the home; a woman's place was thought to be in the home with her family.

baby boomers — That cohort of people born between 1945 and 1960 (the post-war "baby boom") who will begin entering old age between the years 2010 and 2025.

age cohort — A group that has a particular definition by age, such as all people born from 1900 to 1910, or people born during the Depression.

The family was usually large: many rural families consciously attempted to have lots of children so there would be many hands to work on the farm. And, many parents had the thought in the back of their minds that they probably should have a few extra children, since not all infants were expected to live into adulthood. Something that was not mentioned was the fact that couples had no access to birth control. They certainly wouldn't have spoken to their own parents or asked questions about it. So, large families were the norm and also pretty much inevitable. Further, in a Victorian era, women were not supposed to enjoy sex; it was the woman's place to submit to the needs of her husband. Those who did enjoy a healthy intimate relationship probably would never have talked about it. Those raised with Victorian values might be shocked and scandalized by the material that is now commonplace on TV talk shows.

Most people thought of sex outside of marriage as a sin in no uncertain terms. Women who "had to get married" (those who were rushed into a marriage because they were pregnant) were thought of as bad women. There is psychological fallout to this day among older people who were the unwanted children of couples shamed into marriages due to unplanned pregnancies. As children, many were treated as unwanted. And, people who lived together outside of marriage were thought of as only the lowest form of trash: "good" people would have nothing to do with them.

Same-sex relationships were kept in the closet. Gay and lesbian people who today feel unwelcome social pressures might have a hard time imagining how difficult it must have been for same-sex partners during the early 1900s. It was said that Queen Victoria was horrified when Parliament passed laws against homosexuality—not because she was against the laws, but because she had difficulty even thinking of such a thing.

However quaint and strange the values of the very old might seem to us today, we must remember that they grew up in a different era, that their personal history strongly affects how they view the world. Values are transmitted from one generation to the next, of course. Even in the 1950s and 1960s, it was still common to hear a husband say, "No wife of mine will ever work outside the home!"

Not only were women repressed in the home in the early part of the twentieth century, those who did work were often made to feel ashamed of it. Women who worked in factories and in the garment industry were often little better than slaves. Professional careers for most women were out of the question; those who did work as nurses or schoolteachers were routinely exploited in terms of pay and working conditions and expected to give up their profession when they married. And, it often was the expectation that the youngest daughter in a family would remain single so she could live at home and "take care of the folks."

Many people who are now old lived through the Great Depression of the 1930s, a period of poverty for many: the unemployment rate reached 27% in 1931. (Political leaders now get nervous if the unemployment rate gets much above 7%). The values of saving and thriftiness may be ingrained in people who had to make do with next to nothing. If Grandma can't bring herself to throw something out, it may be because of her childhood experience during the Depression. We could call this a *cohort effect*, something that the people who lived through an era all have in common. As an illustration, many people now in middle age remember the summer of 1952, when most public swimming pools were closed because of the polio epidemic that swept the nation; this and other similar experiences could also be called cohort effects.

At the back of many a married woman's mind early in the twentieth century was the genuine danger that another pregnancy might represent: one pregnancy in ten resulted in the death of the mother. It was the sad experience of many young women to attend funerals of friends from school days who had died during the delivery of a child. A brief walking tour of many cemeteries will find family plots with the graves of a man, two or even three wives, and a number of children who had died in infancy.

These grandparents of the current generation of baby boomers provide the image for aging that has been held by people who are now middle-aged. While much is made of the adaptability these old people had—being born into a pre-flight era and living into the space age—their values and the ways they saw life often characterized them as truly from the Victorian era. The current generation of people of retirement age seems very different by comparison. Their horizons are broader, and many have seen different parts of the world and place a greater value on its diversity; they are much more sophisticated than their parents.

We have gone from a generation of old people where only a third of the women ever learned to drive to one that is much less dependent, likely to have their own money, and likely to own their own cars. We now expect to see elders with pensions who own their own houses, are much less dependent upon their children to take them in, and have activities and travel plans of their own.

So the generation of older persons is changing in a number of ways, not just in terms of numbers or percentages. The expectation is that people who retire at age 65 today will have a number of active years of life to enjoy. For the most part, the young old are not really very different from people in late middle age: they have a few aches and pains, perhaps a chronic health condition or two that is under control; many married women expect to be widowed during this decade of life.

Those aged 75 and above have more of the problems of frailty that we usually associate with old age: problems of failing health, sensory loss, chronic dependency and isolation, fears of loss of independence, and the possibility of having to go into a nursing home. Their values in this regard have not changed much from those of their own parents: no one wants to be old and dependent. However, the bulk of the actual problems associated with old age now seemingly come later in life—or perhaps not at all. Despite physical declines, many old people now enjoy a satisfying quality of life right up to or near the very end of life.

glossary

cohort effect — Something people in the same age cohort have in common because of their age; the common experience of living through World War II might be seen as a cohort effect.

Both of my grandmothers were born in 1884. My first memory of my mother's mother was when she was 66. She was entirely grey, but she used a blue rinse in her hair; she used a cane because she'd had a stroke, and she had false teeth. She referred to my bicycle as "your wheel." Her father had been a soldier in the Civil War. Her husband had died of a heart attack when he was 49; I never knew him. She had eight children. In order to support the ones still living at home when Grandpa died, she took in other peoples' laundry. To the best of my knowledge she had no income at all in later life: she didn't qualify for Social Security, and she had no pension. Grandma lived with her youngest daughter for the last ten years of her life. She died in 1960.

My father's father was born in 1880 and came to this country from Norway in 1890 with his parents and nine brothers and sisters. There had been 15 children in that family, but only eleven lived into adulthood. He and my grandmother raised their eight children on a farm, which they lost to the bank during the Depression. They felt that they couldn't have a television in their home in the 1950s because it was "worldly." After all, what would the neighbors think? They were always quick to turn on our TV, though, when they came to visit. They had a small pension from the government: their youngest son had been killed in World War II.

Because the Nineteenth Amendment to the Constitution was not ratified until 1920, neither of my grandmothers could vote until they were 36 years of age.

$g$lossary

demography — The study of populations, usually the facts and figures relating to the size and characteristics of groups of people.

Changing Numbers

Changing values are important, but changing numbers are important, too: they help us to visualize how and why values are changing. If the world is experiencing a gray revolution, we need to know in what ways things are changing. Perhaps we can better prepare for what seems to be on the horizon. And, there may be some practical implications—things we can do or plan for.

Demography is the study of populations: how many people there are, in what proportions, how these numbers and percentages are changing, and what effect these changes will make. When we usually think about the demography of aging, we think of total numbers and proportions of older people in the population as a whole. We also need to consider their longevity, or how long people live, and mortality—what people die of and how that is changing as well. Demography is influenced by three things: births, deaths, and migration. There are a few additional terms we will use as we look at these different concepts: cohort is a term we have already considered. It is a category within a category. The elderly, for example, are a category within the entire population. One could define an age cohort in terms of the years they were born (for example, those born between 1900 and 1920) or in terms of some common experience, such as baby boomers or depression babies. In other words, a cohort is a group with particular boundaries or characteristics that must be defined. The young old and the old old could be seen to be two different cohorts.

Life expectancy is the average number of years of remaining life from a particular point, such as life expectancy from birth or life expectancy at age 65. Life expectancy is usually expressed as an arithmetic mean or average. A 65-year-old white woman, for example, has a life expectancy of an additional 19.1 years, on the average.

Life span is the maximum possible length of life for the species. Most individuals do not live out their entire potential life span: for humans, for example, the life span is about 115 to 120 years (but hardly anyone makes it this long). For elephants, the life span is about 70 years; for the Galapagos tortoise, it's 150. While we usually think of life span as the maximum potential, it is sometimes used in another way: to speak of the practical potential for most people, not just the few at the extreme end. It has been said, for example, that the practical potential life span for most humans is roughly 85 years (Fries & Crapo, 1981).

Mean is the arithmetic average: the mean age of a group is found by adding the ages of each member and dividing by the number in the group. The mean age for a group of two people, say a newborn baby and a ten year-old, would thus be five years.

Median is the midpoint at which half of a group lies above and the other half lies below; the median age for a group is the point at which exactly half are younger and half are older.

Mortality rate (or death rate) is the rate per thousand that die of a particular cause during a certain year.

glossary

life expectancy — The mean or average length of life for a group; the ages at which members of a group die, added up and divided by the number in the group. Life expectancy is often expressed as the average number of years of life remaining at birth or from some particular age.

life span — How long a species lives. Life span is often expressed in terms of maximum life span (115–122 years for humans) or practical life span (about 85 years for humans).

Gradual Change

When we examine the change in numbers of older people, one of the first things we might say is this: we really don't notice it much. That is, while there now are a lot more old people than there used to be, the change doesn't hit you in the face. The change that results from the aging of the population is so gradual as to not be very apparent. Take a look, for example, at Table 1.1.

Table 1.1 lists the median age of the United States population from the year 1850 to 2050. (Remember that the median is the half-way point: half the people are younger than the median age and half are older.) Notice, for example, that the median age in the year 1990 was 32.7 years. Out of a total United States population of 249,975,000 that year, 124,978,500 were younger than 32.7 and 124,978,500 were older than 32.7 years of age. (Of course, there were some who were smack dab on 32.7, but there's no reason to quibble over that: the median is a theoretical point lying exactly between the two halves. For practical purposes, we don't need to worry about the few actually on the point itself.)

TABLE 1.1. Median Age of U.S. Population

Year	Age
1850	18.9
1860	19.4
1870	20.2
1880	20.9
1890	22.0
1900	22.0
1910	24.1
1920	25.3
1930	26.4
1940	29.0
1950	30.2
1960	29.5
1970	28.0
1980	30.0
1990	32.7
2000	35.7*
2025	38.0*
2050	38.1*

*projected
Statistics from U.S. Bureau of the Census (1998b).

For purposes of comparison, the median age in Canada was 35.2 years in 1996, the most recent year from which national data is available (Zapotochny, 1999). It is comparable to the United States figure of 35.7 for the year 2000.

Looking over the list presented in Table 1.1, we notice that the median age has increased gradually. Small increments characterize the changes reported for each ten-year period. The net effect is substantial: the median age of the U.S. population increased from 18.9 to 35.7 over the course of 150 years, but each increase was so slight as to be essentially undetectable.

Even though the median is a type of average, it would be a mistake to assume that the average person in the year 1850 was about 19 years old. Remember that the median is just the midpoint: half the people were under 18.9 years and half were older than 18.9. Some were much older. Stating the population's median simply gives an idea of the relative youth or age during a certain year. In 1850, about half of the population of the United States was made up of children or adolescents.

Now, take a look at the years 1960 and 1970 on Table 1.1. We see a curiosity: the median age for the U.S. population actually went down during those years; it started going up again in 1980 and 1990. What happened?

This downward change in the median age of the U.S. population during the years from 1950 to 1970 could be explained in two ways: either people older than the median were for some reasons dying at younger ages, or there were a lot more babies. This second explanation is in fact the case: the post-World War II baby boom was taking effect; it lowered the median age of the group as a whole for a couple of decades.

Now that this big bulge in the population has aged enough to be past the median point, however, it will begin to have another effect, bringing the median age up. We can see this in the change that took place between 1990 and 2000: a jump of 3.0 years, which is the biggest change on the chart.

So, what we can conclude by looking at the median age of the population is that it is affected by the birthrate (which started going down again between 1960 and 1965) and by the number of survivors. Remember this concept; people often make the mistake of thinking that the average age of the population is influenced only by the number surviving into later life. They often forget that it is also influenced by the rate at which new babies are added.

We suspect that the median age of the population will continue to increase, but we really won't know that without knowing the birth rate in future years. Although we can guess that it will not again become the fashion to have families of five, six, or seven children (which we think is pretty unlikely), we in fact cannot say that with certainty. We can project trends, however. This is what the Census Bureau does when it estimates the future population. It projects what is thought to be the likely trend in both the birth rate and the mortality rate. The median is a useful concept when comparing the relative youth or age of different populations, particularly different countries. Nations in South America, Africa, and Asia generally have lower median ages when compared to the countries of Europe or North America.

Another kind of average, the mode, is less useful. The mode is the most frequent case. For example, if one used the mode, it would be correct to say that the average person in the world is an 18 year-old Chinese female. There are more people who fit into that category than any other. This is a curiosity, but not a very useful.

What we can say for now, though, is that it appears that the average age of the country, expressed as a median, is increasing both due to a birth rate that is lower than it was during the middle part of the century, and also because more people are staying alive into old age. Note that we did not say "people are living longer." We said more people are staying alive into old age. Whether or not old age itself is being extended is something one can't tell from the median; we'll look at that concept a little later on in this chapter. Actually, we can't tell from looking at the median whether the biggest influence upon it is the birth rate or the death rate. We have to look at more detailed data to draw a conclusion.

While the gradually increasing median age of the entire population seems to be difficult to notice, the proportion of the population that is elderly may be more apparent.

Table 1.2 gives the total number of people aged 65 and above, as well as those in the age cohorts from 75 to 84 and those 85 and older for the years from 1900 until 2050. This information relies on data that have been collected through the Bureau of the Census, plus projections based upon their best estimates of the future growth of the population for the decades

TABLE 1.2. Number and Percentage of U.S. Older Population, 1900–2050

Year	65+ Years Number	65+ Years Percent	75–84 Years Number	75–84 Years Percent	85+ Years Number	85+ Years Percent
1900	3,084	4.0	772	1.0	123	0.2
1910	3,950	4.3	989	1.1	167	0.2
1920	4,933	4.7	1,259	1.2	210	0.2
1930	6,634	5.4	1,641	1.3	272	0.2
1940	9,019	6.8	2,278	1.7	365	0.3
1950	12,270	8.1	3,278	2.2	577	0.4
1960	16,560	9.2	4,633	2.6	929	0.5
1970	19,980	9.8	6,124	3.0	1,409	0.7
1980	25,550	11.3	7,727	3.4	2,240	1.0
1990	31,697	12.7	10,349	4.1	3,313	1.3
2000	34,921	13.0	12,318	4.6	4,926	1.8
2010	39,195	13.8	12,326	4.4	6,551	2.3
2020	51,422	17.3	14,486	4.9	7,081	2.4
2030	64,581	21.2	21,434	7.0	8,612	2.8
2040	66,988	21.7	24,882	8.1	12,834	4.2
2050	67,411	21.8	21,263	6.9	16,034	5.2

Numbers in thousands.

Statistics from U.S. Bureau of the Census (1998a).

into the middle of the 21st century. The numbers are expressed in thousands; we need to mentally add three zeros to each of them. Look at the first figure in the first column, for example: the number of people aged 65+ in the United States in the year 1900 was 3,084,000. This represented 4.0% of the entire population that year.

Going across that row, we can see that the number of people between the ages of 75 and 84 in 1900 was 772,000, or about 1% of the population as a whole. There were 123,000 people aged 85 and above in 1900, only two-tenths of 1% of the total.

Our first conclusion from looking at these figures is that there indeed were plenty of old people at the turn of the last century. In Table 1.1, we saw that the median age in 1900 was 22.9 years, but that the half of the total above 22.9 was spread pretty far. There were over three million people 65 and over, and within that group aged 65 and above, there were 123,000 who were 85+.

Now, look again at the first column of figures in Table 1.2, along the left side. Going down it, we see that the total number of older people increased ten times over from 1900 to 1990, from three million to over 31 million. In the 1990 census, there were 31,697,000 people aged 65 and older. This represented a growth from 4% of the total U.S. population in 1900 to 12.7% of the total by 1990.

The middle two columns tell us that the population aged 75 to 84 increased about 13 times over during the years 1900–1990, from 772,000 to 10,349,000. The figures in the last two columns on the right side of Table 1.2 represent those 85+ and show that the total number of this oldest group increased almost twenty-seven times over from 123,000 to 3,313,000 during those same years. These figures show us, then, that the aging population is growing overall, both in terms of numbers as well as the percentage

---

Illustration 1.2.   Some Implications of the Changes in Average Age

What does it mean to say that the average age of the population is increasing? What is the practical value?

In fact, slight changes over time are hardly noticeable, particularly if there are other changes taking place in society. It was predicted in the early 1980s, for example, that there was a coming "Baby Bust" in American colleges and universities. It was thought that enrollments would decline after the post-war baby boomers finished college; since the birth rate had started to drop in the 1960s, it was reasoned that a smaller pool of 18-year-olds entering college would mean lower enrollments in the 1980s.

The total United States population under five years of age in 1960, for example, was 20,341,000. In 1970, it was only 17,166,000, and by 1980, it had declined to 16,121,000. Thus, it was expected that college enrollments would peak around the year 1980, when the large group born in 1960 was of traditional college age, and then enrollments would begin to decline and would continue to decline well into the 1990s.

This didn't happen. Despite projections and a decreasing total number of people of college age, enrollments in higher education actually increased and will probably continue to increase in the near-term future:

Year	U.S. College Enrollment
1970	8,581,000
1980	12,097,000
1990	13,558,000
2000	14,326,000

Despite the shrinking pool of people of traditional college ages, enrollments continued to grow. Why?

Something else happened. Actually, two things happened. Between 1970 and 1996, the overall proportion of American citizens who are college graduates more than doubled (from 10.7% of the population to 22.0%). One of the things we can say about the children of college graduates is that they are more likely to go to college than are the children of people with less education. Their parents value education highly and transmit this message to their children. So, if there are more parents who have gone to college, there should be a higher proportion of children who go to college; this in fact is what happened.

The other thing that happened that also took university administrators by surprise is that an increasing number of people of "nontraditional" ages started coming back to school. Many urban campuses presently find that the majority of their students are older than traditional college students, go to school part time, are working, and have families of their own. In other words, two societal trends—a higher percentage of young people going to college and more older students going to college—together overwhelmed the demographic trend of fewer 18-year-olds. More, not fewer, people are now in higher education than there were ten or twenty years ago.

of the population represented by the aged. They also show us that the category of the oldest old is growing fastest.

Look at the years 1990 through the figures going all the way to the year 2050: it's projected that the whole group 65+ will more than double, from 31.7 million to 67.4 million. Similarly, those aged 75–84 will also double during that 60-year span, from 10,349,000 to 21,263,000. However, those 85 and older will increase almost five times over, from 3.3 million to over 16 million. This gives us an indication of how the population is aging. A category that now represents only slightly more than 1% of the population will make up over 5% of the population by the year 2050.

The percentage of the population represented by the elderly will grow, as will the actual numbers of old people. Percentages, though, depend on the relative size of the rest of the population. If a lot of babies are born, the percentage represented by young people will be larger for a while, which means that the percentage represented by the elderly will then be somewhat less. On the other hand, if the birth rate is very low, then the percentage of the total made up of middle aged and older adults will be greater.

Two broad trends in the population of the United States earlier in this century are having an influence on the relative size of the older population. First, the birthrate was comparatively low during the Great Depression, from 1929 to 1940. The cohort of people born during those years started becoming 65 years of age in 1994. So, the relative size of the cohort of the young old in the years 1994 to 2005 is lower than might have been expected. We can see this reflected in Table 1.2: the percentage of those 65 years of age and over was only from 12.7 to 13.0 during the decade of the 1990s. This is a small increase in comparison to the other percentage increases on the chart: just three-tenths of a percent.

The second great demographic influence of the twentieth century is something we've already mentioned: the Post World War II baby boom. It represents an unusually large birth cohort. These people born between 1945 and 1960 will begin to turn 65 in the year 2010. By the year 2025, all of them will be at least 65, and the oldest of the baby boomers will be around 80. Look again at the years 2010, 2020, and 2030 on Table 1.2. The percentage of people 65+ is projected to jump from 13.8 in 2010 to 17.3 ten years later and then rise again to 21.2 by the year 2030. The baby boomers will have become senior citizens. The low birthrate in 1975–1985 though, will mean only a very small increase of people 65+ in the years 2040 to 2050.

So, by comparison, the decade of the 1990s saw only a very small increase in the percentage of the population as a whole that is elderly: just three-tenths of a percent. On the other hand, the second decade of the twenty-first century is projected to have a increase in the percentage of the aged in the population as a whole from 13.8 to 17.3. The third decade of the twenty-first century is expected see an increase in this percentage to 21.2.

To summarize, the relatively small increase in the percentage of the whole population represented by the elderly during the decade of the 1990s is the result of a smaller number of births during the Great Depression.

The dramatic increase in the proportion represented by the aged during the early decades of the twenty-first century will be due to the greatly increased birth rate that took place during the years following World War II.

The birth rate, then, has an important effect on how many old people there are in two very distinct ways. The obvious one is that the pool of living people is begun at birth; if there are fewer births, there will be fewer people who have become old 65 years later. If, on the other hand, the pool of new babies is relatively large, then a relatively large cohort of older people will be the result 65 years later.

The second reason that the birth rate is an important determinant of the relative size of the older population is this: the percentage represented by those 65+ is always related to the percentage represented by those who are under 65. Simply put, if we have a great many young people, the part of the whole represented by old people must be smaller.

We sometimes forget this very basic point. Low birth rates mean higher percentages of adults, including the elderly. Too often we go on about how people are living longer (and they are, of course, which is a topic we'll discuss later in this chapter) and think this is the only reason that the percentage of the aged is increasing. As we have seen in Table 1.2, however, the main reason for fluctuations in the percentage of the population that is represented by the aged is, at the most basic level, the birth rate. While the survival rate is, of course, important, we can't have a high number of survivors if the cohort we started with in the first place was a small one.

Take a look, for example, at Table 1.3, which lists the countries with the oldest populations. Twenty-one of the top 25 are in Europe, where a postwar baby boom did not occur. In fact, birth rates in most European countries have been very low for several decades. The result is that they have high percentages of their total populations represented by the elderly. The people in these countries do not necessarily live a great deal longer than those elsewhere (although each of these countries does have a good record of keeping their citizens alive so they can reach old age). These countries are the oldest because of the low number of young people being added to the pool at the front end, not the great age of their oldest people.

We can see in Table 1.3 that the United States, with 16.5% of its population aged 60 or above in 1996, is actually a fairly young country by comparison to the others listed. Canada, at 16.4%, just missed getting into the oldest 25. Some of the other countries not listed among the oldest 25 include Mexico at 6.5%, China at 9.5%, and Russia at 16.4%. The majority of the countries making up the list of the 25 oldest are in Europe. Sweden, which led the list in 1991, has had a small baby boom and thus had slipped to third by 1996.

Generally, it could be said both that the developing nations have high birth rates and also a somewhat lower percentage of their populations living into later life. Brazil has only 7.2% of its population aged 60+, India has 6.5%, and Indonesia only 6.3%. Nicaragua at 4.2% and the Ivory Coast at 3.5 are among the youngest countries in the world. For the most part, the

TABLE 1.3. The World's 25 Oldest Countries: Percent of Population Age 60 and Over

Country	Percentage
Italy	22.3
Greece	22.3
Sweden	21.9
Belgium	21.5
Spain	21.2
Bulgaria	21.2
Japan	20.9
Germany	20.9
United Kingdom	20.5
France	20.3
Portugal	20.2
Denmark	19.9
Austria	19.8
Norway	19.8
Hungary	19.6
Switzerland	19.5
Luxembourg	19.1
Estonia	19.0
Finland	19.0
Czech Republic	18.1
Belarus	17.9
Netherlands	17.8
Uruguay	17.3
Georgia	17.0
United States	16.5

Source: U.S. Bureau of the Census, International Programs Center, International Data Base, 1996.

younger countries have a different set of social problems due to their population makeup. Their need to develop schools and public health systems to provide services to large numbers of children overwhelms their ability to provide services to the aged or social security systems. Countries like Sweden and Norway, on the other hand, are able to devote a much greater proportion of their resources to pensions and services for the aged. By the year 2020, China is projected to have a higher percentage of its population 60+ than the United States does now. So, it is a young country, straining to provide education and health services for its current population, that will have to plan to be a relatively old country in just two more decades.

Migration

Like birth rate, migration has an influence on the percentage of the elderly in a particular area. And, as with birth rate, it is mostly the proportion of the young that influences the percentage of the aged when we look at migration. Historically, it has been the out-migration of young people that has resulted in a higher percentage of older people remaining in an area. Likewise, in-migration of the young lowers the remaining percentage represented by the aged. However, the volume of older people themselves moving from place to place has begun to also have an impact. There has been a large loss of older people from New York, Illinois, Ohio, Michigan, and Pennsylvania over the past two decades and a large gain of older in-migrants to Florida, Arizona, Texas, North Carolina, and Arkansas (Crown, 1988). There has been a tendency of older persons to move from the industrial states of the East and Midwest to the sunshine states of the South and West. (Actually, the majority of moves made by older persons relocating are within their same county of residence; in terms of state-to-state moves, however, the pattern generally has been for people to move south or west.)

Expense is another consideration, and for that reason there are as many older people moving out of some states as there are moving in. California is a prime example. During the past two decades, about as many older people move out of California as move in.

There is also a little-known factor involved with return migration. People who leave a state in later life typically do so during their early years of retirement, generally during their 60s. A certain portion of them return to their native state later on, usually when they are in their late 70s or early 80s. These people are more likely to be widowed and in poor health; often they are returning to be near an adult child or other source of personal care as they near the end of their lives. Still, some states attract more return migrants than others. Typically, Hawaii and Florida have the highest num-

---

Illustration 1.3.   Looking Ahead

People born in the year 1980 will be 70 years of age in the year 2050. What will their world be like? In fact, a United States population that has 21.8% of its citizens aged 65+ will not seem strange then; even though the rate in 1990 was 12.7%, this proportion will increase so gradually over time that it will not be possible to note any sudden changes. No doubt things will seem to be more crowded overall: they will be. Conveniences not thought of today will be commonplace. One thing that will be noticeable, though, will be the change in numbers of people in nursing homes. Currently, about 60% of those who live to be 85 or more have spent some time in a nursing home. Note that we did not say that 60% of those 85+ are in nursing homes, just that they have been a nursing home resident at some time in their lives (Kemper & Murtaugh, 1991). That represents about two million of the very old. If the rates stay the same, this figure will increase to over nine and a half million by the year 2050. Nurses and aides in long-term care are in short supply now, but the shortage of nursing personnel to care for the very aged of the future will constitute a genuine crisis.

TABLE 1.4. States with the Highest Percentages of People 65+

1940			1996	
1. New Hampshire	10.0%	1.	Florida	18.5%
2. Vermont	9.5	2.	Pennsylvania	15.9
3. Maine	9.4	3.	Rhode Island	15.8
4. Iowa	9.0	4.	Iowa	15.2
5. Kansas	8.7	5.	West Virginia	15.2
6. Missouri	8.6	6.	North Dakota	14.5
7. Massachusetts	8.5	7.	South Dakota	14.4
8. Oregon	8.5	8.	Arkansas	14.4
9. Indiana	8.4	9.	Connecticut	14.3
10. Washington	8.3	10.	Massachusetts	14.1

Statisics from U.S. Bureau of the Census (1998b).

bers of returns; the lowest proportions of return migrants are to Alaska, Wyoming, and Idaho.

Historically, the out-migration of young people has been a more important factor than the in-migration of the elderly in determining states' relative percentages of the aged. This makes sense: there are a lot more young adults moving about, and they move more often. In Table 1.4 we can see part of the result of this trend over 56 years' time.

These numbers indicate the percentage of people aged 65 and above in the ten states having the highest proportion of elderly people in the years 1940 and 1996. We can see in Table 1.4 the effect of migration, both of young people and old people. It is evident that there were large numbers of young people moving from New England by 1940, leaving older people behind. Out-migration of the young from agricultural states such as Iowa, West Virginia, and the Dakotas has been the reason for their higher percentages of people 65+ remaining in more recent years. In-migration of more elderly people in the past decades has been so great as to now put Florida at the top of the list and to place Arkansas within the top ten.

Projections

U.S. Census Bureau projections of the growth or decline of certain segments of the population are based upon trends and a number of assumptions. The assumptions take into consideration high or low birthrates, trends in migration (including migration of people into the U.S. from other countries), and, to a lesser degree, assumptions about the mortality rate. Table 1.5 contains what are called "Series A" projections about the population of the 50 states and the District of Columbia for the year 2010. "Series A" uses migration patterns for the previous two decades as a basis for projecting into the future.

Table 1.5 shows a listing of the states, plus Washington, D.C., giving the Census Bureau's estimates of what their total population will be in the

TABLE 1.5. Projected U.S. Population in the Year 2010, by State

	Population (in Thousands)		
State	Total Population	Population 65+	Percentage 65+
U.S., total	297,716	39,408	13.2
Alabama	4,798	674	14.0
Alaska	745	55	7.4
Arizona	5,522	807	14.6
Arkansas	2,840	451	15.9
California	37,644	3,789	10.0
Colorado	4,658	611	13.1
Connecticut	3,400	477	14.0
Delaware	817	109	13.3
District of Columbia	560	65	11.6
Florida	17,363	3,235	18.6
Georgia	8,824	974	11.0
Hawaii	1,440	182	12.6
Idaho	1,557	213	13.7
Iowa	2,968	476	16.0
Kansas	2,849	391	13.7
Kentucky	4,170	589	14.1
Louisiana	4,683	610	13.0
Maine	1,323	186	14.1
Maryland	5,657	664	11.7
Massachusetts	6,431	863	13.4
Michigan	9,836	1,276	13.0
Minnesota	5,147	686	13.3
Mississippi	2,974	393	13.2
Missouri	5,864	830	14.2
Montana	1,040	164	15.8
Nebraska	1,806	265	14.7
Nevada	2,131	295	13.8
New Hampshire	1,329	163	12.3
New Jersey	8,638	1,150	13.3
New Mexico	2,155	259	12.0
New York	18,530	2,399	12.9
North Carolina	8,552	1,218	14.2
North Dakota	690	111	16.1
Ohio	11,505	1,624	14.1
Oklahoma	3,639	561	15.4
Oregon	3,803	605	15.9
Pennsylvania	12,352	1,908	15.4
Rhode Island	1,038	146	14.1
South Carolina	4,205	584	13.9
South Dakota	826	121	14.6
Tennessee	6,180	844	13.7
Texas	22,857	2,601	11.4
Utah	2,551	276	10.8
Vermont	651	86	13.2
Virginia	7,627	945	12.4
Washington	6,658	880	13.2
West Virginia	1,851	316	17.1
Wisconsin	5,590	783	14.0
Wyoming	607	82	13.5

Statistics from U.S. Bureau of the Census (1998b).

year 2010 and what the population 65 and older will be, both in numbers and percentages. Again, the numbers are expressed in thousands, so we need to mentally add three zeros: it's projected that there will be 297,716,000 people of all ages in the U.S. that year. Of them, 39,408,000 will be 65+, which will represent 13.2% of the total.

If we compare some of the figures in Table 1.5 with those in Table 1.4, we can see that the Census Bureau's projection actually predicts that the percentage of some states' elderly will go down. Connecticut, Massachusetts, and Pennsylvania, for example, are predicted to have slightly lower percentages of those 65+ in the year 2010 than they had in 1996. This is based on a projection that fewer young people will leave these states; if the population of young people grows, then the portion made up of old people will of course be somewhat smaller.

The projections also predict continued growth among some of the states already having high proportions of the aged. Look at Florida: it's predicted that Florida will increase only slightly in the 14-year period, from 18.5% elderly in 1996 to 18.6% by the year 2010. This very small increase is predicted because more young people are anticipated migrating into the state. Bigger gainers are projected to be Arkansas (from 14.4% in 1996 to 15.9% in 2010), West Virginia (15.2 to 17.1), and North Dakota (14.5 to 16.1). These states will lose younger persons, and, in the case of Arkansas at least, also gain older in-migrants.

So far, we have looked at proportions of various areas made up of aging people and projections of how those percentages might change in

---

Illustration 1.4.   Elderly Ranks Growing Larger

by Sara Rimer of *The New York Times*

Delray Beach, FL—As retirees keep getting older and older, Floridians are taking steps to keep up with a new age.

When Herman and Annette Adelson moved to the Kings Point retirement community 20 years ago, they were happy to pay extra for a condominium on the second floor. The upstairs apartments offered breezes, better views of the golf course and, important to transplanted Northerners, fewer bugs.

There were no elevators, but who needed elevators? 'We used to run up the stairs two at a time,' recalled Herman Adelson, a retired pharmacist from Newton, Mass. 'We didn't even think about them.'

But that was another life, when the Adelsons were in their 60s. Today those same stairs—one flight, 14 concrete steps—loom as an insurmountable obstacle. Now Annette Adelson, who is 83, has severe rheumatoid arthritis. She can negotiate the stairs only painfully, going down backward, with the help of her 85 year-old husband. And she does so only once a week."

From *New York Times*, March 23, 1998.

TABLE 1.6. Leading States in Numbers of Older People, 1996 (in thousands)

State	Total	65–74	75–84	85+	%65+
California	31,878	1,961	1,180	375	11.0
Florida	14,400	1,452	925	281	18.5
New York	18,185	1,335	815	284	13.4
Texas	19,128	1,112	627	212	10.2
Pennsylvania	12,056	1,037	667	208	15.9
Ohio	11,173	834	502	161	13.4
Illinois	11,847	803	510	172	12.5
Michigan	9,594	666	400	126	12.4
New Jersey	7,988	604	376	119	13.8
North Carolina	7,323	527	298	92	12.5

Statistics from U.S. Bureau of the Census (1998b).

the future. In terms of actual numbers of people in their later years, however, California leads in the total number of people 65 and older and in the total number of "oldest old" as well (see Table 1.6).

It's possible to take the number of those aged 85 and older for each state and divide it by the total number of those 65+ that the state has: this gives us an idea of how relatively old the older population of that state is. For example, of the ten oldest states, North Carolina has the youngest older population; only 10.0% of all those 65+ are 85 or older. This might confirm what we said about people moving to a Sun Belt state early on in their retirement years and then going back to their home state later on. That is, North Carolina, more than most states, may have in-migration of the young old and out-migration of the old old. By contrast, New York (11.7% of the 65+ population is 85+), Illinois (11.6%), and Pennsylvania (10.9%) all have a somewhat higher concentration of the very old among their elderly populations. They seem to have out-migration of the young old and return migration of the old old.

In conclusion, migration affects the population of the aged just as the rates of birth and death ultimately reflect how many older people there are in a particular area. Just barely in the list of the twenty-five "oldest" countries, the U.S. will continue to increase in its proportion of older adults. This mainly will be more due to the aging by middle-aged people than because of migration. Most migrants are younger people, and in-migration of younger people have kept Canada and the United States relatively young in comparison to other countries.

The large group of baby boomers living out its allotted span of life will cause the average age in the United States to increase. The real demographic change in the twentieth century has been the change from young people dying of acute illnesses to the more common occurrence of older people dying of chronic illness. In the next section, we will explore just how long people do live and start to explore some of the reasons for these limits.

Longevity

What do most people consider to be "old?" The quasi-official definition of old age beginning at 65 has become less and less realistic over the years. As the age for full retirement benefits from Social Security changes from 65 to 67 in the first decade of the twenty-first century, this usual governmental definition will be changing as well. When asked at what age people become old, most people pick an age between 70 and 80; in fact, most older adults define themselves that way. This has been a fairly common definition for many years—perhaps several thousand years. Even though only about 10% of the population made it that long, this idea of how old "old" is has been around for a very long time indeed.

Notions that years ago, old age began somewhere in the 40s or even earlier are based on misinterpretations of average life expectancy. These mistakes are common, especially in the popular press.

How long would one have to live to set the record? That is, if you set out to get older than anyone else—how old would that be? True, longevity often is hard to verify: not everyone has good proof, like a birth certificate. And long life may not be a real matter of choice. Certainly, some people come from long-lived families; however, it's also evident that there are some things we can do to help ourselves to live healthier, longer lives. It's also evident that some people don't try as hard as others to stay alive. Certainly, no one can do a thing about their genetic background, and recent research indicates that about a third of the variance in longevity is genetically determined (Ljungquist, Berg, Lanke, McClearn, & Pedersen, 1998).

But back to our question. What is the extreme limit of human longevity? If you avoided all the things that might carry you off of this earth, if you were somehow fortunate enough to avoid having a heart attack, if you never got cancer, if your kidneys never failed, if you never stepped in front of a bus—how long could you make it?

In answer to this question, a statistician once looked at the odds of continued life if all natural causes of death were eliminated—including old age itself as a cause of death. In other words, how long would life be if old age as well as every disease and other natural cause was eliminated? This

---

Illustration 1.5.   Who Wants to Live to Be 100?

I'm often asked to speak to groups of older people, and I often ask the audience who among them would like to live to be a hundred. There's always the response from someone: "I'd like to, if I didn't get any older," but generally most older people hoot and say that they wouldn't care to live that long at all. One lady did raise her hand in response to this question, though, and I asked what her reason was. The man next to her spoke up and said, "She's 99."

---

would leave only the unnatural causes of death: accidents, suicides, and homicides. The odds of *survival curve* calculated projected that most people would be dead somewhere between 600 and 700 years of age, with the oldest checking out a bit past 1000.

Fanciful as this might seem, serious people are engaged in research on extension of the life span itself, not just getting more people to live out their potential and thus raising the average life expectancy. Imagine for a moment how valuable a longevity pill might be. The quest for a fountain of youth has been a universal theme. The first recorded literature, the Saga of Gilgamesh, written on Babylonian clay tablets, has the hero ranging across the wilderness in quest of immortality. Well, if we can't have immortality, why not the next best thing? Most of us would like to live longer, *provided that we remain vital and healthy*. That, of course, is the rub. So far, it has been impossible to put the aging process on hold. It would do us very little good to keep on getting older unless the basic process of aging itself might somehow be arrested.

Writing in 1726, Jonathan Swift had Gulliver travel to many different lands; one was the land of Luggnagg, where there were Struldbrugs, people who never died. They continued to age, however. Most were blind, crippled, demented, unable to move, in constant pain, lying in puddles of their own waste, begging for death. This is, of course, the stuff of science fiction.

The study of longevity looks at the parameters of human life span today, at the length of life and the averages. There are common mistakes that are made in dealing with life expectancy figures that tend to mislead many people. In the remainder of this chapter, we will examine them, and we will then look at elements that contribute to longevity and at the prospect of adding years to one's life as well as life to one's years.

Long life has traditionally been a mark of favor and strength among the peoples of the world. For this reason, the *antediluvian* (before the deluge, or before the flood described in the Bible) patriarchs were described

g lossary

survival curve — A graph representing the number or percentage who are still living at certain ages. *Rectangularization* of the survival curve happens when there are few deaths in childhood or adulthood and the line on the graph represents less of a curve and more of a rectangle.

antediluvian — Literally, "before the deluge," or before the Biblical flood described in Genesis 6; usually used to denote a period before the dawn of recorded time; prehistoric.

Illustration 1.6.   In the Land of Luggnagg

"The Struldbrugs were the most mortifying sight I ever beheld, and the women more horrible than the men. Besides the usual deformities in extreme old age, they acquired an additional ghastliness in proportion to their number of years, which is not to be described; and among half a dozen, I soon distinguished which was the eldest, although there was not above a century or two between them.

"The reader will easily believe, that from what I had heard and seen, my keen appetite for perpetuity of life was much abated. I grew heartily ashamed of the pleasing visions I had formed, and thought no tyrant could invent a death into which I would not run with pleasure from such a life."

From Jonathan Swift, *Gulliver's Travels*

How long people live, and why, has caused controversy for hundreds—even thousands—of years. In Psalm 90, it says the measure of man's days is three score and ten or four score by reason of strength. In other words, how old is old? When the psalm was written three thousand years ago, the length of life was three score (three times twenty years) plus ten: 70, or four score (80) if one was especially strong.

How old is old now? About 70 or 80.

as living extremely long lives; Methuselah was said to have lived to the age of 960. Whether or not years were measured the same way back then, the fact is that most primitive cultures describe mythical ancestors as living to great ages: they said that there were giants on the Earth in those days.

Claims of great age today tend to come from societies where there are few literate people and almost no documentation. Such claims are usually thought of as innocent and rather charming in more sophisticated cultures, but they are believed by a few gullible people who would like to think that we can indeed live to outlandish ages. Some years ago, one of the TV networks flew an old gentleman named Javier Pereira from Columbia to New York to appear as a mystery guest on the panel program "What's My Line?" He claimed to be 165 years of age at the time, and said he owed his long life to drinking lots of strong coffee and smoking cigars. Much was made of the fact that he had asked one of the flight attendants for a date. Many people smiled and thought he was cute; perhaps there were some who believed that he actually was 165.

Several years ago, "60 Minutes" featured an older woman from what was then Soviet Georgia dancing and drinking vodka on her 130th birthday. Our tendency is to smile and say, "More power to her." To ourselves we think, "I'd like to believe it's true; perhaps I could live to be 130 and dance and drink vodka on my birthday."

In 1979, a retired circus roustabout, Charlie Smith, died in Florida. He was said to be 137 years of age. During the last period of his life it was a regular story in the newspapers when Smith celebrated his birthday. Reporters would troop out to his little house and ask him to what he attributed his long life. Smith claimed to have been born in Liberia in 1842 and to have been taken in slavery to the United States by a man who lured him onboard ship by promising to show him a "fritter tree."

Smith was charming, and people wanted to believe that living to such a great age was possible, so no serious challenges were made to his stories while he was alive. Indeed, the Social Security Administration took his story at face value. Some of his tales, however, defied credibility: he once said that he taught Jesse James how to use a six-shooter.

And, students of black history would find his claim to have been sold into slavery from Liberia doubtful: Liberia was founded by American slaves who had been freed and returned to Africa (Monrovia, the capital, was named after U.S. President James Monroe, and American dollars are the unit of currency there to this day). Liberia (the place of liberty) would have been a most unlikely place from which to carry on the slave trade.

In 1982, it was revealed that Charlie Smith's marriage certificate had been located in Arcadia, Florida (Freeman, 1982). It gave his age when he got married in January of 1910 as 35, which means he was actually born in 1875. So, at his death in 1979, he was a very old man indeed: he was 104, not 137.

Unlikely claims of longevity are popular, however, and were promoted during the 1970s by at least two journalists (Benet, 1974; Halsell, 1976) and a Harvard Medical School professor who should have known better. Three particular areas of the world were identified as having unusually high numbers of *centenarians* (people over age 100): Vilcabamba, Ecuador; Hunza, a remote region of Pakistan; and the Caucasus Mountain region of Abkhasia in Georgia. Various publications reported that people in these places lived uncommonly long lives; claims of 130 or even 140 were not unusual. The most extreme claim was 168.

Why people in these out-of-the-way places had such long lives was explained in terms of their clean living: they ate diets low in fat and low in total calories, got lots of exercise hiking up and down mountains while breathing nothing but the purest of air, had good sex lives, and had universally high respect from younger members of their communities. It was never explained why people in other primitive places in the world that were long on pure air and exercise and short on available food lived such brief lives by comparison.

The most credible person documenting why people in these areas of the world lived to such incredible ages was Dr. Alexander Leaf, Professor of Clinical Medicine at Harvard Medical School and Chief of Medical Services at Massachusetts General Hospital. He wrote articles that were published in the Scientific American (1973) and The National Geographic (1973) and a 1975 book detailing why people lived so long in Hunza, Vilcabamba,

glossary

centenarians —
People 100 years of
age or older.

Illustration 1.8.   The Record Holders

The oldest person for whom adequate documentation can be presented is Jeanne Calment, who was born in Arles, France, on February 21, 1875, and died on August 4, 1997. She had lived 122 years and 164 days.

The oldest male that has been documented is Christian Mortensen, who was born in Denmark August 16, 1882, and died in California April 25, 1998 at age 115.

As the odds of living to 115 are about one in two billion (Fix & Daughton, 1980), it is exceedingly unlikely that these records will be exceeded any time soon.

and especially Abkhasia. He had visited each place, done extensive interviewing and physical examinations, and documented many centenarians and super-centenarians. His publications explained how they lived such long lives in these places. Readers loved to hear about all of these charming old people riding horses, leading active lives, fathering children after age 100; it all seemed too good to be true.

It was.

The crack in the picture of super-centenarians began with a publication by Russian gerontologist Zhores Medvedev (1974). His article, in a major journal in the field (*The Gerontologist*) exposed Soviet longevity claims as frauds. He listed 13 persuasive arguments as to why these claims could not be taken seriously. He detailed the almost universal practice in use in what was then the Soviet Union of patriotic propaganda, trying to show how life in the U.S.S.R. was best because people lived the longest there.

Next came an article by two reputable gerontologists who did extensive research in Vilcabamba, Ecuador (Mazess & Forman, 1979). They found not only that there were no actual super-centenarians there, but that there had never been a person in Vilcabamba who had lived to be even as old as 100.

In fact, the research began to accumulate reasons why people lie about their age. Essentially, old people who live in areas where great age is respected may have a tendency to add a few years to their reported age, and then add a few more. Many very old people get somewhat forgetful. And, like Charlie Smith, people who claim to be especially old get fussed over. People pay attention to them if they claim to be 125, but those who are 89 or 90 don't get much attention at all.

To his credit, Leaf reversed himself and admitted that he had made a crucial mistake: when they told him how old they were, he had thought they were telling the truth. Perhaps he, like many of us, wanted to believe that it was possible to live to be 140.

Harold Wershow (1981), a gerontologist who edited a book entitled *Controversial Issues in Gerontology*, commented on Dr. Leaf's response when he was asked if one of his articles could be included in Wershow's book:

Illustration 1.9.   Claims About Super-Centenarians Are Abandoned

---

Investigative journalist Dan Georgakas (1980) reported on his visit to Abkhasia in a book, *The Methuselah Factors*. He met there with many older residents and a number of gerontologists, including Dr. Shoto Gogoghian, director of the Institute of Gerontology, a branch of the Academy of Medical Science: "Gogoghian volunteered the view that probably no one in the world had ever attained 120 years of age and that most definitely no one in Abkhasia had. This disclaimer was a stunning departure from many previously published Soviet opinions." This was the first official departure from 30 years of Soviet claims of superlongevity.

Dr. Alexander Leaf took the occasion of a fellow gerontologist's book to update his views of Ecuadorian longevity.

"The Andean village of Vilcabamba in southern Ecuador has received much attention in the past decade as having an unusual number of very elderly individuals and an unusual proportion of elders compared with rural Ecuador generally....

Since the population is of Spanish descent and Catholic, it seemed that ages should be correct in view of the authenticity which written Church and civil records should establish. On my first visit in 1970, Miguel Carpio was pointed out to us by the local authorities and physicians to be the oldest citizen, aged 121 years. When I returned in 1974, I was startled to be told that Carpio was then 132 years old! I then asked to see the baptismal record for Carpio. None could be found. A couple of other instances, such as that of Micaela Quezada, aroused further suspicion about the correct ages. We were told she was 104 years old but careful examination of the baptismal record provided by the local authorities proved it to be that of her aunt who bore the same name; the names of the parents on the birth certificate were indeed different than the names of the parents of the living Micaela Quezada. Thus, without great care, examination even of existing records may be quite misleading."

From Wershow (1981, p. 25). Used with permission of the publisher.

Leaf regrets his enthusiastic and insufficiently critical investigation of the aged of Shangri-La. In reply to our request to use his paper, he ruefully wrote, "Frankly, I would rather give you permission to burn it," and requested that a statement be added, containing newer evidence from Vilcabamba. (p.25)

Too often, we are willing to suspend disbelief, especially if the unlikely claim we hear is something we would like to believe. However, living beyond 125 just is not possible at the present time. The process of physical aging literally wears the body out. This happens pretty much at a constant rate. We don't just age to a certain point and then stop. Thus, another 20 years of the wearing effect that comes with aging does make a difference. We can easily see, for example, the difference between a 60-year-old and an 80-year-old. Similarly, those who have ever met a person 100-years-old can readily tell the difference between him or her and someone who is only 80. If someone lived to 120, we could just as easily tell her from a person aged 100. In fact, most 100-year-olds are exceedingly frail. It is most unlikely that such frail bodies could tolerate another 20 years of the aging process. Extreme longevity that is well-documented, however, has been increasing over the years (Wilmoth & Lundstrom, 1996; Wilmoth, Skytthe, Friou, & Jeune, 1996). New record holders may be established. The practical limits of life span, however, are very unlikely to be expanded in the foreseeable future.

Life Span and Life Expectancy

In the first part of this chapter we pointed out the difference between life span, the limit for the species in terms of length of life, and life expectancy, the average (mean) length of life. Unfortunately, these concepts are easily mixed up by the general public—and by people who should know better as well. One study reviewed 17 different *gerontology* textbooks and found that seven of them had made errors in this regard (Yin & Shine, 1985).

The problem comes with the supposition that people years ago didn't live very long. What's true about that statement is that years ago, only a small percentage lived into old age. However, there still were old people, some of whom in fact lived to a ripe old age. Old age, however, didn't somehow occur at 30 or 40 years of age; people still thought of old age as taking place at around 70, it's just that fewer of them got there.

When we say that the average life expectancy in a society was, say, 30 years, this leaves the impression that a 29 year-old was nearing the limit and a 31 year-old was on borrowed time, so to speak. What actually caused the low average life expectancy over the course of most of human history was high infant mortality. Despite this, there always have been some really old people. Even in Biblical times, remember, "old" was defined as 70 or 80. So, lots of babies dying pulled down the average, but it didn't pull down what most people thought of as "old." Recent evidence from another culture is illustrative: it would seem that in fourteenth century China, about 13% of the population lived at least until age 60 (Zhao, 1997).

Take a look at how this works: the infant mortality rate in some parts of Russia before and during the First World War was about 60%. Let's take a sample of ten people, say, six of whom died by age one and the rest of whom lived full lives of 80 years. We would calculate the mean life expectancy for this group of ten people this way:

6 babies dying by age 1	$6 \times 1 = 6$
+ 4 people living to age 80	$4 \times 80 = 320$
equals	326

Now, divide the 326 by the ten people in the group, and we come up with an average life expectancy for these ten people of 32.6 years. Citing the mean life expectancy from birth, then, actually misrepresents both groups.

Life expectancy, which is always expressed as a mean or an average, can be thrown off by having extremes to account for, which is usually the case when we look at life expectancy from birth. Unfortunately, the uninformed seem to *always* look at life expectancy from birth, or confuse life expectancy with life span. Now, as we can see from Table 1.7, the life expectancy at birth for a male born in the year 1900 was 48.2 years. But, that wasn't how long a male in 1900 was supposed to live; it was the average, all the ages at which people died (including infants) summed up and divided by the number in the group.

Let's say a male in 1900 was 45 years of age. Did he have only 3.2 years to go? Of course not. Table 1.7 shows us that his life expectancy at age 45 was another 24.1 years. In other words, a 45-year-old man at the turn of the century, who had lived past the years of childhood diseases and the risks that young adults were prone to, could reasonably expect to live to 69 at any rate. If he was fortunate enough to escape death for the next 20 years, at 65 he could still anticipate another 11.5 years of life.

Each time we figure the life expectancy for those at a certain age, we're really taking the figures for a new group. When we calculate the life expectancy for people aged 25, for example, we start only with those people who have already made it to 25. We count the years the survivors have yet to live; we don't figure in the ones who have already died: they're no longer in the pool.

The number of younger people who have died before them has no effect on the average years of life remaining for the 25-year-olds. So, it would be silly to take the life expectancy at birth and apply it to those who have already gotten past the high numbers of deaths that took place in childhood.

The real mischief comes when people don't take this into account and assume that average life expectancy from birth is how long most people in fact live. True, it is the average from birth for that entire category, but it has little to do with how long people in adulthood have left to live. By not tak-

TABLE 1.7. Expectation of Years of Remaining Life at Selected Ages, 1900–1996

Age			Year		
	1900	1950	1980	1990	1996
Males					
0	48.2	66.3	70.8	72.7	73.9
15	46.3	54.2	57.1	58.7	59.6
25	38.5	44.9	47.9	49.3	50.2
35	31.3	35.7	38.7	40.1	40.9
45	24.2	26.9	29.6	31.1	31.9
55	17.4	19.1	21.3	22.6	23.3
65	11.5	12.8	14.3	15.2	15.8
75	6.8	7.8	8.9	9.4	9.8
85	3.8	4.4	5.1	5.3	5.3
Females					
0	51.1	72.0	78.2	79.5	79.7
15	47.8	59.4	64.3	65.2	65.3
25	40.1	49.8	54.6	55.5	55.6
35	32.8	40.3	44.9	45.8	45.9
45	25.5	31.1	35.5	36.3	36.4
55	18.4	22.6	26.6	27.3	27.3
65	12.2	15.0	18.6	19.1	19.1
75	7.3	8.9	11.6	12.1	12.0
85	4.1	4.8	6.3	6.6	6.3

From National Center for Health Statistics, Oct. 7, 1998.

ing this into consideration, we see mistakes such as assuming that average life expectancy in some way dictates when people got to be old—saying, for example, that because 40-year-olds were near the extreme of the average life expectancy from birth for their cohort years ago, somehow were getting close to old age. They in fact were not old people, and they were not necessarily nearing the point of death.

People at age 40 a hundred years ago would have been hard to distinguish from the 40-year-olds of today. The physical process of aging itself has not really changed all that much. Portraits of people in middle life from the last century look like, well, people who are in middle life.

One difference would be in their experience of death in their lives: middle aged adults a hundred years ago would probably have experienced the deaths of more of their friends and relatives at an early age. That higher rate of infant and childhood mortality was what pulled down the average for the population as a whole.

True, older people at the turn of the century might have had fewer teeth, and many middle-aged adults would have had some scars from childhood diseases we no longer see. But for the most part, they would seem pretty much like people their age do today. People on the frontier might have been a bit more weather-beaten, but there would have been few real physical differences between old people in the good old days and old people now. In fact, since only the tougher ones survived, people a hundred years ago might actually have been heartier. However, the point is that the onset of old age did not start any sooner in some magical way.

The real difference between now and bygone days is that more children used to die. Tuberculosis and pneumonia were the leading killers in 1900; epidemics of diphtheria, polio, typhoid, and other infectious diseases killed thousands. Unclean drinking water, unsanitary childbirth practices, and a lack of immunization meant that scores of young people never had the chance to be old. We now can inoculate our children and prevent them from getting whooping cough, polio, typhoid, diphtheria, pneumonia, measles, and other diseases that used to carry off thousands. Since 1979, we haven't even had to immunize young people against smallpox; it's been virtually eliminated as a cause of death, which is a public health triumph of the twentieth century.

Only about 75% of the people born in 1900 in the United States lived until age 25. This has changed over the century: 97.5% now live at least that long. In other words, a quarter of the people died before age 25 in 1900, and most of those deaths took place in infancy; that would have pulled down the average life expectancy for the population quite a lot. As we've already seen, though, while it was true that the average was lower, this didn't actually cause the ones who survived to live shorter lives.

At the turn of the century, over 40% of the population made it at least until age 65. There were plenty of old people, and they actually were old—in their 70s and 80s, not just 40-year-olds who for some reason looked old. But the chances of making it into old age were only about half of what they are now. Currently, 76% of males and 87% of females live to age 65, and about 26% of males and 43% of females live to 85 years of age.

The revolution of public health in the twentieth century has been to keep more people alive into old age, not to extend old age itself. For that reason, it is

---

Illustration 1.12.   My Mother's Experience With Death as a Young Person

My mother was born in 1912. Her first experience with death was seeing a cellar door crash down on her Aunt Mary's head during a tornado in 1918. She has told me that one of the frequent social occupations of her childhood was going to funerals. She survived the epidemic of Spanish influenza of 1918; many children did not. Worldwide, more people died of the flu during 1918 and 1919 than had died in World War I. One can tour cemeteries today and see lots of the little "lamb" tombstones on the graves of children who died in the 1918 epidemic.

It was her experience that many young mothers died in childbirth. In 1934, when my sister was about to be was born, my mother took her love letters from my father down to the furnace and burned them. She didn't want anyone snooping into her private correspondence if by chance she should die in childbirth.

not technically correct to say that people are living a lot longer; it more properly should be said that a greater percentage of people are living into old age. Once they get there, old age itself hasn't been extended by much.

Look again at Table 1.7. The average number of years of life remaining for a male aged 85 in 1900 was 3.8; for a female it was 4.1. In 1996 the remaining number of years left for the average 85-year-old male was 5.3 and 6.3 for a female. This represents a gain for that oldest group of only 1.5 years for men and 2.2 for women over the course of the twentieth century. So, the increase in life expectancy that has taken place really has had a greater affect on younger people, not those in very late life.

Until recently, the real progress in extending average life expectancy has taken the form of more children living into adulthood, so that more adults live into old age. The reason that average life expectancy at birth has increased during the century from 48.2 to 73.9 years for men and from 51.1 to 79.7 years for women is not that over 25 years has been added to life, but rather that the average is no longer being pulled down by people dying in childhood. More people are living long enough to get old. It's easiest to see this concept when it is illustrated with a survival curve, a graph of how many people are still alive at certain ages. Take a look at Figure 1.1.

In London in 1688, out of every 1,000 people born, only 417 were still living by age of five (Besant, 1902). This is an extreme comparison, of course; in the U.S. in 1900, the comparable figure would have been more like 855 out of 1,000 still alive at age five. Presently, over 99% are still alive at five years of age. After this initial high rate of death in the London of 1688, survival began to decline less steeply: 360 of the original 1,000 were still living at age ten, and 329 were still alive at age 20. But by age 60, only 119 out of the original 1,000 were still alive.

Notice how the shape of the survival curve has changed: with the passage of time, it has become more rectangular. More people are now living into adulthood and on to old age. This is what gerontologists call the *rectangularization of the survival curve* (Fries & Crapo, 1981). The end point at the right side of the curve hasn't gone out all that much. Almost all in both groups had died by age 90, so we can't say that old age itself has been extended too much. What we can say is that a greater proportion are living out their three score and ten.

Incidentally, if we were to calculate the average life expectancy from these figures for London in 1688, it would be 21.9 years. The high rate of infant mortality at that time pulled the average down by that much.

In order to avoid these common misperceptions, it is best when dealing with older people to use a standard life expectancy chart, such as Table 1.8. That way, the average number of years remaining can easily be seen from any age up to 85, and a more accurate picture can be drawn of what is realistic. Older people are mislead by what's printed in the newspapers, too. A 70-year-old man, for example, might read that the average life expectancy at birth for males is 73.9 and think that he has less than four years left to live. Actually, he has over 12. Those not exactly on one of the five-year

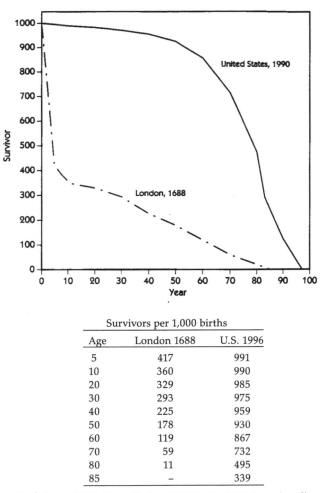

Survivors per 1,000 births		
Age	London 1688	U.S. 1996
5	417	991
10	360	990
20	329	985
30	293	975
40	225	959
50	178	930
60	119	867
70	59	732
80	11	495
85	–	339

From Besant (1902); Peters, Kochanek, & Murphy (1998, November 10).

FIG 1.1.
Survival Curves for London in 1688 and the United States in 1996

intervals given in Table 1.8 must extrapolate a bit, but the point remains the same: those who live as long as their life expectancy at birth still have a substantial expectation of further life.

Table 1.8 includes some interesting figures (although it unfortunately excludes several racial groups). Notice the difference between whites and blacks at birth: white males have a longevity advantage of 7.8 years compared to black males (73.9 compared to 66.1), and white females have an average life expectancy at birth 5.5 years longer than black females. This is largely explained by higher infant mortality among African Americans.

This longevity advantage continues through most years of life, but it narrows as the two groups get older. By age 85, the length of life remaining for males, both black and white, is identical: an additional 5.3 years. By age 85, both black and white women have essentially similar average life ex-

As we have seen, the extreme limit of human life span is about 122 years. Hardly anyone lives that long, of course. What we see instead is an increasing proportion making it through middle life and into their 70s or 80s. But, we're also starting to see a higher percentage making it into very late life. As recently as 1950, only 9.9% of males and 15.6% of females lived as long as 85 years. In 1997, it was more like 25.6% of males and 42.3% of females (Anderson, 1999).

What would happen, though, if the life span itself was extended to 130 years and most people lived to be, say, 95? This might be technically possible in some brave new world of the future.

Most people would probably agree that this would be a good thing, but only under certain conditions. First, the process of aging itself would have to be delayed. Few would buy into a bargain that only kept people alive on respirators in nursing home beds for years and years at the end of life. If youth could somehow be extended, though, and an 85-year-old of the future could have the vital capacity of the typical 65-year-old of today, then most would think the bargain would be a pretty good one.

The next question to be answered, though, would be this: who would support all of the old people? Pension systems and Social Security are currently calculated on people living only to a certain age. What would happen to their means of support if hardly anyone died? The pension plans would go broke in rapid order. The age for retirement would have to be moved up from 65 to 75 or 80. How would this affect the labor market if people didn't retire? Would young people tolerate still being in entry-level jobs at age 45?

And say that the entire life-long process of maturation was somehow delayed in order to achieve this miracle of keeping people alive longer. That is, if we put off old age, maybe we would have to put off adulthood, too. But, who would want a 35 year-old adolescent running around the house, playing his stereo too loud, not doing his homework, and complaining that there isn't anything for him to do?

pectancy. At age 87 there actually is a crossover point at which African Americans have longer to live, on the average, than similarly-aged whites. This racial crossover in longevity advantage might be explained this way: the older black people who have been tough enough to survive all they've had to put up with for 87 years might have had greater resistance to disease and disability and thus are less likely to die.

Mortality

Even a brief look at the obituary page of most newspapers gives us a clear and fundamental perspective on the most basic of human inequalities: some of us live longer than others. Keeping track of the ages in obituaries for several weeks would probably give us an average that is fairly high: most of the people who die do it late in life.

TABLE 1.8. Life Expectancy at Selected Ages by Race and Sex: U.S., 1996

Age	White		Black	
	Male	Female	Male	Female
0	73.9	79.7	66.1	74.2
1	73.4	79.1	66.2	74.2
5	69.5	75.2	62.4	70.3
10	64.5	70.2	57.5	65.4
15	59.6	65.3	52.6	60.5
20	54.9	60.4	48.0	55.7
25	50.2	55.6	43.7	50.9
30	45.6	50.7	39.4	46.2
35	40.9	45.9	35.1	41.6
40	36.4	41.1	31.0	37.1
45	31.9	36.4	27.1	32.8
50	27.5	31.7	23.4	28.5
55	23.3	27.3	19.9	24.5
60	19.4	23.0	16.7	20.7
65	15.8	19.1	13.9	17.2
70	12.6	15.4	11.2	13.9
75	9.8	12.0	9.0	11.2
80	7.3	8.9	7.0	8.5
85	5.3	6.3	5.3	6.2

From Metropolitan Life Insurance Co. (1998, October–December). Used with permission.

The information in Table 1.9 illustrates the differences between males and females and between whites and blacks in their odds of survival from birth to particular ages. Given that these are chances per 1000, it is pos-

TABLE 1.9. Chances per 1,000 of Surviving from Birth to Specific Age, by Race

	Age	White	Black
Males	15	990	978
	25	978	955
	35	963	921
	45	938	864
	55	890	764
	65	779	598
	75	564	376
	85	259	148
Females	15	992	982
	25	988	975
	35	981	960
	45	969	930
	55	941	873
	65	869	764
	75	715	572
	85	429	309

From Metropolitan Life Insurance Co. (1998, October–December). Used with permission.

sible to mentally insert a decimal point and have percentages. For example, 99.0% of white males survive at least until age 15, while 97.8% of black males live at least that long.

One can quickly see that 77.9% of white males and 86.9% of white females survive at least until age 65; the percentages of African Americans living that long are 59.8% for males and 76.4% for females. Thus, we might conclude that the majority of deaths take place in later life (taking a composite of the entire United States population, about 66% of all male deaths take place after age 65 and 80% of all female deaths take place after age 65).

Table 1.10 confirms this: it gives us a picture of deaths and how they differ by age, race, and sex. We need to pay particular attention to death rates, as they give us a way to compare the mortality experience of different groups. Obviously, comparing numbers of deaths among, say, blacks and whites wouldn't be too useful, as there are so many more white people in North America than African Americans. So, let's take a look at the rates, which on Table 1.10 are per 100,000 per year. As an example, along the top row of figures, we see a death rate of 682.4 for white males under one year of age and a rate of 536.4 for white girls of the same age. While we can't compare the numbers in a very logical way (there are more male babies

TABLE 1.10. Deaths and Death Rates by Age, Sex, and Race, U.S., 1997

Age	Number	Rate	Number	Rate
	White Male		White Female	
Under 1 year	10,569	682.4	7,894	536.4
1–4 years	2,161	34.6	1,667	28.1
5–14 years	3,468	22.1	2,327	15.6
15–24 years	16,104	107.0	6,062	43.1
25–34 years	22,449	138.5	9,472	59.7
35–44 years	42,991	234.2	21,867	120.4
45–54 years	69,733	492.5	41,307	285.8
55–64 years	113,211	1,251.3	74,461	765.5
65–74 years	230,031	3,129.9	170,590	1,903.8
75–84 years	299,370	7,121.5	306,787	4,802.8
85+ years	178,452	17,889.9	369,487	14,739.2
	Black Male		Black Female	
Under 1 year	4,548	1,614.1	3,693	1,349.9
1–4 years	793	66.9	590	51.2
5–14 years	1,070	34.6	817	27.3
15–24 years	5,895	211.3	1,674	60.4
25–34 years	7,760	304.2	3,718	131.5
35–44 years	13,206	518.3	8,192	283.3
45–54 years	17,847	1,100.6	11,410	583.4
55–64 years	21,928	2,284.8	16,220	1,294.6
65–74 years	29,474	4,271.4	25,956	2,709.9
75–84 years	26,093	8,178.3	30,433	5,591.6
85+ years	13,599	15,887.2	27,934	13,501.6

Age-specific rates per 100,00 in specified group.
From National Center for Health Statistics, Oct. 7, 1998

born), we can compare the rates. They show us that, for every 100,000 white males in the first year of life, 682 die, while only 536 out of every 100,000 white girls die in the first year of life. Another way of understanding this is to say that white girls under one year die at a rate that is only 78.5% as high as that of white boys.

What does this table tell us? First, males of both races indicated on Table 1.10 had higher rates of death at all ages compared to females. Next, rates of childhood death are higher among African Americans when compared to whites; this has the effect of pulling down the mean for that group, as we learned in earlier in this chapter.

Blacks had higher death rates generally than whites, but this is not true in the oldest age group. At ages 65–74, white males had a death rate of 3,129.9, while black males had a rate of 4,271.4. By ages 85 and above, however, the rate for whites was higher than the rate for blacks: 17,889.9 compared to 15,887.2. Similarly, African American women aged 85+ had a rate of 13,501.6, which was lower than white females' 14.739.2. The implication is that more black people die at younger ages and that more whites die in later life.

Overall, most of the people who die are old people, and death rates in adulthood increase dramatically with age. Among whites in 1997, those 65+ represent 72.4% of male deaths and 80.8% of all the women who died. Those 65 and older, however, accounted for only 48.6% of African American male deaths, and those aged 65+ accounted for 64.5% of deaths among black females. This indicates higher rates of death at younger ages for the black population. Also, it shows that women have a greater chance of surviving into late life, and white women have the best chance of all.

Table 1.11 gives us an appreciation of how important it is to differentiate by gender and race as well as by age when looking at mortality data. It

TABLE 1.11. U.S. Deaths and Percentage of Deaths in Each Age Group, 1997

	Total Deaths	Percentage of All Deaths	Cumulative Percentage
All ages	2,314,738		
Under 1 year	27,691	1.19	1.19
1–4	5,480	0.23	1.42
5–14	8,084	0.34	1.76
15–24	30,962	1.34	3.10
25–34	44,931	1.94	5.04
35–44	88,827	3.83	8.87
45–54	144,093	6.22	15.09
55–64	231,253	9.99	25.08
65–74	464,577	20.07	45.15
75–84	672,221	29.04	74.19
85+	596,193	25.76	99.95
Not stated	476	—	—

From National Center for Health Statistics, October 7, 1998

simply lists the total number of deaths, and the percentage of all deaths for the entire U.S. population, by age. As we can see, about 9% of those who died in 1997 were under age 45, and a little over 25% of deaths that year were people younger than 65. Because this table does not give death rates, however, it would be a mistake to judge probability from it. It doesn't mean that 25.08% of the population dies before age 65; rather, it is just what we said: 25.08% of all deaths are among those under 65 years of age. Because there are so many more younger people than older people, they account for a relatively higher number of all deaths. For our purposes, it is best to compare rates rather than numbers. To sum up Table 1.11, then, most of the people who die are older people, and young people account for only a very small proportion of all deaths.

Conclusion

We can project that the older population is going to continue to increase, both in terms of absolute numbers and in terms of the percentage of the total population that it represents. Also, we can project that increases in average life expectancy will continue to actually add more years to old age, rather than just increase the proportion who make it into old age. In later chapters, when we discuss health and morbidity, we will see that progress in medicine is now starting to decrease the chronic illnesses that old people typically die of, not just the contagious diseases that used to kill children. And, there is some indication that research may unlock the secrets of longevity and begin to extend the life span itself.

As one generation of old people dies off and is replaced by the next, different cohort effects will dictate different values among those who are older. And while older people will not be any more concentrated in the U.S. than they currently are in some of the countries of Western Europe, the greater numbers of the aged may have a practical influence on public policy. This will especially be the case if the elderly begin to live longer and longer with no decrease in levels of disability. There will be comparatively fewer young people to care for the greater number of frail elders in the future. This will not happen until well in the twenty-first century, but it will happen. States to which high numbers of older people move (like Florida) will have greater problems in this regard than some of the states with populations that are comparatively younger.

Countries worldwide, however, will have to devote increasing attention to problems and issues related to an aging population. Most of these issues will revolve around such things as income and services. However, if life span is prolonged, public policy decision-making might become increasingly difficult. What might happen, for example, if average life expectancy for 85-year-olds changes from five or six additional years to 25 or more years, and the absolute limit of life span extends to 135?

Most people might now think that this will represent real progress. However, if conditions such as Alzheimer's disease that increase in prevalence in later life are not controlled at the same time, then science might be creating not a dream, but a nightmare.

However, in an era of cost containment in health care expenditures, there may come a day when public policy choices have to be made as to how much the country is willing to invest in keeping old people alive. At a time when it might be increasingly possible to extend the life span, generational conflict might worsen amid competition for scarce resources, and politicians will argue that greedy senior citizens are taking support away from poor children. Older persons of the future may have no choice but to be self-reliant.

Questions for Discussion

1. How long would you like to live? Why?
2. Who was the longest-living person in your family?
3. Why would people lie about their age to make themselves appear to be older rather than younger?
4. Describe the oldest person you know. What is he or she like?
5. What does "rectangularization of the survival curve" really mean?
6. What cohort effects will influence how you see the world when you are an older person?
7. Speculate on the consequences of extending life expectancy and further reducing infant mortality, both nationally and globally.
8. What are some ways older people of today are different from their own parents?
9. When, in your opinion, does "old age" really begin?
10. Do you see people you know who seem to be aging at different rates?
11. Do you think the birthrate will increase much in the near future?
12. What really has the most to do with the percentage of older people, the birthrate or the death rate?

Sources of Further Information

When searching out statistical information on the demography of older people in the U.S., our advice is to go for the easiest and the cheapest sources first, and then move on to the more technical and expensive information sources, if necessary.

U.S. Census data is reported in a host of publications. The detailed household census publications for each state should be available in most college libraries; ask the Reference Librarian. These data sources are available both in paperback and on CD-ROM.

The most usable compilation of census data, however, can be found in the Statistical Abstract of the United States, which is available in every college library and almost every community library. Paperback copies are available for $30 from the Superintendent of Documents (at the address below) for those who wish to have their own copy.

More detailed information on particular geographical areas can be found in either the State and Metropolitan Area Data Book or the County and City Data Book ($30 and $40, respectively), or, for those who want to find out who died of what and where they did it, the imposing Vital Statistics of the United States—Vol. II: Mortality ($56).

For those who would like to find out the many, many publications of the Census Bureau, subscribe to the Census Catalog and Guide ($15). This and the Census publications listed above can be ordered from:

The U.S. Superintendent of Documents
Government Printing Office
Washington, D.C. 20402-9325

Customer Services of the U.S. Bureau of the Census is a very helpful office indeed and can help point out where the information you need can be found. They can also provide you with information on how to order some of the above documents on machine-readable CD-ROM discs ($150+ each); call them at 301/763-4100 or write to:

Customer Services
U.S. Bureau of the Census
Washington, D.C. 20233

Small requests for Census data often can be handled by request (and at no charge) through the office of one's Senator or Representative in Congress; look up his or her local number in the phone book under "U.S. Government—Congress." It helps them a lot if you know exactly what it is you want: don't just ask for "any information you have on old people."

General data on health and mortality is attractively presented in the Statistical Bulletin ($50 per year for a subscription) available from:

The Metropolitan Life Insurance Co.
P.O. Box 465
Hanover, PA 17331

For those who must have everything right off the press, by far the most up-to-date data on births, deaths, marriages, divorces, and other things, like annual hospital discharge surveys, is available from the National Center for Health Statistics (telephone: 301/436-8500), which publishes the Monthly Vital Statistics Report and Advance Data from Vital and Health Statistics of the National Center for Health Statistics:

U.S. Department of Health & Human Services
Public Health Service
National Center for Health Statistics
6525 Belcrest Road
Hyattsville, MD 20782-2003

An enormous amount of census data is available on the World Wide Web at http://www.census.gov/

Finally, quarterly bulletins reporting on the availability of a very wide variety and number of data sources in the field of aging can be had for free from the:

National Archive of Computerized Data on Aging
P.O. Box 1248
Ann Arbor, MI 48106

The Social World of Older People

2

Chapter Outline

"When Groucho was in his fifties, and about to marry for the third time, I thought to myself, is Father crazy? How could anyone his age possibly think of getting married again, and to a twenty-one year-old at that? How could he have any interest in sex? And even if he did, could he possibly hope to satisfy a wife nearly forty years his junior? And how could she want him for anything but his money?"

—Arthur Marx, born 1921

Was Groucho Marx playing out the cliche "There's no fool like an old fool," or was he merely living his own life the way he wanted to? His son Arthur, now himself in his 80s, saw his father then as engaging in folly inappropriate to an aging man. No doubt Arthur changed his mind as he himself got older as to what might be ***age-appropriate behavior*** for a man in his fifties, and his perspective also changed as to when people actually can be defined as old. Groucho, who lived well into his 90s, had completed a successful movie career with the other Marx Brothers, and was just beginning a second career with a very popular television program when he was in his 50s. And, he probably gave little consideration to what his son—or the neighbors—thought about the way he was living his life.

Contained within this anecdote are several important elements relating to the social world of older people. How one is supposed to act in later life might be influenced by what others think. The roles that are appropriate for people as they age seem to change, and the opinion of others has some importance in the ways aging people feel comfortable behaving. Physi-

glossary

age-appropriate behavior — Acting one's age, doing things that are normal for others at the same age.

cal limitations may also have some influence on how aging people function in society. Arthur Marx as a young adult certainly had difficulty in seeing his father in late middle age as a sexual creature. Norms for aging people might also be seen as being defined by older people themselves; Groucho Marx was certainly not the first man to take on a new career or a new wife at his age. The fact that he succeeded might help others who are aging to see different role models as society itself changes.

On February 20, 1962, John Glenn was the first American astronaut to orbit the earth in a spacecraft. When, in November of 1998, he served as a crew member in the space shuttle, he also provided a different message of what is appropriate for older persons. Senator Glenn was 77 years of age at the time.

These issues revolve around the concept of how older people are seen in our society. Older people, just like younger people, are expected to conform to certain perceptions and norms as they interact in a social world. In this chapter, we will examine some of these perceptions of older people, the expectations that society has for them, and those that they have for themselves. We will look at several theories of social gerontology and see if they have value for predicting how older adults will be seen in their social world, and we will examine the process of *socialization*—how people adapt to social forces in later life.

Attitudes, Norms, and Socialization

The first question we might ask about how a younger Arthur Marx viewed Groucho's plans in his fifties to marry a woman in her twenties is this: whose business is it? Obviously, the way we behave is first and foremost our own business. And, it is apparent that Groucho Marx went right ahead, despite his adult son's concerns, and married the person he wanted to marry. After all, it was his business, right?

At first glace, this seems like a very simple issue. However, we might take a more extreme case. Let's say that there is a widower in his 80s, a man of some wealth who has three adult children. He has a diminishing circle of old friends he sees from time to time, and he has some health problems. It has fallen upon his oldest daughter to look in on him and make sure he is doing all right. She is afraid that he is starting to be a bit confused, and she has discussed with her brother and sister her concerns about how long Dad will be able to live in the old home place. They agree that the services of a part-time, visiting nurse would help to keep him independent and out of an institution. Things go well with the visiting nurse; in fact, they go so well that four months later, Dad announces that he and the nurse, age 27, are to be married and are giving some thought to moving to Palm Springs. When confronted by his adult children, he says, "You're just worried about the inheritance." His friends are drawn into the controversy; some think he's doing the right thing, others think he's gone off the deep end. His adult children are at a loss as to what to do.

The theoretical issues of social gerontology can be translated into very practical, important concerns by looking at such a case study. First, we have issues of socialization, how the older man interacts with his family and friends. We could call these people who are concerned for his welfare his *social network*, those who are providing him with various kinds of support. It is typical for one particular individual in an older person's social network, in this case the oldest daughter, to be a *primary caregiver*, who takes the lead in providing for his social (and perhaps psychological and physical) support.

And, it's not unusual for some issues of conflict to arise, especially if there is disagreement within the social network or between individuals when a crisis arises. These conflict situations often relate to issues of *control*. Is the older man's control internal—that is, does he make his own decisions for the most part—or is it external? In this instance, his family and friends may exert different kinds of pressures upon him to conform to their expectations of what acceptable behavior ought to be for a widower in his eighties. These pressures could be seen as efforts to exert external control. Ideal norms in this instance would be their desire to see Dad conform to what they consider to be appropriate ways that older people are expected to behave. Society's attitudes toward the elderly contain a system of *age norms*, ways in which people of a certain age are supposed to act. We need to look at each of these factors in greater detail.

Socialization is the process by which individuals interact with their society and learn its norms, values, and role expectations and develop attitudes and opinions. This is a lifelong process: we literally learn how to be family members, children, adolescents, and adults—and older adults—by dealing with those around us. Their attitudes and actions influence the ways in which we behave. We learn what expectations are, and we learn what limits society places upon us. Acceptable and unacceptable behaviors are defined through a process of socialization. We learn to act in ways that others expect us to act, and we learn what the punishment is if we behave differently.

Through a system of *norms* or standards of behavior, one learns how to be a member of the society. Breaking these rules usually brings down a number of social sanctions, disapproval from others that can range from being laughed at, mild scolding or questioning, all the way to punishment that can be quite painful. Anyone who has heard questions like "What will people think?" or "What will the neighbors say?" has confronted a potential violation of social norms. The mildest kind of norms are *folkways*. *Customs* are a little more serious; they are traditional or long-lived norms. People usually follow them because they're expected to, like serving turkey for Thanksgiving dinner.

Mores are also norms, but they go beyond customs or folkways. Atti-

social network — The system of family and friends with whom one interacts most.

primary caregiver — The one individual who bears the main responsibility for the care of another; there also may be one or more secondary caregivers.

control — The perception of who is in charge on one's life: people who are internally controlled are independent; those who are externally controlled have lost their independence.

age norms — Markers of what is expected at certain ages.

norms — Rules and guidelines for social behavior shared and accepted by most people within a culture.

folkways — Short-lived, informal norms; fashions or fads.

customs — Long-lived, traditional norms.

mores — Strongly-held norms, often encoded into laws. These beliefs about the proper ways for people to behave within a particular culture are seen as crucial to maintaining the social order; violations of mores are often punished.

tudes associated with mores are more intense in that they actually define what moral behavior is in a culture. In this way, mores carry more weight than customs and folkways. Those mores having the strongest sanctions are the ones that have been made into *laws*. The society will actually take steps to legally enforce its most strongly held mores, as they are seen as vital to social stability.

The structures and values of a society are reflected through its norms, folkways, customs, mores, and laws. As values change, so do the norms. There are strongly-maintained prohibitions in almost every culture against, for example, theft, incest, and homicide. Sanctions or punishments of those who violate these norms will, however, vary from one society to another. And, these sanctions are dynamic (continually changing) in societies. Sexual relations outside of marriage, as an illustration, used to be seen as highly immoral, violating mores as well as customs and folkways. There actually were laws against having sex outside of marriage. Few in contemporary America will now be actually legally punished for it, and while it might be frowned upon by some, sex outside of marriage is increasingly tolerated and has become somewhat less of a violation of social norms during the past several decades.

Similarly, marriage outside one's own race was at one time punishable by law in most parts of the United States. Virtually all of these laws have been abolished. So it might be seen that the rules are subject to change. While we have become less up-tight about some things, other realms of behavior have become less acceptable. Smokers, for instance, have recently felt the sting of social disapproval as well as an increasing network of laws regulating their behavior. Socially acceptable behavior, what is and what is not done, not only changes, but it also varies tremendously among groups within a society.

All of these issues revolve around attitudes and perceptions, which make up our feelings about what is right and what is wrong. Is it socially acceptable for an 80-year-old man to marry a woman who is 27? At one level, it's his own business. Adults in our society have the fundamental right to determine their own marital partners; no one has to give permission. But, on another level, such a marriage would certainly cause tongues to wag. What the neighbors think may be a very important factor for many of us. Would attitudes be different if there was less of a gap in the ages?

Illustration 2.1. Some Things Aren't Done

I once did some interviewing to try to determine why the lowest suicide rates among Americans occur among older women of African American descent. The almost universal response was: "Well, it just isn't done." This is a prime example of how social norms dictate how people will behave at the most basic, life-or-death level.

Illustration 2.2. Looking for Love in All the Wrong Places

In the early 1960s, rock star Jerry Lee Lewis was hooted off of a London stage when it became known that had married his 13-year-old cousin. His explanation, "She wasn't no virgin," was seen as contemptible, and his tour of the United Kingdom had to be cut short. The marriage, only minimally acceptable in the U.S., was seen in England as absolutely unacceptable. The event hurt Lewis's career, badly.

In the summer of 1992, film stars Mia Farrow and Woody Allen divorced. Headlines indicated that Allen, 57 at the time, had admitted to having sexual relations with Farrow's 21-year-old adopted daughter. Allen defended himself, saying that they were both adults and were not blood relatives. Public perception, however, was that Allen had violated more than an age norm; while he was not the biological father, he had in their family life acted in the role of a father. Thus the affair in a way violated society's very strong prohibition against incest, and was seen by many as being hopelessly grotesque.

Probably. What if the genders were reversed: a 27-year-old man marrying a woman in her eighties? Most would probably agree that such a marriage would cause considerable talk. However, it would not now be considered to be nearly so much of a scandal it once would have been. Social norms and values gradually change over time.

Norms not only influence our perceptions of right and wrong, but they also provide a kind of a map for our development across the lifespan. *Age-normative* influences are the expectations of what will happen in our lives at different ages. Going to kindergarten at age five is age-normative; just about everyone in Western society does it. Similarly, finishing school sometime late in the teens or (increasingly) into the twenties is age-normative. Although in the United States and Canada an increasing number of middle-aged adults seek higher education, they are still thought of by university administrators as "non-traditional" students. In other words, the "normal" college student is between 18 and 22 years of age. Similarly, leaving the parents' home and establishing an independent residence is thought of as an adult task and thus is age-normative. Retirement for most people is also age-normative. So is death. These all are typical events and responsibilities that are appropriate for people at particular ages.

Contrasted with age-normative life events are *non-normative* influences on life, such as getting hit by a car, getting cancer, or winning the lottery. These are big events in peoples' lives and will have a profound influence upon them, but they are not necessarily tied to age, nor are they typically expected to happen to most people. Some events that used to be considered to be non-normative, such as divorce, have become so common as to be thought of in a different way. Divorce, in fact, may have become normative; however, it is not tied to any particular age and thus could not be said to be age-normative; that is, there is no particular age when one might

glossary

age-normative — Pertaining to common values of persons at certain ages.

normative behavior — Actions that are common and accepted; non-normative behavior is deviant.

history-normative —
Accepted by all people
who have been
influenced by a
particular historical
event.

expect to be divorced. An increasing acceptance of cultural diversity in American society has made different lifestyles "more normative" as the dynamics of society and social attitudes change over time.

Some life events might be seen as *history-normative*, or appropriate to a particular age cohort or generation (Perlmutter & Hall, 1985). The occurrence of particular historical events, such as World War II or the Great Depression of the 1930s, may have particular influence upon those who were alive at the time. The public perception of each historical event will differ, of course. Men now in mid-life who sought to avoid the military draft during the war in Vietnam have a much different perception of conscription into the Army than did those in the previous generation who were drafted to serve in World War II. "Draft dodging" was something that just was not done during the early 1940s, except by a relatively few conscientious objectors. Working the system to get a draft deferment during the very unpopular Vietnam War, on the other hand, was considered by many in the 1960s and '70s to be a normative activity. So, views of what is history-normative may depend upon the character of the event as well as the age cohort viewing it.

Attitudes toward old people are made up of a wide variety of positives and negatives. We are literally socialized into old age: we see examples around us of what it is to be older. Roles that are appropriate change during the life course. As we mature throughout the course of our lives, we see that we are subject to a number of age-normative influences. In the example used at the beginning of this chapter, there was pressure exerted upon the older man to "act his age" and perhaps to conform to what was seen as age-appropriate behavior. That is, his family and others in his social support network had a vision of what it was to be over eighty. In their view, a man of 80 years didn't go around marrying a 27-year-old.

In a very real way, these influences and pressures dictate what we do and how we behave; we are usually most reluctant to undergo the disapproval of those closest to us. The social sanctions they can place upon us can make life very uncomfortable. And, those sanctions are based upon their (and our) attitudes as to what is appropriate. In the opposite realm, we can be rewarded by our family and friends for conforming to roles thought by society to be appropriate. By the time we are old people, we have thoroughly mastered an understanding of age-normative influences. Over the course of time, we've been told to "grow up," or asked when we are going to get into (or out of) school, marriage, parenthood, and so on. Repetition of these experiences thousands of times during the course of young and adult life makes us specialists in perceptions of acceptable behavior by the time we are old.

Obviously, different personality characteristics and life experiences will make some people acutely sensitive to the feelings of others; at the other extreme, some people just won't really care what others think. There is some speculation that older persons have a tendency to lose inhibitions, especially in very late life, and behave with less concern over the opinion of others. If this is true, it may be as a result of several things—perhaps the social network of the individual is shrinking and is perceived to be less important. Or, older individuals might discover that they can in fact "get away" with more in very late life because expectations for their behavior are lowered. There is little research in this area, unfortunately, to confirm or deny these speculations. The notion of loss of inhibition in later life must also be considered, however, keeping in mind the theory of *continuity of personality over the life course*: people have a tendency to become more like themselves. Perhaps those who "bust loose" always had a tendency to be less restrained by social conventions and the opinions of others. This speculation is all based on practical observation of how social theory applies to individual lives. We might also look at societal perceptions of the elderly as a group.

In a series of studies over the years, we have found that attitudes toward the elderly generally are positive in the United States (Thorson, 1975, 1981; Thorson & Powell, 1991). Although there definitely is *ageism*, prejudice, and discrimination against the elderly (especially in the workplace), overall impressions of older adults held by most people are fairly benign. Older people are thought of generally to be good neighbors, responsible citizens, and thrifty, kind, and generous. On the positive side but patronizing, many describe the elderly as "cute," "little," and "sweet." Ageist attitudes toward the elderly include concepts such as "slowing down" or lacking in energy; older people may also be characterized as more likely to be confused or selfish. There may be a good deal of unexpressed envy among younger adults toward the group of elderly who are relatively prosperous and lacking in responsibilities; retirees who seemingly can devote all of their time to leisure activities are seen both as representing something of a goal for the middle aged to achieve and at the same time as having a soft life. Despite this envy, most younger adults are willing to admit that older people who "have it made" have for the most part worked hard to achieve their life goals.

While ageist stereotypes are prevalent among the aged themselves, and thus often contribute to a lack of self esteem, roles that older people play, such as grandparent, are universally admired in our society. In our research, we have demonstrated that the most positive attitudes toward the elderly are expressed by older people themselves, by women, and by those surveyed who have the most education. Interestingly, a colleague and I have also found that medical students tend to be significantly more positive toward the aged than are other post-graduate students in the same age category, and that the experience of medical school apparently does not change their original attitudes toward old people (Thorson & Powell, 1991). The general public, we can conclude, holds both ageist stereotypes and positive images of the elderly simultaneously.

Role Loss

role transition —
Changing (adding or
subtracting) social
roles, usually over the
course of time as one
develops.

Old age is often characterized as a time of adjustment to loss. This is a different perspective on development than the one into which we have been socialized into from childhood, when many of our plans and actions have been focused on gaining things: status, a family, money, friends, and so on. At some time later in life, the process may be reversed in some circumstances: we tend to lose friends and family through death, lose occupational status (and income) through retirement and perhaps we lose bodily integrity, strength, beauty, or health. Some may lose a sense of purpose in life.

It must be realized that all of life's transitions probably involve some role loss: assuming the mantle of adulthood, one loses the role of adolescent. Getting married by definition means the role of single person is lost. Many *role transitions* involve such trade-offs. However, the losses that are often associated with late-life transitions typically mean giving up a role that is highly valued and, perhaps, replacing it with one that is slim compensation. The loss of the work role and gain of the retiree role is a prime example.

Think of how people define themselves: when people in a group are asked to introduce themselves, they almost always say what they do rather than who they are. Asked to say who they are, nine times out of ten adults will respond with an occupational role. We eagerly seek this occupational role that clearly defines our place in society; it provides us with status, security, meaning, income, and one way of making our unique contribution to our civilization. Many of us have prepared for years, working hard to qualify to take on a desired occupational status with its associated role. We can often speak of this role with a sense of pride. Our occupation also provides us with companions and a set schedule of daily activities. We know what to do with ourselves because of our work; we make friends on the job. If we change jobs at some time in adulthood, the change is usually seen as a major life transition.

Illustration 2.3. The Limits to Accumulation

A cousin, now deceased, was Dean of Arts & Sciences at a university in another state. Visiting him, I admired his fine collection of books. I picked out several I wished to borrow and gave a solemn pledge that I would return them. I was taken aback when he said, "Please don't. I'm now at a stage in life where getting rid of books has become more important that getting books." This was a new perspective for me, as I'd always thought that accumulating more and more books was a good thing. I now find that we no longer have any space on our own bookshelves, or room for any more, and I'm starting to lend out my own books with the hope that they won't be returned.

Now think of how we might feel if this very important part of our lives should be taken away. Most of us give lip service to the notion of having time to pursue leisure activities in retirement. But, most of us also realize that no one can go fishing all the time; if we wanted that, we could have fished for a living, which would have meant a work life of backbreaking labor. And although retirement does have its compensations, most retirees report that there is a period of transition between the work life and adjustment to retirement that often is difficult. Many people have eagerly anticipated retirement, but losing occupational roles and status can be traumatic, and finding worthwhile things to do with one's time may be equally difficult because of a vague understanding of the retirement role.

It is true that there are roles, such as grandparent, that many people look forward to in later life. However, many transitions in old age are not anticipated with any sense of eagerness: the death of one's spouse may be the biggest loss that many people associate with old age, and it certainly involves transition from one major social status to another: from married person to widow. Helena Lopata's research among widows indicates that they often feel devalued by their friends. In addition to all of the grief work involved with the loss, and with all of the inevitable changes in one's life associated with death of a spouse, the new status of "widow" is most often seen as a particularly unwelcome role change in later life (Lopata & Brehm, 1986).

Loss of valued roles that we may have been able to cling to in middle age catches up with us in later life. While some may try to hold onto past glories, and others may successfully make the transition from active to less strenuous sports, "athlete" is a role that only a few can credibly maintain very late into old age. Similarly, for those who take pride and achieve status from their good looks (and, through face lifts and cosmetic surgery, seek to cling to this status), the process of aging almost inevitably decreases what society popularly defines as physical beauty. Certainly, we may make allowances and ascribe to values that many older people are in fact beautiful, or we may hear comments like "She is really good looking for an older person." Inevitably, though, we must realize that the newsstands are not filled with magazines featuring old people on their covers. Our society thinks of youth and beauty almost without exception as going hand in hand. Getting old means a loss of good looks for most people.

Other valued roles may be given up as one ages. For the very old and frail, the loss of the status of "driver" may come as a particular catastrophe. Being able to drive a car means independence in our society, and losing one's driving license or losing one's ability to drive is seen as an important role transition, symbolizing going from independence into dependence. Also associated with loss of independence are a host of physical changes for some older people that prevent them from accomplishing activities of daily living. Sensory losses also might be seen as role losses. Impaired vision for many necessitates giving up reading, an important and often devastating loss; reading substitutes are useful and important, but they in fact do not replace the original ability.

Although the desire and capacity for sexual relations remains strong in most individuals, our roles as sexual creatures are frequently lost in later life. Along with the losses of youth, beauty, and energy that may be inevitable in old age, there is also the loss of opportunity. Further, there is frequently the loss of the perception of oneself as a sexual being; that is, older people themselves often reflect society's attitudes toward them as becoming increasingly sexless. When they attempt to rally against these expectancies, as with the story from Arthur Marx that began this chapter, other people may influence them with negative responses. If the violation of social norms is too extreme, as exemplified in the hypothetical case of the 80-year-old and his nurse, peoples' lives may be disrupted indeed. We might conclude from these examples that in some circumstances status and role loss will actually be imposed by members of the person's social world.

There is no place where this is so clear as in the matter of institutionalization. Hardly anyone wants to enter a nursing home. Whether to "let" an aged parent continue on in her or his own home is a genuine dilemma for many people who may themselves be senior citizens. The loss of the status of independent decision-maker—being in charge of one's own life to the extent of deciding where to live—is seen as devastating.

In the same way that society devalues older people, they often tend to devalue themselves. We all have heard comments like, "I'm too old to try that" or "Get someone younger." Stereotypes of inactivity among the elderly are thus reinforced. Not wanting to attempt new things is not necessarily characteristic of the majority of old people; however, it is descriptive of a large enough minority to have been the basis for a pervasive societal attitude. Perhaps the loss of the status of "person who would try something new," or "adventure seeker" is one of the more subtle losses associated with the aging process. Being "old-fashioned" or "stuck in her ways" are common societal expressions of this prejudice. So we might conclude that status and role losses among the aged are also seen, and expected, by younger people. And they are in this way reinforced. Older people literally may not be allowed to be independent, or sexual, or innovative, because of the expectations of their children and others in their social world.

In summary, then, we might see the loss of status with roles in later life as being (1) enforced in part by younger persons in the society, (2) only partially compensated for, (3) looked upon with dread in certain circumstances, and (4) often requiring a period of transition or adjustment. These constraints are enforced by our conceptions of age norms, and we have our own sense of appropriateness, a "social clock," that keeps us on track with what is age-appropriate behavior (Hagestad & Neugarten, 1985). Role theory can be seen as a particular way to explain how older people interact with their social world. It was one of the earliest ways of explaining social changes in later life (Cottrell, 1942). And it has endured because it is often seen as both applicable and self-evident.

Theories of Socialization in Old Age

The *activity theory* of aging sees aging in many ways as an extension of middle age (Havighurst, Cavan, Burgess, & Goldhammer, 1949). This theory says that the best way to approach aging is similar to the rest of adult life: a full life will find the individual engaged in many different statuses, roles, and activities. A status that is lost through retirement, such as being a worker, will be replaced by things such as being a volunteer. The best way to be happy in later life, in other words, is to be active and to attempt to retain desired roles and status from earlier parts of life. Allowing that physical limitations and circumstances make giving up some things a necessity, the activity theory expresses the concept that age-appropriate replacements should be found, and that the happy older person is an active older person.

This makes a certain amount of sense, of course; it is the opposite of a "rocking chair" approach to retirement. People who give up trying or who become hermits tend to be unhappy in later life. Older people thus have essentially the same needs as middle-aged people; both resist the shrinkage of their social world. Neither wishes to rust out; most would prefer to wear out. Any decline in social interaction results from withdrawal by society away from aging persons rather than voluntary withdrawal of the aged from society. The activity theory stresses that older people seek to maintain their status in later life (Havighurst, 1968). This reflects the worth-through-work norm of the society into which they have been socialized: people should be busy accumulating things, such as wealth, property, and using their time productively. Losing any of these is evidence of decline. Voluntarily giving them up would be seen as a contradiction of activity theory.

Disengagement theory (Cumming & Henry, 1961), on the other hand, is more developmental; it sees old age as a separate period of life, not as an extension of middle age. Values and norms change, and people in later life are more willing to pull back. Some role and status loss is normative and consistent with the physical slowing down that is inevitable among the elderly. Separation from society is seen as more mutual; society has less need for older people just at a time in life when older adults feel that it is appropriate to be taking on less in life. Society and the older person withdraw from each other. Older people desire less interaction. Social withdrawal is accompanied by increased preoccupation with the self and less investment in others: "In this view, the older person who has a sense of psychological well-being will usually be the person who has reached a new equilibrium characterized by a greater psychological distance, altered types of relationships, and decreased social interaction with persons around him" (Neugarten, Havighurst, & Tobin, 1961, p. 134). According to the disengagement theory, the aged do not necessarily have to be active and productive to be well adjusted.

glossary

activity theory — The idea that the best way to approach old age is to remain as active and involved as possible.

disengagement theory — The idea that the most satisfying approach to old age involves a mutual withdrawal of the older person from society.

glossary

The first real test of the activity and disengagement theories came with the Kansas City Studies of Adult Life, taking repeated interviews with 159 women and men aged 50 through 90 during the years 1956 to 1962. Due to deaths and people who either moved or preferred to leave the study for other reasons, just 88 subjects remained in the panel by the end of the study. The researchers concluded that neither the activity theory nor the disengagement theory was adequate to explain the study's findings. It was apparent that high levels of life satisfaction were found among both the active and the disengaged elders. It was suggested that dimensions of personality might better explain satisfactory adjustment in later life. Additional criticism of disengagement theory accumulated during subsequent years, and it no longer sparks the discussion it once did in the field of gerontology (Maddox, 1964; Wershow, 1981; Youmans, 1969).

Neither theory allows for the ***heterogeneous*** nature of aged people: they become less like one another as they age, rather than more alike. This has been a common stumbling block with many studies of the aged: a tendency to lump all old people into one group, not allowing for individual differences. Obviously, some people are happy with an active later life, and some are perfectly pleased with being disengaged. Longitudinal research has suggested that these may be characteristics of younger adults that maintain continuity into late life: people who were active when they were young continue to strive to be active, and people who would have preferred to be less engaged in younger adulthood now have the opportunity to be less active.

This ***continuity theory*** of aging holds that people do not change as they age, that their personalities remain pretty much the same throughout adult life (Neugarten, Havighurst, & Tobin, 1968). Thus, their likes and dislikes will also remain pretty much the same. Those who prefer to remain active will do so, given certain physical limitations; those who desire a lower level of interaction may finally achieve it in later life, just when society places fewer demands upon them. This theory, of course, has some ***face validity***: it seems to be reasonable. Unfortunately, it is also very difficult to test.

Most longitudinal studies of aging have focused upon measures of performance rather than personality or social interaction. Few have set out to directly test the continuity theory itself. There is some evidence from the Duke Longitudinal Study to infer that self image does not change as people age (Back & Morris, 1974). Few studies have been designed specifically to test continuity theory.

Essentially, the ideal of research in the social sciences is deductive: the scientist has a hunch (a theory) and then finds ways to do research that either proves or disproves the theory. Most social science research, however, winds up being inductive: something is found in a study or a series of studies, and then the researcher tries to come up with an explanation of why to form an explanatory hypothesis. As evidence accumulates, one feels more comfortable supporting one theory or another. Critics might charge that gerontology has done little deductive research to adequately test social theories of aging. Much gerontological research has been observational or descriptive, with hypotheses advanced later to help explain what has been observed.

The concept of continuity theory itself, of course, rests on the notion that older people are too diverse to be adequately explained by one theory or another; it merely says that they remain pretty much like themselves as they age. Perhaps this simple explanation is adequate, but it leaves those in search of practical implications somewhat frustrated.

Zena Blau (1981) argues that assigning older people the role of "senior citizen" in effect takes them out of the perceived useful population and puts them into a separate category: people who no longer really matter. She notes that the persuasive body of evidence actually is in the opposite direction; people are living longer, are more involved in their communities, are accomplishing useful roles, have functions beyond what were expected of the aged only a few years ago, and are leading increasingly complex lives. No longer does one have a simple, assigned status such as "worker" or "mother." People have greater freedom to explore their own potentials, to grow, to return to school, to begin new careers or pursue new

subculture — A group within a larger group whose members usually interact mainly with one another; there has been debate over whether or not the aged constitute a subculture.

exchange theory — The concept that older and younger persons maintain a fairly equal balance of interchange of support, both material and emotional; when this gets out of balance, interaction tends to break down.

directions. Simply setting old people on the shelf as those who have lived their lives does them a great disservice.

Blau says that the old are not a *subculture* (people who interact mainly with one another) but have important relationships and roles to accomplish that are intergenerational. The evidence of the past few decades is that people go in all different directions as they develop, and that there is no reason to expect the aged to be any different. Only when illness or frailty dictate it should the lives of older adults be expected to become somewhat constricted. For the most part, though, people move into and out of a succession of different statuses and roles as they age (Riley, Johnson, & Foner, 1972). This age stratification, however, need not be a predictor of how people will approach old age so much as an explanation of the diversity of roles people engage in as they develop through life. Many will continue to blossom until shortly before they wither.

The concept of quantifying the exchange of interpersonal relationships was proposed by psychologists John W. Thibaut and Harold H. Kelley (1959). They saw that interaction could be expressed as a system of investments in others relative to an expected payoff. A person's investment in another would tend to continue if they got something back. Ideally, the payoff would be at or higher than the level of investment. So, if a woman invests in a relationship with a man at the rate of, say, a 90, and she only gets benefits at a level of a 60, she will have a tendency to not make this a long-term relationship. She'll be putting too much in for what she's getting back. On the other hand, if she puts in at a level of an 80 and gets back a 95, she'll seek to maintain the relationship. In other words, we have a tendency to seek to maximize payoff (but not necessarily a corresponding tendency to minimize investment). Very unequal relationships will fall apart: this explains why we may avoid people who are "really a drain" on us. We don't get much back for what we're putting in.

This way of looking at things was essentially confirmed by Stinnett and DeFrain (1985) in their study of marriages that had lasted into old age. Those interviewed who had marriages of 40 to 50 years said that the level of effort invested in the marriage was about equal, and that neither felt that they were putting in 100%. They didn't need to break their backs to keep the relationship alive; just investing at a level of about 85 seemed about right. Relationships where the emotional investments of the two partners was lopsided didn't last.

This is an expression of *exchange theory*, which works as a sort of mental calculation of costs and benefits of social interaction (Blau, 1964). People engage in relationships that they find to be rewarding, and they withdraw from those relationships that they see as too costly. Exchange theory could be applied at any age. However, James Dowd (1975) thought to apply it to later life in an attempt to explain why old people sometimes withdraw from social relationships, especially with younger people. He writes that old people have few resources to bring to such relationships and as a result, decrease their participation in interactions with younger people.

We're starting to see a decline in participation among people eligible to take part in the meal sites for the elderly attached to many senior centers. First authorized as "nutrition sites" in the early 1970s under the Older Americans Act, many of these hot lunch programs grew into full service senior centers over the years. People pay a portion—or sometimes all—of the cost of their meals. The generation of the aged that began participating in these meal sites has been aging in place, getting older year by year and dropping by the wayside. It is not being replaced by the next generation of the elderly. Meal site coordinators are calling to ask us for ideas as to how to attract younger old people; often, their daily count is off by half of what it once was. This might be an example of exchange theory in action: the young old find that the old old have little to offer in terms of equal relationships.

This is not a true expression of exchange theory, which would hold that young people might disassociate themselves from older people who have less to give in a relationship. And, Passuth and Bengtson (1988) note that Dowd's analysis overlooks an emotional component, love, that makes analysis of relationships in strictly economic terms less apt. The relationship of parents with their children, for example, is hardly ever on equal terms. Nor are the changing relationships of older people with their adult children. Most adult children acknowledge a sense of *filial obligation*, a feeling that they ought to care for their parents out a sense of both duty and love. Thus, the strictly objective principles of exchange theory are not always applicable. However, it has been observed that many older people in fact pay a price for relationships with younger adults that might otherwise seem to be unequal. And, Roberto and Scott (1986) have shown that the principles of exchange theory are applicable among older adults and their friends.

Cowgill and Holmes (1972) postulate that as societies become more complex and technically sophisticated, the status of the elderly declines. This *modernization theory* notes that in traditional societies, the aged tend to retain their status and serve in important roles as elders of the tribe. As societies become more modern, elders' roles are less important. This is modified with the realization that in historical terms, relatively few people actually lived into old age, and that there are now many more aged people in contemporary society. High status tended to be, according to this theory, associated with agricultural societies where older survivors not only knew the traditions but also owned the land. Now, older people in urban societies tend to have comparatively less status and fewer important roles.

Palmore and Manton (1974) reviewed data from 31 different countries and found only slight evidence that supported the modernization theory; moreover, in her research in Samoa, Ellen Rhoads (1984) found little support for the idea of elders losing status in a modernizing society. She

glossary

filial obligation — A sense of duty to one's family members.

modernization theory — The view that the more highly industrialized or urbanized a society, the lower the status of the elderly.

reasoned that cultural values may have a greater influence on respect for and status of the elderly than does social change. That is, a tradition of reverence for the aged may be more important than modernization. Further, more recent research by Abel (1992) indicates that rural elders in the nineteenth century United States did not necessarily enjoy high status. This erodes part of the assumption upon which modernization theory is based.

Respect for people in many societies, such as our own, might also be said to be largely a function of economics: we gauge status for the most part by relative income. Poor people get little respect; rich people get a lot of it, almost regardless of their personal qualities. If this is so, we might see the relative status of the aged as having improved in recent decades as their relative economic position has improved.

Role Transitions

Passuth and Bengtson (1988) note the inability of any of these sociological theories of aging to adequately explain the scope of the social relationships of older people. They call for research that views aging through a combination of two or more perspectives, or the development of multi-disciplinary theories of aging. They say that another fruitful approach might be to look at the social context of aging. The implication is that social theories have in the past given us little practical information about the ways that older people live their lives. Passuth and Bengtson point to the work of Rosow (1974), who writes that aging is characterized by a loss of social status, roles, and norms. Lacking status and roles in later life, older people can thus be seen to be in a "roleless role." By contrast, they then note that Hochschild (1973), in her research among a group of elderly widows living in an apartment complex, found that the women did not face this bleak picture of old age at all. Not only were they not "roleless," they appeared to take on many new and satisfying roles as they formed a community within their environment: " . . . these women live busy, purposeful lives within their group. She found an elaborate set of newly defined social roles and experiences among the women, which included numerous norms regarding appropriate social behavior" (Passuth & Bengtson, 1988, p. 349). That is, this group of people in a transitional context did not have to grope for new status or roles; they developed them. Being without appropriate roles or status was not a problem.

This may force us to view aging within a social context as more complex than what any one theory encompasses (Lynott & Lynott, 1996). We might look at aging as a series of transitions. Roles and statuses may be discarded as people leave one period of life and enter another. The giving up of a treasured status such as "worker" is often traumatic. In the practical context of retirement, Palmore and his colleagues looked at six longitudinal data sets to see if people actually have problems when they face the role transition of retirement (Palmore, Fillenbaum, & George, 1984). They found that there indeed was a period of adjustment as well as some decline in income at the time of retirement, but that retirement could not be found to explain any health differences, to have any major effects on social activity, or to have much influence on life satisfaction or happiness.

In other words, this theoretical problem when viewed in context turns out to be not much of a problem at all. For some individuals, of course, there is a significant disruption when they retire. But, for the broad groups studied, it did not seem to be a crisis. Just as Hochschild did not find old widows wandering about roleless, Palmore and his research team did not find the loss of the work role to have much of an effect on social interaction or life satisfaction. From a practical standpoint, we can ask individuals if retirement is a particular problem for them, rather than assume that it is for all retirees in general.

To return to role theory, we might think of later life not so much as a period of role loss as a period of role transition. Particularly with an issue like aging, we have a time to get ready to shed old roles and statuses or to assume new ones. With the exception of widowhood, a special concern that we will deal with more in later chapters, few role changes come suddenly. (And with the death of a spouse, there often is an opportunity to use anticipation; many people expect the inevitable to happen, and when it comes it is no surprise.) Those who are facing later life have ample opportunity to prepare psychologically. They have received warning signs of physical deterioration throughout middle age. They have seen examples of others older than themselves and how they have coped with the transitions that come with the aging process. Many aging people are masters of adaptation: they have seen many changes in their lives, and the gradual changes associated with aging are taken pretty much in stride.

Questions for Discussion

1. Make up a list of terms commonly descriptive of older people. Are they mostly positive or negative?
2. What are several behaviors that would be considered to be non-normative for the elderly?
3. In the case of the 80-year-old wanting to marry his 27-year-old nurse, what can the family do about it?
4. In a practical application of exchange theory between younger and older people, what gets exchanged? Is it usually an equal trade off?
5. What is your own ideal for yourself as an older person? Do you think this may change any as you get older?
6. Cite some examples of people you know who you think are disengaged. For the most part, are they happy or satisfied with life?

7. Do you see the aged as a sub-culture?
8. What adult roles might you be unwilling to give up when you are old?
9. What filial obligations do you feel for older persons in your own family?
10. What history-normative events will influence your own generation that makes it unique from other generations?

Sources of Further Information

The material in this chapter, unlike that in Chapter 1, deals mostly with theory, with research that either supports or conflicts with theory, or with findings that are the basis for development of new ways of looking at society and the elderly. For this reason, articles in scholarly journals are probably the best sources of further information on these topics. In addition to the sources mentioned in the References, here are a few recent articles that might give the reader additional places to look for information on aging and socialization. Obviously, this is not a comprehensive list; it merely represents a place to go to begin finding further information:

Byrd, M., & Breuss, T. (1992). Perceptions of sociological and psychological age norms by young, middle-aged, and elderly New Zealanders. *International Journal of Aging and Human Development, 34,* 145–165.

Ferraro, K. F. (1992). Cohort changes in images of older adults, 1974-1981. *The Gerontologist, 32,* 296–304.

Giles, H., Coupland, N., Coupland, J., Williams, A., & Nussbaum, J. (1992). Intergenerational talk and communication with older people. *International Journal of Aging and Human Development, 34,* 271–297.

Hendricks, J. (1992). Generations and the generation of theory in social gerontology. *International Journal of Aging and Human Development, 35,* 31–47.

Hoskins, I. (1992, March). Gender, aging and development: Emerging issues and policy recommendations. *Aging International, 19,* 12–19.

Ingersoll-Dayton, B., & Talbott, M. M. (1992). Assessments of social support exchanges: Cognitions of the old-old. *International Journal of Aging and Human Development, 35,* 125–143.

Jette, A. M., Tennstedt, S. L., & Branch, L. G. (1992). Stability of informal long-term care. *Journal of Aging and Health, 4,* 193–211.

Krause, N., Herzog, A. R., & Baker, E. (1992). Providing support to others and well-being in later life. *Journal of Gerontology: Psychological Sciences, 47,* P300–P311.

Lynott, P. P., & Roberts, R. E. L. (1997). The developmental stake hypothesis and changing perceptions of intergenerational relations, 1971–1985. *The Gerontologist, 37,* 394–405.

Nelson, E. A., & Dannefer, D. (1992). Aged heterogeneity: Fact or fiction? The fate of diversity in gerontological research. *The Gerontologist, 32,* 17–23.

Okun, M. A., & Keith, V. M. (1998). Effects of positive and negative social exchanges with various sources on depressive symptoms in younger and older adults. *Journal of Gerontology: Psychological Sciences, 53B,* P4–P20.

Shi, L. (1993). Family financial and household support exchange between generations: A survey of Chinese rural elderly. *The Gerontologist, 33,* 468–480.

Stolar, G.E., MacEntee, M.I., & Hill, P. (1993). The elderly: Their perceived supports and reciprocal behaviors. *Journal of Gerontological Social Work, 19*(3–4), 15–33.

Older People and Their Families

3

Chapter Outline

"Yet in those days, families and societies still held together, and the old,
if they survived in good physical shape, had their roles as elders in the
family and community, dispensing wisdom which increasingly fewer
people chose to hear, but at least respected and cared for as if their lives
had a meaning for those around them."

—George Woodcock, born 1912

Introduction

By far, the greatest amount of the care that is given to older people is delivered by family members. There is no greater illustration of the exchange
theory of aging than what we can see around us every day with example
after example of older wives caring for their husbands, husbands caring for
their wives, sons and daughters caring for their parents and grandparents,
and so on. Whether it is a service so simple as stopping by the store for
someone, or as all-encompassing as caring for an Alzheimer's patient for

the rest of his or her life, family members perform countless acts of service for old people. This care goes both directions: it has been found that the primary beneficiary of extended households is the adult child (Speare & Avery, 1993).

Some may perform the services they do out of an expectation of some type of reward or repayment—a clear example of the exchange theory of aging. Actually getting payment or expecting an inheritance may happen less frequently than getting some kind of a psychic reward, feeling good for performing good deeds, getting praise and high regard from others, or simply "building up credits" in the expectation that in the broad scheme of things, they will eventually be repaid. Most people have little expectation of any tangible reward for the services they provide for family members. Rather, they help their loved ones because of a sense of filial obligation, the notion that they are supposed to help them merely because that is the way that members of a family behave.

This family feeling is the cement that holds civilizations together. Call it support for the group, tribal loyalty, family obligation, or norms and values of a culture, the interpersonal regard and care provided within families is among the most important factors in human relationships. As a general rule, in the field of social gerontology, we can say that people in late life who have families seem to do better in many ways than those who are without families. When family systems break down and caregivers under too great a strain get to the end of their rope, the outcome can be abuse and neglect, issues of such importance that we will devote all of Chapter 12 to them. And we will see in Chapter 4 that some ethnic and cultural groups have such strong family bonds that they tend to not call upon public agencies for help in caring for their aged. In the present chapter, we will look at family environments, widowhood and the family life cycle, living arrangements, the need for intimacy, relations of older persons with their adult children and *siblings*, grandparenting, and parent care and the older adult

Families and History

Following an historical life course perspective, it can be seen that one important issue relating to families and aging is the concept of different cohorts moving through time. The events of the times will be different for each cohort and will have a different impact on each cohort as it moves along in time. That is, historical events that occur in families' lives and the changing *zeitgeist*, or spirit of the times, will often have an influence on the ways that families interact. Thus, we should not necessarily expect families to all act a certain way; social networks and patterns of family interaction might be expected to change over time.

This can occur at various levels: for example, on a personal level, one can see the different ways a family might react if the mother dies and the oldest sibling assumes child-rearing responsibilities. That oldest sibling may still be acting (or may still be expected to act) like a mother or a father to their younger brothers and sisters many years later. A personal historical circumstance, then, could be seen to affect a particular family. The members probably behave somewhat differently from those in other families because of it. These individual historical happenings that color the interaction patterns of families are both pretty common and, by their nature, somewhat distinctive.

At a different level, we might look at commonalities of families that have all experienced the same historical events. During wartime, for example, it would be possible to identify all families that had lost children. Although they have much in common, they are somewhat different when compared to other families or other generations that have not had such experiences. A different example might be found among a generation of immigrants. They have certain commonalities one might expect: difficulty in adapting to the new language and customs, establishing ways of making a living, and so on. There are also certain commonalities among the children of immigrants. So, there are a variety of perspectives from which to view family interaction.

An historical life-course perspective would emphasize that values and norms change over time and are influenced by the events surrounding the family. In other words, the ways our parents related to our grandparents probably differed in some ways from the ways we now relate to our parents or the ways our children will relate to us. Times change, and changing fashions and events have some influence upon the ways we live.

As an illustration, not so many years ago, many men were commonly heard to say, "No wife of mine will ever work." The expectation of the time—well up into the 1950s and '60s—was that the woman's place was in the home. And, the norm of the 1950s was caring for the children; three, four, or five children (or more) made up the typical family unit, along with married parents. There were other dominant values: divorce was seen as a kind of disgrace, and people who weren't married didn't live together—at least nice people didn't. Same-sex partnerships were out of the question. Gay and lesbian companions really never felt comfortable coming out.

These elements of family dynamics seem to offer sharp differences from the perspective of the new century. Much has changed in fifty years, of course, and the ways that family members interact have to have changed as a result of these value differences affecting societal norms. It seems, however, that few of the changes in family dynamics over the past several decades have influenced the fundamental ways in which families interact with their elders. That is, it is difficult to identify how recent historical events might have made much of a change in how older and younger family members get along.

Historical events over several lifetimes are perhaps a source of greater change. Probably the most important historical change to have influenced most North American families has been immigration. The United States and Canada are immigrant nations made up of a melting pot (or crazy quilt) of people with ancestors from all over the world. Joining the original residents of the continent, the Native American peoples, have been wave after wave of new arrivals from Europe, Africa, Asia, and Latin America. Adapting to the ways of the new country, and perhaps learning a new language, provided a potent opportunity to abandon or change cultural values and

---

Illustration 3.1. History-Normative Events

It is hard for us to look back much beyond World War II and the Great Depression, historical events that shaped the values of the current cohort of older individuals. We need to remember, however, that great historical events influenced their grandparents. Perhaps the greatest in the history of the United States was the Civil War. Following is an excerpt from a letter written by a young man on the battlefield at Iuka, Mississippi, to his sister back home in Ohio.

Dear Sister,   Sept. 24, 1862
    I seat myself this evening by the cook's candle to answer your kind letter which came to hand last night just at Tattoo. I wrote one yesterday to father and mother. I was waiting for an answer but thought that I would write while I had an opportunity, knowing that you would be apt to hear of the Battle soon and perhaps would be anxious to hear from me.
    Well, Ann, I have seen some of the horrors of war last Thursday morning. We started again in the direction of Iuka. None of us except some of the head officers knew exactly where we were going, but we apprehended that there was something to be done in the shape of a fight. We are getting pretty well used to laying out. We haven't slept in tents but one night since we left Bear Creek.
    Last Friday the 19th about one o'clock we began to find out where Hamilton's forces made the attack. We soon began to hear a few mountain Howitzers open, and then came up within a mile of the battlefield and was ordered to rest. We lay there where we could hear the roar of muskets that sounded like pouring potatoes into an empty barrel. I can not describe my feelings while laying there. It is given up to be the most unpleasant position that man can have in time of battle as far as feeling is concerned. We were double-quicked directly onto the field and drawn up in line of battle, and then I began to feel different. I felt that I would as leave fight as anything else.
    The fight was short, but it was what might be called a regular pitched battle while it lasted. The 11th Ohio battery was captured and retaken again, which caused a heavy loss on both sides. We have learned that about 500 will cover our loss killed, wounded and missing, but the Rebel loss is greater. It is said that not much less than a 1000 will cover their loss. We have reasons to believe this because they were not as well armed as our men, and they also came up in line six deep, and of course would suffer more. They left in the night in a great hurry. Some left their knapsacks and a great many tents. I picked up some writing paper and will finish my letter on it to show you.

    Robert Morral, who wrote this after the Battle of Iuka, was killed the following month from wounds received at the Battle of Corinth. He was 21 years of age.

norms. As a general rule, older immigrants might be seen as less than enthusiastic to see their children and grandchildren adopt new, American values at the expense of traditional customs associated with the old country. We will examine these concepts in more detail in Chapter 4.

Other historical events characterize cohorts of people as they move through history, and they must also have some important influences on family relationships. The industrialization and consequent urbanization of the United States that took place between the time of the Civil War and World War II was an historical phenomenon of great importance. The country went from a nation of farmers to a population that mostly lived in cities. Family life was affected in many ways by this historical trend, and the ways people interacted with their aged members must have been affected as well. There would have been a change, for example, in the traditional tension of who would inherit the family's land, or how the farm might be divided to provide a living for adult children and surviving elders. And big families would no longer have been an economic necessity. Having lots of children on the farm meant more hands to work the fields; in the city, a large family usually meant tighter quarters and more mouths to feed with few economic benefits.

There has been a steady decline in family size over the course of the past century, especially after the introduction of the birth control pill in the early 1960s, and there will be a corresponding change in future relationships between younger and older family members. For one thing, because there has been a decline in average family size over the past four decades, there will be fewer available adult child caretakers for the aged in the future. On the other hand, due to unprecedented mortality decline, there are correspondingly more people than ever before who have surviving parents, spouses, siblings, children, and grandparents (Uhlenberg, 1996).

Other historical facts of life have influenced generations of older Americans. The migration of African Americans from the Deep South to the cities of the North is an example. And for the cohort of people who are now old, living through the Great Depression of 1929 to 1940 and the war years of 1941 to 1945 had profound influences. Movement of younger city dwellers to the suburbs could also be seen as having important consequences for older people, as there has been a tendency for the aged to remain in cities. We are starting to see the aging of suburban communities.

Among generations now still alive, a number of historical events have occurred that may color the way they view relationships between the old and the young. Migration, wars, economic depressions, and more personal historical events no doubt have much influence on the ways generations interact. In the broad picture over many generations, however, one must recognize that there really has not been a great deal of change in intergenerational relations. That is, taking an historical life course perspective, we might see that adult children and their older parents have always faced the same issues of nurture and mutual responsibility. Given that current public health advances have allowed more people to live into late life,

intimacy from a distance — The desired situation of most older people: to live near their children, not with them.

this merely means that more families are confronted with what to do about Mom or Dad. Worries over income, housing, inheritance, health maintenance, and personal control have not changed substantively over the generations; the details are merely different.

There may be too much of a tendency to romanticize "the good old days" when three or four generations lived in big old Victorian houses, when people for some reason were all hard-working, respected their elders, and kept their noses clean. These stereotypes play well at the movies, but they have little basis in fact. Objective assessments of families in prior years indicate a much higher degree of poverty, for instance. The stately Victorian homes that have been preserved to the present day were certainly not the residences of the masses but only of a small minority of wealthy people. The dugouts, sod huts, shanties, lean-tos, and slums that most people were forced to live in were not worth preserving; they were torn down or collapsed years ago.

In fact, there never was an era when most people lived in three-generational households. There may have been an economic necessity, particularly during the Great Depression, for several generations to live together, but that was not the choice of any of the generations. "The great extended families that became part of the folklore of modern industrial society were rarely in existence" (Hareven, 1992, p. 7). When economics and the availability of housing allowed it, the ideal has consistently been *intimacy from a distance*: older people want to live near their adult chil-

---

Illustration 3.2. Historical Perspectives on the Aging Family

"The evidence from a broad range of 14th and 15th-century English sources indicates a considerable tension between the young and the old. The young were desirous of gaining control of the family resources while the old wished to secure care and comfort. In the absence of a binding cultural norm of devoting family resources to caring for the aged, such as is found in China, English peasants resorted to contracts and wills when they doubted that their families would provide adequate care. How one fared in such contract negotiations depended then, as now, on the personal resources one had amassed in a lifetime. Peasants with land and goods could negotiate for their care either with kin or with other parties. Those with nothing depended on private charity. Retirement arrangements were flexible. The aged persons showed a marked preference for staying in their own homes even if it meant that they would have to share it with nonkin. But sharing a home was a choice imposed by economics and not by preference. In addition to anxieties about material comfort in old age, peasants worried about their funeral and prayers for their soul. Again, rather than trusting to family completely for these offices, they formed voluntary associations—surrogate family—that would ensure safe passage through the hereafter."

From Hanawalt (1986), used by permission of the author.

---

dren, but not with them. This has not changed over time. What has changed is relative prosperity and the ability to afford separate dwellings.

The historical trend is a gradual weakening of mutual assistance of kin. This is consistent with the observation above that we are already feeling the influence of the smaller families that emerged as the fashion thirty or forty years ago. Fewer adult family members are now available to care for elders, and this will especially be the case in the future with the maturing of families that have had one or no children. One can only hope that pension savings and personal wealth among the childless elderly of future years will be sufficient to allow them to purchase services from surrogate kin.

Family Status and Living Arrangements

The great majority of people live with others throughout their lives. This has been a fact across the course of history and is pretty much universal. The unfortunate correlate, however, is the implication that people who live alone are somehow odd or different. Because it is expected, living with others has assumed the status of a norm; thus, those who live alone for some reason are seen as somehow not being normal. Single people at all ages might testify to this rather irritating fact of life. In only one age cohort, however, does an actual majority live alone: women aged 75 and above.

An unhappy fact of biology that will be discussed in the Chapter 5 is that men's lives are, on the average, about 10% shorter than women's. And most women who marry usually marry a man several years their senior. The result is normative widowhood. Although it certainly is not necessary in North American society to live the traditional life of marriage to a person of the opposite sex throughout adult life, most people in fact do live that way. And, most women in later life are widows: the percentage of women who are widows climbs from 12.6% of the group aged 55 to 64, to 32.8% of those aged 65 to 74, and it reaches 63.6% for women aged 75 years and older (U.S. Bureau of the Census, 1998b).

Most people consider widows to be at a disadvantage in dealing with a society where being married seems to be the ideal norm. Many widows testify that they lose contact over time with friends who still are coupled. This sometimes leaves them with the impression that they either are no longer desirable companions or that through widowhood they have achieved a status that is somewhat akin to second class citizenship. And, of course, widows also must cope with bereavement.

As we can see in Table 3.1, the majority of men and women in the middle years are married. Of interest, though, this certainly does not apply to all men and women. The percentage of men who are married peaks out at 79.9 for those aged 55 to 64; obviously, 20.1% are in categories other than married. The greatest percentage of women who are married is 72.2%,

Table 3.1. Marital Status by Age—Percentages

	Single	Married	Widowed	Divorced
Male				
18–19 years old	97.5	2.4	—	0.2
20–24 years old	83.0	15.6	0.1	1.4
25–29 years old	51.5	44.2	0.1	4.2
30–34 years old	30.3	61.1	0.2	8.5
35–39 years old	19.2	69.8	0.2	10.7
40–44 years old	15.3	71.5	0.3	12.9
45–54 years old	8.6	76.2	1.0	14.2
55–64 years old	5.8	79.9	3.2	11.0
65–74 years old	4.3	79.1	9.4	7.3
75 years and over	3.7	66.7	25.4	4.2
Female				
18–19 years old	92.2	7.5	0.1	0.2
20–24 years old	70.3	27.0	0.2	2.4
25–29 years old	38.4	55.3	0.3	6.0
30–34 years old	19.6	70.1	0.5	9.8
35–39 years old	13.5	72.2	0.9	13.3
40–44 years old	10.2	72.2	1.7	16.2
45–54 years old	7.1	71.6	3.8	17.5
55–64 years old	4.7	67.1	13.2	15.0
65–74 years old	4.2	53.5	33.2	9.2
75 years and over	4.5	28.8	61.5	5.2

Source: U.S. Bureau of the Census (1998b).

at 45 to 54 years of age. The percentage of men who are married remains at a high level of 79.9% well into old age, and it only drops to 66.7% by age 75. In contrast, the percentage of married women drops to 53.5% in the years 65 to 74 and on down to 28.8% in the group 75 and older. Note that the Table lists current marital status, not the rates of "ever married" or "ever divorced."

Obviously, there is a greater tendency for widowed and divorced males to remarry. Only 1% of all women's marriages take place after age 65, and only a tenth of one percent of all women's first marriages take place after that age. Of those widows who remarry, the average age is fairly young: 54.0 years. Older widows are not very likely to remarry. And there are about five times more widows than widowers.

In terms of living arrangements of persons in later life, the clear trend has been toward increasing home ownership over the years. About 80% of the elderly own their own homes; this declines from 82% at age 65 to 74 to 78% at age 75 and older. The percentage living alone goes from 24% at ages 65 to 74 to about 41% of those aged 75+; correspondingly, the percent living with a spouse at those ages declines from 64% to 41%, respectively. Fewer than 13% of those 65 to 74 live with people other than their spouses; this increases to 18% by age 75 (U.S. Bureau of the Census, 1997).

Associated with these concepts is the increasing freedom older persons now have in their living arrangements compared to earlier generations. The number of older people living alone has increased during recent decades; this is because more and more older people are financially well-off enough to live by themselves. Fewer are dependent on family members for housing or support. Widows increasingly have assets and pensions of their own; fewer are forced to depend only on what their husbands left them. Social Security payments have increased substantially since regular cost-of-living increases began in the early 1970s; this has contributed greatly to the ability of older persons to afford independent living.

Also associated with this freedom, the current generation of older persons are unlike their parents and grandparents in that there is less reliance on kin for assistance. If more and more older people live in their own household, there of course will be fewer day-to-day contacts with family members they might rely upon for assistance. And although researchers have shown that family members remain the greatest source of help for older persons (Brody, Litvin, Albert, & Hoffman, 1994), it has been observed that "The erosion of mutual assistance among kin has tended to increase insecurity and isolation as people age" (Hareven, 1992, p. 9). Another factor that has changed is that more adult daughters work than was the case in previous years. One study, however, has shown that working and non-working adult daughters provide about the same number of hours of assistance to their mothers. The difference comes in terms of less personal care and cooking on the part of working daughters; this is compensated for by purchased help: "Employed and non-working daughters provided equal amounts of help with shopping, transportation, household tasks, managing money, service arrangement, and emotional support" (Brody & Schoonover, 1986, p. 378).

Gay and Lesbian Aged

When discussing family status and living arrangements of the elderly, we also need to recognize that not all families are necessarily made up of people who are related. It has been said that "love makes a family," and there is a meaningful number of homosexual people among older Americans. Of nonfamily households among those over 65 years of age, about 5% of males and 2% of females live with a non-relative (U.S. Bureau of the Census, 1997). Not all of these instances represent gay partnerships, of course, and not all homosexual older persons live with another individual. We in fact have few reliable figures on the extent of same-sex partnerships in later life. Estimates range from 2% to about 10% of older persons (Dorfman, Walters, Burke, Hardin, Karanik, Raphael, & Silverstein, 1995; Quam & Whitford, 1992; Wojciechowski, 1998). However, this is an area that has only recently been researched, and the literature on homosexual aging remains sparse.

Much of the research on gay men and women focuses on younger persons. And much of the research on the aged fails to acknowledge sexu-

"The most obvious lifestyle difference is that among gay people, friendship networks assume equal or greater importance than kinship networks. This is extremely important for service providers and planners to understand.

Most laws, statutes, protocols, and societal norms do not recognize the legal or social standing of same-sex relationships. With few exceptions, neither sociology nor law yet recognize the reality of homosexuality. This social and legal invisibility makes it easy, even inevitable, that human service providers would overlook the presence of this population. Some consequences:

- Mental health care can be totally off track and even dangerous if all clients are presumed to be heterosexual.
- Community services will alienate and therefore fail to serve gay men and lesbians if they are not made—explicitly—to feel welcome.
- Social workers will not be able to discern a bereaved widow/widower behind the mask of someone who has just lost a 'roommate' of 40 years and will probably assume that the client has a 'housing' problem."

From Freedman (1995).

ality, either heterosexual or homosexual. There has been little research on the aged as yet that would challenge popular stereotypes.

Societal attitudes toward homosexuality may combine with negative images of the aged to result in what has been seen among the minority aged: double or triple jeopardy (Kehoe, 1986). In fact, many of the characteristics of minority groups that we will discuss in the next chapter might be applied to homosexual elders. In some ways they are treated as a subculture and are subject to prejudice and discrimination. One nurse-researcher notes that some of the implications of these issues are rejection by adult children and grandchildren, poor quality of care in long-term care settings, and discrimination in housing (Wojciechowski, 1998). In terms of age cohorts, it may be the case that fewer gay and lesbian aged persons have been willing to come out of the closet and publicly acknowledge their sexual orientation; that may be something younger individuals are more likely to do.

There is some indication in the literature that integration into the gay and lesbian community has positive outcomes for many aged persons who might otherwise become isolated (Berger, 1982). Family support system and kinship networks are enhanced by friends. This, however, may be more true of older lesbians than among gay men. One study of 241 gay men in Los Angeles found that social participation dropped dramatically in later life (Kelly, 1977).

The Los Angeles study, however, was done prior to the widespread knowledge of the danger of AIDS. There is some evidence that gay men have had a greater tendency to form partnership relationships in recent years in response to the prevalence of AIDS, and that these single-partner liaisons may well endure into later life.

A more recent study in Minneapolis of both gay men and lesbians found about half of the total respondents of both sexes under 60 and half over 60 years of age shared households. However, the tendency to share housing was somewhat higher among the women: 63% of the men lived alone, compared to 41% of the women. Of those sharing a household, 70% of the lesbians had a partner, compared to 40% of the gay men. Of those of both sexes who were 60 years of age or older, 25.8% reported being separated or widowed from a same-sex relationship, and about 20% were separated or widowed from a heterosexual marriage. Interestingly, 6.5% of the older respondents reported currently being in a heterosexual marriage. Of the older respondents, 66.7% reported having children. In terms of overall satisfaction, the data indicated that the older lesbians seemed to be happier and less lonely than were the older gay men (Quam & Whitford, 1992).

The Need for Intimacy

A considerable body of research has been done on the need for an intimate relationship with another person in later life. This does not necessarily have

---

Illustration 3.4. Older Gay Men

"The sex life of the older man in the Los Angeles study is, characteristically, quite satisfactory, and he desires sexual contact with adult men, especially those near his own age. He is not, however, currently involved in a gay liaison (an emotional and sexual relationship of one year or longer). Of those in the 50–65 age bracket, 50 percent reported satisfactory sex lives; 83 percent of the respondents over age 65 report being sexually satisfied. Content analysis of interviews with older gays indicates that the majority of older interviewees are sexually interested and satisfied in relationships with, or are attracted toward, adult men—oftentimes men in their own age cohort. The number of persons involved in liaisons seems to increase with age, peaking with 59 percent of those 46 to 55 years old being members of gay partnerships. After this apex, partnerships decrease to almost none. Two reasons for this decline often mentioned by older gays were the death of the loved one and the rejection of the notion of having a single life-long lover.

The typical older man in this study neither considers himself effeminate nor likes to define himself in terms of gay age labels, but he remembers the terms that were commonly applied to 'older gays' when he was younger."

From Kelly (1977).

to be a physically intimate relationship; rather, psychological intimacy with a *significant other* seems to be primary. Of greatest importance is the presence of a *confidant,* a person in whom one can confide. A confidant is a trusted other who will listen to one's most intimate and important concerns. Those who have a confidant relationship seem to do much better in later life, particularly in terms of life satisfaction and mental health.

The research on intimacy and isolation in later life was begun by the late Marjorie Fiske Lowenthal (1964; Lowenthal & Haven, 1968). She drew two samples to study: 534 persons aged 60 and above who were first-time admissions to mental hospitals, and 600 people in the same age group in a stratified random sample from the community. Her objective was to determine the extent to which isolation contributed to mental illness and lower morale.

She asked the first group to list or tell her the number of their social contacts two weeks prior to the event of hospitalization; the group that had remained in the community was asked to indicate the number of contacts they had had two weeks prior to their interview. She divided respondents into three categories: pure isolates (those with very few social contacts—urban hermits), semi-isolates (those with a few but essentially a very small number of social contacts, most of which were superficial), and interacters (persons with a high number of meaningful social contacts).

In the hospitalized group, she was able to identify 52 pure isolates, 50 semi-isolates, and 30 interacters for study (the remaining subjects did not fall clearly into any of these categories). She was also able to identify 30 pure isolates and 417 interacters in the community group. About 75% of the isolates were men, while about 75% of the interacters were women. The isolates were four times more likely to be single than others in the population, and 79% were in the lowest socioeconomic group.

A first conclusion that might be drawn from these data is that although pure and semi-isolates in the hospitalized group outnumbered those in corresponding categories in the community group by a ratio of more than three to one, we cannot conclude that all isolates are going to have emotional problems or that all people with high levels of social interaction are necessarily going to be mentally healthy. Isolation, then, is perhaps a correlate of mental illness, but we can't really say that it's a cause of mental illness. More than 5% of the hospitalized group had high levels of interaction with others prior to hospitalization, and 5% of the group remaining in the community consisted of pure isolates. However, we might conclude that people with low levels of social contact with others are more vulnerable to mental problems than are the people who remain integrated into the social fabric and have frequent contacts.

In order to get a clearer picture of the apparent relationship between isolation and mental illness, one would have to investigate the quality of the individual's social interactions as well as the life-long patterns of isolation or integration. Lowenthal did this in a follow-up study four years later with 280 surviving subjects from the earlier research (Lowenthal & Haven,

1968). The first observation was that social isolation seems to increase sharply at about age 75; more of the isolates in this older age group were women who had become widowed. Four patterns of isolation were identified:

Pure isolates

- *The lifelong alienated;* mostly single men who had never attempted to become integrated into society. They represented 28% of the sample; most were alcoholics, and the majority were living in skid-row flop houses.
- *The defeated;* lifelong marginal isolates who had tried and failed to make a place for themselves in society. They represented 24% of the sample; two-thirds of them were men.

Semi-isolates

- *Chronic blamers;* 20% of the group, almost all of whom were single or divorced and had only casual or superficial contacts with others in society.
- *Late isolates* made up the remainder; half of them were over age 80 and a majority were women. About two-thirds were widows who had no children.

Out of the total sample of 280 in the follow-up study, 112 had some form of psychiatric impairment and 60% were depressed. Social losses, such as widowhood, were clearly related to poor morale. An important differentiation, though, must be made here: "Lifelong isolates tend to have average or better morale and to be no more prone to hospitalization for mental illness in old age than anyone else, but those who have tried and failed to establish social relationships appear particularly vulnerable" (Lowenthal & Haven, 1968, p. 108).

It appears, then, that lifelong isolates do not have a higher rate of mental illness, whereas people who become isolated have much higher rates of depression and emotional distress. In other words, people who have been alone all of their lives have adapted to a solitary existence and have no particular adaptation to make in this regard in later life. Those who are used to the presence of others and with interacting with others, though, have an especially hard time accepting the loss of those contacts in later life.

A confidant is a person one can tell one's troubles to, a close, trusted friend or relative who is near at hand and willing to listen. A man's confidant is most often his wife, if he has one. A woman's confidant could be her husband, but is as likely to be an older daughter, a sister, or a close personal friend. The majority (69%) of the mentally healthy persons in

Lowenthal's study had a confidant, while only 31% of the emotionally impaired group had one. The concept of loss is important. It was concluded that the majority of those who lost a confidant were depressed, and the great majority of those who kept one were not depressed.

The implication is that the presence of an intimate relationship serves as a buffer against the forces of isolation. It appears that people who become isolated are quite vulnerable, whereas those who have always been loners perceive no particular change in this regard as they get older. In summary, it is the loss of interaction that causes the problem. People who have at least one close, intimate relationship with another person are better off, since the confidant acts as insulation against social loss. Having a single confidant is as good as having many relationships. Those who maintain a confidant relationship are much less likely to become depressed.

It is clear that family and kin contacts are important sources of confidant relationships, especially among those who are widowed or divorced. Those who have few kin relationships or who have alienated their families are at particular risk in later life. This may be especially true for men, who tend to have smaller social networks, perhaps have greater problems in expressing emotional intimacy, and who have a harder time replacing confidant relationships once they are lost. A number of epidemiological studies have shown that persons without social ties have significantly higher death rates (Berkman & Syme, 1979; Seeman, Kaplan, Knudsen, Cohen, & Guralnik, 1987; Steinbach, 1992). Interestingly, these studies have found marriage to have primary importance for those under age 60, but that friends and relatives assume greater importance for those aged 60 and above. Again, the socially isolated were found to be much worse off than those with close social ties.

Relationships with Adult Children

The sociologists' ideal of a family life cycle, in which the family begins at marriage of two unrelated individuals and develops over time with the birth

---

Illustration 3.5. Confidants

"It is clear that if you have a confidant, you can decrease your social interaction and run no greater risk of becoming depressed than if you had increased it. Further, if you have no confidant, you may increase your social activities and yet be far more likely to be depressed than the individual who has a confidant but has lowered his interaction level."

From Lowenthal and Haven (1968).

and growth of children who ultimately leave the nest prior to the death of one of the parents, is exactly that, an ideal norm. As we begin the twenty-first century, the notion of a family life cycle that can be generalized is increasingly less apt. Many people who are never married have children, many others marry and divorce several times, a significant proportion of American children are raised in single-parent households, and many adult children return to the nest for a time after their own divorce. The patterns are too complex to generalize, and the concept of a traditional family's life cycle is becoming less and less useful.

Given that it is increasingly difficult to generalize about the cycles gone through by most families, it still cannot be denied that the family is the most important social unit for almost the entire population (Atchley, 2000). Whatever the complexities and variations the configurations of families take, our basic identity derives from our family relationships. And the most essential relationship for just about everyone is between children and their parents. Usually, the parent-child unit is called a *nuclear family*—it forms a nucleus from which all other family relationships derive. Extending from the nuclear family are a host of relationships with uncles and aunts, cousins, friends, grandparents, and other kin; this is called the *extended family*. It has been argued that with industrialization the old concept of an agrarian extended family—many generations and many relatives living together or near to one another—has broken down, and the nuclear family is now predominant. Obligations to members of our extended family have declined because they may live in all different parts of the country and we seldom see them. We may have cousins we've never even met. Still, although we may not feel any special kinship obligations to aunts, uncles, and cousins, the relationships between parents and their children remain strong.

This is certainly the case with aged parents and their adult children. Although it is not unusual for children to relocate to different places, and for aged parents to live close to only one of their children, most adults still look upon relationships with their parents as primary. One might lose track of a few cousins, but it's most unlikely that one would lose track of a mother. The strong social bond between most parents and children lasts a lifetime. Frequent contacts between aged parents and their adult children, either through personal visits or, more likely, through telephone conversations, is the statistical norm. A problem area, however, is that about 20% of the elderly are childless, and there is some evidence that the independence now enjoyed by most older persons may be leading, at least in very late life, to their increasing isolation.

An often-quoted study in the field of gerontology was published by Ethel Shanas and her colleagues (1968). About two-thirds of the older persons interviewed in that study said they had seen at least one of their adult children during the 24 hours preceding the interview. About 80% lived within 30 minutes or less travel time from at least one adult child. By 1984, the percentage living within 30 minutes of one child had declined to 66% (AARP, 1998a). In a 1975 research study, Shanas found in a representative sample of 4,553 older persons who had children that only 53% had seen a child within the previous 24 hours. Of those who had children who had not seen one of them within the previous week, 58% had not seen a sibling (a brother or a sister) either. This percentage was 39% among the childless; they evidently have a greater motivation to keep in contact with siblings. Apparently, over 39% of the total sample either had no children or had not seen one of their children during the previous week (Shanas, 1979).

In a more recent study, a colleague and I surveyed a random sample of 500 older residents of Nebraska (Thorson & Powell, 1993b). Almost all of these people were in their 70s or 80s and lived independently in their own residences. They received a mean number of visits from family members of 2.37 per week, but 30% had not received a visit from a family member during the previous week, and 42% had not gone to visit a family member. About 31% had not visited friends, and 26.4% had not been visited by a friend during the previous week. Telephone visiting was more frequent: only 17% had not phoned a family member the previous week, and only 14% had not received a phone call from a family member. About 10% had not received a phone call from a friend.

So, it is evident that most older persons interact socially with family and friends on a regular basis. There remains, however, a core of between 10 and 20% who apparently have little social contact with others, family or friends. These isolated persons generally have greater needs, are more likely to be institutionalized, and they have a higher mortality rate (Seeman et al., 1987). They are also much more likely to enter a nursing home. Freedman (1996) found that those who are socially connected, especially with family members, had lower rates of institutionalization. Married older persons have about half of the risk of nursing home admission in comparison to unmarried persons. Having at least one daughter or sibling reduces an

---

Illustration 3.6. Principle of Substitution a Myth

"By comparing involvement with relatives among the childless unmarried, the unmarried with children, and the married with children, we find little evidence that the principle of substitution operates. For those without a spouse and children, or at least one child in the area, siblings and relatives do not usually become substitutes. Most contemporaries of the respondents, particularly those from their family of orientation, their siblings and cousins, are deceased. In some families, the sibling bond was not strong enough to persist on a close-knit basis after marriage and the formation of families of procreation. Often, too, with the passage of time, links to siblings' children did not persist after the siblings' death."

From Johnson and Troll (1992).

older adult's chances of nursing home admission by about one quarter.

In a study of the oldest old, those 85 and above, it was found that there were widely diverse patterns of family interaction and help from adult children (Johnson & Troll, 1992). Many of those studied were widows or had never married, lived alone, or had no surviving child living nearby. Apparently, there was a risk among the very old of outliving their families. About one-third of those studied had a family member who served as a caregiver and another 35% had one available if needed. The remaining 29% had no one available to meet their needs. In many cases, the situation was of an adult child in her 70s caring for a mother in her 90s.

One of the important variables in later life is the maintenance of social networks, and although women seem to maintain them better than men, there is wide variation. Certainly some women are isolates in later life, just as many older men have wide circles of social contacts and interaction. Maintenance of primary relationships with significant others seems to be of greatest importance for successful aging. We may give lip service to the benefits of extended families that include many relatives and close friends, but recent research would suggest that the nuclear family remains the primary unit that people turn to for help when it is needed.

Gerontologists have emphasized the importance of "aging in place" (Lawton, 1990; Silverstone & Horowitz, 1992). Comparatively few older

---

Illustration 3.7. Family Care for the Oldest Old

Bertha Smaha's family listened to many of her stories over the years, tales about drought, blizzards, sod houses, and what it was like to grow up before the turn of the century.

Mrs. Smaha, who was living at an Alliance, Nebraska, nursing home, died in her sleep Sunday at age 106.

"Her mother died when she was 8 years old, and her father was trying to farm 160 acres near Hemingford," said daughter Betty Eizones, also of Alliance. "Those were horrible years for them. They lived in a sod house."

Mrs. Smaha attended country schools but never received a graduation certificate, Mrs. Eizones said. But she always enjoyed nature and the outdoors, things that would be reflected later in her life.

Mrs. Smaha's husband died in 1959, and she continued to live in their house north of Ravenna. But in 1979, when she was 91, Mrs. Smaha became unable to take care of her daily needs, and various family members took turns taking care of her. Mrs. Smaha lived with family members in Denver, Miami, and Shreveport before moving to Alliance.

Mrs. Eizones said her mother often told stories of walking home from country school during snowstorms. A classmate once left the group to walk home on his own, and his frozen body was found curled up in a snowdrift the next day, she said.

From Henion (1994).

persons permanently relocate in retirement. The stereotype of most older people entering retirement communities or going off to a Sunbelt state certainly has some basis in reality, but it remains a fact that the great majority of retired persons age in place. That is, they remain in the same dwelling they occupied prior to retirement. They may take trips in the years after retirement, they may even get a mobile home and go back and forth for a number of years, but their home base of operations remains the same. Given that most older people remain in the same environment, it must be realized that both the environment and the older person still are constantly changing. Maintaining the big old family house, for example, may become increasingly inappropriate for a widowed older person who is becoming frail. It is clear that family members, especially adult children, may either promote or hinder the ability of older adults to age in place.

Among those retirees who relocate, the tendency is for people in the first stage of retirement to live some distance from adult children, and then move closer to one adult child later on. Often, the event that precipitates this later move is widowhood.

When people do return to their home community or that of one of their adult children, the expectation is that the future holds no further moves. Indeed, it might be said that many people come home to die, or move to be near one of their adult children in the expectation of needing personal care and support. Silverstein and Angelelli (1998) have found that older parents are much more likely to move closer to a daughter than a son. We again would note the dynamic processes going on in later life: what might be true of 65-year-olds certainly is not true of 85-year-olds. Whether people age in place or whether they move away and then later come back, the very old individual is more likely to have trouble maintaining autonomy and be more in need of services. These expected services tend not to come from the extended family; they come from one's children. If an adult child is not available, the services are more likely to come from formal organizations than they are from siblings, friends, or distant relatives.

Being the adult child who is chosen to be the caregiver puts one in an ambivalent position. While this is not always the case, the designated care-

---

Illustration 3.8. Migration in Later Life

"The literature on migration in later life clearly highlights the importance of family considerations in motivating relocation decisions, especially at later life stages. As need for care and support increases, the desire or necessity for kinship proximity represents a significant incentive to move closer to (or back to) areas where family, especially children, are located."

From Silverstone and Horowitz (1992).

taker in the family is generally a woman. At one time there was speculation in the gerontological literature that the youngest daughter might be likeliest to inherit parent care responsibilities, but it seems that this varies greatly in families. During the early years of this century, it certainly was the case that, should one of the daughters remain unmarried, the expectation was that she would remain at home and care for the folks. Now, with fewer children in families and many families with only one child, caretaking responsibilities fall on whomever is available, son or daughter. Care for the aged as "women's work," however, is normative. One study found that when it came to care for older parents, "a) family members adopt cultural assumptions about what constitutes gender-appropriate behavior; b) the lone sister typically is 'in charge' of service provision; c) brothers' actual contributions tend to be considered unimportant by both sisters and brothers" (Matthews, 1995, p. S312). Due to the importance of adult children as caregivers, one can project that in future years couples who now remain childless will have a difficult time.

The Sandwich Generation

As more people are surviving into late life, and as more older persons are living independent lives, it's possible that providing services to help an aged parent remain independent has become normative. The fastest-growing segment of our population is the group 85+ (although the rate for nursing home placement is 25% at that age, obviously there are 75% of people aged 85 and older living outside of nursing homes), and many people that age are only able to live independently with some help and supportive services of family members. There are a number of issues that cause family strain; perhaps the greatest of these is the decision as to whether or not the older parent needs nursing home care. Generally, families go to the limit of their abilities—and beyond—to avoid institutionalization. This often involves heavy work, almost always on behalf of one designated caretaker among the adult children. And, not all caretakers are necessarily capable caretakers. Those with lower levels of mastery in this regard have been shown to be high in depressive symptoms because of their caregiving responsibilities (Bookwala & Schulz, 1998; Schulz, O'Brien, Bookwala, & Fleissner, 1995). Bergman-Evans (1994) has found high levels of both loneliness and depression among spousal caregivers as well.

Known in the popular literature as the "sandwich generation" because they are sandwiched between their own children needing care and older parents needing care, adult children are theorized to be uniquely subject to caregiver strain (Thorson, 1989a). In actuality, by the time most peoples' parents are in the group likeliest to need care—the very old cohort aged 80 and above—most adult children have already accomplished all their g lossary

respite — A chance to take a break, to get some relief from caregiving duties.

empty nest — The period in midlife when the children have all left the home.

child-rearing tasks. What they don't have, however, is a long period of *respite*—years free of child-rearing prior to parent-care responsibilities. It's quite possible for people in their 50s to have just entered an *empty nest* stage before one of their parents is in need of more care. In fact, a phenomenon of the beginning of the twenty-first century in North America is old people becoming responsible for the care of even older people. It is not unusual to hear of a 75-year-old whose principal problem is caring for her 95-year-old mother.

In some cases, there is a mutuality of help. The adult child receives as much back as she gives; this is a practical illustration of the exchange theory of aging in action. An adult daughter who has taken a widowed mother into her home, for example, may welcome the additional income the older woman brings into the household. One study has shown that helping adult children tends to enhance older women's well-being (Spitze, Logan, Joseph, & Lee, 1994).

Too frequently, however, the person responsible for parent care feels stuck and unjustly burdened with more of the parent care duties than is her share. It is common in the gerontological research for caretakers to look to brothers or sisters for help and find little or none there; one study indicates that early in the process, caregivers seek more help than they receive (Karlin & Bell, 1992).

One study found siblings to be as much of a source of stress as they were a source of help when parents needed care. Studying caregiving for demented parents provided by 95 daughters and 1195 members of their social networks, it was found that friends were at least as helpful as other family members. And, siblings were by far the most important source of interpersonal stress. Those who had cared for an elderly relative before were more likely to be a source of support rather than a source of stress; those closest in age to the caregiver were also less likely to be sources of stress. Interestingly, social network members of the same gender were both sources of support and stress (Suitor & Pillemer, 1993).

Illustration 3.10. Some Practical Advice on Parent Care

It's apparent that almost all of the young old are living independently and need no special help. Fewer than 1% of 65-year-olds are in nursing homes. However, the need for help rapidly increases among the old old, especially among those who are in their 80s or 90s and live alone. Our goal, of course, is to keep them independent and living in their own home for as long as possible. This involves providing alternatives to institutional care. While this is discussed in greater detail in Chapter 14, there are several points we need to make here.

It is absolutely vital to know what is going on physically. An assessment at a medical center by an interdisciplinary team trained in geriatrics is the ideal. Short of that, a thorough examination by an internist or family practitioner who is skilled in working with older patients is necessary. If Mom or Dad's physician doesn't seem to be particularly interested in caring for older people, if he or she is too busy to answer questions or explain procedures, find a better doctor. Ask around and find out which physician in your community seems to do well with older patients. Some older patients stick with doctors they're not satisfied with because they're afraid of hurting the doctor's feelings. Explain that the doctor's feelings aren't our primary consideration. Many older people can appreciate this; about 10% of older patients change doctors each year.

Helping older parents is a delicate matter because we don't want to take control or decision-making authority away from them. It could be perceived as an insult to have one's life taken over by an adult child. Better to work with Mom or Dad, letting them make the important decisions if they can, than to move in on them like a steamroller.

When negotiating with siblings, it must be made clear that the individual who obviously is going to provide most of the services has to have the decision-making autonomy and not be second-guessed by a brother or sister who's not on the scene. It often is helpful for that individual to be designated as the one who holds durable power of attorney for health care. It also should be made clear which duties will be shared by those who are in the same geographic area. Making up a schedule often helps.

Our surveys of older persons' needs indicate that what might seem to be relatively minor services make a very big difference in their lives. Having someone do their shopping when they can't get out, or arrange for cleaning or doing their laundry, might be all the help that's needed to keep a person independent and out of an institution. Taking them to the doctor, arranging for home-delivered meals, helping with home maintenance duties, perhaps helping with finances or bill paying—all of these may also help keep an older person living independently.

Ask for help; don't try to take on everything without any assistance. Getting burned out will only put Mom in a nursing home that much quicker. Look for the "Area Agency on Aging" in the Yellow Pages under "Social Services." It can let you know what kinds of services are available for help in your area. Hospital discharge social workers and community visiting nurses are usually very knowledgeable about available services that help keep older people at home and independent.

Grandparenting

The great majority of people ultimately become grandparents, and for most of these people this is a very satisfying role. However, demographic changes that have taken place make drawing a typical picture of grandparenting exceedingly complex if not impossible. It is no longer the case that one can assume that Grandma, for example, is a sweet little widow, living in the old family place, who spends her time knitting and baking cookies. She is just as likely to be a divorcee in midlife, living in a condo, working in a position from which she will receive her own pension, and living with a man who is unrelated to her grandchildren.

Nevertheless, it is satisfying to have grandchildren. They represent the continuity of the generations, the future of the family, and personal immortality in a very real sense. Most of us will not make outstanding contributions that will give us a place in history, but most people can look to their survival—for a few generations, at least—in the memories of their grandchildren and great-grandchildren.

It has been suggested that grandparental roles have evolved in recent generations from authority figure, to burden, to companion (Gratton & Haber, 1996). That is, in a rural economy, the owner of the land—usually the grandfather—wielded great authority. He determined who would inherit the farm, what the family's status in the community would be, and what major decisions would be made. Indeed, he may have been responsible for arranging marriages for his offspring. Grandmother was often seen as a burden after Grandfather died, for she had few possessions and virtually no income. Her children were forced to take her in, and she had few skills other than as domestic help; certainly, no one had ever consulted her on financial decisions. Now, in an era when most women work, her financial acumen may be eagerly sought by her adult children—along with a loan so they can make the down-payment on a first house. With most people becoming grandparents in mid-life, and with most people living into at least their 70s if not their 80s, there is a multi-decade span of time for grandparents to be companions rather than burdens.

The onset of grandparenthood varies considerably, of course, and it extends over a considerable period of time, too. Thus, the relationship with a first grandchild may extend for twenty or thirty years, and the relationship with a last grandchild may last for only a few years. The roles then, could be quite different. Grandparents may survive well into the adulthood of a first grandchild but not their last one (Szinovacz, 1998). Due to increasing survival into later life, about a third of all grandchildren will have all of their grandparents survive at least for their first ten years of life, and about 75% will still have at least one surviving grandparent at least until age 30 (Uhlenberg, 1996). Thus, grandparents now spend at least several decades as grandparents; they also will share the role of grandparent with other surviving grandparents on the other side of the family. And, increasing divorce rates in the twentieth century mean both that more grandparents will be married to people other than the biological grandparent of their grandchildren, and that there may be ambivalent roles and relationships if their son or daughter has a different partner than their grandchildren's biological mother or father.

Grandparents' average age at the birth of the first grandchild is 47.0 years, and the average age at the birth of the last grandchild is 60.5 years (Szinovacz, 1998). We can refer back to Table 1.7 in Chapter 1, then, and extrapolate. The typical grandfather should anticipate about another 30 years of life after the birth of his first grandchild, and on the average, grandmothers can anticipate another 35 years of life after the birth of their first grandchild; the corresponding numbers for grandparents after the birth of the last grandchild are 19 and 23, respectively. This is a considerable amount of time over which to develop and maintain a relationship, and it also represents a considerable change from generational experience in earlier centuries. By age 26, fully 70% of the population still has at least one living grandparent (Szinovacz, 1998).

Illustration 3.11. Some Demographic Trends in Grandparenthood

Maximiliane Szinovacz (1998) analyzed data from a major demographic study among 10,008 persons interviewed concerning grandparenting. The results imply the following expected trends:

1. Most people will become grandparents.
2. Grandparenthood most often has its onset in middle life, but minorities and women become grandparents earlier than whites and males.
3. Most grandparents survive past their grandchildren's adolescence, and grandchildren often have several surviving grandparents after they reach adulthood.
4. There are gender differences in life expectancy; this means that it is more likely that grandchildren will have surviving maternal grandmothers and less likely to have surviving paternal grandfathers.
5. Most families will have at least one surviving great-grandparent, at least while the great-grandchildren are still young.
6. At the onset of grandparenthood, most people will no longer have their own dependent children at home.
7. Only a minority of grandparents with young grandchildren will be widowed.
8. About 20–25% of grandparents will be step grandparents, either because of their own or because of their adult children's divorces and remarriages.
9. Most grandparents, both male and female, will be employed.
10. Fewer than 10% of grandparents reside in the same household as their grandchildren at any one time, but about 20% will have ever lived in the same household as at least one grandchild.

From Szinovacz (1998).

Grandparents as a rule give their grandchildren both time and money. One study indicates that 36% of grandparents shared an average of 13.7 hours of time spent helping grandchildren during the previous week, and almost 20% provided at least some income to grandchildren (Bass & Caro, 1996). Indeed, some grandparents have complete responsibility for their grandchildren, having assumed the role of surrogate parents (Minkler & Roe, 1996; Roe & Minkler, 1999). Szinovacz's 1998 study indicates that a total of 11% of all grandparents surveyed ever had primary responsibility for rearing a grandchild. There were important ethnic differences in this regard, with 14.0% of black grandparents, 5.4% of white grandparents, and 7.3% of Hispanic grandparents ever having primary responsibility for one or more grandchildren.

This can cause role conflict as well as disappointment for some or all of the parties involved. When it becomes necessary to provide care for grandchildren, the children are losing interaction with younger, more active parents, and the grandparents are giving up a great amount of freedom in order to resume a parental role. Conflict can be extreme and continuing if the grandparents have had to step in and take over from an abusive or unfit parent. Cases where the birth parent is an alcoholic or drug addict are all too frequent. Continuing pain is then engendered when the birth parent feels that she or he has turned life around and seeks to regain custody. The grandparents see themselves as providing needed stability in their grandchildren's lives and are often reluctant to step back and let the birth parent give it another try. In situations where the parent has died, of course, then both the grandparent and the grandchild have to confront grief and loss as well as new living situations.

Illustration 3.12. Parenting All Over Again

When Charles Miller moved from Omaha to New Jersey to work on a second master's degree, he and his wife, Chestene, felt young again.

Their three daughters were grown. No diapers to change, toddlers to chase or manners to teach.

But all that changed in 1994.

Their youngest daughter, Colette, the single mother of five children, died of complications from asthma at age 28.

Miller and his wife flew back to Omaha and gained custody of the children. NaTina was 9, Eddie was 7, Johnathon was 6, Branden was 4, and JimNeshia was a month old. The grandparents were close to 50.

"It could be challenging to give up certain things," said Miller, who had wanted to pursue a doctorate in music education. "But if you have to give up this or that, you just do it. You do it without complaining."

From Grace (1998).

Conclusion

Families are the source of the strongest bonds in our social networks. Where those bonds are most effective, they can provide supports and services that help keep the frail elderly out of institutions. Where they do not exist, have been broken, or for some reason are not effective, a downward cycle leading to isolation, homelessness, or institutionalization is not uncommon. People who have not had children are about twice as likely to wind up in a nursing home. One of the real problems we will see, especially in the twenty-first century, will be the aging of people who now have only one child or none at all. They will be forced to rely on public and private agencies for services that otherwise might have been delivered by adult children.

Support in families has been found to have a high level of continuity. As generations travel through time, the faithfulness of adult children in the provision of parent care is constant. Friends, however, fall away in very late life (Field & Minkler, 1988). For the oldest old, it's possible to outlive one's family supports.

Looking at an historical life course perspective, we can see that there has been some modification in roles and responsibilities of family members over the course of the generations. We no longer have large, multigenerational extended families living with or near us but tend to rely more upon nuclear families. Nevertheless, filial obligation seems to have remained constant, and most family members will go to the end of their rope and beyond to keep parents out of institutions (Finley, Roberts, & Banahan, 1988). Having to place a family member in a nursing home is viewed as a crisis. We will deal with this crisis at greater length in Chapters 9 and 14. For now, we might conclude that it causes more family conflict than almost any other issue affecting families and their older members (Brody & Spark, 1966).

Older persons who are coupled tend not to call upon community agencies for services; they care for each other. This care is not only physical, but it is psychological and social as well. The person who maintains a bond of intimacy and has a confidant is much less likely to be institutionalized (Kendig, Coles, Pittelkow, & Wilson, 1988). And older persons who maintain social networks have lower rates of mortality and morbidity (Seeman et al, 1987; Steinbach, 1992). Widowhood is a normative event in our society; most women can anticipate being widows for a good many years at the end of life. Fortunately for them, women tend to be better than men at maintaining social networks in later life. Women are much more likely than men, for example, to maintain multiple confidants, so that replacing one who dies is not so much of a problem. As a result, women tend to have broader and more plentiful networks of support in old age. People who have their own children later and are themselves children of older parents are likely to be caught in a "sandwich generation," where they have care of adolescent children and older parents confronting them at the same time. Finally, most older people ultimately are grandparents, and the demographic changes that have taken place in North American indicate that many can expect to be great- grandparents. Most people find this to be satisfying, but a minority who are forced to take on primary care for grandchildren generally find it to be very disrupting.

Questions for Discussion

1. How have you seen filial obligation work in your family?
2. Does it make sense that most of the services received by older persons are provided by family members? Why?
3. How have the ways that families interact changed in the past several decades?
4. Did your father ever object to your mother working outside the home?
5. How have patterns of family dynamics stayed the same over several generations?
6. Can you see signs of the graying of the suburbs?
7. At what age do the majority of the people live alone?
8. Have any of your grandparents become widowed? If so, how have their lives changed?
9. Can you name one or more people you consider to be your confidants?
10. What problems emerge when grandparents have to take over primary care for their grandchildren?

Minorities and Cultural Diversity

4

Chapter Outline

"I have little patience for people who refer to the elderly as having reached the 'golden age.' Age brings with it deterioration, and deterioration is not golden. The advertisements aimed at 'mature' (read 'old') people usually show a handsome white-haired woman holding hands with a similarly white-haired man while both look off, misty-eyed, to distant and alluring horizons. This is the Mary Poppins approach to age, and while Mary Poppins may entertain me, she does not provide me with wisdom."

—Ira Wallach, born 1913

Introduction

The end of the twentieth century brought with it the increasing realization of the importance of diversity in North American culture. Not only was there an increase of the cultural mix brought about by the migration of

African-Americans —
People who trace their
ancestry to the African
continent, usually
sub-Saharan Africa.

Francophone — A
person whose native
language is French.

peoples, but groups often thought of as minorities increasingly sought to speak out on their own behalf. This has not necessarily led to greater understanding or harmony, but it certainly made clearer the necessity for different groups to learn to live with one another. And although the majority culture has made strides in valuing diversity, much remains to be accomplished in this regard.

Minorities Defined

A curiosity is the changing definition of "minority" when applied to human societies. We may have once thought strictly in racial or ethnic terms when deciding on what constitutes a minority group, but this has been found to be increasingly inadequate. It's entirely possible, for example, to be a member of both minority and majority cultures at the same time. For example, residents of Southern California whose heritage is *African-American* might think of themselves both as a racial minority in a predominantly white United States, but also as part of a native English-speaking majority when compared to immigrant Koreans or Vietnamese. Similarly, French-speaking Haitians of African heritage might find themselves to be part of the *Francophone* (those whose native language is French) majority in Montreal, but in reality find that they are members of quite a small racial minority group in an overwhelmingly white European culture. People who have grown old in the same neighborhood may have seen old friends and neighbors move or die off. Even though the young people who have replaced them may be of the same racial group—the older residents remaining may begin to feel that they have become a minority group—the elderly. Similarly, women, who constitute the numerical majority in our society, almost certainly have confronted discrimination that in some ways has been characteristic of that experienced by minority groups.

In other words, it is possible to be a member of a minority while also being part of the majority culture. What, then, is a minority? Let us define a *minority* as a part of a population differing from others in some characteristics and often subject to differential treatment. "Differential treatment" is the crucial issue for our purposes, and we will focus on it in much of this chapter. To a certain degree, "minority" can also be seen as how people define themselves.

This brings us to the question of whether or not older people constitute a minority. They often do not define themselves as a separate group based solely on age. Getting older is a gradual process of adjustment to a new status: no one starts out old. Since older people have never been old before, it may be common for them to not define themselves that way. It's easier to see members of particular racial groups defining themselves as members of a minority in a majority culture than to find older persons thinking of themselves as a minority.

Another way of thinking of minorities, however, is to define elements of a subculture, a group of common characteristics that differentiate it from others. Although there has been much discussion on this point, it is difficult to maintain that the aged actually take on the characteristics of a subculture in most parts of North America. Due to their heterogeneity, it is hard to identify particular traits that are characteristic of simply being old. Points of personal identification with one's nationality, race or ethnic group, and religion are stronger than is identification as an "old person" for most older adults. Another way of thinking of a subculture is to see members interacting more with one another than they do those outside of the subculture (Rose, 1965). Again, it is hard to argue that this is true for the majority of older people.

It is not strictly necessary to be part of a subculture to be a minority, however. Being treated like a minority or in some ways like a minority at risk is another factor. Older workers who are shoved out of the workplace may indeed be subject to discrimination as members of a minority group, whether they define themselves as members of a minority or not. We might find, then, at least some characteristics of being a minority at risk among many of the aged. Looking different, being treated differently, interacting more and more within one's own group, and encountering discrimination are a few of these elements of identification as a minority at risk.

Not all points of minority identification are necessarily negative, however. Protected minorities are often given certain rights and privileges because of their minority status. Often these benefits are in an effort to compensate for disadvantages that have been associated with being a member of the group. In the case of the elderly, there is an income tax benefit in the United States based solely on age. Those 65 years of age or above get to take a double personal exemption on their federal income tax. This was originally based upon the assumption that "old" meant "poor," and that people 65+ needed economic help simply because they were entering old age. Rather than appropriating funds, Congress thought to give older people a tax break based entirely on their age status, regardless of their actual income. And older people are the only citizens of the United States who are entitled to a guaranteed annual income: Supplemental Security Income (SSI) provides an income base for the poor elderly that most younger people are not entitled to under the law. We will explore these supports and services at length in Chapter 14. A host of discounts are available to older consumers that younger people, in essence, subsidize. Economically, then, the aged are in some ways being treated as a protected minority.

Further, some have seen the emergence of older people as a political force, and this no doubt has elements of identification as a minority group. Lobbying for one's personal welfare is based upon recognition of common interests as a part of a group, and older persons' organizations certainly have emerged as powerful political forces. Few politicians would dream of decreasing Social Security benefits, for example; it would be political suicide. And while the double income tax exemption is of doubtful constitutionality (it clearly violates the Equal Protection clause of the 14th Amendment), political support for removing or changing it is nonexistent. Older voters, identifying themselves as a common interest group, would no doubt punish any office holders who dared to tamper with it. We will deal with these public policy issues at greater length in Chapter 13.

Does all of this add up to defining older persons as members of a minority group? For some, it may be a matter of individual identification. Older people organizing for their own self-interest seem to take on many of the characteristics of a minority group. For many elderly people, however, identification as being part of a group defined as "old" would seem entirely foreign. Generally, minorities at risk are vulnerable due to their disadvantage in relating to a majority in a power position. Some old people may be in power positions; they identify more with the dominant majority than they might with any minority status. As age increases, however, the population of the aged has less access to power: the cohort of the oldest old is increasingly female and poor relative to the young old. Concepts relating to those minorities at risk will be the focus of the balance of this chapter.

Gender Issues

It may seem curious to refer to the numerical majority of the population as a minority, but what we have said about relation to a dominant group and minorities applies especially to women in North American society. There is a particularly potent cohort effect here. For most of their lives, it has been the norm for the present group of older women to be subservient in one way or another to men. That is, women have hardly ever been in power positions. As younger people, most women in North America who are now old were socialized into dependency: men were thought of as being the breadwinners. With changing norms for women encouraging work outside the home, some older women now feel that they were cheated, that the rules of the game were changed on them. Many sought a husband and family as primary goals when they were young women. Now, they see their daughters and granddaughters going on in higher education and into the professions. Schoolteacher and nurse were among the few acceptable occupational roles when women who are now in their 70s and 80s were younger. Now, many perceive that the limits that held them back have been removed for the next generation of women coming along behind them. Women approaching old age may have a particular problem in that many accepted what was normative at one time and now find that there is a new set of norms.

When speaking of norms and values, however, it is difficult to generalize about what is normative for one group or generation of women versus another. A meaningful proportion of women in all generations have worked. Getting married, having a family, and being a housewife may have been

---

Illustration 4.1. Midlife Dependency

"My sister's friend Kathy got married right out of high school; this would have been in, say, about 1952. Kathy never gave a thought to either work or higher education. She married a guy who went on to med school and then became a small-town physician. Being a doctor's wife in a small town was a good job. I remember a woman in Asheville, North Carolina, who won a seat on the City Council with that as her sole qualification. Well, Kathy was able to lord it over the other women and generally be a big frog in a small pond. When the host dies, however, it's bad for the parasite, and the doctor kicked off several years back. Over thirty years of a dependent relationship have made Kathy into a cripple, and she's not been able to do anything since but spend up the life insurance. She's stuck.

"Women in the current generation are playing by a new set of rules, thank God. A Nebraska farmer who was ahead of his time was quoted in our local paper, responding to why he had spent the money to send his seven daughters to college back in Depression days: 'So they wouldn't become slaves to the sons of my neighbors.'"

From Thorson (1989, pp. 22–23).

---

normative for some women, but certainly not for all. Plenty of women in each generation have been single all their lives, and plenty have worked and balanced a family and a career as well. Although it's true that looking toward a career has gained increasing acceptability for women in recent decades, we shouldn't forget that this is not the first generation of women who have worked outside the home. Further—and this is a point we will return to several times in this chapter—when we speak of diversity, we need to remember that people are, well, diverse. It's unfair to generalize and lump all people into groups or categories: we can't say that this is the way it is for older women any more than we can say that this is the way it is for older *Native Americans* or African-Americans. People become more heterogeneous as they age; they are less alike in later life rather than more alike. Some women in late life want to bake cookies, and some want to continue to be stockbrokers—we really can't generalize.

Having said all that, there are certain demographic facts we need to look at to gain a perspective on the cohort of women who are now old. They were born for the most part between 1910 and 1935. Many have vivid memories of the Great Depression and of World War II (and the oldest ones may remember World War I and Prohibition as well). Unlike their mothers, they have been able to vote during their entire adult lives. They have seen, and adapted to, tremendous social change. When they were girls, fewer than 10% of college students were female; now over 50% are. They were born in an era when it was a rare medical school or law school that admitted even a token number of women students; now 37% of medical graduates and 43% of newly graduated attorneys are women (U.S. Bureau of the Census, 1998b). They have lived past an age when 143 out of

glossary

Native Americans — Generally understood to be people descended from those who resided on the North American continent prior to European colonization: American Indians, Aleuts, and Eskimos.

glossary

Hispanics — Any of
those people who
trace ancestors or
language to a Spanish
or Portuguese-
speaking country.

every 1,000 babies died during their first year of life (that ratio is less than 8 out of a 1,000 now). In short, older women have seen a host of changes in their lives and have learned to adapt to change as a part of development across the lifespan.

However, we also need to remember that only a third of the oldest generation of women now living ever learned to drive. This is a continuing source of dependency, and many of these women were expected to be dependent. Helena Lopata, in her studies of American widows, has found that it is normative for them to transfer their dependency to an older son when their husband dies (Lopata & Brehm, 1986). For many women, there has been a life-long financial dependence on one or more relatives (Arber & Ginn, 1991). The fact that this is changing may be slim comfort to the oldest women.

Between 1970 and 1997, the percentage of women heading households increased by 57% and the number living alone also increased by 57% (U.S. Bureau of the Census, 1998b). This in most cases is due to increasing prosperity among older women: they no longer *have* to live with a relative—they can afford their own home. This increasingly is the case for older women.

As we saw in Table 3.1 in the previous chapter, the proportion of women who are widowed increases with age. In this chapter's Table 4.1, we can see that the proportion of people living alone increases by age for whites, blacks, and **Hispanics**. Taking age groups from those 45 to 54 to those 75 years of age and older, the percentage of whites living alone increases from 11 to 42%. The comparable percentages for African-Americans goes from 16 to 40%, and for Americans of Hispanic heritage, it goes from 9% to 31%. The

TABLE 4.1. Living Arrangements by Age and Race in Percentages

	White	Black	Hispanic*
Alone			
Ages 45 to 54	11%	16%	9%
Ages 55 to 64	13	20	12
Ages 65 to 74	24	30	23
Ages 75 and older	42	40	31
Living with spouse			
Ages 45 to 54	74	47	64
Ages 55 to 64	75	50	63
Ages 65 to 74	66	40	55
Ages 75 and older	42	26	32
Living with other persons			
Ages 45 to 54	15	37	27
Ages 55 to 64	12	30	25
Ages 65 to 74	10	30	22
Ages 75 and older	16	35	37

*Persons of Hispanic origin may be of any race
From U.S. Bureau of the Census (1998a).

changes over time for those living with persons other than a spouse—generally, their children—do not change that much. But, the number of those living with a spouse declines because of widowhood. Thus, we see changing patterns that are much different from previous generations. We might conclude that this, for the most part, is due to fewer people having to move in with one of their children in later life.

At one time, it was normative in families to expect a single daughter to remain at home (or return to the home of her parents) and take care of the old folks. This often was a situation of mutual dependency; as time went by, the daughter may even have given up her job to become a full time caregiver. This has become an historical artifact, an anachronism, and cases of it are becoming very infrequent. Now, the daughter often has a good enough job to be able to afford her own household and is no longer dependent upon her parents for housing. With smaller families and changing norms, this increasingly will be the case.

However, older women are about twice as likely as older men to be living with other relatives. So, despite the historical changes we are observing, the chances of a woman in later life living with an adult child or a sibling remain much greater than those of a man. The likelihood of her living alone is much higher as well. There is a much larger proportion of men who live with a spouse (among those 75+, it is 66.7% for men versus 28.8% for women). This is because men tend to marry women younger than themselves, and they are much more likely to re-marry if they become widowed or divorced.

The most dramatic difference between men and women in later life, of course, is income. In 1995, men 65 and older in the United States had a median income of $16,684 while women in the same age group had a median income of only $9,626. This represents an average income for older women of only 57.6% of the average for men in the same age group (U.S. Bureau of the Census, 1998b). There is a stereotype of women ultimately controlling much of the wealth because of inheritance of houses and other assets such as life insurance. It is true that a small minority of old women are relatively wealthy individuals during their final years of life. However, this generally applies only to the top 5% in terms of net worth. For the great

---

Illustration 4.2. An Important Lesson

One of my wife's most vivid memories of her grandmother is going with her to vote. An immigrant, Grandma had come to this country shortly before women became enfranchised. She made it a point to bring her granddaughter with her every time she went to the polls and to carefully instruct her how important it was for a citizen to participate in the democratic process. Women couldn't vote in the old country, and she wasn't about to take her new responsibilities lightly.

majority of women, inheriting a house after their spouse dies hardly classifies them as wealthy.

It might be concluded that while women are a diverse group in older age and there is little basis upon which to generalize, they all face certain issues and problems. Cultural expectations of dependency are changing, but they still exist. Issues of independence, self reliance, and self confidence have less application to older men but remain real issues for older women. Personal safety is an important concern. Differential attitudes toward older men and women are of significance as well. Stereotypes of men as they age becoming "more distinguished" while women become "little old ladies" are a benign expression of these prejudices. At the most extreme, there is in our folk history the notion of old woman as witch: a sinister and perhaps magical hag, wrinkled and ugly. It was not a little old man who was going to eat up Hansel and Gretel. This vision of old woman as witch is not necessarily just a Eurocentric stereotype; African and *Asian* cultures perpetuate it as well (Missinne, 1980). And there are few corresponding stereotypes on the positive side. We have few cultural images of beneficent older women—*Mrs.* Santa Claus doesn't get much press.

Race and Ethnicity

The National Urban League first coined the term "double jeopardy" to the special problems of the minority aged, being members of a racial minority and being old as well (Cool, 1986). More recently, the concept of triple jeopardy has emerged, referring to older women who are members of a racial minority, the likeliest members among the aged to live in poverty. *Ethnicity*, or belonging to an ethnic group, at its most basic level means being defined by shared cultural traits, usually traits that differ from those of the majority culture. Linda Cool (1986) says that the term "ethnic" now is being used for what anthropologists once called tribal or cultural.

Ethnic groups are usually defined by race, nationality, or religion, especially if the group has common norms and values. This shared-culture concept is an important one: it allows a more precise definition than just race. Jacquelyne Jackson (1985), for example, notes the great differences between African-Americans who have lived in North America for many generations and recent immigrants of black people from, say, Nigeria or Haiti. Similarly, Spanish-speaking people might be of any race, but immigrants from Cuba, Puerto Rico, Honduras, or Spain all have important differences. They in turn need to be differentiated from those Americans of Mexican ancestry, for example, whose families may have lived in the United States for many generations. It is actually somewhat imprecise to lump them all into one group labeled "Hispanic."

It is thus possible to speak of minorities within minorities. That is, groups that might be considered to be minorities may encompass numerous smaller groups that make up true subcultures. This may happen as a result of different migration patterns, different customs and values, or geographic differences. In particular, the immigration experience is of exceeding importance to first- and second-generation peoples who are at a distinct disadvantage relating to the majority culture.

The aged among these subcultures may be genuinely isolated in immigrant nations like Canada and the United States. Jackson (1985) points out, for example, that recent African immigrants to the United States may affiliate more on a tribal basis than due to any similarities of race or national origin. Ashantis from Ghana, say, might feel they have little in common with Ibo from Nigeria. And because younger people are the ones who are most likely to immigrate, there may be relatively few older people in a particular ethnic group. The aged are the least likely to feel comfortable with a new language. Thus, older recent immigrants from relatively small groups may find themselves to be very isolated indeed. A study of elderly Vietnamese living in Southeastern Texas, for example, found loneliness, worry, and discouragement to be among their principal problems (Die & Seelbach, 1988). This may be particularly true if the older immigrant is somehow separated from family; wanting to be near adult children is usually a primary motivation in the decision to immigrate. One recent study found little support for financial motivations among aged immigrants (Van Hook & Bean, 1999). Most come to be with family members.

An examination of ethnicity helps us to differentiate among groups and to have a better concept of the particular needs and problems of each. Shared culture probably is a better way to look at groups than is race or religion. We cannot assume that all Protestants are alike; neither can we assume that all Muslims are alike or that all Asians are alike.

Religious affiliation tends to be an imprecise means of group identification, mainly due to the divisions within groups and varieties of national culture that outsiders may not be aware of. A more exact way to view groups is in relation to their norms and values, the things that make up a shared culture, and how they define themselves.

An example of this might be seen with a differentiation of the Hasidic Jews of Brooklyn in comparison to the larger body of Jewish people in the United States. Many Jews in America are bemused when confronted with the ultra-orthodox *Hasidim*, who relate mostly with each other and maintain the dress their ancestors wore in the sixteenth century. By looking at ethnicity, it is possible to see further group differences by national origin or social norms. Other Hasidic Jews in Brooklyn, for example, often view the Lubavitcher Hasidim with some alarm because they tend to be more evangelical (Harris, 1986). So, we can see a subgroup within a subgroup. Adding old age to the equation makes for an even smaller minority.

It is vital to take tradition and values of minority groups into account. Often, what may appear to be subtle differences might seem unimportant to outsiders, but they are very important indeed to the persons who are involved. Cultural differences and the ways that people define themselves

*g*lossary

Hasid (plural: Hasidim) — Ultra-Orthodox Jews with origins in Eastern Europe (especially Poland, Hungary, and Russia) who dress in characteristic garb and strictly follow Jewish law.

glossary

assimilation —
Absorption into the
cultural tradition of a
population or group.

must never be trivialized, nor should groups that might seem to have obvious similarities be lumped together with one another. This is true in terms of race and religion, and it is also true in terms of national origin and language.

It might, for example, seem odd that the Norwegian immigrants of the nineteenth century to South Dakota had, within a very few years after their arrival, organized four separate synods of the Norwegian Lutheran Church (Rolvaag, 1971). All of these people were of the same race, national origin, language, cultural heritage, and religion, but they would have maintained that there were important differences between groups. We need to seek to understand and respect such differences.

We cannot discuss every ethnic group, of course, but in the balance of this chapter, we will examine several of the larger minorities in the North America and how their cultural heritage relates to the topic of aging.

African-American Elderly

As noted above, people whose ancestry goes back to African roots make up very diverse groups in North America. Common in race, they differ greatly in many other important ways. Thus, it is rather unfortunate that census data lump all together in one group, "black." On the other hand, dealing with Census data prior to 1980, we find two categories: "white" and "non-white," which is not only imprecise but downright misleading.

The most common cultural similarity, of course, that most African-Americans share (other than those who are recent immigrants from Africa) is descent from slavery. In 1860, a little over eleven million people lived in the U.S. South, and almost four million of them were black slaves (Patterson, 1982). Slaves made up the numerical majority of people in Mississippi and South Carolina. This common heritage is one of the most distinct cultural factors differentiating any of the groups in North America, for there can be no more debilitating status than bondage. About the only positive aspect of this is that the great majority of black people in the United State have been here for many generations and have fewer of the problems of ***assimilation*** that are experienced by recent immigrants. The prevailing theme of people from Africa during the past century and a half might be best characterized by the title of Booker T. Washington's famous book, *Up From Slavery*. It might be said that no group in America has had greater relative success, because no group started from such a disadvantaged status.

This is not to say that older black people are without their problems, of course. To say that they are very likely to be better off than their parents or grandparents were at the same age may bring little comfort. Historically, African-Americans have experienced a heritage of discrimination, and older black people are likely to have memories of its most vivid manifestations, especially segregation of public facilities in many parts of the country up

TABLE 4.2. Persons 65 Years Old and Over Below Poverty Level: 1970 to 1996

| | Percent Below Poverty Level | | | |
Race	1970	1980	1990	1996
White	22.6	13.6	10.1	9.4
Black	47.7	38.1	33.8	25.3
Asian & Pacific Islander	NA	NA	12.1	9.7
Hispanic	NA	30.8	22.5	24.4
In families	14.8	8.4	5.8	5.6
Unrelated individuals	47.2	25.6	24.7	20.9

From U.S. Bureau of the Census (1998a).

until the 1960s. Many older blacks in fact are among the early pioneers of the civil rights movement in the United States.

Quality of life is relative. We might say that the current generation of older African-Americans is fairly well-off compared to black older people who came before them. We must, however, compare them as a group to other older Americans. Here we find some important differences. As we can see in Table 4.2, the rate of poverty among older blacks is much higher, on the average, than it is among older whites. The data indicates that 22.6% of white aged were living in poverty in 1970, but only 9.4% were below the poverty level by 1996. For black older persons, 47.7% lived in poverty in 1970 and 25.3% in 1996. So there was relative improvement, but not nearly as large a gain as there was for whites, and the poverty rate for older blacks is still almost three times higher than the rate for older whites.

Data in Table 4.3 indicate that mean household income for African Americans 65 and older is about 68% of that for whites. Researchers identify life-long patterns of disadvantage in terms of education, employment, and income of blacks relative to whites (Taylor & Chatters, 1988). Some social scientists are pessimistic about narrowing these gaps, pointing to

TABLE 4.3. Mean Household Income by Age and Race (1997 dollars)

	1987	1997
White		
Aged 65 and older	29,831	32,718
Aged 75 and older	24,078	26,413
Black		
Aged 65 and older	18,466	22,260
Aged 75 and older	15,173	19,805
Hispanic		
Aged 65 and older	21,043	23,206
Aged 75 and older	17,628	18,929

From Income Tables—Households. Last revised December 1, 1998.
Http://www.census.gov/

continuing income inequality in younger age categories and the nature of poverty for those increasingly concentrated in large cities (Markides, 1987).

This points again to the importance of differentiating among which black Americans one speaks about. Many of the problems and concerns of the elderly relate to income and class more than they do race. Obviously, location makes a difference as well. A growing African-American middle class may be seen to have few of the concerns of those persons who live in very rural areas or in inner cities and who are in poverty. And about 72% of black Americans of all ages have incomes that place them above the poverty threshold (U.S. Bureau of the Census, 1998b). Those living in rural parts of the South remain those likeliest to be poor. Still, poverty is relative, even among those experiencing it. One study of older low-income women found that they felt much better off than their parents: "Instead of considering themselves old or poor, the women defined themselves as fortunate and blessed" (Barusch, 1997, p. 269).

Health disadvantages are among the most apparent outcomes of poverty. As we saw in Chapter 1, economic well-being is an important predictor of health, and poverty is one of the most important predictors of disability and mortality. One report documents the conditions of adversity experienced by people living in rural Mississippi: only about 20% had adequate access to health care and other necessary services (Turner, 1992). By contrast, a study done in Cleveland found fewer problems experienced by low-income elderly blacks in terms of access to health care (Pechters & Milligan, 1988). A colleague and I did a study in Omaha that essentially replicated the Cleveland study, and then gathered additional data in rural areas. Our findings showed that there was little frustration expressed in terms of access to services among any of the older respondents, and there was a high level of satisfaction with available health care (Thorson & Powell, 1992). Other research indicates that income, rather than race, is the important consideration in accessing services (Wallace, 1990).

Two of the most important elements in examining relative health are self-rating and level of disability (Idler & Kasl, 1991; Shanas & Maddox, 1985). That is, how well people say that they are is closely related to their clinically rated health, and how well they feel is closely related to how well they can perform everyday activities. The National Health Interview Survey took a sample of 504,000 persons of all ages and races in the United States, seeking (among other things) to find their self-ratings of health and their levels of limitations of activity. Older whites and blacks in this study did not differ significantly in their number of physician contacts (8.6 and 8.9 per year, respectively), but they did vary in the number of their days of restricted activity. Overall, aged blacks had an average of 43.5 days of restricted activity per year, while older whites reported only 30.5 days per year of restricted activity (Ries & Brown, 1991).

People in this study were also asked to indicate whether they thought they were in poor, fair, good, or excellent health. Table 4.4 indicates that a

TABLE 4.4. Self-Assessed Health Status of Respondents Aged 65+, by Limitation and Race

	Limited in Activity		Not Limited in Activity	
	Fair or Poor Health	Good or Excellent Health	Fair or Poor Health	Good or Excellent Health
White	20.1%	17.6%	9.2%	53.2%
Black	32.9%	14.2%	14.3%	38.6%

From Ries and Brown (1991, p. 4).

higher percentage of older African-Americans rated themselves as in fair or poor health and limited in activity compared to older whites in the sample (32.9% of older African-Americans, compared to 20.1% of older whites). Among those not limited in functional activity, a higher percentage of whites rated their health as good or excellent (53.2%) than did blacks (38.6%). Confirming this difference, other studies have found that older blacks tend to rate their health as poorer than do older whites (Mutchler & Burr, 1991). On the other hand, African-American elders are less likely to report unhappiness or depression (Gallo, Cooper-Patrick, & Lesikar, 1998).

The black elderly are at a disadvantage compared to white elderly for a host of degenerative, chronic diseases common in later life. Although the rate of coronary heart disease is similar for older black and white men, it is much higher among African-American women compared to white women. Hypertension is much higher among the black elderly of both sexes. Lung cancer rates for women are similar, but the death rate for lung cancer is 45% higher among older black males when compared to older white males. Rates of death for esophageal and stomach cancer are much higher among blacks of both sexes. African-American women are two and a half times more likely to die of cervical cancer than are white women, and they also have a 33% greater chance of cancer of the uterus. Blacks of both sexes have about one third more incidents of diabetes, and black women are significantly more likely to be obese. Strokes and end-stage renal disease

---

Illustration 4.3. Health Problems of Older African-Americans

"Hypertension is the most serious threat to the health of the black population because of its frequency and its devastating impact on the cardiovascular system, leading to stroke, renal failure, heart attack, left ventricular hypertrophy, and congestive heart failure. According to the Health and Nutrition Examination Survey, 58.8% of black men and 50.1% of black women aged 65 to 74 have hypertension. The comparable prevalence rates for white men is 35.3% and for white women 42.3%."

From Curry (1990, p. 321).

are much more common among African-Americans, as is cirrhosis of the liver (Morrison & Gresson, 1990).

Rates of alcoholism and drug disorders are much higher among black men, although suicide is much lower among blacks of both sexes. In terms of mental health, older African-Americans have higher rates of admission to mental hospitals and higher rates of usage of community mental health programs. There is, however, some criticism of possible racism in different diagnoses of emotional problems, as older whites tend to be diagnosed with depression more frequently and older blacks are more often diagnosed with schizophrenia (Morrison & Gresson, 1990). Given the experience of the cohort of African-Americans that is now aged, having confronted economic strain, living in communities higher in crime and poorer in housing, and experiencing a life-long confrontation with discrimination, one might actually think that depression would be more common.

Religiosity has been an emerging area of research, and the socialization involved in religious activities as well as the psychological benefits of faith have both been found to have important health and mental health correlates among older adults (Koenig, 1998). Levin, Taylor, and Chatters (1994) found consistently higher levels of religiosity among older women, as well as significantly higher levels of religiosity among older African-Americans in comparison to older whites. Other studies have found religiosity to be high among older blacks and an important source of life satisfaction as well as socialization, both in and out of formal religious settings (Taylor & Chatters, 1991).

It might be concluded that many older black Americans live under considerable stress due to economic circumstances, especially inner-city residence with associated higher rates of crime and other social problems. Most studies take some care to point out that white elders living in inner cities with high rates of crime and drug abuse, poor housing, and inadequate services have similar problems. We again need to emphasize that not all African-Americans live in the rural South or in ghettos of cities in the industrial North. Those in good neighborhoods with low rates of crime

---

Illustration 4.4. Powerlessness

"The incidence and prevalence of mental illness among older blacks appears to be related to powerlessness as determined by sex and race, perhaps the safest speculation that can be made from the extremely limited information about sex differences among racial minorities is that aged women tend to be at higher risk than aged men for psychological problems, due largely to their inferior status. That is, the incidence and prevalence of psychological and psychiatric problems not organically induced are inversely related to power, prestige, and economic statuses."

From Morrison and Gresson (1990, pp. 249–250).

and other social problems generally confront fewer stresses. The fact that statistical compilations take entire groups and give averages by group can sometimes be misleading, and it must be remembered that diversity means that people have a wide variety of experiences, and many cope with great stress very well. There is no single typical case.

Social networks are important to the well-being of older people. It has been demonstrated that having adult children is an important determinant of the availability of an informal network of helpers, and most of the black elderly indicate that their children are the first place they would turn in a personal crisis (Chatters, Taylor & Neighbors, 1989). There is some evidence, however, that the importance of family supports has declined in recent years, and that friends and neighbors are taking their place as a support network. One study found that when social support was needed, 80% of those studied said they received help from a close friend, 60% received help from church members, and 50% received help from family members (Taylor & Chatters, 1986). Burton and her colleagues (1995) found that the likelihood of a non-immediate family member among unpaid caregivers was significantly higher among disabled older African-Americans. There is a considerable amount of research indicating that the church is an important source of social as well as spiritual support for many older African-Americans (Taylor, 1993; Taylor & Chatters, 1991). Many people look on the members of their congregation as an extended family.

There can be no doubt of the importance of family networks as sources of social supports. The unfortunate situation among black elderly, as is also the case among the white aged, is that smaller families, higher rates of divorce, and greater geographic dispersion of family members will mean that fewer familial supports will be available in future years. Informal networks outside the family as well as services provided by public and private agencies will increasingly be called upon to fill the gap.

Table 4.5 gives a projection of the relative size and growth of the numbers of older individuals in five ethnic or racial groups in the United States. It can be seen that whites represent the largest group by far, followed by blacks and those of Hispanic heritage; Asian and Pacific Islanders are next, followed by a fairly small population of American Indians, Eskimos, and *Aleuts*. The relative growth of the older groups within these categories is also given, and it can be seen that within the oldest groups that Hispanics and Asian Americans are projected to grow the fastest.

The census of population in the United States lists 22 racial or ethnic minorities, plus "other races" and "other Hispanic" as well. The relative size of these populations and their concentrations in various parts of the nation is also given. For example, African-Americans are spread pretty evenly across the country, although there is a somewhat higher concentration in the South. There is a much greater concentration of Japanese Americans in the West, and some clustering of Asian Indians in the Northeast. More Cubans tend to live in the South, particularly in Florida, while Puerto Ricans are more likely to live in the Northeast.

*g*lossary

Aleuts — Native Americans residing in the Aleutian Islands west of Alaska.

TABLE 4.5. Projections of the Older Population by Race, 2000–2025 (in thousands)

Age and Race	2000	2005	2010	2025
White				
55 to 64 years old	19,039	23,235	27,137	27,490
65 to 74 years old	14,825	14,660	16,653	26,504
75 to 84 years old	10,607	10,868	10,394	15,373
85 years old and over	3,694	4,209	4,788	5,428
Black				
55 to 64 years old	2,301	2,850	3,601	4,498
65 to 74 years old	1,608	1,695	1,921	3,364
75 to 84 years old	862	919	947	1,457
85 years old and over	310	344	381	496
Hispanic				
55 to 64 years old	1,717	2,260	2,997	5,272
65 to 74 years old	1,120	1,308	1,606	3,595
75 to 84 years old	568	748	896	1,771
85 years old and over	183	242	345	763
American Indian, Eskimo, Aleut				
55 to 64 years old	136	164	195	227
65 to 74 years old	82	91	106	176
75 to 84 years old	46	52	34	52
85 years old and over	21	27	34	52
Asian, Pacific Islander				
55 to 64 years old	770	1,046	1,354	2,055
65 to 74 years old	500	615	1,354	2,055
75 to 84 years old	231	311	387	787
85 years old and over	51	78	123	308

Source: U.S. Bureau of the Census, *Current Population Reports*, P25–1130.

What we can only infer, though, is how the interaction of each minority with the surrounding majority population is impacted by geography. That is, each group has a different history and a unique set of relationships according to where it is in the country. Many Cubans, for example, live in the Miami area and migrated there after the Castro revolution in 1958. A second wave of Cuban immigrants came to Florida during the 1970s. This means that many Cuban Americans who are aged were born in another country, but have been in the United States long enough to become acclimated to it. They may not have the problems of loneliness and culture shock that are experienced, say, by Hmong or Thai elderly, who are among the more recent immigrants. They have a much smaller pool of their own group with whom to interact, and they are much farther from ancestral homes.

This is not to say that some particular groups have no problems. However, among the more concentrated, larger ethnic groups, at least there is less likelihood of isolation. And many aged Puerto Ricans, for example, have the opportunity to go home to see their relatives every now and again; this possibility is hardly open to the same degree to older Vietnamese or

Cambodians, most of whom are unlikely to see those they left behind when they came to this county.

Further, pressures to adopt the norms of the majority culture are greater when only a small minority is present; that is, Samoans in the Midwest or Eskimos in the South are not likely to have much support from within their own ethnic group. Minorities that are small in number are forced to interact with persons from the majority culture to a greater degree because they are relatively more isolated from others in their own ethnic group.

These may be exceedingly important concerns to some older people. Not having other people of their own heritage to talk to, not being able to obtain familiar foods, being forced to communicate in a foreign and difficult language—all of these issues lead to higher rates of depression among immigrant elderly. The prospect of being buried in a foreign land may hold a particular fear for some older people.

Table 4.5 gives the data from which to infer percentages of the five categories represented among several different age groupings. That is, it is easy enough to add up the totals and make a few simple calculations. For example, the "white" category totals 48,165,000 for the year 2000, or 82.1% of the total. By the year 2025, it is projected that this group will total 74,795,000 or just 73.9% of the total. Similarly, while black people aged 55 and above in Table 4.4 represent 8.7% of the total in 2000, they will represent 9.7% twenty-five years hence. While American Indian elders will continue to represent about one-half of one percent in both 2000 and 2025, the percentage of those of Hispanic heritage will almost double, from 6.1% of all elderly to 11.2%. In fact, Hispanic elderly will outpace black elderly and become the largest older minority group. Similarly, the proportion of Asian and Pacific Islanders will about double, going from 2.6% to over 4.6% in just 25 years.

We can also see from these data that a number of minority groups in the United States are fairly "young" in that they contain a relatively smaller percentage of very old people. For example, those whites aged 85+ in the year 2000 represent 7.7% of the white population aged 55 and older; the comparable percentage for African-Americans is 6.1% and for Hispanics it is 5.1%; it is 7.4% for Native Americans but only 3.3% for Asians and Pacific Islanders. This is projected to change in 25 years so that the comparative figures calculated from the data in Table 4.4 will look like this: the percentage of those aged 55 and older represented by those 85 and older will be 7.3% for whites, 5.0% for blacks, 6.7% for Hispanics, 10.3% for Indians, and 6.6% for Asians. In other words, the oldest group among Asian Pacific Islanders and American Indians will grow the fastest; it will actually decline slightly for whites and blacks. These are census projections made on people who are already alive, of course, so they tend to have greater accuracy than projections based on an assumed birth rate.

The relative youth of certain minority populations is confirmed in other data (U.S. Bureau of the Census, 1998b). Only 5.2% of the current Hispanic population is aged 65 or above, while 13.9% of the white population is elderly. For purposes of comparison, 6.2% of Asians are 65+; the corresponding percentage for Native Americans is 5.8%, and among African Americans it is 8.4%. The relatively small percentage of older people among the groups that do not have a large number of recent, younger immigrants might be explained by a health disadvantage; that is, as we learned in Chapter 1, comparatively fewer blacks and Native Americans live to become old.

Hispanic Elderly

As we have already noted, Hispanic peoples can be of any race and are more diverse than some of the other ethnic groups in certain ways. This means that they may have less in common with each other than other minorities. Immigrants from Portuguese-speaking Brazil, say, might feel that they have little in common with Spanish-speaking Mexican-Americans, even though both groups might be classified as Hispanic or Latino. Their problems of *acculturation* and getting along within the society may be quite different. Further, race does make a difference, and the darker one's skin, the greater the burden of discrimination, as a general rule.

Usually, those who have been in place for the longest time have the fewest problems with language and customs. People whose families have been in North America for several hundred years obviously have an easier time relating to the norms of the majority culture; recent immigrants who are at a language disadvantage would certainly agree with this. "Americanization" and English language classes became popular offerings in adult education programs sponsored by public schools in response to the large wave of immigration to the United States early in the 1900s. These programs have been reborn in recent years with the influx of more immigrants.

Immigrants unfamiliar with the norms, values, and language in their new country are at a distinct disadvantage. So we need to consider issues of diversity within a minority group that really is a cluster or an umbrella category encompassing several racial and ethnic groups. For example, refugees from Central America who are sponsored by Sanctuary groups, and thus are technically in the United States illegally, may in reality have few things in common with Mexican-Americans who have lived in the United States for many generations, or with Puerto Ricans who are American citizens by birthright.

As we can see in Table 4.6, persons of Mexican heritage represent by far the largest proportion of the overall category labeled "Hispanic." There are over 18 million Mexican-Americans in the United States. Many, in places like New Mexico and Colorado, are not immigrants: their families were here before the country was a nation. Others are recent arrivals, and there is a relatively higher proportion of undocumented immigrants among this group.

TABLE 4.6. U.S. Hispanic Population by Age (in thousands)

Age	Total Hispanic	Mexican	Puerto-Rican	Cuban	Central & South American	Other Hispanic
Total persons	29,703	18,795	3,152	1,258	4,292	2,206
Under 5 years	3,443	2,415	313	77	410	228
5 to 14 years	5,560	3,783	639	126	632	380
15 to 44 years	15,106	9,564	1,532	509	2,394	1,104
45 to 64 years	4,079	2,274	499	286	677	341
65 years and over	1,516	757	167	260	179	154

From U.S. Bureau of the Census (1998b).
Note. Totals are not precise due to rounding.

The census data list 757,000 Mexican-Americans as being age 65 or over; this represents only 4.0% of the entire group. This is because almost all of the large number who have come to this country in recent years are young people. Older persons, as a rule, don't migrate, or at least they don't migrate at nearly the rates that younger people do. For the most part, then, we might conclude that most older Mexican-Americans have been in the United States for a relatively long time (with certain exceptions, of course). This would mean that they might have fewer language and acculturation problems than other minority groups. What will happen in the future, however, is the aging in place of more recent migrants. Mexican-Americans are the fastest-growing minority in the U.S., and there will be a fast-growing group of older people among them in only a few years.

Table 4.2 indicated that 24.4% of the Hispanic elderly lived in poverty in 1996, compared to 9.4% of white and 25.3 percent of black aged persons. But, as we can see from Table 4.5, people within the "Hispanic" categorization are themselves quite diverse. Should we assume that these income figures mainly apply to Mexican-Americans, since they represent over half of all Hispanic elders? That would be a misuse of the data. Unfortu-

---

Illustration 4.5. Illegal Aliens in Nebraska

A colleague and I did some interviewing in Scottsbluff, in the far western part of Nebraska. One of the problems of the elderly we heard about dealt with anxiety over being illegal aliens. Were these people from Mexico, we wondered? Our informants said, no, the Mexican-Americans who live around there had been there many generations. The people most afraid that the Immigration and Naturalization Service might catch on that they have no green cards are German Russians, who came to work the sugar beet fields in 1917–18 and who just stayed on. Some of these people, now quite elderly, are reluctant to apply for services or government benefits because they're afraid they might be sent home if it is discovered that they never became citizens.

nately, we do not have income or poverty figures available that are specific to both age and nationality within ethnic groups.

About the best we can do is look at a comparison of total family income (for all ages) from the United States 1990 census of population, as the 2000 census data are not compiled as of this writing. For example, Cubans had the highest median family income among Hispanic people at $31,439, and Puerto Ricans the lowest at $18,008. Mexican-Americans, people from Central and South American, and "other Hispanics" taken together were in between at about $23,500. Puerto Ricans of all ages had the highest percentage of persons in poverty at 40.6%. By comparison, only 16.9% of Cubans were below the poverty level, and Mexican-Americans had a poverty rate of 28.1% (U.S. Bureau of the Census, 1998b). Remember, these figures are for all ages. Within groups, a reasonable assumption is that older persons have less income and a higher poverty rate. Since these figures are not age-specific, we can't speak with a great deal of precision, but we might be able to generalize a bit. The inference we can draw from these data is that Cubans tend to be the least poor among Hispanics, Puerto Ricans the poorest, and Mexican-Americans somewhere in between. This is probably also true for the aged within these groups.

Beyond these few figures, however, there is little value in generalizing about groups. To say that people are all the same because they speak the same language is, of course, absurd. The needs of poor people, recent immigrants, and illegal immigrants are of course going to be much different from others who have adapted to the language and customs of the majority culture and who have a good income. Middle-class Hispanics really have much more in common with middle-class whites than they do with recent political and economic refugees from Spanish-speaking countries. When working with groups of the aged—of any cultural heritage—their own special needs must be taken into account; we cannot assume that people within groups are all the same any more than we can assume that different ethnic groups are the same.

We must also remember that the aged of particular ethnic groups still are aged, and physically will have the same problems of other older persons. Poverty, though, tends to make these problems worse. And we shouldn't forget the real message of being a minority. Many white, middle-class people can go from day to day without giving much if any thought to issues of race and class: they're comfortable dealing within the majority culture. The same cannot be said for members of minority groups; for them, not a day goes by that they are not reminded in a dozen different ways that they are seen as being somehow different, and, by implication, inferior.

This may be particularly true of people who have come from other countries. Everything must seem different. To the old, especially, the strange language, the different customs (many of which may offend their traditions), and the entire atmosphere must be bewildering. A special problem is seeing their children and grandchildren adopting new ways of speaking, acting, and relating to the family. Delgado (1997), for instance, found a

> **Illustration 4.6. Research Among Puerto Rican Elders**
>
> "The elders described countless personal experiences reflecting the inability or unwillingness of their children and other family members to help them with daily living activities.
>
> "The elders also mentioned that there had been dramatic changes in values concerning the role of caregiver within the Puerto Rican families. Many children were no longer willing to make the necessary sacrifices to help their aging parents. Instead, they wanted to have freedom to enjoy life without the burdens of caregiving. Many elders, in turn, could not depend upon anyone other than themselves. Virtually all of the elders attending the forum knew of a peer who had to be, or was in the process of being, institutionalized in a nursing home because their children were not interested in assuming responsibility for their care."
>
> From Delgado (1997, p. 325).

good deal of disintegration—and resentment—among the families of older Puerto Ricans. It may seem that old, traditional values are being cast aside. Family members are becoming Americans, and elders feel like they are frozen in time. They may consider themselves to be repositories of values and traditions that are no longer regarded as important by younger family members.

One study of older Cubans in the Miami area found these problems to be especially acute. Many felt themselves to be strangers in a strange land. Their children readily adapted to their new environment, but the older people felt a sense of cultural displacement (Linn, Hunter, & Perry, 1979). Other older people from foreign countries must also regard themselves to be displaced persons. In some cases, these perceived cultural barriers may assume greater importance than economic difficulties.

A study comparing Puerto Rican older persons, who tend to be among the poorest within the category "Hispanic," to Cuban elders, who are the least likely to be poor, found more positive patterns of adjustment among the Puerto Ricans. They had fewer problems accessing services, perhaps because they felt more comfortable in dealing within the majority society. The Cubans, even though they were economically better off, were the more recent immigrants and thus at a disadvantage culturally. The study underscored the diversity within and among Hispanic groups (Starrett, Todd, & DeLeon, 1989). This concept holds within Hispanic groups based on how long they have been in this country. Angel and her colleagues (1996 & 1999), for example, found that foreign-born Mexican-Americans had a much greater expectation of living with their adult children than older Mexican-Americans who were born in the United States. However, Levin, Markides, and Ray (1996) found that older Mexican-Americans in Texas were well adjusted, especially among those with high levels of religious attendance.

Of particular note among those who have migrated to this country, relative to the feeling of being displaced, is a high rate of depression (Cuellar, 1990). This has been documented among Hispanic elderly immigrants, and may also be the case among older immigrants from other countries.

Native American Elderly

There are about 149,000 older persons in the United States who are of Native American heritage. This category includes American Indians, Aleuts (natives of the Aleutian Islands), and Alaska Natives or Inuit. This relatively small number of older Native Americans puts them among the smallest groups among the older minorities in the United States. Canada has a somewhat larger Native minority. Native Americans can live anywhere, and many of the cities in North America have a meaningful number of Native Americans, but they are unique among minority groups in that almost half of them live on reservations. It is also the case that people move back and forth, living on a reservation some of the time and elsewhere some of the time. It is difficult to speak of particular issues common to all Native American elderly because they are such a diverse group. Issues such as poverty and a poor record of longevity apply to most older Native Americans, but there is such a wide geographic spread and tribal cultures are so different that it is unfair to lump all of them together and say they are one group with common problems. In Table 4.7, for example, we can see that the overall poverty rate among Navajo people is over twice that of, say, Iroquois or Choctaw people. And only those tribal groups of 50,000 members or over are listed in the table, leaving out somewhat smaller tribes

TABLE 4.7. United States American Indian Population

Tribe	<5 yrs.	Age 18+	65+	Total Number	Poverty rate
Cherokee	6.3%	73.3%	7.2%	369,035	22.0%
Navajo	13.6	57.7	4.6	225,298	48.8
Sioux	12.3	60.0	4.4	107,321	44.4
Chippewa	10.3	64.0	4.7	105,988	34.3
Choctaw	8.2	68.8	8.0	86,231	23.0
Pueblo	10.3	64.2	5.8	55,330	33.2
Apache	10.2	64.7	3.4	53,330	37.5
Iroquois	8.1	71.1	6.7	52,557	20.1
Lumbee	8.3	66.2	5.6	50,888	22.1
Total	9.7	65.8	5.9	1,937,391	31.2

From U.S. Bureau of the Census (1998b).
Note. Total includes others in addition to the nine largest tribes.

such as Creeks or Seminoles. Thus it is difficult to generalize about Native Americans overall.

There is, though, one over-riding generalization that is fair when speaking of Native Americans. Just as we saw that African-Americans share a common heritage in previous generations of slavery, it would be fair to generalize and state that Native Americans share a common heritage of being conquered peoples. That is to say, if one goes back far enough, there is evidence that the majority culture conquered the Native peoples in one way or another. This was literally true in the case of many tribes, which were defeated in one or more wars, but it is psychologically true of the way almost all Native peoples have been regarded by the majority culture: for the most part, it is fair to say that Native peoples in American have been historically treated as people who have been vanquished in combat. Defeating people in a war, especially in previous centuries, often meant that the people who regarded themselves as the "winners"—the majority culture—devalued Native Americans' culture, language, and customs. A prevailing problem of older Native Americans to this day is the preservation of their cultures in the face of pressures of assimilation from the majority culture (Weibel-Orlando, 1989).

Older Native Americans have a health disadvantage in comparison to other older Americans for chronic diseases such as diabetes, liver, and kidney disease, high blood pressure, emphysema, and gall bladder problems (Chapleski, Lichtenberg, Dwyer, Youngblade, & Tsai, 1997). And they have much higher mortality rates for cirrhosis of the liver, diabetes, and accidents. It is a fact that only about 5.9% of all Native Americans are aged 65 or older, which could be accounted for by either a high birthrate or high rates of death prior to age 65. While the American Indian birthrate is somewhat higher than that of other groups, the rates of death at younger ages is so much higher that it provides most of the explanation for their very low percentage of people 65+. Diabetes and alcoholism are especially devastating to middle-aged Native Americans, and accident and suicide rates are much higher among younger Native Americans. Fewer die of heart disease and cancer because fewer live to get old and die of these causes of death most common among the elderly. Only about 42% of Native Americans live until their 65th birthday, compared to over 70% among the population as a whole (Rhodes, 1990).

This is not to say that older Native Americans should be disregarded because they represent such a small group (only four-tenths of one percent of all old people in the United States). Unfortunately, they are sometimes considered to be a hard-to-serve population by service agencies and consequently have a record of under-utilization of the services that are available to most older persons (Kramer, 1991). Assessments of health and social services for older Native Americans have not been particularly positive, and researchers point to the greater importance of informal, family-based service networks (Versen, 1981). It cannot be doubted, though, that a major research agenda should include improved health status and increasing longevity among older Native Americans (Wykle & Kaskel, 1994).

One study of older American Indians found women to note that advantages of aging included greater independence and a feeling closer to their families (Harris, Begay, & Page, 1989). Overall, however, those who have concern with the preservation of traditional values, language, and culture often express dismay at the assimilation of younger persons into the majority culture and the disappearance of traditions, such as respect for the elderly. It might be said that in this regard, Native American elders are similar to many other minority elderly, particularly those of Asian heritage. Problems of poverty, alcoholism and resultant family violence, discrimination, a lack of social and health care services, and a lack of political clout continue among older Native Americans.

Asian-American Elderly

Asian and Pacific Island older people represent one of the fastest-growing groups of ethnic elderly in the United States (Tanjasiri, Wallace, & Shibata, 1995), and, like other minority elders, financial strain is among their principal problems (Ferraro & Su, 1999). Like Hispanic elders, older persons of Asian decent represent a considerable number of ethnic and racial groups, including Chinese, Japanese, Filipino, Korean, Asian Indian, Vietnamese, Cambodian, Laotian, Hmong, Thai, Hawaiian, Samoan, Guamanian, and others.

In the case of Asian-Americans, we might differentiate them on the basis of the country of origin and on how recently they have come to the United States. Largest among those groups of Asian heritage are persons whose families have come from China (1.8 million), followed by those from the Philippines (1.7 million), Asian Indians (1.0 million), and Japan (1.0 million). Of these groups, those whose families have been in the United

TABLE 4.8. Older Asian Pacific Islanders in the United States

Group	Total (thousands)	Age (in percent) 65+	65–74	75+
Chinese	1,809	6.6	4.5	2.1
Filipino	1,171	7.2	4.8	2.4
Asian Indian	1,017	2.0	1.3	0.6
Japanese	1,007	14.6	9.8	4.8
Vietnamese	961	2.3	1.7	0.6
Korean	784	4.4	3.2	1.1
Other API	1,108	3.3	2.6	0.7
All API	7,857	6.0	4.1	1.9

From Kuo and Porter (1998).

States the longest (i.e., the Chinese and the Japanese) have the highest average age, and those more recent immigrants (i.e., Vietnamese and Koreans) tend to have relatively fewer older persons. Among the Japanese, in fact, there is a higher proportion of older persons in the United States than there is among the general population taken as a whole (Kitano, 1990; Kuo & Porter, 1998).

As is indicated in Table 4.8, groups vary widely. Japanese-Americans, 14.6% of whom are aged 65 or older, represent the oldest minority group in the United States. The Vietnamese represent one of the youngest.

The Chinese were the first Asians to migrate to America in appreciable numbers (if one excludes those of Mongol racial heritage who were the forebears of American Indians and who crossed into North America thousands of years ago). Large numbers of Chinese men came to the United States in the middle of the nineteenth century as laborers. Many hoped to prosper and then bring their wives and families in time. The Chinese Exclusion Act of 1882 and the Asian Exclusion Act of 1924 unfortunately restricted Chinese female immigration. Few Chinese males were able to afford to return to their homeland, and the result was a disproportionate sex ratio of four males to only one female among Chinese living in the United States during the earlier years of the twentieth century (Sakauye, 1990). As a result, an unusually high proportion the Chinese-American elderly population still is male. Despite a history of institutionalized discrimination,

---

Illustration 4.8. Assimilation of Older Asian Americans

"In later generations, Asian groups have often been able to assimilate better than most other visible minority groups in terms of occupational achievement, income, and education. For most Asian subgroups, the culture of poverty is not the primary explanatory factor underlying differences. The impact of ethnicity and culture may be more important."

From Sakauye (1990, p. 41).

Illustration 4.9. Elderly Chinese

"Chinese families, both old and new, still cherish Confucian ethics, which espouse the oldest male controlling family economics and maintaining a high prestige in his family as well as in society. The Chinese are more concerned about their families than the average Asian-American in the United States. Although their commitment to family and a filial responsibility to older members are somewhat lessened due in part to modernization and westernization of their children, semiextended family systems have been noticeably developed among Chinese Americans."

From Kim (1990, p. 350).

Chinese-Americans have prospered in the cities of North America. Service programs that have been successful among older Chinese have drawn upon a heritage of family values and respect for the aged (Der-McLeod & Hansen, 1992).

While there is some evidence that traditional values no longer have as much cultural reinforcement, there remains a strong feeling among many Chinese elders that it is the son's responsibility to care for his parents. For this reason, governmental efforts to promote birth control in modern-day China meet resistance among parents who have had a girl as a first child. Their expectation is that their daughter ultimately will marry and go off to care for her husband's parents; thus, they are motivated to continue trying to have a male child. Such birth restrictions in China do not affect Chinese-Americans, but the cultural desirability of having one or more sons must continue to have some influence, especially among recent immigrants.

Illustration 4.10. *Kai* Bonding

"We were aware of the tradition of *Kai* bonding. Sworn brotherhood or sisterhood between individuals of the same age had been a not uncommon pattern in the countryside in years past.

"A variation of this type of relationship that was particularly useful to the single individual who had no children, or to the person whose children had died, was entering into a Kai relationship with a younger person, preferably one who had no living parents. Gifts would be exchanged publicly, and the older individual would provide advice and service to the younger one, with the pattern reversing in the later years of the relationship. Ikles (1980) maintains that the force of public opinion encourages both participants to fulfill their obligations. She also says, however, that increasing pressures of urbanization, particularly in Hong Kong, have made many Kai relationships less stable or more difficult to form."

From Thorson (1984, p. 89).

Japanese-Americans, at least from the point of view of material prosperity, have had the greatest success of all groups of Asian heritage. Although smaller in number than some other Asian groups, the Japanese overall have prospered and have been influential in the United States. There is some feeling among older Japanese, as there is among the aged in other groups, that traditions of care and respect for the aged are not what they once were or could be. Lamenting the lack of respect for the elderly in comparison to some idealized earlier time in life may not, of course, be exclusive to Japanese-Americans. Erdman Palmore (1975) pointed to the fact that Western values adopted in Japan itself have bothered many older persons: they feel that their children just don't give them the respect that they were expected to give their own parents. Nevertheless, there still is a strong expectation among older people in Japan (and among Japanese-Americans) that care will be provided by their children. Palmore relates an interview he had with a 78-year-old woman who was in failing health and who expected to be moving in with her son and his family. Asked if this would not put a strain on her daughter-in-law, her response was, "Her happiness is not our consideration now."

Given the acceptance and place in American society that Japanese people have achieved, it is important that we realize that this is only a recent phenomenon. Like the Chinese, the Japanese were kept from coming to the United States, in particular by the Asian Exclusion Act of 1924. Going even beyond that, racist hysteria during World War II was the basis for the government rounding up Japanese families and placing them in "interment" camps—actually, prison camps—and over one hundred thousand sat out the early 1940s in bleak concentration camps in remote areas of the West. It was only in 1988 that Congress passed legislation offering an official apology for this action and authorizing a one-time payment of $20,000 (which finally was appropriated and paid over the course of the years 1990 to 1993) to individuals still living who had been subject to this treatment. Those who were young people when they were in the camps are now approaching old age, and the memory must be a vivid one that has had a profound impact upon many Japanese-Americans. Not only was the arrest

---

Illustration 4.11. Respect for the Honorable Elders

"Actual beliefs in the power of the ancestral ghosts were probably exaggerated, but it was generally considered important that the ghosts be kept happy through reverence and nourishment. . . . It is but a small step from this ancestor worship to filial piety toward living parents and grandparents. Since reverence and devotion to dead ancestors are of supreme importance, respect and duty toward living parents and grandparents (who will soon become dead ancestors) became the second most important thing in life."

From Palmore (1975, pp. 23–24).

Illustration 4.12. *Issei* and *Nissei*

"Most Japanese elderly are known as *Issei* (first generation Japanese). Unlike their Chinese counterparts, the Isseis came to American with a desire to stay. They do not regret their immigration, in spite of overt and covert racial discrimination, forced dislocation to concentration camps during World War II, and subsequent economic impoverishment. The Japanese-Americans are perhaps most well adapted to the new culture; yet they have retained their latent cohesiveness as a group. While Chinese-Americans value the family, Japanese-Americans transcend family values to group conscience. The Issei in particular believe in self-esteem or self-worth as measured by the degree to which the individual contributes to the Japanese. . . . Although *Nissei*, the second generation, does not fully accept traditional values, the Japanese vision of Buddhism endures through Issei, in that they still cherish filial devotion and loving indulgence between old and young."

From Kim (1990, p. 351).

of United States citizens and imprisonment of them without trial totally unconstitutional, but the message the government gave that it was acceptable to discriminate on the basis of national origin is one that is hard to erase. This message must have been particularly harsh to older Japanese individuals at the time, given their traditions of value and respect for the group.

Sociologist Harry Kitano has observed particular values important among older Japanese persons: first among these is reliance on the group and the opinion of the group. "What will others think?" is very important. He says a practical implication of this is that younger Japanese may go beyond all usual expectations in attempting to care for elders, and that this might result in unusual instances of caregiver strain. Male dominance and traditional family roles may be more important to Japanese and other Asian Americans, as is obligation to the family. Feelings of shame and guilt may result if such obligations are ignored. He also points to strong dependency needs, a sense a fatalism, and submission to authority as characteristic traits (Kitano, 1990).

Because people from the Philippines were American nationals after the Spanish-American War of 1899, and because they were not included in the Asian Exclusion Act of 1924, they were free to immigrate to the United States during the first three decades of the twentieth century. This explains why they are presently the second-largest group from Asia. The Tydings McDuffie Act of 1934, however, was meant to exclude Filipinos, limiting their number of immigrants to the U.S. to only 50 per year. The 1965 U.S. Immigration Act, however, abolished the quota system, reopening Filipino immigration to the United States. This has made for a peculiar configuration in the Filipino-American demographic profile, and Filipino elders can

"One of the more common practices that may lead to misunderstanding and a high degree of frustration among majority group workers is that of indirect communication. It stands in contrast to the American attitude of 'letting it all hang out'. Frustration may come about because communication then becomes long and drawn out, and inferences (often incorrect), nuances, and other cues have to be used to try to understand the situation. Problems and important issues may be presented in an oblique manner so that time and patience may be necessary in order to make the wise decision."

From Kitano (1990, pp. 346–347).

be divided in to two groups: those who came to the United States prior to 1940 and those who came after 1965. Those in the first group are predominantly males who came to this country as laborers in the early part of the twentieth century; they have little education and many are now older urban dwellers in boarding houses or houses shared by a group of older Filipinos. Having experienced harsh racial discrimination, they rely on each other when they need help. Many do not have families, but due to feelings of shame tend not to ask for help from outside agencies. The second group has more women, is better educated, and experiences a lack of support from the first group of older Filipinos; it is, however, more receptive to the use of health and social services (Kim, 1990).

Fast-growing groups of immigrants from Asia include Asian-Indians, Koreans, people from various countries in the Middle East, and refugees from Southeast Asia. They have little in common. Those from India and Korea have migrated to the United States in a steady stream since the passage of the Immigration Act of 1965, tend to be better-educated, and came to the United States with the intention of establishing a better life. Many individuals from Arab countries are in similar circumstances, although their

Illustration 4.14. A Tradition of Respect

"An ethnic value, respect, is the fundamental basis of social interaction among Filipinos, extending to everyone, including parents, older individuals, and persons occupying positions of authority. Listening to others, self-imposed restraint, loyalty to the family, and an unquestioning obedience to authority are culturally prescribed behaviors. Moreover, those who are to be respected receive preferential treatment in Filipino society established even in the United States."

From Kim (1990, p. 456).

numbers of migrants have only grown in more recent years. Many Vietnamese, Hmong, Laotians, and Cambodians, on the other hand, have had no choice about leaving their home countries and had little expectation of living the second half of their lives so far from friends and family (Yee, 1992). As might be expected among immigrant populations, adaptation to a new language, norms, and values of the majority culture are difficulties.

Like many groups that have come to North America over the years, all have tended to follow what is called beachhead migration patterns: pioneers establish a beachhead in a particular city or part of the country, and others follow to join them. This explains the fact that over 300,000 people who speak Arabic live in Detroit and an even larger number of Koreans live in Los Angeles. There is a two-mile stretch of Devon Avenue on the North Side of Chicago that has no fewer than 15 sari shops; people who come from India look on this district as a shopping mecca, and many will travel hundreds or even thousands of miles to shop there.

Conclusion

In summary, North America has proven to be a land of opportunity for most immigrants, racial prejudice notwithstanding. Many have come to the United States and Canada with little except a willingness to work, and many have prospered. Those who are the most recent immigrants tend to have the greatest problems adapting; they have had to learn a new language and get used to new customs and ways of doing things. Many must long for the old country and for traditional norms and values. Loneliness away from their own particular ethnic group has to be a pervasive problem, and those who have immigrated in later life must be acutely aware of their minority status. Those born in North America may have fewer difficulties in terms of adaptation, but they no doubt present their aged parents with considerable concerns as they inevitably distance themselves from traditional values.

Valuing one's heritage is by no means something that is exclusive to minorities who are recent immigrants from other countries. Many African-Americans and Native Americans have been especially conscious of their unique cultural heritage. Many older persons are seen as repositories of generational wisdom and are sought out by younger people concerned with the preservation of their individual cultures. There are, after all, older blacks still living who knew people who were born into slavery and Native Americans who knew ancestors who were free to wander the Plains before the reservation system was instituted. They are living history books, and oral history projects with them have particular value.

In working with groups from whatever minority, we should be particularly conscious of their individual and cultural values, being careful to not offend persons who may not have a particularly Western way of seeing the world. Learning more about the heritage, values, and customs of the groups with whom we work is not only personally enriching, but it makes for a more effective way of dealing with older people. In cases where we have doubts about the values of cultures other than our own, it's always a good idea to ask: inquire of knowledgeable others, the adult children of elders, or the older persons themselves. The diversity of American culture adds a richness from which we can all learn.

Questions for Discussion

1. Which minority group (or groups) do you think have had the hardest time relating to the majority culture in America?
2. Describe some positive stereotypes you might think of that could describe particular older minority group members.
3. What are some reasons that Cuban-Americans have a higher average income than other Hispanic people in the United States?
4. In the earlier years of this century, many Chinese living in America either returned home or wanted to return home. Why do you suppose this was true?
5. Older African-American women have the lowest suicide rate of any group in the United States. Can you offer a possible explanation for this?
6. In what ways have you seen traditional values change over time in your own family?
7. Do you think that older women as a group have the characteristics of a minority? Why or why not?

Sources of Further Information

A number of different organizations produce excellent publications on aging and diversity; write for a list of current publications.

Human Resources & Aging
National Eldercare Institute on Human Resources
c/o Brookdale Center on Aging of Hunter College
425 East 25th St.
New York, NY 10010

Older Women's League
666 Eleventh Street, N.W., Suite 700
Washington, D.C. 20001

Forecasting and Environmental Scanning Department
American Association of Retired Persons
601 E Street, N.W.
Washington, D.C. 20049

National Association of Hispanic Elderly
3325 Wilshire Blvd., Suite 800
Los Angeles, CA 90010

National Hispanic Council on Aging
2713 Ontario Road, N.W.
Washington, D.C. 20009

National Caucus on the Black Aged
1424 K Street, N.W., Suite 500
Washington, D.C. 20005

American Indians Elder Project
220 Strong Hall
University of Kansas
Lawrence, KS 66045

Anyone with access to the World Wide Web can get the most recent United States Census data at: http//www.census.gov/

PART
Physical and Psychological Aspects of Gerontology

Why do we get old? What happens to our bodies and minds over the passage of many years? As we age, we go through several decades of development and then enter a period of decline. Hearing is most acute at around age ten; we never hear better after that. Perhaps this is the first system to begin to decline. Maximum running speed peaks several years after that, and overall physical strength a few years later. Some time around age 40 the eyes begin to change their shape, and many people need glasses—or bifocals—at that age. During the decade of the 40s, the hair begins to turn gray, and many men lose significant amounts of it. Almost all women have completed menopause by age 55. Later, the spinal column begins to become compacted and we actually get shorter. By the 60s or 70s, there is a general physical slowing down that is associated with the aging process. People may complain that they're getting forgetful. By the 80s, genuine frailty sets in for almost everyone who is still living. Hair that appeared in the armpits and groin in early teens now begins to disappear. The immune system begins to fail for the majority of the population. Only 22 in 1,000 women—and 7 in 1,000 men—are still living by age 100.

Why does this happen? Are we programmed to become old? Do we wear out like an old pair of jeans? Is there anything we can do about it?

We'll seek the answers to these questions in this second section of the book, looking at the processes of physical and psychological aging as well as older people and the health care system. First , in Chapter 5, we'll examine several theories dealing with the basics of physical aging; the chapter will conclude with some practical advice on personal aging.

The Aging Body

5

Chapter Outline

"But death eventually comes to all things that live, whether they 'stop' or not. First life, then death. As a physicist, I believe that life is a mechanism that defies the second law of thermodynamics, while death is the ultimate triumph of this law. What is this second law? It states, in effect, that all natural processes tend to degrade, to lower the levels of energy in a very potent system, in an irreversible manner, unless the system is refurbished."

—Dan Q. Posin, born 1909

Introduction

Tennis players and swimmers often seem to peak out while still in their teens. Track and field athletes for the most part are past their prime while still in their 20s. A Nolan Ryan only comes along once in a blue moon; baseball pitchers hardly ever make it past 40. Sandy Koufax hung it up when he was 29. The football career of Gayle Sayers was about typical for an NFL player: around five years. Yet, orchestra conductors, poets, and golfers seem to go on almost forever. Why?

Each of these activities uses different abilities or combinations of abilities, and it is clear that our capacities in different areas develop and decline at different rates. Most of us can hear about as well as we'll ever be able to by around the age of ten; after than, there are subtle declines in hearing ability that continue throughout the rest of life. One can't exercise or build up the ability to hear; about the best we can do is try to preserve as much of it as we can (avoiding jet runways, artillery ranges, and rock concerts all seem to help). By the same token, there's nothing we can do to build up our capacity to fight off skin cancer; the only thing we can do is try to prevent it by using a sun screen and avoiding bright sunlight.

Of course, many physical abilities do respond to practice and repetition. Power lifters don't peak in their teens; they've not had time enough to build up the bulk of muscle that weightlifting requires. In the same way, the physical skill of musicians seems to develop over time; piano players who are good in their 20s can expect to be better in their 30s, if they keep practicing.

So it's apparent that certain physical abilities, combined with practice and experience, can improve over time. This can be true even in the face of simultaneous declines in other abilities. Experience and judgment can, in fact, overcome some decrements in physical ability. Baseball pitchers who last a long time don't continue to rely on their blazing fast ball as much as they did in their younger days. They don't pitch "fast" so much as they pitch "smart." Golf is a game of fine motor control and judgment more than strength or endurance, and golfers whose game is in fine tune seem to play at near their peak ability for many years.

What's involved here is the complex aging of the body and brain. We usually think of physical aging as a downward spiral, an inevitable decline

---

Illustration 5.1. Different Abilities at Different Ages

Don't expect to be a virtuoso violinist if you don't take up playing the instrument until you're 20. Most of the really great violin players started in early childhood. This doesn't mean that you'll not be able to learn to play the violin as an adult; but, you will probably not reach the peak of skill you might have achieved if you'd started earlier.

We've never heard of a painter, though, who was a child prodigy. Most great artists apply their craft for many years before they reach their peak. There are examples of artists like Grandma Moses and Elizabeth Layton who didn't take up painting until later life. Painting isn't so much a test of reproducing visual accuracy (photography can do that), so much as it is communicating a way of viewing the world. Would Elizabeth Layton or Grandma Moses have been better painters if they'd begun as little girls? This is something we can't know; they might have been different painters, but who can say that they'd have been better?

The development of different skills seems to be a combination of when they were begun, the coordination of different abilities that go into their development, and the level of motivation necessary to achieve satisfaction. This kind of development can happen in spite of physical declines associated with aging.

in speed, strength, accuracy, and control. We know that with training some abilities can be maintained or even improved over time. But while practice and exercise can improve particular skills or even one's vital capacity, other systems in the body inevitably decline. No amount of exercise will improve one's vision, hearing, or taste, for example, or make the kidneys or liver work better. About the best we can hope in some areas is to not hasten inevitable losses.

Physical aging, however, does not always mean disability. Different systems of the body change with aging at different rates. Although it is true that the *coordination* of physical and mental functions declines faster than single systems decline, it is also true that some abilities develop over time or decline much later in life, if at all.

Physical Theories of Aging

As we develop over time, changes take place in our bodies. Generally, we think of those changes as development in our younger years and as decline in our later years. This is not always the case: Isaac Stern is probably a better violinist now in his 80s than he was in his 20s—he certainly makes a better living at it now. But, few of us have the abilities of an Isaac Stern, and few of us are willing or able to devote long hours every day to keep our abilities at their peak.

We could practice and exercise our physical abilities constantly, but we would still experience their inevitable decline. Practice and exercise might slow down the rate of decline or even delay its onset, but we know that eventually we slow down in many ways if we live long enough.

Illustration 5.2. Coordination of Physical Functions

"By the year 2002, the number of licensed drivers over age 75 will be 17.5 million. Of these, well over half will suffer from cataracts, dementia, or nervous disorders that can make their hands tremble on steering wheels. Eighty percent will take one or more prescription medicine, including some that make them dizzy or drowsy.

"As a group, they will drive an estimated 84 billion miles a year.

"The potential for disaster is already evident. While older drivers as a group aren't nearly as dangerous as teenagers, their accident rates slowly begin rising at age 60, and start rocketing after age 75. After age 85, they are involved in accidents more than four times as often as the safest drivers, those age 50 to 59, on a mile-for-mile basis. And when they are in accidents, drivers over age 85 are 15 times as likely to die as drivers in their 40s."

From Rigdon (1995, p. 1).

**immune or
immunological** —
Having to do with the
body's immune system
of fighting off infection.

With aging we have less reserve capacity, we become more prone to certain illnesses, and our physical appearance changes. There are several specific theories of physical aging that seek to explain why these changes take place, and we'll discuss them briefly. Overall, however, the entire aging process seems to fit well within a theory of margin. This explains aging as a process whereby we use more and more of our marginal capacity as we age; we don't have as much "left over" ability when we are old.

This theory of margin could have many applications. For example, let's suppose that walking ten miles when you are 20 takes up, say, half of your marginal capacity to walk long distances without collapsing. You're tired after walking ten miles, but you've not reached the absolute limit of your capacity. But, unless you're an accomplished walker, going even a few miles when you're aged 70 might take up more like 80 or 90 percent of your marginal capacity. Or, walking even a block might take up 95 percent. The idea is that older bodies are forced to go nearer to the limit of their marginal capacity to perform life's tasks.

Another example might be in some realm other than physical endurance. Let's say that you have a young, healthy body and that you have high resistance to infection. Your ability to fight off disease is not really being stretched, and you bounce back quickly when you have a cold or the flu. Later in life, you may find that your *immune* system is less efficient and that you're more prone to chronic as well as acute illnesses. We might say that your body's ability to fight off disease is pretty close to the margin of its capacity. That's why a bad influenza season generally is responsible for about 20,000 deaths and most of these people are elderly. They were frail to begin with, they were already close to the edge, and the additional infection tipped the balance for them. Sooner or later, one more straw will break the camel's back. An interesting thing that has happened over the past few

---

Illustration 5.3. Healthier Generations of Older People

"They called it the failure of success. As medical scientists got better and better at treating people with fatal diseases—but not curing them—the nation would be burdened with an accumulation of elderly people who were living longer and longer but were crippled with pain and riddled with disabilities.

"It was a notion that called into question what medicine had wrought. But to nearly everyone's surprise, the predicted pandemic of pain and disability has not materialized. Instead, new information, some not yet published, on studies involving people at all socioeconomic levels show that not only are Americans living longer, but they are developing less chronic disease and disability, and the reasons may have as much to do with changing social circumstances, including events that occur in the first few decades of life, as they have to do with medical advances in treating diseases."

From Kilata (1996, p. B1).

decades is the emergence of a healthier, heartier cohort of older people. One might say that they have more marginal capacity than their parents did at the same age.

Another way of looking at the concept of marginal capacity is to measure the average decline among large groups of people and compare their results with their own records of performance at an earlier age. That's what scientists at the Baltimore City Hospital have been doing with a longitudinal study of aging that began in 1958. "Longitudinal" means measuring the same people repeatedly over time. This kind of study differs from *cross-sectional* research, in which people of different ages are compared to each other at the same point in time. Having both kinds of data helps to verify what actually is going on.

These studies have documented the remaining abilities of a number of physical functions in later life. Taking age 30 as a baseline and assigning it the value of 100%, the remaining capacity at age 75 is shown in Table 5.1. The numbers are the approximate percentages of functions or tissues remaining at 75.

The theory of margin has a certain logic to it, but there are some problems as well. One is that few of us have ever tested our true limits, nor do we want to see how far we can go until we drop. And, our differing abilities obviously are influenced by a number of things: the rate of aging, how we feel, our motivation to develop our varying capacities, the basic mechanisms we were born with, and how much practice we're willing to devote to different tasks. In addition, many of these physical abilities will decline regardless of what we do. About the best we can hope for is that maintaining a healthy body overall will be our best defense against premature decline.

There are runners who are still actively competing in races such as the Boston Marathon who are in their 70s. They are, of course, remarkable individuals, but it might be argued that they have always been remarkable: most of us never could run 26 miles, regardless of how much we trained.

TABLE 5.1. Percentage of Capacity Remaining at Age 75

Brain weight	90%
Blood flow to brain	80%
Cardiac output	70%
Kidney filtration rate	69%
Number of nerve trunk fibers	63%
Nerve conduction velocity	90%
Number of taste buds	36%
Maximum oxygen uptake	40%
Vital capacity	56%
Hand grip	55%
Basal metabolic rate	84%
Body water content	82%

From Shock (1976, p. 244).

These are people who had the basic ability to accomplish the task in the first place, were willing to devote long and strenuous hours to practice, and have been fortunate enough to preserve their remarkable capacities into later life. Could it be said that in some way they have postponed the aging process?

It may be that they had greater marginal capacity to begin with, but people who are able to achieve great things in later life in terms of physical accomplishments have also exercised an uncommon self-discipline. Many people who study physical aging would argue that old marathon runners are so unique as to not be a very good example for use in the study of normal aging—they're not typical of most people. Whether these remarkable individuals have actually delayed the aging process is debatable, but it is certain that they have been able to actualize more of their marginal capacity than most people, and for that reason their marginal capacity may have declined less than that of most people. By developing and preserving their capacity in this way, it could be said that they have in fact delayed one or more of the aspects of physical aging. This illustrates one of the basic principles of gerontology, the "use it or lose it" concept. It's evident that some people in late life intentionally remain active physically—and mentally—and seem to retain more of their marginal abilities.

Marginal capacity differs greatly among individuals, and it varies within individuals as well. We can never be sure how close to the margin of ability a person is, or what proportion of their capacity is being used. We have to be satisfied with the general idea that marginal capacity declines in many ways among most people in midlife. The theory of margin is a description of the aging process but not an explanation of it. However, it is one area of physical aging we can actually do something about. Remaining inactive will do nothing to delay physical aging; taking the initiative to remain active will probably show results in many ways. The best practical implication of the theory of margin is that practice seems to slow down decline: if you use it, you'll be less likely to lose it.

Most theories of physical aging are related to one another; that is, there is not just one correct explanation for why we age—they all may be correct. Closely associated to the marginal theory is the ***wear and tear theory of aging***. This theory holds that the body literally wears out over time, just like a machine or a pair of shoes. The wear and tear explanation has some fairly obvious points: old joints and nerves and organs and skin simply don't function the way they did when they were younger.

The comparison of the human body to a machine is not apt in some ways, however. The first reason is that the body goes through a period of growth and development from birth through childhood and adolescence and into young adulthood. Most declines in function cannot be measured to any great degree until the body is past 30 years of age. Machines don't grow and develop into maturity. With a machine, the mean time to failure can be calculated from the day it's made, and it is never quite as good as it was when it was brand new. The second problem with a comparison of the body to a machine is that the body repairs itself. Machines may now be smart enough to tell us when they need maintenance, but the body actually goes right ahead and heals itself and replaces worn out components. Actually, a good definition of aging is the declining ability of the body to repair itself. The third reason a comparison to a machine is not really appropriate is that the body often responds to stress by getting stronger, whereas the machine that is stressed is just that much closer to a breakdown.

Taking these points into consideration, the wear and tear theory still has the virtue of being obvious and in many cases apparently true. Exposure to light does have something to do with the aging of the skin over the course of the years (Finch, 1990). Years of exposure to bacteria does have something to do with dental deterioration. Posture and eyelids and breasts all begin to droop due to the force of gravity. Repeated environmental insults and trauma to the body take their toll.

However, the wear and tear theory is only a partial explanation of the aging process. It has little relationship to aging processes that are developmental. Men don't get bald because their hair wears out. Eyesight doesn't become less acute because the individual has been looking at too many things. People don't have sex less often because they have used up an allotted number of times. (On the contrary, the best predictor of frequent sex in old age is frequency in young age). So although the wear and tear theory is attractive and explains some parts of aging, it is inadequate in and of itself to be much more than a marker of the aging process.

Descriptive analogies of the aging process like the *margin theory* and the concept of wear and tear come under what biologists might call *stochastic* theories of aging. Stochastic means involving chance or probability. More specifically, a radiation-induced mutation might be seen as a random event that has greater and greater probability of happening over the course of time. If aging is related to genetic damage resulting from background radiation, as some biologists believe, then the process might be called stochastic: the odds of this happening increase as we age.

Among the stochastic causes of aging, a *somatic* mutation theory was popular after World War II, when it became apparent that organisms exposed to atomic radiation seemed to age more rapidly. Genetic mutations caused by exposure to radiation eventually produce functional failure, leading to death. Exposure to ionizing radiation shortens life. And we are constantly bombarded by radiation from a wide variety of sources: electromagnetic fields, ultraviolet radiation and gamma rays, X-rays, and other sources of radiation we encounter in everyday life.

While this concept is logical and can be demonstrated in extreme cases, such as exposure to massive amounts of radiation associated with an atomic weapon or the meltdown of a nuclear reactor, the slight amount of background radiation that most people are exposed to probably has little to do with the aging process. Biologists have shown that there is no real body of experimental research that relates radiation-induced shortening of the life

glossary

margin theory of aging — More and more of our available abilities are used as we get older.

stochastic (mutation) — A random, especially biological, change that results from an environmental cause originating outside the body.

somatic (mutation) — A change in the genetic message of a somatic cell, one that is part of the tissues rather than the germ cells.

lossary

regulatory mechanism — A means of controlling functions; regulatory mechanisms can be genetic or chemical (hormonal).

zygote — A fertilized egg that will develop into an organism.

span to the normal process of aging (Christofalo, 1999). It's apparent that there is one or more other causes of aging, basic processes that underlie the fundamental processes of life itself. The stochastic theories of aging describe aging processes, but they don't say much about why aging takes place.

Biological Theories of Aging

Most living things are subject to a particular *regulatory mechanism*, a time clock or control that dictates stages of development and decline. Trees, grass, birds, and people all begin as *zygotes* that grow in size and complexity. Plants typically grow to maturity, form seeds one or more times, and then die. This is as true of marigolds that live for one season as it is bristlecone pine trees that may live thousands of years. At some point, growth slows down, the plant is mature and seeks to reproduce itself, and then sooner or later it begins to die.

Among the more complex animals, the young grow to maturity, a stage at which they can feed and defend themselves. At the same time, the body has matured to the point that the animal can reproduce. Among some insects and fish, death follows shortly after reproduction. Among most animals, the period of reproductive maturity may last for a number of months or years, or even many years. Animals generally are at their healthiest and most resilient early in the reproductive years. At some point, however, reproduction stops, and the animal shows signs of aging.

Humans are remarkable in that females live for several decades after menopause. Most other mammals live comparatively brief lives after the point when reproduction stops. Perhaps the task of bearing and nurturing children is both so difficult and so important that extra marginal capacity has been given to humans to take them well past the period of reproductivity.

Inevitably, though, signs of aging appear in both men and women. There begins to be less space between the vertebrae, so the spine starts to compact and the person begins to get shorter. The hair begins to gray, it's not unusual for people to begin losing teeth; strength and endurance start to decline. The fat that was beneath the skin during childhood, which acted as an efficient insulator at that time, begins to migrate toward the center of the body. So, the skin wrinkles and the shape of the body becomes thicker. The immune system becomes less efficient. Carried on year after inevitable year, the aging process continues until the point of death. In almost all cases, however, people die from a combination of chronic or acute illnesses rather than from old age itself. But the aging process has made the body less able to defend itself against these chronic and acute diseases.

The causes of death increase or decrease, but the limit of life span based on aging processes remains pretty much the same. Table 5.2 illustrates how the 15 leading causes of death in humans have varied over the

---
Illustration 5.4. Skin Conditions Change with Aging

Dermatitis
- Tends to become chronic and widespread
- Healing is slow and unpredictable
- Higher incidence of seborrheic dermatitis of scalp
- Aggravated by confinement to bed
- Interdigital athlete's foot is more common

Chronic photosensitivity
- Can be especially bad on the face of older men
- Severe photodermatitis can grotesquely thicken skin

Thinning of subcutis on soles of feet
- Increases trauma from walking

Premalignant lesions
- Higher incidence of squamous cell carcinoma

Skin disorders associated with vitamin deficiencies
- Inadequate diet leads to unusual problems, such as scurvy

From Loescher (1995, p. 11).

course of 16 years. Tuberculosis, which is not on the list at all, was the leading cause of death at the beginning of the twentieth century. Despite its decline over recent years, as indicated in the table, heart disease currently is the leading cause of death, followed by cancer. Obviously, everyone eventually dies, so if one leading cause is eliminated, another will rise to take its place.

Given the universality of changes that come like clockwork in normal human beings—adolescence at eleven or twelve, menopause at 45 or 50,

TABLE 5.2 Percent Change in 15 Leading Causes of Death, 1979–1995

Decreases:	Increases:
Heart disease –26.2%	Cancer 3.8%
Cerebrovascular –34.3%	Chronic obstructive pulmonary disease 58.7%
Accidents –24.8%	Pneumonia 29.4%
Suicide –4.6%	Diabetes 33.8%
Cirrhosis –32.8%	HIV infection 189.8%
Homicide –13.6%	Kidney disease 10.0%
Atherosclerosis –61.5%	Septicemia 94.7%
	Alzheimer's disease 1,862.8%
All causes –9.2%	

Adapted from Anderson and Rosenberg (1998, pp. 6–7).

intrinsic — Within the body, as distinguished from environmental, or outside the body.

error theory — Aging that is caused by repeated mutations of cellular DNA.

mutagenesis — The process in which cells replicate themselves with slight errors in their genetic messages; under the error theory, these mutations are compounded with further replication.

TABLE 5.3. Proportion of Survivors After Age 100

Age	Survivors
100	1,010,000
101	505,000
102	233,000
103	98,600
104	44,000
105	12,300
106	3,630
107	830
108	140
109	16
110	1

From Bellamy and Phillips (1987, p. 22).

death at 70 or 80—it's hard to deny that some regulatory mechanism is responsible for these changes. Certainly, some people at the end of the curve seem to be on a different schedule than the rest of us. A small percentage live into their 90s and a few even make it past 100. However, very few people live that long: the body almost seems to be programmed to die. As can be seen in Table 5.3, even among the aging elite (the centenarians), the odds catch up rapidly: it takes over a million people aged 100 to produce even one survivor at 110.

People seem to age at different rates: many of us know active, vital individuals who are in their 80s and others who seem to be worn out by age 60. However, the fundamental fact of the constancy of the process itself cannot be ignored. And, since it is obvious that there is a process of development and aging, it would seem reasonable to conclude that this process is subject to some regulatory mechanism.

Biological theories of aging recognize that aging is influenced by environmental factors such as we have discussed in the wear-and-tear theory. Most biologists now, however, would agree that while the aging process might be accelerated by environmental influences, the basic cause of aging is **intrinsic**, that is, within the organism itself (Christofalo, 1999). If the physical process of aging is intrinsic, it would seem reasonable that researchers might eventually be able to find where in the body or by what mechanism the rate of aging is regulated, and perhaps even be able to slow it down.

A theory of aging that tries to reconcile intrinsic and environmental theories of aging is **error theory**. This view sees the fundamental blueprint of genetic material at the cellular level, the DNA, as possibly giving the wrong message at some point over the life span (Comfort, 1979). If billions and billions of cells are being replicated, the theory goes, it's possible that a mutation appears every now and again. In most cases, the body seeks to correct it, but a few mutations continue to replicate, and these errors of **mutagenesis** ultimately cause the body to replace itself using bad blueprints.

Aging may be a result of the duplication of irregular cells. These mutations may cause tumors or problems in the circulatory or nervous or immune systems. This is an attractive theory, but it needs more research to gain much scientific support (Christofalo, 1999).

Theories that call aging intrinsic are called *developmental-genetic theories*. They view aging as a part of the process of development that is genetically controlled. The first of these is a *neuroendocrine theory* of aging. This combines the words neuro, meaning "nerve," and "endocrine," hormones that regulate many other physical processes in the body.

With a neuroendocrine theory of aging, the process of aging can be seen as a breakdown (or at least a change) in the neurons, or nerve cells that transmit information, and the hormones that regulate their activity (Finch & Landfield, 1985). Closely related to this is the view that a master timekeeper might be within the hypothalamus and/or the pituitary, ductless glands that lie at the base of the brain. They might send chemical messages to other parts of the body controlling when cells or cell complexes grow or decline. The pituitary hormone, for example, regulates growth, and the hypothalamus regulates the onset of puberty. Perhaps hormones regulating the onset of aging could be identified. Neuroendocrine theories of aging may help to provide explanations for the apparent age-related trend for loss of large neurons in most parts of the brain (Finch, 1990).

Another developmental-genetic theory of aging is called the *immunological theory*. Shortly after maturation, many immune system functions begin to decline. The capacity of the immune system is markedly diminished in later life. Older people are more prone to infection, there is a decline in the function of T cells (cells secreted by the thymus gland), and there is an increase in autoimmune diseases, such as arthritis, in old age. There is a loss of cells in the thymic cortex that continues throughout adult life, and a corresponding decrease in thymic hormone. Whether or not this is a cause of aging or a result of the aging process has yet to be determined (Finch, 1990).

The *free radical theory* of aging holds that much of the damage done during the process of aging is chemical (Harman, 1981). *Free radicals* are compounds caused by the process of oxidation or metabolism. They are highly chemically reactive and prone to combine with other molecules and cause damage. They are generally destroyed by protective enzymes, but the theory is that more and more get through as the organism ages, and the damage accumulates. Many studies have demonstrated that chemical antioxidants (superoxide dismutase, selinium, beta-carotene, and vitamin E, among others) can protect against damage from free radicals. There is some evidence of a relationship between antioxidant mechanisms and species length of life (Finch, 1990).

Interesting evidence that the process of aging is intrinsic began to be accumulated many years ago with a now-classic series of experiments on food restriction in laboratory rats and mice (McCay, Crowell, & Maynard, 1935). Fed diets that were nutritionally complete but restricted in overall

g lossary

developmental-genetic theories — Intrinsic views that hold internal physical processes are responsible for aging.

neuroendocrine theory — Aging is caused in part by hormonal changes that regulate cells.

free radicals — Chemical compounds resulting from the process of oxidation that seek to chemically combine with other substances.

ad libitum — At liberty;
rodents fed ad libitum
have food constantly
available and can eat
as much as they want.

caloric intake, some rodents lived significantly longer than others who were allowed to eat similar diets but with no restriction in amount. Patterns have varied in repeating this experiment during succeeding years. In some cases, the caloric intake has been as little as 20% less, and in others as much as 60%. Some researchers fed the experimental rats or mice two out of three days and made them fast the third. Some experimenters began restricting diet while the rodents were infants, others waited until adulthood. Invariably, the rats whose food was restricted lived longer—sometimes 40 to 50% longer—and had fewer diseases than those who were fed *ad libitum* (without limit, as much as they wanted [Masoro, 1988]).

Food restriction and its effect on longevity have grown into a well-developed body of research that is still being actively pursued, in part because it has been among the few experimental methods that have consistently lengthened life (Ferland, Tuckweber, Bhat, & Lacroix, 1992; Masoro, Katz, & McMahon, 1989, p. 417). Why food-restricted mice live longer than controls that get as much food as they will eat is not particularly clear. Several of the biological theories of aging seek to better explain this phenomenon. Perhaps it is a true decrease in the rate of aging; caloric restriction delays the loss of the capacity to reproduce among female mice (McShane, Wilson, & Wise, 1999). What is clear is that calorie restriction does lengthen life, at least among lab rats and mice; why it happens is still subject to debate. It has yet to be demonstrated that this effect consistently takes place among higher mammals such as primates (Cutler, Davis, Ingram, & Roth, 1992; DeLany, Hansen, Bodkin, Hannah, & Bray, 1999)

If dietary restriction is a key to longer life, why hasn't it been demonstrated spontaneously in the population? That is, among all the peoples of the world, there are plenty who've led lives of deprivation and dietary restriction. In fact, getting enough to eat has been the daily work of most of world throughout human history. Aside from the dubious claims in Ecuador, Hunza, and Abkhazia, it would seem that an especially long-lived group of calorie-restricted people could be identified somewhere in the world. Or does dietary restriction work only with rats, not in humans?

Illustration 5.5. The Key to Longer Life?

UCLA Pathologist Roy Walford is doing what he can to extend his life. He eats a nutritionally complete diet, but he doesn't eat very much of it. Consistent with his quest for health and long life, Dr. Walford says he also takes high doses of antioxidants, such as vitamin E, selinium, and BHT, a food preservative. He also exercises vigorously. He was one of a number of people who emerged from living experimentally in the Biosphere II Project in Arizona. Walford wants to be among the first to demonstrate in human subjects—in this case, himself—many of the findings that have encouraged scientists working in the field of the biology of aging. Now in his mid '70s, Walford may have many years yet to go.

There are many problems in answering this kind of question. First, as we have seen, people in very deprived areas of the world often don't keep very good birth records or ways of proving their ages. More important, however, is that people who are deprived in terms of food don't eat a nutritionally complete diet as do the calorie-restricted rats and mice in the experiments. Half-starved people will most often eat anything they can get their hands on, and it usually doesn't have a well-balanced complement of vitamins, minerals, proteins, fats, and carbohydrates. What food in the underdeveloped world often does have, unfortunately, is a host of microorganisms and intestinal worms—hardly the diet to promote long life. In parts of the world where nutritionally complete diets are available, people usually eat them every day, not every other day.

Perhaps, given the chance to eat ad libitum, rats and mice will simply eat more than is good for them. Critics might argue that this is no less true among human beings. That is, the ideal diet for keeping long-lived rodents seems to be about 60% of what they would eat when given unlimited access to food. Few humans actually eat all they possibly can; perhaps it is the case that many people naturally consume on a daily basis about two-thirds of their possible maximum intake. On the other hand, it might be the case that we'd all be healthier by eating about two-thirds as much as we do eat. While the biologists continue to do research that will indicate exactly what mechanisms are affected by caloric restriction, about the best we can conclude at this point is that too much food probably is bad for both mice and men.

More fundamental biological research on intrinsic causes of aging has supported the *programmed theory* of aging, or, in a sense, the idea of a biological time-clock. This has demonstrated that aging takes place at the cellular level. It is an interesting body of research, not only in what it teaches us about the process of aging, but also in the way the research happened and what resulted from it.

A basic question among the intrinsic theories of aging is where the regulatory mechanism for the aging process is located. Actually, it appears that it may be located in numerous parts and functions of the body. But at the most fundamental level, is the process of aging taking place at the organ level, the tissue level, or the cellular level? Or perhaps some system of organs regulates the aging process. If it's at the cellular level, there may be some information within each cell's genetic code that tells it at what rate to age. This is an important question from a practical point of view. If there is a program that controls aging at the cellular level, it might be possible through genetic engineering to in some way manipulate or influence that mechanism.

Up until the late 1950s, it was thought that animal cells were essentially immortal. A series of experiments, beginning in 1911 and continuing until 1945, kept cells from chicken hearts alive in the laboratory (Carrel & Burrows, 1911). Since that length of time was much longer than a chicken's life span, this was taken as evidence that cells themselves were immortal.

programmed theory — The view that dividing human cells will have a limited number of doublings (the Hayflick limit), usually a total of 50 (plus or minus ten).

Most old people have pretty good sense as to how long life should be. I've been speaking on the topic of aging to many different groups during the past 30 years. I often ask audiences, "Who among you would like to live to be 100?" Among groups of children and young people, almost all of the hands shoot up. When I ask this question of older groups, though, there usually is a collective groan. People say, "No, don't make me live to be a hundred! I've got enough aches and pains now!"

Older people realize that aging is a continuous process. Giving an 85-year-old another 15 years of life might not in fact be giving her a welcome gift. Tacking more years onto the end of life is not the goal of biologists working in the field of gerontology. Everyone realizes that for discoveries to have any practical value, qualities of youth would need to be preserved into the later years; the entire process of aging itself would have to be postponed.

Generally there will be one old joker in the audience who raises his hand and says, "I'd like to live to be 100, if I don't have to get any older." The audience laughs, realizing that he's asked for the impossible: more years without paying the inevitable price of more deterioration.

If cells could be kept alive indefinitely, this was an argument that aging and death must be regulated at some higher physiological level. However, repeated attempts to replicate this cellular research had not been successful (Gey, Svotelis, Foard, & Bung, 1974). Some scientists now feel that in the original research, new live cells might have been introduced into the culture from time to time during the feeding process (Cristofalo, 1999).

The process of one direction in research on causes of cancer in humans in the late 1950s necessitated growing fetal tissue in a laboratory setting (Hayflick, 1974). Although this particular series of experiments reached a dead end in terms of cancer research, an interesting finding concerning aging of cells in culture was discovered:

> Until that time, no one had determined that normal human cells could be cultured by invoking a wide variety of criteria, including chromosome analysis. Prior to these studies normal human cells were only presumed to have been cultivated. The major surprise that grew out of these studies was the finding that the normal cell populations grew and divided perfectly for many months, then slowed down, stopped dividing, and ultimately died. (Hayflick, 1974, p. 37–38.)

At first, it was thought that some defect in laboratory method might be responsible, that the cells aged and died because of some inadequacy in the technique or procedures used for their maintenance. But, after repeated study, it became clear that the aging process itself dictated the lives of cells in laboratory culture. Cells from infants grew and doubled about 50 times (plus or minus ten doublings), those taken from young adults about 30 times, and cells from older people doubled about 20 times before they stopped dividing and died. Cells frozen and then thawed years later began to divide again at the point where they had left off, indicating that there was a genetic memory.

This research has been replicated many times in many different laboratories. There can be little doubt that cells are programmed to replace themselves for a certain number of times and then quit. This effect is now called the Hayflick limit, after Leonard Hayflick, the scientist who discovered it. He has said that the limit might be seen as assurance that we will die, but he adds that the absolute limit of cell replication is hardly ever reached in nature: "functional losses that occur in cells prior to their loss of division capacity produce age changes in animals much before their normal cells have reached their maximum division limit" (Hayflick, 1974, p. 38). In other words, there is a biological limit to the life of the organism that is dictated at the cellular level, but few ever live until they reach that limit. Almost everyone dies of something else; hardly anyone dies of old age itself. It seems that the only cells that in fact divide without limit are cancer cells.

Given, then, that there appears to be a genetic program in cells that dictates how long they will retain vital capacity and continue to replicate themselves, is this the biological explanation for the aging process? Perhaps it is part of the explanation, but physical aging is an exceedingly complex phenomenon.

It probably is the case that several things are happening all at the same time. Perhaps all the theories we have examined are true and are working in concert. It is clear that the process of maturation and development is intrinsic. At the same time, each of us is exposed to illnesses and injuries across the course of our lives that may contribute to overall physical deterioration. The physical and psychological stresses that we undergo contribute to environmental aging. Trauma no doubt plays a part. Football players have "old" knees. The lungs of a heavy smoker are in a sense older lungs; in a similar manner, alcoholics have worn out their livers.

As our bodies get closer to the limit of their marginal capacity, we have lost cells and our remaining cells are less able to replace themselves. Environmental (stochastic) and intrinsic causes of aging combine to make us less resilient. Several of the intrinsic theories of aging might work in tandem. Think of what happens when you get a mosquito bite. The mosquito inserts her proboscis into your skin and deposits a tiny bit of protein as she draws out your blood. The body recognizes this protein as foreign to you and seeks to isolate, encapsulate, and destroy it. In other words, your body is rejecting this foreign bit of genetic bad news. This is exactly what happens when the body seeks to reject an organ transplant: the organ is recognized as foreign, and the body attempts to destroy it. It is only through the discovery and use of immunosuppressive drugs that heart and kidney and other organ transplants have proven to be successful in recent years.

Back to the mosquito bite: it takes place right under the skin, so you

Illustration 5.7. Can Aging Be Delayed?

Living a healthy lifestyle well into a ripe old age goes beyond buying the most fashionable jogging outfit. Here are a few pointers based on the research in gerontology that might help:

1. Stay out of the sun. Being bombarded by ultraviolet radiation is a principal cause of skin cancer. This is especially true among fair-skinned people. Little children are particularly at risk of getting skin cancer later on in life if they have had a number of bad sunburns while they were children, so keep your kids covered up. Make sure they have been protected by a sun screen when they're playing in bright sunshine. Aging of the skin appears to be hastened by exposure to the sun. People who have been working for years on getting a good tan shouldn't be surprised when they start to look like an old saddle. If you must have a suntan, consider staying inside and painting yourself.

2. Avoid smoke. This goes beyond just not smoking. Free radicals in the body are formed by the process of oxidation. The process of oxidation not only goes on with metabolism; most oxidation in nature is associated with things that are burning. Smoke generates free radicals. This is the reason you may have heard that it's a good idea to avoid eating smoked meats or a steak that has been grilled until it has a crust on it. Also, your fireplace or wood stove is putting more particulate matter into the inside air than you might guess. The number one source of the smoke most people breathe is automobile exhaust. People riding in cars inevitably take in a lot of it. Joggers along the roadside not only are in danger of being flattened by the drivers, but they're taking in lungs full of exhaust as well. Go to the park to exercise.

3. Eat broccoli and cabbage. Vegetables and fruits high in beta-carotene, vitamin C, and vitamin E act as natural antioxidants.

4. Women who are childless have more incidents of breast cancer.

5. Property is a correlate of longevity. One consistent contributor to longevity is economics. Poor people don't live as long for a variety of reasons, including less overall access to good health care and nutrition.

6. The greatest single predictor of dementia and disability in old age is high blood pressure. Get tested regularly, especially if one of your parents had hypertension. This goes double for African-Americans, who have a greater risk of high blood pressure. If you're on antihypertensive medications, don't go off of them just because you feel better. People who control their hypertension have no greater risk of dementia in later life than those who do not have hypertension.

7. People lacking a long-term relationship have higher rates of death from almost all causes. The value of intimate companionship cannot be overestimated.

8. If you want to have a long sex life, make sure it's a safe sex life.

9. Get up and get moving. This doesn't mean you have to engage in violent exercise; walking or swimming or other activities that involve major muscle groups are best. Try to get in at least 30 minutes of fairly vigorous activity at least three times a week.

10. One of the less shocking findings is that people who are tired all the time probably don't get enough sleep. Too many people live on the ragged edge of exhaustion.

11. Eat less fat.

12. A little wine for thy stomach's sake is fine; just don't drink the whole jug.

13. If you don't wear your seat belt, you're a fool.
14. It's been scientifically proven that watching 30 years of daytime TV will turn your brain into lint. Read a good book now and then, write some letters to friends, go to plays, concerts, and ball games. Talk to people. Find worthwhile things to do with yourself. You've only been given one life; don't waste it on re-runs.
15. People who are religious in life seem to do better in later life than those who are not.
16. Gerontologists always say that you should pick a pair of long-lived parents. Actually, there doesn't seem to be a genetic predisposition toward long life so much as there are family tendencies toward things that shorten life. Families that are long-lived may simply lack a tendency to have these conditions. Heart disease, diabetes, hypertension, and cancer all seem to run in families to a certain degree. It's important to alert your physician if you have a relative who's had any of these diseases.

can observe your body's effort to reject this foreign invader. It swells, feels warmer than the skin around it, darkens, and itches. Eventually the reaction subsides and your immune system has won: it has destroyed the foreign protein.

Let's say that as you get older there are some errors, some mutations, in the genetic material controlling the replication of your cells (Sinex, 1977). Perhaps the mutated genetic material isn't quite different enough to be recognized by the body as foreign. But out of billions of cells duplicating themselves all the time, perhaps a little "genetic noise" gets through (Comfort, 1979).

During the process of aging, these cells might mutate a little bit more, and this might happen thousands of times throughout your body before the processes that seek to destroy them kick in. Then, you have an *autoimmune reaction*, or a great number of autoimmune reactions (Walford, 1982). You get arthritis, gout, circulatory problems, or any of a host of conditions we might normally associate with aging. Your body has literally identified parts of itself as foreign and is seeking to destroy them. Only, this is not caused by a mosquito bite or some other foreign invader such as a microorganism. In the quest to destroy what it perceives to be a foreign invader, your body is destroying itself. This scenario is the combination of a number of different theories of physical and biological aging. We can see how complex a problem the biology of aging presents to scientists. Many processes may all be happening at once.

glossary

autoimmune reaction
— A dysfunction of the immune system, especially when it is either losing its efficiency or is actually attacking another part of the body.

Conclusion

There can be little doubt that the physical processes of aging are supported by several different theories, and that not one of these theories in and of itself gives the entire explanation for what is going on. Defined at the most basic level, physical aging involves cell loss. Tissues and organs are less likely to function efficiently after maturity, and the process of physical repair slows down. The immune functions decline, and the body becomes more prone to infection. Autoimmune reactions become more common.

Collagen, a component of connective tissue that is found throughout the body, becomes less elastic and is more likely to form cross-linkages with other body components. Joints, heart muscle, blood vessels, and many other parts of the body become more stiff. This is the reason that the meat from old animals is tough. The metabolism of glucose may be related in some ways to the formation of these cross-linkages, and it has been suggested that diabetes might be seen as a model for studying the aging process (Cerami, 1985; Kart, 1990; Masoro et al., 1989).

The ability of the body to neutralize free-radicals formed during the process of oxidation becomes less efficient. Cells may form mutations as they replicate themselves that ultimately are not recognized by the body and are attacked in autoimmune reactions. Neurochemical controls become impaired, and complex activities that involve multiple body systems become less efficient.

While we will look in greater detail in Chapter 7 at the resultant physical outcomes of the biological processes, the fundamental issues are clear. Physical decline leads to more health problems, and the body has less reserve capacity, or margin, with which to deal with these health problems. The process of aging is lifelong and cumulative, and aging results in a less efficient physical entity.

Aging appears to be controlled in the cell's genetic material as well as several of the glands and organs of the body. The body has a genetic program to develop up to a certain age and then to decline in function and efficiency over a great many years. Extra marginal capacity seems to be built in during the younger years of life, and the body loses this as time goes by.

Scientists working in the field of the biology of aging are optimistic, although they hasten to add that it is very difficult to predict when breakthroughs might happen. Putting scientific discovery on a schedule never seems to work very well (Thorson, 1990). The causes of aging are multiple, and because of this, work in the field of the biology of aging is exceedingly complex. However, there has been a dramatic increase in the resources devoted to research in biological aging in recent years, and some of these research efforts seem to have begun to bear fruit.

Gerontologists are in agreement that merely extending the life span with no corresponding improvements in health and functioning would be less than worthwhile. If future discoveries have the effect of extending useful life, it seems likely that they will be a result of a slowing down of the processes of physical aging.

Questions for Discussion

1. Have you detected an age-related decline in your own abilities? If so, when did you first notice it?
2. What abilities have you sought to preserve, and how are you going about it?
3. Have any people in your family lived especially long lives? If so, what do you think the explanation is?
4. If you frankly assess your own personal abilities, in what areas have you made improvement over time?
5. Why is comparing the body to a machine not a particularly appropriate way of looking at the aging process?
6. How important do you think research into basic biological processes of aging is, in comparison to, say, cancer research or AIDS research? Why?
7. How old would you live to be if you could live to be as old as you could be?

Sources of Further Information

The biology of aging is such a specific, technical field that you should try to narrow down particular questions prior to going on a fishing expedition. That is, don't expect to get far by writing to a particular agency and asking for "any information you might have on the biology of aging." Instead, go first to some of the books and journals cited in this chapter. You'll see that this material has undergone a good deal of simplifying in the preparation of this text. If you have a fairly good science background, however, there is a wealth of material available in these and other references.

A tip for those new to library research: go to the journal articles first Find the most recent issue of the journal of choice that's available; in this instance, it's the *Journal of Gerontology: Biological Sciences*. *The Journal of the American Geriatrics Society* might also be good, but its articles will tend to be more clinical (oriented toward medical treatment rather than basic biochemistry). Scan the Table of Contents to see if the topic you're interested in is contained in that copy of the journal. If it's not, go back to the next previous issue and so on. Once you've gotten an article that is exactly on the issue you're researching, backtrack from that author's references. That is, look at the Reference section at the end of that article, and see if you can find the journals mentioned there. If you're working in a university library, it's likely that you'll find at least some of them. Obviously, you can continue to backtrack from the references from those articles as well.

Now, there's a tricky part: Up until 1986, the *Journal of Gerontology* was published as a single journal with four sections: Biological Sciences, Social Sciences, Medical Sciences, and Psychological Sciences, and the pages of each were numbered sequentially from Page 1 of the first issue of the volume year right through to the last page of the last issue of the year. With the first issue in 1987, that was changed. The journal still appeared with four sections under one cover each time, but the numbering had been changed to correspond with each section, not each number. Here's how it works: each section was treated like a separate journal (even though it's bound with the other three), so there were four different page numbering systems in each copy of the journal. They're coded: B for Biological Sciences, M for Medical, P for Psychological, and S for Social. So it's possible to have, for example, the May, 1992 number of the *Journal of Gerontology* pages M61–98, followed by P110–220, followed by S98–148, and B63–104. Four different numbering systems for four theoretically different journals all bound up in the same package.

This was done to ease in the transition to two separately bound journals, a move that the publisher, The Gerontological Society of America, made in January of 1995: biological and medical are now bound together under one cover (Series A), and psychological and social sciences are bound with each other (Series B). In January of 1999, these journals became monthlies, rather than quarterlies. Despite this numbering system (it's actually easier to negotiate than it sounds), the *Journal of Gerontology: Biological Sciences* is the single best place to look for information on the biology of aging. It's also pretty tough going if you lack a science background. Most university and virtually all medical school libraries carry it; don't look for it in your community library. Want to subscribe? Contact:

The Gerontological Society of America
1275 K Street, N.W., Suite 350
Washington, D.C. 20005-4006

A better deal by far is a student membership in the Gerontological Society of America (same address). For $65, you'll get the membership plus a subscription to either Series A or B of the Journals of Gerontology, plus The Gerontologist, the more practically applied research journal in the field. Subscribing to one of the journals without joining the organization costs $171 per year, so only a madman would do it.

The Federal agency responsible for research in biochemical aging is the:

National Institute on Aging
Biomedical Research and Clinical Medicine Section
Building 31, Room 5C11
Bethesda, MD 20892

It might be able to handle specific requests, or at least lead you to who's been funded to do research in your area of interest.

Psychological Development

Chapter Outline

> "As I have advanced into old age, hope and praise have become less important, while recollection has become stronger. As I age, I remember more vividly, because the anticipation of death rings the past into sharper focus. I have noted, too, that I remember best when I am melancholy."
> —David Diamond, born 1915

Introduction

One of our assumptions about personal development is that it is a lifelong process. A conflicting stereotype about older persons, though, is that somewhere after a plateau in late middle age, they start to slip back, to develop in a negative direction, so to speak. Myths about older people focus on this concept: "You can't teach an old dog new tricks" is an example. One thing we can observe is that older individuals often accept these negative stereotypes at face value, and their self-image suffers as a consequence.

Although there can be little doubt that people slow down physically as they age, do they also slow down mentally? And if there is a cognitive decline in later life, is it of any real consequence? That is, does the brain have so much reserve capacity that a slight decline in peak mental performance doesn't really matter that much? Perhaps older individuals, who have had a great opportunity to learn over the course of their lifetimes, have accumulated enough of what's actually important to compensate for any performance declines in late life.

If older people have, in fact, discovered what really is important in life, we need to look at the psychological process by which they have done so. Older people as a group seem to be generally high in both life satisfaction and adaptive skills. These and other elements of psychological development across the lifespan will be the focus of this chapter.

Here are two snapshots of an individual we'll call Viola. At age 6, Viola was always selected first when the children were making up teams for playground sports. Naturally swift and graceful, Viola was also looked upon as a leader by the other students in her class. She was never afraid to volunteer an answer when the teacher asked a question, even if she was not positive that she was right. Like many children, she was a bit disorganized and forever misplacing her scissors and her pencil. Nevertheless, she was a self-confident child who did well in school and was happy and outgoing.

Seventy years later Viola is now retired from a successful career. A widow who lives independently, she is surrounded by a wide social network and extended family. Still active in public affairs, she has been seen as a voice for the consumer in her community. She frequently contributes brief articles and opinion pieces to her local newspaper, despite the arthritis that makes typing them more difficult for her. One other problem she has with this activity is hunting down a stamp in order to mail in her contributions. "I'm always losing that book of stamps!" she says, "I must be getting senile." Her daughter wonders if this could be true and perhaps represents the onset of Alzheimer's disease.

Perceptions of Aging

A long-running debate in the field of gerontology is whether—or how much—people change over time (Cavanaugh, 1993). Granted, visible changes in stature, skin, and hair that normally come with the aging process—all of the physical changes we discussed in Chapter 5—are only too apparent. But, what happens inside of us? Do we become different people as we get older? If not, if we stay pretty much the same as we've always been, is there no real prospect for growth over time? And, will the physical (and, perhaps, mental) changes we experience with aging affect how people perceive us and how we see ourselves?

The answers to these questions make up the substance of this chapter.

Perception of the elderly and self-concept are the first topics we'll examine, followed by growth and development across the lifespan, reminiscence and a search for meaning in life, coping and adaptation, and finally, learning and memory.

But, first, let's return to Viola. In these brief sketches, we see a little girl who is outgoing, confident, successful, and perhaps a bit careless. We then look at her again when she's 76. At this age, she's still bright and active, leading what most people would consider to be a good life. She has had some physical and social losses (arthritis and the death of her spouse) that might be considered to be fairly common for a woman of her age. She's fortunate in that she still contributes to her community and that she has a network of people who care about her.

When she can't find her book of stamps, she laughs at herself, which is a very healthy sign. Perhaps she has spent a lifetime misplacing things—a little girl who can't find her pencil may some day be an older woman who can't find her stamps—but she seems to have adapted well over the course of these many years. The fact that she's as outgoing now as she was seventy years before may be some evidence of personality continuity across the lifespan. If she had been a shy little girl, she might very well still show tendencies toward shyness, but she has never been afraid to speak out, and she still independently voices her opinions and point of view. The fact that she contributes opinion pieces to the newspaper leads us to believe that she most certainly is not becoming demented, despite her daughter's concerns. The daughter, like many children of older parents, no doubt dreads the prospect of caring for a confused older person; perhaps she suspects that losing one's mental abilities might be fairly common in later life. Perhaps she has fears for her own aging that are associated with what she may project for her mother in future years.

There are some areas of importance in these snapshots that need to be discussed. We don't have enough detail to tell whether Viola actually thinks

---

Illustration 6.1. It Seems Like Everyone Has Alzheimer's

Once, over dinner, I listened to the late Nathan Shock's remarks about how people throw around the term "Alzheimer's disease." Shock, who for many years had headed the Baltimore Longitudinal Study of Aging, knew better than most the comparative rarity of true Alzheimer's. It seemed, he said, that just about any older person demonstrating some kind of confusion or disorganized behavior got labeled as having "Alzheimer's." He reflected that an earlier label had been "organic brain syndrome," and before that it had been "chronic brain syndrome." Prior to that, he observed, the term had been "senile dementia," or "senile psychosis," or, going back to the 1960s, "cerebral arteriosclerosis." He pointed out that, while negative attitudes toward the elderly have thus demonstrated continuity over time, we have at least been creative enough to change the pejorative terms every decade or so.

she really is getting senile, or if she's merely repeating a saying that she's heard a thousand times before about old people being forgetful. It says something about our society's attitudes toward older people that she has heard this cliché many times, and it indicates that there is some sense of expectation that "old" and "forgetful" are naturally tied together. There may be a tendency to assume that any sign of forgetfulness among the aged means that senility has finally taken hold.

Older persons' own attitudes may be reflected by a not-very-subtle play on the term "Alzheimer's disease," when someone says, "I'm suffering from old-timers' disease." We laugh, but we may think that this is a person whose self-concept is suffering: perhaps he really does see signs of dementia in himself. Attitudes towards oneself, after all, are a *projection* of generalized attitudes in the society. When did old people learn society's attitudes toward the aged? When they themselves were younger persons, of course.

It is difficult to tell how pervasive negative attitudes toward the elderly are or whether negative stereotypes are held by a majority of the population. This type of research is often comparative; that is, it measures one group against another in terms of scores on a scale measuring attitudes toward the elderly. For example, a colleague and I have done studies that found that older people generally score more positively on such scales than do younger people (Thorson & Perkins, 1981). This, unfortunately, doesn't really tell us much about how older people are actually perceived in the society, how much of this societal belief is accepted by older people in general, and, most importantly, how this view of aging and older persons affects how older individuals feel about themselves. Zena Blau (1981) has pointed out that social identity is made up of three elements: the conception of self, the conception of how others view us, and how others actually view us.

It would be possible, say, to defend a hypothesis that: (1) when they were younger, people who are now elderly learned that the aged were, for the most part, poor, sick, and unhappy; thus, (2) now that they are them-

---

Illustration 6.2. Do Attitudes Predict Behavior?

One question psychologists have debated at length is this: to what extent do attitudes predict behavior? That is, if you feel negatively toward a certain group, will this prejudice be reflected in the way you actually behave toward members of that group? Research going back to the 1960s says that yes, there is a relationship between attitudes and behaviors (Fishbein, 1967). It seems to be manifested, however, only in extreme circumstances. That is, a mild like or dislike probably won't be acted upon. A real love or hatred is needed to actually motivate much behavior. This seems to beg the question where the aged are concerned, however; merely being indifferent toward older people usually translates into the behavioral response of ignoring them. It could be argued that this, too, shows prejudice toward the elderly.

selves elderly, they feel that they should be expected to be poor, sick, and unhappy. Or, we might argue that elderly people learned to adopt societal norms valuing youth and beauty above all other things; now that they have lost youth and beauty, perhaps they have come to despise themselves. A third possibility is that today's older people grew up in a generation that held the aged in high regard because of their wisdom and experience; perhaps their self-concept has now improved over time, since they have now achieved this exalted status. Lacking research, we could argue any or all of these points of view without fear of contradiction.

In 1981, the National Council on the Aging contracted with Lou Harris and Associates, a national polling organization, to do a nationwide survey of attitudes toward older people. A total of 3,452 adults were interviewed. Some startling information emerged from that study. First, the aged seemingly did not suffer from overwhelmingly negative attitudes. Most participants in the Harris survey seemed to be fairly positive toward the elderly in general; they were even more positively disposed toward particular elderly people, such as their own grandparents or other older relatives.

Younger respondents, however, held many surprisingly inaccurate stereotypes, perhaps due to their lack of contact to any significant degree with very many older persons. For example, only a quarter of the older persons answering the Harris survey items said that fear of crime was a real problem for them. Fully 74% of the people completing the survey who were between ages 18 and 64, however, felt that fear of crime was a big problem for the aged. By the same token, only 21% of the older people said that poor health presented a problem, whereas almost half of the younger adults thought that poor health was a problem for the elderly.

Perceptions of income represented an even greater disparity: 68% of the younger respondents thought that old people suffered from inadequate income, while only 17% of the older people in the Harris sample said that inadequate income was a problem. Similarly, there was a difference in perceptions of loneliness: 65% of the younger adults thought it was a problem for the elderly, but only 13% of the elderly themselves actually found loneliness to be a problem. Only 9% of the older respondents said that getting adequate medical care was a problem for them; 45% of the younger adults thought it would represent a problem for the older population. And, only 5% of the older respondents found poor housing to be a problem; 43% of the younger adults surveyed thought of poor housing as a problem typical of the aged.

Further analysis of the Harris data divided the respondents up into age cohorts (55 to 64, 65 to 74, 75 to 84, and 85 years of age and above) (Seccombe & Ishii-Kuntz, 1991). It was found that the youngest age group identified the most problems associated with aging, while the oldest-old were surprisingly positive. Interestingly, in answer to the question of "when does a person become old," the respondents aged 55+ said that men reach old age when they are between the ages of 60 and 64, but that women enter old age sooner, somewhere between 55 and 59.

"These gender differences within the (Harris) findings lend empirical support to Bell's (1970) assertion that a double standard of aging exists. She suggests that women, because they are primarily valued for their physical attractiveness and sexuality, are perceived to age at a faster rate than men. Men, on the other hand, are valued for attributes such as power, occupational achievement, intelligence, and their earning potential, and thus are generally enhanced by the aging process. As Bell writes:

> There is a reason why women are coy about their age. For most purposes, society pictures them as 'old' ten or fifteen years sooner than men. Nobody in this culture, man or woman, wants to grow old; age is not honored among us.
>
> Yet women must endure the specter of aging much sooner than men, and this cultural definition of aging gives men a decided psychological, sexual, and economic advantage over women."

From Seccombe and Ishii-Kuntz (1991, p. 533).

This may indicate another problem of perception or self-perception: many people feel that society projects more negative attitudes toward women than men later in life. This is manifested in a variety of ways: sayings such as "Men become more distinguished as they age" (presumably, then, women do not), or "Never ask a woman about her age." If the generation that is now old accepts these clichés, there must be something of a differential in attitudes toward self in later life: if it is more important for a woman to appear youthful, then she has more to lose in terms of self-image as she ages.

This issue of self-perception goes beyond physical image, of course. One study tested for beliefs about age-related differences in memory (Ryan, 1992). It was found to be socially accepted that older people have more memory problems. Most people felt that a typical 70-year-old would rank much lower than a typical 25-year-old in areas such as memory for people and names, rote memory, overall memory, and absent-mindedness. Typically, people said that this memory decline occurs after age 45 but does not begin to accelerate until after age 65.

This societal belief might conceivably have a predictive effect: perhaps older persons believe they are supposed to be forgetful, and that expectation is in some ways predictive of behavior. Cutler and Grams (1988) analyzed 14,783 responses from persons 55+ to the National Health Interview Survey and found that 15% said they'd had trouble remembering things during the past year. This went up with age: about one in four of those 80 or older reported memory problems. About one in five felt that difficulty in remembering things was happening to them more frequently. And, more women than men reported memory problems. Again, this may indicate a self-image problem, since there is no consistent evidence that indicates that either men or women actually have a greater intellectual performance deficit in later life.

There is some evidence indicating that there is a societal attitude linking unattractiveness with poor intellectual performance. In an experiment rating possible reasons for memory failures on the part of hypothetical target individuals, a panel of 72 women (half aged 19–32 and half aged 64–81) attributed memory failures of older and unattractive targets to a lack of ability. But, they attributed memory failures of young or attractive targets to a lack of attention (Erber & Rothberg, 1991).

It may be possible to make too much of this. Certainly, there are some in later life who actually have begun despising themselves because of what they have become. If they in fact received all of their positive strokes in younger life because of their grace and beauty, they may never have had to develop interpersonal skills that most individuals possess. For these few, there must be a special hell in being old: we can see every day the frantic efforts of people trying to stay cosmetically young by dieting, tightening, conditioning, tucking, or coloring various portions of their anatomy. At least one study, however, found not only that people in general adapt pretty well to the changes that come with aging, but that they don't really think of themselves as old (Goldsmith & Heims, 1992). This was a national, random sampling of 607 adults. Most felt that they look, act, and feel younger than others their own age. The percentage who felt this way rose from 53% of those in their 40s to 97% of those surveyed who were in their 80s.

If people don't really think of themselves as being old, the application of untrue stereotypes must be especially irritating. It's one thing to jokingly refer to oneself as getting older; it's something else again when others start to treat you like an old lady or an old man. Stereotypes of older persons may often be well-motivated but nevertheless patronizing. Thinking of the aged as a group that is somehow helpless and in need of our protection is an example. Concepts of all elderly as frail, isolated, demented, or poor are thus damaging even if they are motivated by kindly feelings of altruism. One study analyzed a congressional debate over Social Security. By far, the greatest number of representatives supporting no cuts in the program used inaccurate, patronizing stereotypes of the aged in their arguments (Lubomudrov, 1987). It has to affect peoples' self-respect when consideration of them is motivated mostly from pity.

So we see the dilemma. People socialized all through their adult lives to be independent and self-reliant may start to be characterized as being dependent and in need of help. Just at a time when chronic illness becomes more common, stature decreases, the skin wrinkles, and the senses become less sensitive, every misplaced thumbtack is taken as evidence of the onset of senility, and every bout of heartburn is seen as a possible coronary. Self-concept has to be affected by these kinds of things for many of the elderly.

introspection —
Self-examination.

trait — A
long-standing, stable
element of the
personality that is
characteristic of the
individual.

state — A temporary
emotional condition,
such as mirth or rage.

ego — The self, the
personality.

One analysis of national studies found an overall decline in regard for the aged generally (Ferraro, 1992). Ironically, however, one of the bright spots can be found in the electronic media. Criticized for years for superficial, prejudicial portrayals of the aged, a more recent study has found a dramatic improvement in the stature of older persons on television (Bell, 1992). For evidence of this, one need only contrast the broadly stereotypical character of Granny on "The Beverley Hillbillies" 30 years ago, a cantankerous idiot if there ever was one, with the kind of sophisticated, intelligent character portrayed by Angela Lansberry on "Murder, She Wrote."

Hayslip and Panek (1989) review the history of perceptions of the aged in the U.S. and maintain that they have become less positive as the proportion of the population that is elderly increases. They say that, while the cult of the young that was characteristic of the 1960s is now passed, we currently are experiencing a cult of the adult, and that most adults do not view the elderly positively.

In a review of studies of attitudes toward older persons and stereotypes held toward the aged, Atchley (2000) concludes that ageism and prejudice toward the elderly can lead to age discrimination, social stigma, and poor self-image. If this is the case, then older people have a considerable task, rising above the negative messages they must constantly receive. Although they may have learned that outside of disability, old age is not really so bad, they still have to deal with ego-threatening signals from a thousand different sources.

Growth and Development Across the Life Span

Introspection is the process of self-examination. It occurs naturally over the lifespan, although some people are naturally more introspective than others. Some theorists in the field of psychology have historically seen introspection as a *trait*, an element of the personality itself (Murray, 1938). A trait can be contrasted with a *state*, such as anger or happiness, which is a temporary emotional condition; a trait, on the other hand, is more stable, an element of the *ego*, or the self. Various traits are said to make up the personality, and they differ according to which theorist one wishes to subscribe to, which gets into material we need not delve into here. For our purposes, let's simply say that the personality is made up of a number of different traits.

Psychological theory holds that traits are constant over time, and many older people would say that, despite the image they see in the mirror, they still feel like they are the same person that they have been throughout life. Personality continuity across the life span predicts that shy children probably will be shy adults. Some research indicates that personality affects well-being; Howard Friedman and his colleagues (1993) have shown in a large, longitudinal study that the trait of conscientiousness predicts longevity, perhaps because conscientious people take better care of themselves. This is not to say, however, that all personality traits are locked in over time; there is the prospect of growth as people develop throughout life.

To see how (or if) personality changes over time, let's simply use one of the personality traits, introspection. If one thinks about oneself, there can be little doubt that there is change over time. Are you the same individual you were when you were five or ten years of age? In many ways, you are not. You have gained a great wealth of information and experience, and you've integrated that information and experience into a kind of knowledge that is characteristic of your personhood. You've learned thousands of different things that help you in the process of adaptation: you've discovered in many ways what works for you and what does not. Perhaps this process constitutes the acquisition of wisdom. (Of course, many of us still have a long way to go!) You no doubt have learned much about yourself as well as about the world around you over the course of the years.

Within this context of growth, however, some personality theorists would maintain that you have grown pretty much within the same basic structure. That is, your personality traits probably have remained essentially similar throughout adult life. Without a concerted effort, the basic structure of the personality remains stable and does not change very much.

Let's take a look at some of the personality traits identified by one psychologist, George Murray (1938). He said that there are a number of traits inherent within each individual, and that each trait might be high or low or somewhere in between. Achievement, for example, is a trait that everyone has to a greater or lesser degree, and we can see people at different ages who exhibit a drive to achieve in different kinds of contexts. One student may try harder than all the others in school to be a high achiever. Theoretically, this same child will still be striving to achieve at a high level by the time she has become an older person. Of course, the context for achievement will have changed from kickball and spelling bees to other things more appropriate to individuals in later life. Perhaps she now tries to achieve great things with her investment program. For some who have become physically frail, getting up and getting out of bed may be a real achievement. The point is, of course, that the trait, the characteristic drive, is what has continuity across the lifespan. One wouldn't expect someone who's never been willing to try very hard to suddenly exhibit great levels of achievement late in life, any more than a lifelong high-achiever would be expected to lie down and give up without a struggle. This brings us to a particular point about traits: they're based on comparisons of individuals.

So, when we say a person is high in, say, achievement or aggression, it means that they're higher in these traits relative to others (Cavanaugh, 1993).

Affiliation is another trait that Murray identified. Affiliation is the effort one puts into being outgoing and friendly. A person high in affiliation may be the life of the party—or, more likely, the organizer of the party—surrounded by a circle of friends. Applying a theory of personality continuity across the lifespan here, then, we will expect younger people high in affiliation to have developed a wide social network by later adulthood; on the other hand, young loners will probably become old loners. In other words, trait theory says that certain characteristics of the personality are typical of the individual, and that they are essentially stable across adult life. A younger person high in exhibition stays that way and becomes an older adult high in exhibition. A person high in nurturance remains a person high in nurturance.

The observer will quickly note a couple of things about trait theories of personality. First, they make sense. Things that describe us as individuals do in fact have a certain consistency over time; if they were not distinctive, then they wouldn't really be characteristic of us. Second, they help to explain behaviors. It might well be that a person who is a crabby older person used to be a crabby younger person. Third, however, is that trait theories might be seen as somewhat pessimistic. Taken too literally, the notion that traits are somehow locked in and never change doesn't really allow for growth.

Just as there can be little doubt that we retain an essentially stable personality structure over time, there is little doubt that people do in fact change. In most instances this change is a result of learning and growth. It is possible, for example, for a person to learn to become more assertive. People who don't like the way they are do have the potential to work on certain things; people have successfully learned to control their anger, for example. Disorganized people can in fact learn to be higher in the trait of order. Dependent people can grow in terms of autonomy. This kind of growth, however, usually involves two things: recognition of a trait, or a tendency within one's own personality, and the willingness to work toward change.

What research has not shown is to what extent environmental factors may have on shaping personality structure over time. Accidents of nature and social forces may have profound effects on ways that people react to their surroundings. An individual who might have flourished and developed fully in a warm, supportive family situation, for example, might turn out very differently if raised in an abusive environment. Refugees from wars or persecution might have developed some traits differently if they had not been so unfortunate as to be in the wrong place at the wrong time.

Factors much smaller than wars or depressions affect our lives. It is possible that tendencies develop or are thwarted by the social climate that surrounds us. Further, as the social climate changes, so might our adaptation to it. That is, environmental factors need not be lifelong. Social changes in later life, such as widowhood or relocation, might either force growth

Illustration 6.5. Lifelong Maladaptation

"During her clinical course the patient was noted to suffer with progressive weight loss, losing almost twenty pounds. Initially she declared, 'I have a poor appetite.' Subsequently she claimed she was 'vomiting every day.' When nurses were requested to observe the vomiting process, the nurses were compelled to follow the patient into the bathroom area where the patient was noted to induce vomiting digitally.

"The patient finally admitted she was in the process of a feud with her roommate. The basis for the conflict was not clearly delineated, except, 'I don't like her. I don't want to be here with her.' When the patient was placed in another room the vomiting ceased, weight gain ensued, and ambulation improved to the preconflict level.

"Additional history revealed the patient had been inducing vomiting since early childhood when she learned her father, whom she loved, had been found in the process of extramarital sexual relationships. Thus, the patient was raised in a home split by dissatisfaction and insecurity. The patient's anger was directed towards father, mother, herself, and subsequently others during the course of her life. The patient's anger and anxiety was expressed with digitally induced vomiting."

From Miller and Schumacher (2000, p. 177).

---

toward autonomy or cause individuals to regress into themselves. It is only the basic structure that remains pretty much the same when it comes to personality; patterns of adaptation may instigate changes either positively or negatively. Still, individual patterns seem to be fairly stable across adulthood, given changes in individual circumstances (Costa et al., 1987; Field & Milsap, 1991; McCrae & Costa, 1984; Vaillant & Vaillant, 1990).

One of the things we need to remember about older people is that they have a history. This is not as simple a concept as it sounds. When we seek to answer the question of whether personalities change in reaction to old age, it is important to take lifelong patterns of adaptation into consideration.

Illustration 6.6. Findings from the Kansas City Studies of Adult Life

"Differences between the sexes appeared with age. Older men seemed more receptive than younger men of their affiliative, nurturant, and sensual promptings; older women, more receptive than younger women of aggressive and egocentric impulses. Men appeared to cope with the environment in increasingly abstract and cognitive terms; women, in increasingly affective and expressive terms. In both sexes, however, older people seemed to move toward more eccentric, self-preoccupied positions and to attend increasingly to the control and satisfaction of personal needs."

From Neugarten (1973, p. 320).

One popular cliché about the aged is that they become more like themselves. That is, traits that are characteristic of their personalities become more pronounced. Research on this concept is sparse, but if there is a grain of truth to the stereotype, then one might argue that older people perhaps have fewer forces inhibiting them, such as having to please a boss or pressures of a marriage that may have been in conflict. They have thus become more free to be themselves. What we may not have is the information necessary to understand all the facets of an individual's personality and how they are manifested in order to understand that older self.

Younger people tend to confront the aged without knowing much about their histories. Life prior to one's own life can seem pretty distant, and it is too easily discounted. It is too simplistic to see an older person's life as a snapshot where only what we see is only what there is at the moment. Life is more complex than that: it is not a snapshot but a moving picture, with a beginning, a middle, and an end.

Further, the forces acting upon older people may be things they've never before had to confront. So while we logically conceive of aging as a part of the life cycle, there are distinct things that happen to most older people that must be taken into account. Most people have not previously had the experience, for example, of getting shorter. That is, the body loses stature in later life; although we can remember getting taller in childhood, there is little experience in becoming less tall. Older people are forced to adapt to losses: loss of employment, loss of friends as they die or move, loss of status, perhaps loss of spouse. In most instances, they've never before had to adapt to such losses. In a narrowing social world, it is possible that some people will confront later life by engaging in what Bernice Neugarten (1973) called a preoccupation with inner life, or a shift from active mastery to passive mastery. This introspection, or concern more with the inner self than with day-to-day external affairs, will be the topic of the next section of this chapter.

Well-Being, Meaning, and Reminiscence

In a gerontology text written 25 years ago, a chapter on adult development across the lifespan would have featured a variety of lists of developmental tasks or hierarchies of stages that people go through as they develop during adult life. Philosophically, this kind of approach would see old age as a truly separate part of the life span, and such theories might list stages or tasks appropriate to later adulthood. For example, in his list of adult tasks, Eric Erikson (1982) listed the one appropriate for old age as "ego integrity versus despair." Also, the concept of disengagement that we discussed in Chapter 3 was seen in psychological as well as sociological terms as part of a developmental approach to later life. Many older people seem to psychologically disengage, perhaps before they socially disengage. Looking inward can be thought of as a sign of losing interest in the outward demands of life and becoming increasingly preoccupied with self. In his original work on developmental tasks in later life, Robert J. Havighurst listed the dominant concern of the decade of life from 60 to 70 years as "deciding whether to disengage and how" and of the decade from 70 to 80 years of age as "making the most of disengagement" (1974, p. 25).

Instead, we prefer to view later life as a continuation of adulthood, with few if any tasks or areas of development that are unique only to old age. Although some social events are more common in later adulthood, adaptation to them does not really constitute a separate stage of adult development. And, while diseases common in later life can influence the personality and mental abilities, they are not exclusive to old age nor do they happen to the majority of older people. Processes of adaptation are pretty similar among younger and older adults, and the stage of life we think of as old age comes on gradually. We cannot easily specify an entrance into old age in the same way that we can separate childhood, adolescence, and young adulthood. No doubt there are changes in later life that occur over time, but they are so highly individualized that it would be both inaccurate and unfair to make too many generalizations about psychological changes that occur with aging.

This preoccupation with inner life that Neugarten described, however, may well be characteristic of psychological aging. In a variety of contexts, this perhaps is not really turning inward and becoming less concerned with the details of everyday living so much as it is a personal quest for meaning. Howard McClusky (1976) called it the search for transcendence, going beyond the self to find meaning in life. This may be one interpretation of what Erikson meant by the quest for ego integrity.

Illustration 6.7. Finding Meaning in Suffering

" . . . Hunger, humiliation, fear, and deep anger at injustice are rendered tolerable by closely guarded images of beloved persons, by religion, by a grim sense of humor, and even by glimpses of the healing beauties of nature—a tree or a sunset.

But these moments of comfort do not establish the will to live unless they help the prisoner make larger sense out of his apparently senseless suffering. It is here that we encounter the central theme of existentialism: to live is to suffer, to survive is to find meaning in the suffering. If there is a purpose in life at all, there must be a purpose in suffering and in dying. But no man can tell another what this purpose is. Each must find out for himself, and must accept the responsibility that his answer prescribes. If he succeeds, he will continue to grow in spite of all indignities."

Frankl is fond of quoting Nietzsche, "He who has a why to live can bear with almost any how.'"

From Frankl (1962, p. xi).

Illustration 6.8.

"Know well, Socrates," Cephalus said, "that when a man faces the thought that he must die, he feels fear and anxiety about that which did not trouble him before."

From Plato, *The Republic*

existential — Relating to human existence, especially the understanding one has of the meaning of life.

life review — A period of reminiscence and self-reflection brought on by a realization of impending death.

Viktor Frankl (1962) wrote a moving account of his experiences as a prisoner of the Nazis during World War II. In it, he detailed how he developed his *existential* philosophy, his understanding of why we exist. He sought to make some sense of life in view of the overwhelming suffering he witnessed and experienced, and he concluded that one of our tasks as humans is to find our own interpretation of life's meaning.

This making sense of life can be seen as the overall task of later adulthood. This may be particularly true in view of the losses undergone by so many older people. Frankl concluded that those who were able to survive the Holocaust experience were the ones who had an inner spiritual strength and will to live. Making sense out of loss, like many older persons are forced to do, provides an understanding of meaning in peoples' lives.

One area of the psychology of aging that has been extensively researched is life satisfaction. What brings happiness in old age? Why are some people, even those who have become frail and are experiencing other kinds of losses, apparently happy and satisfied in later life? Early studies of life satisfaction found that it seemed to be most closely related to health and income (Neugarten, Havighurst, & Tobin, 1961) or with social activity with friends (Lemon, Bengtson, & Peterson, 1972). More recent research has found that morale or life satisfaction is interrelated with a sense of meaning or purpose as well as psychological mastery and positive interaction with others (Gray, Ventis, & Hayslip, 1992; Ryff & Essex, 1992; Zika & Chamberlain, 1992). A lack of meaning or purpose in life has been shown to be related to a host of psychological problems (Kish & Moody, 1990).

Life purpose seemed in one study to not vary much by age or sex; themes of involvement related to high purpose in life included love, children, work, and individual activities (Baum & Stewart, 1990). In an extensive study of sources of meaning in later life, Sharon Kaufman (1986) found that they vary widely among individuals; such things as understanding of themes in their lives, interpretation of historical events, and values they had found in life emerged as sources of meaning for the older persons she interviewed.

Interpretation of themes and events is central to the process of the *life review*, a period of reminiscence that takes place in later life. Looking back over life's events and spending a great deal of mental time in the past was once considered to be dysfunctional. However, in 1963, psychiatrist Robert N. Butler described what has become one of the most influential theories

Illustration 6.9. Some Thoughts on the Life Review

Realizing that one is approaching the end of life spurs one into reviewing life, and one can't live 60 or 70 years without thinking at some time about dying. Such thoughts are reinforced among the aging simply by the number of funerals they attend. It may be possible for younger people to go for years without experiencing a death of someone close to them; this is not the case for the aged. And, with each experience, the aging individual must be thinking, "Some day—perhaps sooner than we anticipate—that will be me lying there."

While one might think that this could be depressing (no doubt for some it is!), the realization that we are not immortal more often stimulates older people into taking on unfinished business. This unfinished business may be exactly that: business—cleaning out drawers, putting pictures into albums, documenting family history, planning one's own funeral, going on trips long postponed, preparing a will, taking on good works, doing things one has always meant to do. It's said that the late Justice Oliver Wendell Holmes took up the study of Greek at age 93; asked why, he said, "It's now or never!"

The life review, however, is as likely to bring on a period of reflection, an attempt to sort out one's psychological business, so to speak, and perhaps to come to terms with life and identity. We might think of the life review as putting one's life on the scales to see how things balance out in the long haul: "Did I live a pretty good life, or was I a stinker?" Old stinkers, people who have intentionally harmed others, especially those who find it's too late to make peace with loved ones they've harmed, may have a very hard time when they review their lives. Perhaps this in part explains the high suicide rate among older men. No doubt it's possible for the life review to inspire terror among some old people. To admit that one's life has been a waste must indeed be a late-life crisis.

Most people, however, are able to sort out the good and repress the bad pretty effectively. They might rationalize a bit to convince themselves that they led happy lives. Some people may need to be reassured that they were not really so bad after all. However, the life review is for most a very positive growth experience, something that may bring serenity in later life.

---

of psychological development in later life. The life review, Butler said, was a normal and necessary return to consciousness of past experiences taken on in an effort to make some sense of one's life and to put it into perspective.

The life review is brought on by a realization of impending death; thus, people conscious of the approach of the end of life, regardless of age, may go through a life review. Butler says that this is a normal process; people who spend a good part of their mental time sifting through the past are not abnormal, but merely trying to find themes of meaning in their lives. He also says that it is not only normal but necessary, especially in the context of trying to sort through unresolved conflicts.

Butler says that the life review is both universal—it happens to everyone—and spontaneous. That is, it takes place without being planned. Thoughts of the past come to mind—often without prompting—and their value and meaning is assessed. Those that have had unsatisfactory experiences may try to revise them somewhat and gain a different perspective—or outcome. Stories of the past are related to others; some of these stories are improved upon. Rationalization and revision are characteristic of the life review process. People may be seeking happiness in past memories.

People are often able to put themselves and their lives into a new context or realize the importance of events and patterns in their lives that have been previously unacknowledged. People often will repeat portions of their life story or events and stories from the past, seeking to sort out their significance. Positive influences of the life review include righting old wrongs, learning to find self acceptance, and gaining a new understanding of what really is important in life. In this sense, the life review is a growth process in old age, and it perhaps is the reason we often seek to find wisdom among the aged (Coleman, 1999).

Coping and Adaptation

If reminiscence is part of the process of finding meaning in later life, it can also be seen as one of the mechanisms of adaptation. A prominent geriatric psychiatrist, Carl Eisdorfer (1972), spoke of the process of reviewing and rationalizing that goes on throughout adult life. He described what he called the "Bird Colonel syndrome," using a military analogy. If one's goal has been to make it to the top, to be a full colonel or a general, and he or she hasn't even made it to major or lieutenant colonel (or the equivalent) by the mid-40s, then that individual must do some rationalizing of life goals. And, of course, most of us never make it to general or president or even sales manager. We have to adapt to how well we have achieved our goals—and perhaps change the goals. Part of this process of adaptation is to review life as we go along and rationalize that getting to be a captain or a member of city council or assistant sales manager is pretty good. Part of this reevaluation of goals might be to set them in perspective, saying something like, "Well, I never got too far in business, but I raised three fine kids" or "I never wrote that novel I had planned, but I've always dealt honestly with my customers."

Rethinking and revising goals is a process of adaptation throughout life. So when people become older and review their lives, they've already had a good deal of practice in terms of putting things into perspective.

Learning what life goals are in fact important and what is of little consequence is a part of growth over the lifespan, too. It also has much to say about the process of adaptation to life, of learning to cope, and this is another realm where we should expect to find both stability and growth.

In her review of the coping literature, Ilene Siegler (1980) concluded that uses of adaptive mechanisms across the adult lifespan remain essentially stable. This does not deny the prospect for growth, but, like the re-

---

Illustration 6.12. Doctors on Their Death Beds

I once had the experience of team-teaching a session on death and dying for med students with Father James Hopf, who is now President of Xavier University. He was Acting Dean of the Medical School at Creighton University at the time, and he opened his remarks by saying, "Let me tell you about counseling doctors on their death beds." This, of course, drew rapt attention from the medical students, as it was a new thought for some of them that physicians in fact have to die, too. He went on, "As a chaplain, I've found that many doctors, when they are dying, feel like they've wasted their lives." This was an even more unique thought for the med students. "They say things to me like, 'I've not led the kind of life I'd anticipated. I thought I was important, I thought money was important. I worked 60- and 80-hour weeks, and I ignored my family. My kids grew up without me, and they're strangers to me now.'"

Thus, Father Hopf gave a lesson not in how to die but in how to live. It's a sad thing when an individual finds out too late what really is important in life.

defense mechanisms
— Characteristic
patterns of behavior
that people use to
adapt in their lives.

hypochondriasis —
Being obsessed with
health, drugs, or
doctors, or misusing
illness for dependency
needs; one of the
immature adaptive
mechanisms.

search in overall personality, the research on adaptive mechanisms indicates a stable framework throughout much of adult life. Adaptive mechanisms or *defense mechanisms*, the means we use to adapt, are characteristic of our personalities and are unlikely to change as we enter old age. Some are more useful than others in promoting well-being in adult life; some are downright maladaptive. As we grow toward maturity, we learn which ways of coping are most successful for us. We typically use a variety of mechanisms, orchestrated in a pattern that is characteristic of ourselves. In order to see how this works, let us take a closer look at some common coping mechanisms.

Interesting longitudinal research has been done on defenses. George E. Vaillant has continued on-going research with a panel of subjects that was originally formed in 1940 (Vaillant, 1977; Vaillant, Bond & Vaillant, 1986; Vaillant & Vaillant, 1990b). He has been able to categorize adaptive mechanisms by their level of maturity. At the lowest level are defenses characteristic of the mentally ill: distortion and delusional projection. Those who rely on these mechanisms are out of touch with reality.

Next among the immature mechanisms are denial and projection, attributing one's own unacknowledged feelings to others. Use of fantasy, acting out, *hypochondriasis* (obsession with drugs or doctors, or misuse of illness for dependency needs), and passive-aggressive behavior are also among the immature mechanisms.

Illustration 6.13. Repression in Later Life

When I was a younger gerontologist and still fairly innocent, I used to think that retirement was a crisis. When I'd give my talk to the Lions or the University Women or whatever group that had invited me, I often would be approached afterward by a person in their 60s, and I would think, "Ah ha! Here comes someone who is anxious about impending retirement."

I was always wrong.

Their question usually had to do with problems with an older parent, and it usually went something like this, "My mother is in her late 80s and is still living in our big old home place. She's got it packed full of newspapers and magazines and I'm afraid it's become a fire trap. She can't handle the stairs any longer and sleeps on the living room sofa. I tell her we ought to get the place cleaned out—or, better yet, move her into retirement housing or at least an apartment that's all on one level—but she just won't listen to me. She's just not in touch with reality! What can I do?"

Being reluctant to see problems that are perfectly obvious to everyone else is an example of repression. Whether it was a mechanism that always dwelled within the individual or whether it emerged in later life is something we probably can't tell for sure.

Oh, in terms of the problem itself: I didn't have a good answer then. I still don't, although my inclination is to let the older person do whatever keeps her happy, unless she's a genuine danger to herself and others. I'm not convinced that repression is always a bad thing. Sometimes reality can be a drag.

Note that it's quite possible for some of the defenses older people use to come from these psychotic or immature mechanisms. Getting older does not always mean that the defenses one uses will be more mature. However, there is no expectation that people normally will regress in the level of the mechanisms they use, either. Like personality traits, a repertoire of adaptive mechanisms seems to remain fairly constant and stable throughout adult life. In Chapter 8, we will look more at psychological problems, but for now, we can say that the immature mechanisms are among the least attractive ones, and that people who use them usually have real problems interacting with others.

Vaillant's categorization of traits at the intermediate level includes intellectualization or isolation and rationalization, including "magical thinking" and mental busywork. Originally listed among the "neurotic" defenses, *repression* might be the most common of these intermediate defenses. Repression occurs when things that seem obvious to others are not acknowledged.

People adapting at the most mature level, according to Vaillant, seem to retain their typical cluster of coping mechanisms well into later life. The mature mechanisms include behaviors we often find to be attractive, such as humor and generosity. Anticipation, being able to plan for the future even if the future is unpleasant, is another mature mechanism. As an illustration, many older persons are fairly matter-of-fact about their own death and are able to anticipate a world without themselves. Putting one's affairs in order and taking care of unfinished business are examples of healthy anticipation. Similar to anticipation are *sublimation*, channeling emotions into acceptable outlets such as artistic expression, and *suppression*, a conscious decision to postpone dealing with an impulse or conflict. Suppression is what keeps people going despite their aches and pains.

True well-being in later life can be found among those older people who typically use these mature adaptive mechanisms. We have to admire those who continue to do things for others despite their own problems, people who are able to laugh at themselves, and those who are able to rise above their losses and continue make the most of life.

Robert Atchley (2000) says that continuity in old age is itself a pattern of successful adaptation. Keeping the same roles and lifestyle has the effect of maintaining people in later life in much the same way that they have adapted in earlier adult life. One of the important facets of continuity often

---

Illustration 6.14. Using Humor and Anticipation in Late Life

When my mother was 82, her refrigerator conked out, and I was sent to buy her a new one. As I was going out the door, she said, "Oh, and don't bother getting one with a 20-year guarantee."

overlooked is the maintenance of personal control. This is a topic we will discuss at greater length in Chapter 9, as control is often taken away from the aged—with disastrous consequences—in health care institutions. First, though, let us look at the concept itself.

Maintaining control is one of the best ways of retaining continuity in later life. Control is developmental. Visualize a continuum that has "dependent" on one end and "independent" on the other. Or, we could call these poles "externally controlled" at the one end and "internally controlled" at the other. Now, think in terms of growing up from childhood to adulthood: in a way, we travel along that plane as we grow up, going from dependent or externally controlled toward the direction of independent or internally controlled. Normal, healthy adults achieve a sense of internal control with maturity: they are no longer dependent upon their parents to meet their daily needs. Because of individual personality traits, some people are naturally more dependent than others, but hardly any healthy adult still has the dependencies that were normal in childhood or adolescence. We've grown as we've progressed along the continuum from dependence to independence. So, gaining internal control can be seen as one of the developmental processes of maturation that's normal in adulthood.

Generally, we cherish the signs of gaining independence. We want to be out from under the control of our parents when we are adolescents. We put away childish things and take on the roles and activities of adults. We learn to be independent and even gain a sense of mastery in life.

Now, here comes the rub: in very late life, when older people are likely to develop physical dependencies, it is all too easy for those concerned about them to assume some elements of psychological control along with helping with activities of daily living. Not involving older people in decisions that affect them is a classic sign of a conflict over control. Think of

---

Illustration 6.15. Free Choice and the Will to Live

"Nelida Ferrari, in her dissertation research, described a group of 55 women (mean age: 82) who had applied for admission to a nursing home. They were asked how much freedom of choice they had over the decision to enter a nursing home as compared to pressure from relatives, or others, to be admitted. Seventeen said that they had no alternative, that it was not their decision. After ten weeks, 16 of these 17 had died. Of the remaining 38 who had perceived that they had some choice in the decision, only one died.

"In other words, those who had control over their own destiny were less likely to give up or lose the will to live; they were less likely to become helpless. The perception of loss of control was for some more disruptive than the move itself. In consequence, it is an axiom of good nursing care to maximize the number of choices patients have to make for themselves. The patient who feels in control of his or her own life situation is more likely to buy into the world of the living."

From Thorson (1988, p. 33).

how stressful it must be for people who have made their own decisions for sixty years suddenly to have their decision-making power taken away. They must perceive themselves as regressing, against their will, back down the scale toward helplessness.

Some of the early literature on life satisfaction indicated that it was related to a perception of internal control (Palmore & Luikart, 1972). Often referred to as the *locus* (location) of control concept, in more recent research, personal independence has been shown to be a durable construct (Lefcourt, 1992). It has been shown to be a correlate of physical functioning as well as psychological well-being in later life (Kaplan, Strawbridge, Camacho, & Cohen, 1993). A sense of mastery and a feeling of perceived control is necessary for maintaining functional ability in later life (Kempen, van Sonderen, & Ormel, 1999). Letting older persons make their own decisions may be a vital component of maintaining independence.

glossary

locus — Location, as in locus of control, which can be internal or external.

Learning and Memory

As we began this chapter, we discussed the common stereotype of elderly people as becoming forgetful or losing the ability to remember things. At this point, we need to differentiate learning from memory. While both are aspects of intelligence, we need to realize that learning is the acquisition of new information, while memory is an element of learning: the retention of the information that has been acquired. Without learning, of course, there can be no memory, but the concepts should be thought of as distinct. The content has to reach the mind and be recorded in order to be remembered.

Two important things about learning are (1) that it is dependent upon the senses, especially hearing and sight, and thus persons who have sensory impairments in later life are literally taking in less information, and (2) that it depends on an intact cognitive structure in the mind, a system of categorization whereby new information is placed in context and integrated with existing information. Older people who have an intact cognitive structure thus have a greater opportunity than do younger persons of integrating knowledge. If, however, their cognitive structure is impaired in some way—and this is particularly common among people who have had uncontrolled hypertension—then the older individual will not perform as well.

Part of this integration of new learning probably includes an assess-

---

Illustration 6.16.

"Old people remember what interests them. I never heard of an old man forgetting where he buried his money."
—Cicero

"What does an old man think? If he has kept his health and is not obsessed with contemplating his illnesses, his thoughts will not be significantly different from what he has thought through most of his mature life."

From Berman (1989, p. 287).

ment of the importance of knowing. This fact can frustrate researchers in that some older research subjects might not appear to be trying as hard as younger people when tests of cognitive performance are given. More than one project has been frustrated when younger and older persons are tested on the same material, and some of the older subjects ask why they should complete the task. Also, older people seem to have a higher fear of failure in testing situations and have a tendency to leave items on tests blank if they are not sure of the answers. Younger test-takers know that it is often good strategy to take a guess even if they are not absolutely sure of the answer. Atchley (2000) points out that it is hard to tell whether cognitive deficits in later life are due to failing memory or from a declining ability to learn. Also, it appears that there may be a greater loss in recent, short-term memory among the aged than there is in long-term memory. One reason could be that older persons who reminisce, who spend much of their mental time in the past, are preoccupied with reintegrating the past, which is where the important events of their lives lie for them. The present and the future might be of little interest.

Most of the research in learning and memory ignores practical and adaptive skills acquired through a lifetime of experience. Instead, tests measure tasks that are typically the same as those presented in an academic setting. And, as might be expected, older people often do poorly in comparison to younger ones in most testing situations. This does not mean that the large body of research on mental abilities in old age is not useful. However, one has to be somewhat selective in looking at the research and aware of constraints and subtle distinctions in the data.

There is little real doubt that, given enough time, cognitive performance does decline. It is difficult to determine whether the decline is sudden or gradual (which seems more likely), or is related to disease, trauma, disuse, or just to the aging process. The testing of older subjects usually does not inquire into what is going on in their lives. Few old people are continuously monitored, and even if this could be done, it wouldn't tell us much: someone taking tests continually would be stimulated by the test-taking process itself. Regardless of whether decline comes at a regular or an accelerated rate, though, and regardless of the fundamental cause, it eventually does come. People who live long enough do experience some slowing of mental processes, and declining cognitive functioning has been shown to be predictive of mortality (Maier & Smith, 1999). For most of the aged, however, some slowing of mental processes does not affect their ability to adapt to their environment.

One study of extreme old age took 166 men and women aged 100 years or more and required them to do a series of basic tasks (Beard, 1968). Twenty percent of them could not tell what they'd had for their previous meal, 40% could not count forward five digits, and half could not count backward four digits. Half could not remember the interviewer's name, and over a quarter of the women could not name the current president. Only 54% could follow a sequence of four or more steps. It was very clear that, either because of disease or simply because of aging itself, these very old people could not for the most part perform even relatively simple mental tasks. Another, more current, study of 165 centenarians also found steep declines in fluid and crystallized intelligence and in both short and long-term memory (Poon et al., 1992). Interestingly, problem-solving ability among those centenarians did not differ from that of test subjects in their 60s.

We sometimes think of learning as the retention of general rules, while memory is the retention of events. Most of the centenarians in both studies had failure of memory: they could not recall (or they never knew) the president's name, they could not count backward from a specific number, and they could not perform a variety of test topics satisfactorily. Yet, all still retained language and its rules of usage, which is a fairly complex series of intellectual tasks. They could carry on a conversation, and many had interesting things to say; some could still perform most of the tests perfectly. Some abilities seem to be very deep-seated and are so interwoven with different parts of our mental functioning that only the most massive kind of a trauma, such as a major stroke, can knock them out. Even then, many capacities can be regained through rehabilitation.

This hints at the complexity of the task when assessing changes in cognitive ability over the course of the later years. Several longitudinal studies have been able to sort out a number of different kinds of intelligence and demonstrate that some decline at a fairly rapid rate in very old age, while some seem to remain stable throughout life (Hultsch et al., 1992;

Illustration 6.18. Special Events

Special events, in particular those that are unique, are retained better than ordinary ones. My son clearly remembers his first and only streetcar ride, while I only remember streetcar rides in general because I took so many of them. I can remember vividly, though, what I was doing when I heard that President Kennedy had been shot in November of 1963, just as my mother clearly remembered what she was doing when she heard the news of the bombing of Pearl Harbor in 1941. Particular, unique events, such as the date of a marriage or the birth of a child, are used as milestones in our lives.

$g$lossary

plasticity — Reserve capacity; capacity to grow.

Schaie & Willis, 1993). In general, abilities that are used seem to decline the least, if at all, and abilities that are not used appear to decline more rapidly. There seems to be little measurable mental decline up until the seventh decade of life; in some individuals, there is not very much even after that. Much of the measurable decline may be related to disease. One very important practical implication is that hypertension needs to be controlled across the adult lifespan in order to prevent mental deficits later on. Also, practice effects are important: if you don't use it, you'll lose it.

There are some other practical implications. First, we should not anticipate that severe memory loss is normal. Too often, failing abilities among the aged are taken merely as a sign of aging. Sudden confusion is an important symptom and should be a indication that a comprehensive medical evaluation is in order. Conversely, we shouldn't be patronizing with the aged who show no signs of a mental lapse; saying that someone is just as sharp as they ever were is something of an insult. We should *expect* him to be just as sharp as he ever was. It should never be forgotten that most psychological changes have physical causes; changes in cognitive ability are symptoms that should be assessed by a competent geriatrician or neurologist.

Next, we should realize that diversity in old age means that older adults will retain different mental abilities and retain them at different rates. The population of older people is too heterogeneous to allow us to generalize very much in this regard. Some people actively involved in interesting tasks can be counted on to continue to mentally improve and grow throughout life. Others who lack mental stimulation will have difficulty retaining what they once had. People react to trauma differently, and there may be differential physical or social traumas that affect an individual's cognitive ability.

There is a considerable *plasticity* (ability to stretch) of the intellect in aging. Not only are most people not tested to anywhere near their limits in their daily patterns of adaptation, but they have an unexplored capacity to learn in later life. Further, these abilities to grow cognitively will differ greatly among the aged (Backman, 1990; Baltes & Kliegl, 1992; Baltes, Kuhl, & Sowarka, 1992). Some older persons are capable of great achievements in later life.

Finally, there are implications for educational programming for and with older persons. Elderly people are used effectively as tutors and mentors in the schools, and have been for many years. There should be no reason to think that older learners should not be integrated with younger adults in continuing education classes. Specialized educational opportunities for older adults, such as the Elderhostel program, also draw on the continuing cognitive capacity of older adults. Keeping an active mind is therapeutic, and educational interventions with the aged have great potential (Thorson, 1990).

Conclusion

Self-perception has a profound impact on how the aged perform (Kempen, van Sonderen, & Ormel, 1999). If they are expected to withdraw mentally from an active life, they may pick up on this expectation and be all the more likely to psychologically disengage. We have seen that there may be a double standard in this regard; women may be especially vulnerable to stereotyping and ageism. It may be necessary to both give special encouragement to keep older people involved mentally as well as to guard against the application of unfair bias against the aging. Most older people do not "slip" or slow down to any measurable degree in terms of cognitive skills: there is a great reserve of mental capacity throughout life, and the processes of adaptation and problem-solving are the least likely areas to expect decrements.

Growth and development across the lifespan means exactly that: we don't get to a certain point of mental achievement and then start to slip backwards. While some older people do exhibit some forgetfulness, particularly for recent knowledge and facts, their abilities to use concepts tend to have a great deal of stability. Personality and patterns of adaptation especially should be seen as having continuity across the life span.

A search for meaning in later life should be seen as part of the life review, a normal, universal process. Putting one's life in order or finding perspective on one's life is part of a process of learning and growth. Learning to live with oneself and who one has been should not be seen as a crisis so much as a time to reflect and grow. Life reviewing can be done more effectively if there is another person willing to listen and help enable the individual reminisce. Learning from older people what has been important to them in life can be a process of growth for younger people as well.

Questions for Discussion

1. What personality traits would you say generally characterize you?
2. Are there traits that you would say are particularly attractive or unattractive?

3. Do you think that there are any elements of personality that are more typical of the elderly?
4. Among the older persons you know, are there any adaptive mechanisms that are more common than others?
5. Have you noticed any personality or behavioral changes among older people you know?
6. Can you give an example of an older individual of your acquaintance who is doing some life reviewing?
7. If you've been able to hear an older person reminisce, is there anything that has surprised you?
8. Can you cite an instance when control was taken away from an older person?
9. If you're aware of an older individual who has shown any kind of cognitive decline, what is the nature of it? What elements of cognitive ability have remained?
10. Based on the material in this chapter, can you give some implications for adult education with the elderly?

Health and Illness in Later Life

Chapter Outline

"During World War II, I was in a U.S. Navy guerilla army—12 American marines and sailors and 250 Chinese soldiers based in northwest China, in the Gobi Desert in Inner Mongolia. What a wonderful life I would have missed if I had been killed at age 24 in another of the senseless wars brought on by incompetent political leaders and military 'heroes.'"
—Dr. Henry J. Heimlich, born 1920

Introduction

Prior to the twentieth century, most people died before they were old. A longevity revolution that was discussed in Chapter 1 has changed all that: for the first time in human history, a majority of the population lives into old age. This is more true for some groups than for others. White women, for example, have a health advantage when compared to other groups. It could be said, in fact, that gerontology is in many ways a women's issue.

In this chapter, we will see that some conditions in later life tend to be either more gender-specific or more *race specific*. That is, some conditions that occur in later life happen to one group more than another: examples are arthritis, which happens to older white females more than any other group; *hypertension*, which occurs more among African-American women; and non-insulin-dependent diabetes, which occurs much more frequently among Hispanics and Native Americans.

In addition to this, we will look at frequencies and outcomes of the major health conditions that occur among all people who live to be old, including disease processes, breakdowns of the autoimmune system, and sensory loss. We'll also discuss at some length the meaning of health and illness to older persons, and we will focus on functional ability: the ability to carry out activities of daily living. There are some special health conditions, like *hypothermia* and fractures, that particularly threaten older individuals. We will take a look at some warning signs and point out some practical implications.

While the content of this chapter may be problem-focused, we also want to emphasize that the adaptation older persons make to the health conditions that take place in later life is remarkably positive. Most older people cope very well, and the majority of older people in surveys rate their health as good or excellent. It could be said that it is after 75 when we see most of the *chronic* health problems usually associated with old age, and it is only among those 85 and above that the majority have a serious disability. Studies of the aged as a group indicate that most are able to live independent lives in spite of disability.

Morbidity and Mortality

The inevitable physical decline we discussed in Chapter 5 leads to *morbidity* and *mortality*. In only a very small percentage of cases do people "die healthy," or essentially drop off while they are symptom-free. Instead, we realize that there almost always is a period of illness and disability that comes prior to the end of life. This chapter will look at illness and its outcomes, as well as to focus on the implications of health and illness.

Even a brief look at the obituary page of any newspaper gives a clear and fundamental perspective on the most basic of human inequalities: some

---

Illustration 7.1. The Human Condition

The human condition is that we get old and die, if we're lucky.

---

of us live longer than others. It is no surprise in a gerontology text to learn that some live extraordinarily long lives. What is surprising is the differential in *death rates* associated with social elements. Looking at Table 7.1, for example, it is clear that death rates for married people are much lower than for the never married, as well as those who are widowed or divorced.

In gerontology, it is often observed that there is an especially close relationship between the physical, psychological, and social elements of older peoples' lives. The late Stanley Brody used the illustration of an older woman in a very poor Philadelphia neighborhood who refused to get her cataracts removed, despite the fact that Medicaid would pay for the operation. She felt that as soon as it was known that she was not at home, her apartment would be stripped clean; indeed, she had ample reason for this belief. Thus, it was her social circumstance, poverty, that led to her blindness.

The relationships in Table 7.1 give the most fundamental physical data—death rates—and illustrate how they differ by the social factor of being coupled or uncoupled. The rates are expressed in deaths per hundred thousand in the population by age and race. Thus, going across the top line, we

glossary

death rates (or mortality rates) — Amount of deaths for specific causes (or by race, age, or sex) expressed as a rate rather than a number; as an illustration, a percentage is a rate (so many per hundred) and a batting average is a rate (so many hits per thousand at bats); death rates are often expressed as so many per 10,000 or per 100,000. The important concept is that rates can be more easily compared between groups than can numbers of deaths.

TABLE 7.1. **Death Rates by Age, Sex, Race, and Marital Status***

	Age in Years			
	45–54	55–64	65–74	75+
White Males				
Never married	1,103	2,399	5,162	14,037
Married	361	1,050	2,737	7,786
Widowed	1,205	2,292	4,415	12,404
Divorced	1,015	2,554	5,170	11,075
White Females				
Never married	541	1,238	2,794	10,969
Married	229	618	1,478	4,037
Widowed	573	1,286	2,410	8,814
Divorced	425	1,046	2,613	8,125
Black Males				
Never married	1,914	3,712	**	**
Married	823	1,827	3,912	8,103
Widowed	**	**	4,124	13,917
Divorced	1,509	3,365	**	**
Black Females				
Never married	847	1,421	**	**
Married	456	995	2,065	4,766
Widowed	1,011	1,694	3,355	8,874
Divorced	666	1,639	2,824	**

*Per 100,000 population
**Figure does not meet statistical standards of reliability
From: National Center for Health Statistics (1998, November 10, p. 2).

see that of every 100,000 white males aged 45 to 54 who have never married, one can anticipate 1,103 deaths annually. About twice as many, 2,399, men in that category who are between the ages of 55 and 64 die per year, and so on.

The increase in death rates with older age should of course be anticipated, and the grim arithmetic of living and dying indicates that death rates continue to increase with age until there is no one left to count. The surprising and dramatic differences shown in the table, however, are seen in the columns. Note that the "ever married" category includes those who are currently married, widowed, or divorced, and then these particular categories follow and perhaps contain the more useful figures to compare. Look, for example at that first group, white males aged 45–54. It is evident that divorced men have a death rate about three times higher than married men, and the death rate of widowed men is almost four times higher. The relationships are similar in the other age categories, as well as the blocks of information for white females, black males, and black females.

There is really no doubt that those who have a life companion do better, on the whole, and some might argue that the best thing one can do for one's health is be in a long-term committed relationship. Others point out, though, that the entire reason for the difference is difficult to pin down. Perhaps the kind of person who gets married is stable and practices good health habits. Those who are widowed or divorced no doubt have to cope with a great amount of stress. The people who have a confidant have a better overall quality of life and greater psychological and social stability. There is much to debate on this topic, but the fundamental point here is that something as basic as who lives and who dies is reflected in a social factor—being coupled—that may be as important or more important than many physical factors. Among black women aged 75 and older, for example, those who are widowed die at a rate twice as high as those who are married. This magnitude of difference would have health empidemiologists scurrying if one group had a rate of death from, say, meningitis, that was twice as high as another's. Again, we cannot overemphasize the point in gerontology that economic, social, and psychological factors all interrelate with physical factors and outcomes.

Another basic correlate of survival is socioeconomic status. The differences in economic status are frequently illustrated by educational level and income. Table 7.2 gives a stark differential. Those with four or more years of college have death rates in the ages from 25 to 64 that are less than half as high as those with less than a high school education, and those at the lowest income level are much more likely to die than those at the highest. We will see later in this chapter that the same relationships hold for disability by socioeconomic status. Prosperity correlates with longevity. While the data in Table 7.2 are for younger and middle-aged adults, similar ratios may be found among the elderly. Again, better health habits and lower levels of life stress may be the explanation.

TABLE 7.2. Death Rates by Years of School Completed, by Sex*

Years of School Completed	45–54 years	55–64 years
Males		
Under 12 years	933.5	1,759.5
12 years	789.6	1,657.5
13 or more years	330.5	831.2
Females		
Under 12 years	321.4	820.1
12 years	391.3	943.0
13 or more years	212.5	515.8

From National Center for Health Statistics (1998, November 10).

Causes of Death

Table 7.3 gives recent overall totals and rates of deaths for persons aged 65 and older. Heart disease at 35% and cancer at 22% are by far the most frequent causes. Cerebrovascular disease (*stroke*) remains as the third leading cause of death for older people, but it has shown a dramatic decline in the past two decades due to improvements in treatment. Lung diseases—chronic obstructive pulmonary disease, pneumonia, and influenza—have actually climbed on the list of the top ten killers of older people. This is probably not so much due to the popular explanation of air pollution as it is because fewer people are dying of cardiovascular and cerebrovascular diseases, which inevitably increases the relative importance of the other

TABLE 7.3. Deaths and Death Rates for the 10 Leading Causes of Death, Ages 65+

Cause	Number	Percentage	Rate*
Diseases of heart	607,703	35.1%	1,783.4
Malignant neoplasms	381,810	22.0	1,120.5
Cerebrovascular disease	140,693	8.1	412.9
Chronic obstructive pulmonary disease	95,997	5.5	281.7
Pneumonia and influenza	79,395	4.6	233.0
Diabetes mellitus	47,109	2.7	138.2
Accidents	30,934	1.8	90.8
Motor vehicle accidents	7,786	0.4	22.8
All other accidents	23,148	1.3	67.9
Alzheimer's disease	22,209	1.3	65.2
Nephritis	21,962	1.3	64.5
Septicemia	18,263	1.0	53.6
All other causes	286,996	16.6**	842.2
Total	1,733,070		5,086.0

*Per 100,000 in specified population
**Exceeds 100% due to rounding.
From: National Center for Health Statistics (1998, October 7).

causes. Remember, everyone has to die of something, so if one cause goes down, something else has to go up.

Alzheimer's disease probably was always with us, but it has increased in popularity as a diagnosis within the past few decades. In 1970, for example, Alzheimer's would not have appeared on the list. Nephritis means kidney failure, perhaps an inevitable cause of death among the very aged. Septicemia means infection, usually bacterial infection, and this represents the decline in immune function typical in older bodies.

One of the sobering facts related to health and illness among the elderly is that what people are being treated for and what they die of are not necessarily the same thing. As we saw in our earlier discussion of declining social value of the aged, older individuals are not often seen as the most important patients in many health care settings. Contrast, for example, the death of an older person and a child. When an older person dies, even if the death was unexpected, the typical response is to say, "Well, perhaps her old heart finally gave out," or something on that order. Further investigation usually is not done. If a young person dies, however, we will often make great efforts to determine the exact cause of death. Young people are not supposed to die; they are of high social value in our society. More often than not, when a young person dies, a postmortem examination will be done to find out why.

Autopsies of older people are, on the other hand, comparatively rare (Soloman & Adams, 1993). We say things, illogical as they might sound, such as, "Well, she's suffered enough," while thinking different thoughts entirely: "She's dead; does it really matter from what? And why go to the trouble and expense of an autopsy? Besides, I don't want my mother to be cut open by a pathologist." These and other unspoken attitudes in fact might be seen as indicators of the lack of importance of older individuals. We expect old people to die, and by our actions indicate that we don't really seem to care very much from what.

Illustration 7.2. Miracle Cures Among the Elderly

A friend who is now retired from his position as professor of medicine at a major university used to tell me about his two keys to success in treating older patients. He said it was often the case that other doctors had never taken the time to actually talk with and listen to them. Frequently, he could hear out an older person's problems over the course of 45 or 50 minutes and then send them on their way without a prescription, perfectly happy and satisfied with the care they'd received. He noted that, too often, other physicians would listen for two minutes and then pull out the prescription pad. And, he attributed many of what he jokingly called his "miracle cures" to taking people off of the medications that other doctors had prescribed. He maintained that many people in later life are over-medicated and said that he often was able to reduce the number of drugs they were on from six or seven down to one or two.

Studies have found that exceptionally few autopsies are done subsequent to the deaths of elderly people. One study in New York, for example, followed deaths in nursing homes during a four-year period; out of 58,985 deaths, autopsies were performed in only 499 cases, a rate of only 0.8%. By comparison, autopsies in the general population usually are done at a rate of about 14% of all deaths. Fewer than one in ten of the nursing home physicians surveyed in that study indicated that they routinely discussed autopsies with patients or families, and 19% actually said they saw little value in autopsy studies of deaths in nursing homes (Katz & Seidel, 1990).

This tendency and the great complexity involved in diagnosis of the multiple conditions older people often have unfortunately lead to sloppy medicine, in some cases, when it comes to care of the aged. It is not unusual, especially in small towns, to be unable to even find a doctor who really is interested in caring for older patients. Geriatics has only recently emerged as a specialty area within internal medicine, and there is a chronic shortage of trained geriatricians. Other practitioners, particularly those who have been out of medical school for some years, may never have had any special training in the care of older patients, and medical practitioners, too frequently voice the same negative attitudes toward the aged that one hears from others in the society.

The tendency may be to hurry older people through their visits to the doctor: they may be seen as demented or chronic complainers. Physicians may not think they can do much for them. Admittedly, geriatrics is a difficult, challenging area of medicine. It often takes a great deal of time to sort out the various problems old people have. And, time is often the commodity that the doctor has the least of. There is hardly ever a "quick fix" for the health care problems that older individuals present. Chronic conditions by their nature demand monitoring and control; they don't lend themselves to a fast cure. Thus, some physicians who treat older people may receive little psychic gratification.

Even less encouraging is the fact that many older people die from an undiagnosed condition. A number of studies indicate that cause of death listed on the death certificate and cause of death revealed by an autopsy do not always correspond. In fact, it has been shown that between 20 and 30% of those who had an autopsy are shown to have actually died from something other than what they had been treated for (Katz & Seidel, 1990; Sarode et al., 1993). Those with cancer had the most accurate diagnoses; those who died from cardiovascular problems the least (Lanksa, 1993). We should point out, however, that many cases where an autopsy is called for happen when there is some doubt about the exact cause the death.

It is with some caution, then, that we continue with a discussion of what people die from in later life, as the data on deaths in the population are taken from a national registry of death certificates. If the death certificates themselves give accurate information only 70 or 80% of the time, then the numbers we generate from them might not be nearly as precise as they seem to be.

external causes of death — Accidental deaths, suicides, and homicides.

acute — Having a sudden onset and a short course; most infectious diseases are acute.

We can only rationalize, then, that the best information we have as to cause of death is the one that's recorded on most death certificates, even if this does not reflect the primary cause in every instance. And, it works both ways: many death certificates may, for example, list heart disease or cancer when the immediate cause of death was pneumonia or an undiagnosed infection that happened as a result of the underlying condition. Or, pneumonia or septicemia might be listed when the underlying condition that actually caused the person to be ill in the first place was diabetes or Alzheimer's disease. We need to remember that while the numbers may seem precise, there is some room for interpretation. Finally, about 10% of all deaths are listed as "other diseases" and "symptoms, signs, and ill-defined conditions." The actual cause is unknown.

Mortality and Chronicity

Having said all that, how do the causes of death in late life differ from those of younger people? Basically, the answer is that young people are most likely to die of *external causes*—accidents, homicides, and suicides—while older persons are most likely to die of chronic causes, such as heart disease, cancer, and stroke. (This represents a historical change: at the beginning of the century, most deaths were the result of *acute*, usually infectious, illnesses such as tuberculosis or pneumonia.)

Let's look at the numbers. Each year for the past decade or so, slightly more than 2.3 million people died in the United States (Ventura, Anderson, Martin, & Smith, 1998). Out of that total, only an annual number of 13,515 were aged from 1 to 14 years, a little more than one-half of one percent of all deaths. Within that group of young people, 5,288 (39.1%)

Illustration 7.3. HIV Often Overlooked in the Elderly

Recent studies indicate that elderly patients are not screened adequately for HIV infection. A retrospective review of the charts of 32 HIV-positive elderly patients in a major teaching hospital in the South identified 24 patients over age 60 who presented with signs or symptoms of AIDS, but were not tested for HIV until months later. Almost one-third of the patients with AIDS symptoms had been screened for cancer or diagnosed with dementia. Only as their disease progressed, especially with pneumocystis carinii pneumonia, were they tested for HIV. Another study in a teaching institution in the North found that of 170 patients between the ages of 60 and 79 who died during 1992–1993, 6% of the men and 9% of the women were HIV-positive. Only a few had documented risk factors for HIV exposure, and most had been misdiagnosed.

From Metropolitan Life Insurance Company (1996, p. 18). Used with permission.

---

died from accidents. Other causes were much less frequent: cancer was second, but represented only 1,545 (10.8%) out of the 13,515. Birth defects were next, accounting for 7.5% of childhood deaths, followed by homicide (only 782 in total) at 5.7%.

Accidents were also the leading cause of death for the 30,945 who died between the ages of 15 to 24; this represented 12,958, or 41.9%, of all deaths for that group. About three quarters of these accidents were automobile accidents. Homicide moved up to the second leading cause of death for these young people, but only represented 5,793 (18.7%) out of the 30,945 who died. The third leading cause for this group was suicide: 4,146 (or 13.4%). In contrast to previous generations, where acute diseases such as tuberculosis, pneumonia, and influenza were major killers, external causes now account for the majority of deaths in this age cohort.

In the next older group, those 25 to 44 years of age, the total number of deaths represented only a little more than 5% of deaths at all ages. Accidents were still the leading cause of death: 25,477, or 19% of the total of 133,612 deaths for those aged 25 to 44. In this age category, cancer (16.1% of the total for the group) moved into second place, and heart disease was third, accounting for 11.8%. Suicide, at 12,008 (9%) was the number four killer, and *HIV* infection (or *AIDS*, Acquired Immunodeficiency Syndrome) was the fifth leading cause of death in that age group, representing about 8.4% of the deaths (a total of 11,166). HIV deaths had declined from 11.5% of the total—which had made it the third leading cause within this group—in the previous seven years.

By late middle age, 45 to 64 years, the two major killers are chronic conditions. There were 375,454 people in this age group who died, and 130,894 (or 34.8% of the total of 375,454) of them died of *malignant neoplasms* (cancer). The second leading cause of death was heart disease, accounting for 100,051 (or 26.6%). Third, at 16,689 (4.4%) was accidental death. Almost as many (15,267 or 4.0%) died of strokes.

By the time we reach the age category 65+, the top six causes of death are chronic conditions. Fully 74.9% of all deaths in the country are accounted for by people 65 or older (1,733,070), and of these, 35.1% are caused by heart disease. The second leading cause of death for older persons is cancer (22.0%), followed by stroke (8.1%), chronic obstructive pulmonary disease (5.5%), pneumonia and influenza (4.6%), and diabetes (2.7%). Accidents account for just 1.8% of the deaths of older persons, but it is interesting to note that, because older persons account for most of the total deaths, older people actually account for a higher number of accidental deaths: 30,933 for those aged 65+ versus 12,958 for those 15 to 24 years of age (Anderson & Rosenberg, 1998).

We'll discuss some of these relationships further in Chapter 9, but for now we need merely note that the causes of death for most of the younger people who die are external (accidents, suicide, and homicide), while those most common in later life are chronic. And, the implication that we might draw from this is that illnesses in late life, at least the ones so serious as to

HIV — Human immunodeficiency virus; the underling cause of AIDS.

AIDS — Acquired immunodeficiency syndrome; a failure of the immune system to fight off both infections and chronic illness.

malignant neoplasms — Cancerous tumors.

lead to the older individual's ultimate death, typically are drawn out rather than sudden, and are often disabling.

As we noted, acute (having sudden onset and a short course) illnesses—usually infectious diseases—accounted for the leading causes of death at the beginning of the twentieth century. Many more young people died then; over half of reported deaths were among people 14 years of age or younger (DeSpelder & Strickland, 1992). To explain that point a bit further: we did not say that half of the population was dead by age 14 (a common misinterpretation of that statistic); we already know from our discussion in Chapter 1 that was not the case. Since the birth rate was high, and infant mortality was also high, half of the deaths that took place at the turn of the century were accounted for by the deaths of children.

Presently, 74.9% of all deaths are accounted for by people 65 or older, and this gives us a very different message when we think of death. Since most of the people who die are old, and most deaths take place in institutions, dying has become something of a foreign concept to much of the population. We don't see death very much any more, except in fictionalized accounts in the movies or on television. As a result, we have come to the attitude, in some ways, of viewing death as unnatural or deviant, as

---

Illustration 7.4. Religious Elderly Have Lower Blood Pressure

It could be the fellowship, the ceremonies, or the connection with a higher power, but whatever the reason, religious practices have a beneficial effect on physical and mental health.

More than a dozen studies by Harold Koenig, MD, and his associates have shown how religious activities can improve health, from boosting immune function to speeding recovery from depression. Now, they have discovered yet another health benefit of religious activity: it maintains lower blood pressure.

Their study of 4,000 North Carolinians ages 65 and older found that the more religious people are, the lower their blood pressure is. Specifically, they found that people who attended religious services and prayed weekly, or studied the Bible at least once a week, were 40% less likely to have high diastolic pressure or diastolic hypertension—associated with heart attacks and strokes—than those who didn't participate in either activity regularly. Religious participants also experienced smaller increases in blood pressure over the years than their non-religious counterparts.

"Our studies have repeatedly shown that the emotional effects of religious activities have physical consequences throughout the body," Koenig said. "In this case, the effect we found was on blood pressure. If you cope with stress better, your blood pressure isn't going to be as high."

Co-author Linda George offered a similar theory: "Religious people have better support systems which keep them healthier. The sense of meaning and kind of comfort that religious beliefs provide make them more resistant to stresses both physical and social."

From *The Center Report* (1998).

---

something foreign to everyday life. And we have a tendency to associate the concept of aging with the concept of death.

Children still have more acute illnesses than older people, but they don't die from them (as a rule) as they did in earlier times. Persons under 18 years of age average 2.86 acute conditions per year, whereas persons over 65 have built up immunity to many acute illness over the course of their lifetimes and average only 1.002 per year (Ries, 1991). Most of the serious infectious illness, such as polio, measles, diphtheria, and typhoid, are prevented by immunization. Other infectious killers like pneumonia and tuberculosis can often be cured with antibiotics. As a result, we now associate illness and death in later life with chronicity, something that is long-term and drawn out.

This is not to say that all chronic illness results in death. Most older people have at least one chronic condition; many have multiple chronic illnesses. The health experience of the majority of older persons is to cope with progressive illness that, at least among the young old, usually is not disabling.

Table 7.4 differentiates the rates per 1000 individuals under 65 and those aged 65 and above for a number of common chronic conditions. Almost half (483 out of every thousand) of those 65+ have arthritis, an inflammation of the joints that is usually painful and may be disabling. The frequency of arthritis increases with age, going from 498 per thousand among the group that is aged 75 to 84, up to 520 per thousand among those 85 years and older.

Next highest in frequency is hypertension or high blood pressure, at 380.6 per thousand; unlike arthritis, it does not seem to increase in frequency among the very old. Hypertension is a condition that is more race-specific than are many of the chronic illnesses seen among the elderly: the rate of high blood pressure among black women aged 65+, for

TIA — Transient ischemic attack; a spasm or spontaneous narrowing of a blood vessel in the brain that can cause stroke-like symptoms and that often precedes a true stroke.

TABLE 7.4. Chronic Conditions per 1,000 Americans by Age

Chronic Conditions	Under 65	65 Years and Over
Heart disease	48.3	278.9
High blood pressure	77.2	380.6
Cerebrovascular disease	4.5	57.0
Varicose veins	24.5	78.1
Emphysema	4.3	36.3
Arthritis	78.8	483.0
Visual impairment	25.6	81.9
Cataracts	5.2	156.8
Glaucoma	3.3	54.1
Hearing impairment	55.4	286.5
Frequent constipation	12.7	61.7
Diabetes	18.3	88.2

From National Center for Health Statistics (1991).

example, is 643 per thousand, compared to a rate of 429 among white women 65 and older (Metropolitan Life Insurance Company, 1988).

High blood pressure can lead not only to stroke (the rupture or obstruction of one of the cerebral arteries, which results in damage to the part of the brain affected), but it can also lead to heart and kidney damage, and it can contribute to transient ischemic attack (**TIA**), a spasm of a blood vessel in the brain that temporarily cuts off the blood flow and leads to dizziness or unconsciousness. Such an attack obviously could lead to injury from falling or to accidental injury or death while driving.

Illustration 7.6. Some Implications of Hypertension

The normal range for blood pressure increases with age, but it doesn't increase all that much. There are two measures: the systolic (the first number given) and the diastolic. The ideal range for adults should be a systolic reading somewhere around 120 and a diastolic of around 80. For older persons, an upper figure above 140 and a lower higher than 90 might be considered to be hypertensive.

High blood pressure is the principal cause of stroke among the elderly. While the rates of stroke death have gone steadily down over the past three decades, stroke is still the third leading causes of death among the adult population. Blood pressure should be monitored regularly, especially among groups prone to have hypertension including African-Americans and Native Americans. Women seem to be somewhat more likely than men to be hypertensive, but that doesn't mean that men are immune: among those 65+, the rates for white men are 317 per thousand and for black men 371 per thousand. A common mistake that people being treated for hypertension sometimes make is to go off of their medication when they feel better. Most patient education programs address this issue of compliance. However, it still should be verified among people who have been diagnosed with hypertension and whose physicians want them to continue on a maintenance dosage.

Although people who have had strokes can often regain much of their abilities through rehabilitation, the process often is a long, painstaking, and expensive one. Further, hypertension is the principal cause of *multi-infarct dementia* (a series of small strokes that damage many parts of the brain), one of the most common causes of cognitive impairment. Of the chronic health problems common in later life, high blood pressure is one of the most controllable. Unfortunately, one of the most frequent conditions charted among nursing home patients is "CVA" (cerebrovascular accident, or stroke); it is the most common disabling condition among the

---

Illustration 7.7. Woman, 84, Dies After Being Locked Out of House

A retired Omaha schoolteacher died in the cold Friday evening when she was locked out of her house, the Douglas county Sheriff's Office said.

Lucille Hammond, 84, was found about 5 p.m. sitting on a bench in front of her house near 146th and Cumming Streets, Sgt. Bill Jackson of the Sheriff Office said Saturday.

"She froze to death,' Jackson said. 'It looks like she let her cat out,' he said. 'When she stepped out, the door locked behind her. She just sat down. It's real sad."

The sergeant estimated that Hammond, who wasn't wearing an overcoat, had been out in the cold for about two hours. Temperatures were in the low teens and wind chills were below zero.

Hammond lived alone but next door to her daughter and son-in-law, Jill and Joe Hartnett. They were not at home at the time.

"She was healthy, but her mind was failing," Jill Hartnett said.

From the *Omaha World-Herald*, January 10, 1999

Accidental Hypothermia

The hypothalamus, the body's thermostat, sometimes does not operate effectively among older persons. Hypothermia, an abnormally low internal body temperature (below 96 degrees Fahrenheit or 35.5 Celsius) may result. Older people exposed to prolonged cold, even those who are not able to keep their house or apartment warmer than 60 or 65 degrees Fahrenheit, may be prone to get hypothermia. Older persons have less subcutaneous (beneath the skin) fat to insulate the body, they have less water in their tissues (water is a good insulator), and they may be less likely to have an effective shivering response (the movement from shivering tends to warm the body). If the body temperature falls below 80 degrees Fahrenheit (26.6 degrees Celsius) there is little likelihood that the individual will survive.

Signs of hypothermia, in addition to low internal temperature, include uncharacteristic confusion or drowsiness, slow or irregular heartbeat, weak pulse or low blood pressure, or sluggishness or a lack of coordination. Older people showing any of these signs who have been exposed to prolonged cold should receive immediate emergency medical treatment. It has been estimated that about 10% of persons found dead at home during the winter months may have died of accidental hypothermia.

elderly, often resulting in paralysis or speech impairment. Hypertension also contributes to heart disease.

Heart attack, the most frequent killer among the elderly, most often is caused by a blockage of the coronary arteries, the blood vessels that feed the heart muscle itself. About 14% of the elderly have coronary disease. Other circulatory problems include peripheral vascular disease, which is an obstruction of the blood supply to the extremities (especially the legs), arrhythmias (irregular heartbeat), and congestive heart failure, where the heart becomes too weak to maintain an adequate supply of blood to the rest of the body. This often results in swelling, particularly around the ankles. Most types of cardiovascular disease are related to coronary artery disease—caused by atherosclerosis (clogging of the arteries with fatty deposits)—with resultant angina (painful, reduced blood flow to the heart). A significant minority of older adults are among the "walking wounded," in that they have had at least one heart attack, but typically they are getting along pretty well. They are continually anxious, of course, as to whether they may have another coronary incident and whether the next heart attack might be fatal. Cardiac rehabilitation is possible through a program of carefully-monitored diet and exercise, but prevention is obviously preferable.

While only 82 out of a thousand persons have a serious visual impairment at age 65, this increases to 219 per thousand by age 85. Cataract, a clouding of the lens of the eye, increases with aging, from 15.6% of those 65 to 32.7% of those 85 and above. This is the one particular area that has yielded the most dramatic improvements in outcome: surgery to correct cataracts is almost always successful and is now most often done on a out-patient basis.

Glaucoma, an increase of pressure within the eyeball, is one of the principal causes of blindness in later life. It is not preventable, nor can it be reversed or cured. But it can be arrested by the use of eyedrops. All aging people should be checked regularly for glaucoma.

Among the sensory losses, hearing impairment is the most frequent and the most likely to get worse with aging. At age 65, 28.6% of the elderly have a measurable hearing impairment (this is somewhat more common

---

Illustration 7.8. In All Things, Moderation

There is no doubt that diet and exercise have an important, positive, preventative influence on health in later life. Fairly vigorous exercise for at least 20 minutes three times a week seems to be ideal for younger and middle-aged adults. It's been shown that even moderate stretching exercise among the aged and rhythmic activities such as walking or swimming have measurable benefits. More vigorous exercise, even weight lifting, has also been show to be beneficial (Porterfield & St. Pierre, 1992)

Illustration 7.9. Examples of Anatomic Age-Related Vision Changes

Many of the visual effects of age are a direct result of anatomical changes that characterize the older eye.

- Cornea: Generally remains clear. However, as some of the endothelial cells (which maintain clarity) drop out, the cornea may become more likely to scatter light.
- Lens: Invariably becomes denser, more yellow and less elastic, accounting for subtle visual changes as well as the loss of accommodation.
- Pupil: Becomes smaller, admitting less light to the eye. Decreased capacity to adjust to changing levels of illumination.
- Vitreous gel: Tends to condense and collapse. Bits of dense gel may appear as floaters against the sky or a white wall.
- Retina: Embryonically a part of the brain (which loses cells). The number of nerves cells within the retina and visual cortex gradually reduces over time.
- Retinal vasculature: Ages along with vasculature throughout the body.

From The Lighthouse National Center for Vision and Aging (1999).

among men than women). This figure increases to almost 50% by age 85. Hearing loss, unfortunately, is often progressive. Deafness is probably the most prevalent isolating condition in later life, and hearing aids can help only a minority of those who have a hearing impairment. The sense of hearing does not regenerate, and much of what we know about prevention involves avoiding continuous loud noises.

Adequate nutrition in late life is sometimes as much a social or economic problem as it is a physical problem. Some authorities maintain that the diet older people eat must have been adequate or the individual wouldn't have lived to get old, but there is a particular problem with changes in diet. Some older people may lapse into eating poorly because they don't feel motivated to prepare balanced meals when they are eating alone. Or, some may simply no longer be able to afford an adequate, balanced diet.

Particular eating patterns make some health conditions worse. Those with angina may suffer when they eat a large meal; the blood supply is drawn to the digestive organs and away from the heart. They would do better eating smaller amounts more frequently rather than a few large meals. Diabetics are also generally better off eating a number of smaller meals.

Cancer is the second leading cause of death among the older adult population; in 1997, there were 536,580 cancer deaths in the U.S. (Anderson & Rosenberg, 1998). Of these, lung cancer was the cause of the greatest proportion of cancer deaths: 152,450, or 28.4%. Lung cancer is associated with cigarette smoking, and many of these deaths might have been prevented. There is good evidence to indicate that fewer older persons now smoke than was the case even a few years ago, and that quitting smoking

Illustration 7.10, Sensory Loss in Later Life

Think of how it would be to be isolated due to sensory impairment. Some gerontology classes have students stuff their ears with cotton and wear glasses with clouded lenses in order to simulate what sensory deprivation must feel like and give the students an appreciation of how older persons might feel.

One thing that can be done to help the aged who have a visual impairment is to be sure their environment has plenty of light. The melanin within the eye darkens over time with exposure to sunlight. The dimming of vision that comes with aging is a result of literally less light getting through to the optic nerve. Bright interior lighting often helps, especially around staircases and thresholds where barriers may be difficult to perceive. Also, older people have a particular problem in adjusting to changes in light. Going from a bright lobby into a darkened movie theater, for example, may be bewildering. Give them a hand and let them take a little more time to adjust to changes in brightness.

Those with even a partial hearing impairment must miss a lot of what goes on around them. Help people who have a difficulty hearing you by looking straight at them when you speak so they can follow your lips as well as the sounds of your speech. Speak slowly and clearly (but don't shout); if you're not understood, repeat yourself, but rephrase your sentence into different words in order to maximize the cues you're giving. Eliminating background noise often improves communication, especially for those who wear a hearing aid.

Older people lose nerve endings in the skin and have poorer perception of hot and cold. Some residences for the elderly have thermostats on the showers to control how hot the water gets and thus prevent scalding.

People with hypertension or congestive heart failure often become dizzy when they change position suddenly. Standing up quickly, especially if the individual was lying down, may precipitate loss of balance and a fall. Help people when they rise. In particular, when someone gets up from a prone position, let them sit for a moment on the side of the bed before they stand up. Much of what we perceive as "slowing down" among older people is really caution, their process of coping with and compensating for sensory changes.

can have a positive effect even very late in life (LaCroix, Guralnik, Berkman, Wallace, & Satterfield, 1993).

Cancer of the colon accounts for a little over 10% of all cancer deaths (55,660 in 1997). The next leading cause of cancer deaths is breast cancer (43,830, or 8.1% of all cancer deaths). It is important that older women get a regular mammogram and also that they learn to perform monthly breast self-examinations. Prostate cancer is the next most frequent cause of cancer death (33,460 or 6.5%); it represents a serious health problem among older men. Annual examination by a physician can aid in early detection of cancer of the prostate.

As we saw earlier, what people are sick from and what they die from are not necessarily the same thing, and we would be remiss to look at health among the aged only in terms of mortality. Table 7.5 is taken from the Na-

Illustration 7.11. Adult-Onset Diabetes

Diabetes is an abnormality in the metabolism of glucose, sugar in the blood. Type I diabetes requires the individual to administer shots of insulin (usually several times a day) in order to help metabolize the sugars that are a product of digestion. They must obviously carefully restrict their intake of starches and sugars and carefully monitor their glucose blood level.

Most diabetics, about 80%, have Type II—adult-onset—diabetes. This is caused not by a lack of insulin being produced by the pancreas (as in Type I diabetes), but by an inability of insulin receptors on the surface of the cells to respond as efficiently as they once did. This is a result of the aging process and genetics and often is apparent sometime between 40 and 50 years of age. Type II diabetics must also watch their diet, but they do not have to give themselves insulin shots; the condition often can be controlled with medications. About 9% of the elderly have diabetes. Research has shown that Hispanics are 3.5 times more likely than others in the population to have Type II diabetes (Marshall et al., 1993). American Indians and African-Americans are also at higher risk.

Vigorous daily exercise and weight loss are the best ways for Type II diabetics to control their blood glucose levels. This is especially important in that the drugs used to manage Type II diabetes may have a diminishing effect over time, and there is a danger of the condition turning into Type I (insulin-dependent) diabetes.

Uncontrolled diabetes can lead to kidney failure, lack of blood to the extremities, poor healing of wounds (and, perhaps, resultant amputation of limbs), and blindness caused by diabetic retinopathy. Diabetes is the sixth leading cause of death among the elderly.

TABLE 7.5. U.S. Hospital Discharge Rates per 10,000 Population, by Age

Condition	Age			
	Under 15	15–44	45–64	65+
All conditions	382	870	1,172	3,460
Infection	26	19	25	88
Cancer	7	28	114	244
lung	—	1	14	36
breast	—	1	10	17
Diabetes	4	10	30	58
Mental disorders	14	96	75	93
psychoses	6	56	48	76
alcohol dependence	—	12	10	3
Heart disease	3	21	232	804
myocardial infarction	—	4	53	148
coronary atherosclerosis	—	4	77	171
other ischemic heart disease	—	3	26	66
dysrhythmias	1	4	26	126
congestive heart failure	—	2	28	203
Cerebrovascular disease	—	3	35	215
Pneumonia	33	12	32	206
Fractures	12	22	29	154

From Graves and Owings (1998).

glossary

subcutaneous —
Beneath the skin.

osteoporosis — Loss
of calcium in the
bones.

tional Hospital Discharge Survey; it gives hospitalization rates by age per 10,000 in the population (Graves & Owings, 1998). Going across the top line of figures, out of every 10,000 people under age 15, 382 had been hospitalized; of every 10,000 people 15 to 44 years of age, 870 had been hospitalized, and so on.

We can see immediately that over a third of the older population (3,460 out of every 10,000 who were aged 65+) had been hospitalized that year. Recognize that older people are more likely to have multiple health conditions, have lower immune defenses, and are more likely to be frail; thus, there is a greater probability that an illness will put them into a hospital. Because of greater resistance, many younger persons who were ill can be treated on an outpatient basis and remain at home. Still, hospitalization rates are a good indicator of morbidity, as they indicate illness serious enough to cause hospitalization.

As shown in the figures in Table 7.5, older individuals have much higher rates of illness. Of every 10,000 older people, 3,460 were hospitalized for some reason: 88 because of infections, 244 because of cancer, 58 because of diabetes, 93 for mental disorders, 804 because of heart disease, 215 because of cerebrovascular disease, 206 because of pneumonia, and 154 because of bone fractures.

The severity of bone fractures among the elderly is such that they are much more likely to cause hospitalization than are broken bones among younger people. Older people fall more often, and their falls are more likely to lead to a fracture. Older peoples' bones are, for the most part, more brittle than younger peoples' and are less likely to be padded by *subcutaneous* fat in the arms and legs. Older peoples' bones take longer to heal. A study in Canada found that several factors are associated with more frequent falls among the aged: dizziness, trouble walking and bending over, and other associated health problems (O'Loughlin, Robitalle, Boivin & Suissa, 1993). The fractures most likely to lead to hospitalization are of the upper femur or the hip.

Of the 200,000 people in the United States each year who break a hip, over three-quarters are elderly white women. *Osteoporosis*, a decrease in bone mass and density, is thought of as an underlying cause of hip fracture, and older women are often advised to add calcium supplements to their diet (which is generally too late to be of much help). Women on estrogen

---

Illustration 7.12. The Implication of Table 7.5

The dramatically higher hospitalization rates among the elderly compared to other age groups makes one point very clear: those preparing for health care careers should be prepared to deal with older people, for that is who they will see in health care institutions. This is true now, and it will be even more the case in future years.

therapy have a lower incidence of osteoporosis. There is seemingly no adequate explanation as to why this condition is more prevalent in white women than in black women.

There is some speculation that the upper end of the femur, or thigh bone, may break and cause the fall, rather than the fall happening and causing the fracture. Prior to the 1970s, a broken hip was often considered to be a death sentence for the very old: it kept people bedfast for prolonged periods of time, typically leading to pneumonia. This is now prevented for most by good nursing care; many individuals, even among the very old, now have the break surgically pinned and are soon up and walking again as a part of an aggressive program of rehabilitation. Research on falling gives some indication that older women are more likely, when they lose their equilibrium, to fall on their bottoms, whereas older men are more likely to fall forward and break their wrists. An Australian study has shown that older people who fall are more likely to have decreased sensation in the lower limbs, decreased visual contrast sensitivity, decreased stability, or muscle weakness (Lord, Clark, & Webster, 1991). This indicates that those who exercise regularly are less likely to fall and fracture a bone. Encouragingly, the death rate from falls for persons aged 65 and older dropped from 137 per 100,000 in 1948 to just 33.1 in 1996 (Metropolitan Life Insurance Company, 1998). This probably is a result of better care of people who have broken a hip.

Frequent falls are an important sign of underlying health problems and may lead to institutionalization (Dunn, Furner, & Miles, 1993). One study of falling and fear of falling in a community-dwelling sample of older persons found that 43% had fallen in recent years and 28% had fallen in the year prior to the study. Of those who fell, 65% were injured, and 15% required hospitalization. Fear of falling among the participants in this study ranked higher than fear of crime and other common fears (Howland et al., 1993)

Males actually have a slightly higher rate of death from falls than females at ages 65 and above: 30.7 per 100,000 versus 27.4 (Metropolitan Life Insurance Company, 1990). This is true for deaths from all types of accidents; males have a rate at age 65+ of 108.6 compared to an accidental death rate of 71.2 for women. By age 85, accidents have become the fourth leading cause of death for both men and women, accounting for about 2.2% of deaths (compared to heart disease at 53.6%, cancer at 14.1%, and stroke at 13.1% of all deaths among those 85+). At ages 65 and older, deaths from motor vehicle accidents for men are about twice as high as those for women (31.4 per 100,000 versus 16.2); older men not only drive much more, but death in an automobile accident may be a preferred (but unrecorded) means of suicide for older men.

Accidental deaths from all causes for the elderly have declined in recent years, and this is particularly true for automobile deaths; this has led at least one researcher to point out that many older drivers in the past were probably not very good drivers in their younger years (Evans, 1993).

Functional Ability

The strongest association with high life satisfaction among the elderly is the maintenance of good health (Hirdes & Forbes, 1993). But we need to take a look at conceptualizations of health held by most older people. As a general rule, health in late life is usually not defined as staying out of the hospital so much as it is the ability to do things. That is, one important way to define health among the elderly is level of functioning (Shanas & Maddox, 1985). It is common to hear from an older adult statements such as "I don't feel old as long as I can still get around. The minute I can't do things for myself—that's when I'll feel old."

Recognizing, then, that few older individuals are in fact disease-free—most have one or more chronic conditions—one way to look at relative health or illness in later life is to assess functional ability, the way that people can perform the activities of daily living. A number of *ADL* (activities of daily living) and *IADL* (instrumental activities of daily living) schedules have emerged in recent years (Ranhoff & Laake, 1993). Some are more or less reliable depending on who does the assessment, but all focus on different day-to-day tasks that relate to the ability to function independently.

As an illustration, a colleague and I surveyed a random sample of 500 non-institutionalized older persons on questions related to health care, health attitudes, and health care satisfaction (Thorson & Powell, 1993b). Their responses gave us some indication of the relative level of disability among community-dwelling older people. Here are their responses to a list of 14 questions that combines ADLs and IADLs:

1. Can you get to places out of walking distance to your home?
   No = 75, Yes = 425
2. Can you go shopping for groceries?
   No = 40, Yes = 460
3. Do you go shopping for necessities (clothes, etc.)?
   No = 45, Yes = 455
4. Do you prepare your own meals?
   No = 44, Yes = 456

Illustration 7.13. The Implication of ADL Scales

One important, practical outcome of ADL scales is this: insurance companies typically will not sell long-term care insurance to persons who cannot perform a set number of the activities of daily living (usually three out of five ADLs). The most crucial activity of daily living that qualifies or disqualifies applicants for nursing home insurance: being able to go to the bathroom by oneself.

---

5. Do you do your own housework?
    No = 63, Yes = 437
6. Do you take your own medicine?
    No = 9, Yes = 491
7. Do you handle your own money?
    No = 10, Yes = 490
8. Do you dress and undress yourself?
    No = 2, Yes = 498
9. Do you take care of your appearance; for example, combing your hair or (for males) shaving?
    No = 5, Yes = 495
10. Do you walk around without assistance?
    No = 34, Yes = 466
11. Can you get in and out of bed without assistance?
    No = 2, Yes = 498
12. Do you take a bath or shower without assistance?
    No = 9, Yes = 491
13. Do you ever have trouble getting to the bathroom on time?
    No = 435, Yes = 60
14. Do you feel that you need help with your daily activities?
    No = 468, Yes = 32

The people who answered these questions ranged in age from 60 to 94; the mean age was slightly less than 75 years. Their incomes ranged from $200 per month to $12,000 per month, with a mean of about $1050 monthly. There were 362 women and 138 men among the respondents; 259 of the 500 were married and living with a spouse.

The first thing we noticed with responses to the 14 questions is that about 12–15% of the entire sample (about 60 to 75 out of the 500) have some restrictions in their activities of daily living: getting away from home, getting to the bathroom on time, doing housework, and so on. About half of that restricted group (between 32 and 44 of the total sample of 500) have more serious restrictions: going shopping is a problem, as is preparing meals, walking without assistance, doing housework, or help with some other activity of daily living. But, only a very small group has severe ADL restrictions: 2 out of the 500 interviewed can't get in and out of bed without assistance, 5 need help shaving or combing their hair, 2 need help with dressing. Doing further analysis, we found that males and African-Americans tended to have the most ADL restrictions of those in this sample.

Turning these data around, we could conclude that 85–88% of a random sample of Americans in later life report that they are able to live without any significant restrictions on their activities of daily living. In other words, despite their inevitable health problems, they are living independently and can carry on their everyday lives without any help. Asked to give a self-assessment of their health, between 10 and 11.5% in this study said it was poor, and self-rated health was one of the few independent predictors of disability. It has been found that each disability has its own set of predictors (Furner, Rudberg, & Cassel, 1995). Difficulty with managing money, for example, has visual impairment and stroke as independent predictors. Difficulty with using the telephone has hearing impairment and health status as predictors. Suburban respondents in our sample were somewhat more likely to rate their health as good or excellent when compared to rural or urban subjects. We found in an earlier study that there is something of a tendency for rural elders to give a more negative self-assessment of health (Thorson & Powell, 1992a, 1999b).

A study by the National Center for Health Statistics gives a similar perspective on relative level of disability among persons 65 and above (Ries & Brown, 1991). Among the ADL limitations, about 6% of the aged had some difficulty bathing, a little over 4% had some problem with dressing, slightly over 2% with toileting, and less than 1% with eating. Among the IADL limitations, about 4% had difficulty preparing meals, 7.5% with shopping, about 3% with money management, and about 5% with doing light housework.

Researchers at Duke University have demonstrated declining levels of disability among older Americans over a period of years (Manton, Stallard, & Corder, 1995). Analyzing data from the National Long Term Care Survey covering disability rates of older people during a seven-year term, they found significant declines in 10 out of 16 medical conditions. There was an overall decline of 11% in seven years. The largest decreases were seen in heart and circulatory problems, as well as in dementia, pneumonia, hip fractures, and Parkinson's disease. The total decline in disability rate indicated about 540,000 fewer old people with chronic disabilities than the number that could have been predicted by the data at the beginning of the study. This trend could significantly impact the future need for long term care institutions and Medicaid spending in the future.

Dependencies may or may not restrict the performance of activities of daily living. For example, in many studies that survey the aged for health conditions or sensory impairments, there will be a large discrepancy between health conditions and actual inability to perform particular func-

---

Illustration 7.14. Mature Sexuality

"Men and women who have had satisfying sex in a long-term marriage have likely learned to satisfy each other in many ways besides traditional intercourse. Now that I am older, I know that those who dare to love again in a caring, thoughtful way are apt to find great comfort in a tender embrace, a great sense of support from being loved again by another mature person for whom one also has a great love and respect."

—Marion Pease Davis, born 1918
  The Courage to Grow Old

Table 7.6. Level of Functional ADL and IADL Dependencies, Ages 65+

Group	All Dependencies	5–7 ADL	3–4 ADL	1–2 ADL	IADL
White	28.4%	4.9%	2.5%	14.0%	6.9%
African-American	36.4	5.2	3.4	18.2	9.6
Hispanic	30.3	6.0	4.1	14.5	5.6
Married	21.5	2.7	1.8	11.7	5.2
Not Married	37.5	7.5	3.5	17.2	9.3
Above Poverty	25.4	3.4	2.3	13.0	6.7
Below Poverty	49.5	13.7	4.8	21.5	9.6

From Hing and Bloom (1990).

tions. This may be due to the questions that are asked, as common health impairments may not actually translate into disabilities. Many of the aged need eyeglasses or contact lenses, for example, and these may appear in the data as visual impairments, yet only a comparatively few are actually so visually impaired as to be disabled. Hearing loss is another common impairment, but it is hardly ever so severe as to keep a person from, for example, going shopping or carrying out most other ADLs or IADLs.

The message we get over and over from the aged is one of coping and adaptation: doing what they can do when they can do it. Some, easily exhausted, will anticipate their needs and plan their activities within the boundaries of the capacity of their energy. They may decide which activities to give up and which to expend their energy upon.

As we can see in Table 7.6, the level of functional dependency varies by social characteristics. In this study done by the National Center for Health Statistics, it is clear that minority elders have a higher level of dependencies and have more total restrictions on activities of daily living. This is also true of those not married compared to those who are married. But the greatest differential in levels of disability in performing the activities of daily living in later life shown in the table is economic: those with incomes below the poverty line are much more likely to have multiple ADL dependencies.

The correlation of social and psychological characteristics with health has been observed for some time. It is established, for example, that a low score on intelligence tests is predictive of mortality in mid-life (O'Toole & Stankov, 1992). Studies of elderly populations document a relationship between mortality and a low level of social activities or between mortality and a weak level social support (Falk, Hanson, Isacsson, & Ostergren, 1992; Rozzini, Bianchetti, Franzoni, & Zanetti, 1991; Welin, Larsson, Svardsudd, & Tibblin, 1992). In a study of changes in health and physical functioning over six years among 356 members of the Alameda County Study aged 65 and over, declines in functioning were significantly associated with age, income, self-assessed health, number of chronic conditions, exercise, marital status, social networks, and perceived health locus of control (Kaplan, Strawbridge, Camacho, & Cohen, 1993).

Analysis of data from the Established Populations for Epidemiologic

Studies of the Elderly revealed similar findings. One report from this longitudinal study focused upon maintaining mobility, rather than ADL loss (Guralnik et al., 1993). "Mobility" for the purposes of this study was defined as the ability to climb and descend stairs without assistance and to walk a half mile without assistance. A total of 6,981 persons 65 and older who met these criteria were followed for four years. During that period of time, 55% maintained mobility as it was defined for the study, 36% lost it, and 9% died. Significant risks for loss of mobility included lower educational level as well as physical factors: previous heart attack, stroke, high blood pressure, diabetes, leg pain, and shortness of breath.

The best predictor of health and survival, however, seems to be the individual's own assessment. Those rating themselves in poor health have, for the most part, a very accurate perception of what is going on inside of them; it is the wise physician who questions patients closely as to their own ideas of what is happening. Studies have repeatedly shown significantly higher mortality among older persons who rate their health as fair or poor as compared to those rating it as good or excellent (Helmer, Gateau, Letenneur, & Dartigues, 1999; Menec, Chipperfield, & Perry, 1999).

One study in Great Britain followed 1,203 people aged 75+ for seven years (Jagger, Priers, & Clarke, 1993). By the fifth year of the study, 42% had died, and by the seventh year, 58% had died. Of those free of ADL impairment when the study began, 34% were still independent seven years later. Those rating their health as fair or poor were much more likely to lose independence and subsequently die. This study gives a graphic picture of the inevitability of decline and death among the very old.

Among the predictors of longevity demonstrated by the Longitudinal Study of Aging at Duke University were: for men—health self-rating, work satisfaction, intelligence, and frequency of sexual intercourse; for women—health satisfaction, health self-rating, and enjoyment of sexual intercourse (Palmore, 1982).

To summarize this section, it is evident that people live with multiple chronic conditions in later life, and that the number of these conditions increases with age. Many of these conditions become disabling, but most older people are not in fact disabled to such a degree that they cannot carry out the activities of everyday life. Most older people continue to live independently, and only a minority report either poor self-rated health or serious disability. Those most at risk are older, poorer, and more isolated. Many older people are able to husband their energy and accomplish meaningful tasks even in the face of declining vigor. Most seem to know what is going on with their health, even in the instance of approaching death.

Conclusion

The preceding content has gone over quite a few facts and figures dealing with relative mortality and morbidity. Some of this material might seem pretty gloomy, given the inevitable decline of the body's resources and defenses. Although we've drawn practical implications along the way, there really is no way to avoid or postpone many of the conditions that affect the health of older people. Maintaining an active lifestyle, exercising, avoiding products of combustion, eating a balanced and nutritious diet, and being surrounded by a wide social network all contribute to health throughout the lifespan, old age included. It also helps to be intelligent and prosperous. Will accomplishing all these things put off death? Based on the sum of our knowledge to date, we can answer that question this way: in most cases, yes. It certainly improves the odds over leading a sedentary, isolated lifestyle focused on junk food and drug abuse.

Life and death can be arbitrary, of course. Fitness advocate Jim Fixx dropped dead while jogging in July of 1984; he was 52-years-old. On the other hand, baseball star Joe DiMaggio, who died in March of 1999, was a heavy smoker and lived to be 84.

A certain unpredictability remains in the realm of health. Overall, though, the odds are inexorable and relentless: with modern public health and preventive medicine, most people in the developed world live into the decade of their 70s; many then die during that decade. About half live into their 80s, and most of them die during that decade. Fewer than 20% remain to live into their 90s and fewer than 1.5% to 100. Most by those ages are so severely disabled that many would argue that there is no particular point in living that long.

The inevitability of universal chronic illness and disability led James Fries and Lawrence Crapo (1981) to write an intriguing book in which they argue that the role of health care is to eliminate premature disease, to make the survival curve increasingly rectangular. They suggest that most people have the inherent capacity to live about 85 years and then essentially have multiple system failure. By that age, the immune system is so inefficient that even those who avoid circulatory problems and cancer can be counted upon to have repeated infection and autoimmune illness.

Arthritis is the principal cause of disability in later life (Hughes, Edelman, Singer & Chang, 1993). Hearing, taste, and vision loss affect the well-being of increasing percentages of the population as great age is achieved. The majority of those surviving past age 85 have multiple disabilities (Zarit, Johannson, & Berg, 1993). Even those so fortunate as to have dodged the bullet of bad health in younger years face dependencies, and even those few lucky souls in perfect health ultimately face the loss of confidants and a deteriorating social network as friends and family die off. And no amount of exercise and clean living is going to do away with all of these problems.

Having said all that, the goals of health care in late life obviously are multiple. Preservation of life, of course, is primary, except in those instances we will discuss in Chapter 10, where the life is not being extended so much as the process of death is being drawn out. Next, the treatment and prevention of debilitating disease is an important goal of health care and maintenance in old age. Rehabilitation and restoration of function are also exceedingly important. Overall, though, contributions to the quality of life might be seen as the ultimate objective of health care in later life: preservation of function to maximize independence, to allow older persons to live the best lives they can in the face of the inevitable (Strain, 1993).

A long-term research project, the Aging in Manitoba Study, followed 4,317 older individuals and examined perceived barriers in the management of health problems. Three types of barriers were identified: control barriers—the perceived lack of control over health care and the management of health; personal barriers, such as memory deficits; and social barriers, such as transportation and financial problems. Over the course of 12 years, control and personal barriers were shown to be predictive of mortality, even after controlling for initial health status, age, sex, income, and education (Chipperfield, 1993). It's interesting to note that social barriers such as finance and transportation were not significant correlates of 12-year mortality in this Canadian study. These participants, of course, were eligible to participate in the Provincial health plan in Manitoba. Just as important in a geographic area that large, though, is that transportation was not a barrier. A colleague and I found the same thing in the study of a random sample of 500 older people discussed earlier in this chapter (Thorson & Powell, 1993b). None of the respondents had postponed needed health care because of a transportation problem; in fact, 12 who had postponed health care said they did so because they were too busy.

To return to the control issue identified in the Manitoba study, though: older persons must inevitably feel or fear the loss of control in health care situations. As we will discuss in Chapter 9, they are confronted with powerful others who often attempt to assume control of their health care, just at a time when the natural processes are making control of health all that more difficult. Maintaining independence must be all the more difficult. Health well-being, however, must in most cases be related to individual responsibility.

Recognizing that quick cures are not in the cards for most health conditions that affect the elderly is important. So is the concept of rehabilitation: many older people are able to come back to a state of good health after a serious bout with illness or disability. Most important, however, is to realize that by far the majority of the aged are able to cope with multiple health conditions, some of which are disabling, and still maintain their independence and carry out their activities of daily living.

Questions for Discussion

1. What activities of daily living do you find essential? Do these differ from the ADLs for older persons? If so, how?
2. What are some race-specific or gender-specific health problems?
3. When—at which ages—do most deaths take place?
4. Why do causes of death listed on death certificates and causes revealed by autopsy not agree 100% of the time?
5. What is the implication of the fact that causes of death have changed
6. If acute causes of death are eliminated, chronic causes increase. Why?
7. What health practices do you think will have the greatest long-term benefit? Why?

Sources of Further Information

For specific information on a disease or health condition, local affiliates of national organizations may be the quickest source of information. Try the white pages of the local phone book (or the telephone book of the nearest big city), for such organizations as the American Cancer Society, American Heart Association, American Lung Association, the American Diabetes Association, and so on. And, in the yellow pages, look under "Health Agencies" for similar listings. Of course, a web search using your favorite search engine will produce a wealth of material as well.

For statistical information, most local libraries will have a current *Statistical Abstract of the United States*. For specific information on mortality by cause, subscribe to *Advance Data* from:

U.S. Department of Health and Human Services
Public Health Service
Centers for Disease Control and Prevention
National Center for Health Statistics
6525 Belcrest Road
Hyattsville, MD 20782

The National Institute on Aging issues occasional *Age Pages* on various topics (pneumonia, vision, flu, Alzheimer's disease, stroke, osteoporosis, and so on) as a part of their public education mission. These are large print, non-technical, and short publications on specific health topics of interest to older adults. It helps to specify the condition you want information on. Contact:

NIA Information Center
P.O. Box 8057
Gaithersburg, MD 20898

For conditions not covered by a recent *Age Page*, a specific request to this address might help:

National Institute on Aging
Public Information Office
Building 31, Room 5C27
Bethesda, MD 20892
301/496-1752

Specific information on osteoporosis or arthritis can be obtained from:

National Institute of Arthritis and Musculoskeletal Diseases
NIAMS Clearinghouse
Box AMS
Bethesda, MD 20892

Information on menopause and osteoporosis is available from:

The American College of Obstetricians and Gynecologists
409 12th St., S.W.
Washington, D.C. 20024

Another source of osteoporosis information is:

National Osteoporosis Foundation
1625 Eye Street, N.W., Suite 822
Washington, D.C. 20006

A substantial list of publications is available from the National Cancer Institute; they have early detection materials and other patient education materials, including Spanish language materials. Request their latest Publications List for the Public and Patients:

Office of Cancer Communications
National Cancer Institute
Building 31, Room 10A 24
Bethesda, MD 20892

Research on aging and blindness or low vision is summarized by the Aging & Vision News, available free from:

The Lighthouse, Inc.
111 East 59th Street
New York, NY 10022-1202

Information on talking books for the blind is available from:

Talking Book Topics
CMLS
P.O. Box 9150
Melbourne, FL 32902-9150

And, finally, don't neglect texts on geriatrics; many have been written for nursing and medical students and provide more detailed information than we have been able to cover in this chapter.

Aging and Mental Health

8

Chapter Outline

"Surely the most devastating among the many upsetting changes I've experienced thus far was the tragedy of watching my first wife deteriorate from the meaningless ravages of Alzheimer's disease. For two years, I watched her deteriorate into little more than a vegetable. The task of caring for her and teaching full time became an almost unbearable load. The folly of judging the situation to be good or bad became increasingly clear the worse things seemed to get. There could, after all, be no rational justification to account for such a tragedy."

—Alfred Painter, born 1914

glossary

cognitive — Having to do with cognition, the ability to think and learn.

schizophrenia — A mental illness characterized by disintegration of personality, gross delusions, and loss of contact with the environment; often accompanies paranoia.

depression — A persistent mood disorder characterized by loss of interest, sleep disturbance, anxiety, fatigue, or thoughts of worthlessness.

dementia — A loss of intellectual abilities.

affective disorders — Mood ailments, such as depression or bipolar disorder.

developmental disabilities — Chronic disabling conditions that occur prior to age 22 and limit the individual's ability to lead an independent life. Usually, the developmental disabilities are grouped in the categories of mental retardation, cerebral palsy, epilepsy, autism, and other neurological impairments.

Introduction

One of the most universal fears of older people is the loss of mental ability.

As a defense against this fear, people often make little jokes about it; "I'm starting to lose it," "They say the mind is the first thing to go," "I wouldn't remember my head if it wasn't screwed on"—that kind of thing. Or, old age might be used as an excuse for forgetfulness: "I can't remember things like I used to," or, "I used to be sharp as a tack." In fact, these and comments like them are often the basis of stereotypes of older people: you can't teach an old dog new tricks, for example.

Slowing down mentally is often considered to be a parallel to slowing down physically in later life. However, as we've already seen in Chapter 6, *cognitive* decline in normal aging among healthy people is almost imperceptible until very late in life. Even then, it usually is not a serious problem among the well elderly.

Not everyone in later life is well, though. Mental illness affects people at all ages of life, old age and young. Causes of emotional distress such as *schizophrenia*—things that usually come to mind first when we think of mental illness—are joined by problems more common in later life: *depression* and *dementia*.

Emotional problems such as depression may be more common as people are forced to adapt to loss in later life: loss of spouse, loss of companionship, loss of income, loss of status, loss of health. Those who lose their social support network may be especially vulnerable. Because it is so common, depression has been called the common cold of emotional illness in old age.

More than depression, however, people fear dementing illness. This is especially the case if they've seen it in their parents or older relatives. The little jokes about forgetfulness have at their heart the fear of becoming senile and losing all of one's mental abilities.

These are serious health issues for the elderly. In this chapter, we will see that mental deterioration affects a relatively small percentage of the older population; on the other hand, it is a catastrophe for those it does affect. Family members of older people with a mental illness have their lives disrupted as well.

First, we'll look at prevalence rates—how many people are affected by which condition. Then, we'll get into the conditions themselves: *affective disorders*, such as depression, and organic disorders, such as the various types of dementia. We'll learn that not every situation is hopeless; in fact, there are many conditions where improvement and rehabilitation should be expected. In the most serious cases, there still are things that can be done. The chapter will conclude with some practical advice for caregivers from a social worker and from a nurse, both of whom work with old people who are cognitively impaired. And the chapter will conclude with an emerging issue of critical importance to a small group of people: the aging of those with a *developmental disability*.

Cognitive Impairment in Later Life

We saw in Chapters 5 and 6 that the older body and mind go through a normal course of development and growth over time, and, especially with the body, there is an inevitable course of slowing and decline—if the person lives long enough. To a certain degree, there is also a normal course of growth and decline in mental abilities, although, as we have seen in Chapter 6, those who utilize their mental abilities to their best capacity probably will not have much measurable decline until very late in life. Reserve capacity in terms of mental abilities is such that most older persons will have little noticeable decline, if they are healthy.

But that's a pretty big "if."

As we saw in Chapter 7, there are a host of chronic and infectious conditions that affect older people. Although we couldn't really say that it is normal to be sick in later life, we certainly could justify saying that illness is common—and perhaps inevitable—among the elderly. And, as we also learned in the last chapter, among the illnesses that affect mental abilities, hypertension (high blood pressure) is probably the one that affects the greatest number of older people (Sands & Meredith, 1992).

When high blood pressure is kept under control, people affected are no more likely to have ill effects than are others who do not have hypertension. Unfortunately, though, there are many people who go undiagnosed for a variety of reasons: perhaps they just don't like seeing doctors, or they feel that they have no symptoms, or they go off of their medicine because they are feeling better. Uncontrolled hypertension can lead to strokes and resulting impairments; it can also lead to vascular dementia.

There are a host of causes for decreased mental abilities in later life. Controlling hypertension is probably the most effective way of offsetting one of the most preventable physical illnesses that affects mental health. There are other conditions that cannot be prevented, however, and we'll review them as well. Most can be thought of as cognitive impairments—conditions affecting the abilities of thinking and learning. Most of these conditions can also be thought of as abnormal; they are not part of the normal aging process. We will look at their frequency, some indicators of their presence, differences between them, and some practical implications of what can be done to help the person who is cognitively impaired.

Overall, the message of this chapter is that people who begin to act differently or in a disorganized manner in late life are not necessarily mentally ill or hopelessly senile. Some of the conditions we'll discuss can be prevented, reversed, or controlled. Even when the condition is progressive and cannot be reversed, there are practical considerations and things that can be done to either slow the progress of the illness, make the individual more comfortable, or be of assistance to caretakers and family members.

Two Cases

First, though, let's look at the experiences of two individuals, both of whom began to have problems late in life:

Mrs. Peake was a piano teacher, and her friends and family always considered her to be an accomplished musician and professional. In addition to making a good living (she attracted many students), she was often called upon to accompany other artists in recital. She continued these activities very successfully past normal retirement age, and bragged that she was just as active at 75 as she'd been at 25. She had thoughts of slowing down but said she was having too much fun and would slow down when she got old. Because she felt so healthy, she'd not seen a doctor in years.

One afternoon she realized that she was so dizzy that she had to sit down; she feared that she was on the verge of blacking out. She felt better after a while and put her concerns down to "just getting old," and continued to have a busy day, full of activities. This happened several more times, but Mrs. Peake did not go to the doctor. Then one morning she had real trouble getting out of bed, and she felt a peculiar weakness in her left arm and hand. This got better and she forgot about it. Then, one day playing the piano, she seemed to forget how to move her hands in the proper sequence; she was able to play the melody all right, but the notes in the lower range seemed all out of kilter.

Then she began to forget her piano students' names and the pieces they were working on, and sometimes they had difficulty understanding her when she spoke. Her daughter noticed this and asked her what the name of her doctor was; she said, "It's funny, I can see him in my mind's eye, but I can't seem to spit out his name: it's right on the tip of my tongue." Then Mrs. Peake started to cry. Her daughter called her own doctor and said, "I'm afraid Mother's showing signs of senility."

Contrast Mrs. Peake's situation to that of Mr. Rich. A retired merchant, he found at age 67 that he could no longer balance the family checkbook; when his wife looked over their records, she was shocked at what a mess he'd made of them. He didn't object when she insisted on taking over the family finances, even though he had prided himself on his abilities; he'd even done the tax work for friends, but found that they no longer asked for this help. This was the first of many signs of deterioration and disorganized behavior his wife noticed over the next few years. Once she found his underwear and his balled-up socks in the refrigerator.

Things went from bad to worse, but for the most part, Mr. Rich maintained his usual happy disposition. His wife often helped him compensate, laying out his clothes, taking over many of the decision-making responsibilities, doing all the driving and shopping. Sometimes he would do things like go outdoors without his shoes on or act vague and uncertain with people who seemed to know him. He was skillful, though, at covering up these lapses and continued to carry on conversations that for the most part made sense. He had problems, though, with specific facts. He did very badly, for example, when his doctor asked him a series of questions. One was "name the president of the United States." His reply was, "To be perfectly honest with you, doctor, I don't pay that much attention to politics."

Both of these people show signs of cognitive impairment in later life. Although we shouldn't jump to too many conclusions on the basis of the few facts we know, there are several signs to be aware of that would be useful clues when reported to their physicians. Neither one of these people should be dismissed as irreversibly senile, nor should their problems be thought of simply as signs of "getting old."

Both Mrs. Peake and Mr. Rich have certain abnormalities that affect their mental processes, and mental abnormalities should never be ignored among the elderly any more than they should among younger adults. Mrs. Peake shows a "stepwise" regression in her abilities, that is, her problems don't seem to occur in a regular, gradual decline so much as more sudden downward shifts in her cognitive skills, like walking down a staircase. From the little we know about her situation, it might be reasonable to suppose that her dizziness could be caused by hypertension that has led to a series of small strokes (multi-infarct dementia); she seems to have losses in motor abilities on one side of the body but not the other, and facts are in the proper context for her but she has them "just on the tip of her tongue." At least, these are important signs that her physician would want to take into consideration.

If what we've suspected about Mrs. Peake is true, it's entirely possible that good medical attention can prevent further deterioration and, with rehabilitation, she might regain many of her seemingly lost abilities. The same might be concluded for many stroke patients: people can regain lost facilities with a comprehensive rehabilitation program and proper medical supervision. Mrs. Peake may also be showing some signs of depression, which is very common in stroke patients and which also can respond well to treatment.

Mr. Rich seems to have deteriorated along a more steady path, constant and gradual rather than stepwise. His characteristically skillful way of responding in conversation when he really has no clue as to specific facts can often be found among people with Alzheimer's disease. The reason his doctor was asking him questions like "who is the president?" was part of a mini-mental status exam, one thing a physician or a psychologist would want to use in arriving at a diagnosis. If the doctor is a good one, however, then she or he will not rush to the conclusion that Mr. Rich has Alzheimer's disease. Other possible causes for his apparent regression should be eliminated one by one. The physician should find out, for example, if Mr. Rich has a family history of organic brain disorder, a personal history of head trauma or alcoholism, or any particularly troublesome losses in his life. The physician will also want to determine what medications Mr. Rich has been taking, and will also do a thorough physical examination,

Illustration 8.1. A Little Diagnostic History

When I worked in a nursing home back in the 1960s (when dinosaurs roamed the earth), it seemed like Alzheimer's disease hadn't been invented yet. That is, the condition we now know as dementia of the Alzheimer's type (which in fact had first been identified back in 1907) still was not a commonly used diagnosis, although plenty of our patients surely had it. In retrospect, I can think of many who showed signs of Alzheimer's. Multi-infarct dementia was better recognized, but it wasn't called that, either. Patients who'd had a stroke were diagnosed and had "CVA" on their charts, for "cerebrovascular accident." But those who were demented from multiple strokes were not necessarily described that way. Usually they had *"arteriosclerosis"* or "atherosclerosis" written on their charts, the idea being that a reduced blood supply to the brain was the cause of senility.

In order to improve the cerebral blood flow, people in the 1970s started getting their carotid arteries surgically reamed out. This seemed to help the few who survived the operation, but many died of an *embolism* (a particle, such as a blood clot, that travels to the brain) after the surgery.

Going on the theory that oxygenated blood flow to the brain needed to be increased, the people at Duke University and other medical centers tried hyperbaric therapy in the late 1960s and early 1970s: people sat around in high-pressure tanks to see if squeezing more oxygen into their heads helped.

It didn't.

Recognition of organic mental problems has improved greatly since that time, of course. Few patients have "chronic brain syndrome" or "arteriosclerosis" as the only diagnosis written on their charts any longer.

My hunch, though, is that too many are listed as having "Alzheimer's disease." Dementia of the Alzheimer's type is a tricky diagnosis, even for geriatricians or neurologists who see quite a lot of it. They usually try to eliminate other causes before deciding on Alzheimer's, which is a clinical diagnosis: there's no lab test yet for dementia of the Alzheimer's type. It's possible that the condition underlying the apparent dementing behaviors might be something that is reversible, or that it's not a dementia at all. Depression, for example, can present signs of dementia in some older people.

If I had a relative who a family doctor diagnosed as having Alzheimer's disease, the first thing I'd do is make an appointment for a comprehensive geriatric assessment at a university medical center. I'd get a second opinion.

particularly to determine if there is any infection or signs of congestive heart failure. Only after a thorough physical, neurological, and social assessment should the diagnosis of dementia of the Alzheimer's type be made.

If that diagnosis is arrived at, then certain things might be done to help with Mr. Rich's safety and comfort. Mrs. Rich should also be assisted: support groups and respite programs can help her in her role as primary caretaker. This is vital, because she may be facing several very unhappy years ahead as Mr. Rich's condition deteriorates. She may find that at some point he doesn't know exactly who she is, but she may also find that he still responds positively to her loving touch and the warm tone of her voice. She'll bear a heavy burden, and she'll need help.

Although many people seemingly have a mental impairment in later life, and the problems of individuals such as the two we have described are all too common, it should not be expected that abnormal declines in cognitive ability or confused behaviors should occur among most older people. Cognitive disorders increase with age, but it still is only a small proportion of older people who are troubled with them. Do a simple reality check: think of the number of older people you know who show some signs of disorganized behavior. It is probably very low.

glossary

arteriosclerosis —
Thickening and hardening of the arterial walls; once thought to be the main cause of dementia.

embolism — A particle, such as a clot, that is transported in the blood vessels to the lungs or to the brain; a frequent cause of stroke.

Epidemiology of Mental Disorders in Later Life

As we look at the prevalence of mental problems among the aged, we should remember that the conditions that affect older people are not unique to them. Organic problems such as those that may be affecting the lives of Mrs. Peake and Mr. Rich can happen to adults at earlier ages. It's just that these kinds of illnesses become more common in later life (and they increase in prevalence among the oldest old). Still, it is only a very low percentage of the aged who experience anything beyond the normal (and very slight) declines we have discussed in Chapter 6.

We should also be aware that mental illnesses such as schizophrenia, psychoses, and phobias occur in later life, but they might often have been present earlier in adulthood and persist into old age. We will deal with these and other forms of mental illness later in this chapter, but first let's look at a number of studies and some epidemiologic data on the prevalence of cognitive problems most common in later life.

To put mental problems in later life into context, we first need to look at prevalence rates in the entire adult population.

TABLE 8.1. Number and Percentage of U.S. Adult Population with Serious Mental Illness

Age	Adults with Serious Mental Illness			Percentage Currently Limited
	Number*	Percentage	Rate**	
18–24 years	361	11.1	14.2	80.6
25–34 years	707	21.7	16.5	70.8
35–44 years	744	22.8	20.7	80.6
45–64 years	919	28.2	19.9	81.5
65–69 years	142	4.4	14.3	70.0
70–74 years	102	3.1	12.9	79.8
75 years and older	288	8.8	25.3	86.6

*In thousands
**Per thousand
From P. R. Barker et al. (1992, p. 5).

Table 8.1 gives the number and percentage, by age group, of the United States adult population that has any serious mental illness, as well as the rate of mental illness per thousand in the population at particular ages. In the far right-hand column, it also gives the percent of those with a mental illness who are currently limited in their activities of daily living by that condition.

Going across the top line, of those aged 18 to 24 yeas, 361,000 have a serious mental illness; this represents about 11% of all adults who have a serious mental illness, a rate per thousand of 14.2 (or, in percentage figures, about 1.42% of those aged 18 to 24 have a serious mental illness). Currently, 80.6% of those 361,000 mentally ill 18–24-year-olds are so ill as to have their activities limited by that illness.

Looking at the older population, Table 8.1 gives us three age groupings: those 65 to 69 years of age, those 70 to 74 years old, and those 75 years of age and above. We can see in these groups the dramatic increase of mental impairment as age goes up. Among the youngest old, those 65–69, the rate of mental illness per thousand is 14.3 (just about what it is for young adults aged 18–24).

The situation is much the same (or, actually, a little better) for the next age group: adults aged 70 to 74 represent 4.4% of the adult population, but they account for only 3.1% of the mentally ill adult population. Their rate per thousand of serious mental illness (12.9) is actually the lowest on the chart; it's less than two thirds of the rate for adults aged 35 to 44. This might lead us to conclude that the two groups making up the young old are relatively less troubled with mental illness than the rest of the adult population: mental problems of younger years may have declined somewhat for those aged 65 to 74, and the degenerative mental impairments that are more common in very late life have yet to become serious, relatively speaking. That may be too simple a conclusion, however; we will look more in detail at this concept later on in this chapter.

Now, look at the bottom row of figures on Table 8.1, and we see a dramatic increase in the rate per thousand as well as the percent with a mental illness who are currently limited by it. Adults 75 and older represent 6.3% of the adult population, but they account for 8.8% of the mentally ill adult population; their rate per thousand (25.3) is about twice as high as the next younger age group. And, their rate of functional limitation (86.6% of those who have a mental illness currently find their lives limited by it) is the highest on the table.

To put this all into perspective, we can't say that all or even most people who are very old (75+) are impaired by a serious mental illness. Even at that advanced age, only 2.53% of the population is troubled by a mental problem. True, this is a rate that is higher than that for the other age groups listed, but it still is only a small proportion of the population.

The last thing that is important to note on Table 8.1 is the increase of mental impairment among the oldest age groups. The young old have rates that are less than most of the rest of the adult population. It's only among those 75+ that the rates go higher.

Much of the difficulty in putting mental illness into perspective has to do with attitudes and prejudice. Older people who forget things may indeed have signs of some kind of mental impairment, but as likely as not they are entirely normal, or they may have some *transient* problem that may be self-limiting. Too often, however, we rush to the conclusion that someone is "losing it"; she may herself jokingly say things such as, "I'm getting old-timers disease." Perhaps we're too ready to believe unfair stereotypes of older people. Part of our cultural folklore is that old people get absent-minded or that it's normal to get a little dotty in later life. What is characteristic of a small percentage, though, is hardly descriptive of the group as a whole.

Another difficulty in getting a true perspective of the scope of mental problems late in life is the difficulty of determining exactly what mental illness is. Dan Blazer (1980) of the Duke University Medical Center has said that a problem with getting an accurate epidemiology of mental illness in late life is that most data is based on chart reviews or case registries. This obviously is based on a clinician's evaluation of the patient. This is influenced by a host of biases: variations in the patient's socioeconomic status (and, thus, their perceived social worth), the clinician's diagnostic criteria (and skills)—which may vary from doctor to doctor—and the difficulty of determining an accurate diagnosis among older patients. One condition may mimic another among the elderly, there may be psychological outcomes from other physical illness, and *co-morbidity* (multiple illnesses compounding one another) is often a problem. Self-administered symptom scales, which force the researcher to assume that a valid response is given on every item, can also introduce bias into the data.

By no means are all of the elderly with a mental problem getting treatment, nor are all so badly off as to need institutional care. Many are functioning pretty well in the community. Many who are receiving treatment are able to live at home and, especially if they have a caretaker, survive pretty well outside of a hospital or nursing home. Because psychiatric prob-

*g*lossary

transient — Coming and going.

co-morbidity — Afflicted with more than one condition.

lems tend to be disabling, however, people with them often end up in nursing homes. One study found that 47% of those in long-term care facilities have significant psychiatric impairment, and another 39% have mild to moderate psychiatric impairment (Blazer, 1980).

The most frequent psychological problem of later life is depression, followed by various kinds of dementia. Dementia should be distinguished from depression, although they can go hand in hand: a demented person certainly can be depressed as well. Both can have some of the same features: social withdrawal, moodiness, loss of memory, loss of interest. Following depression and dementia are other conditions that can affect cognition: alcoholism or other substance abuse, HIV, misuse of medications, schizophrenia, and *paranoid* disorders (Molinari, 1991).

One study found depression to increase with physical illness (Katon, 1992). While about 2 to 4% of the population is clinically depressed at any one time, it is estimated that this increases to 5 to 10% of primary care patients and 6 to 14% of hospital patients. This study, done at the University of Washington Medical School, estimates that at any one time, there are two to three times as many individuals with symptoms of depression who fall short of criteria for major depression. In about a third to a half of those diagnosed with major depressive disorder, the symptoms persist over six to twelve months.

It may be even more difficult to determine the true number of people with dementia (a loss of intellectual abilities) than the number of those with depression. The problem is that (1) much of it goes unrecognized: many people may show signs of dementia, but an undetermined number actually go on to develop a clinically diagnosed dementing condition; (2) it is difficult to diagnose and can be confused with other conditions that present similar symptoms; and (3) the various dementias generally are not listed as causes of death in the monthly mortality data issued by the Centers for Disease Control. Alzheimer's disease, which some consider to be the fourth leading killer of old people, is considered to be an *underlying* rather than a *primary* cause in the way these statistics are compiled, and has only been added to the CDC listing in the past few years. So, there is the problem of registration of deaths from a major cause of dementia.

Based on case ascertainment studies, it appears that fewer than 5% of the elderly have a dementing condition. A Johns Hopkins University study, for example looked at a group of 3,841 adults aged 65–92 years. The prevalence rates estimated from this sample were 2% for Alzheimer's disease, 2% for multi-infarct dementia, and 0.5% for mixed dementias. In this sample, women had higher rates of dementia of the Alzheimer's type, while males had higher rates of multi-infarct or vascular dementia. Non-whites had higher rates of dementia than did whites (Folstein et al., 1991). In another study that made racial comparisons, however, no racial differences were found in types of dementia or reported length of illness. Persons of lower socioeconomic status, though, were found to be more likely to have a dementing illness (Cohen & Carlin, 1993). Recent mortality data indicate that white women as a group have the highest death rate from Alzheimer's disease (Hoyert, Kochaner, & Murphy, 1999).

Similar results were found in a study done by researchers at the Mayo Clinic: the prevalence rate for all types of dementia was 4%; the rate for dementia of the Alzheimer's type was 2.6% (Beard, Kokmen, Offord, & Kurland, 1991).

The Framingham study is a famous investigation of heart disease, among other things, that has been going on in a Massachusetts community for several decades. In one analysis, which involved 2,180 individuals, rates of dementia are reported. Of those examined, 90 cases of definite dementia were identified. The prevalence rate was 3% for men and 4.8% for women, and it increased with advancing age. Among those cases that the examiners rated at probably being dementia of the Alzheimer's type, the prevalence rate was 1.2% for males and 3.0% for females. Alzheimer's disease accounted for slightly over 55% of all cases of dementing illness (Bachman et al., 1992).

Dementia is more likely in very old age. A Swedish study published in the *New England Journal of Medicine* reported on 143 men and 351 women aged 85 or older. The overall prevalence of dementia was almost 30%; it was mild in 8.3% of the cases, moderate in 10.3%, and severe in 11.1% of the cases. Among those who were demented, 43.5% were reported as having Alzheimer's disease and 46.9% had a vascular (multi-infarct) dementia; almost 10% had dementias that were due to other causes (Skoog et al., 1993). It has been found that the prevalence of dementing illness declines dramatically as educational level of the subject increases (Gagnon et al., 1990).

If the figures seem imprecise, we must remember that there is no chemical test for many of the dementias. Cranial x-rays can determine brain shrinkage and multi-infarct dementia in some instances, but there is no corresponding lab test for dementia of the Alzheimer's type. Detecting Alzheimer's is said to be a *clinical diagnosis*: it's based on the signs and symptoms the physician detects, not on laboratory analyses. The classic way of determining if a person had Alzheimer's is a brain autopsy after death, something one obviously can't do with a living person. And even some of the best clinicians admit that their diagnoses of probable Alzheimer's are correct only about 70% of the time. For studies that are compilations of the diagnoses of many different clinicians, then, we should expect some variation.

One way to reconcile differences is to do a *meta-analysis*, a review of many case ascertainment studies to see what the trend is. Two such analyses, reported in Table 8.2, indicate that the prevalence of Alzheimer's disease is 1% or less at age 60 but over 30% by age 90 (Brayne, 1993).

As we look over the figures reported in Table 8.2, we must note two things: first, the numbers are pretty close together for the younger age

glossary

clinical diagnosis —
An assessment made on the basis of physical signs and symptoms rather than lab tests or x-rays.

meta-analysis — A large-scale compilation of many studies.

TABLE 8.2. Results of Two Meta-Analyses of Studies of the Prevalence of Dementia of the Alzheimer's Type

Age Group	Analysis 1	Analysis 2
60–64 years	1.0%	0.7%
65–69 years	1.4	1.4
70–74 years	4.1	2.8
75–79 years	5.7	5.6
80–84 years	13.0	10.5
85–89 years	21.6	20.8
90–94 years	32.2	38.6

From Brayne (1993, p. 289).

groups, and they begin to become more divergent for the older subjects in the various studies. More important, however, is the clear message that dementia of the Alzheimer's type is not very common among the young old and that it increases dramatically in very late life. This is an important point.

These meta-analyses of many different studies makes several additional points: it is noted, for example, that the features of both Alzheimer's disease and vascular dementia are sometimes found in populations that are not demented, and that postmortem (after-death studies, that is, autopsies) findings of Alzheimer's disease do not always agree with the known clinical findings. Taking these difficulties into consideration, looking at the results of many studies of dementia of the Alzheimer's type in many different parts of the world, it was found that there was a consistent doubling of the prevalence of Alzheimer's disease every 5.1 years in later life. So, this type of dementia appears to be relatively unlikely among the young old, but it affects about a third of those who have attained the age of 90 years (Brayne, 1993).

Among the various types of dementia, Alzheimer's disease seems to represent the majority of cases (55%), although this again varies from study to study. One well-accepted analysis agrees with the 55% figure for Alzheimer's and gives the following percentages for other dementing conditions: 15% for stroke or multi-infarct dementia, 12% for multiple causes, 8% for Parkinson's disease, 4% for brain injury, and 6% "other" causes (Goldstein, 1993). These percentages may differ with slight up or down variations in other analyses, and they may not be exactly precise, but their exactness is not important at this point in our discussion.

Suffice it to say, half or more of the individuals who have an organic dementing illness probably have Alzheimer's disease, and though the young old are very unlikely to have signs of a dementing illness, about a third of the oldest old do. As we continue in our examination of mental problems that affect older people, however, we need to look more closely at exact signs, possible causes, and care issues.

Illustration 8.3. Misdiagnosis and Alzheimer's

There is a kind of paradox in today's high-technology environment. On the one hand, we collect mountains of evidence from high-technology imaging, scans, and ultrasounds. This can be particularly important in the elderly patient, who may have a serious abdominal infection with very few physical signs or a subdural hematoma that only manifests itself with a change in mental status. On the other hand, the physician must be attuned to the subtlety of the change in mental status that prompts the search for a cause in the first place. An 80-year-old patient of mine was taken to the emergency room because she had developed confusion. She was sent home with a diagnosis of Alzheimer's disease. The next day, she came to the office. An emergency CT (for computed axial tomographic imaging) scan showed a probably meningioma (a benign brain tumor). Twenty-four hours after surgery, she was back to normal.

From Kavesh (1996–1997, pp. 55–56).

Affective and Mood Disorders

One way to categorize cognitive impairment in later life (or at any time of life) would be to look at *organic mental disorders* (those that are the result of a physical problem) and affective disorders, those that have to do with the affect, one's feelings or emotions. We get the word "affectionate" from the term "affect"; obviously, in that context, it has to do with positive feelings. Affective disorders, disorders of the affect, have to do with emotions. Affect is defined as "An immediately expressed or observed emotion. A feeling state becomes an affect when it is observable, for example, as overall demeanor or tone and modulation of voice. Affect is to be distinguished from mood, which refers to a pervasive and sustained emotion. Affect is to mood as weather is to climate. Common examples of affect are euphoria, anger, and sadness"(American Psychiatric Association, 1994, p. 353). More recently, psychologists seemingly are equating mood disorders and affective disorders as pretty much the same thing.

Both organic and mood disorders can result in *delirium*, which the *Diagnostic and Statistical Manual of Mental Disorders, Fourth Edition* (**DSM-IV**) defines as "a disturbance of consciousness that is accompanied by a change in cognition that cannot be better accounted for by a preexisting or evolving dementia. The disturbance develops over a short period of time, usually hours to days, and tends to fluctuate during the course of the day" (American Psychiatric Association, 1994, p. 124). To complicate matters, people with organic problems can have delirium, and they can also have an affective disorder as well; in fact, depression probably goes hand-in-hand with stroke. But, stick with us and we'll sort this out.

First, let's look at the most common mood disorders in later life: depression, *bipolar disorder*, and major depression.

glossary

organic mental disorders — Ailments having a physical cause, such as head trauma or a disease such as Alzheimer's.

delirium — Mental confusion or disorientation, frenzied excitement, or delusions.

DSM-IV — The *Diagnostic and Statistical Manual of Mental Disorders, Fourth Edition*, published by the American Psychiatric Association (1994).

bipolar disorder — Alternating phases of serious depression and "manic" or overly excited activity.

glossary

dysthymia — Mild depression.

dysphoria — Feeling unwell or unhappy.

Depression in later life goes beyond periods of sadness. One might see the process of adaptation in old age as adjustment to a series of losses and, thus, a kind of continual grief reaction. Just as one does not simply "get over" grief so much as one learns to live with it, one does not necessarily get over other losses associated with old age. One learns to cope with them. Part of the adjustment process of coping with loss has to do with mourning one's lost youth and all that means. In particular, old people lose their companions and life-long friends; bereavement is part of the aging process. In a sense, then, depressed mood could be seen not only as common but as normal at some times in later life.

There are some clear characteristics that differentiate actual depression from moods that occur now and again among all older persons: "although older people often worry, worry that cannot be stopped tends to indicate depression. Loneliness when not socially isolated, general rather than specific past regrets, inactivity preceded by a loss of interest, and long pauses before speaking also indicate depression rather than advanced old age" (Kermis, 1986, p. 195). Sleep disturbances, fatigue, and inactivity uncharacteristic of the individual might also be signs of depression. This might particularly be the case when the person wakens feeling tired and having gloomy thoughts, and the fatigue is constant, going beyond tiredness after exertion. Lack of interest is an important sign of depression. Kermis continues, "When the intention to respond—rather than the action itself—is slowed, depression usually exists. The impression one gets in interacting with a depressed older person is that the person is 'stuck'—unable to decide whether to say or not say, do or not do, something" (p. 196).

As an emotional disorder, depression often has a related component of cognitive impairment, but this may not be significant unless the depression is severe. One might think of the depressed person as not trying as hard cognitively: they're apathetic rather than demented. Depressed people are more likely to complain of memory loss than people with one of the dementias, and they are more likely to give "don't know" answers to questions. Demented people might be more likely to attempt to cover up, make up an answer, or give a wrong response.

Older people who are depressed are more likely to experience weight loss and paranoid symptoms (fears and suspicions that have no basis in fact), express less guilt, and rarely report feeling depressed, in comparison to younger adults who are depressed (Gomez & Gomez, 1993).

Two signs of depression among older persons might be an apparent lack of interest in their usual activities and a lack of energy. They may become more dependent upon others. It is not unusual for them to have physical symptoms such as headaches or pain in the neck, back, or stomach. Older depressed persons are more likely than younger ones to refuse to eat or drink.

Depression can range from mild (**dysthymia**) to major depression. The criteria for a major depressive episode include dysphoric mood (feeling unwell or unhappy: **dysphoria** is the opposite of euphoria) and a loss of

> **Illustration 8.4. _DSM-IV_ Criteria for a Major Depressive Episode**
>
> Five or more of these symptoms present during the same two-week period constitute a major depressive episode:
>
> • Depressed mood most of the day, nearly every day.
> • Diminished interest or pleasure in almost all activities most of the day.
> • Significant weight loss or a decrease in appetite nearly every day.
> • Sleeplessness nearly every night.
> • Agitation or motor retardation nearly every day that goes beyond restlessness or slowing down.
> • Loss of energy or fatigue.
> • Feelings of worthlessness or excessive guilt.
> • Inability to concentrate or indecisiveness.
> • Recurrent thoughts of death or suicide.
>
> From American Psychiatric Association (1994, p. 327).

interest in one's usual activities. This mood is persistent over time and may include feelings of irritability, being sad or blue, or feeling hopeless or down in the dumps. Moods can switch around, for example from one dysphoric mood to another, such as from depression to anger to anxiety.

Major depression can be thought of as going hand in hand with a number of other medical problems, particularly cancer, stroke, or Parkinson's disease. In fact, some researchers say that physical illness should always be considered when signs of depression are evident among the aged (Caine, Lyness, & King, 1993)

Depression, physical illness, and cognitive impairment all influence each other, perhaps more directly among older people than in any other group. We've already noted that physical illness can cause depression. Social losses can, too. Aside from frequent major stresses, though, of greater impact may be a chronically stressful environment. Those who are already suffering from an organic mental disorder are prone to react to the frequent losses associated with later life by becoming depressed as well. That is, it is entirely possible to be both demented and depressed.

Physical illness may not only be a cause of depression, it may also be a result of depression. This relationship is not just theoretical: a Duke University study found a significant correlation ($r = .55$) between physical and mental health, as well as a significant correlation ($r = .61$) between mental impairment and an inability to perform activities of daily living (Blazer, 1980). In another study, a nurse researcher studied depression in a group of community-dwelling older people and found depression to correlate significantly with physical health, social resources, and a sense of mastery. Those low in mastery or control believed they had minimal ability to control outcomes in their lives (Badger, 1993).

glossary

involutional —
Shrinking and
entangling;
downwardly spiraling
with age.

Since loss of internal control and physical illness are associated with depression, it would be reasonable to conclude that it is a common condition among institutionalized elders. Various studies have found this to be the case. Research done at the Philadelphia Geriatric Center, for example, followed a population of 868 nursing home patients (mean age = 84 years) for one year and found that 16.5% of them displayed minor depressive symptoms and 15.7% had major depression. Most showed no remission of symptoms over the course of the year, and persistence of depression indicated greater health decline (Parmelee, 1992a).

A number of studies have found that cognitive disorder predicts death among the elderly (Arfken, Lichtenber, & Tancer, 1999; Takeida, Nishi, & Miyake, 1997; Zubenko, Mulsant, Sweet, Pasternak, & Tu, 1997). This is especially true of organic mental disorders, but it is also true of depression.

Following up on the same sample 30 months later, for example, the researchers from the Philadelphia Geriatric Center found that the depressed individuals were about twice as likely to have died, although this could be because of co-morbid conditions—the depressed people were also more seriously physically ill (Parmelee, 1992b). These results were confirmed by an Australian study that followed 72 patients hospitalized for psychiatric morbidity and physical dependency. At the end of one year, 44% of the patients had died. It was determined that their previous scores on a measure of depressive signs was the only significant predictor of mortality (Shah et al., 1993).

As long ago as 1964, Marjorie Fiske Lowenthal found isolation and depression to be associated among older people. She also found that mental illness in later life is isolating: it's hard to be around people with an emotional problem—they're a drain on their caretakers. So we might look at the social nature of depression in one of two ways: it might be *involutional* in that the physical illness present limits one's life and influences depressive outcomes, just as the depression makes the physical condition that much worse. Or, we might also think of the isolating characteristics of emotional illness in later life in the same manner: the depression causes isolation, and the isolation causes depression. As a social outcome, isolation might also be related to emotional problems in a kind of chicken-and-egg proposition, and we are left to wonder if the emotional problem caused the isolation (it's no fun to be around depressed people) or if the isolation—say, widowhood—caused the depression.

Whichever way makes sense, there is more recent research to support what Lowenthal found. One study followed a panel of 1,070 subjects aged 65+ longitudinally. Within this group, 44 cases of depression were identified, an incidence rate of 4.1%. The risk factors for developing depression were determined to be a lack of satisfaction with life, loneliness, and being female and bereaved (Green et al., 1992).

Although we often think of major life stresses such as widowhood as being associated with depression, a constantly stressful environment may be a better predictor. Two Canadian researchers followed 200 people aged

55+ to determine the influence either of major life event changes or daily hassles on physical and psychological well-being. The best predictors of negative psychological and physical well-being were found to be age, self-rated health, limitations in activities of daily living, and frequency of daily hassles. Frequency of life changes was not a significant variable, whereas frequency of hassles was (Landreville & Vezina, 1992).

In terms of the epidemiology of depression, another Canadian study, this of 1,274 older persons, found 2.4% to be clinically depressed and 5.6% moderately depressed. Women were significantly higher in depression than men. Social factors associated with depression in this study were recent death or serious illness of a relative or close friend, being divorced or widowed, and lower education (Stephenson-Cino et al., 1992).

Results found in a Johns Hopkins study of 810 adults in Baltimore were that 5.9% were depressed and 1.1% had a major depression. Women and widows were higher in depression. One inference we might make from this particular study of the overall adult population is that the number of depressed people is higher in later life because there are so many more women and widows in the very old population (Romanoski et al., 1992).

Another study of depression among older people found that it typically began in later life and did not readily resolve. This research followed 102 patients aged 64 and above for one year. A high prevalence of depression was found among the physically ill individuals—and a low rate of treatment by mental health professionals. Greater physical impairment was consistently associated with psychiatric co-morbidity (Rapp, Parisi, & Wallace, 1991). Other research suggests that depression in later life may have had roots in earlier adulthood. About half of the depressed patients identified in this particular study had late-onset depression. Life-long personality disorder was often associated with early onset (before age 60) depression (Kunik et al., 1993).

Treatment of depression, even among the very elderly, is often successful through a variety of therapies and antidepressant medications or with the use of electroconvulsive shock therapy in the case of depressive psychosis (Benbow, 1991; DasGupta, 1998). The tragedy is that older people who are depressed often go untreated, even if they reside in a health care facility. Either their condition goes unnoticed or remains untreated because people seemingly expect mental distress to go hand-in-hand with old age.

Affective or mood disorders are not organic, but they can be influenced by organic conditions such as physical illness. They can also be influenced by social disruption or a chronically stressful environment. Usually, we think of affective disorders as a disturbance of mood; thus, depression resembles normal sadness but lasts longer and is more intense. Loss may trigger depression, but depression may also occur in the absence of any trigger event. Depression may often become disabling before the individual or the family notices. Major depressive disorder may be the result of a building up of depression over a long period of time; depression can become chronic and life-threatening. Kermis says that depression of-

> ### Illustration 8.5. *DSM-IV* Criteria for a Manic Episode
>
> One or more distinct periods with a predominantly elevated, expansive, or irritable mood. The elevated or irritable mood must be a prominent part of the illness and relatively persistent, although it may alternate or intermingle with depressive mood.
>
> Duration of at least one week (or any duration if hospitalization is necessary), during which, for most of the time, at least three of the following symptoms have persisted (four if the mood is only irritable) and have been present to a significant degree:
>
> - increase in activity (either socially, at work, or sexually) or physical restlessness
> - more talkative than usual or pressure to keep talking
> - flight of ideas or subjective experience that thoughts are racing
> - inflated self-esteem (grandiosity, which may be delusional)
> - decreased need for sleep
> - distractibility, that is, attention is too easily drawn to unimportant or irrelevant external stimuli
> - excessive involvement in activities that have a high potential for painful consequences (buying sprees, sexual indiscretions, foolish business investments, reckless driving.
>
> From American Psychiatric Association (1994, p. 362).

g lossary

manic — Frenzied, overactive.

ten accompanies illness late in life, and that "older persons can tolerate the loss of love objects and prestige better than they can a decline in health. The reasons are fairly straightforward. Physical disability often restricts the individual's mobility. Mobility restriction, in turn, leads to social isolation. Social isolation leads to decreased self-esteem which, when combined with the physical illness and its losses, leads to depression" (1986, p. 191).

In addition to major depression, the *DSM-IV* lists bipolar disorder as a mood disorder. If the person has ever had a manic episode, then the condition is classified as bipolar. Bipolar disorder used to be called "*manic*-depressive illness," in that it can be characterized by mood swings from elation to depression. A person showing manic behavior often is seemingly uncharacteristically active, can't stop talking, has mixed-up ideas, sleeps less, and is impulsive and often irritable. A period of mania usually begins suddenly, escalates rapidly, and varies from days to months in length. An individual with bipolar disorder may swing back and forth from "down in the depths" to "way up on high." Older people tend to stay disturbed longer than younger people, and their symptoms are more likely to recur. Also, in contrast to younger individuals with bipolar disorder, older people may seem more confused, paranoid, and agitated.

Major depression, a unipolar disorder, is more common in the elderly than is bipolar disorder. Apparently, from 5–10% of those seen for treatment show an excited phase to their condition. Bipolar disorder generally does not occur for the first time in old age. About 60% of first attacks take place between ages 20 and 35, and it is rare for a first episode to take place after age 65 (Kermis, 1986). Most bipolar disorder among the aged, then, is a recurrence of earlier illness. Like unipolar depression, bipolar disorder does not tend to diminish spontaneously in the elderly, can become chronic, gets worse, and becomes more resistant to treatment. This is another reason that older individuals with mood disorders should receive competent psychiatric and medical examination.

Paranoia and Schizophrenia

Terms for older people who act out or act in a manner inconsistent with society's norms have varied over the years. We've already mentioned how "chronic brain syndrome" and "senile dementia" have been supplanted by the more precise diagnosis of Alzheimer's disease (or another of the organic dementias). Similarly, "senile psychosis," which was the term for a fundamental mental derangement (usually paranoia) is no longer in use.

Paranoia usually consists of irrational suspiciousness or delusions of persecution. Kermis offers a brief case study of paranoid disorder:

> Mrs. M., aged 72, was in an acute care hospital recovering from major heart surgery. She had a persistent delusion that CIA agents were spying on her and her roommate. She kept tedious notes on the occurrence of CIA visitations and often regaled the staff with her descriptions of the visits. When carefully examined, her CIA visits were found to correspond to security guard checks of the floor. When this was explained to her, the delusion vanished, although she subsequently became quite depressed; it appeared that she missed the excitement her delusion had offered. (1986, p. 184)

The *DSM*-IV has gotten away from terms like psychosis and neurosis. Also abandoned is *paraphrenia*, a term used to designate delusional disor-

---

Illustration 8.6. Not All Delusions Are Paranoid

Back when I worked in a nursing home, we had a gentleman who had us get him all spiffed up one Saturday morning because he said that he was going to be picked up and taken to his granddaughter's wedding. We had him scrubbed and in his best suit, and nobody came to pick him up at the appointed hour. We called the family and they said that, no, there was no wedding that day. In fact, the granddaughter had been married for several years. Another patient one time said she was expecting to go out on a date with Clark Gable that night. Clark Gable had been dead for seven years at that point, so we didn't bother to check that one out further.

Mild delusions or flights of fancy are pretty harmless.

My father, who had Parkinson's disease, was planning at one point to reorganize the Chicago and North Shore Railroad, which had gone bankrupt several years previously. He got over it.

---

ders of older persons. Several researchers in the field of geriatric psychiatry, however, feel that this has been too hasty a decision (Laitman & Davis, 1994). One review from England, for example, argues that disuse of the term paraphrenia has been premature. It has been used to describe those with a well-organized system of paranoid delusions or hallucinations among older people with an intact personality and affective response. Most patients with paraphrenia are now described as being schizophrenic with delusional or paranoid disorders. It is argued that paraphrenia is a distinct clinical entity and that the underlying pathology differs from paranoia and schizophrenia. Also, it is noted that unlike paranoia or schizophrenia, with paraphrenia there is an absence of negative symptoms. It has been found that paraphrenia is also associated with hearing loss, and that it occurs more frequently among women than in men by a ratio of about seven to one (Almeida, Howard, Forstl, & Levy, 1992; Hassett, Keks, Jackson, & Copolov, 1992; Laitman & Davis, 1994).

Psychiatrist Carl Eisdorfer (1980) notes the likelihood of deafness in late paraphrenia, and points out that the condition almost always has its onset in late life (unlike paranoid schizophrenia), and that individuals diagnosed with it usually have no prior history of psychiatric illness or signs of dementia at the time of diagnosis. He cites one study where 111 out of 132 persons with late paraphrenia were hearing impaired. For this reason, he characterizes it as an illness of isolation in later life. He also notes that it does not have the characteristic deterioration associated with schizophrenia.

People with paraphrenia in later life may have delusions that are quite harmless, or that border on paranoid delusions, which probably is the basis for the confusion between the two terms; those with mild delusions might be thought of as having paraphrenia, and those with more serious ones probably border on paranoia. A study from the University of London Institute of Psychiatry details the difficulty of sorting this out: the research was on the prevalence of "partition" delusions in late paraphrenia. Partition delusions are thoughts of permeable walls, floors, ceilings, and doors. They are much more common in people with late paraphrenia than among schizophrenics who grow old. Such thoughts often are associated with persecutory beliefs, thus the implication that people who have them are paranoid (Howard et al., 1992).

The fundamental characteristic of paranoid disorder is belief in irrational thoughts, delusions that are not grounded in reality. Commonly associated features of paranoid disorder include "resentment and anger, which may lead to violence. Grandiosity and ideas or delusions of reference are common. Often there is social isolation, seclusiveness, or eccentricities of behavior. Suspiciousness, either generalized or focused on certain individuals, is common. Letter writing, complaining about various injustices, and instigation of legal action are frequent. These individuals rarely seek treatment, and often are brought in for care by associates, relatives, or governmental agencies as a result of the individuals' angry or litigious activities."

Some psychiatrists maintain that deafness should always be considered a potential risk factor for the development of paranoid ideas in later life (Stein & Thienhaus, 1993). Kermis outlines the path between deafness and paranoid reactions: after loss of auditory input, the individual begins to rely on an "inner world." Misinterpretation of auditory stimuli leads to a projection of inferiority from deafness, and the individual begins to have delusions of persecution ("people are talking about me" or "people are laughing at me"). It is common for those with low self-esteem related to sensory impairment to then develop active delusions of persecution.

Negative beliefs about others, cynicism, mistrust, anger, and disgust are all characteristics that lead to active hostility among those with a paranoid disorder. A study from the Duke University Department of Psychiatry found that hostile beliefs about others were highest in late life (Barefoot et al., 1993). Suspicion of others might, of course, have some basis in reality; when it does not, however, suspicion may be a sign of paranoia. Blazer and his colleagues (1994) found symptoms of paranoia to be present in 9.5% of a sample of elderly people. African-Americans, people with lower income, and people with fewer years of education had more paranoia.

Paranoia is not often entirely disabling: there are many people who are able to maintain themselves pretty well in independent living situations later in life. While some may be hostile to others or have irrational suspicions, this is not necessarily always the case. We would argue that late life paraphrenia could be seen at one end of a continuum, and that full-blown paranoid psychosis would be at the other. More serious cases might have

---

Ilustration 8.7. Diogenes Syndrome

We had an engineering professor, now deceased, who exhibited signs of social breakdown in his '60s. Always an isolate, he was personally neat and clean but lived in an environment that was horrific. His office was so stuffed full of papers and trash that he was literally unable to move around in it, and his associates joked that he would die in there some day and no one would be able to find him. His collecting took a turn for the worse after his mother died and he became even more isolated. He filled his house to the point of overflowing: odds and ends and bundles of old newspapers stacked to the ceiling with narrow paths through the mess that led from one room to another. He had two old cars in his driveway that were also stuffed full and couldn't be driven. The city mowed his lawn about twice a year, after complaints from the neighbors and resultant fines. The house got so full that he moved out of it and into an apartment. The Health Department was summoned when a neighbor saw a family of raccoons take up residence in the abandoned house. What inspectors found upon investigation brought a summons to the police: they removed 204 guns and rifles (as they said it: they brought out the ones they could get to). Aside from this, however, he functioned quite well on the job and in the community. Regarded by people who knew him as something of an oddball, he was not considered a threat to himself or others, and no intervention seemed to be wanted or needed. Unless they present a hazard to the public health, people have a right to live in a mess if they want to.

glossary

Diogenes syndrome
— Breakdown of
self-maintenance,
often characterized by
messiness or
hoarding.

hallucinations or delusions, but most people with a degree of paranoia have an intact personality and, other than their irrational fears or suspicions, are able to go about their daily business in a fairly logical manner. This is not to say that the disorder does not cause problems in everyday life: paranoid people can drive off others and further isolate their condition. However, the condition by itself is fairly rare—less than 1% of the older population—and it is not often disabling. Paranoid disorder in later life responds to treatment, including counseling and anxiety-relieving drugs. It often helps to explain to older persons showing some signs of paranoia of what is happening to them.

In addition to interpersonal difficulties—people with paranoia can be hostile and drive off friends and relatives—there can be social problems related to paranoid disorder. Self-neglect or disorganized behavior late in life often has features associated with suspicious beliefs about others that might seem to have paranoid features. Like many conditions, this varies in severity, from seemingly harmless eccentricities to almost total social breakdown. At the extreme, social breakdown among the elderly can be characterized as total self-neglect and refusal of help. In this way, it might have features of the apathy related to depression. It usually is not explained by physical illness or social situation (Ungvari & Hantz, 1991).

The British refer to self-neglect among the elderly as *"Diogenes syndrome,"* after the ancient Greek cynic who went about with a lantern and peered into peoples' faces saying, "I'm looking for an honest man," and who supplied his minimal needs for food and clothing by begging. This label doesn't exactly stack up, as many people with Diogenes syndrome actually are hoarders. In this respect, the condition might seem to be related to an addictive disorder: some people are addicted to collecting, and they may have delusions that their hoard of stuff actually has some value. Senile self-neglect is described as "a breakdown of standards of personal and environmental hygiene, social withdrawal, and an apathetic attitude to the resulting squalor" (Cole, Gillett, & Fairbairn, 1992, p. 839). A group of Israeli researchers maintains that hoarding, a characteristic of senile self-neglect, is a result of an obsessive-compulsive disorder, and that it often is characterized by fears of theft and other paranoid delusions (Greenberg, Witztum, & Levy, 1990).

Hoarding becomes dysfunctional when the garage is so full of *National Geographics* that the car will no longer fit in it. That is, many people have collections or neglect to discard useless stuff. This does not present a problem unless the hoard becomes so overwhelming as to indicate a grossly disorganized personality. The British medical journal *The Lancet* gave a description of what we might think of as end-stage Diogenes syndrome:

> All patients lived in a state of domestic squalor, disorder, and extreme self-neglect. Their homes were filthy on the outside—peeling paintwork and dirty, often broken, windows with dingy net curtains serving as external markers to conditions within. Inside there was a characteristic

strong, stale, and slightly suffocating smell. The patients were usually dressed in layers of dirty clothing sometimes covered by an old raincoat or overcoat, and, when confined to bed, they lay beneath a pile of ragged blankets, clothing, or newspapers. They never appeared to undress or wash, the hair being long and unkempt, with exposed surfaces of skin deeply engrained with dirt. Only two patients apologized about their personal or domestic state. Several hoarded useless rubbish (syllogomania)—newspapers, tins, bottles, and rags, often in bundles and stacks—and in six instances the size of the collection seriously reduced living space" (Clark, Mankikar, & Gray, 1975, p. 366).

The researchers noted that these individuals usually had many cats. They concluded that if their mess was cleaned up, these people often restored it within a few months or even weeks.

Schizophrenia is a serious mental illness characterized by loss of contact with the environment, deterioration in the level of functioning, and disintegration of personality. It often involves hallucinations and social withdrawal. Paranoia may be a feature of schizophrenia, but schizophrenia is not necessarily a feature of paranoia, as people with a paranoid disorder often have few other problems other than their peculiar delusion. People with schizophrenic disorder, on the other hand, often withdraw from society entirely, have a serious impairment in their ability to function in everyday life, and have peculiar behavior (e.g., collecting garbage, talking to self in public, or hoarding food) (American Psychiatric Association, 1994, p. 189). This kind of hoarding differentiates the schizophrenic from the hoarding that might be seen with other disorders: many collectors, for example, really intend to read all those newspapers some day, or the things they hoard may actually be of some value. People with a schizophrenic disorder, on the other hand, may collect actual garbage with no particular thought to

---

Illustration 8.8. *DSM-IV* Criteria for Schizophrenic Disorder

Signs of schizophrenia include at least one of the following:

- Bizarre delusions (content is patently absurd and has no possible basis in fact), such as delusions of being controlled, thought broadcasting, thought insertion, or thought withdrawal.
- Somatic, grandiose, religious, nihilistic, or other delusions without persecutory or jealous content.
- Delusions with persecutory or jealous content if accompanied by hallucinations of any type.
- Auditory hallucinations (hearing voices) having no apparent relation to depression or elation.
- Hearing voices where either a voice keeps up a running commentary on the individual's behavior or thoughts of two or more voices conversing with each other.
- Incoherence, loosening of associations, illogical thinking, especially if associated with flat affect, delusions or hallucinations, or grossly disorganized behavior.

From American Psychiatric Association (1994, p. 285).

mental retardation —
A diminished ability to
learn. There is no
single cause of mental
retardation; it may
result from a number
of factors, including
premature birth,
genetic abnormalities,
malnutrition, trauma,
exposure to toxic
agents (including fetal
alcohol syndrome), or
social deprivation.

its ultimate use; indeed, they may not even be aware that they have a hoard of garbage.

People with schizophrenia may also have a blunted or inappropriate affect (laughing or crying that's unrelated to the circumstances around them), make no sense when they speak, have bizarre ideas or magical thinking, and experience delusions, where they sense the presence of forces or persons not actually present. Schizophrenia may be present in *mental retardation*. People with a personality disorder or with paranoia often return to a usual level of functioning in a few hours or days, whereas people with a schizophrenic disorder don't get better, they get worse.

Kermis says that there are few if any cases of new schizophrenia in old age: "Those individuals who are schizophrenic are predominantly chronic, 'burnt out' cases who manifest the symptoms of 'institutionalism' rather than schizophrenia"(1987, p. 188). Researchers at Northwestern University point out that aging persons with schizophrenic disorder usually have a condition that began before old age, and that they often find active delusions and hallucinations to be less troublesome in later life. They say that only 4% of male and 14% of female schizophrenic patients have an onset of symptoms after age 65 (Trinkle, 1992).

Illustration 8.9. Causes of Schizophrenia

Our current model of the causation of schizophrenia is very similar to that used to understand cancer. That is, schizophrenia probably occurs as a consequence of multiple "hits," which include some combination of inherited genetic factors and external, nongenetic factors that affect the regulation and expression of genes governing brain function or that injure the brain directly. Some people may have a genetic predisposition that requires a convergence of additional factors to produce the expression of the disorder. This convergence results in abnormalities in brain development and maturation, a process that is on-going during the first two decades of life.

The symptoms and signs of schizophrenia are very diverse, and they encompass the entire range of human mental activity. They include abnormalities in perception (hallucinations), inferential thinking (delusions), language (disorganized speech), social and motor behavior (disorganized behavior and abnormal or stereotyped movements), and initiation of goal-directed activity (avolition), as well as impoverishment of speech and mental creativity (alogia), blunting of emotional expression (flattened affect), and loss of the ability to experience pleasure (anhedonia). These symptoms and signs occur in patterns that may not overlap: one patient may have hallucinations and affective flattening, whereas another has disorganized speech and avolition. The diversity and nonoverlapping pattern of symptoms and signs suggest a more basic and unifying problem: abnormalities in neural circuits and fundamental cognitive mechanisms. Patients with schizophrenia also have impairment in may different cognitive systems, such as memory, attention, and executive function.

From Andreasen (1999, pp. 645–647).

It would appear, then, that schizophrenia is more often a life-long problem, rather than one that develops in later life. Cases emerging late in life that formerly were diagnosed as "senile psychosis" might more properly be described among the dementias or affective disorders and not be true schizophrenia. Chronic schizophrenia, however, can also be dementing, either because of the disease itself, or as a result of the regimen of high-powered drugs that the adult schizophrenic has been subjected to over the years.

A team of pathologists from the Mount Sinai Medical Center presented autopsy data on brain specimens from 13 elderly schizophrenics who had shown evidence of dementing disorders, and compared them to 12 aged-matched cases who had been diagnosed as having Alzheimer's disease and 12 controls without impairment. None of the schizophrenia patients showed the characteristic senile plaques and neurofibrillary tangles found among people with Alzheimer's disease. Nor were other conditions such as multi-infarct dementia identified. So, the severe cognitive impairment often seen in older persons with schizophrenia was not due to a concurrent dementing disorder. Their demented and disorganized behavior was evidently explained by long-term schizophrenia itself (Purohit et al., 1993).

Organic Mental Disorders, Delirium, and Dementia

The *DSM-IV* has an elaborate "decision tree" for differential diagnosis of mental problems, including those more common in later life. This provides detail beyond the scope of this chapter, but it indicates the difficulty in determining the exact *etiology* of mental problems that are ultimately diagnoses by clinical signs and symptoms rather than specific laboratory tests or x-rays.

As we've already noted, the problems seen in older adults with disorganized behaviors may have many causes, but they may also present many of the same outward signs.

A group of symptoms typical to many mental problems more common in later life is listed under the heading delirium, which is categorized within the organic mental disorders but can be manifested within the affective disorders, paranoia, and schizophrenia as well. The *DSM-IV* defines delirium as consisting of five different symptom categories:

1. clouding of consciousness or reduced awareness of the environment and reduced capacity to shift focus or sustain attention;
2. at least two of the following:
   - misinterpretations of perception, illusions, or hallucinations
   - incoherent speech
   - disturbance of sleep, especially the normal sleep cycle
   - increased or decreased physical activity;

glossary

polypharmacy — Overuse of drugs.

iatrogenic — Caused by medical treatment, such as drug intoxication.

3. disorientation and memory impairment;
4. symptoms that develop over a short period of time (a few hours or days) and which fluctuate over the course of the day; and,
5. evidence of a specific organic factor related to the disturbance.

Two decades ago, we might have listed the signs of delirium under a category called "pseudodementia," or false dementia. This was because memory disorientation, reduced awareness, and incoherent speech found in delirium often led to a diagnosis of an organic mental disorder that was commonly called "senile dementia." While this term may still be in use, it is less in favor nowadays. However, the distinction of delirium having recent onset or developing over a short period of time is still a useful one.

The principal causes of cognitive impairment in later life come under the categories of organic mental disorders and affective disorders. We have already extensively reviewed the affective or mood disorders, and we will cover organic mental disorders in this section of the chapter, but we need a bit more discussion on delirium.

Listed in *DSM-IV* under the organic mental disorders, symptoms of delirium can be found among all cognitive problems in later life. Signs of delirium can be found in depression and bipolar disorder, just as they can in other affective disorders and the organic ones, too. Delirium is really a complex of symptoms, however, not a specific disease entity.

It is listed as organic because most of the causes of delirium among the elderly are physical, not mood related. However, it is not a physical illness in the same way as Alzheimer's or Parkinson's disease. Usually, causes of delirium come from functional impairments external to the individual.

For example, one leading cause of delirium among the aged is misuse of medications. Careful pharmaceutical monitoring has for the most part reduced much of the ***polypharmacy*** (drug interactions and overdoses among the elderly) common a decade or two ago. The problem, however, remains. Many older people, particularly if they are confused, misuse their medications: they may take medications their physician or pharmacist is unaware of, may take too much or too little, or may take drugs in combination with inappropriate substances, such as alcohol. Many drugs build to a level of toxicity in old people who have kidneys and livers that are inefficient in removing them. Some geriatricians begin treatment of new patients by taking them off of medications prescribed by other doctors. The message is that many medical conditions among the aged should be approached conservatively rather than aggressively to avoid precipitating an *iatrogenic* problem, a medical problem caused by the treatment itself.

Changes in environment (especially relocation into a hospital or nursing home), social trauma, or grief might precipitate delirium as well. Most causes, however, are not social, but physical: in addition to misuse of prescription and over-the-counter medications, drug abuse among the elderly includes the use of illegal substances. One study describes the difficulties of prolonged crack cocaine addiction and subsequent psychiatric symptoms among the aged. We probably can look for future psychiatric impairment among some elderly as the group of young adult drug abusers ages (Nambudiri & Young, 1991). Alcohol addiction is an organic mental disorder that results in delirium, as is HIV infection (Whipple & Scura (1996). Other physical problems can result in delirium: any fever or infection, congestive heart failure, head trauma malnutrition or dehydration, vitamin deficiency, or electrolyte imbalance.

Some physical problems may be less obvious. *Hyperthermia* (body temperature that is too high) can be the result of a physical environment that is too hot: the body's temperature regulating mechanisms don't work as effectively late in life. This can lead to dehydration, confusion, and, in some cases, death. Hypothermia is the opposite condition: commonly seen in northern climates in the winter, it is the result of being in too cold an environment for too long a period of time. In fact, some senior center directors report older clients coming in on cold days seemingly confused; after a few hours in a warm place and a hot meal they've become more lucid. Perhaps they're coming from a house or apartment that's kept at too low a temperature because they can't afford to stay as warm as they'd like. Thus a social or economic problem can result in a psychological symptom (confusion) that in some instances can result in a physical outcome—death.

Although the causes of delirium often are physical (and thus the condition is listed under the organic mental disorders), there is no reason to think that the outcomes are permanent. This was the point of specifying "pseudodementia" as a condition: the message was that these are the dementias that can be reversed, and it would be a pity to institutionalize someone as organically demented if the cause of the problem was reversible.

This is still true: if the onset of confusion is recent or sudden, prompt medical attention is vital. For one thing, the individual may have an undi-

---

Illustration 8.10. Guarding Against Delirium

Geriatricians know that a preoperative evaluation for an older person differs from that for a younger person. It is important to look at the a priori risks affecting the likelihood of a successful surgical outcome, but it is also critical to advise the surgeon to put into place preventive measures for delirium and other complications that can occur due to the medicines used and other measures taken.

Geriatric assessment involves the "incessant collection of evidence" in spheres where traditional medicine rarely treads: detailed examination of mental status, functional status, and social support systems that may be critical to the maintenance of independence in the elderly patient. This is an area well served by the use of multidisciplinary geriatric teams, but it is a time-consuming task that is usually poorly reimbursed—another factor that limits the interest of the average physician in such a comprehensive approach.

From Kavesh (1996–1997, pp. 55–56).

agnosed physical illness that needs treatment; cure of an infection might result in cure of the delirium. And physical and social causes for cognitive impairment should always be considered. Signs of delirium are associated with organic mental disorder, but not all people with delirium have an organic mental disorder.

Delirium or signs of delirium are often seen among older individuals in acute care, and are not, of course, always the result of a reversible condition. Long-term alcoholics, for example, often have delirium associated with dementia. Sometimes delirium is the result of a head injury, which may or may not be reversible. One study done at UCLA examined 24 patients aged 60 and older who had developed their first psychotic episode after age 45; they were compared to 72 healthy older persons in a control group. Both groups were given MRI (magnetic resonance imaging) and a variety or psychological tests. The psychotic patients were shown to have more clinical abnormalities on the MRI test, especially large brain lesions. They also had a greater frequency of metabolic illness. On the mental tests they did much poorer than the people in the control group in terms of cognitive ability and verbal memory. The researchers concluded that structural brain injury is associated with the onset of delirium in later life (Miller et al., 1991).

A team from Beth Israel Hospital in Boston screened 325 patients 65 or older who had been admitted over the course of a two-year period to an acute care hospital or a nursing home. They found a strong, significant association between incidents of delirium and functional decline. At a three-month follow-up, it was found that in most instances the delirium had persisted, and 51.4% of the patients with delirium had become worse off. The authors questioned whether delirium should be considered to be a transient cognitive disorder (one that comes and goes), since they found that symptoms persisted in 95% of patients who developed it in the hospital. Instead, it might more accurately be seen as a syndrome that has acute onset and long-term consequences (Murray et al., 1993). This particular study, then, continues the debate as to whether delirium should be seen merely as a group of symptoms, or as a condition in its own right. No doubt further research will continue to address these issues.

We often think of Alzheimer's disease and multi-infarct or vascular dementia as the two principal causes of dementia in later life. There are others as well. Brain injury from a variety of causes can be dementing. As we have seen, the UCLA study of brain lesions found signs of dementia

Illustration 8.11. Dementia Pugilistica

A "pugilist"—a boxer—runs a grave risk of head trauma that will be dementing. After all, the whole point of boxing is to inflict injury, usually to the head. Getting knocked out is pretty clear evidence of brain injury. Old boxers often are "punch drunk."

and delirium (Miller et al., 1991). Other brain damage might be caused by disease, such as encephalitis, or by neurological illness, brain tumor, or head trauma, resulting in **subdural hematoma**, a blood clot within the skull that presses on the brain. One cause sometimes listed is "dementia pugilistica," which is the result of repeated blows that boxers have received to their heads. This might more properly be thought of as multi-infarct dementia caused not by small strokes, but by big punches.

There can be little doubt that becoming demented is one of the greatest fears of older persons. Many will continually monitor their own mental performance, and signs of forgetfulness sometimes will be interpreted as the onset of dementia. As we have already seen in this chapter, only a small percentage of older people, particularly the young old, actually have any kind of dementing condition. However, given the importance and seriousness of the dementing conditions—and their prevalence among the oldest old—we need to look at them in some detail.

According to the National Institutes of Health's Consensus Development Conference Statement on Differential Diagnosis of Dementing Diseases, "Dementia is a clinical state with many different causes, characterized by a decline from a previously attained intellectual level" (1987, p. 2). It is sustained over months or years rather than weeks or days. The decline involves memory, learning, and adaptive behaviors. The individual may or may not be aware of the condition. In all cases, there is a deterioration of the ability to remember things, as well as declines in intellectual functions such as orientation in time, verbal ability, reasoning, and judgment. The onset is usually gradual: minor forgetfulness is noticed, and there may be a tendency to misplace things. There may also be repetitious conversation, and the individual may appear to become increasingly disorganized. People with dementia may get lost, not recognize others, sleep during the day and be awake all night, and have delusions. Dementia is progressive when it is the result of a degenerative disease, or it may be static, such as among people with head injury. The course of decline is usually slow, ranging from several months to many years.

There are many causes of dementia, such as Alzheimer's disease, Huntington's disease, Pick's disease, and Parkinson's disease, all of which are progressive. Other illnesses, such as liver disease, hypothyroidism, syphilis, or HIV infection, may also be dementing. "Virtually all of the chemicals used in substance abuse from heroin to glue are capable of producing dementia. Other chemicals include carbon monoxide, carbon disulfide, lead, mercury, and manganese" (National Institutes of Health, 1987, p. 3). Like other substance abuse, long-term alcoholism is dementing.

Whereas "depression is primarily a disturbance of mood, dementia is basically a disorder of intellectual function" (American Psychiatric Association, 1994). Mood disorders are less frequent and less serious in dementia in comparison to depression, and people with dementia score poorly on mental status exams consistently, while people with depression will more likely have ups and downs in their scores. Among people who are depressed,

subdural hematoma
— A blood clot between the skull and the brain.

mental ability will improve as the mood improves; this is not true of people with dementia.

People with dementia may also have delusions and paranoia, and this may be the reason that they have so often been diagnosed in the past as having schizophrenia or "senile psychosis." One study found that 48% of people with dementia interviewed have delusions of theft, and 21% had a belief that "one's house is not one's home." Twenty-one percent had delusions of abandonment. Other common delusions were "imposter" syndrome (thinking that someone has replaced a familiar person), the "phantom boarder" syndrome (someone else living in the house, sometimes having loud parties), or fears that one's spouse is having an affair. One of the strangest delusions is the Charles Bonnet syndrome: hallucinations of odd-looking little people living in the home; sometimes they are thought to be friendly and allow the person to assume a caregiving role. According to researchers at Northwestern University, these kinds of delusions are identified as one

---

Illustration 8.12. Reisberg's Stages of Alzheimer's Disease

Level 1—No cognitive decline or complaints of memory deficit.

Level 2—Very mild cognitive decline; forgetfulness or complaints of memory deficit.

Level 3—Mild cognitive decline (early Alzheimer's disease). Patient may have gotten lost, friends become aware of declines in word and name finding, decreased facility in remembering names, loses things.

Level 4—Moderate cognitive decline. Decreased knowledge of current and recent events, forgets some personal history, cannot do serial subtractions, decreased ability to handle finances. However, the individual often is oriented as to time and person, recognizes familiar faces, is able to travel to familiar locations, but is unable to perform complex tasks and withdraws from challenging situations.

Level 5—Moderately severe cognitive decline, moderate Alzheimer's disease. Patients can no longer survive without assistance; they can no longer recall their address or phone number, names of close family members, time, or place. They remember their own names, many major facts about their lives, and a few names.

Level 6—Severe cognitive decline (moderately severe Alzheimer's). Patients may forget the name of their spouse and are largely unaware of all recent events and experiences, but may retain a few facts about their past lives. Unaware of their surroundings, the year, cannot count to ten, but remember their own name. May become incontinent and require travel assistance. May undergo personality changes and may have delusions or talk with imaginary figures or to themselves in the mirror. May have anxiety and be agitated and may become violent. Requires help with all activities of daily living.

Level 7—Very severe Alzheimer's disease. Ability to talk is lost, they are incontinent, require help with eating, lose the ability to walk and can no longer smile or hold up their heads.

From Reisberg, Ferris, Leon, & Crook (1982).

of the symptoms of dementia and are present in 62% of Alzheimer's disease patients and about 12% of multi-infarct patients (Trinkle, 1992).

Alzheimer's disease results from the destruction of neurons in particular parts of the brain. "Senile plaques" (blotches of darkened pigmentation) and "neurofibrillary tangles" (bunched-up nerve cells) are characteristically found upon postmortem examination of the brain in the laboratory. So far there is no complete understanding of what causes Alzheimer's disease, no reliable lab test to confirm clinical diagnosis, and no cure; several drugs have some value in slowing down the progression of the disease. The condition ultimately leads to death—whether or not the ultimate cause of death is actually Alzheimer's disease may be debatable; it is often an upper respiratory infection secondary to Alzheimer's. Thus, many people who in fact die because they have Alzheimer's have pneumonia listed as the cause on the death certificate. So, while the annual CDC report on deaths in the United States lists Alzheimer's as responsible for 22,154 fatalities (Hoyert et al., 1999), it may actually be responsible for 90,000 to 100,000 deaths per year, which would make it the fourth leading cause of death among the elderly (after heart disease, cancer, and stroke).

Alzheimer's disease is more common among women than men, perhaps because so many more women live into very late life and Alzheimer's is much more common among people in their 80s and 90s (Bachman et al., 1992; Brayne, 1993). There also is a strong familial tendency (Masters & Beyreuther, 1998). According to the DSM-IV, "first-degree relatives are four times more likely to develop the disease than members of the general population" (American Psychiatric Association, 1994). Alzheimer's disease also has an apparent genentic link to Down's syndrome (Cooper, 1992).

The earliest detectable sign of dementia of the Alzheimer's type is usually a personality alteration, especially paranoia and depression, followed by mood change. Mood change can be especially distressing for family members, as it can take the form of outbursts and aggressive behaviors. The person becomes increasingly distractible, and failure of memory for recent events become more obvious. The ability to learn new things declines. The individual becomes disoriented as to where she or he is in terms of place, time, or even season.

As the disease progresses, the occurrence of *confabulation* is common. Confabulation is the individual's response to a question with a fabricated answer in an attempt to present normal conversation when they actually have no actual clue as to the appropriate response. This is especially the case when the response that would be correct involves a specific fact; the individual often gives a seemingly logical answer that is evasive because the memory of the particular fact is lost.

As Alzheimer's disease progresses, motor unrest follows. The person may be agitated and unable to sit still, or may wander and get lost. The onset of total intellectual dullness may occur next; the person is apathetic and seems to have lost all memory, both short and long-term. The individual may at this point become completely disoriented and may lose all

*g*lossary
confabulation —
Making up stories;
from the word "fable."

ability to communicate. The last phase of illness, shortly before death, involves urinary incontinence. The duration of Alzheimer's disease varies from a few years to almost a decade.

The symptoms of Pick's disease, which is much rarer than Alzheimer's, are similar, and the two can be differentiated with brain scans: instead of widespread shrinking, those with Pick's disease show localized atrophy of the frontal lobe of the brain. On autopsy, it does not show the typical senile plaques and neurological tangles characteristic of Alzheimer's disease. People with Pick's disease are more likely to be manic and obsessive, and show sexually inappropriate behaviors, fits of rage, and language dysfunction. Pick's disease appears to be genetic (Crook, 1987).

Parkinson's disease, which may affect as many as 250,000 persons, mostly in later life, is a neurological problem that affects movement; those with it have a characteristically flat affect: their faces are expressionless and masklike. They walk with a shuffle, and some have a shake or tremor that appears first in the hands: there is a particular "pill-rolling" hand mo-

---

Illustration 8.13. Late-Onset Alzheimer's Disease

"One can never be quite certain when or how Alzheimer's will begin. We often speak of it as being a disease of late life, which indeed it is. We know that there are some cases that begin quite early, and we often think of the early onset cases as being familial. It turns out, however, that late onset cases (after age 65) can be familial as well. That is illustrated by an experience I had when a colleague of mine, a professor emeritus in neurology at Harvard, brought his wife to see me. She was, I think, about 87 years old at that time, and his chief compliant was that she could no longer help him out by doing their 1040 tax form. I thought that was curious and amusing because I had once unsuccessfully tried to do the form myself. Indeed, my colleague admitted that he couldn't do the taxes and had always relied on his wife to do theirs.

"But he had correctly identified a change in her mental status. Besides the tax form example, he gave me a number of others where she simply wasn't performing as she had been a few years before. It became clear that indeed the lady had a very subtle, very early dementia. When I asked about the family history, my colleague said that he had played cards with his mother-in-law, an excellent bridge player, each fortnight for decades. But at age 93, she began reneging on occasions, and sometimes mis-bidding. By the time she was 95, she was quite demented, and she died in a nursing home just short of her 100th birthday. It turned out that another of her daughters, my patient's sister, developed this disease around age 85.

"So, if my patient's mother had died in a car accident at 93 after beating everyone at bridge the night before, we certainly would have thought, "Well, there's one case where we can say it wasn't inherited from the mother's side," when in point of fact, the mother did have Alzheimer's disease. We obtained brain tissue from the mother who had died way back in 1959 at close to 100 years old. She had flagrant Alzheimer's. So, we now know that Alzheimer's can be genetic not just when the onset is in middle life, but even when it appears in the very elderly."

From Selkoe (1993, p. 11).

tion characteristic of people with Parkinson's disease. It is progressive, and is caused by degeneration of the neurons in the upper midbrain. About 30 to 50% of people with Parkinson's disease become demented, and the symptoms and course of the dementia are said to be difficult to distinguish from dementia of the Alzheimer's type. It is possible for the conditions to coexist (Rajput, Rozdilksy, & Rajput, 1990). It appears that Parkinson's disease is not genetic but may be in response to environmental factors.

About 15% of dementias in later life are the result of multi-infarct or vascular dementia, which literally is the death of portions of the brain due to small strokes or insufficient blood supply. It has been estimated that in about 25% of cases, multi-infarct or vascular dementia coexists with dementia of the Alzheimer's type (Crook, 1987). In multi-infarct dementia without Alzheimer's, the course of the illness is typically an abrupt onset and "stepwise" one, rather than gradual, decline in cognitive ability. By no means are all stroke victims demented, and many individuals affected by multi-infarct dementia have areas of cognitive ability that are left intact. The condition has a fluctuating course. Rehabilitation is a possibility with multi-infarct dementia as the brain learns to take over functions that have been lost. Controlling hypertension in the middle years of life is by far the most successful way to prevent multi-infarct dementia (Sands & Meredith, 1992). When it is left untreated, those with it usually survive for only two or three years after diagnosis.

Survival ultimately is an important issue for all persons with a cognitive impairment in later life. In a Swedish study of 324 persons aged 84 to 90, more than half of those with a moderate or severe rating for cognitive impairment had died by the end of two years, compared to only 18% of those who had been rated as normal. The degree of impairment was shown to be progressive over time and was related to likelihood of dying (Johansson, Zarit, & Berg, 1992). Another study that followed older persons with a cognitive impairment over the course of two years found that those with an organic dementia were 2.5 times more likely to die than those who had been diagnosed with a major depression only (Hoch et al., 1993). This has been confirmed by other researchers: cognitive impairment predicts mortality, and organic impairment is a more certain predictor than affective disorder (Arfken, Lichtenberg, & Tancer, 1999).

The Developmentally Disabled Elderly

People with developmental disabilities used to die in early or middle adulthood—often in state hospitals or other institutions. Better medical care and community services have lengthened their period of independent life. We are now starting to see people with a developmental disability live into old age (Holland, 1998).

Developmental disabilities are usually defined as chronic, disabling

$g$lossary

cerebral palsy — A group of neurological conditions resulting in impaired movement, usually caused by injury to the brain before or during birth. People with cerebral palsy often have severe speech problems and difficulty in muscle coordination; they may also have seizures or the inability to see, hear, or learn.

autism — "Absorption in self-centered mental activity (as daydreams, fantasies, delusions, and hallucinations) especially when accompanied by marked withdrawal from reality" (*Webster's Ninth New Collegiate Dictionary*, 1988). Those severely affected may withdraw into themselves and display instances of repetitive, unusual, or aggressive behavior. Constant rocking, scratching, or chewing on a finger are examples.

epilepsy — Abnormal electrical discharges in the brain that result in seizures and muscle convulsions as well as partial or total loss of consciousness.

MR/DD (Network) — Multicounty agencies supported by federal funding that provide services to the developmentally (*continued next page*)

conditions that have their onset prior to adulthood and that will last life-long. Mental retardation, *cerebral palsy*, *autism*, and *epilepsy* are examples. Custodial care was the norm one or two generations ago. People with disabilities now have supports allowing them to live more independent lives in the community.

A particular problem they have, however, is the death of family. This is especially troublesome for aged parents who have been providing care for their disabled adult child. They have great anxiety over what will happen after they die.

In this section, we will look at this dual issue: aging of people with disabilities and the aging of their parents. We'll also explore some public policy options and look toward what the future may hold.

Generally, we think of a developmental disability as either a physical or mental disability from the time of birth rather than something caused by disease, but this is not true in every case. To be designated as a developmental disability under the Federal legislation (the Developmental Disabilities Act of 1984), it must:

1. Be the result of a mental or physical impairment (or both)
2. Occur prior to age 22
3. Be likely to continue throughout the person's life
4. Cause the person to need specialized treatment
5. Result in functional limitation in at least three of these areas: self care, self direction, economic independence, learning, mobility, communication, or independent living.

In other words, these are chronic disabilities that began early in life, have little prospect of a cure, and are serious enough to threaten the person's independence. Generally, the developmental disabilities are grouped into five categories.

Mental retardation accounts for about 80% of those who have a developmental disability. The literature in service delivery often shortens or abbreviates the beginning letter of conditions, so that it is not uncommon to see references to "DD individuals" (developmentally disabled people), "MR individuals" (persons who are mentally retarded), or even *"MR/DD"* (mentally retarded/developmentally disabled). While spelling out the words in their entirety may seem a bit clumsy, we prefer to use the whole words rather than initials when referring to human beings: the only instance where we will be using "DD" is in reference to the "DD Network," the system of services for persons with one or more of the developmental disabilities.

Mental retardation is a catch-all term that includes a host of conditions, all of which result in a limited ability to learn and put what one has learned to use. Not all mentally retarded persons are the same. Some may be so seriously disabled as to have essentially no functional capacity; others may be living very independent lives with little apparent impairment. There is no single cause of mental retardation; it may be genetic, it may be a result of social or physical deprivation, or an injury to the brain, it may be a result of exposure to environmental pollutants such as the heavy metals (lead or mercury poisoning, for example), or to cocaine or alcohol while in the mother's womb.

Many types of mental retardation do not limit length of life; people may have a life expectancy similar to that of those in the general population. However, one of the most recognizable causes of mental retardation, Down's Syndrome, has until recently been the cause of very limited life. Better treatment has extended the prospect of life for many who used to be expected to die at a young age. Only a few decades ago, people with Down's Syndrome commonly died in their 20s or 30s; it is only recently that many are living into their fifth or even sixth decade of life.

Neurological impairments group disabilities of the brain and central nervous system that result in an impairment of the use and development of language, attention span, memory, muscle control, and the ability to master adaptive behavior. People with a neurological impairment need special care due to problems with muscle control and resultant social or behavioral problems.

Epilepsy results in abnormal electrical discharges within the brain that cause muscle convulsions, seizures, and partial or total loss of consciousness. However, most epileptics are not mentally retarded.

Autism is a disorder of communication and behavior that impairs the way sensory input is taken in. This causes problems in communication and learning as well as social behavior.

Cerebral palsy is really a group of neurological conditions that are associated with injury to the part of the brain that controls movement. It is usually caused by brain damage at the time of birth. People with cerebral palsy commonly have difficulty with fine motor control and balance; their large opposing muscles frequently overpower their counterparts, so the person's arms may be pulled back by the biceps involuntarily, for example, or the legs may kick out in convulsive jerks over which the person has no control.

Birth defects such as spina bifida (a congenital cleft of the vertebral column) might also be called developmental disabilities.

In addition to those listed above, other conditions may technically be developmental disabilities in that they have their onset in childhood, are chronic, and are disabling. Cystic fibrosis, some types of arthritis, and muscular dystrophy are examples. Persons who have brain or spinal injuries in accidents prior to age 22 might also be seen as developmentally disabled. It is possible for a person to have multiple developmental disabilities, cerebral palsy and mental retardation, for example. And individuals with a developmental disability may also have it in combination with other conditions. One survey has indicated that 14.3% of the mentally retarded population also had a mental illness (Eaton & Menolascino, 1982). The main distinction lies in the notion of early onset: most disabilities affecting the older population are only seen in later life: stroke, for example, or dis-

glossary

continued

disabled. Services to people who qualify as having a developmental disability under the definition of the law might include case management, in-home services, group homes, ICF/MR placement, or other services designed to assist in making the person's life as independent as possible in the least restrictive environment.

neurological impairments — A catch-all term that describes a number of conditions—disorders of the brain and central nervous system that impair the use and development of language, understanding, memory, attention span, fine muscle control, or adaptive behavior.

abling heart disease. The developmental disabilities, on the other hand, do not first appear in later life; they are lifelong.

For our purposes, disabling conditions in childhood that result in early death, such as muscular dystrophy, will not be included in our discussion. Instead, we will focus upon two particular populations: one includes the developmentally disabled who live into late life, the other is the aging parents who serve as caretakers of adult children with a developmental disability. As they go through old age and approach death, they have less capacity for the often heavy work of caretaking. And they fear for the future when they can no longer take care of their disabled child.

While it is common to hear that developmentally disabled persons in the past just didn't live long enough to get old, this is not entirely the case. One survey of an institution for the mentally retarded looked at records of patients who were known to have died by the year 1965 (Hamilton & Mestler, 1969). It found a survival rate of 45.1% at age 60 and 28.2% at age 70 among these people who were born at or before the beginning of the twentieth century. So there were at least some mentally retarded people living into later life several generations ago. This was not apparent to most people, however, because most of these people lived in institutions—out of sight.

Although their survival rate is still lower than that of the general population, there can be no doubt that many more people with a developmental disability now live into old age than was true even a few years ago. There are now about 200,000 mentally retarded people aged 60 and above living in the United States. Estimates of the number of people with other developmental disabilities who are getting older vary, but they seem to be much smaller in number.

Studies within the mentally retarded population indicate that those who have the best chances of survival into later life are women, those who

---

Illustration 8.14. Nickie Schmitt

A family named Schmitt lived across the street from us during the 1950s; they had a teen-aged son named Nickie who was developmentally disabled, although we didn't know what to call it at the time. Nickie was mentally retarded, and I can now see that he also had cerebral palsy. Although he could walk, his arms jerked up to his chest convulsively with his palms facing out. Nickie couldn't talk (he made sounds that we thought were more like mumbles than like speech), but he could understand much of what was said to him. He knew enough to not to go out in the street. We knew that he couldn't be toilet trained, but his mother always kept him neat and clean; in fact, he was a handsome boy. We little kids liked Nickie and would call out and wave to him, but we didn't know if it would be all right to go over and play with him, so we didn't. I can't recall that we were ever afraid of him, although we knew he was different. I think we were more afraid for him, because it was obvious that he could easily be injured. Nickie didn't go to school; he stayed in the house or out in his own yard in good weather. Nickie died when he was 19.

This is taken from a series of interviews I've done with aging parents of developmentally disabled adult children:

"My daughter is 46-years-old and has Down's Syndrome. When she was a baby, all the doctors said we should put her in an institution, but we resisted. My late husband and I cared for her at home all these years. She has had cancer and also a stomach obstruction, and all of her food has to be put through a blender in order for her to swallow it. When she was born, they told me not to expect her to live past her teenage years.

She's lovable and happy and especially likes watching TV. I'm really glad for the TV because it gives her some kind of mental stimulation that she wouldn't otherwise get. Left to her own devices, she'd be perfectly happy to sit in the corner all day and fool with a handkerchief.

"I'd like to put her in a group home, but she doesn't want to live anywhere but here with me. She doesn't realize that I'll die some day and then where will we be? I resent that the people who have priority at the group homes are the ones who are getting out of institutions. Here we saved the state all that money by caring for her for all these years, and they don't seem to appreciate it, while people who were in institutions get right into the group homes without being on the waiting list.

We don't have any immediate needs; my greatest fear is what kind of a place she'll have to go when I can't take care of her any longer. My greatest hope is that she'll die before I do."

are ambulatory (not in wheel chairs), those who have less severe retardation, those who do not have Down's Syndrome, and those who live in the community (Walz, Harper, & Wilson, 1986).

Most surveys have found mental decline in later life to be more rapid among the developmentally disabled and that signs of aging have an earlier onset. For this reason, some would argue that a definition of aging at age 60 or even 50 would be more appropriate for the developmentally disabled population.

The Social World of the Disabled

Among older adults, holding on to what they have may be an increasingly dominant life task. Adapting to the changes taking place around them may also be increasingly difficult. How much more of a strain is adaptation to change in later life for the developmentally disabled? In our interviewing with the older parents of people with a developmental disability, an overall message we have heard is the desire to keep things the same, to hold on to what they have for as long as they possibly can. If the individual lives at home with family, the hope is to keep living at home for as long as possible and to put off the prospect of institutionalization for as long as possible. If

failure to thrive — A
syndrome common in
institutionalized
children, now
recognized to be
prevalent among the
institutionalized aged
as well; it involves
undernutrition,
depression, lack of
growth, and higher
rates of illness and
death.

the person is in a group home, the desire is to maintain that placement for as long as possible. If the person works in a sheltered workshop, the prospect of retirement from that activity and taking on other activities may be perceived as a threat. The life changes associated with the prospect of having to enter an institution are viewed as an impending disaster.

In late life, people with a developmental disability face the almost certain prospect of loss of independence: a good group home placement is seen as the very best choice. Going to a nursing home or to a state hospital is seen as distinctly less desirable. At the very worst is the prospect of care breaking down and the developmentally disabled person ending up as homeless (Cohen, 1999). These are real fears: people with developmental problems can readily be seen among the homeless people in American cities.

The message of the institution as being an asylum lingers in memory for many older people. They recall the poor farm or the state asylum as a dumping ground, and they may translate this message into their images of modern care facilities. The treatment of choice for persons with disabilities in this country up until very recently has been to put them away. In fact, some critics charge that social policy was that when a social problem was identified, a building was erected for it. No matter that orphanages and prisons and asylums didn't work very well; at least the people were out of sight and out of mind.

By mid-century, it had become obvious that orphanages were a social failure. Children raised in institutions exhibited what is called *failure to thrive* syndrome (Bullard, Glaser, Hegarty, & Pivchik, 1967). It was demonstrated that children with failure to thrive syndrome did not gain weight, were shorter, had lesser ability to learn, were likelier to become ill, and had a higher mortality rate. Orphan asylums closed down during the 1950s and 1960s and the emphasis was changed to foster care and adoption.

Similarly, it was seen that mental hospitals often make people worse. Especially for long-term patients who were receiving no real care, the mental hospital truly could have been seen as an asylum where patients in the back wards were abandoned. Mentally ill and mentally retarded people were warehoused in pitifully inadequate state hospitals. Mental hospitals often were overcrowded and under-staffed, and the best of them often offered little more than custodial care (Luchins, 1988).

The rate of mental hospitalization for persons with an emotional illness began to decline in 1945, and the actual number of people in mental hospitals in the United States has been going down since the year 1955 (U.S. Bureau of the Census, 1998b). Outpatient treatment with family support has been found to be much more effective than isolating people in strange environments that may have contributed to their problems rather than making them better.

In more recent years, a team of nurse researchers has drawn the parallel between failure to thrive among institutionalized children and a similar syndrome among institutionalized older people (Braun, Wykle, & Cowling, 1988). Undernutrition, physical and cognitive problems, and depression are hallmarks of old people in institutions. Because of this, we now have a national policy of trying to keep the elderly out of institutions and to provide services that are effective alternatives; the ideal is to maintain independence for as long as possible.

This is no less true for the aging individual who has one or more of the developmental disabilities, but maintaining an independent lifestyle could be seen as a much more formidable challenge. Not only are people facing life challenges with fewer resources, they may also have lived in a very restricted social world for many years. And, they may have memories, often unpleasant memories, of past experiences with living in an institution. They well may fear losing present independence and adapting to unwelcome changes in their living environment.

Most developmentally disabled people who are now in their 40s and 50s grew up in a social world where "different" meant "deviant." There was—and still is—a stigma attached to having a child with a disability. This may have been even more the case years ago. Pressures to put disabled children into institutions often resulted in long-term separation from families. Public schools had neither the interest nor the programs available to help keep developmentally disabled children integrated in the community. Many developmentally disabled people spent the early years of their lives in hospitals and state or private institutions. Many, of course, continue to be institutionalized, especially those without family who are able to assist in their care. Those with especially severe disabilities cannot be cared for at home, however willing the family is to provide care, if their needs exceed the family's ability to provide care for them.

In the early 1960s, the Administration of President John F. Kennedy brought new energy to programs and treatment for persons with a developmental disability, in part because Kennedy had a mentally retarded sister, and family members were familiar with the issues and problems that disabled people confront. The Kennedy family, for example, has been in-

---

Illustration 8.16. News Account: Retarded Man Shot by Mother

"Last October, a 51-year-old suburban man with mental retardation was shot by his 81-year-old mother. The mother, who was in poor health, attempted to murder her son and take her own life. Fortunately, both were found by a neighbor and survived. This tragedy occurred because the mother feared her son would not be properly taken care of after she died. Although this action was extreme, her plight reflects the concerns of many older parents caring for offspring with developmental disabilities at home. Because they have not planned for their child's future, there is often a crisis when they die or become too infirm to provide care."

From Factor & Haller (1989, p. 3).

Medicaid — A welfare
program in the United
States that pays
hospital, medical, and
nursing home costs
for those unable to pay
for their own care.

ICF/MR —
Intermediate care
facilities for the
mentally retarded;
specialized nursing
homes.

deinstitutionalization
— A movement that
began in the United
States in the 1960s
and 70s to provide
services in the
community that would
allow mentally ill and
developmentally
disabled people to be
released from state
hospitals and to lead
more normal lives in
the community.

Medicaid Waiver — A
plan agreed to by the
U.S. Health Care
Financing
Administration and
many of the states
whereby Medicaid
dollars that might have
gone to pay for
nursing home care
can be used to provide
in-home services to
help keep people out
of nursing homes.

strumental in promoting the Special Olympics as a vehicle for enhanced self-esteem among the disabled.

In 1962, a study supported by the White House recommended movement away from institutional care for the developmentally disabled. Custodial care would be replaced by active treatment and rehabilitation leading to lifelong development. People would be released from the back wards and reintegrated into the community. Group homes would replace asylums. Supports for families would allow more people to remain at home.

After President Kennedy's death in November of 1963, the Administration of Lyndon Johnson continued efforts to formulate and pass through Congress a host of social programs to benefit the poor, elderly, unemployed, and disabled. As a part of this Great Society movement, legislation was passed to provide services to developmentally disabled people to help them remain independent. At this time, the **Medicaid** program was passed into law; it provides reimbursement for doctors and hospitals caring for people unable to pay for their own care. Funding and regulations have since been implemented that provide for services to developmentally disabled children through the public schools. With this combination of programs and funding sources, it became more of a possibility to keep a retarded or physically disabled child at home with support from service agencies and the schools. Day centers and sheltered workshops for adults with a developmental disability grew up, as did specialized transportation programs and other community-based services.

The MR/DD (Mentally Retarded/Developmentally Disabled) Network, a federally-funded system of community programs offered by the states, now provides a fairly effective program of case management. Adults with a disability in many instances have a case manager employed by a community program; the case manager's responsibility is to assist in keeping the individual independent and functioning. Case managers orchestrate available programs, group facilities, and medical care in an effort to keep developmentally disabled people out of institutions. For those who cannot make it in the community, a number of **ICF/MR** (intermediate care facilities for the mentally retarded—nursing homes especially designed for those with disabilities) have been established (Lakin, Hill, White, Wright, & Bruininks, 1989; Redjali & Radick, 1988).

The real growth of the **deinstitutionalization** movement began in the early 1970s. It became clear that it was possible to move some people out of state hospitals, where care was not appropriate for many and was actually harmful for some. Getting people out of hospitals and back into the community meant developing a system of group homes and supportive services.

Keeping people independent who were already in the community became a better possibility. Special education classes in schools helped to keep children who might otherwise have had no real education or training more in the mainstream of community life. In many states, it is now possible, through **Medicaid Waiver** programs, to use dollars that might otherwise have gone for institutional care to instead provide in-home services that help to keep people out of institutions.

glossary

OBRA — The Omnibus Budget Reconciliation Act of 1987.

There is, unfortunately, a less benefical side to the deinstitutionalization movement. In some states, it was seen that pressures on the state budget could be relieved, often considerably, by emptying and closing down state institutions. It was reasoned that 100% of the cost of care came from the state budget when a person was in a state hospital, but only 40% of the costs came from the state budget for persons out in the community (Medicaid provides 60% of the funding from federal sources and requires the states to provide the other 40%). And, it is often cheaper to keep people in settings other than state hospitals—in nursing homes for example.

In the early 1970s, many retarded and mentally ill people who had been deinstitutionalization from state hospitals wound up in nursing homes, on Medicaid, and received no more treatment than they had back at the state hospital. This influx of "different" people also often caused objections from older nursing home residents who saw the disabled and emotionally ill as less than desirable companions.

Regulations under **OBRA** (the Omnibus Budget Reconciliation Act of 1987) have since restricted nursing homes from admitting Medicaid patients who have a primary diagnosis of mental retardation. However, these regulations are sometimes bent or disregarded altogether; this is especially true when there seems like there is nowhere else for an individual to go. It is possible, for example, for a retarded person to be admitted with a primary diagnosis of "organic brain syndrome" or Alzheimer's disease, thus getting around OBRA regulations.

Further, it is often the case that inadequate or fragmented services in the community make it next to impossible to keep some disabled persons independent. The Aging Network, the system of community-based services for older people in the general population, is often ill-prepared to assist in the delivery of services to the developmentally disabled. (The Network is discussed at length in Chapter 14).

Service Goals

The concept of rehabilitation involves restoration of functional ability and moving the disabled individual toward independent living. Central to the philosophy of rehabilitation in services to the developmentally disabled of all ages is *active treatment*. This gets away from passive or custodial care and involves an active, organized effort to make the most of each individual's potential. Improving health, life skills, functional abilities, and mental health are all goals of active treatment. An individual plan of programs and services leading toward achieving measurable goals is central to these goals. People served by the MR/DD Network are supposed to have an active treatment plan that leads to rehabilitation goals. This plan is to integrate avail-

> **Illustration 8.17. Does Everyone Want to Be Independent?**
>
> "An often neglected factor needing consideration independent of specific setting characteristics is the desire of the client being considered for alternative placement. Clients who have been institutionalized for years develop routines, adjust to the safety of the institution, create a social network, and develop a sense of permanency and stability. All too often, major decisions that affect a client's life situation are made by persons other than the individual that the change will most directly affect. The disruption of a life situation caused by relocating the target individual may be severe. . . . Professionals must be aware of the possibility of displacement shock and develop means to alleviate its impact."
>
> From Malone (1990, p. 12).

able social and health services and to piece together the means toward achieving maximum independence in the least restrictive environment.

These service goals for the developmentally disabled individual are accompanied by a series of goals that come under the heading of family support. This is supposed to be a comprehensive range of services for the families of those with a developmental disability to strengthen their ability to provide care at home for the disabled individual. Some success has been achieved in training family members to be informal case managers, helping the disabled to receive available supports and services in the community (Seltzer, 1992). Family support services include advocacy, information services, home care, crisis intervention, respite care, and supportive coun-

> **Illustration 8.18. Issues in Service Delivery**
>
> "Outliving one's parents also raises the issue of the need to transfer guardianship for the developmentally disabled, assuming the parents were the designated guardians. This transfer of guardianship comes at a sensitive time, when the parent's estate is probably being probated. Any sort of inheritance will also complicate the individual's transfer income and medical insurance status.
>
> "For developmentally disabled adults in residential care, their impending geriatric status tests the preparedness of the setting to address these needs. Most community care systems have been child- and young adult-oriented. Few are prepared and perhaps even interested in dealing with geriatric considerations. . . . There is also the similar question of the preparedness of traditional geriatric services to serve the aging developmentally disabled person. Neither aging network agencies nor nursing homes appear anxious to deal with the different and complex needs of MR/DD clients."
>
> From Walz, Harper, & Wilson (1986, p. 626).

seling. This is important, as family caregivers are under high levels of stress, often with little positive reinforcement (Greenberg, Seltzer, & Greenley, 1993).

Clearly, these goals of active treatment, independence in a least restrictive environment, and family supports are in danger of breaking down in later life. The individual who has been maintained at home with the help of family and supportive services cannot continue to be maintained at home forever. Developmentally disabled persons may outlive their parents, and the loss of a caregiver often is devastating. Fortunately, there is some evidence that mentally retarded older people, at least, may adjust to placement in long-term care as well or better than older people in the general population (Cotton, Sisson, & Starr, 1981).

A problem noted in Chapter 1 was the increasing pressure of the expanding population of aging people on the limited number of available nursing homes, and especially the limited number of people available to work in those nursing homes. It would seem that limitations in community services for the developmentally disabled are a fact of life, and that more and more of the aging developmentally disabled will become candidates for long-term institutional care in nursing homes in the future as they outlive their family caregivers. Strains on the informal support networks of the aging developmentally disabled seem to indicate that increased pressure upon already overburdened institutions of long-term care are pretty much inevitable. About the best option for the short term is the development of specialized ICF/DD institutions, where the care of the developmentally disabled elderly is more likely to have appropriate goals, and the personnel are better prepared to deal with special problems. Re-institutionalization of persons once they have successfully adjusted to life in the community, however, might be seen as particularly unfortunate.

In summary, the population of developmentally disabled is growing dramatically. More and more infants with a disability now survive, and more and more people who once might have been expected to die in their teens are now living into old age. This is not necessarily due to any particular breakthroughs in medicine, but is simply a result of the application of good care principles to the developmentally disabled. Many in this population are difficult to serve medically; they are more prone to infections, certain kinds of cancers, and respiratory illness. Many are vulnerable to health problems related to their disabling condition, and providing good health maintenance should be seen as the first of a series of goals for people with a developmental disability.

The concept of "habilitation" takes the individual's needs and wants into account and might be seen as particularly applicable to older disabled people (Raia, 1992). While it is desirable and necessary for the younger developmentally disabled person to have an active treatment plan, some older people with developmental disabilities indicate that they find additional rehabilitation efforts to be exhausting. It would seem that there comes a time in life to ease up a little and relax. Similarly, some aging people who have worked in sheltered workshops have expressed the desire to retire. These are new issues for the service community to address, as only a few decades ago people in day programs and sheltered workshops didn't usually live into retirement age.

Clearly, families who are at all able to provide care at home should be given every possible support in order to assist them in continuing to hang on. In an ideal world, aging parents of people with developmental disabilities should be given some choice in working out the best possible placement for their child when this becomes a necessity. Unfortunately, the situation now is that there is usually a crisis, there are no choices, and the individual winds up in whatever facility is available at the moment.

Integration of the programs of services available through the MR/DD Network and the Aging Network is something that is happening currently. There are problems associated with the lack of training among the DD personnel in working with the aged and of the Aging Network personnel in working with the developmentally disabled, but these are being overcome with cross-training programs. What remains unanswered is the ability of the Aging Network to take on much of the load in providing services to the developmentally disabled aging population, and the willingness of other older people to accept the disabled into their programs.

Care Issues

In this final section of the chapter, we discuss care issues that apply to older people with cognitive difficulties, including the developmentally disabled—those with Down's syndrome are much more likely, for example, to develop Alzheimer's disease by age 45—as well as older people in general who are depressed, delirious, or have an organic cognitive degenerative disorder.

In many instances, there are few risk factors or preventive measures for causes of organic mental illness in later life, other than the control of high blood pressure, as already mentioned. In actuality, there is little that can be done other than that in terms of prevention. For those with a genetic predisposition to Alzheimer's or Pick's disease, reassurance that they are not necessarily certain to develop the illness may help; their odds are just higher than those with no family history of the particular illness. Other than people with Down's syndrome, there are no groups that can be said to be definitely fated to develop Alzheimer's. In a few instances, the few risk factors that can be identified, such as lack of education or earlier exposure to environmental toxins, seemingly make little difference by very late life (Katzman, 1993).

This is not the case with the affective or mood disorders. Here, prevention and identification of higher risk groups might lead to intervention. A report from the Institute of Psychiatry at the University of London, for example, notes that psychosocial distress often follows negative life events and stressful environments, especially among those who lack social support networks (Murray, 1992). Given that cognitive disorders often predict physical decline and, perhaps, institutionalization, it is important to do what can be done (Colantonio, Kasl, & Ostfeld, 1992). This is especially the case with those who appear to be at the greatest risk; there is a wealth of research, for example, demonstrating the association in late life between emotional illness, poverty, and homelessness (Cohen, 1999).

In terms of post-traumatic stress disorder, a study from Finland is illustrative. A total of 562 World War II-era combat veterans were compared with controls who were veterans but who had not seen combat. Both groups were followed for 25 years. A significant association was found for those who had been in nine or more battles with such things as depression, sleeplessness, paranoia, hallucinations, schizophrenia, and other forms of mental distress (Molgaard et al., 1991). People with a history of such stressful events in their lives might be seen as prospects for preventive measures.

It would seem obvious that those individuals with fewer social supports and more frequent and serious life events should be prospects for intervention. Those with an alcohol-related disorder, for example, are definitely more likely to be demented in later life (Rains & Ditzler, 1993). Intervention, unfortunately, usually depends on having concerned caregivers, and a lack of a social network is predictive of alcoholism and depression, as well a host of other disorders (Adams & Waskel, 1993). Self-esteem, self-rated health, morale, life satisfaction, and internal control all seem to rest on a secure relationship with a confidant. The removal of one's confidant can lead to hopelessness, depression, and, in some instances, suicide (Blazer, 1991; Hayslip, Lopez, & Nation, 1991).

So, we are faced with the dilemma that isolated people and people under stress are more likely to experience an affective disorder in later life. But the fact that they are isolated and lack social supports may in fact be the cause of their emotional distress. And, they often are seemingly invisible people; they most likely have lost their confidant and in many instances have no one else to turn to for emotional support.

Further, there is the problem of resources. We in fact have not done a good job in the United States of providing services for either older people with mental health problems or people with a developmental disability. Given this record, preventive efforts in terms of identification of those at greatest risk for developing problems in later life might seem to be an all but unattainable goal.

Providing supports for caregivers might be more likely. Spouses, children, and friends of older persons with mental illness carry a heavy burden. They provide by far the greatest amount of the services that mentally ill older people receive, are under constant stress themselves, and they often need assistance in coping. Older couples in particular should be seen as candidates for assistance. Often the caregiving spouse is faced with his or her own health problems and declining energy. Partners intimately in-

Illustration 8.19. Advice from a Social Worker on Coping with Alzheimer's

Get a thorough, multidisciplinary diagnosis for your loved one. Many physicians and hospitals are not equipped to do a full diagnostic procedure. A thorough diagnostic evaluation ensures identification of any reversible causes of dementia and will help the family plan effectively for the future.

Plan for the legal and financial future of your loved one and yourself. As the disease progresses, your loved one will not be able to make competent legal and financial decisions for him/herself. Many issues are easier and less costly if dealt with while your loved one can participate in the planning. Both you and your loved one should at least have Durable Powers of Attorney (one for health care decisions and one for financial/legal matters) on record.

Educate yourself so that you can educate health and social service personnel. There are many myths about dementing illness; however, accurate information and resource materials are available.

Develop a good working relationship with your patient's attending physician. Be willing to work to educate your doctor, but also be willing to change doctors if yours is not responsive.

Learn about and use community resources. Diagnostic centers, day care programs, support groups, nursing services, and other services will be valuable for support, and will help make it easier to cope with Alzheimer's disease.

You don't have to do it alone, so don't. It will help you and your loved one if you develop partnerships with others. Look to your family, your friends, and neighbors. Share your information with them. Many of them would like to help; let them. Now is the time you need them.

Take care of yourself. It is tempting to always put the patient's needs ahead of your own. Remember that your loved one needs you to be healthy—physically and emotionally. If you want to be there for your loved one, you must take care of yourself. Keep doing things you enjoy and remember to laugh.

Make arrangements for regular time off (respite) for yourself. Family members and friends may be willing to relieve you for a few hours on a regular basis. Perhaps the best option is to enroll your loved one in an adult day care program. Or you may have to hire someone to come in to relieve you.

Attend family support groups. You are not alone! It helps to talk with people in similar situations. They will understand your problems and may have useful suggestions. For further information on where you may attend a coping/support group, contact the Alzheimer's office for a listing of local groups.

Learn creative problem-solving techniques. Your loved one will engage in behaviors that distress you at times (not bathing, wandering, not sleeping, etc.). Rarely will there be a single or simple answer to the problem. Some behaviors you will simply have to accept. Others will require you to think of possible causes and experiment with various solutions. Be patient with yourself and your loved one and be willing to experiment with possible solutions."

From Hart (1992).

fluence each others' quality of life. One study in fact found that the husband's health directly and strongly predicts the wife's mental health (Simonsick, 1993).

The gerontological literature, especially during the past several years, has seen the emergence of many studies of caregiver burden. We will not review them at length: they're pretty obvious. Those who care for a family member who is depressed or demented are under severe stress. A study from the School of Social Work at the University of Wisconsin sums it up: a group of outpatients, average age 74, who had Alzheimer's disease were surveyed along with their caregivers. Both patients and their caregivers reported the presence of interpersonal family stress in a number of areas, especially in terms of disrupted relationships, anger, and frustration. Personality changes associated with the disease were especially upsetting, as was the typical change in sleep patterns (Kramer, Gibson, & Teri, 1992).

"Sundown syndrome" is a term that describes increased agitation and delirium among older demented patients at the end of the day. It is particularly irritating to caregivers who are awakened at night by the demented person or who are anxious about the individual wandering or becoming endangered (Exum, Phelps, Nabers, & Osborne, 1993). In particular, disoriented persons are much more prone to falling, and injury from a serious fall may be the event that triggers institutionalization (van Dijk, Meulenberg, van de Sande, & Habbema, 1993).

People with dementia may also engage in abusive or violent behavior—or be the recipients of abuse. One study examined the relationship between abusive behavior and dementia among 342 demented individuals and their caregivers. Thirty-three of the caregivers reported they had physically abused the patient they were caring for; these were the caretakers that had been providing care for more years and who cared for patients who functioned at a lower level. Reversing the direction of abusive or violent behavior, 92 caregivers (27%) reported that the patient was abusive toward them; they in turn were more likely to direct abusive behavior back toward the patient (Coyne, Reichman, & Berbig, 1993). Another study followed 184 people with Alzheimer's disease and their caregivers; it found that 15.8% of the patients had been violent in the year since they had been diagnosed, and that 5.4% of the caregivers had been violent toward the patient. Caregiver depression was predictive of violence (Paveza et al., 1992). The most difficult behaviors occur during bathing (Burgener, Jirovec, Murrell, & Barton, 1992).

Having a disabled or a demented family member is a major life crisis—one that, unlike most crises, is not resolved in a short period of time. Caring for a person with dementia is difficult not only because they are prone to personality change and thus become a different person, but also because the deterioration caused by the illness goes on for many years. Working with a person with Alzheimer's disease or any of the dementing disorders demands a great deal of patience on the part of caregivers.

In terms of interaction with a demented individual, several things have been found to be more effective. People with dementia should never be treated in a harsh or abrupt manner. Even if they have difficulty understanding what's being said to them, they will often be able to pick up the tone of the conversation. Shouting will always result in a negative response from people who may already be agitated. Most will respond well to warmth and loving attention, especially touching. Also, many people with dementia have lucid moments when they seemingly understand things clearly. It is best to try to maintain eye contact when speaking to a demented individual, and to speak slowly and clearly. Part of the frustration of caring for a person with dementia is that they seem to constantly need attention; they respond poorly to isolation. One study emphasizes the soothing influence of music on Alzheimer's patients (Lord & Garner, 1993). And, people who are less in touch with their environment always do better in familiar surroundings.

As the condition degenerates, nursing home care is an inevitable prospect. This is a step that no family is eager to take. Most of our efforts at service delivery to the aged focus on keeping people out of institutions and providing alternatives to nursing home care. Contrary to stereotype, families do not "dump" their elders in nursing homes. In fact, the opposite tendency is often the case: they go to the end of their rope and beyond to do almost anything to avoid that final step. Almost all confronted with such a decision see it as a family crisis (Brody, 1985). It is a sad, but usually necessary, final outcome to dementing illness.

We will be discussing the dynamics of institutional care and placement further in the next chapter, but for now, we should recognize that for many families, it is inevitable to turn to nursing home care for their demented family member. Caregivers burn out. It has been shown that perceptions of caregiver burden is a predictor of institutionalization; the caregiver ultimately cannot continue to devote every waking hour to someone else's care (Cohen et al., 1993a).

When all forms of outside support and community-based services are not enough and the decision to turn to institutional care has been made, some deliberate planning is called for. If possible, it would be best to take the individual to several different care facilities to see if they have any input as to a preference. This is not always possible, of course, if the person is seriously demented and cannot express his or her wishes. However, just letting people feel that they have some control over where they will be living can have positive psychological effects (Thorson, 1988). But if the individual is unable to participate in decision-making, the primary caregiver should still shop around to look at the various features of different facilities, talk to the staff, and determine which environment seems best. It should be remembered that this will be the patient's home, and that comfort at this point is more important than high-tech amenities.

Preparation for the move might include several visits to the facility, perhaps taking a meal there or participating in a variety of the care center's

---

Illustration 8.20. Advice for Nurses on Helping Patients Cope with Change

---

- Place identifying labels on the patient's room, bathroom, and closet doors.
- Ask the family to bring in some familiar personal items, such as a bedspread, slippers, family pictures, and so forth.
- Provide structured routines, based as closely on the patient's normal daily routine as possible (you may need to ask family members for input).
- Always approach a patient with Alzheimer's disease from the front and move slowly so you don't startle him. Never touch him without speaking first.
- Be sure he's wearing his glasses and hearing aid if he needs them.
- Begin conversations with orienting information. For example, you'd identify yourself, call the patient by his name, and explain what you're going to do or want him to do.
- Talk with him at his level of ability—remembering to remain respectful at all times. Always use a calm and gentle voice.
- When giving the patient directions, use short, simple sentences with clear and familiar words. Be sure to give only one direction at a time, and allow time for him to respond.
- To give him a sense of personal control and maintain his self-esteem, offer realistic choices whenever possible, and praise him when he completes a task successfully.

From Lewis (1993, p. 75).

---

programs prior to the move itself. It helps to get the patient familiar and used to the environment.

Conclusion

Cognitive impairment among older people is usually a grave, life-disrupting problem. Although there may be disagreement as to how many older people are demented, there can be no doubt that the number itself is increasing as more and more people survive to very late life. Dementia affects relatively few of the young old, but it becomes much more serious among the oldest old; about a third of those 85 and older have some type of cognitive impairment.

Dementia is most frequently caused by Alzheimer's disease, a degenerative, fatal condition that usually lasts from about three to ten years. It is not transmissible—one cannot "catch" Alzheimer's disease. There is evidence that there is a genetic predisposition for dementia of the Alzheimer's type, as there is for some of the other degenerative neurological conditions of later life. This does not, however, appear to be related to a dominant gene, and children of people with Alzheimer's are not necessarily fated to get it, although they are somewhat more likely to develop it than others.

There is no known cure, nor are we aware of any preventative measures that can be taken to avoid it.

Other forms of dementia caused by head trauma or heavy metal poisoning are obviously things that one tries to avoid in earlier life. Abuse of alcohol or crack cocaine are inevitably dementing over time and are, of course, avoidable. The second-leading cause of organic cognitive impairment in later life is multi-infarct dementia or vascular dementia, and it can be prevented by control of hypertension.

Affective disorders such as major depression and bipolar disorder also can be dementing in later life. Unlike most of the organic dementias, depression can be treated with some success and should always be considered as a problem with older people who are showing cognitive deficits. Depression is frequently associated with physical illness as well as breakdown of the social network. Organically demented people are often depressed, and the depression can be treated even if the dementia cannot.

Delirium, or pseudodementia, is often reversible and should be considered before concluding that the individual is organically demented. Signs of delirium include reduced awareness, incoherent speech, disturbed sleep, decreased level of activity, and disorientation of memory. It can be caused by misuse of medications, drug or alcohol abuse, any illness or infection, dehydration, hypothermia or hyperthermia, changes in the environment, malnutrition, social trauma, or heart attack. It is characterized by a recent onset of symptoms, rather than the gradual building up of symptoms more typical of organic dementia.

People with schizophrenia live into later life as well. While there are few cases of new schizophrenia that develop in old age, those who have it and survive into later life are often burned out and need institutional care. This is particularly the case when community mental health programs can no longer help maintain them outside of institutions; eventually, their care networks and social supports break down. In some instances, there is a decrease in symptoms; some older schizophrenics may tend to mellow out late in life.

Institutional care should be seen as an option for those with organic degenerative disorders. The prospect of rehabilitation, however, should always be considered as a possibility for those with conditions such as multi-infarct dementia and depression. For those with delirium who are not in fact organically demented, it would be a shame to turn to institutional care when the underlying condition might be successfully treated.

Finally, most older people have no real prospect of becoming senile. Conditions influencing cognitive ability affect only a fraction of the older population. Signs of forgetfulness usually are not serious symptoms or the onset of organic dementia. While there is some cognitive decline in normal aging, measurable decline is usually not seen until the eighth decade of life, and even then, reserve mental capacity for the great majority of older persons is such that mental decline does not represent a serious difficulty. We should also remember that there is plasticity of intellectual abilities in later life—people can still learn (Baltes, Kuhl, & Sowarka, 1992; Raykov, 1995). People who continue to use their mental abilities are most likely to maintain them into later life.

Questions for Discussion

1. Describe the principal differences between organic and affective mental disorders.
2. What signs of cognitive deficits have you seen among older people you know?
3. Do you have any friends with a developmental disability? Describe what their condition is and how it affects them.
4. How do you remember people in your school felt toward the kids who were in special education classes?
5. What forms of care would you think are best for older people with dementia?
6. If you have ever been depressed, describe how your mood might have been disorienting.
7. In what ways do you think older developmentally disabled people differ from other older people who are disabled?
8. Put yourself into the situation of a disabled person. What would you want out of life? In what ways would your world be different?
9. Why do people consider nursing homes to be a last resort for care?
10. Are you aware of any services of local community mental health centers?
11. Why do you suppose older people in the general population might resist integrating the developmentally disabled into their programs?
12. If you were destined to have a degenerative organic mental disorder in later life, would you want to know it?

Sources of Further Information

Over a dozen brief publications on a variety of mental disorders can be obtained at no cost from:

Consumer Information Center
P.O. Box 100
Pueblo, CO 81002

More detailed publications on 95 different aspects of mental illness, many of which are also available in Spanish, can be ordered from the National Institute of Mental Health. Request a catalog from:

Information Resources & Inquiries Branch, Room 7C-02
Office of Scientific Information
National Institute of Mental Health
5600 Fishers Lane
Rockville, MD 20857

A wide variety of publications on Alzheimer's disease is available from two different sources:

Alzheimer's Disease Education and Referral Center
P.O. Box 8250
Silver Spring, MD 20907
800/438-4380

Alzheimer's Association
919 North Michigan Avenue
Suite 1000
Chicago, IL 60611
800/272-3900

Publications on Parkinson's disease can be received from:

Parkinson's Disease Foundation
650 West 168th Street
New York, NY 10032-9982
800/457-6676

One of the state offices in the MR/DD Network that has done the most in terms of the aging developmentally disabled population is the one in New York:

New York State Office of Mental Retardation and Developmental
    Disabilities
44 Holland Avenue
Albany, NY 12229-1000

There is a federally-funded Clearinghouse on Aging and Developmental Disabilities; they publish a quarterly newsletter entitled "ADDVANTAGE." Write to:

The Rehabilitation Research and Training Center Consortium
    on Aging and Developmental Disabilities
Department of Disability and Human Development
University of Illinois at Chicago
1640 West Roosevelt Rd.
Chicago, IL 60608-6904

Information on available publications can be found by writing the following organizations:

The Arc
P. O. Box 1047
Arlington, TX 76004
817/261-6003

National Resource Center on Homelessness and Mental Illness
Policy Research Associates, Inc.
262 Delaware Avenue
Delmar, NY 12054

National Mental Health Consumer Self Help Clearinghouse
311 S. Juniper St., Suite 1000
Philadelphia, PA 19107

The Mental Illness Education Project
P.O Box 470813
Brookline Village, MA 02147
617/621-9700

National Alliance for the Mentally Ill
2101 Wilson Blvd., #302
Arlington, VA 22201

National Depressive and Manic-Depressive Association
730 N. Franklin, Suite 501
Chicago, IL 60610

National Mental Health Association
1021 Prince St.
Alexandria, VA 22314
703/684-7722

The Association for Retarded Citizens of the United States
Publications Department
P.O. Box 1047
Arlington, TX 76004

Pilot Parents
2150 East Highland, No. 105
Phoenix, AZ 85016

Older People and the Health Care System

Chapter Outline

"Certainly the late Helen Hooven Santmyer deserved better than a nursing home when she published her lifelong effort, *And Ladies of the Club*, the greatest best-seller since *Gone With the Wind*. She should have had TV interviews and cocktail parties, a radio show and autograph sessions at bookstores. All this would have killed the old girl, but she would have had fun! Isn't fun what we are told life is all about? She deserved the rewards of publication, but she died at 87, within a year, in the nursing home anyway."

— Margaret Coit Elwell, born 1919

Introduction

Older people make up about 13% of the United States population, but they account for over 38% of hospitalizations (U.S. Bureau of the Census, 1998b).

There were a little over 30.5 million persons of all ages who were hospitalized in 1996; however, this is down from 37.8 million since 1980—a decline of 19%—despite the growth of the population during those years. The average length of stay declined by about 29%. This is the first fact of health care in the final two decades of the past century: hospitalization rates are declining, and the average length of hospital stays is declining

glossary

Medicare — The
health insurance
program for the aged
(and younger disabled
people) through the
Social Security
program; 99.5% of
people 65 and older in
the U.S. have
Medicare coverage.

faster. Uses of hospitals are lower for the entire population, mainly because of the use of diagnostic-related groups and preferred provider arrangements among health insurers, including *Medicare* and Medicaid. Conditions one routinely required several days of hospital care for are now done on an out-patient basis; recovery is more likely to be at home than in a hospital.

Disability rates among the aged are also declining (Manton, Stallard, & Corder, 1995), which means that lengthy stays in the hospital that once were the norm are becoming less and less likely. Older people who once would have received hospital care for the length of their treatment and rehabilitation now are faced with recuperation either at home or in a nursing home. Thus, rates and numbers of nursing home utilization are growing. Growing even faster, though, are home care and hospice programs (Haupt, 1998).

Older people tend to view the health care system in the United States positively. They rate satisfaction with their doctor and with the hospital care they have received higher than do other groups in the adult population. They do have two particular fears, however: no one wants to enter a nursing home, and people have a special fear of dying in an intensive care acute hospital setting, isolated from their loved ones, hooked up to tubes and monitors, surrounded by machines.

How likely is either prospect?

In this chapter, we will look at older people as they confront the health care system. In particular, we'll look at the odds of entering a nursing home, of spending one's own resources to pay for nursing home care, and at some of the problems with long-term care.

Acute Medical Care

There were just over 11.7 million people aged 65+ hospitalized in 1997 (National Center for Health Statistics, 1998). Many if not most of those older individuals had multiple hospitalizations within the same year. Uses of hospital care among the aged are much higher than other adult groups in the population.

As we can see in Table 9.1, the hospitalization rate for those aged 65–74 is over twice that of the population as a whole (257 per thousand versus 116 per thousand), and the rate for those aged 75+ (455 per thousand) is almost four times higher. The rate of days of care is highest among the older categories, and the average length of stay is also significantly higher.

Many conditions for which older people are treated, of course, do not require hospital care. Rates of ambulatory surgery are about twice as high for those 65+ as for other adult groups. By far the procedure with the greatest frequency is treatment of cataracts, extraction of lens and insertion of prosthetic lens, surgery that used to require hospital care for as long as a week (Metropolitan Life Insurance Company, 1997).

TABLE 9.1. Hospitalization Rates, By Age

Ages	Number of patients (thousands)	Rate per thousand in population	Days of care per thousand persons	Average length of stay (days)
All	30,545	116	606	5.2
25–34 yrs	4,077	102	360	3.5
35–44 yrs	3,399	79	373	4.7
45–64 yrs	6,294	117	624	5.3
65–74 yrs	4,804	257	1,604	6.2
75+ yrs	6,914	455	3,075	6.8

From U.S. Bureau of the Census (1998, p. 137).

While it is true that older persons typically indicate that they are well-served by hospitals, there remains a fear that any acute care procedure or admission may get out of control, deplete their savings, or, among the oldest old, be their last hospitalization. In particular, older people have a fear of an isolated death in intensive care (Kaufman, 1998). Most physicians have no particular training in geriatric medicine (Warshaw, 1997), and there is the problem of the "technological imperative," the tendency to use every machine and procedure available, sometime without really finding out what it is that the older patient really wants. Some older people may feel bowled over by aggressive care in acute settings.

The word "juggernaut" comes from the Hindi *Jagannath*, "lord of the world," which comes from the Sanskrit for moving and living world. Webster's dictionary defines it as, "a former belief that devotees of Vishnu sometimes allowed themselves to be crushed beneath the wheels of the car on which his image was being drawn in procession, or a massive inexorable force or object that advances irresistibly and crushes whatever is in its path" (*Webster's*, 1986, p. 653). One has this vision of a juggernaut as a massive steamroller that cannot be stopped, that rolls over everything in its way.

Older people who confront the world of high-tech health care, expensive beyond belief and characterized by teams of anonymous professionals hurriedly going about their business, must at times feel like a juggernaut is about to roll over them. Lines, monitors, tubes, strangers in a strange place, flashing lights, and beeps from machines taken together all bewilder and confuse people who may already have trouble remaining in touch with their surroundings. Frequently, this juggernaut of modern medical care has the net effect of extending death rather than life, of giving a few more days or weeks of life at the cost of thousands or even hundreds of thousands of dollars.

Beyond this vision of intensive care in the modern acute-care hospital is the alternative of the nursing home, where days may turn into years of dreary existence, surrounded by companions who have lost their mental abilities, among bored and sometimes incompetent staff members who are underpaid and overworked.

Illustration 9.1. On Watching an Old Man Die

I did a bit of a field placement in gerontology the week before this chapter was written. Jerry, an old friend, called one evening to tell me of the frustration he was having with the hospital care received by his 85-year-old father. His dad had emphysema and congestive heart failure; he'd been in a nursing home for three months. When he had a respiratory arrest there they sent him to the hospital. Now, he was in the intensive care unit, there was a tube down his throat, he was barely clinging to life, semi-conscious, and the docs wanted to do a tracheostomy—to cut a hole in his throat and put the old man on a ventilator.

I asked Jerry if he knew that once on the ventilator there would be little chance of ever getting his dad off of it. He did. I then asked him why they wanted to go ahead with the procedure on a man who was so obviously at the end of his life. Jerry said, "Well, he went into the nursing home three months ago they had him fill out a Living Will. On it, there was an item asking if he wanted to be resuscitated if the situation arose, and he checked it off, saying that yes, he did want it." Now, the doctor at the hospital took that as an advance directive that he wanted all available means to keep him alive. I asked Jerry if that was what he thought his father in fact would have wanted. No, he didn't think so. In fact, he was sure that he specifically did *not* want to spend his last weeks or months on a machine breathing for him. Several times he had already tried to pull out the tubes that were in his nose and mouth.

So, I told him, "First thing in the morning, you go and meet with the doc. Tell him that you are the person responsible for your father, that the situation has changed since he was in the nursing home, that you do not authorize him to go ahead with the surgery, and that you want only comfort measures for your father. If he gives you any trouble, tell him you have power of attorney (Jerry did in fact have Power of Attorney for his father's financial affairs, but he didn't have a specific Durable Power of Attorney for Health Care). He won't ask to see it. If you want someone to go with you to meet with the doc, I'm willing."

He thought he could handle it without having me along. I told him not to be surprised if his dad lingered on for a few more days.

This was on a Sunday night. That Thursday I got a call from Jerry's wife. She said the medical staff had been only too willing to go along with Jerry's request; they'd actually been waiting to hear something from the family to prevent what they thought probably would be a useless procedure. Dad was out of intensive care, he was in a regular hospital room, his daughters were in from out of town, and everyone was reconciled to this being the end of Dad's life. Only, Jerry's son was going to perform in his last high school program that evening, and they'd like to go see . . .

I picked up on where that was going. "And you don't want Dad to die alone," I said. "What time do you want me to be there?"

So, I took a stack of term papers with me to grade and went over to the hospital that evening to sit with an old man while he died.

He was lying there on his back with his mouth open, puffed up like a blister from the congestive heart failure, obviously close to the end. His breathing was labored, short little puffs that weren't doing him any good. He wasn't conscious, but he wasn't comatose, either. Jerry told me earlier that his dad hadn't been able to recognize or respond to him for some time. When I went over and took his hand to tell him who I was, one eye did open for a moment. It didn't focus on me, but it did open. And, he squeezed my hand.

As I sat there next to him, reading my papers, it was clear that he wouldn't be able to keep breathing like that for much longer; he would die of exhaustion. I timed him. At 7:00 he was taking 23 breaths per minute; at 8:00 it was up to 30. By nine o'clock he was taking 43 breaths per minute. I shouldn't say breaths, they were pants. Try taking 43 breaths per minute and see what I mean.

There was a monitor hooked up to him: the top number gave his blood oxygen levels, the bottom his pulse. He had an oxygen tube in his nose and an intravenous line giving him saline or glucose. Respiratory therapy people came in twice while I was there to give him some help and to suction the gunk out of his trachea. I turned off the TV; it seemed to be just one final indignity to have to die to a Matlock rerun. When the light on the monitor indicating his heart-beat slipped below 50 it would turn from green to red and a beeping noise would sound. I asked the nurse if she could turn down the volume of that, as the noise seemed to agitate him.

"But if I turned off the sound, we couldn't hear it."

"That's right. It's all right if you don't hear it."

She understood, and she turned off the sound. She agreed that all that was wanted now was "comfort measures," and that he had "no code" written on his chart. In other words, we were in an open awareness: the man was dying, it was all right, and they wouldn't do cardiopul-monary resuscitation on him when he did die.

On the other hand, he still was hooked up to an antibiotic drip. Damned if I know what good *that* was going to do.

The readings of both monitors gradually slipped down and down; the pulse monitor was red much of the time now, reading in the 40s for the most part. His breathing became even more labored, if possible. The first time both monitors went flat and read zero I figured that was it. The old man continued to pant along, though, and I began to have less faith in electronic moni-tors and more in the basic instinct to cling to life. The monitors went down to zero several more times while I was still on shift.

Jerry and his sister came in to relieve me late that evening; they'd enjoyed the program at the high school and were most appreciative. The old man died at 1:00 that morning.

He'd wanted a Dixieland band at his funeral. He got it.

Neither of these visions is entirely true, but neither is entirely untrue. In order to understand the older individual confronting the health care system as it exists in our society, we need to appreciate elements of both of these fears. Older people, like everyone else, have seen and heard horror stories of health care run amok, of life-sustaining procedures and machines inflicted upon people who merely want to die with some sense of peace and dignity. Alternatively, press accounts of deaths by neglect in nursing homes also rivet our attention.

When most people who are now among the oldest old were children, what they heard from their parents and grandparents in part shaped their images of health care institutions. Some of these impressions persist to this day. Hospitals were thought to be for poor people, and they were seen as places that housed the impoverished and homeless who were destined to die there (Luchins, 1988). People who had any resources at all would do everything in their power to avoid hospitals. This usually involved hiring private nurses and being attended to at home by a doctor who made house calls. Those who were *really* down and out, who had no one to care for them and who may have been thought of as mentally ill or senile, were sent to the county poor farm, an asylum far outside the limits of the city. The poor farm was characterized by the neat, anonymous row of tombstones out back, resting on the graves of those who'd made a one-way trip (Luchins, 1989a). The image of the county farm remains in the minds of many older people when they think of hospitals or nursing homes.

As we saw in Chapter 8, one of the greatest fears of older persons is ending life in a nursing home. A more compelling fear, if we were to ask many older people, would be to end life in an intensive care unit of an acute-care hospital, hooked up to tubes and monitors, isolated from human contact, alone and dying. Something many older people might not be aware of—something that would exacerbate these fears—is the fact that pain control is a frequent problem, particularly for those with chronic illness or diminished cognitive capacity. Numerous studies have indicated inadequate pain control among older hospital patients (Kaasalainen et al., 1998).

There has been a tendency to hospitalize nursing home patients who are nearing the end of life. In a 1991 study, Teresi and her colleagues reviewed data collected from 286 patient transfers to hospital from 10 different nursing homes. They tended to be the more chronically ill, physically frail patients, those with infection, and those less likely to survive in the long-term care setting.

Long-Term Care

The thrust of community-based services to the elderly is to keep them independent for as long as possible, at home, and to provide alternatives to institutional care. However, no amount of home-delivered services will keep everyone independent all the time. At some point, caregivers give out, and visiting nurses around-the-clock cost more than nursing home care. Furthermore, not everyone has available caretakers to help keep them at home. Social networks break down. And many people never had a partner or children to begin with.

People who need care on a continuing basis (for more than a few days or weeks) are candidates for long-term care. We should emphasize from the beginning that long-term care and nursing home care are not necessarily the same thing. Many frail older adults are being taken care of at home by family members, friends, visiting nurses, and others; if they are sufficiently disabled, this should be seen as long-term care. Most older persons who need help, in fact, receive most it from family caregivers: spouses and adult children. These caregivers deliver the majority of the services received by older individuals in need of it (Shanas, 1979). Families often maintain their elder members at home for months or years, most without the help of formal services from outside agencies.

People prefer to stay at home, not only because of the images they have of institutional care, but because they are better off psychologically and socially in familiar surroundings. They are also better off financially, as long-term care in a nursing home can easily top $4,000 a month these days in many urban areas, and most nursing home care is not paid for by insurance.

Over the past three decades, there has been a movement in the field of health and social services to place people at the least restrictive level of care. It has been observed that people—not just the elderly, but people at all ages—function better outside of institutional environments. This has been graphically seen in the fields of child care and mental health. Orphanages began to close down in the 1940s and 1950s due to the realization that children fail to thrive in institutional environments. A system of foster care in most parts of the country has grown up to replace the orphanages once common in most cities. Similarly, due to the recognition that mental hospitals often caused as many problems as they helped, the number of people in them has declined, from about a half million in the mid-1950s to a little over 70,000 in 1998 (U.S. Bureau of the Census, 1998). The focus has been on community mental health care. However, it has not been entirely successful, either. Many homeless people are former mental patients who receive little in the way of care.

These concepts combined with the sobering fact of the high cost of nursing home care, result in the dramatic expansion in recent years of home health care programs. Many insurers have realized that it is often cheaper to provide home nursing care and in-home therapists than it is to pay for hospital or nursing home care. Psychologically and socially, the individual is almost always better off at home. As a result, home health is the fastest-growing means of the delivery of long-term care.

There are some 13,500 home care and hospice agencies in the United States; 7,400 of them are *proprietary* (for-profit), 4,600 are voluntary nonprofit agencies, and 1,500 are governmental. A total of 6,400 home health programs are part of national chains. Of all the home care agencies, about 2,900 are certified for hospice care. In 1996, there were almost 2.5 million home care patients served by these agencies: 72% of them were aged 65 or older. There were 59,400 hospice patients, and 46,100 of the hospice patients were 65 years of age or above (Haupt, 1998).

glossary

proprietary — Profit making.

Due to the availability of more home health care programs, as well as the awareness of the difficulties associated with institutional care, inappropriate nursing home placement is not as serious a problem as it once was. A generation ago, it was not unusual for nursing homes to house people who really didn't need nursing services. Misuse of nursing home care now is not only discouraged by the escalating costs of care in an institution; there is also a system of utilization review that seeks to prevent inappropriate placement. Nursing homes themselves, for the most part, will no longer take people who don't need their care, and some now sponsor their own community services and outreach programs to serve people who formerly would have been candidates for their institutional services.

Most long-term care facilities do a good job, generally without overly adequate resources, and the job they do is a necessary one. However, as we have mentioned with the vision of the poor farm that some older people may cling to, the nursing home industry suffers from an image problem. It is not uncommon to hear older people say that they would rather die than live in a nursing home (Kuhn, 1998). Thought of as "warehouses for the dying," many care centers are characterized as sterile, impersonal, and smelly. New nursing graduates generally hope to go into critical care jobs such as neonatal intensive care, cardiac care, surgery, or emergency care, rather than positions in less-glamorous long-term care settings. Families commonly say, "We'll do anything to keep Mom out of a nursing home," or "I hate to see Dad in *that* place." Even though most facilities carry out legitimate rehabilitation programs and return many people to the community, the impression still remains of the nursing home as the place where older people go to die.

And there are the news stories of nursing homes that do not do a good job. Tales of neglect, unsafe facilities, and owners who are found guilty of gouging the Medicaid program may apply to a relatively few facilities, but the images created by such headlines remain in the public consciousness. The *Wall Street Journal* ran a series ("Older People Will Do Anything to Avoid Life in a Nursing Home") that profiled people who preferred homelessness to living in a care center:

> "Berenice Bradley has lived on a Greyhound bus for most of the past four years. The 65 year-old widow, who has high blood pressure and is incontinent, periodically visits her post-office box in Chicago, cashes her pension checks and buys a $429 monthly bus pass. Between homeless shelters, home is wherever Greyhound takes her. The bus lady has been trying to dodge what she dreads most: a nursing home" (McCarthy, 1992, p. A1).

Perhaps at this point it would be helpful to actually define what a nursing home is; too many people confuse nursing homes with senior housing or board-and-care facilities. Nursing homes in the United States and Canada provide a sheltered environment for disabled people, the elderly included (but not restricted to only the elderly), under medical supervision and employing a staff of registered nurses and trained care staff members. Nursing homes provide not only housing and all meals for their residents, but they should also have programs of rehabilitation, therapeutic activities, and consultation with professional social workers and pharmacists. Each person there should have a written care plan, and drugs and therapies should be administered under the supervision of professional nurses.

Nursing homes should be distinguished from residential care facilities, which range from institutions where assisted living may be provided by a professional staff (but at a step below the level of care provided by nursing homes), down to little more than boarding houses for the aged. There are 9,258 residential care facilities in the U.S. at last count (U. S. Bureau of the Census, 1998b). Over seven thousand of them average 15 beds or fewer.

In contrast, there are 16,700 nursing homes in the United States; a little less than 5% of them are under government auspices, two-thirds are proprietary, and the remainder are not-for-profit. Their average size is 106 beds, and they serve 1,706,400 people per year, 11% of whom are under 65 years of age. Only 15.6% are between 65 and 74; fully 73% are aged 75 or older, with half of that group being over 85 (Strahan, 1997). Less than 5% of nursing homes are not certified to receive either Medicare or Medicaid (U.S. Bureau of the Census, 1998b).

The greatest trend among nursing homes in recent years is to add assisted living units. Assisted living is a lower level of care, almost always paid for by the individual; the number of nursing homes with their own assisted living units (1,910) has doubled in a decade (Metropolitan Life Insurance Company, 1998). Assisted living residents may need some help with getting their meals or in monitoring their medications, but they lead fairly independent lives and have few ADL impairments. By contrast, 96.3% of nursing home patients need help with bathing, 86.6% need help with dressing, 57.8% with getting to the toilet, and 45.1% with eating (Dey, 1997).

Public housing for the elderly under the sponsorship of local housing authorities is not nursing home care; these are apartments rented to older people. They may provide a safe environment and some social services, but the residents receive no nursing care from the housing authority (though some may receive it from visiting nurse or home care organization, just like any older person living in the community).

Neither should specialized housing for the elderly on the private market be considered nursing home care. Continuing care retirement communities (CCRCs) that older people buy into may contain a nursing home as part of the facility, but by far the great majority of their residents live independently in condos or apartments—or, in some instances, in free-standing single family dwellings. They may opt for this sheltered retirement housing because it provides welcome security as well as opportunities for socialization. Many CCRCs give assurance to residents that rehabilitation and nursing care is available if and when the time comes.

The level of care in nursing homes can be either skilled or intermediate, depending on the number of hours of actual nursing care the individual receives. We used to designate facilities as being either skilled nursing homes or ICFs (intermediate care facilities), but most facilities now have both skilled and ICF beds under one roof and change the designation according to the needs of the current patient population. Nursing homes come under a variety of state regulations usually enforced by a unit of the state's department of health, as well as a host of federal regulations that come mainly as a package under the authority of the Omnibus Budget Reconciliation Act (OBRA) of 1987. OBRA regulations, for example, specify that certified care staff members must receive a particular number of hours of training in order to be employed, and that they must update that training annually through continuing education programs.

Many nursing homes are owned by large corporations that enforce their own standards and have their own inspectors as well. In fact, the current movement in the industry is for independently-owned nursing homes to be bought up by the large corporate entities; 55% of nursing homes are now owned by chains (Strahan, 1997).

The research is somewhat cloudy as to whether better care is given in the proprietary or in the non-profit nursing homes. The difference is clearer among the continuing care retirement communities. A Stanford University study, for example, stated that quality of care in residential facilities is related to its ownership. Non-profit facilities provide a more comfortable

---

Illustration 9.3. Nursing Home Chain Proscecuted

Laura Morgan's marching orders were simple. As a social worker at a nursing home owned by Vencor Inc., she was to ensure that as many beds as possible were filled with residents covered by generous private insurance or by Medicare. Patients whose high-paying benefits expired, and who thus ended up on lower-paying Medicaid, were to be moved out as soon as possible.

One of her tasks was smoothing the way with relatives. "I had to sit across from family members and lie to them, manipulate them, tell half- truths," says Ms. Morgan, who resigned in June after alerting state authorities to the practices.

A month later, Vencor did a complete flip-flop. Facilities in Savannah and other Southeastern cities suddenly were sent a memo that told them to "just say yes to admissions." After years as one of the nation's most selective nursing home chains, Vencor switched almost overnight to one that was focused on keeping its beds full.

This sweeping reversal, coupled with an apology the chief executive had already issued for evicting Medicaid patients at a handful of homes, vindicated critics of the company's intently profit-focused admissions policy. But it also was emblematic of hard times that have befallen a once high-flying company that dived ambitiously into an industry it barely knew, and sought to pioneer new strategies as it did so.

From Adams & Moss (1998).

physical environment and more resident control than did proprietary settings matched for size (Lemke & Moos, 1989). This also applies to the nursing care units attached to the retirement facilities. Another study pointed out that residents of continuing care retirement communities ultimately spend fewer days in nursing homes (Cohen, Tell, & Wallack, 1988).

This is an important public policy issue, since about half of the total national cost of nursing home care is provided through Medicaid, a public welfare program. Medicaid pays health care costs for people (at all ages, the elderly included) who cannot pay. Nationally, 35.4% of Medicaid dollars goes for long-term care for the elderly (Older Americans Report, 1998). It is thought that many older people who enter nursing home care pay for it themselves until their money runs out (they "spend down"); at that point, Medicaid kicks in and pays for all or a portion of their nursing home costs. About a quarter of private-pay nursing home patients spend down and are forced to go on Medicaid (Adams, Meiners, & Burwell, 1993). A study of nine years' experience of patients in Connecticut, for example, found that there was a lifetime risk of Medicaid spend down of 21.5% (Liu & Manton, 1991). A similar study in Wisconsin found that 12% of discharges from nursing homes had spent down to Medicaid eligibility, and that about 23% of persons admitted as private pay had spent down. It was also found that 40% of those who spent down did so within six months, and 58% did so within a year (Arling, Buhaug, Hagen, & Zimmerman, 1991). Obviously, programs that keep people out of nursing homes for as long as possible lessen the burden of government in terms of tax dollars devoted to long-term institutional care. In Chapter 14, we will look at a variety of these programs and their effectiveness at lessening this burden. For now, however, we might conclude that most programs, including continuing care retirement communities paid for by older people themselves, ultimately do tend to reduce the overall level of governmental expenditure on nursing home care by preventing ultimate Medicaid expenditures for nursing home care.

A common misconception is that Medicare, the health insurance program sponsored under the U. S. Social Security Administration, will pay nursing home costs. In fact, many older people are bitterly disappointed when they find out that in most instances it does not. Only under carefully defined circumstances does Medicare pay for long-term care (it was designed, after all, to pay only for hospital and doctors' bills). As a result, only between 1 and 2% of total national nursing home costs are paid through Medicare. Hospice care is an important exception to this general rule.

The complexities of the various programs—and their changing details—are such that we cannot be too specific in this context. Those who need to know would be well advised to consult a hospital social worker; our experience is that they rapidly become experts on what will be paid for by whom, and they tend to serve as advocates rather than gatekeepers.

Also difficult to pin down with accuracy is the actual number of people in nursing homes: it of course varies from day to day. The *1998 Statistical Abstract* lists 1.55 million (U.S. Bureau of the Census, 1998b). The rate varies by age from less than 1% at age 65 to a little more than 20% of men and almost 30% of women by age 85. Older men are likelier to have a caretaking spouse still living, so they are less likely to be cared for in an institution. Married people have only half the risk of entering a nursing home; having at least one sibling or daughter reduces the risk by about a quarter (Freedman, 1996).

In the field of gerontology, we used to make much of the fact that fewer than 5% of the aged are in nursing homes, forgetting that the greatest number of people 65 or older are actually in the cohort aged 65 to 74 (which has the lowest institutionalization rate among the elderly population overall). This was cleared up by Kastenbaum & Candy (1973, p. 423), when they pointed out that 23% of deaths recorded in metropolitan Detroit took place in nursing homes. Harold Wershow's research in 1976 demonstrated that as many as 44% of nursing home deaths occur within a month after admission, and that "short-lived patients are necessarily under-represented in cross-sectional studies, giving rise to the myth that only a small proportion of the elderly end their lives in nursing homes"(1976, p. 52). In his study of nursing home deaths, Wershow found that 3% took place within 24 hours after admission. "It seemed to us to be worth noting that of those 460 (total nursing home) deaths, 20% of the males and 10% of the females died within a week after admission; 58% of the males and 40% of the females were dead within a month after admission."(1976, p. 54) Despite these and other facts we will examine shortly, the happy myth of only 4 or 5% of the elderly being in nursing homes has persisted. True, the percentage may be that low at any one time (it varies by region: lower in the South and higher in the Midwest; it's even higher in Canada), but we need to realize that people constantly move *through* nursing homes.

This point was made best by Mary Ann Lewis and her colleagues (1985) at the UCLA School of Public Health. They followed a random sample of 197 persons admitted to 24 different nursing care facilities for two years. This was a difficult task: people move in and out of nursing homes, go from the hospital to a nursing home and back again, from the nursing home to the hospital and back either to the same or a different nursing home, and they go back and forth from home to the same or different nursing homes. Keeping track of a random cohort of nursing home admissions over time had never previously been accomplished. At the end of the two years, slightly over 9% of the 197 had been discharged home without further institutional care. Thirty-seven percent had died in the nursing home, and 54% transferred frequently between hospitals and nursing homes. The end result: two years after being admitted to a nursing home, about 15% were still living there, slightly less than 15% were living at home, and about 70% had died. Overall, 60% died in the first year, and 28% died during the first 30 days after the initial admission to a nursing home. The length of stay varied from 65.3 days for those who had a single admission and lived, up to 300.7 days for those with a single admission who died.

So, we can see how difficult it is to answer the seemingly simple question: what's the average length of stay in a nursing home? It depends. A number of researchers have addressed this problem, as well as the question of lifetime risk of nursing home entry.

A national study from the Agency for Health Care Policy Research found that, of those who die at age 25 or older, 29% have at some time in their lives been residents of a nursing home. About half of those who entered a nursing home spent a cumulative total of at least one year in one or more nursing homes. It was also found that the probability of being in a nursing home increases with age: 17% of those aged 65 to 74, 36% of those aged 75 to 84, and 60% of those who died between ages 85 and 94 had spent some time in a nursing home. It was projected that 43% of current 65-year-olds will enter a nursing home some time before they die; of that group, 55% will be institutionalized for over a year and 21% for over five years. Further, it is projected that more women than men will utilize nursing home care at some time in their lives: 52% versus 33%. Finally, more women than men will have a total lifetime use of nursing home care for five years or more: 25% compared to 13% (Kemper & Murtaugh, 1991).

Somewhat different are figures from a study done by the Agency for Health Care Policy and Research of the U.S. Public Health Service. Rather than lifetime risk, the experience of patients already institutionalized was analyzed. It was found that 9% of patients utilize at least five years of care or more; they account for 64% of the aggregate cost for their cohort of nursing home patients. By contrast, fully 68% of patients use less than three months of care. They account for only about 1% of costs (Kemper, Spillman, & Murtaugh, 1991).

How long someone stays in a nursing home is of course directly related to their physical and mental condition. Alzheimer's and AIDS patients stay longer than people with conditions that might respond more readily to rehabilitative therapies—or that might be fatal in a shorter length of time. One study of stroke patients found that by 90 days after nursing home admission, 27.4% remained in the nursing home, 22.4% had gone home, 25.7% had been readmitted to the hospital, 8.7% had gone to another nursing home, and 15.6% had died (Berg & Mor, 1995).

Length of stay in a nursing home is dependent on physical condition; less obviously, it also may be dependent on the type of home. A study of Veteran's Administration (VA) nursing homes in the U.S. is illustrative. A sample of 4,918 persons admitted to VA nursing homes was examined. They were broken down into three groups by length of stay: 1,139 were there for less than one month, 1,947 stayed from one to six months, and 1,832 stayed for over six months. The median length of stay overall was 104 days; 26% died during the seven-month period of the study, 59% were discharged, and 15% remained institutionalized (Williams, Fries, & Mehr, 1993). These figures vary somewhat from those in the study by Lewis we have already reviewed. Perhaps admission to a nursing home has less to do with physical impairment than it does with a lack of community supports—or with the availability of institutional care. That is, it is possible that more of the veterans for some reason lacked the caregiver support available to the community group Lewis surveyed. Or, given that the VA care was provided without cost, it might be that those who have to pay for nursing home care resist admission for a longer period of time than those who get it for free. This is an important public policy issue that needs further study.

There is additional current research in terms of predicting outcomes in nursing homes. A study at the University of Tennessee College of Nursing, for example, followed 647 newly admitted residents in eight nursing homes (Engle & Graney, 1993). They were evaluated at admission and again three and six months later. The most important predictor variable for death at three months was a cancer diagnosis. On the other hand, being a *first* nursing home admission was the most important predictor for discharge to home within three months, and not having a dementia diagnosis was the second most important predictor of discharge within three months. This study implies what people who work in nursing homes already know: patients vary greatly in terms of their condition, level of functional ability, and adaptation to the facility. Some (in this instance, those with a cancer diagnosis) may be there for the last few weeks of their lives. Others are there for a brief time and are discharged home, for example, those there for recuperation after surgery or rehabilitation after a stroke. And some, those with a diagnosis of dementia, will probably be in a nursing home for the rest of their lives; this could range from a few months to many years. Thus, it would be incorrect (and unfair) to categorize nursing home residents into one single group.

One thing we do know from the research is that current nursing home patients are sicker than typical nursing home patients used to be (Fischer & Eustis, 1988; Garrard et al., 1993). That is, the effect of payment plans for hospitals using diagnostic related groups (*DRG*s) has been to make for a heavier load of nursing care in nursing homes. The DRG system is used by many insurance and governmental health payment plans. It works like this: the third party (the insurance company, Medicaid, or Medicare) will pay the hospital a certain number of dollars for a specific condition or diagnostic-related group of conditions. Say, taking out an appendix is worth six thousand dollars. The patient can spend one day in the hospital or ten, the pay's the same for the hospital. Naturally, it's in the interest of the hospital to move people on out in the minimum amount of time. A stroke patient who in the early 1980s might have been in the hospital for 30 or 40 days is now typically in the hospital for only a few days and they then convalesce in a nursing home. Care for this kind of patient requires more hours of work for the nursing home nurses than is required by many other patients. The situation is similar for people who have had heart attacks or been in surgery; their care puts a heavier load on the nursing staff. A study of nursing home outcomes in Wisconsin found that mortality data increased 16.6 percent between the years 1982 and 1985, and the number of patients dying within the first 30 days after admission increased by 59%. These results were attributed directly to Medicare's prospective payment system that was instituted between those years (Sager, Easterling, & Leventhal, 1988).

The prospect seen by these patients who may have once been cared for in the acute-care hospital setting may be discouraging. Few people want to enter a nursing home under any circumstances, and they may wonder if they will ever be able to leave the institution. However, they do have a greater probability of recuperation and rehabilitation in the long-term care setting. And, they have a greater probability of returning home than do most other nursing home patients. The possibility of returning home, of course, depends for many on the presence of a caregiver at home. We know that the likelihood of nursing home admission for most patients depends on several things: the older the age, obviously, the likelier they are to be admitted; admission also depends on level of impairment, the availability of in-home services, and the perception of burden or strain on the care-taker (McFall & Miller, 1992). Similarly, the possibility of returning home having once been institutionalized depends upon these same variables. Those without much prospect of help at home may have nowhere else to go and remain in the nursing home, at least until they are able to care for themselves without help.

Nursing Home Problems

If we were to ask administrators of nursing homes what their greatest problem areas were, they probably would not focus on patient problems. Areas

glossary

DRG — Diagnostic related group; used by prospective payment systems as a basis to pay hospital and medical costs.

identified would most likely be centered around personnel problems, problems with regulations, and problems with finance.

Regulations are an inevitable fact of life for all health care institutions. Corporate homes need to not only satisfy governmental regulators, they have their own corporate inspectors to satisfy as well. This is also true of the larger not-for-profit chains. And whether the institution is proprietary or non-profit, it can't lose money for long and stay in business.

Expensive as long-term institutional care is, most facilities actually run on a pretty tight margin. Between 10 and 20% of nursing homes are "private pay only," which means that they do not accept patients who cannot pay for their own care. And, many facilities will go so far as to move people out when their resources are exhausted. Almost all other nursing homes have a mix of private-pay and Medicaid patients, ranging from a few on Medicaid up to all on Medicaid.

The ideal from the administrator's point of view usually is to have a maximum number of private pay residents because the facility receives a higher amount from them than from Medicaid. Each institution has a Medicaid rate per patient day that is calculated by the particular agency that regulates Medicaid in their state (Medicaid dollars come from both the state and from federal sources). This Medicaid reimbursement rate in almost all cases is less than the rate received from private-pay patients. Often it is much less. Thus, private-pay patients in effect subsidize the costs of care for Medicaid patients. Care centers that let their percentage of patients on Medicaid get too high tend to get into financial trouble, and something has to give. Nursing homes with financial difficulties by necessity provide a lower level of service.

From a public policy point of view, Medicaid is both a blessing and a nightmare. A colleague and I did a study for the State of Nebraska some years ago that projected Medicaid expenditures from state dollars as the

---

Illustration 9.5. Testifying Against a Nursing Home

I was approached by the Legal Services program in a nearby city to be an expert witness in a court case against a nursing home that wanted to give the boot to a patient who had been there seven years. The patient, a retired telephone operator, had spent all of her resources on her care; now that she was broke, she had to go onto Medicaid. The home said they had too many Medicaid patients and that she would have to be transferred to the county home. The people with Legal Services wanted to know if I'd be willing to testify that this would endanger her life. I said that I couldn't do that, but that I could testify that, in my opinion, the thrust of the research in the gerontological literature was that people who were moved out of familiar environments against their will were in greater jeopardy. That was good enough, and they had me swear out an affidavit. They went and waved this under the administrator's nose; she backed down, and the patient wasn't moved.

fastest-growing item in the state budget for many years to come (Thorson & Horacek, 1986). Looking back, we were right about it being the fastest-growing, but we underestimated its actual growth by about a third. This is also the case in most other states. The blessing is that indigent peoples' health care is paid for by the program. The nightmare is that rising health costs can seem to be virtually uncontrollable. One of the "generational equity" issues now being raised is that public services for young people in the population are having to be cut back in order to devote a greater share of tax dollars to the care of the indigent aged.

"Certificate of need" panels are one response by some state governments; they regulate where and when new hospitals and nursing homes can be built—or change hands. Nursing homes have a way of filling up; one way to limit Medicaid costs is to limit the number of facilities built. Change of ownership of existing homes also presents a financial burden to the state. The problem is this: a portion of the cost of the mortgage for the building is included in the calculation of the facility's Medicaid reimbursement rate, along with the cost of heat, lights, food, personnel, and so on. It's possible for an investor to purchase a nursing home, let Medicaid pay for it over a period of years, and then sell it. The next owner then naturally wants Medicaid to help pay off the new mortgage. The state winds up paying for the same building twice—or more than twice.

A fear that administrators—and patients—have is that private-pay patients will spend down: they'll enter with enough money to pay for their care, spend until it runs out, and then remain in the nursing home, perhaps for many years, on Medicaid. Although this represents a potential financial burden to the home, it's not a universal phenomenon—less than a quarter of nursing home patients admitted on a private-pay basis spend all their assets and have to go onto Medicaid. Nursing home administrators generally try to restrict the number of people who are admitted on Medicaid in the first place, but they can't do much about those who spend down (other than kick them out). So, they will try to designate only a certain proportion of their available beds as "Medicaid" beds.

Illustration 9.6. Medicaid Beds

Nursing homes try to limit the number of people they admit on Medicaid. Hospital discharge social workers tell me that in Omaha, a metropolitan area of over a half million people that has 34 nursing homes, on any given day there may be only one or two Medicaid beds available. This means that patients seldom have much choice as to where they are placed, and families have no option either. Inevitably, some people are placed in institutions on the other side of the city from their family, making visitation that much more difficult. In rural areas, where there are few institutions to begin with, this can be a critical problem; it's not uncommon for families to find their older member placed in a nursing home in the next county.

Families anticipating nursing home placement of an older member sometimes will transfer assets in an attempt to have the person's care paid for by Medicaid. The response of many states has been to prosecute these family members for fraud.

In terms of personnel problems, many nursing homes are plagued with staff turnover. This is probably more true in urban areas than in rural ones, where jobs are scarcer and the population is more stable. The "nursing" staff of nursing homes actually contains very few registered nurses. Most of the care is delivered by certified care staff members—aides and orderlies. These are often minimum-wage or little more than minimum-wage jobs. The work is hard, it's often messy, and it usually is very demanding. It takes a special kind of person to do it. Some homes experience a turnover of their non-professional staff several times a year, on the average. Research on the lives of care staff members has found that they frequently feel trapped in a self-perpetuating negative cycle (Tellis-Nayak & Tellis-Nayak, 1989).

Nursing homes are difficult places to work in. The majority (67.4%) of people in nursing homes are there because of a diagnosis of dementia (National Center for Health Statistics, November 10, 1998). This means that behavioral difficulties among patients are not infrequent. Problems of wandering, violent outbursts, and delirium must be dealt with. Patients who once would have gone to state mental hospitals are now routinely admitted to nursing homes. Patients who are lucid often are depressed because of the circumstances they find themselves in, especially if their roommate is demented. Despite regulations, many times patients must have restraints; they are tied into bed or into chairs to reduce wandering and falls. Death is also a daily fact of life, and the numbers of deaths in nursing homes has been shown to have increased dramatically since the introduction of DRGs in the mid-1980s (Lindberg et al., 1989; Wood & Estes, 1990). Incontinent patients must be constantly tended to or the home will smell of stale urine. It's no wonder that many facilities have high staff turnover.

The response of some patients to involuntary nursing home placement is to turn their face to the wall and die (Thorson, 1988). The mortality statistics after entry into nursing homes are startling, as we have seen in

---

Illustration 9.7. Deaths Caused by Physical Restraints

"A retrospective analysis of 122 deaths caused by vest and strap restraints found that most victims were women (78%) and a median age of 81. Victims were found suspended from chairs (42%) or beds (58%); 83% were in nursing homes. Detailed analysis of 19 cases showed that all were demented, 13 had impulsive or involuntary movements, and 14 had recently tried to escape."

From Miles & Irvine (1992, p. 762).

the studies by Wershow (1976) and by Lewis (1985) discussed earlier in this chapter. How much of the increase in mortality rate is due to the transfer itself remains an issue of debate within the field of gerontology; obviously, healthy people are not placed in nursing homes, and many of the early deaths could be of sick people who might otherwise have died in the hospital or at home. Overall, those who are able to adapt to a different environment often do pretty well in nursing home settings and are fairly realistic about the stresses associated with living in an institution (Stein, Linn, & Stein, 1986). Those who perceive that they can maintain some control over their environment seem to respond best (Mikhail, 1992). Some research demonstrates that those moved within a nursing home do better if they are carefully prepared for the move (Grant, Skinkle & Lipps, 1992).

Conclusion

Quality of nursing home care is subjective; in a way, it's like beauty: we all know it when we see it, but it's difficult to describe in objective terms. The response of governmental agencies to the maintenance of quality in nursing homes is, of necessity, the issuance of increasingly tighter regulations (Shaughnessy, 1989). Some gerontologists argue that the pendulum of relying on regulations has swung too far, that staff are virtually hamstrung in decision-making. Energy is taken away from therapeutic work in order to concentrate on meeting regulations and avoiding liability (Wiener & Kayser-Jones, 1989). One effort at response is the Long-Term Care ***Ombudsman*** program that each state agency on aging has. An ombudsman is a mediator who tries to resolve conflicts between two parties. This program tries to respond to complaints informally and settle them without interference from regulatory bodies or litigation. This may work well in some instances. However, research is lacking to indicate a thorough evaluation of the program's effectiveness (Netting, Paton, & Huber, 1992).

Older people in the United States find themselves in a peculiar position: they are the only group, as of this writing, that is entitled to national health insurance—the Medicare program. Yet that program for all intents and purposes does not cover the health care need many of them ultimately have—long-term care.

Long-term care at home and long-term nursing home care become the only options for the very old who are frail or disabled. For those without a caretaker at home, entry into a nursing home ultimately becomes almost inevitable. It is impractical to expect hospitals to care for people who do not need acute care, and, as we saw in Table 9.1, hospital use already doubles with each decade in late life.

Families tend to look to nursing home care as a last resort after their own resources are exhausted. We will see in Chapter 14 that private and governmental agencies have made an increasing variety of services available to help keep people at home for as long as possible. This maintenance of independence, however, usually relies on the presence of a capable caretaker in the home or nearby. This is not always likely. Not everyone has a capable caretaker, and caregivers under too much of a burden may become abusive.

The modern nursing home fills a need for families and their older members who need care. Regardless of the headlines that expose scandals and neglect in some facilities, the majority do a good—and often thankless—job. The expectation of restoration to independence of every nursing home resident is not a realistic one. After all, lives do end. It happens that the nursing home is where a large proportion of the lives of older people meet their end. In a sense, then, the nursing home has a dual role: rehabilitation of people who have been hospitalized, and hospice care for those who will die in the institution.

Through effective advocacy, older people caught up in the health care system need not be helpless. The real problem is that so many reach very late life without a social support network and have no advocates.

Questions for Discussion

1. Do you think that families should be forced to pay for nursing home care of their older family members?
2. If you have a family member in a nursing home, are you aware of how much the monthly cost is?
3. What is meant by the reference in the chapter to a "juggernaut?"
4. Why do so many older people look upon entry into a nursing home as the end of the road?
5. Do members of your family provide long-term care for an older family member? If so, what's involved?
6. What do you think the best options are for avoiding nursing home care?

Sources of Further Information

Many area agencies on aging have listings of support groups for family caretakers of older individuals, as well as support groups specifically for bereaved persons and for those who care for a person with Alzheimer's disease. In addition, the Area Agency on Aging can put one in touch with the Long-Term Care Ombudsman employed by the state department or commission on aging in each of the states. Look in the Yellow Pages of your local phone book under "social service organizations."

The National Eldercare Institute on Long Term Care is funded by the U.S. Administration on Aging to disseminate materials on nursing homes; a publications list can be requested from that organization:

c/o National Association of State Units on Aging
1225 I Street, N.W., Suite 725
Washington, D.C. 20005
202/898-2578

A number of other organizations are funded to administer advocacy projects on behalf of at-risk older people:

Alzheimer's Association
919 N. Michigan Ave.
Chicago, IL 60611-1676
800/272-3900

National Association of Area Agencies on Aging
1112 16th St., N.W., Suite 100
Washington, D.C. 20036
202/296-8130

American Association of Homes for the Aging
901 E Street, N.W., Suite 500
Washington, D.C. 20004
202/783-2242

National Committee for Prevention of Elder Abuse
Medical Center of Massachusetts—Institute on Aging
119 Belmont St.
Worchester, MA 01605
508/793-6166

Older Women's League
666 11th St., N.W., Suite 700
Washington, D.C. 20001
202/783-6686

There is a monthly journal targeted to nursing home administrators and directors of nursing on current issues in the field. A one-year subscription can be had for $39.95 from:

Contemporary Long-Term Care
c/o Bill Communications, Inc.
P.O. Box 7689
Riverton, NJ 08077-9189

The End of Life

10

Chapter Outline

"The transience of life gives it its reality. Death is part of life. Those close to me, both alive and dead, are part of myself. These objects will be here when I'm not, part of the mystic flow that outlasts the giver and the given, the living and the dead. The persons who have composed both the discords and harmonies of my life continue in me, and from me, to the people whose lives I help compose the discords and harmonies of theirs."

— Charlotte Zolotow, born 1915

Introduction

One surprising finding in research on how people feel about death is that older persons seem to have less fear of it and younger people have higher levels of death anxiety. This may be because young people have more to lose—they've not yet had a chance to live their lives. It also may be because older people are more likely to have gone through a life review process; while they have looked at the meanings of their lives, they have also be-

glossary

terminal — Literally "the end;" a terminal illness is one that is expected to result in the individual's death.

come reconciled to the impending end of life (Butler, 1963). We'll look in this chapter how the meanings of death differ among older and younger people. This may lead to some practical implications as to how best to help people who are dying.

We'll also look at grief and the process of bereavement in this chapter, as well as the shocking information on suicide among older white males.

Helping the dying will be our focus, for all of us some day will be involved in care for a dying person. Some, of course, will work with those who are **terminally** ill on a professional basis. Others will be faced with the death of a loved one. In either event, there are some practical considerations that may help in terms of providing support and advocacy for people who are dying.

On the Nature of Death

Death is a natural part of the life cycle, a fact that we all know objectively, but, on a feeling level, have a difficult time adjusting to. However, those closest to death, the aged, seem to fear it least. This is true despite the fact that they are closer to it and are the ones who have the most experience with it. Most death takes place in late life.

Many younger persons are, in effect, shielded from personal encounters with death: if a young person dies, it is most likely from a sudden cause, such as an accident. Few young people have the experience of someone they are close to dying over an extended period of time from a chronic illness. And the young are often segregated from the old in our society. Many young people have little experience with death. It is not unusual to find a young adult who has never been to a funeral.

Older people, on the other hand, come from an age cohort where childhood death was not uncommon. Early in this century, it was typical to grow up and know persons of one's own age who died of diseases such as tuberculosis, polio, diphtheria, or pneumonia. Death was more likely to take place in the home, where it could be seen; now, almost 80% of deaths take place in hospitals or nursing homes, and we are thus separated from the personal encounter of seeing a loved one die day by day. And of course, it is the aged in our society who have the most experience with death throughout the lifespan. The elderly have had to face the deaths of contemporaries, friends, and relatives over the course of the years. They are the likeliest to be widowed and the likeliest to have had to work through the loss of those closest to them into their lives. The old are no strangers to death and grief.

The aged are also increasingly in the situation of anticipating their own death. One cannot experience the deaths of siblings or peers without thinking about personal survival. Needs of the aged thus may turn to memories and memorials, reflecting on life's meaning, and seeking to leave a personal legacy. Confronted with the inevitability of one's own death, the thoughts of older people must also turn to necessities: taking care of unfin-ished business, resolving interpersonal issues, and being concerned over matters of personal care.

As we saw in Chapters 1 and 7, the nature of death changed over the course of the twentieth century. Leading causes of death at one time were for the most part sudden, acute illnesses. Now, except for accidents, most of the leading causes of death are chronic and occur in late life. This means that the death *trajectory*, the path of development that most dying people go through, is extended: it usually takes some time to die, and death is characterized in most instances by an inevitable downward progression. This means that dying people may face steadily declining levels of func-tional ability over the course of months or even years. It also means that terminal care has emerged as a specialty area in recent years.

The emphasis of terminal care should be to allow individuals to live until they die, to provide comfort measures and support in such a way as to maximize life's possibilities even as life draws to a close. The unfortunate situation—something we need to guard against—is that too often terminally ill people are consigned to a lesser status, that of "dying person," and are treated as if they are no longer fully human. This is an issue we'll discuss at some length in the next section of this chapter. For now, though, we need to keep it in mind as the most important implication of our entire discus-sion of death and dying in later life.

Table 10.1 reinforces the point on chronic causes of death. Note that the causes (given per 100,000 per year for different age groups) that imply chronic illness—such as heart disease, cancer, and cerebrovascular causes—are the most frequent in that they continue to grow proportionally into very late life. The odds are overwhelming that older people will die of a

*g*lossary

trajectory — A downward-sloping line; a *death trajectory* describes the process over time of nearing the end of life.

TABLE 10.1. Death Rates by Age and Cause

Cause	Age			
	55–64	65–74	75–84	85+
Heart disease	315.2	776.2	2,010.2	6,314.5
Cancer	406.5	861.6	1,351.5	1,798.3
Cerebrovascular	45.3	135.5	477.0	1,612.7
Chronic obstructive pulmonary	47.0	161.6	385.3	540.9
Accidents	32.2	47.0	102.0	276.2
Pneumonia and influenza	16.9	56.8	230.6	1,010.9
Diabetes	39.5	88.7	166.1	288.0
HIV	8.4	2.7	0.8	—
Suicide	13.7	15.0	20.0	20.2
Liver disease	24.9	30.7	30.7	21.4
Kidney failure	7.9	24.8	73.1	209.6
Septicemia	8.2	21.7	59.3	172.7
Alzheimer's disease	1.3	11.0	72.8	284.7
Homicide	4.1	3.0	2.9	3.0
Atherosclerosis	2.7	10.1	43.0	241.7

From Peters, Kochanek, & Murphy (1998).

chronic cause, and these odds get all the greater among the oldest old. Note also that, with the exception of pneumonia and influenza, there are few acute conditions listed among the natural causes.

Setting the statistics aside, dying is a very human issue, and death has a potent meaning—or a number of meanings—to all of us, older people included. The end of one's personal existence, the dissolution of the personality, the idea of missing out on things going on after one's death, the loss of personal control, concern for those who survive us, what happens to the body, and the uncertainty of life after death all are issues that confront us when we contemplate death.

As the merchant Cephalus said to Socrates, when a man faces the thought that he must die, he feels fear and anxiety about that which did not trouble him before (Thorson & Powell, 1988). Most of us are able to objectively acknowledge that we will die sooner or later, but the "later" part dominates our thinking; we successfully repress thoughts of death most of the time. This might not be a possibility for the elderly. Not only are they reminded day in and day out that their bodies are nearing a point of failure, but the concept of personal death is reinforced by the experience of friends and relatives of the same generation who have died. One can't see one's sister or brother die without thinking, "I may be next."

The idea that meanings of death might be different among older persons in comparison to those of younger people led us to do a research project on elements of death anxiety and meanings of death (Thorson & Powell, 1988). We gave a 25-item death anxiety scale to 599 people ranging from 16 to 86 years of age and analyzed the factors and responses to the items of the scale to answer the question: what is it in particular about death that people fear most? The first difference we found was that older subjects as a group had much less overall death anxiety, a finding that has been confirmed in the many different studies we've done (e.g., Thorson & Powell, 1990, 1991, 1993a, 1994; Thorson, Powell, & Samuel, 1998a, 1998b). Next, we found that women had a significantly higher score on the death anxiety scale than men, mostly because they expressed higher fears of pain and bodily decomposition.

The elements of death that most concerned older people were fear of a loss of control and concerns with the uncertainty of an afterlife. Young people, by contrast, showed higher anxiety on many different aspects of death: bodily decomposition, immobility, fear of pain and helplessness, and isolation. The most universal fear, expressed by over 80% of the total sample, was concern over an afterlife.

The finding on anxiety over the uncertainty of an afterlife came as something of a surprise; when doing research, one often finds things one was not looking for. It was evident from our findings that our respondents had concerns over elements of death that others had not investigated. The meaning of existence, something that people who have gone through a life review might have resolved, apparently was a primary concept when people thought of death. This led us to another study, this time on relationships between death anxiety and religiosity.

We gave the death anxiety scale and a measure of intrinsic (inward) religiosity to a sample of 346 people ranging in age from 18 to 88 years (Thorson & Powell, 1990). Intrinsic religiosity deals more with beliefs and spiritual well-being, as apposed to extrinsic religiosity, the outward activities of religion, such as going to church. Again, we found older persons to be significantly lower in death anxiety and significantly higher in intrinsic religiosity. Further analysis revealed that those higher in religiosity were lower in death anxiety. However, there is no relationship for those who are not religious: this does not appear to be a construct, and might explain contradictory findings in some previous studies of death anxiety and religion. Lower death fear appears to apply only to those high in intrinsic religiosity.

Most older people cope pretty well with the prospect of death, and we are only now learning about some of these coping mechanisms. Another

---

Illustration 10.2. Some Practical Implications from the Death Anxiety Research

Death obviously means different things to different people, and it would be a mistake to go in and assume that all dying people have the same needs. Nurses, social workers, chaplains, and others who work with dying people should, I think, feel free to be fairly direct in asking people who are dying what concerns them most. For those who express fears of the pain involved in the dying process, reassurance should be given that everything possible will be done to keep them out of pain (and this should be followed up with advocacy, letting the medical staff know that particular efforts in pain management need to be made on the individual's behalf). Many people may have unfinished business; perhaps it would be possible to help them resolve some of the affairs that are concerning them. Sometimes these concerns may come as a surprise. Elisabeth Kubler-Ross (1969) wrote of a woman dying of cancer who could never quite get to the point of death. Asked by her daughter what was the matter, she said, "I hate the thought of being eaten up by worms!" The daughter suggested that arrangements could be made to have her body cremated. This put the woman at ease, and she died peacefully that night. No one would have known of the woman's anxiety over decay and bodily decomposition unless her daughter had asked the question.

social death — A
decline in individual
social worth so drastic
that the individual
begins to be treated
mechanically, like an
object rather than as a
person.

study we did involved giving a large sample of adults the death anxiety scale and a scale that measures different dimensions of sense of humor (Thorson & Powell, 1993a). We found both that the factor of coping humor increased into old age, and that those high in coping humor were significantly lower in death anxiety.

So, we have clues at least that older people may use both religiosity and humor as they face death. No doubt there are additional adaptive mechanisms characteristic of individual personalities that may be useful in helping the aged adapt to the end of life. As a practical matter, the caretakers of the dying unfortunately know little of their patients' personal histories. Likes and dislikes, things that people enjoy, fears that they might have, and other personal matters too often are given little consideration in the often-impersonal environments of institutions. Older people usually can speak in a fairly matter-of-fact way about death; it is only through personal inquiries that we can learn how best to serve the needs of those who are terminally ill.

On the Nature of Dying

It is possible to differentiate the prospect of death from the process of dying. Many people who are in their last illness say that they don't have that much fear of being dead, it is the process of dying that gives them the greatest concern. Those who may have little anxiety for the prospect of the hereafter might be greatly concerned with the present and with pain. The sad fact is that unless patients ask for pain medication, there may be an assumption that they don't need it. And despite all the things that are now known about pain management, many people near the end of life in a great deal of discomfort. One study of the deaths of 200 older people found that most had a great deal of pain in their final year of life. Pain increased over the course of that last year, and by the final month, 66% felt pain often or all the time (Moss, Lawton, & Glicksman, 1991). Pain contributed significantly to depression among these individuals.

The unfortunate fact is that while techniques exist to ease even the most intractable pain, they are not always used (Coyle, 1990). Patient advocacy in this regard involves careful questioning to determine if the individual is uncomfortable; some older people may not want to bother the nurse or the doctor about how they feel, or they may think that they will be categorized as chronic complainers if they ask for pain relief.

A major issue in care of the dying—and this is especially the case with older people who are dying—is a status differential. The social value of people who are dying can decline to such a point that *social death* may occur long before actual physical death. Social death involves being treated as if one were already dead. It can be characterized by such things as talking about people in their presence without acknowledging that they can hear, or treating people in a dehumanizing way, more like objects than as individuals (Sweeting & Gilhooly, 1992). People who are dying often receive the most mechanical care, as if developing a personal relationship will somehow infect the caretaker. In effect, social death means that social value has become so low that the person is no longer considered to be a part of the world of the living, but has been more or less consigned to the world of the dead.

As we saw in Chapter 2, it is not uncommon for older people to be victims of ageism, of prejudice and discrimination due to their perceived unimportance in a society that values youth. This can be even more the case with the terminally ill, who may be characterized by a loss of essential personhood in a society that values health. This in effect blames the victim. The attitude is that older people who are terminally ill represent all that is negative in contemporary society: perhaps they are wrinkled, toothless, or helpless; they may be depressed, confused, cranky, or ill-smelling. The result is that they often are isolated, especially in institutions where it is not uncommon to segregate dying patients off into one part of the building where they will be out of sight. In effect, dying older people have minimal status both because they are dying and because they are old (Glaser & Strauss, 1968). This can be especially apparent among those who are demented.

Institutionalization can be seen as something of a status passage in itself, in that people entering a hospital or a nursing home are leaving the world of the healthy and entering the world of the sick. And, the older individual entering an institution must wonder if going through the doors will be a one-way trip. This may be especially true for long-term care. With hospitalization, the expectation usually is that the person will be treated and then released. This might not be the expectation at all with entry into a nursing home. The family (and the individual) may well see entry into long-term care as a message that a dying trajectory has begun. With the understanding of this message, the person might be regarded as less "alive" and less of a player in the world of the living. This affects how they are treated, and it influences how people see themselves. It is not uncommon for institutionalized people to draw into themselves and lose interest and contact with the outside world.

Signs of social death vary. Making decisions for people that they are perfectly capable to make for themselves can be an indication of the onset of social death. Not talking to the individual or, especially, talking about the individual as if he or she is not there can be a sign. Medical staff are often guilty of this, and it is almost always resented by the individual. Even comatose patients have been able to repeat conversations about them that took place while they were apparently unconscious. Any behavior that treats people as less than individuals can be an indication of impending social death.

Expectancies relating to death sometimes can be predictive of behavior. Taking decision-making power away from people, giving them only the most mechanical of care, not making attempts to involve them in the outside world—all of these things can communicate the message that death is expected. Those treated this way may conclude that there is little left to live for. If personal control is taken away, people may go into a failure-to-thrive syndrome, become helpless, and enter a downward spiral ending in death (Braun, Wykle, & Cowling, 1988; Verdery, 1997).

There are other, related signs of impending death. Decreasing functional ability and life satisfaction may be predictive of oncoming death (Parker, Thorslund, & Nordstrom, 1992). Cognitive disorders are also predictors, as is depression. Especially, those who express a wish to die are more likely to do so (Ashby, Amers, West, & Macdonald, 1991). Epidemiological evidence indicated that people may have some control over when they die; one study demonstrated that people may often hold on until after religious holidays (Idler & Kasl, 1992).

Bereavement and Widowhood

Loss of one's spouse is one of the most catastrophic life changes that one can experience, and loss of spouse is, of course, most likely to happen in old age. Just when people become most physically and economically vulnerable, they are also at a point in life where the death of their husband or wife is most likely to happen. This may represent the end of a relationship that has lasted many years, and its impact cannot be underestimated. Other changes in life might have major outcomes, but widowhood not only represents the obvious loss but also any number of additional losses that combine to change the survivor's life in unexpected ways. Loneliness and grief are the primary manifestations of widowhood, but the loss of the role or status of married person can have a major impact, as can the lack of availability of a willing sexual partner. Companionship, daily activities, social networks, and the availability of a confidant all change with the loss of one's partner.

The most obvious statistical fact about widowhood in the United States is the gender difference: women live about 10% longer than men, and it is typical for women to have married a man who is several years older. There were 2.11 million widowed men aged 65+ in the U.S. in 1997 (15.7% of the total male population in that age group) and 8.54 million widowed women. This represented 46.3% of all women aged 65 and above (U.S. Bureau of the Census, 1998). Among those 75+, 25.4% of men are widowers and 61.5% of women are widows. Males are much more likely to remarry, an option that most women don't have; women who are widowed in later life are confronted with a lack of available partners.

Widowhood for older women can, in a way, be seen as normative or expected. Oftentimes men whose wives die say that they expected to be the first to go. Some research points to the loss of a husband as a status passage: it's expected, there are many other women in the same situation, and there is an understood role for widows in American society (Howie, 1993). Widowhood represents an orientation to inevitable death, but there are so many women who live for a considerable number of years as widows that there is a growing sense of living beyond bereavement. Widows often retain or develop considerable social networks (Lopata, 1988). This has several important implications.

A classic study of bereavement published in 1963 followed 4,486 widowers aged 54+ for the year after the death of their wives. There was an increase of death of almost 40% during the first six months over what the anticipated rate should have been for men in the same age group. This elevated mortality rate trailed off rapidly thereafter and was back to the anticipated rate by the end of the first year (Young, Benjamin, & Wallis, 1963). One outcome of this research was that it was for many years felt that the stress of the loss of spouse led to higher than anticipated levels of illness and death among survivors.

It was only in 1981 that this apparent mortality effect was clarified. Knud Helsing and his colleagues did a 12-year follow-up of a sample of 4,032 adults and found that mortality rates were about the same for widowed as for married females. The rates were, however, significantly higher for males who were widowed compared to those who were married. Mortality among widowed males who remarried were much lower than for those who did not remarry. No significant difference was found among widowed females who did or did not remarry. This left the question as to why older men seemed to adapt so poorly to the loss of a spouse in comparison to the experience of older women who had been widowed.

A third epidemiological study of widowhood, social networks, and mortality provides some of the answers. Teresa Seeman and her colleagues (1987) reported on a 17-year study of 7,000 adults. They found widows' highest relative mortality to be among those aged 38 to 49. The rates were lower among women who lost their spouse in later ages, going down to what the expected rate would be among those aged 60 to 69, and only slightly higher among those 70+. The big difference they found had to do with the importance of a social network. Those of both sexes who had a large number of contacts with friends and family and who belonged to church groups and voluntary organizations were much less likely to die after the loss of a spouse.

A 1996 study in Finland followed 1,580,000 married persons aged 35 through 84 for five years. Excess mortality among those who were bereaved during the period of the study was greatest during the first six months after the death of the spouse and greatest among younger subjects than among older ones. Unanticipated death was most closely related to excess mortality among survivors, and the excess mortality was most likely to be a death from accidental, violent, or alcohol-related causes (Martikainen & Valkonen, 1996). Another longitudinal study found that the likelihood of mortality actually declined among older female survivors who had been caring for a spouse during an extended illness (Smith & Zick, 1996). One additional study found that it is typical for bereaved older men to experience declines in mental health, morale, and social functioning (Bennett, 1998).

We might draw two conclusions from these studies. The first has to do with the element of anticipation. Older men are expected to die first. Older women seem to be able to work this into their lives. When the wife dies

first, however, it is unexpected, and the man may be poorly prepared. Indeed, one study of gender differences in bereavement found that among
women, the main element linking widowhood to depression was financial
strain; among men, it was the difficulty of household management
(Umberson, Wortman, & Kessler, 1992). Perhaps the members of this generation of older men are not able to cope very well on their own. The second implication we might draw from the epidemiological studies is that
women maintain and develop social networks more readily than do men
do. Widows have more people to turn to for support; the man whose wife
dies may have lost his only confidant and be truly isolated.

Another study of older widows found that the loss of spouse among
women is not a predictor of either community integration or the lack of it
(Pellman, 1992). Women seem to maintain their social networks well into
very late life whether they are widowed or not. This is not the case for male
widowers.

It was once thought, due to the anticipation of death of spouse in later
life and the corresponding opportunity to accomplish grief work during
the spouse's final illness while he was still alive, that the impact of grief on
older women was less than that upon younger persons who were bereaved.
The notion was that caregiver strain was lifted from the responsibilities of
the surviving spouse, and life was that much less stressful for her despite
the fact of bereavement. More recent research contradicts this. One study
of younger and older widows found that the older women showed more
intense grief at the time of the interview than did the younger women.
They had greater feelings of depression and anxiety. This is explained by
the life-long relationship that is lost by the older women, in spite of the
element of anticipation (Sable, 1991). The basic loss with bereavement continues to exist like a phantom limb after an amputation (Horacek, 1995).

The process of bereavement is a familiar one, although there are some
misconceptions about it. Some writers have proposed stages of grief that
persons must go through and accomplish prior to bereavement resolution,
and it has been suggested that one year is probably a reasonable time to
expect this process to last. There is in fact little research to support any

---

Illustration 10.5. Generational Changes Among Widows

We are now beginning to see differences in the generation of women who are becoming widowed. The principal one is that they are much likelier than their mothers to have worked outside the home, and have that much greater an opportunity to form broader social networks.
One study of 157 women aged 55–75 whose husbands had died suggests that those who had
paid work during their married years coped much better with bereavement (Aber, 1992). They
were more self-confident in their own abilities and had greater adaptive skills. They also had an
identity with their worker status in addition to their spousal identity.

staging theory of bereavement; there may be wavelike patterns of different, complex emotions affecting the grief-stricken person. These come and go, but they may be combined in different ways and certainly do not represent a hierarchy. Among these emotions are sadness and depression, sleeplessness, guilt, anger, loneliness, inability to concentrate, and fatigue. Thoughts of the departed one that may dominate the consciousness shortly after the death become less frequent over time, but one doesn't get over grief: one learns to live with it.

One study of bereaved older persons found their eating behaviors to be disrupted and that they had consequent nutritional deficiencies (Rosenbloom & Whittington, 1993). Another found that most experienced loneliness and feelings of unhappiness and ill health (Grimby, 1993). Most of those studied also experienced illusions or hallucinations of the deceased, which were described as pleasant and helpful. Marital happiness was related to the frequency and good quality of these illusions, but length of marriage was not. As might have been expected, the quality of life among those who had been recently widowed was lower than controls who were married or single.

In general, there are several practical implications that can be drawn from the grief research. First, it helps to talk about it. Attempts to enter the personal world of the bereaved person are usually appreciated, even if these efforts seem awkward. Getting the person to ventilate in a non-judgmental atmosphere usually is healthy. On the other hand, assurances such as "I know just how you feel" or "You'll get over this in time" or "It was God's will" are usually of little help and may be resented. We should try to let people express feelings, not tell them how to feel.

It should be no surprise if grief has physical outcomes, such as feeling ill or having headaches or fatigue. Grief is often compared to doing hard work; it can be exhausting. Feeling better for a while may be followed by a totally unexpected downward swing later on. More than one emotion can be felt at the same time. Guilt and anger, emotions that are difficult to

---

Illustration 10.6. Findings from a Two-Year Study of Surviving Spouses

A study done at the University of Utah College of Nursing (Lund, Caserta, & Dimond, 1986) followed 192 men and women who had lost a spouse, gathering information from them at six different intervals over the course of two years. The findings included these points:

• Men and women did not differ substantially in their bereavement adjustments.
• As a group, the bereaved elderly were found to improve gradually over time.
• There is evidence that bereavement is a long-term experience; it does not end in one or two years.
• Bereavement is characterized by competing and conflicting behaviors that occur simultaneously.
• There is no evidence for specific stages of grief.

express in our society, are often present. Finally, pain doesn't always diminish, it just becomes less frequent.

To sum up, while grief outcomes for older and younger men and women may differ, the process itself seems to be similar. The situational context in our society is such that the majority of older women are or will be widows. Their husbands are likelier to die before they do, and men who have lost a spouse are likelier than women to remarry in later life. Widowhood is thus normative among older women; it involves a status change, but this usually is an accepted status change. Older women seem to adapt better than men to the loss of a spouse, probably because they are more likely to have a support network. Older men who lose a confidant are likely to be vulnerable, and they may be suicidal; depression and hopelessness predict suicide (Uncapher, Gallagher-Thompson, Osgood, & Bongar, 1998). The process of bereavement itself is not resolved in a set period of time; one doesn't get over grief so much as one learns to live with it. We can support people who are bereaved by being good listeners and encouraging them to share their feelings.

Suicide

Suicide is a major public health problem among older white males. Contrary to the accepted stereotype, teenagers do not commit the most suicides in American society; as a group, the suicide rate for teens is less than that for the population as a whole. The social value of teenagers is such that teen suicides tend to grab the headlines, and suicide rates among teens have increased in recent decades, but their rates are relatively low in comparison to adult groups. Men, especially white men, commit the most suicide (73% of all suicides are accounted for by white males), and their rate increases dramatically with age (Peters, Kochanek, & Murphy, 1998). The very highest rates are found among white males aged 85 and over.

Table 10.2 demonstrates that there are large variations in suicide rates by age, sex, and race. As a general rule, the suicide rate for women at any age is never even half as high as the corresponding rate for males of the same age and race. And, the rates for African-Americans at most ages are significantly lower than suicides among whites. Table 10.2 reports deaths from suicide per 100,000 in the population for whites, blacks, Native Americans, Hispanics, Pacific Islander, and those whose heritage is Asian. As we can see, the rates for white women increase until middle life and then decline slightly in older age groups. Among black women, there are very few suicides, especially in later life, which is also true of Hispanic women. Native American women commit suicide at relatively higher rates in comparison to the other groups shown in young and middle adulthood, but their suicide rate then declines in later middle age and is so low in late life as to be unreliable statistically. Asian and Pacific Islander females are the only

TABLE 10.2. Suicides per 100,000 Population by Age, Sex, and Race, 1996

Age	White	Black	Native American	Hispanic	Asian, Pacific Islander
Males					
15–24	22.8	18.4	37.3	17.4	14.3
25–44	26.0	18.4	35.0	15.6	11.9
45–64	24.3	11.3	13.7	13.7	8.9
65–74	29.8	13.6	11.8	18.5	18.1
75–84	47.8	14.7	*	*	*
85+	68.2	14.6	*	*	*
Females					
15–24	3.8	2.4	7.7	2.8	4.6
25–44	5.4	3.1	7.1	2.7	4.2
45–64	6.9	2.2	4.8	2.5	5.1
65+	5.5	2.1	*	2.4	8.1

*Data not available

From Pamuk, Makuc, Heck, Reuben, & Lochner (1998).

group among women in the United States to have a suicide rate that increases in later life. Still, it is less than half of the rate for Asian or Pacific Islander men aged 65+.

Native American men commit the most suicide in younger ages; their rate trails off after age 45 and becomes the lowest of the five groups shown by age 65. Note that statistical standards of reliability are not met after age 75 for Native American, Hispanic, and Asian or Pacific Islander males, so no data is reported in those instances in Table 10.2. African-American males start off with a relatively high rate of suicide in younger adult years and then commit relatively few suicides later in life. The rate for Hispanic or Latino men does not show a clear pattern by age, declining a little in mid-life and then increasing somewhat after age 65. Similarly, Asian or Pacific Islander men have a suicide rate in mid-life that is rather low; it then more than doubles in later life.

The group in American society that has by far the highest suicide rate is older white males. Higher than the other groups by age 45, it then begins to climb so that it is by far the highest (29.8 per 100,000 in the population) by age 65 to 74. By ages 75 to 84, it has increased to 47.8; it then skyrockets to 68.2 by age 85.

Suicide rates have shown a 20-year increase for the male age categories, black and white, but there have been only slight increases over time for younger females, and there have been significant declines in the rate of suicides among those in young adulthood and the middle years for both black and white women (U.S. Bureau of the Census, 1998b). The overall total number of suicides in the United States declined by about 10% in the final years of the 1990s.

One wonders what the explanation is for the dramatically differing suicide rates by age, race, and sex. One basic explanation might be that the most stressful time of life for women comes in the middle years, while it comes in young adulthood for African-American males and in the later years for white males. However, there is little in the way of research to connect this hypothesis of stressful times of life with suicide; we need to take a closer look at motivations and causes of suicide.

Some of the earliest survey research in the social sciences was done by French Sociologist Emile Durkheim. First published in 1897, Durkheim's book *Suicide* points to **anomie** as an underlying explanation for most self-destructive behavior. Defining anomie is one point where sociologists and psychologists differ. From a sociological point of view, anomie is defined as normlessness, social instability resulting from a breakdown of standards and values. A psychologist, on the other hand, would understand anomic behavior as a tendency to view the future with pessimism and to feel controlled by hostile outside forces, or perhaps as alienation resulting from a lack of purpose in life. Other commonly understood motivations for suicide include egoistic, where the person seeks to destroy the self, and altruistic, where the individual sacrifices himself for some greater good; these probably represent only a small minority of suicides.

One recent study of geriatric suicide points to the primary motivation being a desire to escape from intolerable life circumstances (Courage et al., 1993). Most research associates suicidal behavior with depression and hopelessness, and it is accepted that suicidal motivation often can be seen as wavelike, coming and going in varying degrees of intensity (Uncapher, Gallagher-Thompson, Osgood, & Bongar, 1998). A review of studies on suicide among the elderly found that the likeliest group to commit suicide is, as we have already seen, the oldest category of white males; within that group, though, it is those who are widowed or divorced who are much more likely to kill themselves (McIntosh, 1992). Another study found that suicide in later life was associated with more determined and planned self-destructive methods and fewer warnings of suicidal intent (Conwell et al., 1998).

Making sense of suicide can be difficult, but there is at least some logic that might explain self-destructive behaviors among older white males. If one thinks of the concept of locus of control that was introduced in Chapter 6, it is white males who are the most likely to have enjoyed an internal locus of control during adult life. The lives of the other groups we have discussed—women, African-Americans, and other minority groups—have been much more likely to have been externally controlled (although this of course is changing). Old age may bring real prospects of change in the location of one's control from internal to external; for many people, old age represents helplessness and isolation. Having others in control of one's affairs may be perceived as intolerable. For those who have not had much of a say in societal decision-making, however, this prospect in old age may represent no real change: many members of minority groups have had little power to lose.

glossary

anomie — Viewing the future with pessimism and feeling controlled by hostile outside forces; normlessness or helplessness.

Older white males, on the other hand, have pretty much been the decision-makers in the business and social worlds that they lived in; the prospect of the loss of this internal control may be a motivation for suicide. This is particularly true for those who have few social supports and who have lost their confidant through widowhood. The concept is a grim one: the statistics demonstrate, however, that some people would rather be dead than old, powerless, and alone. Haight (1995) found that those who commit suicide in nursing homes are over 85, want to retain control of their lives, and have a high degree of self-esteem.

By this theory, groups such as African-Americans and women, who are gaining power and internal control, may in the future demonstrate higher rates of suicide in late life when they are faced with the prospect of losing that power. But this is something we may have to wait for a generation or two to find out.

One other facet of the control theory of suicide motivation is that older men are those in society who have had the most life-long internal control, and suicide may thus be a demonstration of a last act of independence. They have had control throughout their lives, and by self-destruction are taking control over the end of their lives.

This kind of theorizing does not lend itself to proof by experimentation, of course, and suicide research by necessity is descriptive, giving rates, trends, and figures. Obviously, there is no one cause for self-destructive behaviors, and we can only extrapolate from the data to speculate on motivations and explanations. We can, however, put suicide into perspective: despite its highest rate among the oldest group of white males, it actually represents only a tiny proportion of deaths (less than 1%) when compared to major killers, like heart disease and cancer that increase rapidly in later life. Because of these increases in other causes, suicide is not in the top ten causes of death for white males aged 65+. It is far behind accidents, for example: for the year given, 13,543 white males 65+ died in accidents, while only 4,715 were suicide deaths. This compares to 248,511 deaths from heart disease for white males 65+ that same year (Peters, Kochanek, & Murphy, 1998).

Nevertheless, it does represent a commentary that old age is intolerable for some in our society, and it is certainly important for the lives and the families affected. Older men tend to use more lethal methods of killing themselves, and are also more likely to use multiple means (Conwell et al., 1998). This can be seen as an indication that they really do want to die, not just make a dramatic gesture or a cry for help. In a five-year study of suicide of males aged 60+ in Maricopa County, Arizona, Marv Miller (1978) found that the cause of death for 85% was a gunshot wound, most often to the head. Over a quarter of them had purchased the gun during the last month of their lives. Fewer than 5% in that study took drugs or inhaled lethal gas, means more typical of those who are uncertain as to whether or not they actually want to die.

Not everyone who wants an end to life goes about it so directly. Suicide statistics are thought to under-represent the actual number of deaths from self-destructive behaviors. Many accidents, for example, might well have resulted from suicidal intentions. There is also the phenomenon of *passive suicide*, letting oneself die. This can be manifested by such things as refusing to eat, forgoing medical treatment, or altering dosage of medications (Courage et al., 1993). Those who have given up the will to live may show clear signs of wanting to end life. This does not have to be as obvious as the person with kidney failure who decides to go off of dialysis; signs of it might also be seen in the diabetic who binges on candy or who continually misplaces or misuses her insulin, or the person with emphysema who continues to smoke. Passive suicidal behaviors can be manifested in a variety of different behaviors on the part of those who are ambivalent to whether they wish to continue to live.

glossary

passive suicide — Not taking an active means to kill oneself, but allowing oneself to die over the course of time.

Advocacy and Professional Roles

An increasing number of those in the health care and social service professions will spend a significant part of their careers working with older people, and this inevitably means that they will also spend a good deal of their professional lives working with people who are dying. There are some prac-

---

Illustration 10.8. Enjoying Each Day as "The Night Cometh"

"The paradox of time in maturity is that we can be vividly conscious of our inevitable temporal finitude and yet enjoy its abundance, because we are in no great hurry. To know that 'the night cometh' may actually be to sense a liberation from worry about lack of accomplishment, rather than the sadness which we usually associate with those sacred words. If I have only a few years in which to live, as is certainly the case, then the intelligent thing to do is to enjoy each day as though it were the last."

—D. Elton Trueblood, born 1900

---

tical outcomes related to this. Beyond the obvious implications of guarding against behaviors that lead to social death, of treating the terminally ill with the same kindness and consideration that is due to any living human, there are a number of ethical and professional considerations that are of importance.

Those who are not necessarily preparing for careers with the elderly will also confront care issues relevant to death and the process of dying: we all have parents, grandparents, or other older relatives. It is likely that almost all adults will, sometime in their lives, be caught up in the drama of another person's death. Whether one is a professional directly involved in service delivery or a daughter or son concerned with the care of a parent, it helps to have thought through some implications of terminal care.

The first of these issues is what it means to be an advocate for the patient. Not everyone is prepared or able to indicate their needs during their final illness. The old and frail may be at a particular disadvantage in this regard, and the comatose and the cognitively impaired obviously have no way to assert their needs. Family members, health care professionals, social service professionals, chaplains, or friends may need to serve as patient advocates to speak on their behalf.

Speaking for another may be difficult. In some cases, the needs may be obvious: if a person needs pain medication or nursing attention, then it is incumbent upon his or her advocate to request it. There usually isn't much controversy about such simple requests. The difficulty comes when decisions need to be made on such thorny issues as continuing further treatment. Families may go through much anguish over such matters, and professionals in health and social service can be of great assistance to them

---

Illustration 10.9. Living Will Declarations

If I should lapse into a persistent vegetative state or have an incurable and irreversible condition that without the administration of life-sustaining treatment will in the opinion of my attending physician, cause my death within a relatively short time and I am no longer able to make decisions regarding my medical treatment, I direct my attending physician, pursuant to the Rights of the Terminally Ill Act, to withhold or withdraw life-sustaining treatment that is not necessary for my comfort or to alleviate pain.

Signed this _____ day of _____, 20___.

(Signature)_____

Witness_____

Witness_____

---

by trying to outline different options and alternatives. Difficulties may arise, however, when not all of the family members are at the same level of acceptance.

A typical case is for those most closely involved in the situation to come to a realization that further curative efforts are no longer doing any good and it is time to move on to comfort and pain control measures to make the last days or weeks more livable. In effect, the goal of patient care at that point has moved from efforts to cure to efforts to care. A relative who has not been involved in the day-to-day decision making may enter the picture at this point and demand that further surgery or chemotherapy be attempted. It may fall on the nurse or social worker to try to work with the family to come to a consensus, or to urge them to select just one spokesperson who can speak with authority.

What helps more than anything else in this kind of a situation is to know what the individual affected would want. The best way to be sure of this is to make an *advance directive*, such as a Living Will or a statement appointing someone to have *durable power of attorney for health care*. The federal Patient Self-Determination Act of 1991 requires Medicaid-participating hospitals, nursing homes, home health agencies, hospices, and health maintenance organizations to provide information to patients on their rights to make advance directives for their care; indeed many such institutions now require that they do so. (Note, however, that not all nursing homes or other agencies and institutions are Medicaid-participating, nor is actually making an advance directive required—the law only specifies that people must be informed of their right to do so.)

Essentially, an advance directive is a written statement showing that the individual has made a particular health care decision or has appointed another individual to make such decisions for them. The most common form of an advance directive is a Living Will; it states the kind of medical care those involved want (or do not want), should they become unable to speak for themselves. The statement can be as simple as the one illustrated (Ill. 10.9), or it can be more elaborate. Some states have a special form that the Living Will should follow; a copy of it should be contained in the admissions packet given to new hospital or nursing home patients. In many instances, the person can specify particular treatments or details of care that are not included in a standard form; it is permissible to write additional comments on a Living Will.

In any event, however, it should be considered critical that the person's physician has a copy of the Living Will and that she or he understands the patient's wishes. Executing a Living Will and then keeping it in a desk drawer or safety deposit box will do little good: copies should be given to one's personal physician, lawyer, and next of kin. It is best if all family members are aware that the individual has executed a Living Will, and that they are in accord with the individual's wishes. Unfortunately, many older people are reluctant to prepare or sign such a document until confronted with its necessity (High, 1993).

g lossary

advance directives — A written statement such as a living will or a signed statement appointing someone to have durable power of attorney for health care; one gives preferences for terminal care, the other appoints an agent to determine appropriate care.

hospice — A program designed to serve the needs of people who are dying.

The SUPPORT project was a four-year clinical trial conducted in five teaching hospitals in the United States that followed 9,105 adult patients who had life-threatening illnesses. These patients had a six-month mortality rate of 47%. The objective of the study was to improve end-of-life decision making and to reduce the utilization of mechanical life supports at the very end. Phase I of the study, during the first two years, indicated genuine problems in patient-doctor communication: only 47% of physicians knew when their patients preferred to avoid cardiopulmonary resuscitation, 46% of all do-not-resuscitate (DNR) orders were written within two days of death, 38% of patients spent ten days or more in an intensive care unit at the end of their lives, and over half of the patients who died in the hospital were in moderate to severe pain at least half the time (the SUPPORT Principal Investigators, 1995).

The Phase II intervention sought to improve communication and understanding of patient preferences with regard to their final care. Nurse advocates worked with patients and families to educate them about advance directives and to encourage attention to pain control. However, the outcome of the project showed no improvement in incidence or timing of written DNR orders, physicians' knowledge of patients' preferences not to be resuscitated, number of days spent in intensive care, receiving mechanical ventilation, or being comatose before death. The conclusion of the project was that substantial shortcomings in terminal care remain the norm in American hospitals: "To improve the experience of seriously ill and dying patients, greater individual and societal commitment and more proactive and forceful measures may be needed" (the SUPPORT Principal Investigators, 1995, p. 1591).

Illustration 10.10. What Is Wrong with Care Near the End of Life?

SUPPORT documented serious problems with terminal care. Patients in the study experienced considerable pain: one half of the patients who died had moderate or severe pain during most of their final 3 days of life. Communication between physicians and patients was poor: only 41% of patients in the study reported talking to their physicians about ***prognosis*** or about cardiopulmonary resuscitation (CPR). Physicians misunderstood patients' preferences regarding CPR in 80% of cases. Furthermore, physicians did not implement patients' refusals of interventions. When patients wanted CPR withheld, a do-not-resuscitate (DNR) order was never written in about 50% of cases.

Other studies also have found serious deficiencies in pain control and with physician-patient communication. When describing CPR to patients, physicians use jargon, fail to provide quantitative information about outcomes, and miss opportunities to discuss the patient's goals and values. Unrealistically optimistic expectations lead patients to request interventions that physicians believe are inappropriate. Patients have overly optimistic estimates about the outcomes of CPR. After their misunderstandings are corrected, fewer patients desire CPR.

From Lo (1995, pp. 1634–1636).

One wonders, then, how Living Wills can have efficacy if they are routinely ignored by medical personnel. While there is some evidence that older persons often do not understand the full implications of advance directives, there is also evidence that older people trust their physician to carry out specific instructions about their dying (Huber & Evans, 1998).

Because no document can anticipate every eventuality of what might be wanted or not wanted in all of the circumstances that can arise during terminal care, an alternative is to appoint a trusted individual to have "Durable Power of Attorney for Health Care."

A Durable Power of Attorney for Health Care is a written directive naming another person (often a husband, wife, or adult child) to act as the individual's agent or representative, making health care decisions for those unable to make them for themselves. The person so designated obviously is to be guided by the individual's wishes, so it is a good thing to discuss those wishes beforehand.

The health care institution is required by law to indicate in writing its policy regarding advance directives. It is important to note that it is not federal law that the health care provider follow such directives, only that the provider follow state laws or court decisions that deal with advance directives. It is therefore advisable to have a clear, complete understanding with one's physician regarding what one's wants and needs are, and to

---

Illustration 10.11. Durable Power of Attorney for Health Care

Should I become disabled or incapacitated, I designate and authorize:

_____ (name)

_____ (relationship to me)

to consent on my behalf to all medical, surgical, and hospital treatment that in his or her opinion may be necessary or advisable for my health and benefit, and likewise to refuse to consent to and to waive and terminate such treatment, if he or she thinks it is advisable to do so. This designation and authorization shall be effective only in the event I become disabled or incapacitated to such an extent that I am unable to participate in decisions about my treatment.

_____ (signature)

_____ (date)

witness signature_____

witness signature_____

find out what the hospital and nursing home's policies are, prior to the need for any advance directive. The Living Will might in some cases be considered to be more of a statement of wishes than a legal document. However, the Durable Power of Attorney for Health Care is legally enforceable. Again, good advocacy for the patient involves explaining matters dealing with advance directives and the institution's policies.

Some nursing homes now include a statement with their admissions packet that, unless otherwise directed in writing, it will be assumed that there will be "no code" for the patient. This means that should the patient quit breathing or his or her heart stop, no efforts will be made to provide cardiopulmonary resuscitation (CPR); the staff will not "call a code" to initiate CPR. In other nursing homes or hospitals, this kind of order must be written in the patient's chart if that is what's wanted.

In either event, this kind of statement is also an advance directive, an understanding of what should be done in a particular set of circumstances. There is good evidence to indicate that many CPR efforts in nursing homes either are unsuccessful or provide a merely temporary stretching out of the dying process (Applebaum, King, & Finucane, 1990). Making a statement that CPR will not be initiated at least gives clarity and sanction to what otherwise may or may not be understood.

We have anecdotal evidence of instances where a *slow code* is called: the nurse is obliged to call a code for CPR because there is no written DNR directive, but the patient is clearly not going to respond, or bringing them back to life will only prolong their misery. In the instance of a "slow code," the nurse takes her time in alerting the CPR team in order to allow the person to be "good and dead" prior to going through the motions of attempting a revival (Wolfe, 1998). Nurses tell us they have heard of such things, and that they are often uncomfortable with assuming the decision-making when the matter of response should have been determined earlier.

Illustration 10.12. Resuscitation: When is Enough, Enough?

With the widespread training of health care providers and the lay public and the development of code teams and arrest protocols, CPR has come to be used for virtually anyone found in a pulseless state, unless explicit documentation exists that the patient should not be resuscitated. Yet, survival rates have not improved dramatically in the past 30 years. Initial success with resuscitation ranges from 30 to 50%. Although survival to discharge has been reported to occur in as many as 29% of patients suffering cardiac arrest and undergoing cardiopulmonary resuscitation in the hospital, most studies report less encouraging results, with survival to discharge occurring in about 15% of resuscitated patients. Of the survivors, 10 to 20% have evidence of moderate-to-severe neurologic dysfunction.

From Hamill (1995, pp. 515–522).

> **Illustration 10.13. Slow Codes**
>
> Of all the code scenarios, the most ethically charged is the slow code. This type of resuscitation "effort"—in which staff members take their time responding to a code call, or even in calling one, in the hopes that lifesaving measures will be started too late to do any good—though decreasing, remains an entrenched practice in healthcare. One in five respondents say they've taken part in a slow code during the last year—compared to one in four in 1988. Among nurses working in critical care or the emergency department, about two in five participated in a slow code in the previous year.
>
> From Wolfe (1998, p. 52).

In some instances, patient advocacy may mean asking the family and the physician to come to a prior resolution on these kinds of matters.

Decision-making in this regard is not often easy. Deciding to forgo CPR when the patient has ceased breathing, however, may be much simpler than, say, deciding to withhold feeding from a comatose patient. This is a excruciating ethical dilemma, and it goes beyond the scope of this chapter. Those involved in terminal care, however, need to discuss when life extension measures turn more into the process of extending the process of dying (Wurzbach, 1990). Again, it is always helpful to find out what the individual's wishes would be in different circumstances.

Ethical decisions must be made when the situation becomes extreme. Some argue that allowing terminally ill, comatose patients to die of dehydration is ethically and legally acceptable (Taylor, 1995). Others describe "terminal weaning" from ventilators, which essentially removes life support and provides patients with enough morphine to keep them in comfort

> **Illustration 10.14. 71-Year-Old Man Shoots Aged Mother**
>
> Chicago (AP)—A 71-year-old man who had been caring for his 98-year-old mother was accused Saturday of fatally shooting her in the head.
>
> "He said he's tired of seeing his mother suffering, and he shot her," police spokesman Pat Camden said.
>
> Terry Hutson, who was charged with first-degree murder, was arrested just after midnight Friday after police discovered the body of his mother, Georgia Hutson.
>
> She was shot once in the head with a bullet from a .22-caliber revolver.
>
> Hutson had been caring for his mother, who had had a stroke, for about 10 years and had prostate cancer himself, Camden said.
>
> From: Man Charged in Killing of His Mother, 98 (1999).

while they die from lack of oxygen (Sorenson & Thorson, 1998). Recently, assisted suicide among the terminally ill has been newsworthy. In one study of nurses' opinions on assisted suicide, a paradox was found: while the majority supported the concept of assisted suicide, most were opposed to the actual practice (Beder, 1998). After two affirmative plebiscites, the state of Oregon became the first political jurisdiction in the United States to condone assisted suicide.

Given that most older people in fact die peacefully without controversy over their treatment (Lawton, Moss, & Glicksman, 1990), it still is incumbent upon us to face the issues involved in terminal care. At the extreme, headlines are made by people like Dr. Jack Kevorkian, who has assisted many terminally ill people to commit suicide (Gibbs, 1993). As of March 29, 1999, Kevorkian had been convicted of second-degree murder in a Michigan court and was sentenced to from 10 to 30 years in the penitentiary. It shouldn't have to come to that. Effective pain control and good nursing care can give necessary support to those who are dying; this should be accepted as the norm (Meek, 1993). Those in the social services likewise should be prepared to provide counseling and personal support to individuals who are terminally ill.

Unfortunately, not all professionals who are involved in providing care to people who are dying feel that they have adequate preparation for the task. One study of nursing home social workers indicated that 71% of those studied said no policies on terminal care were available to them where they worked, and 59% reported that the role of social workers had not been discussed in terms of support for those who are dying (Remsen, 1993). Again, professionals need to discuss their roles in terms of providing care for people who are dying.

Illustration 10.15. Physician-Assisted Suicide

Oregon officials reported Wednesday that in the first year of the only legally sanctioned assisted-suicide program in the world, 15 terminally ill people in the state ended their lives with lethal medication.

The average age of the eight men and seven women who took their lives was 69, the state said; 13 had cancer, and the other two had heart or lung disease. Fourteen had lived in the state for at least six months and one came to the state to be with a family member. Eight other people also received prescriptions for drugs to end their lives in 1998, but six died from their illnesses before taking the drugs, and two were still alive as of January 1, 1999.

The state Health Division's official report on the states Death with Dignity Act was quickly hailed by advocates of doctor-aided dying as evidence that the law had not led to abuses, botched suicides or a widespread rush among the sick or suffering to move to Oregon for the right to be put to death, as many critics of the law had contended.

From Verhovek (1999).

Conclusion

glossary

catalyst — Someone who makes things happen.

The need for special efforts at care and support for people who are dying has been recognized, and much has been accomplished in this respect during recent years. There are now over 3,200 hospice organizations in the United States—institutions and agencies designed to provide specialized care to the terminally ill (Johnson & Slaninka, 1999). Hospice programs can be free-standing institutions, or they can be programs that are a part of hospitals, nursing homes, or home health agencies. The goal of the hospice is to maximize the quality of life for people who are dying through pain control, comfort measures, spiritual understanding, and interpersonal support. Especially, the hospice organization seeks to reassure dying people that they will not be abandoned once the possibility of a cure has passed. As a result of this open awareness of impending death, many superficialities and rituals of denial can be dispensed with, and the focus becomes the care that is wanted and needed by the individual.

Support groups are also available in many communities for people who are dying, for survivors, and for those responsible for caregiving. It often is helpful to share one's burdens with others who have had similar experiences and thus a special understanding of what one is going through.

Illustration 10.16. Guidelines for Those Visiting a Person in an Institution

1. Establish presence; be at the same eye level; don't be afraid to touch; dying people are often starved for human touch.
2. Eliminate distractions: turn off the television. Realize that excessive small talk can also be a distraction; so is pain. Frail people may not have the energy to spend long periods of time with you.
3. Deal with the person at their level; don't insist on acceptance if he or she wants to deny the reality of the situation. On the other hand, don't insist on denial if the patient is accepting.
4. Allow the expression of anger or guilt; encourage the expression of feelings. Realize that a depressed person may simply want your silent presence.
5. Don't be afraid to ask what the prognosis (the expected outcome) is. Discuss alternatives, especially unfinished business.
6. Realize that your role may be as a *catalyst*, someone who makes things happen. Ask if there are others the person wishes to speak to.
7. Encourage reminiscence, especially of any memories you may have in common.
8. Sit down and talk with the person when he or she wishes to talk. If this is impossible, make an appointment—and keep it.
9. Share your feelings, but realize that few dying persons have the time or energy to be bereavement counselors for their visitors.
10. Express your regard for the individual; don't be afraid to express love; don't be afraid to say goodbye.

Area Agencies on Aging and hospital social service departments should have lists of local support groups and how to contact them.

We need to realize that death and the process of dying have different meanings for different individuals. We shouldn't assume that all people who are facing death have the same needs or feelings. Listening to people is the first step in determining how to provide help. This often takes patience and understanding; many dying people are depressed. It is normal to go through a process of grieving for one's own future loss. And, depressed people don't necessarily have a ready list of things that would assist them. It may be important to treat the depression, something that modern psychiatry has been quite successful at doing. People who are dying may often be receptive to suggestions, ideas for things that would be of comfort. And those who wish to assist the dying should realize that they might need to suppress their own feelings in order to be effective helpers.

Questions for Discussion

1. It is sometimes said that people who are dying have a narrowing social world. Who are some of the individuals you would want to have around if you were nearing the point of death?
2. Why might suicide in later life be said, for some, to be a rational decision?
3. How has death changed during this century?
4. Why do we refer to grief "work"?
5. How do concepts of death differ for older people compared to those held by younger people?
6. What are some important ways to help people who are dying?
7. What are some signs of impending social death?
8. List some important considerations in deciding whom to appoint to have Durable Power of Attorney for Health Care?
9. Speculate as to some of the reasons for the great difference in suicide rates between older white males and older black females.

Sources of Further Information

Research studies on the topics of death and dying can be found in many different psychology, sociology, or nursing journals. Five journals that specialize exclusively in matters related to death are: *Death Studies, Omega; Mortality, The Journal of Near-Death Studies;* and *Suicide and Life-Threatening Behavior,* which ought to be available in most university libraries. Such libraries ought also to have an assortment of recent books on various death topics. Personal assistance might be sought from members of the clergy, particularly hospital chaplains, who deal with dying on a day-to-day basis. Hospital social work departments can also point one to resources, particularly support groups and hospice programs. *Hospice,* the journal of the National Hospice Organization, can be obtained by writing to the organization at: 1901 N. Moore St., Suite 901, Arlington, VA 22209.

PART
Societal Issues
and Responses

We have seen how the body and mind age, how older people interact with their families and in society in general. In previous chapters, we have examined the special issues of being aged and a member of a racial minority. And, we have discussed the growth of the aging population, physical and mental health and illness, older peoples' interactions with the health care system, and the end of life.

In this third section of the book, the topics covered are more applied and less theoretical. Chapter 11 covers the economics of aging: work and retirement. The next chapter includes information on a special issue of importance to older people: abuse and neglect. How people relate to the political world is discussed in Chapter 13. And the concluding chapter in the book looks at intergenerational relationships, especially at services and programs designed to address the problems and needs of older individuals.

Economics, Work, and Retirement

11

Chapter Outline

"I live in a free-standing home, and when something in it needs repair, I fix it myself or pay to have it fixed. Since the death of my husband, I have learned how to install a new ribbon in my typewriter, how to change the chimes of my grandfather clock, found out that there are two kinds of screws and screwdrivers, what it means when the little light in the circuit breaker glows red. I have discovered that galvanized gutter systems will rust, while aluminum ones will not."

— Vera A. Cleaver, born 1919

Introduction

Retirement from work might be seen as a two-edged sword. On the one hand, it provides time to do what people say they've wanted to do all their lives: travel, visit the grandchildren, go fishing, pursue leisure activities and hobbies, perhaps volunteer and do good works. On the other hand, it disrupts one's daily pattern of activities, income usually goes down, retirees lose the role of "worker" that has provided them with identification and status during their work lives, and all that leisure time may be hard to fill with meaningful activities.

career jobs —
Long-term work, for
the majority of one's
working life, that the
individual has been
trained or educated to
do.

social convention —
Something usually
thought of as the
norm.

Most retirees, though, report high levels of life satisfaction after they leave the world of work. However, one can also see many people who are dissatisfied with their new role of "retiree." A good many seek to return to work, at least for the first several years after retirement.

Only a minority of American workers are covered by private pension plans; the greatest source of income for most retirees comes from Social Security. On the other hand, most retired people own their own home and have fewer expenses than they did while they were working. Overall, the present generation of American retirees is a fairly prosperous one, which is evidenced by the fact that the majority have retired from their *career jobs* prior to age 65.

Work and Role Identity

Think about a group of people who are strangers to each other who are asked to introduce themselves. Typically, they'll say things like, "My name is Joe Smith and I'm an auto mechanic," or "My name is Sally Jones and I'm a high school principal," or "My name is Sam Black and I manage a Burger King." Asked to say a little more about themselves, they might give their age, whether or not they are married, whether or not they have kids and the children's ages.

Almost all the time, when asked to say who we are, we give our occupation in the first sentence. Even such things so close to us as our family status come in second or third in terms of priority. We typically give information not on who we are, but on what we do. One doesn't say, "My name is Joan Brown and I'm a child of the universe"; instead, one is more likely to say, "I'm Joan Brown and I do market research." In fact, this is a *social convention* or norm, something that we're expected to say. If we define ourselves by something other than occupational status, the other person might assume that we have no occupation, or that for some reason we're ashamed to mention it.

Job status tells us a lot about other people. It gives us a rough sense of where to place them on in a scale of importance: most people would rank a judge higher than, say, a garbage collector. If we know peoples' occupation, in an instant we know their social status and have an idea of how much their income is, how much education they have, and to a certain degree how valuable or important they are thought to be in our society.

We jealously guard these status markers. If you don't believe this, go over to the medical school and ask if there's a difference in the hem length for the lab coats worn by the students and the faculty members. It's been observed that in the in the Chinese army, in the days when no outward signs of rank were permitted to be shown on uniforms because everyone was supposed to be equal, one could tell status differences by the number

of ballpoint pens carried in the breast pocket. Lieutenants might have had
just one, but full colonels had a whole pocketful.

In a society that has values tied up with work and proving one's worth
through contributions that for the most part revolve around work, taking
occupational status away might be seen as a threat to a person's worth. Of
course, this is exactly what happens with retirement. Some people may try
to hang on to the status markers from their former occupation, but this
may not always be an entirely successful strategy. The individual who re-
tires, then, is faced with what we might call a role transition, going from a
"worker" role to a "retired" role (or, actually, to a "former worker" role). In
theory, this status passage, this role transition, is seen as stressful and traumatic. It could be especially tough on those who define their worth on the
basis of their occupational role.

On the other hand, there are plenty of people who can't wait to retire.
Regardless of status loss, they're ready to grab that check and run, and this
can be for a variety of reasons. In fact, the decision to retire is as individual
as is the retiree. Some may be threatened by employers they feel are pres-
suring them to leave, others may have failing personal health, or family
obligations could be a consideration. Some who retire no doubt do it as
early as they possibly can because they hate their job or their boss. On the
other hand, there are those who would prefer to continue to work if only
they could gradually diminish the pace or the amount of work that's expected. The result is earlier retirement among American workers over the
past several decades, a trend that has continued in the past decade. In
1990, fully 74% of workers had retired prior to the usual retirement age of
65; by 1996, this had increased to 75% (AARP, 1998).

Increasingly, people opt to retire because they are able to financially.
As we can see in Table 11.1, the median retirement age steadily declined
during the second half of the twentieth century, and this trend is projected
to continue. This is despite the passage of legislation—the Age Discrimina-

**TABLE 11.1, U. S. Median Retirement Age
by Sex, 1950–2005**

Period	Men	Women
1950–1955	66.9	67.7
1955–1960	65.8	66.2
1960–1965	65.2	64.6
1965–1970	64.2	64.2
1970–1975	63.3	63.0
1975–1980	63.0	63.2
1980–1985	62.8	62.7
1985–1990	62.6	62.8
1990–1995	62.7	62.6
1995–2000	62.3	62.0
2000–2005*	61.7	61.2

*Projected
From: Forecasters say the average American
worker will retire even earlier (1999, p. 4).

g lossary

*mandatory
retirement* — Forced
retirement, usually at a
specific age.

tion in Employment Act of 1986—that has made *mandatory retirement* for most employees at a particular age (usually 65) illegal. People aren't being forced out of their jobs by mandatory retirement so much as they are retiring early because they can afford to.

While retirement is the principal event in later life that shapes (or is shaped by) economics, there are other things happening in the lives of older adults that relate to work and money. In addition to the social meaning of retirement, in this chapter we will deal with older people and their income, where their money comes from, work-related issues, and things that directly relate to retirement and what it means, such as uses of leisure and retirement housing.

Work and Retirement

There are conflicting forces: retirement means a loss of status to many people, but most leave the labor market prior to the usual retirement age, usually because they can afford to do so. Despite the perception of role loss, many people will retire even though the law says they can continue to work. Social Security and most pension plans are presently set up to give full benefits at age 65, but many people will opt for partial benefits and leave the labor force earlier. There are fewer and fewer persons aged 65+ who continue to work. In 1960, over 36% of males 65 and older were employed; by 1997 this had declined to 18.3% (U. S. Bureau of the Census, 1998b).

Recall that we've been stuck with 65 as a more-or-less official beginning-point for old age—or retirement—ever since the Social Security Administration was established back in the 1930s. The precedent originated in Germany in 1884. We realize, though, that 65 has increasingly become a less appropriate definition over the years. Many gerontologists would argue that age 70 or 75 is actually a more meaningful beginning point for the onset of old age.

Realizing this, the National Budget Reconciliation Act of 1984 changed the definition for workers who will retire in the future. On a graduated scale, persons who retire during the first decade of the twenty-first century will have to be 66, and, a few years later, 67, in order to receive full Social Security benefits.

This was done more in an effort to keep the Social Security system actuarially sound than because of a realization that the 65-year-old worker is not really "old." Lip service was given to the latter concept, but in fact it was necessary to readjust the numbers of retirees who will be drawing from the system in a few years when the post-war babies become post-war senior citizens. Those who retire at age 65 in the year 2010 will receive only partial benefits; if they want full coverage, they'll have to wait until age 67. Thus, aging has in a way been redefined legislatively.

Other programs use other definitions. Certain vocational rehabilitation programs look on those 45+ as older workers. This applies to most of the programs administered by the U.S. Department of Labor. Eligibility to participate in different programs sponsored by the Older Americans Act generally begins at age 60.

Governmental definitions, however, ignore a fundamental concept of gerontology: people age at different rates. And variability within populations increases as age increases. Over a generation ago it was pointed out that compulsory retirement at a specific age disregards important individual differences in capacity (Donahue, Orbach, & Pollack, 1960).

We all know those who are still going strong at age 75 and who can out-work many younger people. Other people seem to be "old" at 60. Just as people live to different ages, people age at different rates. And, some want to retire as soon as they can, while others may feel that they have important work remaining.

About 83.6% of males and 64.6% of females aged 45 to 64 are working (U.S. Bureau of the Census, 1998b). Many, however, have been able to retire "early," and the trends we saw in Table 11.1 confirm that more people are retiring before age 65. We might speculate that these trends will continue, despite the increasing age to receive full Social Security benefits and removal of the legal cap on mandatory retirement. This, of course, assumes that there will be no drastic economic reversals for retirement-age people in the coming years.

A study of new retirees done by the U.S. Social Security Administration (1992) indicates that among first-time beneficiaries, 76% of the men and 84% of the women retired before age 65; half of them filed for benefits by age 62. Asked why they retired early, the most frequent response given was simply "a desire to retire." Health reasons were the second most-frequent response.

Questioned further, some of these early retirees might have elaborated on why they left their jobs. Motivations would vary, no doubt: some felt that they were being shoved out, others couldn't wait to be liberated from drudgery. One study found that older workers are more satisfied with jobs that require a higher level of attention and carry a significant level of responsibility (Fleisher & Kaplan, 1980). At the other extreme, many people leave jobs they see as meaningless as soon as they can.

Two conclusions can be drawn at this point: first, many people can, and do, continue to work past the age at which retirement is thought of as appropriate. Workers late in their careers can be divided into two groups: those who want to work and those who don't. More to the point, however, is the second conclusion: no one definition of "older" is going to be adequate in every situation.

Most of us probably do not think of 45 as "older," yet those workers aged 45+ who feel that they have been discriminated against because of age may file complaints with the Equal Employment Opportunity Commission (EEOC). On the other hand, one review of research indicates that persons 65 to 74 are more similar in terms of health profiles to the group 45 to 64 than they are to persons 75 and older (U. S. Senate Special Committee on Aging, 1985). Definitions of when "old age" begins vary.

Since 55 is the age at which many people begin to retire, and since 75 is the age at which almost all workers in fact have retired, let us then focus on this cohort of people aged 55 to 74. Most of the transitions from full-time work to full-time retirement occur during these two decades. Most of these people are facing the issues associated with aging and work. They are the older workers.

Myths and Realities About Older Workers

A number of stereotypes have influenced common perceptions of older workers. In many cases, these stereotypes are based on little evidence, outdated information, half-truths, or mythology. Commonly accepted attitudes hold that all older workers are sick of the job and just waiting to retire, are less productive, are more interested in personal benefits than in the good of the organization, are less creative and show less initiative, are more likely to have accidents, use all of their sick leave for real or imagined illnesses, show less willingness to cooperate with supervisors, and are generally slower, especially in terms of learning new things such as applications of technical innovations.

No doubt there is a worker some place in the country to whom all of these things are applicable. But these stereotypes are not true for most older workers. On the contrary; older workers are less likely to be characterized accurately by any of these stereotypes (Halachmi, 1998).

Perhaps an actual case would be instructive at this point to examine the different things that may be going on in the life of an older worker and his problems.

Fred was just 62 by the time he had literally worried himself sick over his job. He was a skilled technician for the phone company. He began his career as a lineman, and he had worked his way up in the organization to a point when, by his early 50s, younger technicians would come to him when they had a problem that was too complex for them to handle.

Fred had been the master of his trade, the grand old man of the shop who knew how to fix everything. After he had reached this peak, however, technical changes came quick and fast in the telephone industry—so fast that he had difficulty keeping up. Satellite technology and a host of computer-age innovations made many of Fred's skills obsolete. By the age of 61, Fred was entering a profound period of depression. He realized that others in the shop had surpassed him in terms of expertise. Younger workers seemed to keep up with the changes better than he did; they no longer brought him the tough problems to solve. He felt that the other workers were taking it easy on the old man and doing the difficult parts of the job for him.

He began to be absent more often because of illness. His pride in his work and his status on the job suffered. By the time he sought counseling, he was a nervous wreck. He said that he planned to retire at 62 with partial benefits, although he had no clear plan as to what he would do with himself in retirement. The younger men and women in the organization were good to him, and his supervisor was understanding and gave him assignments that he could handle, but the situation as he saw it had become intolerable. He felt that he had to get out.

A few months after this crisis, not long before he was to start receiving his pension, Fred fell ill at a dinner party; his wife took him home. That night, Fred suffered a massive stroke, and he died in the hospital the next morning from a second stroke.

This is a true case. Its details could be interpreted in a number of ways, and Fred's situation could confirm a number of stereotypes of older workers. He in fact did feel less able to learn new things, and as a result he felt that he was less productive on the job (although there were no complaints from his employer); he was off work more often than was usual for him (but no more often than the younger people in the shop). In his own mind, though, Fred had become a problem worker.

There are two alternative explanations for Fred's situation, and both may have some bearing on what was really going on. Fred may have suffered declining work skills because of ill health. He may have been having a series of small strokes for several years prior to the massive one than killed him. He could have been in a downward health spiral sometimes called *terminal drop*, a decline in performance that is noticeable six months to a year prior to death (Botwinick, 1973). It sometimes is apparent prior to the diagnosis of illness. That is, Fred may have been a dying man, and the performance of a terminally ill person could hardly be expected to be at its peak.

Something else was going on, though, that would not have come as a surprise to anyone who knew Fred. He had a long history of emotional illness. Various breakdowns in his younger years had put him into the hospital for months at time. He had become more stable during his 50s, his highest years of productivity. Anxious over his apparent difficulty in learning new technology, he again began to be troubled by his old mental problems. His worries compounded themselves. Stress he felt on the job was then complicated by stress associated with the approach of an unwelcome retirement. Fred may literally have worried himself into an early grave.

However, we still lack critical information. Fred was less productive in his own mind—less productive, he thought, than he had been a few years previously, by his own standard. Was he, in fact, less productive than the others on the job? Was he no longer fulfilling a useful function? His boss felt that Fred was still pulling his own weight, even though he no longer was the superstar in the shop. He took a few more sick days, but he was not a chronic absentee. He actually was out less than he had been years before. Was he no longer interested in the goals of the organization? To the contrary: he worked himself into a snit because he couldn't be the absolute master of his craft and be of even more value to the company. Was he a calendar watcher, just waiting to seize a pension the minute it was available? No, he actually dreaded the prospect of leaving his beloved company. The anxiety associated with this prospective loss may have contributed to his untimely end.

We must realize that these kinds of complexities—and we have barely begun to go into the intricate factors of Fred's case—are the rule rather than the exception. Each individual's situation can be as complex as Fred's. Putting all older workers into one category is stereotyping; it is unfair to characterize all with the traits of a few. We need to look at objective studies on the various elements we've touched on with Fred's case study.

There is a great deal of research in *industrial gerontology*, the study of older workers. First, let's examine a series of studies on the work ethic (Doering, Rhodes, & Schuster, 1983). That is, how committed are various groups, generally, to the fundamental idea that we must work for a living? One study of 131 manufacturing workers, 129 food service workers, and 75 police officers found that there was a clear and significant relationship between age and the work ethic (Aldag & Brief, 1977). The older the worker, the greater the attitudinal commitment to the ideal of work. Another study of over 3,000 employees in 53 different manufacturing concerns found that the older the worker, the greater the pride in the work (Cherrington, 1979).

A study of 1,058 employees of governmental and private organizations found a *negative correlation* between age and the perceived importance of money. The older the respondent, the less importance placed on material rewards. That is, the older workers were more interested in other things they found rewarding about the job; they weren't there just for the paycheck.

On-the-job problems are often related to the inability or unwillingness of employees to follow the direction of superiors. Satisfaction with supervision and willingness to comply with directions were found to be more characteristic of older workers in a study of 385 female and 1,682 male manufacturing employees (Schwab & Heneman, 1977).

How interested one is in one's work may be related to performance, and one study found a positive, significant relationship between age and job involvement (Hall & Johanson, 1980). It also found age to be related to internal motivation to work. Further, older workers have a greater organizational commitment; this was not only true for older executives, but applied as well to janitorial and food service workers. Older employees express more loyalty to the organization.

So, in terms of attitudes and loyalty, a variety of studies indicate more positive characteristics among older workers than among younger workers. Senior employees are more committed to the work ethic, take greater pride in their work, are less interested in monetary rewards, have greater satisfaction with both their jobs and the work involved in them, are more willing to respond positively to supervision, are more involved with their jobs, and have a greater commitment to the organization.

Further research has gone beyond these subjective variables into investigation of physical indicators of productivity: job performance, absenteeism, accidents, and job-related injuries. These studies of industrial gerontology provide information on the quantity of work as well as its quality.

One review of the research examined a number of studies of aging and job performance, and concludes that, while speed does decline somewhat with age, steadiness and experience more than make up for it. Given that there is wide variance in capabilities at all ages, "Older workers are generally capable of performing as well as younger workers, if not better in some areas" (Bourne, 1982, p. 42). In all but the most physically demand-

---

Illustration 11.2. Problem Workers

An article in the *Wall Street Journal* (Burrough, 1986) reported 200 arrests in the General Motors plant at Mansfield, Ohio:

> Drug and alcohol abuse can seriously affect worker productivity, plant safety, and product quality. . . . At some of the nation's largest steel mills, nuclear power plants, and offices, the authorities say, drug, gambling and theft rings flourish. . . . Pilferage of company equipment and merchandise by workers costs industry an estimated $33 billion a year. Drug abuse, moreover, costs companies about $70 billion a year in lost productivity and health expenses, a congressional report says" (p. 11).

Older workers are less likely to use or sell illegal drugs, gamble on the job, or rip off their employers. The attitudinal qualities enumerated in the research—commitment to the work ethic, job satisfaction, stability, loyalty to the organization—are characteristic of a generation more willing to give a day's work for a day's pay.

ing of jobs, people have ample reserve capacity to compensate for decrements in speed or strength. In a similar manner, another study of piece-work employees' overall productivity found: "On work tasks requiring a fair amount of manual dexterity, older workers were no more or less productive than younger after differences in experience were taken into account" (Doering, Rhodes, & Schuster, 1983, p. 249)

Other studies have differentiated speed from judgment: one found, for example, that machine operators who were younger were in fact faster, but that the older workers still were more productive (Gupta & Beehr, 1979). Speed and strength tasks tend to be performed better by younger workers, while experience and judgment-related activities are done more effectively by older workers (Bourne, 1982). Since very few jobs actually require employees to work at their absolute limit of physical capacity, physical decline may not be particularly important in assessment of workers' abilities. One foreman observed that he didn't need someone who could lift 200 pounds; what he really wanted was someone who would show up every day to lift two pounds.

Regularity and faithfulness are areas where older workers excel. A number of studies indicate a negative correlation between age and unavoidable absence from work; that is, absence goes down as age goes up (Blumberg, 1980; Constas & Vichas, 1980; Spencer & Steers, 1980). Other research has found lower rates of avoidable absence among older workers (Froggatt, 1970; Nicholson & Goodge, 1976). That is, older workers are less likely to be off the job when there is some reason to be absent, and are also less likely to be away from work when there is no reason at all. Older workers tend to not lay off and take sick leave just because they have it coming. Older workers have lower turnover, fewer accidents, and are less likely to be injured on the job. This body of industrial research is very well documented, and it goes back all the way to 1921, when Hewes did a study of 2,891 silk mill workers and found negative relationship between age and accident frequency.

So, the data indicate that older workers have lower rates of absence and accidents, lower turnover, and are more productive in tasks requiring judgment. They are somewhat less capable than younger workers in jobs that require speed and strength, but this is compensated for by steadiness and faithfulness to the job.

Most jobs require more brainpower than physical strength and speed. Unfortunately, there are few areas where stereotype and misinformation have done more to lower the image of the older worker. Phrases such as "you can't teach an old dog new tricks" have generally been accepted by the populace as a whole, older persons included. Older people who believe that they can no longer be effective learners thus may have little incentive to learn new things, and some may cease to try to continue learning. However, as we have already seen in Chapter 6, there is evidence that demonstrates that where physical illness is not a problem, older people can continue to be efficient learners well into the eighth decade of life.

> **Illustration 11.3. A Functional Approach to Job Suitability**
>
> A reasonable approach to matching people and jobs would be to look at abilities rather than be guided by misleading stereotypes. The repetitive production-line work that requires speed or strength might be better accomplished by the younger worker, although research indicates that due to lower absenteeism and turnover, the older worker might in fact be more productive in the long run. If we take a look at most jobs, however, we see that the majority of functions in the employment setting are not piecework manufacturing. The majority of all jobs are, in fact, in service functions. Such qualities as experience, judgment, and regularity tend to be of much greater importance in such areas. And simply in terms of equality of opportunity, if the person can do the job, then he or she should have the opportunity to do it. Age has less to do with functional capability than many other qualities and characteristics of employees.

Retirement and Preparation for Retirement

Mandatory retirement, having to leave the job at a particular age, is no longer the issue it was a generation ago. The age for mandatory retirement for most occupations was raised by an action of Congress from 65 to 70 in 1978, and it was eliminated altogether by other legislation in 1986. As we saw in Table 11.1, however, most people do not in fact remain in the labor force even until age 65: the median age at retirement in 2000 was projected to be 61.7 for men and 61.2 for women. Despite the role loss associated with retirement, and despite the fact that most employees are fully capable of working more years, at least half have in fact retired by their early 60s. This raises the question of whether workers late in their careers are lured into retirement because of pensions and available benefits, or whether some are "shoved" into an earlier retirement than they might wish.

Almost 25,000 complaints are filed each year with the Equal Employment Opportunity Commission (EEOC) charging age discrimination in the workplace. Many of these are from workers who felt pressured into retirement.

This is not to say that all early retirement plans or buy-outs are sinister. Many such plans offer material benefits and freedom of choice to the person who wishes to opt for something that may be beneficial to both the employer and employee. Sometimes such plans will provide for partial retirement or a gradual disengagement from the work role that is attractive to the older worker.

Pressure to retire early, however, can also border on age discrimination, and many older workers find themselves for all practical purposes forced out of a job with little choice in the matter. The unfortunate fact for some is that there is no real decision; they're forced to take what they can

The Supreme Court in California ruled on November 10, 1997, that employers have the right to replace older workers with younger ones to save money. The justices said that doing so did not amount to age discrimination because the motivation was economic. According to media reports (British Broadcasting Corporation, 1998):

> Employers now have the right to take on a younger worker and sack anyone over 40 years of age if a younger employee would be cheaper, regardless of ability. The court ruled it is right and proper for an employer to run a business as profitably as possible. But critics say the decision gives bosses the perfect excuse to fire older employees they no longer want.

> Is a miser's approach to human resource management likely to enhance productivity? Can veteran employees trust managers to avoid compromising possible long-term productivity gains, let alone important aspects of their welfare, for the sake of short-run economic gains in operation?

From Halachmi (1998, p. 6).

in terms of benefits or separation compensation. They don't have the resources to pursue a court case, and an EEOC complaint may take years to be resolved.

There is also the prevailing social message that despite the loss of occupational role and job status, retirement should be seen as a time for freedom and pursuit of leisure activities and travel. Some workers who are essentially forced out of their jobs are in the position, then, of putting the best face on it and telling friends that they now can do the things they want to do, even if what they really wanted to do was remain on the job.

Illustration 11.5. Pre-Retirement Anxiety

I had a grant from the U.S. Administration on Aging to develop televised pre-retirement education programs. We did eight half-hour shows on different aspects of retirement planning; then, in cooperation with the community colleges around the state, we organized pre-retirement seminars. Groups got together at the colleges, watched the shows once each week as they were broadcast over the statewide educational television network, and then they discussed each week's particular topic. We thought this was an effective way to provide continuing education programming, and over 900 people participated. The program evaluations showed, though, that what people really appreciated was the discussion period. They said the content was fine, but the real value of the seminars was finding out that other people were anxious about retirement, too.

Further, the economic impact of changing legislation may make continued work less worth it. In 1993, retired individuals with an adjusted income of $25,000 and couples with an income of more than $32,000 paid tax on half of their Social Security benefits. In 1994, however, because of changes in the income tax laws, individuals with more than $34,000 in adjusted income and retired couple with more than $44,000 paid tax on 85% of their benefits. The impact is complex, but it means for some people that continued working may not be worth the trouble. A single taxpayer in this example would actually lose $70 if she or he made an additional $2,000 in earnings; the married couple would only gain $431 from $2,000 in additional earnings (Rowland, 1993). The Administration released figures indicating that 5.5 million of the 43 million Social Security retirees in the nation would pay more in taxes on their benefits as a result of the change.

There are, then, many incentives to retire, some of which are internal and some of which are external. Some workers tend to perceive their jobs negatively and are thus more than happy to take these incentives and leave the world of work. There is a great deal of individual variance in the retirement decision, however, and we should not rush to conclusions as to whether or not people are being forced out of their jobs late in life. For example, a nine-year study of 1,365 workers aged 50 to 69 years found that participants evaluated their jobs as more burdensome the closer they came to retirement, regardless of their age (Ekerdt & DeViney, 1993). This is evidence for what the researchers called a "preretirement dynamic," psychological preparation for the retirement event.

Also, there is evidence that job strain increases relative mortality risk. That is, some jobs in fact create such stress that health—and survival—are affected. An interesting study on this was done in Sweden: 477 elderly men were followed, and it was found that relative mortality risk associated with their jobs continued even after retirement (Falk, Hanson, Isacsson, & Ostergren, 1992). In this study, it was found that social network contacts acted as buffers against the negative effect of job strain, but that those who had been in stressful jobs continued to have higher rates of mortality after retirement.

Studies of social networks among retirees, not surprisingly, indicate that they change, not in number but in composition. Relationships with fellow workers tend to be terminated and replaced with others. Reciprocal relationships (where people help each other) are the ones most likely to be maintained (VanTilburg, 1992). Those who remain involved in activities and in relationships with other persons tend to have the highest levels of life satisfaction in retirement (Mishra, 1992). Other research, however, has found that individual personality may be more important to life satisfaction in retirement than other variables (Ries & Gold, 1993). Obviously, personal resources and outlook are important determinants of coping with any major life change.

$g$lossary

There is some evidence to indicate higher levels of satisfaction among those who have planned for retirement (Singleton & Keddy, 1991), and that participatory discussion of retirement issues is a more effective means of successful pre-retirement planning than is a straight lecture type of program (Connolly, 1992). Still, most employees receive little from their employer in terms of retirement preparation, other than the traditional meeting to discuss potential benefits.

Not every employee wants to retire, of course; many say they would prefer to taper off by working fewer hours per week or by going from full-time to part-time employment. Continuation with the same employer on a reduced-hours basis, unfortunately, is not often a possibility; more typical is formal retirement from one employer and then part-time employment with another. An obvious problem here is that those who are less educated and have the lowest incomes have the greatest financial need to continue in some kind of work after formal retirement, while those who have the greatest accessibility to post-retirement employment are the better-educated workers who have the least financial need for further employment (Podgursky & Swain, 1987). It has been shown that there is little in terms of gender difference in the rates of exit from or return to work before and after retirement (Henretta, O'Rand, & Chan, 1993).

The situation has developed that an actual majority of older workers tend to leave their career job before traditional retirement age and then pursue other types of work (Fontana & Frey, 1990). Career jobs are the ones that take up the majority of one's work life, the job for which the person trained or prepared for academically. After the end of the career job, the older worker typically can be involved in a variety of things, such as self-employment, part-time work, temporary employment, or "off the books" work (payment in cash not reported to the government). These are often described as **bridge jobs**, in that they serve as a bridge between career employment and full retirement (Christensen, 1990).

A fair number of those who retire return to paid employment, especially those who retire before they are 65. Often the prime motivation is financial: they need more money. They return to work because they in fact have few pension benefits, and their Social Security payments are stretched too thin. Going in and out of the labor market is fairly typical for those in the first five years of retirement (Ruhm, 1990). So we might not see a picture of people in later middle life working full time until a particular retirement age and then going on a pension for the rest of their lives. The more typical picture may be of people retiring at different ages after about 55 and of going into and out of the labor market in a variety of ways for several years thereafter.

Some labor economists see the trend in downsizing of corporations as having the greatest impact on older workers, making them more vulnerable to being forced out of career occupations (Useem, 1993). There may no longer be a neat boundary between work and retirement for workers in the future.

Pensions and Retirement Income

It may be that many individuals who would like to consider themselves to be retired are—and will continue to be—forced back into the labor market for economic reasons. One need only observe the staff at fast food restaurants during the daytime hours to see this in action: those older workers are not there for their health—they need money. Being forced back into

---

Illustration 11.6. Myths and Realities of Social Security

Myth: Retirees get nothing they haven't "earned."

Reality: The average beneficiary (collecting $858 a month for an individual retiring last January at age 65) will get back all the money he or she contributed, with an allowance for interest, in three and a half years or so. This retiree, given a normal life expectancy, will collect nearly a decade's worth of benefits "free." Earlier retirees, including millions still living, did even better. Ida May Fuller of Ludlow, Vermont, who got the first monthly check in 1940, collected more than $20,000 in benefits after paying $22 in taxes.

Mistakenly believing that they're getting no more than they're owed, recipients often resent the suggestion, however correct, that their benefits include a portion that is a gift, or to use the pejorative, welfare.

From Hershey, Jr. (1995).

The *New York Times* article cited above looks at the average recipient. Let's look at an example for individuals who have paid in the most to Social Security that they possibly could have during the course of their working years:

The 1998 maximum Social Security benefit was $1,342 per month, for a retiree leaving work at age 65 who had paid into the system at the maximum level for at least 35 years. That's a total of $16,104 per year, which is not much to retire on, but it will grow somewhat with future cost-of-living increases and, if the individual lives a normal life span for a 65-year-old (15.7 additional years for a man, 19.0 for a woman), a bonanza is in store.

Assuming a 45-year work life, and assuming maximum payments into the system all of those years, a 65-year-old retiring in 1998 would have begun work in 1953 (when the most one could have paid into the system was $54 a year) and paid a total of $75,349 in Social Security withholding.

At a $16,104 per year maximum payout, he or she will receive those contributions back in 4.68 years. For a male, the additional 11 years of life remaining beyond that period will mean payments in excess of contributions of $177,144. For a woman, the additional payments beyond what she contributed will equal $230,287 (plus future cost-of-living increases). Those who paid in at lower than the maximum rate will reap even greater rewards, proportionately.

These figures are calculated on future life expectancy for a 65-year-old now; life expectancy may increase in the future. There are those among the recipients who will live to be 110 and collect for 45 years. And, of course, there are those who will drop dead the day they qualify for benefits. That's their tough luck.

low-paid, part-time work is particularly the case for those persons who rely only on Social Security for their support in later life.

Social Security was never designed to be the sole means of income for older persons; rather, it was to be both a retirement safety net and an insurance program to take care of the widowed, orphaned, and disabled.

As of 1996, the total number of Social Security recipients in the United States had grown to 47.3 million; of these, 26.8 million were retired workers, 3.2 million were wives and husbands of retired workers, and another 5.2 million were widows and widowers. There were 4.4 million disabled workers and their dependents. The average monthly benefit of retirees was $745; it was slightly less than that for widows and disabled workers (note that this includes many retirees who took reduced benefits by retiring prior to age 65). The average for a retired worker and spouse was $1,262 per month (U.S. Bureau of the Census, 1998b). This had grown to $1,288 by 1998 (AARP, 1998a). In addition to the $369.2 billion that went to Social Security recipients, a total of $31.8 billion was paid out to those receiving Supplemental Security Income (SSI), a form of aid to the aged who have no other income; the maximum SSI payment to an older person. In 2000 the maximum was $512 per month; the maximum for a couple was $769 per month.

The complexities of the Social Security system are such that it's almost impossible to keep current on the programs and their changes, so we will not go into program details here, but instead refer the reader to the Sources of Further Information section at the end of this chapter. For now, though, our purpose is to look at economics of retirement and income of retirees. Social Security no doubt is a mainstay of the elderly people of the United States in terms of income. The proportion of retirement income that Social Security represents, of course, is dependent upon the amount of other sources of income that each individual has.

For older people who are officially classified as in poverty (about 10.8% of the older population as a whole), Social Security represents about 71% of personal income, on the average. Among the elderly poor, earnings and wages account for only about 1% of household income. Food stamps account for 2%, and pensions account for only 3%. Means-tested cash assistance, or SSI, accounts for about 9%. So, for those who have either very small private pensions—or no pensions at all—Social Security is a vital portion of personal income. For many, it is their only income (U. S. Bureau of the Census, 1998b).

For the non-poor elderly, Social Security represents a relatively smaller proportion of personal income: about 39%. Surprisingly, pension income represents only about 18% of the personal income of the group of non-poor elderly. After Social Security, the next largest part (28%) of the household income of the non-poor aged is accounted for by interest and dividends on personal savings and investments. Earnings account for 12% of the income of the non-poor elderly.

The relatively small amount of total household income that is accounted for by pensions comes as a surprise; it is explained by the fact that only a minority of all workers have any pension coverage at all. In 1996, for example, only 41.9% of all workers had pension coverage through their work. This varied by age, sex, and race: the highest rates of coverage were for white males aged 45 to 64, and in that group, 56.9% had jobs with pension plans. The rates were 49.8% of white women in the same age group. African-American males aged 45 to 64 had a pension coverage rate of 55.9%; black females had a higher rate than white women—56.1%. But only 37.9% of Hispanic males and 39.6% of Hispanic females in that age group had pension coverage through their work (U. S. Bureau of the Census, 1998b).

In 1996, the median household income of people aged 65+ in the United States was $19,448 (compared to a median figure of $35,492 for all households). Fully 4.48 million had incomes below $10,000 per year (20.9%), and only 6.5% of the elderly households had annual incomes in excess of $75,000 (U. S. Bureau of the Census, 1998b).

Where the aged differ most dramatically from younger people is in savings and home ownership. Fully 79.1% of those aged 65+ in the United States live in a house that they own (compared to a 65.7% home ownership rate for adults of all ages). And only 11.0% of those 65 to 74 years of age (and only 4.5% of those aged 75+) are still paying on a home mortgage (U.S. Bureau of the Census, 1998b). This varies by location; a colleague and I found a home ownership rate of 86.9% among elderly people in the Omaha area (Thorson & Powell, 1998). In an earlier study, we had found among the 500 people surveyed that 452 (90.4%) lived in a single family dwelling that they own, and that they had lived there an average of 29.3 years (Thorson & Powell, 1992a).

Of those 55 years of age and above who consider themselves to be retired, 82.2% owned a principal residence, and about 25% also have other investments in real estate. About 5% own a business. Among those in this group of retirees aged 55+, mean net worth was slightly over $200,000. On the other hand, there were 3.3 million older people who lived below the poverty level in 1997; 700,000 of them were black and 384,000 were Hispanic. Among African-Americans aged 75 and older, the poverty rate is 29.3%; it is 28.2% among similarly-aged Latinos. The median household income among all Americans aged 75+ was only $17,079 in 1997 (U.S. Bureau of the Census, 1998b). As a general rule, older people have a higher net worth but a lower level of income when compared to most other Americans.

Income and assets vary widely among the aged, as might be expected. We have seen in Chapter 4 that income is likelier to be lower among racial minorities; it is also lower among those older persons who live outside of metropolitan areas. In fact, the income gap between rural and metropolitan elders widens with age (McLaughlin & Jensen, 1993). This is not to say, however, that there is no urban poverty among older Americans. The problem of older homeless persons has been increasing in recent years (Cohen, Teresi, Holmes, & Roth, 1988). Certain risk factors compound the likelihood to live in poverty in later life: being female, being widowed, being black, and being 75 years of age or over.

Illustration 11.7. Fat Cats or Hungry Victims?

Just how well off are the nation's elderly?

Endless oratory from debates over Medicare, Social Security, and other programs illustrate just how polarized opinions are on this subject. Republican Senator Alan Simpson of Wyoming called the 65-plus crowd "greedy geezers"—oldsters in Bermuda shorts teeing off near their second homes in Florida. Old people "care most about themselves—even at the cost of future generations," concluded a study by Third Millennium, a young-adult group that is lobbying for Social Security reform.

On the other side of the debate, older people are seen as helpless victims—frail folks saving coins for what sometimes is the best meal they can buy—dog food. They "live on low incomes and they know where every penny goes," Democratic Rep. Pete Stark of California has said.

From Duff (1995, B1).

In summary, we might say that there appears to be a widening gap among retirees. While most live and own their own home, income and assets among retirees are quite diverse. The minority have pension plans in addition to their Social Security (and these individuals tend to have been among higher income employees prior to retirement and thus receive higher Social Security payments as well). For these people, money in retirement tends to be less of a problem; indeed, they are the ones most likely to retire sooner than the usual age of 65 because they can afford to do so. Others may retire prior to 65 for reasons of ill health, and they are likelier to have less income than the norm.

Many may feel that they have been forced out of the labor market. These individuals are more likely to return to part-time, non-career jobs for several years post-retirement because they need the extra income.

For all retirees, though, whether their separation from the world of work is one neat event or, as it is for many, a less clear separation that occurs gradually over time, retirement represents an important transition in life. It means a loss of the status our society accords to the role of "worker," and many retirees complain that they no longer feel that they are performing a useful role in life. This perception of role loss can, and does, vary from individual to individual.

Added to this loss of role is an important change in each person's schedule of daily activities, and learning to adapt to increased leisure time may be difficult for those who had few interests other than their work. Another important transition that comes with retirement is whether or not to relocate one's household.

Retirement Environments

We have seen that most people in their retirement years prefer to remain in their own home. In fact, the majority of household moves after age 65 are within the same county. Yet, retirees are confronted with an increasing array of options of where to live after they have left the world of work.

About one half of 1% of the nation's older people live in retirement communities. We often think of these communities, such as Sun City, Arizona, or Leisure World in Laguna Hills, California, as whole towns that have been built entirely for the elderly. These actually represent only a small fraction of the environments that have been built to serve retirees.

More common, and housing many more older people, is the ***continuing care retirement community*** (CCRC). Many of these are in the Sun Belt states, but continuing care retirement communities can be anywhere in the country, and most metropolitan areas of some size are likely to have many of them.

The typical CCRC houses between 100 and 200 retired individuals; they usually live in their own apartments. What characterizes these communities is that: (1) they have congregate housing on an identifiable campus, providing secure living space, (2) they typically are built with architectural features that make them user-friendly for older persons, and (3) they most often are characterized by providing a ***continuum of care***.

The continuum of care found in most continuing care retirement communities goes from independent living in one's own condo or apartment, to assisted living for those who need some help and supervision, to nursing home care for those who need it. While all of the elements of a continuum of care are not necessarily present in every CCRC, it is usually the case that the facility is set up to assist people as they become more frail. Most living units, for example, will have "panic buttons" available in the bedroom and bathroom that can be used to summon help. Many will have nursing staff and recreational programs available. Most CCRCs have a health care center, on-campus or at least under the same organizational umbrella, that provides rehabilitation services and long-term nursing care. The idea is that a higher level of service may be needed only temporarily, and that residents, once restored to health, can then return to their independent condo or apartment. Others progress along the continuum of care from independent living to assisted living to long-term nursing care. As we will see in Chapter 14, the goals in services to keep older people as independent as possible involves a great variety of programs with home-delivered services, step-downs to lower levels of care, and a general blurring of distinctions between home care and institutional care (Kane, 1995).

There are literally thousands of CCRCs in the country. The majority are under the auspices of profit-making corporations, although there is some evidence that those sponsored by denominations, fraternal organiza-

glossary

Sunbirds — People who continue to live in the North but who reside in the Sun Belt during the winter months.

Snowbirds — People who move in retirement to one of the Sun Belt states.

tions, or other not-for-profit groups provide a higher level of service (Lemke & Moos, 1986, 1989). The feature that attracts residents most is security; the facility is essentially a sheltered environment.

Together, public housing for the elderly and continuing care retirement communities house the great majority of the aged who no longer maintain their own homes. The difference is that public housing for people with very limited incomes tends to provide fewer services and is confronted with an "aging in place" phenomenon. People move in while relatively healthy and need more and more supportive help as they become more frail. This is planned for in the CCRC; provision is made to take care of people as they move along a continuum of care. While a few CCRCs are luxurious, most are not, and in image they contrast sharply with the stereotype held by many of retirement resorts.

While a small minority of the well-to-do elderly are in fact able to afford luxurious accommodations in various retirement resort communities in Florida and Arizona, by far the greatest number who do relocate to another state during their retirement years sell their house in one part of the country and purchase a similar one in another. Or, there are the *Sunbirds*, who keep their principal dwelling in the Northeast or Midwest and go to temporary accommodations in the South or Southwest during the winter months. The area around Phoenix, Arizona, for example, expands by thousands of people each winter, most of whom live in mobile home parks.

Sunbirds, or seasonal migrants among the elderly, have been shown to be significantly higher in both education and income than are non-movers. Krout (1983b) points out that one in seven of the elderly is a seasonal migrant, and that 86% of them chose a Sun Belt state as their destination. He concludes that statistics on elderly migration often undercount the temporary movement of elderly people between regions, and that seasonal migration can be seen as part of the preparation process for eventual residential location.

For *Snowbirds* (those who relocate principal residence entirely), Florida has continued to be the largest gainer among the states (Sanders & Long, 1987). And in terms of overall growth, California, Texas, and Florida have gained the most people in recent decades (Raymondo, 1987). Florida receives the highest proportion of the nation's migrants who are aged 60 and above (23.8%), followed by California (6.9%), Arizona (5.2%), and Texas (4.1%) (Longino, 1995).

The Sun Belt states are usually defined as being composed of California, Arizona, New Mexico, Texas, Oklahoma, Missouri, Arkansas, Louisiana, Mississippi, Alabama, Georgia, North and South Carolina, Florida, and Virginia (Biggar, 1980). The flow of more affluent migrants into the Sun Belt states initially enhances economic expansion and thus contributes to the development of the South and the Southwest in the United States. In the Sun Belt, retirees are seen as important consumers; they tend to be home owners and broaden the tax base. Retirees put minimal pressure on the job market or on local institutions such as schools, and they increase the receiving states' share of federal funding for aging services.

Although the Sun Belt migrants initially contribute to the economic well-being of most receiving states, as they continue to age, their increasing need for health care and aging services increases the local demand for these services. The long-term effect of this migration to the Sun Belt is an increased demand for social and health care services.

Significant emigration of elderly people from Sun Belt states has taken place for at least two decades (Longino, 1995). This may be because of a scatter effect: older people seeking less populous retirement areas—being squeezed out of Florida into Georgia or South Carolina, for example, or from California into Oregon or Arizona. Or, it may be due to the return migration of now-frail, older retirees to their original states of residence, seeking to re-establish a social network now that personal care needs have increased. Both are important effects. In some states, such as California, there are almost as many emigrants as immigrants among the aged. Older people have moved to California in such numbers for so long that: (1) it may no longer be attractive economically or socially as a retirement state, as property costs and taxes present barriers, especially in comparison to places like Arizona and Oregon, and (2) there is now a growing back-flow of the very old who are leaving to go home for terminal care.

Studies confirm that retirement moves for amenity destinations (better climate and recreational opportunities) are associated with being younger, married, and more affluent (Meyer & Speare, 1985). On the other hand, moves for assistance reasons (to be near a caregiver, usually a family member such as an adult child) are associated with older age, widowed status, declining mobility, and less likelihood of being a homeowner. Thus, return migrants are more likely to be poor, widowed, and older. They are also more likely to be heavy consumers of health care and social services. Litwak and Longino (1987) provide data to confirm that the first move in retirement is of people who are younger, healthier, and wealthier, and the second move is more likely to be of an older, poorer, widowed individual who is relocating to be near family. A third move, for some, is into an institution.

Conclusion

Compared to previous generations, retirees in North America are much more prosperous, healthy, and mobile. They are no longer forced to live with their adult children for economic reasons; indeed, the opposite problem is now being seen: adult children who cannot afford to live outside the residence of their parents. By far the great majority of retired persons, though, have their own home, and most of them own that home free and clear.

Most people now retire prior to the traditional age of 65. Some are essentially forced out of the labor market, but it is probably the case that most of the people who retire prior to 65 do so because they can afford it. While only a minority of the aged have private pensions in addition to their Social Security, among the non-poor elderly, fully 28% of personal income comes from interest and dividends. This means that older people are prodigious savers. A substantial portion of individual wealth in the United States is accounted for by Individual Retirement Accounts and other retirement investment plans owned by older people.

Many older people continue to work. For some, this work consists of taking advantage of volunteer activities they were too busy to engage in while they were working. For a substantial number of retirees, though, this work represents bridge jobs they have taken in transition from full-time career occupations to full-time retirement. Bridge jobs often are seen as a supplement to other retirement income, and individual earnings represent a total of 12% of the personal income of the non-poor elderly.

Although retirement is touted as a time to enjoy leisure activities and hobbies, it also represents a loss for many of the important role of worker while they are still capable of making contributions. On the other hand, many older workers are increasingly dissatisfied, and they psychologically prepare for leaving the world of work. American society, unfortunately, has not made effective provisions for easing people from the world of work. Many would like to continue with their career employment and work fewer hours per week as they go though a transition into retirement. Only a few forward-thinking employers allow this. The pattern in industry, with a few exceptions, has been to downsize; older workers frequently are among the first to be eliminated when a company downsizes its workforce.

As the pool of available skilled workers shrinks in the future, there may be a demand for more older workers to remain on the job. Companies may be forced to engage in innovative plans to attract and keep mature workers. Older workers have been shown to have fewer on-the-job accidents and injuries, to be more productive, and to have greater loyalty to the employer.

Despite the seeming popularity of communities built exclusively for retirees, the great majority of older people continue to live in single family dwellings in the same place they've always lived. A minority are Snowbirds, people who move to a Sun Belt state; many of these people move back later on when they are older and in need of care from an adult child. A growing number are Sunbirds, who move back and forth with the seasons, at least for the first few years of retirement. However, the research indicates a decline in retirement migration, probably due to less economic mobility (Fuguitt & Beale, 1993).

Permanent movers among retirees often have an important economic impact on the Sun Belt state they retire to: they tend to be more prosperous than other retirees. Local communities in the South and West, however, have also found both that these immigrants are reluctant to vote for such local improvements as school bond issues, and that as they age, the immigrant elders require added health and social services that the locality may not be prepared to provide. This may lead to a number of public policy problems, ones that we will explore in the final chapter of this book.

Questions for Discussion

1. Do you think that there is an "ideal" way to retire?
2. What are the advantages—and disadvantages—of early retirement?
3. Do you think people aged 65 and above should receive tax benefits based on their age?
4. Where would you like to live in retirement? Why?
5. What is the difference between a continuing care retirement community and a nursing home?
6. Why do you suppose that the majority of workers do not have pension coverage?
7. Discuss the pros and cons of the multigenerational households typical of previous years. What has changed this living pattern?

Sources of Further Information

Much of the current data on workforce participation, income and assets of older people, Social Security recipients and amounts received, housing and home ownership, and pensions of retirees can be found in the current *Statistical Abstract of the United States*, available in almost every college and community library. It can be purchased from the:

U.S. Government Printing Office
Superintendent of Documents
Washington, DC 20402
202/783-3238

A host of questions can be answered in a single visit to the local office of the Social Security Administration; they have good informational booklets describing technical details that seemingly change with the seasons. Look for the address in the white or blue pages of the phone book under "U.S. Government, Department of Health and Human Services."

The Select Committee on Aging of the U.S. House of Representatives frequently publishes hearings on age discrimination in the workplace and other issues of importance to older workers and retirees. Individual copies of the hearing reports are available from the Superintendent of Documents, but a simple phone call to the office of one's Congressional Representative can get a variety of recent hearing reports at no cost.

An information packet is available from:

Business Partnerships
AARP Worker Equity Department
601 E Street, N.W.
Washington, D.C. 20049
202/434-2090

A publication list of items dealing with finances, work, and retirement is available from:

Boettner Institute of Financial Gerontology
University of Pennsylvania
3718 Locust Walk, McNeil 254
Philadelphia, PA 19104-6298
215/573-3414

And by far, the most informative continuing publication on older workers and retirement issues is *Working Age*, available without cost from the AARP Work Force Programs Department at the above address (or telephone: 202/434-2041).

Abuse and Neglect

Chapter Outline

"Worse than the fear of death is the fear of being left alone. If you live long enough you will experience the awful silence of an empty house when your long-time companion, husband or wife, is suddenly no more. And more loneliness comes as your friends disappear."

— Paul Arthur Schlipp, born 1897

Introduction

Headline accounts and televised news stories would have us believe that the elderly are uniquely prone to being victims of frauds, rip-off artists, and abusive relatives. Further, the people we know or hear of who have been abused in later life tend to reinforce these concepts: old people abandoned at hospital emergency rooms, grandmothers forced to care for the children of their crack-addicted daughters, widows cheated out of their savings.

Although we realize that most older people have not been victimized, we are left to wonder what happens to those who are. It is slim comfort to a battered or exploited older person to know that he or she is the statistical exception.

elder abuse —
Harming an older
person either
physically,
psychologically, or
materially.

neglect — To
disregard or leave
unattended; in the
context of elder
neglect, to allow
personal care to
deteriorate without
corrective action.

We'll look at the scope and extent of *elder abuse* and *neglect* in this chapter, examine some underlying social conditions, and seek some practical implications of what can be done to prevent it. We will begin with a case study.

Alice Kaiser was found naked on the floor of the house on her ranch in Hermosa, South Dakota, covered only by a dirty Army blanket. By the time the ambulance got her to the local hospital, she was in critical condition. The nurses had to soak off the dirt on her hands and feet and clip off her matted hair. She was malnourished, dehydrated, and confused. There were bruises and stains on her legs, the ambulance attendants said, and her cluttered house was littered with her own excrement. She died twelve days later; her death was listed as complications from a broken hip. She was 89.

"If this was a child of the same mental capacity as Alice Kaiser, we'd obviously have a child-abuse case," according to Custer County Sheriff DeWayne Glassgow. "If you treated your horse the way Grandma Kaiser was treated, I could charge you with a crime."

Her 66-year-old son, Don Kaiser, and her grandson Herb, 36, were charged with murder; the state said, in effect, that they had killed Alice Kaiser by neglecting their duty to her. Eight months later, a judge threw out the case, saying that the grand jury had been misled. Three months later, the state's attorney again charged Don and Herb Kaiser, this time with second-degree manslaughter.

About ten years before her death, Alice Kaiser had stopped cooking. Edna, Don's wife, would fix her dinner and either Don or Herb would run it over to Grandma's place. Edna died four years before Alice's death; the job of caring, doing the cooking, cleaning, and washing fell to Don. By this time, Alice was increasingly disorganized; she once tried to start a wood fire in her propane heater when it ran out of gas. She hid her sheets and laundry so Don would have to search them out before he could wash them. She turned down a chance to have indoor plumbing installed in her little house. Don would bring her buckets of water, but for reasons of modesty never stayed to see that she would use them to wash. She used an outhouse, or the pot by her bed, but during the last year of her life she lost control of her bowels. Although Don would bring her meat and potatoes, during her final months she was eating only ice cream and cinnamon rolls.

When Don found his mother on the floor two weeks before her death, she was in too much pain to move; he covered her with a blanket until the ambulance arrived. Later, Custer County deputies took pictures of her house; there were dead mice all over, wads of stained laundry, excrement and clutter everywhere. "The elderly still have their rights," according to Custer County social worker Rosemary Sayers. "If they lived that way all their life, you have to respect that person's right. But there comes a time when you have to be a parent and them a child" (Carrier, 1985).

Neighbors rallied around Don and Herb at the trial. "Who is the sheriff or the state's attorney to come and tell Alice Kaiser she has to have indoor plumbing and three hot meals and visitors," Herb's lawyer asked.

Women outside the courtroom said that their own mothers had taken over-doses of medications, or wet their beds, yet wanted to continue living at home alone. Was the state going to arrest them if mother died? Many looked at Don Kaiser and said, "There but for the grace of God go I." They swarmed around Don and Herb when they were found innocent. Later, the state's attorney said that manslaughter was too strong a charge, but that there was no law on the books in South Dakota against elder abuse or neglect.

"I've got no regrets of how I took care of my mother," Don said. "I done what she wanted done, took care of her to the best of my abilities. She told me many times, 'Don't take me out of my house; I want to die right here'" (Carrier, 1985).

The Prevalence of Elder Abuse and Neglect

This case points to many of the problems associated with the topics of elder abuse and neglect. Defining exactly what elder abuse *is* is one of them. Perceptions may vary, and attitudes toward the rights of elders complicate the matter. There is no doubt that inadequate care led to an intolerable situation for Alice Kaiser. The jury evidently agreed that she had a right to be left in her own home, though, eating what she wanted and living how-ever she wanted to. Unanswered is whether or not she had the mental capacity to make decisions for herself. Her son and grandson could hardly be seen as capable caretakers, but we are left to decide whether or not they were expected to be capable caretakers. As things deteriorated, Don, an older person himself, no doubt was increasingly concerned over the wel-fare of his mother. She was still his mother, a person who throughout her life was an independent individual who presumably did not look to her son for supervision. He no doubt was at a loss as to what to do or how to handle the situation. It might be argued that we recognize that every parent is not a capable caregiver; why do we think that every adult child should be?

This still leaves us with a number of serious questions. Does the state have a responsibility to monitor the lives of older people? Do people have a right to live in a mess? At what point should some kind of intervention be made? No one would argue that Alice Kaiser should have been left in the circumstances in which she was found. Should she have been placed in a nursing home? Who is responsible for making such a decision?

One of the first tasks in clarifying how we view elder abuse and ne-glect is to differentiate one from another. Elder abuse is harming an older person intentionally, either physically or psychologically. Neglect also re-sults in harm to an older individual, but it usually is inadvertent, caused more by inattention or incompetence than on purpose. The British term for elder abuse, "granny bashing," gives the connotation that most abused older people are getting hit in the head. Actually, in terms of prevalence, neglect is much more common than actual abuse.

Illustration 12.1. Sherman and Cora

I only met my great-Uncle Sherman once, in 1956. He was, I thought, a bizarre old man even then. Almost toothless, with hair coming down to his shoulders, he was cheerfully drunk at a large family gathering. Later on, my older sister told me why she had not been present at this affair; at a family gathering that took place some years previously, Sherman had come up behind her at the kitchen sink and fondled her breasts. She didn't care to see him again. A family joke was that Sherman's wife, Aunt Cora, was the only one in the family who could prove she wasn't crazy—she had her discharge papers from the insane asylum.

Family lore has it that Sherman and Cora in very late life had boarded up the windows in their old house on the north side of Chicago and lived like hermits, fending off officials from the Health Department who periodically responded to neighbors' complaints about the forty or more cats that they kept. Childless, Sherman and Cora wouldn't open the door when any of their nieces or nephews came to see how they were doing—so they quit trying. Not only did no one in the family think to call for social services assistance (which were minimal at the time), none felt that they had the particular duty to intervene in Cora and Sherman's lives. Furthermore, nobody in the family liked Sherman and Cora very much, so there was little incentive to take on the responsibility for their care.

It was no real surprise when, early in the 1960s, a cousin called to say that Sherman and Cora had been found in their house, unheated in the dead of winter, either frozen or starved to death. He was in a wheelchair; she was on the floor. The house was an unholy mess, and the cats had been nibbling on the bodies. The Coroner said they'd been dead for at least a month. Uncashed pension checks were found on the table. It was suggested that the bodies be cremated. Old Uncle Meredith, Sherman's only surviving brother-in-law said, "Good idea! Let's burn 'em up!"

There are difficult problems in determining actual prevalence of either elder abuse or neglect. Those doing the abusing are hardly likely to come forward with information (although it has been found in surveys that they may be surprisingly candid when asked) (Pillemer & Finkelhor, 1988). Older people who are abused may be embarrassed or fearful of retaliation, however, and thus the incident may go unrecorded. There usually is no central place or registry to gather information on cases of abuse; police data and emergency room reports may be inadequate or incomplete. Protective service workers frequently have such large case loads that thorough investigation of every suspected case of abuse or neglect is impossible. And cases where no actual abuse is present, such as in the instance of the presence of bruises on the body of an individual who falls frequently, may be inappropriately recorded as abuse. So it is likely that there is no one source that has completely accurate information on elder abuse. Cases where no actual abuse are present may get recorded, while genuine instances of abuse may go unreported. A three-year study of reported cases of elder abuse in Forsyth County, North Carolina, for example, found 123 cases. Upon investigation, only 23 were confirmed as elder abuse. Of the confirmed cases, 46% were of exploitation of resources rather than of actual physical abuse. Only 3% of charges of physical abuse were substantiated (Shiferaw et al., 1994).

Because traditional ways of gathering information (police reports, emergency room records, data from protective service workers) are often inadequate, the only real way to determine the true prevalence of elder abuse would be to do a survey. The first really comprehensive study of the frequency of elder abuse was done in Boston by sociologists Karl Pillemer and David Finkelhor (1988). They took a random sample (in a random sample, each individual within the boundaries of the study has an equal chance of being selected) for their study. This is important, because only results from random samples can be generalized to the population as a whole (in contrast to convenience samples, where the researcher simply reports data from whoever is available to be questioned). Further, Pillemer and Finkelhor's sample was stratified, that is, efforts were made to include groups in proportion to their representation in the population. With a large, stratified random sample, one can be fairly confident that an accurate picture is being presented.

They took a listing of all community-dwelling persons 65 years of age and older residing in the Boston metropolitan area for their population; the sample contacted totaled 2,813, and 72% of them could be interviewed, giving a total of 2020 respondents in the survey. These people were then interviewed to determine whether or not they had ever been a victim of maltreatment; a follow-up interview was done with abuse victims. The final sample was quite similar to the population of older people in metropolitan Boston generally in terms of gender, race, religion, and income.

The results of the study indicated 63 out of the 2,020 had been maltreated one way or another. In total, there were 40 individuals who had experienced physical violence (a rate of 20 per 1000), 26 who experienced chronic verbal aggression, and 7 who were victims of neglect. Surprisingly, physical violence was the most widespread form of abuse or maltreatment uncovered by this study: 45% of those who reported physical violence had something thrown at them, 63% had been pushed, 42% had been slapped, and 10% had been hit with a fist, bitten, or kicked. The identities of those who had mistreated them were determined: the most frequent category of abuser was wives (23 of the 63 incidences of abuse), followed by husbands (14), sons (10), daughters (5), and other persons (11), such as siblings or grandchildren. The researchers concluded that comparing elder abuse to spouse abuse was thus a much more accurate model than comparing it to child abuse; 43% of the cases of physical violence consisted of a wife abusing a husband and 17% of the physical violence cases involved a husband abusing a wife.

Pillemer and Finkelhor also determined characteristics of elders most likely to be abused. Those older people living alone had much lower rates of abuse, only about a quarter as high as the rate of those who lived with

---

Illustration 12.2. Some Myths About Elder Abuse

Myth 1: Elder abuse is rising at alarming rates.

"Those driving the elder abuse issue regularly contend there are some 2 million reportable cases of abuse each year, up from 1 million a decade ago. The figure comes from a distortion of the research by Pillemer, who concluded that no more than 1.1 million older Americans have been abused—ever. In fact, even Pillemer himself says there are no sure numbers—which suggests that it makes more sense to be cautious rather than alarmist when examining the problem. Although it is logical that abuse will become a more urgent problem in a rapidly graying America, it is not clear that abuse is occurring with greater frequency. More likely, with rising awareness by health care workers and the public, is that more cases are being reported."

Myth 2: Physical abuse is most common.

"Most elder abuse laws—following the child abuse model—focus on physical, psychological, and sexual abuse, as well as neglect. But new research suggests the elderly are more probably victims of financial exploitation. Pillemer found financial abuse was the primary problem in 50% of cases in Canada, although it is much tougher to detect: a forged check is far harder to spot than a black eye. Contrary to popular perception that the elderly are victimized most by door-to-door con men and get-rich-quick schemers, the typical abuser is frequently a somewhat distant relative or an acquaintance. Spouses are rarely involved, since most money and property are jointly held."

Myth 3: Stressed caregivers are the most likely abusers.

"The first wave of research suggested that it was usually well-meaning family members who hit older relatives when care giving became difficult. This echoed theories that child abuse resulted from stress on the parents. New studies, however, debunk this. According to Rosalie Wolf of the National Committee for the Prevention of Elder Abuse, abusers of older people tend to be relatives or acquaintances with their own histories of problems, such as mental illness and alcoholism. Douglas Kaplan, the public guardian for Yolo County, California, says a growing group of offenders is children and relatives who take money to support drug habits."

From Shapiro (1992, pp. 26–28). Reprinted with permission.

---

others. The widowed, divorced, and never married were less likely to be abused, which makes sense, if the most frequent abusers are spouses. Another factor was health: those in poor health seemed to be three to four times more likely to be abused. Gender was another factor: males were much more likely to be abused physically and psychologically than were females; females were more likely to be neglected. The researchers concluded that there is substantial under-reporting of elder abuse; only a fraction of actual cases comes to public attention. Given the confidence limits of their statistics, they estimate that if the experience in the nation as a whole is comparable to their Boston data, there are between 701,000 and 1,093,000 abused older people in the United States.

Another approach was taken in a study that followed up on some 17,355 reports of elder abuse in South Carolina during a ten-year period. It was found that about three-quarters of all reports were cases of maltreatment. Types overlapped: 85% of the cases involved neglect, 17% involved physical or psychological abuse, and about 20% involved exploitation or material abuse. In this study, the most frequent victims were women (Cash & Valentine, 1987). It is important to note that neglect was far more frequent than the other types of abuse among these cases that were reported to adult protective service workers.

A study similar to the South Carolina and North Carolina longitudinal studies was done in New York by Lachs and his colleagues (1997). They followed a cohort of 2,812 community-dwelling older adults; adult protective service records were reviewed over a nine-year period. Protective service workers had seen 184 of the individuals (6.5%) for any indication of abuse or neglect. There were 47 cases (1.7%) where the charge of abuse or neglect was corroborated. Older age, minority racial status, poverty, functional disability, and cognitive impairment were significant risk factors for mistreatment. A recent study by Wolf and Li (1999), however, indicates that the credibility of an adult protective service worker's report of elder abuse depends on how well that worker has been trained. In that study, it was found that lower socioeconomic status was the best predictor of a report of elder abuse.

Material Abuse

The Boston study by Pillemer and Finkelhor did not investigate financial exploitation and, according to the South Carolina data, that type of abuse may have a greater involvement of adult children with their parents than does physical abuse. The most common type of financial abuse is probably

---

Illustration 12.3. Elder Abuse in the Good Old Days, circa 1895

"John and Leo Koelbel, well-to-do farmers residing in the town of Newton, had a hearing in Manitowoc in the county court before Judge Anderson, having been cited there on the charge of contempt for failing to comply with an order of the court commanding them to pay 60 cents a week each for the support of their aged parents. The two sons have positively refused to give a single cent toward the support of their father and mother. The court ordered them both to be committed to the county jail until they saw fit to comply with the order."

From Lesy (1973).

glossary

guardian — A court-appointed individual who is responsible for overseeing the physical or financial welfare of another.

loans from an older person to an adult child that are not repaid. There is no source of information to indicate how often this happens, but we suspect that it occurs with some frequency. Older adults have little leverage in collecting such loans, and their adult children may figure either that they have it coming as a birthright or that they would eventually receive the money anyway through inheritance. People in financial trouble would probably repay other creditors before paying back their parents.

If exchange theory is applied to this type of transaction, older lenders might reason that they in fact have less in the way of services and advice to give their adult children, that they need to keep on the good side of those who may be their eventual caretakers, and that the funds will ultimately go to their children anyway. Better to not make waves and complain about unpaid loans. So, the exchange of funds in the hope of ultimate support may be seen by both parties as having some rough justice if not entire fairness.

This is not to say that material abuse of the elderly is not a serious problem. Nor is it uncommon. Stealing from older persons, particularly relatives, takes many guises. Nonpayment of loans probably involves more actual dollar losses, but stealing from old people can range from petty theft to grand larceny. This is particularly true when older individuals have diminished capacity for management of their own affairs. In most cases, material abuse is committed by a relative or other caretaker who knows the older person well and has the opportunity to rip them off. Larceny by strangers and con men tends to make the news more often, but being taken advantage of by relatives no doubt occurs with greater frequency. Ultimately, if the abuse is unchecked, some older people may lose most of what they have. Adult protective service workers sometimes recommend a court-appointed ***guardian*** to take over management of assets of potential victims (Wilber, 1990).

After psychological abuse, material abuse by relatives may well be the most frequent type of abuse. Since it really is impossible to determine the extent of it, however, most studies other than the survey by Pillemer and Finkelhor are based on reports of complaints, either to the police or to adult protective service workers with local welfare agencies. These kinds of studies, of course, do not provide information that indicates the actual scope of elder abuse as a problem, nor do they give us much to go on with in terms of determining the actual proportion of the elderly who are victims of material abuse. This abuse is truly invisible: older victims are unlikely to complain, those guilty of material abuse certainly are not about to step forward, and there are no outward signs such as bruises, fractures, or malnutrition that an emergency room nurse might spot. As a consequence, only the most extreme cases reach the public eye. Unfortunately, there is also the problem that persons unjustly accused by the confused elderly may be almost as frequent as are genuine cases of abuse.

Self-Neglect and the Social Context of Abuse

Anthropologist Madelyn Iris (1988) presents the case of a 78-year-old woman, living alone, who has no known family. She talks to herself, dresses strangely, and will have nothing to do with the neighbors, whom she accuses of stealing her food, mail, and money. Hospitalized for malnutrition and dehydration, she accuses the hospital staff of trying to poison her. A psychiatrist diagnoses her as paranoid. The court appoints a guardian to assist her, and she accuses him of trying to locate her bank accounts and steal her money. Because of her total incapacity to make financial decisions or care for herself, it is recommended that she be placed in a nursing home; when she arrives there, she is agitated and hostile. The court-appointed guardian finds that she receives minimal supplemental security income checks monthly and has a bank account of about $500. The sad outcome is that she dies in the home after two years, convinced that she is a victim of multiple thefts and frauds.

In this case, there was an extensive investigation, and there never was any overt abuse. The fact is, unfortunately, that society has imperfect mechanisms for dealing with people who do not seem to fit in very well. The woman was mentally ill and abused herself. Her neighbors, while concerned about the woman, probably saw her as a crazy old lady and didn't really want to get involved with her problems. If she was neglected, we have to wonder by whom. Who had the responsibility to see to her well being?

This case in not necessarily typical of those who are living increasingly unsatisfactory lives in old age, but it is an example of a person who feels that she is abused when in fact there is no way to pin down where abuse might be taking place. She is unhappy, alone, suspicious of others, and looking for somewhere to place the blame.

Of course, just because there seemingly was nothing much to steal in this case, we cannot determine conclusively that there was no abuse. The woman was in no condition to testify rationally, and all of her complaints were dismissed as paranoia. Perhaps some of them were legitimate. She may have been exploited for years; some of the suspicions she had might have been legitimate, while others were blown out of proportion. This is the sad case in the narrowing social world of some isolated elderly people. Their social value is so low that there really is no one interested in being their advocate. The neighbors no doubt thought of her as a pest. It could be possible that children harassed her psychologically, tipped over her garbage cans, stole her garden hose, and threw rocks at her cat. Having no means to defend herself, and few personal qualities by which she might have found friendship among her neighbors, she became a true urban hermit. Afraid of those immediately around her, she had no place to turn. Ultimately, she trusted no one, and felt that everyone was out to get her. Perhaps from her point of view, this was a rational way to react; it really did

glossary

Gray Panthers — An
activist group that
speaks out on behalf
of older people.

seem like everyone was out to get her. About the best that society could do in this instance was to place her in an institution.

This account expands our vision of the scope of elder abuse; it seemingly is a broader issue that goes beyond merely finding somewhere to put the blame for an older person who is physically hurt, whose care has been neglected, or whose money or property has been misused. Going beyond the model of the incapable caretaker who either lashes out against a demanding, helpless person or whose incompetence results in criminal neglect, we might see elder abuse as a problem in a society where elderly people have little value. That is, if old people in our society really are unimportant, then they are in a way victims. They might be considered to be the invisible aged.

In recent years, we have seen successful efforts to uphold human dignity by at least avoiding demeaning labels and images. Women, people with disabilities, and people of color have rightly demanded greater respect and have reacted against prejudicial and insulting characterizations. There has been an associated decline in public ageism in recent years. Gone are the televised depictions of senile older people. Television comedian Johnny Carson, who retired in 1992, had retired his "Aunt Blabby" character early in the 1980s; she was a woman who bordered on senility who would take an occasional belt of whiskey from the flask concealed in her cane. This program change by Carson was in response to complaints from the ***Gray Panthers*** an activist group that campaigns for the rights of older people. Similarly, the Children's Television Workshop program *Sesame Street* at one time had a Muppet character, Professor Arid, who was so old and dull that he would nod off to sleep during his own lectures. He represented a demeaning image of an older person and was also eliminated.

However, social prejudice is subtle and goes beyond labeling or ridiculing people. It became evident during the 1980s that fewer and fewer older people were appearing on television at all (Almerico & Filmer, 1988; Bishop & Krause, 1988). In other words, if it was not socially acceptable to portray old people as confused, poor, or mean, then perhaps they could be ignored altogether. Denying peoples' existence is potent way of saying that they are unimportant. Eliminating images of aging—whether positive or negative—denigrates the aged as non-persons.

Illustration 12.4. Self-Neglect

"Ida died in 1924. On her deathbed, she couldn't rest easy, she worried, she fretted. She said, 'Oh, who'll make Charley change his underwear now?' She was right. No one ever did. Two of his sons had become doctors, so they sent their dad all sorts of new clothes, but he never wore them; he stuffed the packages away. By the time he was ninety, he was walking around town with a sweet smell coming off him, stuffing trash in his pockets."

From Lesy (1973).

There may have been a recent reversal of this trend. In response to a realization by sponsors that older individuals have a significant amount of disposable income, shows featuring older people are now being produced. Noting the buying power of older viewers, television producers may be seeking to gain markets previously unaddressed. Relatively few images of old people appear on the screen, however; certainly their depiction is much less frequent that their place in society would justify.

Much of the research on elder abuse to date points to the fact that dependent people in need of care are often a source of stress and strain to their caregivers (Pillemer & Wolf, 1986). The theory is that those responsible for caring for frail elders reach a saturation point and either lash back in frustration or begin to fail in their duties, which results in neglect.

This is in contrast to an older theory of family violence that held that the abused elder was once an abusive parent, and the adult child harbors resentment over the past and now has an opportunity to get even. This explanation of elder abuse has a certain logic to it, and perhaps rests on a notion of an adult abuser getting his or her own licks back. However, the research in fact does not support this model. Those adult children who resent past abuse are not often the ones relied upon in a caretaking relationship. Instead, spouses are much more likely to be caretakers of frail older persons. Caregivers who are without any help may reach the limit of their patience.

We need to be cautious, however, in identifying one overall theory explaining all abuse. Family violence does seem to form a pattern; where it is the norm that arguments might be settled with force, there of course is a greater potential likelihood for physical abuse. And there may well be instances where someone who has been abused as a child does indeed have festering resentments stored up that come out later when his or her parents are least able to defend themselves.

Illustration 12.5. Fake Wedding Is Part of Plan to Bilk Widow

"A former Philadelphia stockbroker pleaded guilty this week to masterminding an elaborate scheme—including a sham marriage—to defraud a 90-year-old blind widow of $1 million. Lee Alderton, 47, tried to carry out the scheme by asking a 52-year-old associate to pose as the elderly woman in a marriage ceremony at the older woman's house so he could eventually inherit her estate.

"The scheme unraveled when the younger woman told the older woman about the plan, and both went to police. The younger woman later wore a body wire so she could secretly record conversations with Alderton for the FBI. In one conversation, he asked her if she knew any other 'rich old ladies' and suggested they could engage in similar schemes as a 'small-time career.' He could 'spend the rest of my life marrying people'."

From: Fake Wedding Is Part of Plan to Bilk Widow (1992).

"An unexpected finding not considered by most other studies is the double direction of violence. While violence perpetrated on elders has been sensationalized in the media, violence by elders on their adult children has remained hidden. . . . The authoritarian father who ruled his children with an iron fist and dealt with a loss of authority or control by a beating apparently still resorted to these techniques at age 90. When the father found it to be more difficult to maintain control over children, he resorted to temper tantrums and physical outbursts. It is not difficult to understand why these elders resorted to physical violence since they had no other mechanism, such as money, prestige, mobility, or independence, with which to assert their will and gain their wishes. They had to depend on manipulations or physical control if their children were unwilling to meet their needs or their demands."

From Kosberg (1983, p. 14).

There is the almost pervasive social pathology of drug abuse: recent research reports the increasing likelihood of alcoholic or drug abusing adult children exploiting or physically abusing a parent. In fact, one of the signs leading to possible elder abuse is involvement of alcohol or drugs (Hwalek, Neale, Goodrich, & Quinn, 1996). One study says that, contrary to popular belief, abused elders tend to be functioning at a fairly high level and generally are abused by emotionally disturbed or violent family members (Bower, 1989). Benton (1999) points to a culture of violence among African-Americans as an explanation for higher rates of physical abuse among minority populations. Similarly, Carson and Hand (1999) refer to cultural forces as a partial explanation for neglect and exploitation of Native American elders.

No doubt there are instances where all of these theories might be applicable. It is important to remember that social science research looks for broad trends in large groups and tends to be inclusive rather than exclusive; there may be many variations and exceptions within general principles. All the needed research on elder abuse has not been done. It may be the result of relatives pushed to the edge and beyond by the strain of constant care, the result of a generations-long pattern of family violence, or the act of emotionally disturbed or drug abusing family members. Or, it could be the result of a combination of any or none of these factors.

The research can give us a pretty good idea of risk factors for abuse. Those identified in adult protective services records are typically female and have low incomes (Cash & Valentine, 1987). This may be because persons of very low income may come into contact with social service departments more frequently. However, it may also be because financial strain is one of the most potent factors contributing to an overall pattern of stress in families. If the family or caregiving-caretaking unit is running out of resources, money obviously is one of the most important elements to take into consideration. Those who have money can buy services.

Jordan Kosberg (1988) has identified a number of elements common to the caregiver and has also identified several typical aspects of the care recipient that seem to be associated with a potential for elder abuse. High-risk factors among the aged include being female, being of advanced age, being dependent, and having a drinking problem. Risk factors for caregivers include inexperience with caregiving, economic problems, and alcohol or drug abuse. Overall family problems are also considered to be risks; these include a lack of family support, marital conflict, and economic problems.

Older people, especially helpless or combative older people, might also be seen to be subject to abuse in nursing homes and other institutional care settings. Again, prevalence rates are difficult to determine. One study interviewing 477 nurses and aides in skilled and intermediate care settings

---

Illustration 12.7. Granny Dumping

Elderly and often confused Americans are being shockingly abandoned in small but growing numbers on hospital emergency room doorsteps across the country. Sometimes they are abandoned by children who have come to regard aging parents as a nuisance. And sometimes they are dropped off by family or friends who are simply exhausted by the pressures of caregiving. Whatever the reasons, people increasingly are leaving the elderly at emergency rooms and, at times, bolting, as one doctor puts it, telling hospitals they are relinquishing all responsibility for their aging relatives.

Reports indicate that this "granny dumping" is much more routine than had been thought. Investigators are hearing about cases like these:

In Boston, a physically and emotionally exhausted daughter and son-in-law cajole an emergency room into admitting the daughter's severely disabled mother after two months of around-the-clock home care. "They were just worn out," a doctor explains, noting that she sees several cases a week and frequency is on the rise.

In Tampa, an elderly woman in a wheelchair suddenly materializes at the triage desk of Tampa General Hospital's emergency department, in the brief absence of the nurse. "She's sick," says a note pinned to her bag. "Please take care of her." The hospital sees two or three cases a week, up from practically zero two years ago.

In New Jersey, a woman of about 60 asks a hospital emergency department to admit her confused father. Finding no acute condition that would justify admission, the doctor questions her. She breaks down, says her father wanders, is more than she can care for, and that she hopes the hospital will find some pretext to admit him.

Some people don't even bother to explain. They drop off elderly relatives outside emergency rooms, summon hospital staff by blowing their car horn, and drive off when nurses appear. Staff at Tampa General call this a "positive taillight sign" as the car flees.

It isn't that people are necessarily callous. Many caregivers feel overwhelmed. The fact they are unable to continue doesn't mean they don't care for the person; it means they have reached the point where they can't go on.

From Hey & Carlson (1991, pp. 1–3).

found that 10% admitted engaging in physical abuse and 40% in psychological abuse of patients, usually in response to patients who were themselves perceived to be abusive (Pillemer & Moore, 1990). The general reasons given for patient abuse again revolved around caregiver strain, lack of adequate help and resources, and poor preparation for the caregiving role. And the double direction of violence has been noted in studies of institutionalized as well as community-dwelling elderly (Paveza et al., 1992; Pillemer & Suitor, 1992; Shiferaw et al., 1994).

Gerontologists have also speculated that part of the reason for inadequate or abusive care in institutions can be found in the disrupted lives of the people hired as caregivers (Tellis-Nyak & Tellis-Nyak, 1989). Many nurse's aides, the people who in fact deliver the bulk of personal care, are poorly trained, are working at or near minimum wage, have families at home they are responsible for caring for, and may have additional personal problems that are frequently overlooked. They may themselves be living lives of considerable stress and be near a personal breaking point. Given that the job is not often especially rewarding, it may be no wonder that some lash back at abusive treatment from the very people they are hired to care for. After psychological abuse or neglect, personal larceny from older patients is probably fairly high in frequency, although it is seldom reported.

Illustration 12.8. Daughter Charged in Elderly Man's Abandonment

Morgantown, Ky. (AP)—John C. Kingery, an Alzheimer's disease patient who in March was taken from a nursing home and left at an Idaho racetrack with a bag of diapers next to his chair, died Monday.

Kingery, 82, whose daughter is accused of leaving him at the track, died of natural causes at a nursing home.

He had been removed from an Oregon nursing home and left at the Coeur d'Alene dog track with a note taped to his wheelchair that identified him as John King. His children recognized him from news accounts and in May brought him to Morgantown to live near them.

"Hillsboro, Ore. (AP)—The daughter of an Alzheimer's patient left at a dog racing track goes on trial this week for allegedly abandoning the 82-year-old man to get his pension.

Sue Gifford, 40, faces charges of kidnaping, theft, unlawfully obtaining public assistance, and a related perjury charge. A nonjury trial begins Tuesday.

She denies kidnapping her father or stealing his pension money.

Her father, John Kingery, was found in March at a dog track in Idaho. All identifying labels had been cut from his clothing. He was left with a bag of diapers and a nametag that read: "John King."

From: Man Left at Racetrack Dies in Kentucky and Woman Faces Trial for Abandoning Father (1992).

Also, there is the point of view that unnecessary institutionalization of the aged is in itself a type of abuse (Pillemer & Wolf, 1986).

In response to the perceived need, all 50 states have now passed legislation to protect elderly victims of domestic abuse and neglect. Nurses and emergency room doctors are increasingly aware of signs of abuse and of reporting requirements. One study of state health departments, however, detailed difficulties in the reporting process (Erlich, 1991). As we have already seen, getting the true facts of the case is generally quite difficult: relatives are often reluctant to testify against one another, the staff responsible for investigations are frequently overwhelmed, and the majority of cases constitute neglect where no one in particular may actually be at fault.

Congress appropriated funding for elder abuse prevention for the first time in 1991. It also added an amendment to the 1992 reauthorization of the Older Americans Act that established a national center on elder abuse. This, in addition to the recently-adopted legislation in all 50 states, is an expression of concern over the scope an importance of the issue.

Crime and the Elderly

A pervasive stereotype of old people is that they either are: (1) unusually vulnerable to crime, particularly to personal larceny such as purse snatching or fraud perpetrated by con men, or (2) not really the victims of much crime, but so afraid of it that they hide behind multiple locks in personal fortresses that have become more like jails than homes. The fact that neither of these myths is supported by the facts seems to have no real effect on the people who report the news. A cliché with almost every local TV news program is the annual story about fraudulent chimney inspectors or pyramid scheme operators who have defrauded some poor old widow out of thousands of dollars.

There is no doubt that some old people have been suckers in various get-rich-quick scams, pigeon drops, and other kinds of personal frauds. The question is: are older people more likely than younger adults to fall for such schemes? There is little research that says they are. In terms of documented crime, the trend of the research is exactly the opposite. Old people are much less often the victims of all types of crime than are younger persons (Webb & Marshall, 1989).

As can be seen in Table 12.1, the rates of crime (given as number of crimes per 1,000 individuals in the population) for persons aged 65+ are the lowest of any adult group. The number of murders, for example, is too low to be accurately reported as a rate, so it is not given in the table. The number of rapes of persons 65+ has averaged about 2,200 per year during the past two decades, and thus calculates to a rate of only slightly above zero (Bureau of Justice Statistics, 1998). Personal assault among the elderly is only a tenth as high as the rate for all adults, and theft is only about a third as high.

Even crimes against households, rather than against individuals, are much lower among the aged: burglary is only about half as high and car theft is less than half as high among older people, compared to the adult population in general (Bureau of Justice Statistics, 1998).

These data are consistent, year in and year out. The aged are much less likely than any other adults to be the victims of any type of crime. Why, then, the stereotype of helpless old ladies having their purses snatched or being hit in the head by heartless ruffians? Perhaps it's because of the fact that it is particularly poignant when an older person is the victim of a crime. They do present the image of being helpless and defenseless, although they are no more nor less likely to resist than are other adults (Webb & Marshall, 1989). The story of an older person being defrauded strikes a sympathetic chord in the consciousness of the public. The event becomes newsworthy, whereas crime against younger adults may not make the papers. As awful as rape is, the brutality of an older woman being raped is seen as that much more of an outrage. Aged, presumably helpless people being mugged stirs up more of a public outcry. In a way, this perception of older people as helpless is patronizing and might itself be seen as a kind of abuse.

Earlier gerontological research, while recognizing that the aged are the least frequent victims of crime, painted them as being particularly afraid of it. That is, the real victimization of the elderly was said to be the *fear* of crime rather than crime itself (Janson & Ryder, 1983; Sundeen & Mathieu, 1976). That is not to say that fear of crime is an insignificant factor among some older people. Security from crime has been found to be a predictor of well-being, particularly among those who have sought out congregate housing because they have a personal concern over possible victimization (Lawton & Yaffe, 1980). There is some research to indicate that older people are more intimidated by actual events of crime (Fox, 1991; Muram, 1992). Sometimes the belief in victimization goes to illogical extremes; a colleague and I surveyed 700 older people in Nebraska, and 14.3% of them said that it was likely or very likely that they would be murdered (Powell & Thorson, 1994). In actuality, the odds are that none of them will be a victim of homicide.

TABLE 12.1. Rates of Violent Crime Victimization by Age*

Age	All Crimes of Violence	Rape/Sexual Assault	Robbery	Assault	Theft
12–15	87.9	2.5	8.2	77.1	2.8
16–19	96.2	5.6	10.2	80.4	3.5
20–24	67.8	2.4	7.4	57.9	1.8
25–34	46.9	2.3	4.7	39.9	1.1
35–49	32.2	0.6	3.7	27.9	1.6
50–64	14.6	0.2	2.2	12.2	1.1
65+	4.4	0.2	0.9	3.4	1.2

*Per 1,000 in population
From Rand (1998, p. 4).

However, the most comprehensive study of older people as a group finds that they actually have no more fear of crime than do younger people (Ferraro & LaGrange, 1992). We need to remember that there are now over 34 million people aged 65 and above, and opinion among such a large group varies quite a lot. Although we may know some individuals who seem to live with a great fear of victimization, the elderly as a group have been shown to be no more fearful than the general public. It has been found that those who live in high-crime neighborhoods are rightly fearful, but that location, rather than age, is the biggest determinant of fear (Janson & Ryder, 1983).

Conclusion

Although older people are the least likely people in U.S. society to be the victims of crime, there is a growing awareness that there is a potential for them to be abused, either physically, psychologically, or materially. Public agencies are increasingly aware of their responsibilities for monitoring signs of potential abuse and reporting and documenting cases where it occurs. While the victimization rate seemingly is very low, life in fact can be a living hell for those individuals who are subjected to continual abuse. Merely because of their status as citizens and human beings, they deserve to be treated with decency and kindness. The most frequent type of abuse seems to be neglect when care is needed, usually of an old person by another old person. And, while patterns of family violence no doubt contribute to the problem, the issue of elder abuse is more similar to spouse abuse than it is to child abuse. All 50 states have now passed legislation dealing with elder abuse and neglect.

Caretaker strain and burnout are at the heart of much elder abuse. For this reason, we can identify some symptoms of potential abuse. Abuse may occur when the elder adult:

- is in poor health
- is overly dependent on an adult child
- was (or is) excessively dependent on spouse
- persists in directing or controlling caretaker

And, there are several signs of abuse as well. Such as when the elder adult:

- has unexplained or repeated injury
- shows evidence of dehydration or malnutrition
- has been given inappropriate food or drugs
- is noticeably passive and withdrawn
- has muscle contractions from being restricted

Further, there are a number of caregiver risk dynamics. Caregivers may be likely to abuse or neglect their charges if the caregiver:

- was abused as a child
- has a poor self-image
- has a limited capacity to express own needs
- abuses alcohol or drugs
- is psychologically unprepared for dependency of spouse or parent
- shows a loss or a fear of loss of control
- gives a history full of contradictions
- denies parent's or spouse's illness
- has delayed seeking care
- reacts inappropriately to the seriousness of the situation
- complains continually of unrelated problems
- refuses consent for further diagnosis or treatment

In summary, much abuse and neglect can be seen as a family problem, a breakdown in the ideal interaction between spouses or between older parents and their adult children. Where no apparent caretaker is present, this of course is not the case: older isolates are more prone to neglect than actual abuse. Society has a responsibility to intervene in cases of abuse, but we must be careful to investigate and document instances and differentiate them from false claims or paranoia. Caretakers who have reached the end of their rope should be given support and help with care rather than condemnation and punishment.

Questions for Discussion

1. Do you think that ageism is at the heart of elder abuse?
2. Have you ever been responsible for the care of another person? If so, what difficulties did you encounter?
3. The story of Don and Alice Kaiser began the chapter. Was it just that Don was found innocent of all charges?
4. Are you familiar with any cases of elder abuse?
5. How could it be said that elder abuse is more like spouse abuse than like child abuse?
6. What actions might best prevent abuse in nursing homes?
7. Were you surprised to learn how low the rates of crime against the elderly are? If so, why?
8. Should adult children be held legally accountable for the welfare of their aged parents?

Sources of Further Information

There are at least three sources of information nationally on the topics of elder abuse and neglect.

Criminal Justice Services
American Association of Retired Persons
1909 K Street, N.W.
Washington, D.C. 20049

They have published a guide, *Domestic Mistreatment of the Elderly: Towards Prevention,* single copies of which are available free. Ask for any additional material on elder abuse that they might have developed recently.

The College of Human Resources, University of Delaware, Newark, Delaware 19716, has regularly published a newsletter: *C.A.N.E. Exchange* (Clearinghouse on Abuse & Neglect of the Elderly), which is quite good and informative. Ask for available materials that can be ordered.

A new advocacy organization has been formed. Those wishing to join it should write to:

National Committee for the Prevention of Elder Abuse
Institute on Aging
The Medical Center of Central Massachusetts
119 Belmont St.
Worcester, MA 01605

Request a copy of *Elder Abuse: Questions and Answers* from:

National Center on Elder Abuse
810 1st Street, N.E., Suite 500
Washington, D.C. 20002-4267

In addition, local or state information might be received by contacting the adult protective services division of your state's department of welfare or human services.

Older People and  the Politcal World

Chapter Outline

"I believe that it is tremendously important for the elderly to organize for political power and clout. We need to sign petitions to pass new laws, to improve existing legislation, and to check on current regulations in the health field. We need to keep watch on congressmen and other public officials and must make our desires known."
— Sarah McClendon, born 1910

Introduction

Would it be a surprise to learn that an organization of older people has been called one of the three most powerful political lobbies in Washington? During the 1993 budget debates, Senator Daniel Patrick Moynihan, Chairman of the Senate Finance Committee, dismissed consideration of Social Security out of hand, saying that to even talk about the program would be "political suicide?" Why is this?

And why are groups of people in their 20s campaigning against benefits for the elderly?

We will deal with aging and politics in this chapter. We'll look at the relationship between political action and the formation of public policy, at the voting behavior of older adults, and at the formation and uses of political clout. In particular, we'll look at organizations providing advocacy for the interests of older people, and how these organizations might at times get out of touch with their own membership. In particular, we'll examine the politics of self-interest. And we will look a bit to the future, which may hold increasing conflict between the generations. First, though, we'll discuss how the aged fare in the political process.

In the study of the social world of older people, how they interact with society and how society interacts with them, there can be no more important realm than politics and the formation of public policy. The welfare of the aged as a group, over the course of time, is largely dependent on public policy. Income of the aged is, to a great degree, determined by what happens to the Social Security program. Financing the health care of the aged is to a considerable degree determined by what happens with the federal Medicare and Medicaid programs. Other areas of life are not so clearly dependent on public programs, but nevertheless are influenced by policy decisions made in the political arena.

Housing is an example. While only a very small fraction of housing for the aged is provided through public housing sponsored by the U.S. Department of Housing and Urban Development, the way older people live still is greatly influenced by public policy. In the United States, buyers of houses are able to take the amount of the interest they pay on a home mortgage as a deduction from their income tax. In this way, the federal government subsidizes individual home ownership. This is a public policy decision, and it has a great influence on how people live. As we saw in Chapter 11, the great majority of old people in the United States live in houses that they own. They have for the most part lived in the same dwelling long enough to pay off the mortgage, and for most, their house is their principal asset. In Canada, where home mortgage interest is not deductible from income taxes, the majority of older persons live in apartments. Thus, a public policy has had a great influence on where older people live. Older people probably did not come to mind when the U.S. Congress decided to exempt home mortgage interest from income taxes, but the net result of that action was to make a house affordable for ordinary people, and ordinary people eventually become old.

Further, and more intentional, most states and local governments give older home owners a break on their real estate taxes. This has the effect of allowing more older people to stay in their own homes, and is the direct result of a public policy decision.

That decision was made by elected representatives, and these public leaders got elected—and remained in office—when the voters perceived that their needs and aspirations were adequately represented. Older people make up an important bloc of the electorate, and many wise politicians are aware of this fact.

There are many interrelationships between the aged and access to political power. Many elected representatives, for example, age in place: they get older while they are in office, and they for that reason may ultimately represent the point of view of elders. Of greater importance, however, is the responsiveness of elected representatives to the needs of older voters. Political leaders believe that pleasing the elderly voter is good business. And, in a variety of ways, older people have shown they have the ability to communicate their needs to politicians.

Older people have been able to organize themselves into politically effective groups. Due to their stature in the community, older people might be more likely to get a sympathetic hearing from political leaders than other interest groups. Older individuals might simply know more elected representatives; personal friendship could give them an "in" that others might not have. Also, while every politician is not necessarily old, every politician aspires to become old. Good public policy for the elderly might be part of enlightened self-interest for many elected officials. Whatever the reason, older citizens have fared very well in the political arena.

In this chapter, we will look at older people in the political process, how they interact in the public policy-making realm, and some of the difficulties they may have in the future. First, we will review research on the older voter, and then we'll look at political beliefs of the aged as a group. Finally, we will examine interest groups and organizations of older persons and how they impact the political process.

The Older Voter

One of the reasons older people have fared well in the political realm is the belief held by most politicians that older adults vote more than any other group. While there may be a tendency to believe that older people also vote

---

Illustration 13.1. Subsidizing the Older Taxpayer

U.S. taxpayers are confronted each year by forms from the Internal Revenue Service. At the top of the first page of each individual income tax form is a block where exemptions are to be checked off. A personal exemption is a set number of dollars on which taxes need not be paid; the system in effect gives families with children a break on their taxes. Many younger voters, however, don't take much notice of the wording at the top of that first page: individuals are able to check off two exemptions if they are either over 65 or blind. In 2000, the personal exemption was $2,800; a nominal tax rate of 28% of that amount is $784. In other words, U.S. tax policy is to subsidize most 65-year-old taxpayers by the amount of $784 each for no other reason than that they have become officially old.

Some observers might criticize this as being blatantly discriminatory and contrary to the Equal Protection Clause of the 14th Amendment to the U.S. Constitution. Will it be changed? We have yet to see the politician who has the courage to embrace this issue.

in a bloc, which has less evidence to support it, the contention that they are faithful voters is, to a large extent, true.

Table 13.1 lists the percentage, by age, of those who said they voted in the most recent U.S. presidential elections for which data is available (U.S. Bureau of the Census, 1998c). For our purposes, the interesting comparisons are by age. We can see that the youngest voters had a consistently poor turnout. Fewer than half of the eligible voters under age 21 had even registered to vote. Fewer than a third of them voted. We know that there are several social correlates of voting behavior:

- voting goes up with age
- females are somewhat more likely to vote than males
- whites are more likely to vote than blacks
- consistently, a higher percentage of people in the Midwest vote, compared to people in the Northeast, South, or West
- employed people vote much more regularly than do the unemployed
- voting goes up with years of education.

We can see that the most frequent voters listed in Table 13.1 were the oldest group and those aged 45 to 64. It is sometimes said that voting behavior increases across the lifespan, and the oldest voters participate at a slightly higher level than the next-oldest group. The data in Table 13.1 provide some evidence that older persons are able to get out and get to the polling place in relatively high numbers, and that their level of voting is high compared to other adult groups.

Political scientist John Strate and his colleagues give a number of reasons for this high level of political participation by the elderly (1989). They maintain that the aged have an increasing sense of community attachment and civic participation. In a sense, the older voters embrace the proposition of citizenship to a greater degree than others; they're less likely to be alienated from the participatory process. This leads to a theory of civic development across the lifespan. Older people have a greater sense in this regard for a number of reasons, including changes in community attach-

TABLE 13.1. Voting-Age Population and Percent Registered and Voting

Age Group	Voting-Age Population*	Percent Reporting They Registered, 1996	Percent Reporting They Voted, 1996
18 to 20 years	10.8	45.6	31.2
21 to 24 years	13.9	51.2	33.4
25 to 34 years	40.1	56.9	43.1
35 to 44 years	43.3	66.5	54.9
45 to 64 years	53.7	73.5	70.0
65 years & over	31.9	77.0	70.1
Total	193.7	65.9	54.2

*in millions
From U.S. Bureau of the Census, 1998.

ment and civic competence. Predictors of voter participation that Strate's group found in their study of the older voter included community attachment, strength of partisanship, more regular church attendance, a sense of government responsiveness, family income, and an understanding of the process. These variables accounted for over half of the variance in voter participation. Studies of older black voters have found essentially the same predictor variables, and that older blacks vote about as frequently as older whites (Bazargan, Barbre, & Torres-Gil, 1992; Bazargan, Kang, & Bazargan, 1991; Powell & Thorson, 1990).

In an earlier review of research on the older voter, Hudson and Strate (1985) demonstrated that political interest increases across adult life, although there may be some evidence that the aged have a lower sense of personal efficacy in politics compared to younger voters. Older people seem to have about the same level of trust in government, although it also has been demonstrated that the aged have a greater sense of attachment to political institutions. This may be a cohort effect, in that as children the people who are now old were taught to have a greater respect for government and public officials. There appears to be little research evidence to support a contention that people identify themselves as more conservative as they age (Campbell & Strate, 1981).

Table 13.2 gives stated party affiliation by age. It can be seen that the majority of those 65 and older declare themselves to be Democrats, although identification with either party appears to increase by age. The numbers in Table 13.2 do not add up to 100% because a relatively small number of respondents indicated that they were apolitical. One might argue, also, that the stronger affiliation with the Democratic party among the 65 to 74 year-olds may be a cohort effect; these people were young during the Great Depression of the 1930s and may still have an identification with Franklin Roosevelt and the New Deal programs.

Party attachment may be said to be weakening, but Campbell and his colleagues found the aged to have the strongest party attachments a generation ago (1960). The data in Table 13.1 seem to confirm this.

Overall political opinions of the aged appear to be much like those held by middle aged adults, although the aged have been found to be some-

TABLE 13.2. Political Affiliation, in Percentages, by Age

Age Group	Strong Democrat	Weak Democrat	Independent	Weak Republican	Strong Republican
17–24 yrs	9	44	10	27	10
25–34 yrs	11	33	12	27	16
35–44 yrs	13	32	12	25	18
45–54 yrs	15	31	7	28	17
55–64 yrs	18	40	8	28	15
65–74 yrs	28	45	8	27	15
75–99 yrs	19	35	9	22	13

From U.S. Bureau of the Census (1998b).

what more traditional on law-and-order issues (Campbell, 1971; Hudson & Strate, 1985). The elderly also have been shown to have higher levels of racial prejudice. Robert Kastenbaum, for example, found that the defeat in Arizona of the statewide Martin Luther King holiday could be attributed to older voters (1991). He argued that racism and pragmatic self-interest might have accounted for less of the opposition than what he calls a "fortress mentality" that has developed through a combination of circumstances.

The aged as a group, not surprisingly, appear to be motivated by self-interest (Hudson & Strate, 1985). This should come as no surprise; other groups are motivated by self-interest as well. It would be unusual if the elderly were an exception.

However, identifying candidates who clearly support issues embraced by the elderly or identifying issues that are uniquely beneficial to the elderly may be difficult. Most politicians run on a platform of multiple issues, and most seemingly make sure that support of the welfare of the elderly is one of the planks in that platform. The older voter motivated by self-interest, then, is often in something of a dilemma as to which candidate to choose, since no politician is likely to run on an anti-aging platform. In fact, the first thing that most candidates for national office seem to say is that they are in favor of a strong Social Security program, whatever their party or ideological affiliation.

Campbell and Strate contend that older voters are not necessarily more conservative. Yet, there is contradictory evidence in this regard. Haas and Serow (1993) point out that most retirement migration is amenity migration: that is, people are seeking out more pleasant environments when they move to another state late in life. In addition to warm weather and sunshine, the amenity many older persons may be seeking is lower taxes. This may be the reason that California, with relatively high local taxes, loses about as many retirees as it gains (Ahmed & Smith, 1992; Longino, 1995; Longino & Serow, 1992). Perhaps the type of older person who makes an amenity move in later life is seeking to preserve other things, getting away from the hustle of the city and back to a more peaceful environment. It could be that these individuals are more conservative. There is some evidence to demonstrate that they are less likely to vote for local initiatives such as school bond issues. Preston (1984) has pointed out that states that have the highest growth of their elderly population have the largest declines in teacher salaries. Conservatism of older immigrants would also help to explain the findings of the Arizona study by Kastenbaum.

Interest Groups

Organizations of older people have grown faster and larger than any other type of voluntary association in the United States during the past three decades. By far the most successful among them has been the American

Association of Retired Persons (AARP), which claims 33 million members (Novack, 1991). At first glace, this is an absurd number; there are only 34 million people 65 and older in the United States. But, it is possible to join the AARP at age 50 rather than 65, and this accounts for some of the discrepancy. A more realistic membership number may be the one printed on the annual audit report that appears in the Association's monthly magazine, *Modern Maturity*—a little over 19 million. Still, at 19 million, that makes the magazine by far the largest print run of any publication in the United States, far outpacing the *Reader's Digest* at 11 million. Printing the magazine costs the Association $107 million per year, which means that the AARP is big-league by anyone's standards (Silber, 1991).

The organization grew out of the National Retired Teachers' Association (NRTA), which leveled out in terms of membership at about a half-million by the early 1970s. The AARP by that time had over three million members, and it was obvious that it would far outgrow its parent; for many years, the masthead of the combined organizations appeared as "NRTA-AARP," but the NRTA part was dropped over a decade ago.

The appeal of the AARP has been member benefits and low cost. Annual dues are a bargain just for the magazine itself. In addition, AARP members can receive special publications published by the organization and they can participate in insurance programs, travel opportunities, and a discount mail-order pharmacy. The AARP has run special continuing education programs promoting driver safety, and it has been a leader in combating elder abuse. It develops a wide variety of educational materials and offers a free audio-visual library on issues of interest to senior citizens. Its Andrus Foundation provides millions of dollars each year to support research in applied areas of gerontology. In recent years, the AARP has formed its own credit union and, of greater consequence, one of the fastest-growing mutual funds in the country, with over ten billion dollars in assets. The AARP has also grown into one of the country's most effective and powerful political lobbying organizations (Hornblower, Holmes, & Riley, 1988; Mitchell, 1992; Schurenberg & Luciano, 1988; Smith, 1988).

Illustration 13.2. AARP Insurance

Consumer advocates once were critical of the AARP as being little more than a front for Leonard Davis's Colonial Penn Insurance Company. At one time in the early 1970s, it was not uncommon for Association staff to leave the AARP and go to work for Colonial Penn. The Association didn't even control its own mailing list in the early years; mailings for NRTA-AARP were handled by Colonial Penn (Van Atta, 1998). The available insurance offerings were criticized as being overpriced for what older consumers got. The AARP moved to avoid further controversy by making a conscious decision to disassociate itself from Colonial Penn early in the 1980s; it now markets insurance underwritten by Prudential.

This might be seen as a curiosity, as the organization's roots were anything but political. Founded by retired school teacher Ethel Percy Andrus, the NRTA-AARP appeared at one time to be quite a conservative organization. For example, it refused to endorse the passage of Medicare legislation in 1963–64. Democrats, needing older advocates to lobby for the passage of the program, turned to the United Auto Workers, which organized the National Council of Senior Citizens (NCSC) out of a core of its retired union membership. The NCSC at one time had grown to about three million members and was seen as the Democratic organization of older people to the more characteristically Republican NRTA-AARP. The AARP has moved to the left in recent years, so much so that a profile of the Association in *Forbes* magazine charges that the organization has left its many conservative members behind. It claims that only 14% of the membership join to support the organization's lobbying efforts (Novack, 1991).

During the 1970s, the AARP was an enthusiastic sponsor of the National Interfaith Coalition on Aging (NICA), a collective of civic and denominational bodies with a common interest in religion and aging (Thorson & Cook, 1980). Some might argue that religious institutions are essentially socially conservative. Current AARP Executive Director Horace Deets, who was ordained as a Roman Catholic priest, ironically has distanced the organization from NICA and other religious groups in recent years (Van Atta, 1998).

The AARP faces a dilemma in that it has a role in educating its membership in terms of civic issues, but it cannot be seen as leading them. If AARP support is seen as being either too liberal or too conservative, then potential membership may be lost from one end or other of the political spectrum. Oftentimes, the AARP seeks to be somewhat in the middle-of-the-road on issues and, particularly, candidates. It does not usually endorse persons running for public office, nor does it sponsor a Political Action Committee to make campaign donations. Its lobbying efforts,

---

Illustration 13.3. Catastrophic Coverage

"The 1988 Medicare Catastrophic Coverage Act was designed to protect the elderly and disabled from staggering medical bills. Enthusiastically backed by the American Association of Retired Persons, the law would have benefitted seven million persons with no coverage other than Medicare and another several million privately insured individuals who could have switched to public assistance. Proponents of the legislation failed to consider, however, that some elderly might object to the selective income surtax intended to finance the program. Legal complexities and misinformation campaigns contributed to the widespread belief that everyone eventually would have to pay the top premium. Less than 18 months after its passage, protests from senior citizens and lobbies representing their concerns forced the repeal of the law."

From Rhodebeck (1993, p. 343).

however, might be seen as surprisingly far-reaching to many of its members. For example, the organization was embarrassed in 1992 when it was revealed that it and the American Bankers Association had been in secret negotiations on possible legislation allowing banks to enter the insurance business (Brostoff, 1992). This might be seen as straying rather far from AARP's expected role of being an advocate for no reductions in Social Security, say, or fighting cuts in the Medicare program (Arndt & Harrington, 1993).

As the Medicare Catastrophic Coverage debacle demonstrated, the AARP staff at times finds itself in the position of advocating legislation that many of the organization's members are against. Catastrophic Coverage would have had the most benefit for the poor elderly. Most AARP members, however, are middle-class and already carry private health care insurance that supplements their Medicare coverage. They perceived that the Catastrophic Coverage Act would cost them something and do them little good, and they bombarded their representatives in Washington with protests. The AARP, which had strongly advocated Catastrophic Coverage, had to backtrack, and Congress reversed the legislation the year after it was passed.

The AARP thus has to pick and choose among lobbying efforts that will support its members, not just some of the elderly. For this reason, it has been equivocal in terms of the "notch" issue, which was of great interest to the several million elders affected but of hardly any interest to others. (People born in the "notch" from 1917 to 1921 recieve slightly lower Social Security benefits than those born before them and have actively campaigned—without success—to have the Social Security legislation changed.) The overall integrity of the Social Security trust fund seemingly is of greater overall importance to the elderly as a group than increased benefits to a minority of their number, however vocal they might be.

Early in April of 1994, a first-class letter signed by AARP Executive Director Horace B. Deets went out to a select 600,000 members of the organization. It contained a "Long-Term Care Action Alert," and began:

> The cost of long-term care—in nursing homes, in the community, or at home—is a daily threat to the economic security, peace of mind, and stability of millions of American families. You or I could face the crushing cost of long-term care at any time. Right now, Congress is debating

"The notch issue arose after Congress corrected a 1972 legislative miscalculation that eventually would have provided some retirees with benefits amounting to over 100% of their working wages. The 1977 correction left the accidental windfall in effect for retirees born before 1917 but gradually scaled down the extra benefits for retirees born in the notch between 1917 and 1921. Angry about their inability to share in the full unintended windfall, 'notch babies' expressed their discontent (without success) by sending half a million written complaints to Congress, encouraging lobbyists and state and local governments to pressure Washington on their behalf."

From Rhodebeck (1993, p. 343).

whether new coverage for home and community-based long-term care should be included in the health care reform package. *But behind closed doors, special interest lobbyists are telling Congress that this coverage for long-term care has no place in health care reform.* Only you can open those doors and get the debate out in the open . . . where it belongs . . . and only if you take action now. Your direct line to action is as near as your phone. AARP has set Tuesday, April 26th as "Long-Term Care Day." On that day, I urge you to call your Representative and your Senators and tell them that you want long-term care to be part of health care reform.

The letter included names, addresses, and phone numbers of individual senators and congressmen, directions on what to say or write in support of the inclusion of nursing home care in a comprehensive health care bill, and a self-addressed mailer to report back to Deets that the recipient had indeed contacted his or her legislative representatives in Congress. The organization evidently felt that the Administration ultimately would be successful in winning the passage of health care reform and wanted to use its influence to be sure that long-term care was an element included in the plan. One might conclude then that the price of AARP's support for health care reform was that nursing home costs would be included. This was front-page news in the organization's monthly newsletter (Health care reform volunteers use buses, valentines, cellular phones to get messages to Congress, 1994). The Clinton health plan ultimately flopped, of course; long-term care coverage—or any other kind of health coverage—never was passed by the Congress.

The AARP is the largest, but by no means the only organization that speaks out on behalf of the elderly. In addition to the AARP, the National Council of Senior Citizens and other membership organizations, such as the National Council on the Aging, voluntary associations, and groups not specifically focused exclusively on aging, often support legislation or programs for the aged. There are also professional organizations of people working in the fields of aging, higher education, nursing, medicine, hous-

> **Illustration 13.6. Gray Panther Maggie Kuhn**
>
> "We want to give old folks a new sense of power and worth. We've been brainwashed by the youth cult to keep up youthful appearances, to be ashamed of our age. I say we should admit we're old and take pride in it, instead of attempting to cover up our wrinkles and our gray hair to look young—which we can't do. Instead, we have to express—in our persons and our lifestyles—a sense of moral outrage against the injustices perpetrated on people."
>
> From Offen (1972, p. 33).

ing, and nursing home care, and hospitals and social welfare organizations that make their needs known and provide advocacy for issues affecting the elderly.

One of the smaller, but nonetheless effective, organizations is the Gray Panthers, founded by the late Maggie Kuhn. Organized in Philadelphia, the Gray Panthers now draws members from throughout the country. They have been particularly vocal and creative in speaking out on aging and intergenerational issues. In one demonstration on the sidewalk outside the annual meeting of the American Medical Association in Chicago, for example, they had an emergency medical squad administer aid to a dummy dressed as a doctor. Opening up the dummy's shirt to give it cardiac resuscitation, Gray Panthers found its chest to be stuffed with money, but to have no heart.

Generational Equity

The success of older persons in the political arena has been apparent. Only a generation ago, the words "poor" and "old" could commonly have been equated. This is no longer the case. The economic status of the aged has improved to such a degree that a smaller percentage of the aged have incomes below the poverty level than the rest of the population. As recently as 1970, about a third of those aged 65+ lived below the official poverty level; now only 10.8% are officially poor (U.S. Bureau of the Census, 1999). Much of this economic improvement has come through cost-of-living increases in Social Security retirement payments.

Indeed, the aged in some ways have an image problem: they may be seen as being too wealthy. This is less important in a booming economy with low unemployment, but it could be particularly apparent in a stagnant economy burdened with a relatively high percentage of people who are unemployed or underemployed. Not long ago, a common plea for sympathy could be made for "those on a fixed income," meaning pensioners whose livelihood was being eaten away relentlessly by soaring inflation. People who retired on a set amount of annual pension and Social Security payments often found their income to be inadequate only a few years after they left work.

Succorance-seeking on behalf of the elderly no longer works. Older people are no longer seen as poverty-stricken in the public eye. On the contrary, they are often envisioned as the new leisure class, those able to afford recreational vehicles and snowbird migration. Whether it is generally true or not, older people are now often perceived to be the likeliest to be wealthy. In actual fact, the group with the highest median family net worth is in the cohort aged 55 to 64, followed next by those 45 to 54 years of age (U. S. Bureau of the Census, 1999). Nevertheless, the more adequate incomes enjoyed in recent years by the aged have, to a large degree, removed the elements of pity and victim status that once were used with some success by advocates for the elderly.

Perhaps this is due to the more rapid improvements made in recent years by the aged as a group relative to other age groups. Critics now point to the relatively large portion of the federal budget devoted to the elderly in comparison to other groups, most notably children. In actuality, this differential can be accounted for because Social Security is now listed in the main federal budget—it used to be a separate, non-budget item. Service expenditures on behalf of the elderly have not grown in recent years, nor do they approximate in any reasonable way the level of services received by children or adolescents. This is especially true if one looks at all governmental expenditures: by far the greatest expense item in local budgets is for the public schools, dollars that are spent almost exclusively on behalf of younger people.

Illustration 13.7. Generational Accounting

"Generational accounting is a 90s creation, the brainchild of three economists: Laurence J. Kotlikoff of Boston University, Alan Auerbach of the University of Pennsylvania, and Jagadeesh Gokhale of the Cleveland Federal Reserve Bank. Adding to the political-economic dictionary, they created a new economic yardstick, lifetime tax rates. By these measurements, Mr. Kotlikoff predicts, the lifetime tax rate for Americans born in 1900 was 21.5%. For Americans born in 1990, the lifetime tax rate will be 33.5%.

"In these calculations, which define taxes as total tax payments minus total income transfers like Social Security, the trajectory is relentless: the later people are born, the more they will work for everyone else and the less for themselves. 'This', Mr. Kotlikoff said, 'is the natural outgrowth of four decades of Government pursuing a variety of different policies—most of which don't show up on the Government's books—to expropriate the young and future generations for the benefit of older generations'."

From Barringer (1993, p. 32).

Minkler and Robertson (1991) did a review of attempts to disclaim legitimate needs of the elderly through advancement of the ideology of "generational equity." They pointed out that this in fact represents potential generational conflict; it in effect blames the old for poverty among the young. They document growing resentment of programs aiding the aged among minorities and young people, who may perceive that older people are getting more than their fair share of the pie.

Perceptions of the aged may indeed include notions of greed and selfishness. Each time a school bond issue is voted down by older voters, ammunition is added to the criticism of "greedy geezers." Claims of the "Notch Babies" that they deserve greater Social Security payments and of those middle-class elderly who protested the Catastrophic Coverage that would benefit the poor elderly add fuel to what may emerge as a genuine fire in years to come.

An organization called Americans for Generational Equity is devoted to restructuring the Social Security system (Quadagno, 1990). Its claim is that the country is wasting its resources on payments to the elderly while children live in poverty. It advocates a system of reduced benefits and means-testing of Social Security. Arguing that the wealthy have no need for retirement benefits under Social Security, it is maintained that Social Security is a bonanza for most of the elderly, whereby they receive back many times what they and their employers paid into the system.

Lead . . . or Leave is another organization against high payments to older persons who may not deserve them (Barringer, 1993). Not critical only of the elderly but also of the middle-aged, this organization purports to support the generation following the Baby Boomers. It points to the AARP as one of its principal targets among special interest groups. Its message is that the generational birthright of younger adults is being mortgaged through the selfishness of those who have come before it.

Conclusion

Whatever the ultimate success of organizations such as Lead . . . or Leave and Americans for Generational Equity, it is evident that unquestioned support of programs and benefits for the elderly is no longer a certainty. Universal, all-encompassing programs like Social Security and Medicare, however, continue to enjoy broad public approval. Not only can most of the public see the need for such programs, but most people have older relatives that benefit from them. And, many look to the day when they may be beneficiaries.

Political action and interest groups advocating programs of benefit to the elderly may anticipate difficulty in the years to come. The elderly do not speak with one voice. They are a heterogeneous group. All older people do not have the same needs. Like other interest groups, they may not necessarily work only for the greatest good for the greatest number. Some no doubt are motivated by civic-mindedness and the welfare of the population as a whole; others, like many people in all other age groups, are out to take care of themselves first.

Older people continue to endorse the idea of participatory democracy. They vote in high numbers compared to other age groups in the population, and they are interested in public issues. More than other age groups, they tend to be motivated by a sense of civic participation. They do not necessarily go to bat only in support of their own narrow self-interests. They have, however, shown themselves to be effective advocates for their needs, and no doubt this effective advocacy will continue. Others may resent their success; no doubt this resentment will continue as well.

Questions for Discussion

1. How do federal and local tax policies affect housing of the elderly?
2. In the broadest sense, how is public policy established?
3. What are some reasons that explain why older persons have fared well in the political arena?
4. Do you think double exemptions for the elderly on federal income tax should continue? Why?
5. What age group votes the most?
6. Name several predictors of voting behavior.
7. Why would old people hold the strongest party attachments?
8. Do you think the aged receive too many benefits?

Sources of Further Information

Below are addresses for a number of organizations involved in advocacy in different aspects of aging:

American Association of Homes for the Aging
1129 20th St., N.W., Suite 400
Washington, D.C. 20036-3489

American Association of Retired Persons
1909 K St., N.W.
Washington, D.C. 20049

American Bar Association
Commission on Legal Problems of the Elderly
1800 M St., N.W.
Washington, D.C. 20036

American Health Care Association
1200 15th St., N.W.
Washington, D.C. 20005

American Nurses' Association
Division on Gerontological Nursing Practice
2420 Pershing Rd.
Kansas City, MO 64108

American Public Health Association
Section of Gerontological Health
1015 15th St., N.W.
Washington, D.C. 20005

American Society on Aging
833 Market St., Rm. 516
San Francisco, CA 94103

Asian and Pacific Coalition on Aging
1102 S. Crenshaw Blvd., Rm. 43
Los Angeles, CA 90019

Association Nacional Pro Personas Mayores
2727 W. 6th St., Suite 270
Los Angeles, CA 90057

Canadian Association on Gerontology
1080-167 Lombard Ave.
Winnipeg, Manitoba R3C 0B1
Canada

Concerned Seniors for Better Government
815 16th St., N.W.
Washington, D.C. 20006

Council of Home Health Agencies
National League for Nursing
10 Columbus Circle
New York, NY 10019

Elderhostel
80 Boylston St., Suite 400
Boston, MA 02116

Gerontological Society of America
1030 15th St., S.W., Suite 250
Washington, D.C. 20005-1503

Gray Panthers
1424 16th St., N.W., Suite 602
Washington, D.C. 20036

National Alliance of Senior Citizens
2525 Wilson Blvd.
Arlington, VA 22201

National Association of Area Agencies on Aging
600 Maryland Ave., S.W., West Wing 208
Washington, D.C. 20024

National Association of Foster Grandparent Directors
195 E. San Fernando St.
San Jose, CA 95112

National Association of Hispanic Elderly
2727 W. 6th St., Suite 270
Los Angeles, CA 90057

National Association of Retired Federal Employees
1533 New Hampshire Ave., N.W.
Washington, D.C. 20036

National Association of State Units on Aging
2033 K St., N.W., Suite 300
Washington, D.C. 20006

National Caucus on the Black Aged
1424 K St., N.W., Suite 500
Washington, D.C. 20005

National Citizens' Coalition for Nursing Home Reform
1224 M St., N.W., Suite 301
Washington, D.C. 20005-5183

National Committee to Preserve Social Security and Medicare
2000 K St., N.W., Suite 800
Washington, D.C. 20036

National Council on Senior Citizens
925 15th St., N.W.
Washington, D.C. 20005

National Council on the Aging
600 Maryland Ave., S.W., West Wing 100
Washington, D.C. 20024

National Hispanic Council on Aging
2713 Ontario Rd., N.W., Suite 200
Washington, D.C. 20009

National Indian Council on Aging
P.O. Box 2088
Albuquerque, NM 87103

Older Women's League
730 11th St., N.W., Suite 300
Washington, D.C. 20011

Senior Action in a Gay Environment
208 W. 13th St.
New York, NY 10011

Women's Equity Action League
1250 Eye St., N.W., Suite 305
Washington, D.C. 20005

There are many other organizations that have an interest or are involved in aging issues that are not included here. For a list of over 200 associations and organizations involved in some aspect of aging, write to:

NIA Information Center/Directory
P.O. Box 8057
Gaithersburg, MD 20898

Programs and Services

Chapter Outline

Introduction
Family Obligation and the Aged
The Idea of Services
Taking Days Off for Mom
She Ain't Heavy, She's My Mother
Social Security
Social Security at the Max
Medicare
Medicare Participants' Drug Costs
The Aging Network
Nutrition Sites

Community-Based Services
Activities for Seniors
Reminiscence: Seasons of the Year
Low-End Recreation
*The Senior Citizens School Volunteer
    Program*
Conclusions and Some Thoughts on the
    Future
Questions for Discussion
Sources of Further Information

"To be aging and ill requires the greatest courage, it seems to me. To see someone taking care of a wife or husband with Alzheimer's disease, for example, opens the door to a particular kind of hell that must take extraordinary courage to confront every day. For those who must take care of the afflicted, it is a life haunted by financial fears as well as the agony of a loved one's life ending. To face this kind of aging, day after day without faltering, demands courage of the highest order."
— John Tebbel, born 1912

Introduction

If we were to take a close look at everyone who is 65 years of age or older, we would probably find a fairly shocking thing: most of them don't need any help. Especially among the young old, those under age 75, the great majority of people are not disabled or functionally limited in any way that affects independent living.

People who have autonomy want to keep it; they don't want others butting in and running their lives. This includes outsiders from service agencies, and it also includes their adult children. As people age, however, functional disabilities inevitably increase; frailty is common among the oldest old. People still want to maintain their independence, but they need some help doing it. In most instances, that help comes from family members: first the spouse (if there is one), then one of the adult children. Only after seeking these kinds of informal helps will most older people turn to formal service programs.

The biggest service program in the country is Social Security: putting money in peoples' pockets certainly is a service. In this chapter, we'll look at Social Security, but we'll also survey other formal services designed to keep people out of institutions and independent for as long as possible.

As we saw in Chapters 9 and 10, few people want to enter a nursing home or see their aged relative enter one. For most, the alternative is care at home, and we've also seen that the likelihood of care at home usually depends on the presence of a capable caregiver. We've seen that older men are less likely to be in nursing homes because they are more likely to have a surviving spouse. By the same token, those older people who have adult children are less likely to be institutionalized. About 20% of older women never had children, and they tend to be the ones most vulnerable to nursing home placement.

When there is no surviving spouse—or when both parents need care—the caregiving role most often falls to the closest daughter (Scharlach, 1987). This is not to say that many sons are not nurturant and willing caregivers. It just happens that in North America at the present time, adult daughters are more likely than sons to take on the burden of the caregiving role. This may cause conflict in the family: the individual who feels stuck with the bulk of the work may often resent her brothers and sisters who contribute less.

At one time, a typical pattern of caregiving was for an unmarried daughter to stay at home and live with the parents, ultimately becoming their caretaker. This is no longer the case. Family caregivers of the elderly more often than not maintain their own household, have their own families, and the majority have jobs; all of these demands must be balanced. When adult children do live with their aged parents, the direction of the service is more likely to be from the older individual to the adult child (Speare & Avery, 1993). This changes over the course of time. However, most older people no longer have an adult child living in their household, nor do many older people live in their children's households.

Statistically, older women are the most likely to live alone. And, the responsibility for caregiving most often falls to a daughter who lives near, but not with, her mother.

Regardless of the gender of the caregiver, families do feel an obligation to help their oldest members. This goes beyond kinship bonds and role expectations: adult children are genuinely concerned for the welfare of their parents, want to see them do as well as possible, and want to do what they can to keep them independent for as long as possible. A sense of filial obligation is present in almost all families (Finley, Roberts, & Banahan, 1988; Kosloski & Montgomery, 1994). This means that family members often feel a shared obligation to one another; this bond is especially strong between parents and children throughout life. We have already seen in

---

Illustration 14.1. Family Obligation and the Aged

In October of 1993, *Health* magazine published a poll it commissioned from the Gallup organization on attitudes and choices of adult children of aging parents ("Tough Choices for American Families," 1993). Here are the responses to several items in the poll from 601 adults who have at least one living parent:

Do you think it's an adult child's responsibility to care for his or her parents as they grow older?
    Yes. 85%
    No 6%
    Don't know 9%

Do you feel it is the child's responsibility to care for his or her parents even if the parent(s) and child have never gotten along well?
    Yes 66%
    No 20%
    Don't know 14%

Would you favor or oppose your parents using up their savings to provide their own long-term care, even if it meant you would get no inheritance?
    Favor 84%
    Oppose 13%
    Don't know 3%

Would you consider placing your parents in a nursing home if they were too sick to care for themselves?
    Yes 52%
    No 39%
    Don't know 9%

Would you consider asking your parents to move in with you if they could no longer live alone?
    Yes 85%
    No 12%
    Don't know 3%

Respondents over age 50 were the ones most likely to say they would consider nursing home placement for their parents. Perhaps they're the ones most in touch with the reality of the burden of caregiving. We're reminded of the 75-year-old friend who finally threw in the towel and gave up caring for her mother, who was 93 at the time she entered the nursing home. The mother was sore as a boil about it, too, but her daughter said, "Mom, I'm an old lady!"

Chapters 3 and 9 that family members will go to the end of their rope and beyond to see that older parents are not institutionalized. This most often involves caregiving in one way or another, which often involves physically and emotionally-draining hard work, and this caregiving generally becomes burdensome to the caregiver.

There is a strong emphasis in the gerontological literature on the concept of providing support for caregivers: if they get to the end of their rope in providing care, try to give them a little more rope. If they are at the point where they can no longer maintain the older relative independently, perhaps the addition of a visiting nurse service or some respite for the caregivers might keep them going a little longer. The delivery of services from the outside might reduce some of the caretaker burden. If older people have trouble living independently due to the inability to perform some of the activities of daily living, perhaps a home delivered meal, chore services, or help from a homemaker/home health aide might keep them out of an institution. Maybe taking the older person to an adult day care center will allow the family member to continue providing care and still keep her job. In this way, community-based services have a way of extending the service base already present through the individual's family and social network.

The nature of this assistance is the focus of this chapter. There is a wide variety of programs and services available from a number of different kinds of agencies. All seek to provide what was originally stated as a national policy on service delivery to the elderly at the 1971 White House Conference on Aging: to provide supportive services to help keep older people independent and in their own homes for as long as possible and to provide alternatives to institutional care.

The emphasis of this chapter will be on programs, how they work and are accepted, barriers to their use, and the likelihood of services being helpful. In a sense, then, this chapter is about public policy and caregiving. Our aim will be to see how programs and services for the elderly can stretch or supplement what the family and other informal caregivers are already doing to help older people remain independent.

The Idea of Services

The desire of older people to remain independent sometimes includes a desire to remain independent of outside help. This means that there may be attitudinal barriers to accepting help, especially help from public agencies or sources from outside the immediate family. Some 30 of the 50 states have laws on the books mandating that families care for their elders in one way or another. This reinforces our basic societal value that people should care for their parents. However, we saw an example in Chapter 12 of an older person who didn't want any services, either from her son or from outside agencies. This can be a delicate issue, particularly if the older person is paranoid or demented. Some families may be reluctant to turn to outsiders for what they consider to be their own business. Or, more likely, families and elders may not be aware of the existence of available services.

An important current issue in the field of gerontological services is individual autonomy, or freedom. The independent living movement that has grown up over the past several decades tends to view services less as compensating for disabilities than as a means of enhancing independence (Cohen, 1992). Service providers—and family members—need to exercise caution that services in fact do contribute to autonomy. The whole point of the services, after all, is to maximize the independence of the individual. Services should go beyond helping to keep people out of institutions; they should enhance independent living. This may be a difficult goal to accomplish. Services are by their nature controlled by the agencies (and the people) that deliver them. Often, trained professionals on the agency staff feel that they "know better" with regard to what is good for the older person. However, letting the individual have control is one of the best ways of ensuring that the services themselves will actually be received and appreciated. This means that the older person and his or her family will not necessarily follow every recommendation; it takes a mature professional to work with people without taking over their decision-making power.

Another issue related to autonomy and decision making has to do more with the family than with outside agencies. One study of caregivers speaks to this point. Gathering a sample of caregivers, it was found that they were made up mostly of women, and their average age was 79 years (Tennstedt, Crawford, & McKinlay, 1993). Problems of decision-making arose not only due to the reluctance to remove autonomy from the person being cared for, but also to the social roles and relationships that had existed between spouses. Many of the older women had relied on their husbands to make important decisions, especially in terms of family finances. Some were unable or unwilling to take on unaccustomed decision-making roles and responsibilities.

Reversing the gender roles, it may be that the older man must care for his spouse, and he may be unprepared to perform care duties or make important decisions about care. And there may of course be mutuality among older couples who are deteriorating together without the resources to provide their own care. When both partners survive, patterns of co-disability among the oldest old become normative (Zarit, Johansson, & Berg, 1993). Finally, whether living alone or with a companion, some older people, especially the demented, are in no way capable of making decisions about their own care (Smyer, 1993).

In some instances, family members need to step in and make decisions for their older relatives. In the event that there is no family, public agencies end up having this responsibility. If the older person's behaviors are too disorganized, or the individual is in personal danger, a legal guardian may need to be appointed to oversee care and personal well-being. Courts tend to take this action somewhat reluctantly, as the guardianship

Faith Meurrens sees the work force of the future when she looks around her Omaha, Nebraska, office.

The 12 software designers she manages at U.S. West Communications, Inc. are experienced, highly skilled, and, at an average age of 42, about five years older than the typical U.S. worker. Only two have small children, but most have missed work lately to care for an aged relative.

Jerrie Cippera took time off to move her father from his Nebraska farm to a nearby town. Linda Smith rushed to Wyoming after her father had a stroke. Candace Sorenson's mother had a hip replacement. Duane Skaff wound up being with three aged relatives. Two others, plus Ms. Meurrens and her boss, took time off when parents were hospitalized.

"Elder care is the biggest personal issue we face in maintaining productivity from day to day," Ms. Meurrens says.

The tip of a very disruptive iceberg has surfaced in the workplace, and is changing people's lives and job performance to a degree few had anticipated. "In the coming years, elder care will have a greater impact on the workplace than child care," or any other work-family issue so far, says Sally Coberly, an aging specialist at the Washington Business Group on Health. "As the baby boom moves deeper into middle age, the need for elder-care services will simply explode."

From Shellenbarger (1994, p. 1).

process by its nature can be abused. Most courts carefully monitor the process and ask for periodic reports from the guardian. However, in many cases, the older individual who has a legal guardian is able to continue to live independently, often with services arranged to help maintain as much autonomy as possible (Iris, 1988).

Fears of a loss of control and of people coming in and taking over one's personal business and decision-making authority, combine with a desire for independence to make formidable barriers to the acceptance of services among some older people. A Canadian study, for example, looked at barriers to receiving health care among a sample of 4,317 older people. The research examined the influence of control barriers (perceived lack of control over health care), personal barriers (memory deficits), and societal barriers, such as transportation and financial problems. It turned out that control barriers and personal barriers were predictive of survival over the 12 years of the study. "Control and personal barriers predicted the likelihood of dying within 12 years, even after controlling for initial health status, age, gender, income, and education" (Chipperfield, 1993, p. 123).

It has been known for some time that belief in personal control is one of the principal components of life satisfaction among the aged (Palmore & Luikart, 1972). This has to be balanced against the expectancies some older people have in the health care setting concerning the belief in control by powerful others (Smith et al., 1988). That is, older people—perhaps more than younger adults—have been socialized into a world where one did not question a doctor's decision, much less seek a second opinion. Older individuals who are unwilling to give up personal autonomy in a health-care transaction may avoid getting necessary health care. This might explain the commonly-observed problem of getting older men in to see their doctor. They fear that entering the medical system will compromise their personal autonomy. In addition, older people themselves often attribute their ills to being a part of the normal aging process, reasoning that they're supposed to feel bad in old age (Rakowski & Hickey, 1992). In a similar manner, some older people are reluctant to turn over personal autonomy to professionals delivering community-based social services, and thus they do not get the services they really need.

Barriers to the utilization of available services go beyond fears of loss of autonomy. One obvious explanation for low utilization rates is more ba-

---

Illustration 14.3. She Ain't Heavy, She's My Mother

When I was a young gerontologist, I began to notice an interesting phenomenon. I'd give my spiel on pre-retirement planning, field the questions from the audience, and then figure that I'd done my evening's work and start to pack up to go. Invariably, I'd be button-holed at this point by one of the older participants as the others were heading for the door. The situation was always the same. At first, I'd assume they had some personal anxiety concerning retirement that they didn't wish to raise in front of the whole group. That's fine: the after-class questions are often the real teachable moments. I was always wrong, however, about the problem; it took me a while to wise up.

The scenario usually went something like this: a person planning his or her own retirement, in other words, a 64-and-a-half year-old, would come up, usually with a look of concern and anguish, and say: "I've got a real problem."

Me: "Ah, yes. You're about to retire . . . "
Pre-retiree: " . . . and I need a rest. I've struggled to get four kids through school, one got divorced and moved back home for a while . . . "
Me: " . . . and it took some time to actually empty the nest . . . "
Pre-retiree: "It took *forever*! But, that's not my problem."

At this point, I would shut up and start to listen actively. "No, my problem is with Mother." Then, the gory details would start to spill out: "She's 83, strong as an ox, and mean as a snake. She moved in with us six months ago after she broke her hip. Now that she's walking again, she wanders at night. She snaps at my husband (wife) and he (she) is about to kick us both out. I don't want to put Mom in a home, but I need some *rest*!"

Now, when confronted with a similar problem, I let them ventilate for a bit and share their concerns, and—for many—feelings of guilt. Usually, there's nothing else to do but seek appropriate institutional care. Other options, of course, must be explored. But, many people in this kind of a fix have run out of other options.

From Thorson (1989a, pp. 18–20).

sic than negative attitudes toward outside help: many older people (and their families) are simply unaware that community-based services even exist (Krout, 1983a). This is especially unfortunate in the era of DRGs: due to diagnostic-related group prospective payment systems, more people are released from hospitals sooner and sicker (Wood & Estes, 1990). It stands to reason that these are the older people who are most in need of help and most vulnerable to nursing home placement. Other factors have emerged to make the need for home-delivered services even more evident: ten percent of all AIDS patients are aged 50 and above (Gutheil & Chichin, 1991). Many will become chronic-care patients in need of home-delivered services, and they are no different from any other older people who either fear loss of autonomy or who may be unaware of services available to them.

Older people as a general rule will rely first on family helpers before they turn to outside services (Montgomery & Kosloski, 1994; Tennstedt, Crawford, & McKinlay, 1993). A major predictor of the utilization of services is the lack of an available caregiver or the breakdown of a fragile helping network. One study of people who receive formal services found that they also receive help from informal sources, such as family, friends, or neighbors, but that these networks were not strong. Only 18% had a helping spouse, and only half had more than one helper. Few had a helper living with them, and several had only nonkin helpers (Wilcox & Taber, 1991).

The use of in-home services has obvious advantages. Keeping people at home and out of a nursing home is worthwhile not only in terms of their perception of individual autonomy, but also in their essential physical and psychological health. As we have seen in Chapter 9, people just tend to do better outside of institutional settings, regardless of how good the institution might be. Even the best of nursing homes are still nursing homes, and residents must conform to the regular pattern of the facility and its norms and schedule. Entering an institution means giving up a lot of freedom. Long-term care in the home has for these reasons become an identifiable trend during the past two decades (Kane, 1995).

Depending on the level of impairment of the individual, home care is often less expensive. A study of 141 dementia patients and their caregivers found that the average cost of care (including physicians, hospitals, nursing costs, and in-home services) totaled $7,772 during a six-month period (Weinberger et al., 1993). Nursing home care for the same individuals could easily cost $18,000 or more for the same period of time. Another study estimated that in-home long-term care would cost about $9,600 annually (Harrow, Tennstedt, & McKinlay, 1995).

One interesting development has to do with extending the ability of caregivers by providing them with training in how to best to serve frail elders. A study in Australia looked at 91 dementia patients and their caregivers who had participated in a program on home management of dementia (Brodaty, McGilchrist, Harris, & Peters, 1993). They were followed for five years. When compared to comparable family units caring for an older demented patient who had *not* received specialized training, it was found that training of caregivers was associated with delayed nursing home admission and reduced mortality.

Before getting into more detail on home-delivered services for frail elderly people, however, we need to take a step back for a perspective on services overall. In this section, we've suggested that many older people, especially men, may be reluctant to seek assistance, particularly from sources outside the family. Some older people and their families are ignorant of the services that are available. Giving assistance to the family care network seems to help; it may prevent unnecessary institutionalization and its resultant economic, social, and psychological costs. But, we need to take a look at national policy toward the elderly. First, we will look at a very large and very well established program to supplement older peoples' incomes; next, we'll look at a comparatively recent and much smaller federal effort to provide formal services to older people.

Social Security

The Social Security Act was signed into law by President Franklin Roosevelt in August of 1935. It originally had two principal components: Title I, which was a welfare program—Aid to the Aged, and Title II, an insurance program, Old Age Insurance. In 1939, amendments to the Act renamed the Old-Age Reserve Account to the Old-Age and Survivors Insurance (OASI) Trust Fund. This trust has subsequently been changed over the years to "OASDHI," for " Old Age and Survivors, Disability, and Hospital Insurance," since widows and survivors of recipients and disabled persons were added under Social Security coverage. The Medicare program then was included in 1965.

It was only in 1950 that older persons receiving Social Security pensions through Title II of the program finally began to outnumber those who received Old Age Assistance under Title I (Koff & Park, 1993). We sometimes forget that the main motivation for passage of the program during the Great Depression was to provide relief to impoverished older people. It is only in subsequent years that Social Security has become to be thought of mainly as a pension program that people contribute to during their working years and then receive payments from during retirement. It is much more than that, of course: 31% of Social Security recipients are widows, survivors, and disabled workers.

In 1972, Title I Old Age Assistance was replaced by the Supplemental Security Income (*SSI*) program. It guarantees a minimum amount of monthly income for all older people regardless of whether or not they worked and contributed to Social Security. SSI federal payments went to 5.9 million older persons in 1997; the average monthly payment for an individual was $261 (U.S. Bureau of the Census, 1998b). Thirty-seven of the states add a supplementary amount to this. Our discussion of Social Security, though, will focus mainly on the original Title II of the program, pensions and insurance for those who have contributed, their survivors, and their dependents.

Almost all wage earners in America have *FICA* (Federal Insurance Contributions Act) deductions withheld from their paychecks. These contributions are matched by their employers and go into the Social Security Trust Fund. Self-employed persons pay both the employer's and the employee's share. People are currently entitled to receive a pension at age 65 (or at age 62 at a reduced rate) based on the relative size of their average contributions over their working life. (The details of this are necessarily complex and we are forced to generalize a bit on how this works; full details can be found in publications available from any local Social Security office.) So, people who pay in more because their wages were higher get back more when they retire. One can't, however, just pay into Social Security for a short period of time and then expect to get a pension: since 1991, the minimum work credit needed for retirement benefits has been ten years.

The 1998 maximum monthly benefit a retiree could receive from Social Security was $1,342 or a maximum of $2,013 for a worker and his or her spouse. Obviously, both the worker and the spouse could have their own earnings and receive individual Social Security retirement benefits on their own behalf up to the maximum for each individual.

The average monthly benefit for all retired workers in 1998 was $765, and the average monthly benefit for an older couple was $1,288. Benefits are raised every year by annual cost of living adjustments (*COLA*s). Thus it is apparent that Social Security, while an important safety net in terms of older peoples' incomes, is not really adequate to rely on for the principal amount of income for most people. For the non-poor elderly, Social Security accounts for only 39% of personal income. For poorer people, it accounts for a higher proportion. Social Security was never designed to be the sole source of income for older people. For some, however, it is the only income they receive.

The Social Security withholding rate for employees in 1999 was 7.65%. This breaks down to 6.2% of the first $72,600 of wages (or a total of $4,501.20) and 1.45% (designated for Medicare) of all wages (without limit). "Unearned" income—interest and dividends and gains from investments—is not taxed for Social Security purposes.

While the amount paid *in* determines the amount paid *out*, the payback system is graduated to favor lower wage earners (Koff & Park, 1993). That is, Social Security isn't as good a deal for higher wage earners. In 1998, for example, a person who had retired at a salary of $20,000 received Social Security benefits of $9,408 per year. This works out to a replacement ratio of 47% of his or her income. Someone with annual wages of $65,000 who retired that same year, however, would receive a Social Security pension of $16,104—a replacement ratio of only 25%. Also, individuals with a

Illustration 14.4. Social Security at the Max

The Social Security retirement program is a good deal, but it isn't as good a deal as it used to be. Let's look at some possible examples:

Mona, who's done very well for herself, retired the first day of January, 1994, when she turned 65. She was born in 1929 and began working full time in 1949; she's always been a smart, hard-working person. Let's say that she's always made the maximum possible salary taxed by Social Security. In 1949, that amount was 1.0% of the first $3,000 of her wages, or $30 a year. The rate went up to 1.5% of the first $3,000 the next year, so in 1950 she had to put in $45. The rates and the amount of wages taxed increased each year until she retired, so by the end of 1993 she had contributed a lifetime total of $55,851.49 (the only way she could have put in more would be if she'd started work earlier; even if she'd started working in 1937 when she was eight years old, her lifetime maximum still would only have been $56,211.49).

When she retired, she got back the top amount, $1,147 a month, or $13,764 annually. By 1998, this had increased with COLAs to $1,342 per month, or $16,104 per year. She got back what she'd put in within four years. Since her life expectancy at 65 was another 18 years, Mona figures to be on the gravy train for 14 years. True, her employer matched her contributions, so the actual amount that went into the trust fund on her behalf was equal to twice her own contributions, but, she figures that wasn't money out of *her* pocket.

Her sister Annie the Actuary points out that if the contributions from Mona and her employer had been taken and invested in a conservative mutual fund in the same amounts over the years, Mona would actually have a much bigger pile. However, Mona points out to Annie that Social Security will pay her for life, no matter how long she lives; savings in an investment program could run out after a while. And, the Social Security program also provided her and her kids with disability and survivors' insurance coverage for a lot of those years, too, so she's still pretty happy about it.

Mona's Mom Margaret sniffs and says that she did better. It so happens that she started paying in at the max when the program started in 1937. By the time she retired in 1974, Margaret had contributed a total of only $6,043.20 in FICA taxes. Although the top payment when she retired wasn't as much as it is today, those cost-of-living increases have been good to her, and now she also gets the top amount: $1,342 a month. She figures that she got back her contributions in less than a year and a half. And, she points out to the girls, since she's over 70 she won't be penalized if she decides to go back to work at the foundry; if Mona went back to work, she could only make $13,500 before she started to lose some of her Social Security.

Mona's daughter Mary, whose own high salary began to be taxed at the max in 1974, figures that she'd put in a total $79,193.70 by the end of 1999, and she doesn't even want to think about how long she'll have to live past her planned retirement in the year 2021 in order to get it all back. Margaret reminds Mary that Uncle Bruno retired in 1940 after putting in a grand total of $60; he collected the top monthly payment for 35 years until he died in 1975 at age 100. Mary remembers Bruno's poverty (the top amount wasn't all that great during those years, and Bruno had no other income), and she resolves to call her broker to look into investing in tax-free municipal bonds.

retirement income of over $25,000 a year (and couples with an income of over $32,000) must pay income tax on half of their Social Security benefits.

As is shown in Table 14.1, people born after the year 1937 will not receive the full amount of Social Security retirement benefits when they reach age 65. Beginning in the year 2003, two months will be added each year to the age of eligibility for full benefits. People born in 1938 will reach age 65 in 2003 but can't get full benefits until they're age 65 years and two months. Those born between 1943 and 1954 will have to be 66 before they can get full benefits, and those born in 1960 or thereafter will have to wait until age 67.

The penalty for early retirement will also increase. People who retire at age 62 prior to the year 2003 receive 80% of what they would have gotten if they'd waited until 65 (the amount then stays the same—it doesn't increase to what it would have been when they turn 65). In the future, those born between 1943 and 1954 will get 75% of the full amount if they retire at age 62; those born in 1960 (or thereafter) who retire at age 62 will get only 70% of what they'd have gotten if they waited until 67, which will be their age for full benefits.

This is only a brief overview of the program, which gets very technical very quickly. Suffice it to say that Social Security has been a boon to America's older population and is the main reason that their poverty rate has been cut in half over the past three decades. It is by far the government's largest program that benefits the elderly; in fact, it is the government's largest program, period. Changes made in the program in 1983 make it economicly sound at least until the year 2030. The power of the program, however, is such that politically it virtually cannot fail; politicians who wish to survive in office will see that it does not.

TABLE 14.1. Changes in the Full Retirement Age, 2003–2027

Year of Birth	Year to Reach Age 65	Starting Age of Full Amount (Year/Month)	Age 62 Benefit as % of Full Benefit
1938	2003	65/2	79 1/6%
1939	2004	65/4	78 1/3
1940	2005	65/6	77 1/2
1941	2006	65/8	76 2/3
1942	2007	65/10	75 5/6
1943–54	2008–19	66/0	75
1955	2020	66/2	74 1/6
1956	2021	66/2	74 1/6
1957	2022	66/4	73 1/3
1958	2023	66/8	72 1/2
1959	2024	66/10	70 5/6
1960+	2025+	67/0	70

From *Making Sense of Social Security* (1992, p. 47).

Medicare

Medicare is health insurance for the aged; it was passed into law in 1965 under Title XVIII of the Social Security Act. Medicare should not be confused with *Medicaid*, which pays for health care for those in poverty at any age; about 3.2 million older people receive Medicaid.

Prior to the passage of Medicare, only about half of the elderly in the United States had any form of health insurance. Many could not afford it, and many were denied coverage by private health insurers because of their age. In 1972, the program was extended to people under age 65 who had chronic kidney failure and those who had received disability benefits from Social Security for at least two years.

Medicare currently covers about 38 million people—33 million old people and 5 million disabled persons. It consists of Part A, hospital insurance, which requires no premium, and Part B (Supplementary Medical Insurance), which is voluntary and cost $45.50 a month in 1999. Over 97% of the elderly choose to receive Part B as well as Part A. Participants may opt for HMO care in certain circumstances rather than the original Medicare Parts A and B (about 14% of beneficiaries are in a Medicare HMO). Usually, this is in conjunction with an extra-cost "medigap" insurance policy.

Participants in the Part A hospital insurance part of Medicare who are hospitalized must pay an annual front-end deductible of $768 for a hospital stay of 1 to 60 days, $192 per day for days 61 through 90, $384 per day for days 91 though 150, and all costs for hospital stays after 150 days. Obviously, few people are willing to chance the catastrophic cost of an extended hospital stay, and only 8% of Medicare enrollees do not have additional, private, "medigap" policies.

After an annual deductible of $100, Medicare Part B pays 80% of the cost of physicians' services, diagnostic tests, physical and speech therapy, surgical services, and durable medical equipment. Outpatient prescription drugs are not covered, nor are dental services, hearing aids, or eyeglasses.

Most people purchase a "medigap" policy from a private insurance company to supplement the benefits received under Medicare. About 65% of medigap policies have some sort of drug coverage. The average cost of medigap policies without drug coverage ranges from about $920 to $1,500 per year; with drug coverage, the cost of most policies is in the range of from $1,950 to $3,400 annually. It has been estimated that adding prescription drug coverage to Medicare itself would increase the cost of the program by about 7 to 10% (Gluck, 1999).

Under certain circumstances, nursing home care is paid for by Medicare (although the qualifications are surprisingly hard to meet, and many an enrollee is disappointed to find that Medicare isn't really designed to pay for nursing home care). If they meet the qualifications, for each benefit period in a nursing home, patients pay nothing for the first 20 days of care,

"Like other health spending, total and out-of-pocket expenditures on drugs are skewed; a large fraction of beneficiaries spend relatively modest amounts on drugs and a minority spends a great deal. The median out-of-pocket expenditure is about $200. About 29% of beneficiaries have out-of-pocket drug expenses of more than $500, 14% (about 4.5 million beneficiaries in 1999) have out-of-pocket expenses of more than $1,000, and 4% (1.3 million beneficiaries) have expenses that exceed $2,000."

From Gluck (1999, p. 1).

up to $96 per day for days 21 through 100, and the entire cost after day 100. On the plus side, Medicare generally pays for home health care and hospice care, thus allowing home care as an alternative to institutionalization. Again, the details of the program are complex and change; one must rely on individual state Medicare carriers for precise current information.

Medicare has proven to be of great benefit to the elderly and is, after Social Security, no doubt the most popular of governmental programs with the older populace. Estimates of how actuarially sound the program is vary, with speculation on it becoming financially insolvent sometime during the first decade of this century. Continuing political debate focuses on how best to preserve the program on a firm financial foundation. This is particularly important in view of the large numbers of baby boomers who will begin to qualify for Medicare in the year 2011.

The Aging Network

The federal government sponsors a host of programs for the benefit of older persons in addition to income maintenance through Social Security and health insurance through Medicare. Programs to provide services for older people who need them derive from a variety of different laws, some of which were designed to aid only the elderly, and some, such as programs for the blind and services for veterans, that are not age-exclusive but that by their nature benefit a significant number of older people. Many states and localities sponsor programs for their citizens as well.

In 1965, a first effort was made to coordinate programs for the aged and to create local agencies that could put together information for those seeking services. The Older Americans Act created the Administration on Aging (*AoA*), an organizational unit of what is now the U.S. Department of Health and Human Services.

Various titles of the Older Americans Act authorized the Administration on Aging to initiate several different programs. One title authorized Career Training programs, funding a number of universities to begin gerontology training programs for professionals who planned to go to work with older people. At the local level, the main effect of programs sponsored by the Administration on Aging was the funding of information and referral agencies, councils on aging that were to organize and coordinate locally available services so that older people and their families could have one-stop shopping: they wouldn't have to become experts at how to find and access every available service agency.

At first, programs were funded only minimally, and while every state government received funds for a state office on aging, many communities had no AoA-funded programs at all. Local agencies that were funded often had little to offer other than information and referral. Some were able to get funding through what was then Title XVI of the Social Security Act to provide transportation and in-home services, but, again, coverage was spotty. The 1973 Amendments to the Older Americans Act gave the agencies something to coordinate. Two main provisions affected localities. First was the organization of multi-county Area Agencies on Aging (*AAA*s). There are now 664 of these AAAs throughout the country. Their job is to coordinate and sponsor service programs for older people in their geographical areas. Second, what was then Title VII of the 1973 Amendments to the Older Americans Act funded "nutrition sites," places where people could gather for a low-cost (or free) hot meal and socialize. This helped to confront two issues: malnutrition among those who weren't getting a balanced diet and isolation among those who needed human contact.

The AAAs were to become brokers, taking funds supplied by the Administration on Aging, funneled through state commissions on aging, and

---

Illustration 14.6. Nutrition Sites

The congregate meal program now accounts for nearly half of AoA's total funding. It has been one of the government's most politically popular programs. There are thousands of nutrition sites throughout the country; many have been the core around which senior centers have been organized. And, these senior centers have often become focal points for service delivery, especially in neighborhoods and small towns.

We hear from site directors, however, of the phenomenon of "aging in place" among meal site participants. Places that once had 60 or 70 older people coming in for noon lunch now have 30 or 40. The original participants are getting older and dying off, and they're not being replaced by the next generation of the elderly. Doubts continue, as well, as to the real effectiveness of the program. Critics maintain that meal sites, for the most part, serve the older people who are easiest to get to, and that the dollars invested in lunch programs for the aged might be better spent on in-home services for the frail elderly.

purchasing services for older people from existing service agencies. This worked in places where other agencies were in existence; in some locations, however, the AAAs have had to organize and run their own services programs.

The kind of services sponsored and coordinated by AAAs runs the gamut: home-delivered meals; chore, handyman, and winterization services to help maintain older peoples' houses; transportation for people who can no longer drive; adult day care centers; senior centers; congregate meal sites; community advocacy and legal aid; telephone reassurance; respite care; case management; information and referral on housing; employment; health care; counseling; adult protective services; and in-home services, such as visiting nurses and homemaker/home health aides. As perceptions of the need and the imaginations of program personnel have both grown over the years, Area Agencies on Aging find themselves offering a host of services that may not have been envisioned when the Older Americans Act was first passed. As these programs have grown, the agencies have had to seek new sources of funding. Program administrators complain that federal dollars through the AoA have been essentially "flat" for over a decade: programs and needs have grown but the federal support has not. Many AAAs now receive funding from grants received from other state and federal agencies. Some receive funds through state and local appropriations as well as through fees charged for their services. Typically, charges are set up on a sliding fee scale, so that those who can afford to pay more do so.

Those working with state agencies on aging, AAAs, and their affiliated agencies and organizations make up what has come to be called the aging network, professionals committed to the provision of services to older people who need them. Those in the aging network often find that they have an advocacy role, both in terms of going to bat for individuals who are not getting a fair shake with local problems and in providing testimony and expertise at the legislative level. They have an important public education role, too. For example, it's not unusual to find professionals from the aging network teaching gerontology courses.

This growth of a system of agencies and service programs where no services or programs existed before has happened over the course of the past 35 years, and this might be seen as a fairly remarkable accomplishment in terms of public policy. Despite the popularity—and the obvious need—for aging network programs, however, the U.S. Administration on Aging remains a relatively small unit of the federal government (Binstock, 1991). Its 1999 appropriation was $882,020,000. Below are the levels of funding for the principal titles of Older Americans Act programs:

Program Administration	$14,795,000
Title III	
Supportive Services & Centers	300,319,000
Preventive Health	16,123,000
Congregate Meals	374,412,000

Home-Delivered Meals	112,000,000
Frail Elderly In-Home Services	9,763,000
Title IV	
Training and Research	18,000,000
Title VI	
Native American programs	18,457,000
Title VII	
Elder Rights	12,181,000
Alzheimer's Initiative	5,970,000
Total	882,020,000

Although some of these amounts may appear to be formidable, taken in comparison with other federal programs, the AoA's funding is modest at best. Moreover, it has not grown much in recent years: the total is only up five million dollars over what it was five years previously. Many of the smaller line items are little more than token efforts. It is difficult to see, for example, what good the Alzheimer's initiative could do, funded at less than six million dollars. Hardly any genuine training and research can be done for $18 million; those funds mainly go to keep the doors open for a few advocacy organizations. The Older Americans Act, however, is by no means the only source of funding for programs that provide services for the aged. Block grants to communities (the successor to what was first Title XVI and then Title XX of the Social Security Act), for example, may fund in-home services to the frail elderly. Medicaid waivers and Medicare are also important sources of funding for in-home services.

Gerontological research is funded by other federal agencies, as well as by AARP's Andrus Foundation and other private sources. The 1999 appropriation for the National Institute on Aging, part of the National Institutes of Health, was $597 million. Also, the National Institute of Mental Health is an important source of funding for research into cognitive disorders of the aged; that agency received an appropriation of $861 million in 1999. Similarly, other units of the National Institutes of Health fund research into conditions that affect the aged, such as arthritis, kidney disease, AIDS, cancer, heart disease, and stroke.

In the next section of this chapter, we will go into more detail on some of the programs that have emerged in recent years that have been particularly effective in aiding the frail elderly and helping to maintain older individuals' independence. They are sponsored by a variety of aging network agencies as well as hospitals and nursing homes, local government, churches and voluntary organizations, and educational institutions.

Community-Based Services

We have already mentioned the potential in cost savings of utilizing community-based services that keep older people in their homes and out of nursing homes. How much is saved has been a subject of some debate in the field of gerontology. Some in-home services are exceedingly cheap; at the other end of the continuum, there are other services that are extremely expensive. Telephone reassurance is an example of the first type of service. Volunteers call older people at a predetermined time each day. If they don't answer the phone, the volunteer calls for help. Lives of people who've had a heart attack or stroke have been saved by this service that is essentially free. The cost of services increases as they become more complex and require professional staff: around-the-clock in-home nursing, for example, is nearly always more expensive than nursing home care. Traditionally, people have been able to access such services if they are willing to pay for them. But, we are increasingly a society that depends on third-party payers—insurance companies and governmental programs—to assist with care for people who can't pay for it out of their own pocket.

Paying for services is often a good investment from the government's point of view. If the cost of nursing home care can be avoided by using in-home community services, the individual and the society are both better off. It is only recently that we have had hard data, however, to demonstrate the cost-effectiveness of services. A report from a group of researchers at Syracuse University, for example, details a marginal cost analysis applied to the National Long Term Care Channeling Demonstration project. They found that 41% of the individuals had some potential for net long-term care cost reduction through the use of services (Greene, Lovely, & Ondrich, 1993). Other studies have demonstrated that services also have an important effect in decreasing distress among older persons and their families (Harper, Manasse, James, & Newton, 1993).

Services, as already mentioned, range from the very simple and inexpensive to the highly technical and expensive. Think in terms of a continuum of services (a continuum might be seen as a gradation along a line, from lower to higher, like a thermometer). In terms of health care, one end of a continuum of service would be older people living at home, healthy, with no need for any particular services other than occasional visits to the family doctor. Going up the scale, they might need more specialized care from physicians; next might be living at home with occasional visits from a nurse. Going up the scale further still would be living at home with regular care from visiting therapists, nurses, or homemaker/home health aides. After that, a higher level of care might be living with a relative and attending an adult day care center. Next would be going into a facility that provides assisted living: meals, maid service, and supervision of medications, along with therapeutic services delivered from the outside. The higher levels of care would be at the top end of the scale: skilled nursing home care and then hospitalization. Hospital intensive care would be at the extreme end of the continuum. The complexity and the cost of the care go up as one goes along the scale from its lowest end to its highest.

A variety of services might fit into the continuum at different places, or several places.

Senior Centers

Depending upon the older person's level of functional ability, multipurpose senior centers can be a valuable service. Most senior centers are accessible for persons with handicaps or who are in wheelchairs, but they do not as a general rule have the capability or the staff to cope with the seriously ill or disabled. Most senior center participants live independently and get to and from the program site on their own.

There are several thousand senior centers in the United States, some dating back to the 1940s. Their programs range from the simple to the elaborate. Centers typically provide a warm, friendly environment for socialization; many offer noontime meals, and most offer recreational programs and craft activities. Larger programs sponsor day trips and adult education classes. Many have volunteer programs that serve to empower the elderly (Parkinson, 1992). And the best-developed senior centers serve as community focal points, where other services for older people are coordinated and delivered (McClain, Leibowitz, Plummer, & Lunt, 1993).

Many senior centers began as congregate meal sites and have expanded their facilities and programs since their beginning. Others are sponsored by churches, clubs, or civic groups. Studies of participation at senior center activities have varying results. One done by Krout (1991), for example, analyzed three different dimensions of participation: number of activities, duration, and frequency of attendance, among 235 senior center participants from eight different centers. Surprisingly, demographic characteristics, health, morale, accessibility, and social contact were not significantly related to these three participation dimensions in any consistent way.

Apparently, the motivation to participate in center activities is a complex phenomenon. It may have to do with personal characteristics or situational variables. For some retired people, going to a *senior* center would be the last thing on their minds. A study of 623 participants in 15 senior centers in the Midwest found that those who participated in activities tended to have higher educational levels, and those who used services were less mobile. All reported that they had made friends at the senior center, and participants tended to rate high in life satisfaction. Those who participated at a higher level were, not surprisingly, those who lived closest to the site.

More frequent participants were also more likely to rate the importance of the noontime meal highly. It was concluded that variability in the centers themselves, rather than the characteristics of the participants, had the largest effect on the dimensions of senior center involvement (Ralston, 1991). Other studies have demonstrated that activities at senior centers tend to be more attractive to women, who are often more frequent participants (Horswill, 1993).

Adult Day Care

A survey of program needs in the state of Michigan found that adult day care was assessed as being one of the most needed but least available services (Shope et al., 1993). Adult day care is a higher level of service than that provided by senior centers. In adult day care, skilled professionals are available to attend to personal care needs of more frail elderly. Many of the

---

Illustration 14.8. Reminiscence: Seasons of the Year

Goals: The changing of seasons has many meanings according to each individual's experiences. This aging cycle of nature becomes a metaphor for the life cycle, which is safer to discuss than human mortality, yet allows expression of feelings.

Process: this theme can be used quarterly at the beginning of each season or as an overview of all seasons. If all members have adequate dexterity, ask them to make a basic drawing of their favorite season. In presenting the picture to the group, encourage the artist to talk about the objects, scene, or choice of color and why it represents a certain season. Ask members what seasonal activities they recall doing during a certain season as children and as adults. Those who grew up on farms will have different memories than those who grew up in the city. Talk about traditional events that each person associates with a certain season, such as fall hayrides and harvest parties, snow and sledding in winter, first flowers of spring, and trips to the beach in the summer. Encourage vivid word pictures for the enjoyment of everyone. If the group seems ready for a deeper level, the leader introduces discussion about the planting, growing, harvesting, and completion of crops or flowers and how this relates to stages of life.

Outcomes: Seasons are about change and transition. The leader and group members can take this topic to a variety of levels, depending on the group's capability and interest.

Equipment list: color photos or posters that depict seasons. Local travel agents and elementary school teachers will have a wealth of seasonal material to lend. Bring typical seasonal items, such as knitted gloves and hats, fall leaves, spring flowers, or a beach ball

From Erwin (1996, p. 35).

---

participants are demented, and there are limits on the types of activities they can engage in; thus, therapeutic recreation for day care participants often needs to be more deliberately planned and carefully delivered.

The idea behind adult day care is that many caregivers of the aged work during the day. The older person can often live outside an institution if there is a safe environment for him or her during the day; adult day care is for people who shouldn't be left home alone. Day care is seen as a substitute for hiring an in-home companion or quitting one's job to stay home to provide care. Many leave off older family members on their way to work and pick them up on the way home. The adult day care center provides a safe environment and a program of activities matched to the individual's capacity.

A research review, however, notes the scarcity of evidence demonstrating benefits to clients and caregivers (Engstrom, Green, & O'Connor, 1993). Perhaps this is because adult day care participants often come from situations where the family is forced to deal with a continuing crisis of care; adult day care may serve as a stopgap, as the last program to try before turning to nursing home care. A study done at Bryn Mawr College found that family members performed a significantly higher level of service over the course of the time that their older family member participated in adult day care (Kirwin & Kaye, 1991). In other words, these people may be in a downward spiral, degenerating in terms of functional ability. The family is working harder and harder to keep them out of an institution. The day care center serves to give families some respite along the way, but it is not a permanent solution. However, if it helps for a period of months or perhaps for a few years, it is a service that is of great assistance to the family. Adult day care is generally viewed very positively by family members. This is especially the case with adult hospice day care, which is designed to give respite to caretakers of the terminally ill (Corr & Corr, 1992).

An obvious problem with adult day care is its cost. A more highly specialized service, it requires more professional staff, and it is a fairly expensive type of service. Most insurance will not pay for it, so fees must generate much of the center's income. Most adult day care centers lose money during their first few years of operation (Reifler, et al., 1992).

Some nursing homes and Veterans Hospitals are now offering inpatient dementia respite programs, where older, demented patients can be admitted for a few days or weeks in order to give their caregivers a break (Hirsch, Davies, Boatwright, & Ochango, 1993). Thus, day care, temporary institutional respite care, and nursing home care might be seen to follow each other on a continuum from a lower to a higher level of service.

Some companies are beginning to sponsor both child day care and adult day care services as benefits for their employees (Thornburg, 1993). These are often combined. One study of an intergenerational day care center found that older clients consistently demonstrated more positive behaviors when the children were present (Newman & Ward, 1993).

glossary

SCORE — The Service Corps of Retired Executives.

RSVP — The Retired Senior Volunteer Program.

Case Management

Social casework with the elderly, or case management, has been increasingly recognized as a service of vital importance (Morrow-Howell, 1992). This is partially in response to the problems found with simple information and referral services. The situations of many elders in need of services are more complex than something that can just be handled over the phone with a clerk or a volunteer. With case management, a professional social worker deals with the older person and his or her family to explore service options and access programs, be an advocate for the individual and family, and design an array of services that best meet the individual's needs. Thus, the family has someone on their side who is skilled at working within the system and who may know of programs and eligibility requirements of which the family is not knowledgeable. Older people who have benefitted from case management often receive more services and more appropriate services; they usually are more satisfied with the services they receive. In particular, service recipients have reported a greater sense of control with case management (MaloneBeach, Zarit, & Spore, 1992). One study has found case management to be particularly important for the demented elderly and those with greater functional limitations who need an advocate within the system (Ginther, Weber, Fox, & Miller, 1993).

Educational and Voluntary Organizations

Area Agencies on Aging often serve as local sponsors for federally-funded voluntary organizations, such as the Service Corps of Retired Executives (*SCORE*), the Senior Companions Program, and the Retired Senior Volunteer Program (*RSVP*). These programs can have other local sponsorship as well. For instance, hospitals and long-term care facilities for the developmentally disabled might sponsor an RSVP group. All have similar motives: allowing older volunteers to help serve their communities in a variety of ways. Retired Senior Volunteers provide loving companionship to populations in need, such as hospitalized children; Senior Companions help other older persons and provide respite for their caregivers. In both instances, the federal funding helps with paying for staffing the program and providing the volunteers with transportation costs and expenses. The Service Corps of Retired Executives works with people who want to start a business or who need the advice of someone who is experienced in the business world.

Similar efforts go on, of course, without federal sponsorship. For example, in some cities, the Junior League has helped to organize groups called "Volunteers Intervening for Equity," where retired lawyers and business executives work as advocates for older persons who need help with such things as filing Social Security claims or with landlord-tenant issues. Volunteers become specialists in particular areas of business or with particular governmental agencies. It is not unusual for them to serve as guardians for disabled older people, helping them keep their finances organized and paying their monthly bills. Other programs like this in different parts of the country call on older persons to serve as volunteer mediators to assist other older people who have conflicts with agencies and with consumer problems (Cox & Parsons, 1992). Similarly, local Bar Associations frequently sponsor legal aid programs that benefit the elderly.

Many schools and hospitals have organized groups of older volunteers to perform a variety of functions, from tutoring children to peer counseling other older adults. With intergenerational programs, the direction of the service may go the other way as well. It is not unusual for school classes to adopt older people in nursing homes or visit homebound elderly.

Educational programming on behalf of the elderly is a major effort in the United States and Canada. Local school districts and institutions of higher education frequently develop special classes for older persons or offer extension classes at senior centers. Many seek to recruit older learners into their regular adult education programs, and universities in some states now allow people 65 and older to take university classes without cost on a space-available basis.

Illustration 14.10. The Senior Citizen School Volunteer Program

The senior citizens who volunteer in the program are over the age of 55 and come from diverse socioeconomic and racial backgrounds. As volunteers, they give half a day per week to work with a variety of kindergarten through 12th graders, including special needs students. They serve as tutors, teacher's helpers, listeners, career models, oral historians, resource people, artists, and crafts people. Volunteers reinforce students' basic skills, share lifelong skills and experiences, and help students achieve academically and socially by providing support and enrichment.

From McCrae and Smith (1997, p. 96).

The real news in lifelong learning and adult education for seniors, though, is the Elderhostel program. Courses designed for older persons are organized, often as two-week summer classes, on college campuses throughout North America and Europe. Elderhostel, which began in 1975, now involves over a quarter of a million participants each year at over 1500 different institutions. Retired persons are able to take Elderhostel study tours throughout the world. And many enjoy traveling to campuses in different parts of the country to take courses that interest them. Adult education is a major, and often overlooked, vehicle of recreation and enrichment for older people (Thorson, 1990).

Also overlooked in a secular society is programming done through churches (Thorson & Horacek, 1987). Religious institutions constitute what has to be the largest collective voluntary effort among all organizations. Sponsorship of senior centers, golden age clubs, home-delivered meals, "adopt a granny" programs, classes, trips, volunteer programs, health ministries such as parish nursing, and worship services all provide opportunities for older adults under the auspices of churches and synagogues.

There is some debate over whether religious orientation becomes stronger throughout life or whether this is a cohort effect. That is, some would argue that a spiritual dimension gains greater importance as people mature and seek meaning in their lives. Or, perhaps the greater religiosity observed among the aged has been lifelong—they grew up in an age when family church participation may have had a greater emphasis. Regardless, older people have high rates of participation in religious activities, tend to rate religion highly in terms of importance in their lives, and continue to seek spiritual well-being despite physical frailties that may limit their organizational participation. A variety of researchers have found positive correlations between personal religiosity and such variables as adjustment, mental and physical health, life satisfaction, and freedom from anxiety and depression (Holt & Dellmann-Jenkins, 1992; Idler & George, 1998; Koenig et al., 1993; Levin & Chatters, 1998; Van Haitsma, 1986). And, people who do not ordinarily participate in other voluntary organizations may oftentimes find social outlets and confidants through church contacts.

Home Health Care

Chapters 9 and 10 contain more extensive discussions of the importance of care in the home, but we should also mention it here as a major, perhaps the principal, means of keeping functionally disabled persons out of institutions. Most of the care received at home is provided by family members. Their services can be extended by visiting nurse services that take care of the more complex medical needs and which can train family caregivers on methods to more effectively assist the older homebound person. In addition, a variety of professionals—from speech therapists to respiratory care practitioners and physical therapists—can assist with home health care.

Fairly sophisticated care can be provided in the home this way (Haddad, 1987). One study followed 367 adult patients who received services from a certified home health agency. It was found that 61% could manage independently only with the help of family caregivers (Helberg, 1993). This implies that teamwork is required between the home health provider and the family caregiver. The assistance to caregivers often takes the form of education, teaching family members technical skills with monitors and other therapeutic devices (Sorenson & Thorson, 1998). Another study evaluated a personalized health promotion program over the course of three years. Nurses provided a personal health plan, including health care, exercise, nutrition, and stress management. By the end of the program, 75% of the participants (compared to only 59% of a control group) remained at home; it was apparent that the intervention helped prolong living at home for a meaningful proportion of these functionally impaired older people (Hall et al., 1992).

Home health care is increasingly seen as an effective way to reduce overall patient care costs: in most instances, it is less expensive than nursing home care, and it is almost always less expensive than hospitalization (Kaper & Riley, 1992). It is often a viable alternative and a more appropriate level of service (McCoy, Kipp, & Aheern, 1992). Most of the states, in fact, have programs available where, in special instances, they will pay family caregivers in order to extend the time before institutionalization is necessary (Linsk, Keigher, & Osterbusch, 1988). In terms of financing home-delivered health care services, one study has shown that, of total home care costs, Medicare pays 37.8% of all the dollars spent on home care and Medicaid pays 24.7%. Private insurance accounts for only 5.5% of all home health care payments; the remaining costs are paid out-of-pocket by individuals and families purchasing services (Romano, 1994).

Community Mental Health

In contrast to many of the services we have reviewed in this chapter, community mental health care for older people has *not* been particularly successful. Many older people were released from state mental hospitals during the deinstitutionalization movement that began early in the 1970s. The idea was that care in state hospitals often caused more problems than it solved, and that people were better off in familiar environments. They could be maintained at home, it was said, through the use of community-based counseling and drug therapy. In many instances, though, community mental health centers were never adequately funded to provide specialized geriatric services. It *has* been demonstrated that their services work: in one particular case, a federal court order forced Massachusetts to establish a continuum of services for the chronically mentally ill elderly. Evaluation of that program found services to be highly effective at keeping people from going back to state mental hospitals (Fisher et al., 1991). However, most other states, lacking a mandate from the federal courts, have provided less in terms of support for geriatric community mental health.

There are other barriers to the effective utilization of mental health services. People have fears of the loss of freedom—and these may be realistic fears. On the other hand, this is a population that may have unrealistic fears concerning authority figures. Families and older individuals often have negative attitudes toward mental health care (Qualls, 1991). Community programs serving the general population usually demonstrate little in terms of programming for the aged (Vinton, 1992). This may be true of professionals as well as agencies: many psychologists feel out of their depth when confronted with geriatric problems (Gatz, Karel, & Wolkenstein, 1991).

This may be because of a realistic assessment of just what mental health care can in fact do for some older people. Needs of the mentally ill geriatric population are so complex that community-based programs might not be adequate to cope with them (Cohen, Onserud, & Monaco, 1993b). In fact, few studies have found evidence that geriatric services have improved the mental state of aged patients (Cole, 1993).

Many psychiatrically impaired older persons wind up in nursing homes. They are often seen as difficult, undesirable patients (Mosher-Ashley, Turner, & O'Neill, 1991). One study found that only 4.5% of nursing home patients with a mental disorder receive appropriate care (Burns et al., 1993). Some recent studies in fact have detailed the need for specialized residential services for older mentally ill people, implying that mental hospitalization may not be all that bad, and that it certainly has a role in the continuum of care (Mosher-Ashley & Allard, 1993). The alternative may be a cycle of in-and-out care in hospital emergency rooms, homelessness, or suicide (Courage et al., 1993; Puryear, Lovitt, & Miller, 1991).

This is not to say that community mental health services for older people are useless. When funded adequately, specialized geriatric community mental health services have proven to be highly effective. The program in Massachusetts we mentioned is apparently successful. And examples from other countries demonstrate effective approaches to community-based mental health care for the aged. One study from England, for example, assessed case management services provided by community psychiatric nurses for 96 older persons; the program has enjoyed considerable success (Waterrus, 1992). In the Netherlands, psycho geriatric day care and foster care have both been shown to be effective (Diesfeldt, 1992; Haveman, Maaskant, & Brook, 1992). It may be that fresh approaches need to be attempted in this country.

Conclusions and Some Thoughts on the Future

We've seen that the older population is the fastest-growing segment of our society. This is true at the present time, and it will be true for a considerable period into the future. Organized services for the aged in some ways might be seen as a comparatively recent development, and it might be said that our collective response to the emergence of a larger aged population has lagged behind the demographic realities.

This is not because of a lack of will. In terms of public policy, the United States has demonstrated commitment to the needs of older adults. In fact, the aged also are in many ways a preferred group, and this has in a number of instances generated political resentment. The primary purpose of the country's largest governmental program, after all, is to provide income support for older people. At the time this is written, no other group has national health care comparable to the Medicare program for the aged. Nor does any other group have a guaranteed annual income such as that provided to the elderly through the SSI program. There is no corresponding public commitment of effort—or dollars—to any other segment of the population.

Despite the emergence of complaints about generational inequity, service delivery to the aged will be a growth industry for many years into the future. The needs of the population and the political realities of the situation demand it. Not only will an increasing number of gerontologically-trained professionals be needed in employment settings, but members of the general public will increasingly be aware of needs of the older population.

Service programs have, for the most part, demonstrated their effectiveness in their goal of maximizing the independence of older disabled persons. The problem is not *ineffective* services, so much as services that are inadequate due to the lack of available funding. More services and more comprehensive services for the aged can be predicted for the future.

While a higher level of governmental intervention probably is necessary, other means of accessing services have always been with us and will continue to be utilized. One study points to the effectiveness of older women in rural areas as "active manipulators of the social support system" (Shenk, 1991). That is, people's own initiative in developing informal services when they are seen to be needed should never be underestimated.

And if the success of the Elderhostel program has demonstrated anything, it is that people will pay for services out of their own pockets if they value them highly enough.

Older Americans are increasingly prosperous and well-educated. Twenty-five years ago, only 24% of the U.S. population aged 65+ had completed four years of high school. Current figures demonstrate a change in this regard: 34.3% have completed high school, and 14.8% are college graduates (U.S. Bureau of the Census, 1998b). We have already seen that the poverty rate for older people is now the lowest of any group in the population. Both of these trends will continue: older people in the future will be increasingly sophisticated and economically powerful. They will continue to wield considerable political clout as well. As the current generation of adults ages, it most likely will become a group of assertive older people. We predict that they will devote imagination and energy to the development of their own programs, most likely with considerable success.

Questions for Discussion

1. What are the differences between senior centers and adult day care centers?
2. How would you feel about restricting Social Security payments to only those older people in greatest financial need?
3. Some critics of congregate meal programs consider them to be mere soup kitchens for the aged. Do you agree or disagree?
4. Are you or members of your family involved in home care for an older person? If so, what are the problems and advantages that you have seen?
5. Why are some older people resistant to the idea of receiving services?
6. The chapter says that services for the elderly are a "growth industry." Why is this so?
7. Why do you think community mental health services are so difficult to deliver to the elderly?

Sources of Further Information

A host of explanatory booklets is available from the AARP; ask for an order form from:

AARP Resource Services Group
Dept. QD
601 E Street, N.W.
Washington, D. C. 20049

Up until 1996, articles in *The Gerontologist* tried to keep up with web pages and Internet resources on aging (Post, 1996). With the subsequent proliferation of such resources, they haven't been able to keep up and have pretty much thrown in the towel. Now, any good search engine such as WebCrawler or Alta Vista will give hundreds of hits on key words such as "aging" or "gerontology." Two particularly useful web addresses ones are the AARP's: http://www.aarp.org and the Administration on Aging's: http://www.aoa.dhhs.gov.

We have mentioned several times that Social Security in particular tends to have highly technical details and changing eligibility requirements and levels of payment. This is true as well for the Supplemental Security Income program and for Medicare. There is no substitute in terms of current information on the various programs administered by Social Security for a visit to a local Social Security office. Every city of any size, including all state capitals, has one. Look in the telephone directory under U.S. Government, Department of Health and Human Services. Each office makes available publications that describe in simple terms the provisions of the various programs, including retirement benefits, Medicare, SSI, payments to widows and survivors, and disability coverage, in both English and Spanish.

A variety of publications on legal aspects of aging are available from:

Publications Coordinator
Legal Counsel for the Elderly
601 E Street, N.W.
Washington, D.C. 20049
202/434-6464

Locations of Area Agencies on Aging can usually be found in the Yellow Pages of city telephone directories under "Social Service Programs." If that doesn't work, one can find out the location and number of any local Area Agency on Aging by calling the National Association of Area Agencies on Aging at 202/484-7520 or looking up the information on the AoA web page above.

AARP's *Horizons,* a monthly newsletter of research briefs on aging, and especially on programs and services for the elderly, can be obtained from AARP's Research and Information Center. Call: 202/434-6240.

Information on senior centers can be obtained from:

National Eldercare Institute on Multipurpose Senior Centers and
    Community Focal Points
The National Council on the Aging, Inc.
409 Third Street, N.W.
Washington, D.C. 20024

There is a national advocacy group for persons interested in the Social Security program:

National Committee to Preserve Social Security and Medicare
2000 K Street, N.W., Suite 800
Washington, D.C. 20006
202/822-9459

A number of publications on adult day care and other services for the aged can be obtained from:

NCOA Publications
Dept. 5087
Washington, D.C. 20061-5087

A variety of publications on programs for the aged can be had from:

National Eldercare Dissemination Center
2033 K Street, N.W., Suite 304
Washington, D.C. 20006
202/785-0707

Resources on programming in rural areas can be obtained from:

The National Resource Center on Rural Elderly
University of Missouri-Kansas City
5245 Rockhill Road
Kansas City, MO 64110-2499

Information on hospice care is available from:

Foundation for Hospice and Homecare
519 C Street, N.W.
Washington, D.C. 20002-5809
202/547-6586

Additional information on aging network programs can be had from:

National Aging Dissemination Center
National Association of State Units on Aging
1225 I Street, N.W., Suite 725
Washington, D.C. 20005

Specialized publications and media on adult day centers for people with dementia are available from:

Dementia Care and Respite Services Program
Department of Psychiatry & Behavioral Medicine
Bowman Gray School of Medicine
Wake Forest University
Winston-Salem, NC 27157-1087

Information on housing alternatives for older people can be obtained from:

National Shared Housing Resource Center
431 Pine Street
Burlington, VT 05401
802/862-2727

Finally, information for those having difficulty in organizing a case for qualifying for disability under Social Security can purchase the *Disability Workbook for Social Security Applicants* from:

Physicians' Disability Services
P.O. Box 827
Arnold, MD 21012

Glossary

(This glossary is provided to assist the reader. The definitions were not taken from a standard dictionary, but are provided to highlight specific examples in the text.)

AAA — Area Agency on Aging.

acculturation — Adapting to traits from another culture.

activity theory — The idea that the best way to approach old age is to remain as active and involved as possible.

acute — Having a sudden onset and a short course; most infectious diseases are acute.

ADL — Activities of daily living.

ad libitum — At liberty; rodents fed ad libitum have food constantly available and can eat as much as they want.

advance directives — A written statement such as a living will or a signed statement appointing someone to have durable power of attorney for health care; one gives preferences for terminal care, the other appoints an agent to determine appropriate care.

affective disorders — Mood ailments, such as depression or bipolar disorder.

African-Americans — People who trace their ancestry to the African continent, usually sub-Saharan Africa.

age-appropriate behavior — Acting one's age, doing things that are normal for others at the same age.

age cohort — A group that has a particular definition by age, such as all people born from 1900 to 1910, or people born during the Depression.

age-normative — Pertaining to common values of persons at certain ages.

age norms — Markers of what is expected at certain ages.

ageism — Prejudice and discrimination against the elderly.

AIDS — Acquired immunodeficiency syndrome; a failure of the immune system to fight off both infections and chronic illness.

Aleuts — Native Americans residing in the Aleutian Islands west of Alaska.

anomie — Viewing the future with pessimism and feeling controlled by hostile outside forces; normlessness or helplessness.

antediluvian — Literally, "before the deluge," or before the Biblical flood described in Genesis 6; usually used to denote a period before the dawn of recorded time; prehistoric.

AoA — Administration on Aging; a unit of the U.S. Department of Health and Human Services.

arteriosclerosis — Thickening and hardening of the arterial walls; once thought to be the main cause of dementia.

Asians — Strictly, people whose ancestors come from any part of the Asian continent, from the Middle East to Siberia. Because people from Asia cover such a vast array of races and ethnic groups, it is often more accurate to specify country of origin, such as India, Korea, China, the Philippines, or Japan, for example.

assimilation — Absorption into the cultural tradition of a population or group.

autism — "Absorption in self-centered mental activity (as daydreams, fantasies, delusions, and hallucinations) especially when accompanied by marked withdrawal from reality" (*Webster's Ninth New Collegiate Dictionary*, 1988). Those severely affected may withdraw into themselves and display instances of repetitive, unusual, or aggressive behavior. Constant rocking, scratching, or chewing on a finger are examples.

autoimmune reaction — A dysfunction of the immune system, especially when it is either losing its efficiency or is actually attacking another part of the body.

baby boomers — That cohort of people born between 1945 and 1960 (the Post-War "baby boom") who will begin entering old age between the years 2010 and 2025.

bipolar disorder — Alternating phases of serious depression and "manic" or overly excited activity.

bridge jobs — Transitional jobs, often part-time work, taken after leaving career work and prior to full-time retirement.

career jobs — Long-term work, for the majority of one's working life, that the individual has been trained or educated to do.

catalyst — Someone who makes things happen.

centenarians — People 100 years of age or older.

cerebral palsy — A group of neurological conditions resulting in impaired movement, usually caused by injury to the brain before or during birth. People with cerebral palsy often have severe speech problems and difficulty in muscle coordination; they may also have seizures or the inability to see, hear, or learn.

chronic — Having a slow onset and long course; many health problems of the elderly are chronic and characteristically do not have a quick cure.

clinical diagnosis — An assessment made on the basis of physical signs and symptoms rather than lab tests or x-rays.

cognitive — Having to do with cognition, the ability to think and learn.

cohort effect — Something people in the same age cohort have in common because of their age; the common experience of living through World War II might be seen as a cohort effect.

COLA — Social Security cost-of-living adjustment.

co-morbidity — Afflicted with more than one condition.

confabulation — Making up stories; from the word "fable."

confidant — The primary individual in whom one confides.

continuing care retirement community (CCRC) — Congregate housing for the elderly (apartments or condos), on an identifiable campus and having a continuum of care.

continuity theory — The idea that one's personality and ways of seeing the world stay pretty much the same into old age.

continuum of care — Multilevel services to assist people in living as independently as possible, ranging from totally independent living all the way to nursing home care.

control — The perception of who is in charge of one's life: people who are internally controlled are independent; those who are externally controlled have lost their independence.

cross-sectional — A research method in which people of different ages are tested at the same time and the results are compared.

customs — Long-lived, traditional norms.

death rates (or mortality rates) — Amount of deaths for specific causes (or by race, age, or sex) expressed as a rate rather than a number; as an illustration, a percentage is a rate (so many per hundred) and a batting average is a rate (so many hits per thousand at bats); death rates are often expressed as so many per 10,000 or per 100,000. The important concept is that rates can be more easily compared between groups than can numbers of deaths.

defense mechanisms — Characteristic patterns of behavior that people use to adapt in their lives.

deinstitutionalization — A movement that began in the United States in the 1960s and 70s to provide services in the community that would allow mentally ill and developmentally disabled people to be released from state hospitals and to lead more normal lives in the community.

delirium — Mental confusion or disorientation, frenzied excitement, or delusions.

dementia — A loss of intellectual abilities.

demography — The study of populations, usually the facts and figures relating to the size and characteristics of groups of people.

depression — A persistent mood disorder characterized by loss of interest, sleep disturbance, anxiety, fatigue, or thoughts of worthlessness.

developmental disabilities — Chronic disabling conditions that occur prior to age 22 and limit the individual's ability to lead an independent life. Usually the developmental disabilities are grouped in the categories of mental retardation, cerebral palsy, epilepsy, autism, and other neurological impairments.

developmental-genetic theories — Intrinsic views that hold internal physical processes are responsible for aging.

Diogenes syndrome — Breakdown of self-maintenance, often characterized by messiness or hoarding.

disengagement theory — The idea that the most satisfying approach to old age involves a mutual withdrawal of the older person from society.

DRG — Diagnostic related group; used by prospective payment systems as a basis to pay hospital and medical costs.

DSM-IV — The *Diagnostic and Statistical Manual of Mental Disorders, Fourth Edition* published by the American Psychiatric Association (1994).

dysphoria — Feeling unwell or unhappy.

dysthymia — Mild depression.

ego — The self, the personality.

elder abuse — Harming an older person either physically, psychologically, or materially.

embolism — A particle, such as a clot, that is transported in the blood vessels to the lungs or to the brain; a frequent cause of stroke.

empty nest — The period in midlife when the children have all left the home.

epilepsy — Abnormal electrical discharges in the brain that result in seizures and muscle convulsions as well as partial or total loss of consciousness.

error theory — Aging that is caused by repeated mutations of cellular DNA.

ethnicity — Cultural differences (norms and values) belonging to a particular ethnic or national group; defined by shared cultural traits or values.

etiology — Underlying cause.

exchange theory — The concept that older and younger persons maintain a fairly equal balance of interchange of support, both material and emotional; when this gets out of balance, interaction tends to break down.

existential — Relating to human existence, especially the understanding one has of the meaning of life.

extended family — Relatives, including cousins, aunts, uncles, and grandparents; the term is sometimes broadened to include close family friends.

external causes of death — Accidental deaths, suicides, and homicides.

face validity — The property of seeming to be obvious or being apparently true.

failure to thrive — A syndrome common in institutionalized children, now recognized to be prevalent among the institutionalized aged as well; it involves undernutrition, depression, lack of growth, and higher rates of illness and death.

FICA — Federal Insurance Contributions Act; law requiring that funds be taken from wage-earners' paychecks to fund the Social Security system.

filial obligation — A sense of duty to one's family members.

folkways — Short-lived, informal norms; fashions or fads.

Francophone — A person whose native language is French.

free radicals — Chemical compounds resulting from the process of oxidation that seek to chemically combine with other substances.

generation — A group that has lived long enough to reproduce (usually we think of a generation as about 20 years); a generation might often be described as an age cohort—for example, the generation of people representing baby boomers.

gerontology — The study of old age.

Gray Panthers — An activist group that speaks out on behalf of older people.

guardian — A court-appointed individual who is responsible for overseeing the physical or financial welfare of another.

Hasid (plural = Hasidim) — Ultra-Orthodox Jews with origins in Eastern Europe (especially Poland, Hungary, and Russia) who dress in characteristic garb and strictly follow Jewish law.

heterogeneous — Combinations of dissimilar or diverse elements; the opposite of homogeneous.

Hispanics — Any of those people who trace ancestors or language to a Spanish or Portuguese-speaking country.

history-normative — Accepted by all people who have been influenced by a particular historical event.

HIV — Human immunodeficiency virus; the underling cause of AIDS.

hospice — A program designed to serve the needs of people who are dying.

hyperbaric chamber — A tank in which people are subjected to oxygen at a higher than normal atmospheric pressure.

hypertension — High blood pressure.

hyperthermia — Abnormally high body temperature.

hypochondriasis — Being obsessed with health, drugs, or doctors, or misusing illness for dependency needs; one of the immature adaptive mechanisms.

hypothermia — A disorder of temperature equilibrium where the inner body temperature falls below 96 degrees Fahrenheit (or 35.5 degrees Celsius), which may lead to confusion, delirium, and death.

IADL — Instrumental activities of daily living.

iatrogenic — Caused by medical treatment, such as drug intoxication.

ICF/MR — Intermediate care facilities for the mentally retarded; specialized nursing homes.

immune or immunological — Having to do with the body's immune system of fighting off infection.

industrial gerontology — The study of older workers and retirement.

intimacy from a distance — The desired situation of most older people: to live near their children, not with them.

intrinsic — Within the body, as distinguished from environmental, or outside the body.

introspection — Self-examination.

involutional — Shrinking and entangling; downwardly spiraling with age.

life expectancy — The mean or average length of life for a group; the ages at which members of a group die, added up and divided by the number in the group. Life expectancy is often expressed as the average number of years of life remaining at birth or from some particular age.

life review — A period of reminiscence and self-reflection brought on by a realization of impending death.

life span — How long a species lives. Life span is often expressed in terms of maximum life span (115–122 years for humans) or practical life span (about 85 years for humans).

locus — Location, as in locus of control, which can be internal or external.

longitudinal — A research method that tests people over and over again as they age and compares their scores to their own results when they were younger.

malignant neoplasms — Cancerous tumors.

mandatory retirement — Forced retirement, usually at a specific age.

manic — Frenzied, overactive.

margin theory of aging — More and more of our available abilities are used as we get older.

Medicaid — A welfare program in the United States that pays hospital, medical, and nursing home costs for those unable to pay for their own care.

Medicaid Waiver — A plan agreed to by the U.S. Health Care Financing Administration and many of the states whereby Medicaid dollars that might have gone to pay for nursing home care can be used to provide in-home services to help keep people out of nursing homes.

Medicare — The health insurance program for the aged (and younger disabled people) through the Social Security program; 99.5% of people 65 and older in the U.S. have Medicare coverage.

mental retardation — A diminished ability to learn. There is no single cause of mental retardation; it may result from a number of factors including premature birth, genetic abnormalities, malnutrition, trauma, exposure to toxic agents (including fetal alcohol syndrome), or social deprivation.

meta-analysis — A large-scale compilation of many studies.

modernization theory — The view that the more highly industrialized or urbanized a society, the lower the status of the elderly.

morbidity — Illness.

mores — Strongly-held norms, often encoded into laws. These beliefs about the proper ways for people to behave within a particular culture are seen as crucial to maintaining the social order; violations of mores are often punished.

mortality — Death.

mortality rate — Rate of deaths at certain ages or from certain causes, most often expressed as deaths per 100,000 per year in the population.

MR/DD Network — Multicounty agencies supported by federal funding that provide services to the developmentally disabled. Services to people who qualify as having a developmental disability under the definition of the law might include case management, in-home services, group homes, ICF/MR placement, or other services designed to assist in making the person's life as independent as possible in the least restrictive environment.

multi-infarct dementia — Dementia caused by many small strokes. Vascular dementia.

mutagenesis — The process in which cells replicate themselves with slight errors in their genetic messages; under the error theory, these mutations are compounded with further replication.

Native Americans — Generally understood to be people descended from those who resided on the North American continent prior to European colonization: American Indians, Aleuts, and Eskimos.

negative correlation — A direct relationship where as one variable goes up as another goes down; health and age are an example: usually as age increases overall health goes down; thus, these two variables have a negative correlation.

neglect — To disregard or leave unattended; in the context of elder neglect, to allow personal care to deteriorate without corrective action.

neuroendocrine theory — Aging is caused in part by hormonal changes that regulate cells.

neurological impairments — A catch-all term that describes a number of conditions—disorders of the brain and central nervous system that impair the use and development of language, understanding, memory, attention span, fine muscle control, or adaptive behavior.

normative behavior — Actions that are common and accepted; nonnormative behavior is deviant.

norms — Rules and guidelines for social behavior shared and accepted by most people within a culture.

nuclear family — The nucleus: parents and their children.

OBRA — The Omnibus Budget Reconciliation Act of 1987.

old age — Sixty-five years of age and above is the most common definition of the point at which old age begins.

old old — Those persons 75 years and older.

oldest old — Those persons aged 85 and above.

Ombudsman — A mediator who investigates complaints and who meets with both parties to try to resolve conflicts.

organic mental disorders — Ailments having a physical cause, such as head trauma or a disease such as Alzheimer's.

osteoporosis — Loss of calcium in the bones.

paranoid — Unfounded or unreasonable fears or suspicions.

paraphrenia — A well-organized system of personal delusions without other negative symptoms.

passive suicide — Not taking an active means to kill oneself, but allowing oneself to die over the course of time.

plasticity — Reserve capacity; capacity to grow.

polypharmacy — Overuse of drugs.

primary caregiver — The one individual who bears the main responsibility for the care of another; there also may be one or more secondary caregivers.

prognosis — The expected outcome (such as dying or getting well) of a medical condition.

programmed theory — The view that dividing human cells will have a limited number of doublings (the Hayflick limit), usually a total of 50 (plus or minus ten).

projection — An immature adaptive mechanism in which one's own unacknowledged feelings are attributed to others.

proprietary — Profit making.

race specific — Likely to happen more to one racial group than another. To a certain degree, for example, hypertension affects more African-Americans, and for that reason could be said to be somewhat race specific. Some conditions, such a sickle-cell anemia, are entirely race specific.

regulatory mechanism — A means of controlling functions; regulatory mechanisms can be genetic or chemical (hormonal).

repression — An unexpected innocence or failure to recognize reality.

respite — A chance to take a break, to get some relief from caregiving duties.

role transition — Changing (adding or subtracting) social roles, usually over the course of time as one develops.

RSVP — The Retired Senior Volunteer Program.

schizophrenia — A mental illness characterized by disintegration of personality, gross delusions, and loss of contact with the environment, often with paranoia.

SCORE — The Service Corps of Retired Executives.

siblings — Brothers and sisters.

significant other — Another individual, such as a spouse or a parent, who is important to one's well-being.

Snowbirds — People who move in retirement to one of the Sun Belt states.

social convention — Something usually thought of as the norm.

social death — A decline in individual social worth so drastic that the individual begins to be treated mechanically, like an object rather than as a person.

social network — The system of family and friends with whom one interacts most.

socialization — The learning process of social interactions with others that teaches us the culture and norms of the society.

somatic mutation — A change in the genetic message of a somatic cell, one that is part of the tissues rather than the germ cells.

spontaneous remission — Getting better for a period of time for no apparent reason; arthritis and cancer are examples of conditions that sometimes have spontaneous remissions.

SSI — Supplemental Security Income; federally guaranteed income for the impoverished elderly.

state — A temporary emotional condition such as mirth or rage.

stochastic mutation — A random, especially biological, change that results from an environmental cause originating outside the body.

stroke — A blockage or rupture of one of the blood vessels in the brain that kills part of the brain tissue; sometimes also referred to as a *CVA* (cerebrovascular accident).

subculture — A group within a larger group whose members usually interact mainly with one another; there has been debate over whether or not the aged constitute a subculture.

subcutaneous — Beneath the skin.

subdural hematoma — A blood clot between the skull and the brain.

sublimation — An adaptive trait that allows one to rechannel emotion into socially acceptable outlets, such as artistic creativity.

Sunbirds — People who continue to live in the North but who reside in the Sun Belt during the winter months.

suppression — A conscious decision to postpone emotional reaction to a more appropriate time.

survival curve — A graph representing the number or percentage who are still living at certain ages. *Rectangularization* of the survival curve happens when there are few deaths in childhood or adulthood and the line on the graph represents less of a curve and more of a rectangle.

terminal — Literally "the end;" a terminal illness is one that is expected to result in the individual's death.

terminal drop — Sudden decline in perception or performance, usually associated with impending death.

TIA — Transient ischemic attack; a spasm or spontaneous narrowing of a blood vessel in the brain which can cause stroke-like symptoms and which often precedes a true stroke.

trait — A long-standing, stable element of the personality that is characteristic of the individual.

trajectory — A downward-sloping line; a *death trajectory* describes the process over time of nearing the end of life.

transient — Coming and going.

wear and tear theory of aging — The view that physical decline is associated with environmental factors such as disease or radiation.

young old — People 65 to 74 years of age.

zeitgeist — The spirit of the times.

zygote — A fertilized egg that will develop into an organism.

References

AARP. (1998, April). *Working Age, 13*(6).

Abel, E. K. (1992). Parental dependence and filial responsibility in the nineteenth century: Hial Hawley and Emily Hawley Gillespie, 1884–1885. *The Gerontologist, 32,* 519–526.

Aber, C. S. (1992). Spousal death, a threat to women's health: Paid work as a "resistance resource." *Image: Journal of Nursing Scholarship, 24*(2), 95–99.

Aciman, A. (1998, December 21). In search of Proust. *The New Yorker,* p. 81.

Adams, C., & Moss, M. (1998, December 24). The business potential of nursing homes is elusive, Vencor finds. *The Wall Street Journal,* p. 1.

Adams, E. K., Meiners, M. R., & Burwell, B. O. (1993, January). Asset spend-down in nursing homes: Methods and insights. *Medical Care, 31*(1), 1–23.

Adams, S. L., & Waskel, S. A. (1993). Late onset alcoholism: Stress or structure. *The Journal of Psychology, 127,* 329–334.

Ahmed, B., & Smith, S.K. (1992). How changes in components of growth affect the population aging of states. *Journal of Gerontology: Social Sciences, 47,* S27–S37.

Aldag, R., & Brief, A. (1977). Age, work values, and employee reactions. *Industrial Gerontology, 4,* 192–197.

Almeida, O. P., Howard, R., Forstl, H., & Levy, R. (1992). Late paraphrenia: A review. *International Journal of Geriatric Psychiatry, 7,* 543–548.

Almerico, G. M., & Fillmer, T. (1988). Portrayal of older characters in children's magazines. *Educational Gerontology, 14,* 15–31.

American Association of Retired Persons (1991). *A profile of older Americans: 1991.* Washington, DC: AARP.

American Psychiatric Association. (1994). *Diagnostic and statistical manual of mental disorders* (4th ed.). Washington, DC: American Psychiatric Association.

Anderson, R. N. (1999, December 13). United States life tables, 1997. *National Vital Statistics Reports.* Hyattsville, MD: National Center for Health Statistics, Center for Disease Control and Prevention.

Anderson, R. N., & Rosenberg, H. M. (1998, October 7). Age standardization of death rates: Implication of the year 2000 standard. *National Vital Statistics Reports.* Hyattsville, MD: National Center for Health Statistics, Centers for Disease Control and Prevention.

Andreasen, N. C. (1999). Understanding the causes of schizophrenia. *New England Journal of Medicine, 340,* 645–647.

Angel, J. L., Angel, R. J., McClellan, J. L., & Markides, K. S. (1996). Nativity, declining health, and preferences in living arrangements among elderly Mexican Americans: Implications for long-term care. *The Gerontologist, 36,* 464–473.

Angel, R. J., Angel, J. L., Lee, G-Y., & Markides, K. S. (1999). Age at migration and family dependency among older Mexican immigrants: Recent evidence from the Mexican American EPESE. *The Gerontologist, 39,* 59–65.

Ansello, E. F., & Eustis, N. N. (1992, Winter) A common stake? Investigating the emerging intersection of aging and disabilities. *Generations, 16*(1), 5–8.

Applebaum, G. E., King, J. E., & Finucane, T. E. (1990). The outcome of CPR initiated in nursing homes. *Journal of the American Geriatrics Society, 38,* 197–200.

Arber, S., & Ginn, J. (1991). *Gender and later life.* New York: Sage.

Arfken, C. L., Lichtenberg, P. A., & Tancer, M. E. (1999). Cognitive impairment and depression predict mortality in medically ill older adults. *Journal of Gerontology: Medical Sciences, 54A,* M152–M156.

Arling, G., Buhaug, H., Hagen, S. H., & Zimmerman, D. (1991). Medicaid send down among nursing home residents in Wisconsin. *The Gerontologist, 31,* 174-182.

Arndt, M., & Harrington, L. M. (1993, June 12). Enraged seniors fighting back to shield Medicare. *Chicago Tribune,* p. 1.

Ashby, D., Amers, D., West, C. R., & Macdonald, A. (1991). Psychiatric morbidity as predictor of mortality for residents of local authority homes for the elderly. *International Journal of Geriatric Psychiatry, 6,* 567–575.

Atchley, R. A. (2000). *Social forces and aging* (9th ed.). Belmont, CA: Wadsworth Publishing Co.

Bachman, D. L. (1990). Plasticity of memory functioning in normal aging and Alzheimer's disease. *Acta Neurologica Scandinavica 82*(129, Suppl.), 32–36.

Bachman, D. L., Wolf, P. A., Linn, R., Knoefel, J. E., et al. (1992). Prevalence of dementia and probable senile dementia of the Alzheimer type in the Framingham study. *Neurology, 42,* 115–119.

Back, K. W., & Morris, J. D. (1974). Perception of self and the study of whole lives. In E. B. Palmore (Ed.), *Normal aging II.* Durham, NC: Duke University Press.

Badger, T. A. (1993). Physical health impairment and depression among older adults. *Image: Journal of Nursing Scholarship, 25,* 325–330.

Baltes, M. M., Kuhl, K. P., & Sowarka, D. (1992). Testing for limits of cognitive reserve capacity: A promising strategy for early diagnosis of dementia? *Journal of Gerontology: Psychological Sciences, 47,* P165–P167.

Baltes, P. B., & Kliegl, R. (1992). Further testing of limits of cognitive plasticity: Negative age differences in a mnemonic skill are robust. *Developmental Psychology, 28,* 121–125.

Barefoot, J. C., Beckham, J. C., Haney, T. L., Siegler, I. C., et al. (1993). Age differences in hostility among middle-aged and older adults. *Psychology and Aging, 8,* 3–9.

Barker, P. R., Manderscheid, R. W., Hendershot, G. E., et al. (1992). Serious mental illness and disability in the adult household population: United States, 1989. *Advance data from vital and health statistics* (No. 218). Hyattsville, MD: National Center for Health Statistics.

Barringer, F. (1993, Mar. 14). 'Lead . . . or Leave' asks: Who's spending our inheritance? *New York Times,* p. 14.

Barusch, A. S. (1997). Self-concepts of low-income older women: Not old or poor, but fortunate and blessed. *International Journal of Aging and Human Development, 44,* 269–282.

Bass, S. A., & Caro, F. G. (1996). The economic value of grandparent assistance. *Generations, 20*(1), 29–33.

Baum, S. K., & Stewart, R. B. (1990). Sources of meaning through the lifespan. *Psychological Reports, 67,* 3–14.

Bazargan, M., Barbre, A. R., & Torres-Gil, F. (1992). Voting behavior among low-income Black elderly: A multi election perspective. *The Gerontologist, 32*, 584–591.

Bazargan, M., Kang, T. S., & Bazargan, S. (1991). A multivariate comparison of elderly African-Americans' and Caucasians' voting behavior: How do social, health, psychological, and political variables affect their voting? *International Journal of Aging & Human Development, 32*, 181–198.

Beard, B. B. (1968). Some characteristics of recent memory of centenarians. *Journal of Gerontology, 23*, 23–30.

Beard, C. M., Kokmen, E., Offord, K., & Kurland, L. T. (1991). Is the prevalence of dementia changing? *Neurology, 41*, 1911–1914.

Beder, J. (1998). Legalization of physical-assisted suicide. A pilot study of gerontological nurses. *Journal of Gerontological Nursing, 24*(4), 14–20.

Bell, I. P. (1970). The double standard of aging. *Trans-Action, 6*, 75–80.

Bell, J. (1992). In search of discourse on aging: The elderly on television. *The Gerontologist, 32*, 305–311.

Bellamy, D., & Phillips. J. G. (1987, Autumn). Mechanisms of aging. *The University of Wales Science and Technology Review, 2*, 20–29.

Benbow, S. M. (1991). ECT in late life. *International Journal of Geriatric Psychiatry, 6*(6), 401–406.

Benet, S. (1974). *Abkhazia: The long-living people of the Caucasus.* New York: Holt, Rinehart, and Winston.

Bennett, K. M. (1998). Longitudinal changes in mental and physical health among elderly, recently widowed men. *Mortality, 3*, 265–278.

Benton, D. M. (1999). African-Americans and elder mistreatment: Targeting information of a high-risk population. In T. Tatara (Ed.), *Understanding elder abuse in minority populations* (pp. 49–64). Philadelphia: Brunner/Mazel.

Berg, K., & Mor, V. (1995). Medicare nursing home residents with a stroke: Characteristics and 90-day outcomes of care. *Journal of Aging and Health, 7*, 384–401.

Berger, R. M. (1982). The unseen minority: Older gays and lesbians. *Social Work, 27*, 236–242.

Bergman-Evans, B. F. (1994). Loneliness, depression, and social support of spousal caregivers. *Journal of Gerontological Nursing, 20*(3), 6–16.

Berkman, L. S., & Syme, S. L. (1979). Social networks, host resistance, and mortality: A nine-year follow-up study of Alameda County residents. *American Journal of Epidemiology, 109*, 186–204.

Berman, P. L. (1989). *The courage to grow old.* New York: Ballentine.

Besant, W. (1902). *London in the eighteenth century.* London: A. & C. Black, Ltd.

Biggar, J. C. (1980). Reassessing elderly Sunbelt migration. *Research on Aging, 2*, 177–190.

Biggar, J. C., Flynn, C. B., Longino, C. F., & Wiseman, R. F. (1984). Older Americans head south. *American Demographics, 6*(12), 27–29, 45.

Binstock, R. H. (1991, Summer/Fall). From the Great Society to the aging society—25 years of the Older Americans Act. *Generations, 15*(3), 11–18.

Bishop, J. M., & Krause, D. R. (1988). Depictions of aging and old age on Saturday morning television. *The Gerontologist, 28*, 91–94.

Blau, Z. S. (1981). *Aging in a changing society.* New York: Franklin Watts.

Blazer, D. G. (1980). The epidemiology of mental illness in later life. In E. W. Busse & D. G. Blazer (Eds.), *Handbook of geriatric psychiatry* (pp. 249–271). New York: Van Nostrand Reinhold.

Blazer, D. G. (1991). Suicide risk factors in the elderly: An epidemiological study. *Journal of Geriatric Psychiatry, 24,* 175–190.

Blumberg, M. (1980). Job switching in autonomous work groups: An exploratory study in a Pennsylvania coal mine. *Academy of Management Journal, 23,* 287–306.

Bookwala, J., & Schulz, R. (1998). The role of neuroticism and mastery in spouse caregivers' assessment of and response to a contextual stressor. *Journal of Gerontology: Psychological Sciences, 53B,* P155–P164.

Botwinick, J. (1973). *Aging and behavior.* New York: Springer.

Bourne, B. (1982). Effects of aging on work satisfaction, performance, and motivation. *Aging and Work, 5,* 37–47.

Bower, B. (1989). Relative downfalls behind elder abuse. *Science News, 135*(18), 276–277.

Braun, J. V., Wykle, M. H., & Cowling, W. R. (1988). Failure to thrive in older persons: A concept derived. *The Gerontologist, 28,* 809–812.

Brayne, C. (1993). Research and Alzheimer's disease: An epidemiological perspective. *Psychological Medicine, 23,* 287–296.

British Broadcasting Company. (1998). California court allows bosses to trade old for young. http://www.bbcnews.org/hi/English/world/newsid%5f299000/29768.stm

Brodaty, H., McGilchrist, C., Harris, L., & Peters, K. E. (1993). Time until institutionalization and death in patients with dementia: Role of caregiver training and risk factors. *Archives of Neurology, 50,* 643–650.

Brody, E. M. (1985). Parent care as a normative family stress. *The Gerontologist, 25,* 19–29.

Brody, E. M., Litvin, S. J., Albert, S. M., & Hoffman, C. J. (1994). Marital status of daughters and patterns of parent care. *Journal of Gerontology: Social Sciences, 49,* S95–S103.

Brody, E. M., & Schoonover, C. B. (1986). Patterns of parent-care when adult daughters work and when they do not. *The Gerontologist, 26,* 372–381.

Brody, E. M., & Spark, G. (1966). Institutionalization of the aged: A family crisis. *Family Process, 5,* 76–90.

Brostoff, S. (1992, Oct. 5). AARP, ABA clash over leak about their talks. *National Underwriter, 96,* 27–35.

Bulcroft, K., Van Leynseele, J., & Borgatta, E. F. (1989). Filial responsibility laws. *Research on Aging, 11,* 374–393.

Bullard, D. M., Glaser, H. H., Heagarty, M. C., & Pivchik, E. C. (1967). Failure to thrive in the neglected child. *American Journal of Orthopsychiatry, 37,* 680–690.

Bureau of Justice Statistics. (1998, December). *Criminal victimization 1997.* Washington, DC: U.S. Department of Justice.

Burgener, S. C., Jirovec, M., Murrell, L., & Barton, D. (1992). Caregiver and environmental variables related to difficult behaviors in institutionalized, demented elderly persons. *Journal of Gerontology: Psychological Sciences, 47,* P242–P249.

Burns, B. J., Wagner, H. R., Taube, J.E., Magaziner, J., et al. (1993). Mental health service use by the elderly in nursing homes. *American Journal of Public Health, 83,* 331–337.

Burrough, B. (1986, February 27). How GM began using private eyes in plants to fight drugs, crime. *Wall Street Journal,* pp. 1, 11.

Burton, L., Kasper, J., Shore, A., Cagney, K., LaVeist, T., Cubbin, C., & German, P.

(1995). The structure of informal care: Are there differences by race? *The Gerontologist, 35,* 744–752.

Butler, R. N. (1963). The life review: An interpretation of reminiscence in the aged. *Psychiatry, 26,* 65–76.

Caine, E. D., Lyness, J. M., & King, D. A. (1993). Reconsidering depression in the elderly. *American Journal of Geriatric Psychiatry, 1*(1), 4–20.

Camargo, O., & Preston, G. H. (1945). What happens to patients who are hospitalized for the first time when over sixty-five years of age. *American Journal of Psychiatry, 102,* 168–173.

Campbell, A. (1971). Politics through the life cycle. *The Gerontologist, 11,* 112–117.

Campbell, A., Converse, P. E., Miller, W. E., & Stokes, D. E. (1960). *The American voter.* New York: Wiley.

Campbell, J. C., & Strate, J. (1981). Are old people conservative? *The Gerontologist, 21,* 580–591.

Carrel, A., & Burrows, M. T. (1911). On the physicochemical regulation of the growth of tissues. *Journal of Experimental Medicine, 13,* 562–570.

Carrier, J. (1985, January 27). South Dakota tragedy points up lack of laws on neglect of elderly. *Omaha World Herald,* pp. 1, 7.

Carson, D. K., & Hand, C. (1999). Dilemmas surrounding elder abuse and neglect in Native American communities. In T. Tatara (Ed.), *Understanding elder abuse in minority populations* (pp. 161–184). Philadelphia: Brunner/Mazel.

Cash, T., & Valentine, D. (1987). A decade of adult protective services: Case characteristics. *Journal of Gerontological Social Work, 10,* 47-60.

Cavanaugh, J. C. (1993). *Adult development and aging.* Pacific Grove, CA: Brooks/ Cole.

The Center Report. (1998, winter). *The Duke University Center for the Study of Aging and Human Development, 18*(4), 4–5.

Cerami, A. (1985). Hypothesis: Glucose as a mediator of aging. *Journal of the American Geriatrics Society, 33,* 626–634.

Chapleski, E. E., Lichtenberg, P. A., Dwyer, J. W., Youngblade, L. M., & Tsai, P. F. (1997). Morbidity and co-morbidity among Great Lakes American Indians: Predictors of functional ability. *The Gerontologist, 37,* 588–597.

Chatters, L. M., Taylor, R. J., & Neighbors, H. W. (1989). Size of informal helper network mobilized during a serious personal problem among black Americans. *Journal of Marriage and the Family, 51,* 667–676.

Cherrington, D. (1979). Age and work values. *Academy of Management Journal, 22,* 617–623.

Chipperfield, J. G. (1993). Perceived barriers in coping with health problems. *Journal of Aging and Health, 5,* 123–139.

Christensen, K. (1990). Bridges over troubled water: How older workers view the labor market. In P. B. Doeringer (Ed.), *Bridges to retirement: Older workers in a changing labor market* (pp. 35–47). Ithaca, NY: ILR Press.

Clark, A. N. G., Mankikar, G. D., & Gray, I. (1975, February 15). Diogenes syndrome: A clinical study of gross neglect in old age. *The Lancet,* pp. 366–368.

Cohen, C. A., Gold, D. P., Shulman, K. I., Wortley, J. T., McDonald, G., & Wargon, M. (1993a). Factors determining the decision to institutionalize dementing individuals: A prospective study. *The Gerontologist, 33,* 714–720.

Cohen, C., Onserud, H., & Monaco, C. (1993b). Outcomes for the mentally ill in a program for older homeless persons. *Hospital & Community Psychiatry, 44,* 650–656.

Cohen, C. I. (1999). Aging and homelessness. *The Gerontologist, 39,* 5–15.

Cohen, C. I., & Carlin, L. (1993). Racial differences in clinical and social variables among patients evaluated in a dementia assessment center. *Journal of the National Medical Association, 85,* 379–384.

Cohen, C.I., Teresi, J., Holmes, D., & Roth, E. (1988). Survival strategies of older homeless men. *The Gerontologist, 28,* 58–65.

Cohen, E. S. (1992, Winter). What is independence? *Generations, 16*(1), 49–52.

Cohen, M. A., Tell, E. J., & Wallack, S. S. (1988). The risk factors of nursing home entry among residents of six continuing care retirement communities. *The Journal of Gerontology: Social Sciences, 43,* S15–S21.

Colantonio, A., Kasl, S. V., & Ostfeld, A. M. (1992). Depressive symptoms and other psychosocial factors as predictors of stroke in the elderly. *American Journal of Epidemiology, 136,* 884–895.

Cole, A. J., Gillett, T. P., & Fairbairn, A. (1992). A case of senile self-neglect in a married couple: "Diogenes a deux"? *International Journal of Geriatric Psychiatry, 7,* 839–841.

Cole, M.G. (1993). The impact of geriatric medical services on mental state. *International Pschogeriatrics, 5,* 91–101.

Coleman, P. G. (1999). Creating a life story: The task of reconciliation. *The Gerontologist, 39,* 133–139.

Comfort, A. (1979). *The biology of senescence* (3rd ed.). New York: Elsevier.

Connolly, J. (1992). Participatory versus lecture/discussion preretirement education: A comparison. *Educational Gerontology, 18,* 365–379.

Constas, K., & Vichas, R. (1980). An interpretive policy-making model of absenteeism with reference to the marginal worker in overseas plants. *Journal of Management Studies, 17,* 149–163.

Conwell, Y., Duberstein, P. R., Cox, C., Herrmann, J., Forbes, N., & Caine, E. D. (1998). Age differences in behaviors leading to completed suicide. *American Journal of Geriatric Psychiatry, 6*(2), 122–126.

Cool, L. E. (1986). Ethnicity: Its significance and measurement. In C. L. Fry & J. Keith (Eds.), *New methods for old age research* (pp. 263–280). South Hadley, MA: Bergin & Garvey.

Cooper, S-A. (1992). The psychiatry of elderly people with mental handicaps. *International Journal of Geriatric Psychiatry, 7,* 865–874.

Corr, C. A, & Corr, D. M. (1992). Adult hospice day care. *Death Studies, 16,* 155–171.

Costa, P. T., Zonderman, A. G., McCrae, R. R., Cornoni- Huntley, J., et al. (1987). Longitudinal analyses of psychological well-being in a national sample: Stability of mean levels. *Journal of Gerontology, 42,* 50–55.

Cotton, P. D., Sisson, G., & Starr, S. (1981). Comparing elderly mentally retarded and non-mentally retarded individuals: Who are they? What are their needs? *The Gerontologist, 21,* 359–365.

Cottrell, L. (1942). The adjustment of the individual to his age and sex roles. *American Sociological Review, 7,* 617–620.

County holds mass funeral for forgotten. (1995, August 26). *The Washington Post,* p. 35.

Courage, M. M., Godbey, K. L., Ingram, D. A., Schramm, L. L., et al. (1993). Suicide in the elderly: Staying in control. *Journal of Psychosocial Nursing, 31*(7), 26–31.

Cowgill, D. O., & Holmes, L. D. (1972). *Aging and modernization.* New York: Appleton-Century-Crofts.

Cox, E. O., & Parsons, R. J. (1992). Senior-to-senior mediation services project. *The Gerontologist, 32,* 420–422.

Coyle, N. (1990, December). The last four weeks of life. *American Journal of Nursing, 90*(12), 75–76.

Coyne, A. C., Reichman, W. E., & Berbig, L. J. (1993). The relationship between dementia and elder abuse. *American Journal of Psychiatry, 150,* 643–646.

Cristofalo, V. J. (1999). Biological theories of senescence. In V. L. Bengtson & K. W. Schaie (Eds.), *Handbook of theories of aging* (pp. 118–127). New York: Springer.

Crook, T. (1987). Dementia. In L. Carstensen & B. Edelstein (Eds.), *Handbook of clinical gerontology* (pp. 96–119). New York: Pergamon.

Cuellar, J. B. (1990). Hispanic-American aging. In M. S. Harper (Ed.), *Minority aging,* (DHHS Publication No. HHS P-DV-90-4, pp. 365–413). Washington, DC: U.S. Government Printing Office.

Cumming, E., & Henry, W. E. (1961). *Growing old.* New York: Basic Books.

Curry, C. L. (1990). Hypertension in the black elderly: Implications for geriatric education. In M. S. Harper (Ed.), *Minority aging* (DDHS Publication No. HRS P-DV-90-4, pp. 321–339). Washington, DC: U.S. Government Printing Office.

Cutler, R. G., Davis, B. J., Ingram, D. K., & Roth, G. S. (1992). Plasma concentrations of glucose, insulin, and percent glycosylated hemoglobin are unaltered by food restriction in rhesus and squirrel monkeys. *Journal of Gerontology: Biological Sciences, 47,* B9–B12.

Cutler, S. J., & Grams, A. E. (1988). Correlates of self-reported everyday memory problems. *Journal of Gerontology: Social Sciences, 43,* S82–S90.

DasGupta, K. (1998). Treatment of depression in elderly patients: Recent advances. *Archives of Family Medicine, 7*(3), 274–280.

DeLany, J. P., Hansen, B. C., Bodkin, N. L., Hannah, J., & Bray, G. A. (1999). Long-term calorie restriction reduces energy expenditure in aging monkeys. *Journal of Gerontology: Biological Sciences, 54A,* B5–B11.

Delgado, M. (1997). Interpretation of Puerto Rican elderly research findings: A community forum of research respondents. *Journal of Applied Gerontology, 16,* 317–332.

Der-McLeod, D., & Hansen, J. C. (1992). On look: The family continuum. *Generations, 17*(3), 71–72.

DeSpelder, L. A., & Strickland, A. L. (1992). *The last dance.* Mountain View, CA: Mayfield.

Dey, A. N. (1997). Characteristics of elderly nursing home residents. *Advance data from vital and health statistics* (No. 289). Hyattsville, MD: National Center for Health Statistics.

Die, A. H., & Seelbach, W. C. (1988). Problems, sources of assistance, and knowledge of services among elderly Vietnamese immigrants. *The Gerontologist, 28,* 448–452.

Diesfeldt, H. F. (1992). Pschogeriatrics day care outcome: A five-year follow-up. *International Journal of Geriatric Psychiatry, 7,* 673–679.

Doering, M., Rhodes, S., & Schuster, M. (1983). *The aging worker: Research and recommendations.* Beverly Hills, CA: Sage.

Donahue, W., Orback, H., & Pollack, O. (1960). Retirement: The emerging social pattern. In C. Tibbitts (Ed.), *Handbook of social gerontology.* Chicago: University of Chicago Press.

Dorfman, R., Walters, K., Burke, P., Hardin, L., Karanik, T., Raphael, J., & Silverstein, E. (1995). Old, sad, and alone: The myth of the aging homosexual. *Journal of Gerontological Social Work, 24,* 29–44.

Dowd, J. J. (1975). Aging as exchange: A preface to theory. *Journal of Gerontology, 30,* 584–594.

Duff, C. (1995, September 28). Profiling the aged: Fat cats or hungry victims? *Wall Street Journal,* B1.

Dunn, J. E., Furner, S. E., & Miles, T. P. (1993). Do falls predict institutionalization in older persons? An analysis of data from the Longitudinal Study of Aging. *Journal of Aging and Health, 5,* 194–207.

Durkheim, E. (1951). *Suicide.* New York: The Free Press.

Eaton, L. F., & Menolascino, F. J. (1982). Psychiatric disorders in the mentally retarded: Types, problems, and challenges. *American Journal of Psychiatry, 139,* 1292–1303.

Eisdorfer, C. (1972). The impact of scientific advances on independent living. In J. Thorson (Ed.), *Action now for older Americans* (pp. 44–51). Athens: University of Georgia Center for Continuing Education.

Eisdorfer, C. (1980). Paranoia and schizophrenic disorders in later life. In E. W. Bussse & D. G. Blazer (Eds.), *Handbook of geriatric psychiatry* (pp. 329–337). New York: Van Nostrand Reinhold.

Ekerdt, D. J., & DeViney, S. (1993). Evidence for a preretirement process among older male workers. *Journal of Gerontology: Social Sciences, 48,* S35–S43.

Engle, V. F., & Graney, M. J. (1993). Predicting outcomes of nursing home residents: Death and discharge home. *Journal of Gerontology: Social Sciences, 48,* S269-S275.

Engstrom, M., Green, R., & O'Connor, M. C. (1993, Winter/Spring). Adult daycare for persons with dementia: A viable community option. *Generations, 17*(1), 75–76.

Erber, J. T., & Rothberg, S. T. (1991). Here's looking at you: The relative effect of age and attractiveness on judgments about memory failure. *Journal of Gerontology: Psychological Sciences, 46,* P116–P123.

Erikson, E. H. (1982). *The life cycle completed.* New York: Norton.

Erlich. P. (1991). Survey of state public health departments on procedures for reporting elder abuse. *Public Health Reports, 106,* 151–154.

Erwin, K. T. (1996). *Group techniques for aging adults.* Washington, DC: Taylor & Francis.

Estes, C. L. (1993). The aging enterprise revisited. *The Gerontologist, 33,* 292–298.

Evans, L. (1993). How safe were today's older drivers when they were younger? *American Journal of Epidemiology, 137,* 769–775.

Exum, M. E., Phelps, B. J., Nabers, K. E., & Osborne, J. G. (1993). Sundown syndrome: Is it reflected in the use of PRN medications for nursing home residents? *The Gerontologist, 33,* 756–761.

Factor, A. R., & Haller, T. (1989, February). At risk families: Elderly parents caring for aging offspring with developmental disabilities. *ADDVANTAGE, 1*(3), 3.

Fake wedding is part of plan to bilk widow. (1992, October 22). *Omaha World-Herald,* p. 7.

Falk, A., Hanson, B. S., Isacsson, S-O, & Ostergren, P-O. (1992). Job strain and mortality in elderly men: Social network, support, and influence as buffers. *American Journal of Public Health, 82,* 1136–1138.

Ferland, G., Tuckweber, B., Bhat, P.V., & Lacroix, A. (1992). Effect of dietary restriction of hepatic vitamin A content in aging rats. *Journal of Gerontology: Biological Sciences, 47,* B3–B8.

Ferraro, K. (1992). Cohort changes in images of older adults. *The Gerontologist, 32,* 296–304.

Ferraro, K. F., & LaGrange, R. L. (1992). Are older people most afraid of crime? Reconsidering age differences in fear of victimization. *Journal of Gerontology: Social Sciences, 47,* S233–S244.

Ferraro, K. F., & Su, Y. (1999). Financial strain, social relations, and psychological distress among older people: A cross-cultural analysis. *Journal of Gerontology: Social Sciences, 54B,* S3–S15.

Field, D., & Milsap, R. E. (1991). Personality in advanced old age: Continuity or change? *Journal of Gerontology: Psychological Sciences, 46,* P299–P308.

Field, D., & Minkler, M. (1988). Continuity and change in social support between young-old and old-old or very-old age. *Journal of Gerontology: Psychological Sciences, 43,* P100–P106.

Finch, C. E. (1990). *Longevity, senescence, and the genome* (pp. 182–196). Chicago: University of Chicago Press.

Finch, C. E., & Landfield, P. W. (1985). Neuroendocrine and automatic functions in aging mammals. In C. E. Finch & E. L. Schneider (Eds.), *Handbook of the biology of aging* (pp. 567–594). New York: Van Nostrand Reinhold.

Finley, N. J., Roberts, M. D., & Banahan, B. F. (1988). Motivators and inhibitors of attitudes of filial obligation toward aging parents. *The Gerontologist, 28,* 73–78.

Fischer, L. R., & Eustis, N. N. (1988). DRGs and family care for the elderly: A case study. *The Gerontologist, 28,* 383–389.

Fishbein, M. (1967). *Readings in attitude theory and measurement.* New York: Wiley.

Fisher, W. H., Geller, J. L., Pearsall, D. T., Simon, L. J., et al. (1991). A continuum of services for the deinstitutionalized, chronically mentally ill elderly. *Administration & Policy in Mental Health, 18,* 397–410.

Fix, A. J., & Daughton, D. (1980). *The odds almanac.* Chicago: Follett.

Fleisher, D., & Kaplan, B. (1980). Characteristics of older workers: Implications for restructuring work. In P. Ragan (Ed.), *Work and retirement: Policy issues.* Los Angeles: University of Southern California Press.

Folstein, M. F., Bassett, S. S., Anthony, J. C., Romanoski, A. J., et al. (1991). Dementia: A case ascertainment in a community survey. *Journal of Gerontology: Medical Sciences, 46,* M132–M138.

Fontana, A., & Frey, J. H. (1990). Post-retirement workers in the labor force. *Work and Occupations, 17,* 355–361.

Forecasters say the average American worker will retire even earlier. (1999). *Working Age, 9*(3), 4.

Fox, J. A. (1991). Homicide against the elderly: A research note. *Criminology, 29,* 317–327.

Frankl, V. E. (1962). *Man's search for meaning.* New York: Simon and Schuster.

Freedman, M. (1995). We are everywhere. *Aging Today, 16*(5), 7–8.

Freedman, V. A. (1996). Family structure and the risk of nursing home admission. *Journal of Gerontology: Social Sciences, 51B,* S61–S69.

Freeman, J. T. (1982). The old, old, very old Charlie Smith. *The Gerontologist, 22,* 532–536.

Friedman, H. S., Tucker, J. S., Tomlinson-Keasey, C., Schwatrz, J. E., Wingard, D. L., & Criqui, M. H. (1993). Does childhood personality predict longevity? *Journal of Personality and Social Psychology, 65,* 176–185.

Fries, J. F., & Crapo, L. M. (1981). *Vitality and aging: Implications of the rectangular curve.* San Francisco: W. H. Freeman and Company.

Froggatt, P. (1970). Short-term absence from industry. *British Journal of Industrial Medicine, 27,* 199–210.

Fuguitt, G. V., & Beale, C. L. (1993). The changing concentration of the older nonmetropolitan population, 1960–90. *Journal of Gerontology: Social Sciences, 48,* S278–S288.

Furner, S. E., Rudberg, M. A., & Cassel, C. K. (1995). Medical conditions differentially affect the development of IADL disability: Implications for medical care and research. *The Gerontologist, 35,* 444–450.

Gagnon, M., Dartigues, J-F., Letenneur, L., Barberger-Gateau, P., et al. (1990). Risk factors in Alzheimer's disease: Results of an epidemiological study in the area of Bordeaux, France. *Psychologie Medicale, 22,* 1248–1251.

Gallo, J. J., Cooper-Patrick, L., & Lesikar, S. (1998). Depressive symptoms of whites and African-Americans aged 60 years and older. *Journal of Gerontology: Psychological Sciences, 53B,* P277–P286.

Garrard, J., Buchanan, J. L., Ratner, E. R., Makris, L., et al. (1993). Differences between nursing home admissions and residents. *Journal of Gerontology: Social Sciences, 48,* S301–S309.

Gatz, M., Karel, M. J., & Wolkenstein, B. (1991). Survey of providers of psychological services to older adults. *Professional Psychology: Research & Practice, 22,* 413–415.

Georgakas, D. (1980). *The Methuselah factors.* New York: Simon & Schuster.

Gey, G. O., Svotelis, M., Foard, M., & Bung, F. R. (1974). Long-term growth of chicken fibroblasts on a collagen substrate. *Experimental Cell Research, 84,* 63–71.

Gibbs, N. (1993, May 31). Rx for death. *Time,* 35–44.

Ginther, S. D., Webber, P., Fox, P. J., & Miller, L. (1993). Predictors of case management for persons with Alzheimer's disease. *Journal of Applied Gerontology, 12,* 139–154.

Glaser, B. G., & Strauss, A. L. (1968). *Time for dying.* Chicago: Aldine.

Gluck, M. E. (1999, April). A medicare prescription drug benefit. *Medicare brief* (No. 1). Washington, DC: National Academy of Social Insurance.

Goldsmith, R. E., & Heims, R. A. (1992). Subjective age: A test of five hypotheses. *The Gerontologist, 32,* 312–317.

Goldstein, A. L. (1993). Welcome and introduction. In A. L. Goldstein (Ed.), *A town forum on Alzheimer's disease* (pp. 1–2). Washington, DC: Institute for Advanced Studies in Immunology & Aging.

Gomez, G. E., & Gomez, E. A. (1993). Depression in the elderly. *Journal of Psychosocial Nursing, 31*(5), 28–33.

Grace, E. (1998, November 29). Parenting all over again puts a strain on kids, grandparents. *Omaha World-Herald,* pp. 1–2.

Grant, P. R., Skinkle, R. R., & Lipps, G. (1992). The impact of interinstitutional relocation on nursing home residents requiring a high level of care. *The Gerontologist, 32,* 834–842.

Gratton, B., & Haber, C. (1996). Three phases in the history of American grandparents: Authority, burden, companion. *Generations, 20*(1), 7–12.

Graves, E., & Owings, M. F. (1998, August 31). National hospital discharge survey. *Advance Data from Vital and Health Statistics, 301,* 6.

Gray, G. R., Ventis, D. G., & Hayslip, B. (1992). Socio-cognitive skills as a determinant of life satisfaction in aged persons. *International Journal of Aging & Human Development, 35,* 205–218.

Green, B. H., Copeland, J. R., Dewey, M. E., Sharma, V., et al. (1992). Risk factors for depression in elderly people: A prospective study. *Acta Psychiatrica Scandinavica, 86,* 213–217.

Greenberg, D., Witztum, E., & Levy, A. (1990). Hoarding as a psychiatric symptom. *Journal of Clinical Psychiatry, 51,* 417–421.

Greenberg, J. S., Seltzer, M. M., & Greenley, J. R. (1993). Aging parents of adults with disabilities: The gratifications and frustrations of later-life caregiving. *The Gerontologist, 33,* 542–550.

Greene, V. L., Lovely, M. E., & Ondrich, J. I. (1993). The cost-effectiveness of community services in a frail elderly population. *The Gerontologist, 33,* 177–189.

Grimby, A. (1993). Bereavement among elderly people: Grief reactions, post-bereavement hallucinations and quality of life. *Acta Psychiatrica Scandinavica, 87,* 72–80.

Gupta, N., & Beehr, T. (1979). Job stress and employee behaviors. *Organizational Behavior and Human Performance, 23,* 373–387.

Guralnik, J. M., LaCroix, A. Z., Abbott, R. D., Berkman, L. F., et al. (1993). Maintaining mobility in late life. *American Journal of Epidemiology, 137,* 845–857.

Gutheil, I. A., & Chichin, E. R. (1991). AIDS, older people, and social work. *Health & Social Work, 16,* 237–244.

Haas, W. H., & Serow, W. J. (1993). Amenity retirement migration process: A model and preliminary evidence. *The Gerontologist, 33,* 212–220.

Haddad, A. (1987). *High-tech home care.* Rockville, MD: Aspen.

Hagestad, G., & Neugarten, B. (1985). Age and the life course. In R. Binstock & E. Shanas (Eds.), *Handbook of aging and the social sciences* (2nd ed.). New York: Van Nostrand Reinhold.

Haight, B. K. (1995). Suicide risk in frail elderly relocated to nursing homes. *Geriatric Nursing, 16,* 104–107.

Halachmi, A. (1998). Dealing with employees over fifty. *Public Productivity & Management Review, 22,* 6–14.

Hall, A., & Johanson, T. R. (1980). The determinants of planned retirement age. *Industrial and Labor Relations Review, 33,* 241–254.

Hall, N., de Beck, P., Johnson, D., Mackinnon, K., et al. (1992). Randomized trial of a health promotion program for frail elders. *Canadian Journal on Aging, 11,* 72–91.

Halsell, G. (1976). *Los Viejos: Secrets of long life from the sacred valley.* Emmaus, PA: Rodale Press.

Hamill, R. J. (1995). Resuscitation: When is enough, enough? *Respiratory Care, 40*(5), 515–522.

Hamilton, J. B., & Mestler, G. E. (1969). Mortality and survival: Comparison of eunuchs with intact men and women in a mentally retarded population. *Journal of Gerontology, 24,* 395–411.

Hanawalt, B. A. (1986). *The ties that bound: Peasant families in Medieval England.* New York: Oxford University Press.

Hareven, T. K. (1992). Family and generation relations in the later years: A historical perspective. *Generations, 16*(3), 7–12.

Harman, D. (1981). The aging process. *Proceedings of the National Academy of Sciences of the United States of America, 78,* 7124–7128.

Harper, D. J., Manasse, P. R., James, O., & Newton, J. T. (1993). Intervening to reduce distress in caregivers of impaired elderly people: A preliminary evaluation. *International Journal of Geriatric Psychiatry, 8,* 139–145.

Harris, L. et al. (1981). *Aging in the eighties: American in transition.* New York: National Council on the Aging.

Harris, L. (1986). *Holydays: The world of a Hasidic family.* New York: Collier Books.

Harris, M. B., Begay, C., & Page, P. (1989). Activities, family relationships, and feeling about aging in a multicultural elderly sample. *International Journal of Aging and Human Development, 29,* 103–117.

Harrow, B. S., Tennstedt, S. L., & McKinlay, J. B. (1995). How costly is it to care for disabled elders in a community setting? *The Gerontologist, 35,* 803–813.

Hart, V. (1992, September). Coping with Alzheimer's disease: Things to do that will help you survive. *Alzheimer's Association Omaha Chapter Newsletter.* Omaha, NE: Alzheimer's Association.

Hassett, A. M., Keks, N. A., Jackson, H. J., & Copolov, D. L. (1992). The diagnostic validity of paraphrenia. *Australian & New Zealand Journal of Psychiatry, 26,* 18–29.

Haupt, B. J. (1998). An overview of home health and hospice care patients. *Advance data from vital and health statistics* (No. 297). Hyattsville, MD: National Center for Health Statistics.

Haveman, M. J., Maaskant, M. A., & Brook, O. H. (1992). The Dutch system of psychiatric care for adult patients. *Community Alternatives: International Journal of Family Care, 4*(2), 121–133.

Havighurst, R. H. (1974). *Developmental tasks and education.* New York: McKay.

Havighurst, R. J. (1968). Personality and patterns of aging. *The Gerontologist, 8,* 20–23.

Havighurst, R. J., Cavan, R., Burgess, E. W., & Goldhammer, H. (1949). *Personal adjustment in old age.* Chicago: Science Research Associates.

Hayflick, L. (1974). The strategy of senescence. *The Gerontologist, 14,* 37–45.

Hayslip, B., Lopez, F. G., & Nation, P. (1991). Hopelessness in community-residing aged persons: A viable construct. *Journal of Personality Assessment, 57,* 498–505.

Hayslip, B., & Panek, P. E. (1989). *Adult development and aging.* New York: Harper & Row.

Health care reform volunteers use buses, valentines, cellular phones to get messages to Congress. (1994, May-June). *AARP Highlights—The Newsletter of AARP Volunteers, 12*(3), 1–12.

Helberg, J. L. (1993). Patients' status at home care discharge. *IMAGE: Journal of Nursing Scholarship, 25,* 93–99.

Helmer, C., Gateau, P. B., Letenneur, L., & Dartigues, J. (1999). Subjective health and mortality in French elderly women and men. *Journal of Gerontology: Social Sciences, 54B,* S84–S92.

Helsing, K. J., Szklo, M., & Comstock, G. W. (1981). Factors associated with mortality after widowhood. *American Journal of Public Health, 71,* 802–809.

Henion, T. L. (1994, May 17). Bertha Smaha, 106, Dies; Endured Pioneer Life. *Omaha World-Herald,* p. 17.

Henretta, J. C., O'Rand, A. M., & Chan, C. G. (1993). Gender differences in employment after spouse's retirement. *Research on Aging, 15,* 148–169.

Hershey, R. D. (1995, August 26). Misunderstanding Social Security. *The New York Times,* p. 4.

Hewes, A. (1921). Study of accident records in a textile mill. *Journal of Industrial Hygiene, 3,* 187–195.

Hey, R. P., & Carlson, E. (1991, September). "Granny dumping": New pain for U. S. elders. *AARP Bulletin,* pp. 1–3.

High, D. M. (1993). Advance directives and the elderly: A study of intervention strategies to increase use. *The Gerontologist, 33,* 342–349.

Hing, E., & Bloom, B. (1990). Long-term care for the functionally dependent elderly. *National Center for Health Statistics Vital Health Statistics, 13*(104), 23.

Hirdes, J. P., & Forbes, W. F. (1993). Factors associated with the maintenance of good self-rated health. *Journal of Aging and Health, 5,* 101–122.

Hirsch, C. H., Davies, H. D., Boatwright, F., & Ochango, G. (1993). Effects of a nursing home respite admission on veterans with advanced dementia. *The Gerontologist, 33,* 523–528.

Hoch, C. C., Reynolds, C. F., Buysse, D. J., Fasiczka, A. L., et al. (1993). Two-year survival in patients with mixed symptoms of depression and cognitive impairment. *American Journal of Geriatric Psychiatry, 1,* 56–66.

Hochschild, A. (1973). *The unexpected community.* Englewood Cliffs, NJ: Prentice-Hall.

Holland, A. J. (1998). Down's syndrome. In M. P. Janicki & A. J. Dalton (Eds.), *Dementia, aging, and intellectual disabilities: A handbook* (pp. 183–197). Castelton, NY: Hamilton.

Holt, M.K., & Dellmann-Jenkins, M. (1992). Research and implication for practice: Religion, well-being/morale, and coping behavior in later life. *Journal of Applied Gerontology, 11,* 101–110.

Horacek, B. J. (1995). A heuristic model of grieving after high-grief deaths. *Death Studies, 19,* 21–31.

Hornblower, M., Holmes, S., & Riley, M. (1988, Jan. 4). Gray power! AARP emerges as the nation's most powerful special-interest lobby. *Time, 131*(1), 36–37.

Horswill, R. K. (1993). Are typical senior center group activities better suited for women than for men? *Journal for Specialists in Group Work, 18*(1), 45–48.

How groups of voters divide. (1992, October 31). *New York Times,* p. 21.

Howard, R., Castle, D., O'Brien, J., Almeida, O., et al. (1992). Permeable walls, floors, ceilings and doors: Partition delusions in late paraphrenia. *International Journal of Geriatric Psychiatry, 7,* 719–724.

Howie, L. (1993). Old women and widowhood: A dying status passage. *Omega, 26,* 223–233.

Howland, J., Peterson, E. W., Levin, W. C., Fried, L., et al. (1993). Fear of falling among the community-dwelling elderly. *Journal of Aging and Health, 5,* 229–243.

Hoyert, D. L., Kochanek, K. D., & Murray, S. L. (1999, June 30). Deaths: Final data for 1999. *National Vital Statistics Reports.* Hyattsville, MD: National Center for Health Statistics, Center for Disease Control and Prevention.

Huber, R., & Evans, V. C. (1998). Trust in physicians to honor death related instructions. *Omega, 36,* 9–21.

Hudson, R.B., & Strate, J. (1985). Aging and political systems. In R. H. Binstock & E. Shanas (Eds.), *Handbook of aging and the social sciences,* (2nd ed., pp. 554–585). New York: Van Nostrand Reinhold.

Hughes, S. L., Edelman, P. L., Singer, R. H., & Chang, R. W. (1993). Joint impairment and self-reported disability in elderly persons. *Journal of Gerontology: Social Sciences, 48,* S84–S92.

Hultsch, D. F., Hertzog, C., Small, B. J., McDonald-Miszczak, L., & Dixon, R. (1992). Short-term change in cognitive performance in later life. *Psychology and Aging, 7,* 571–584.

Hwalek, M. A., Neale, A. V., Goodrich, C. S., & Quinn, K. (1996). The association of elder abuse and substance abuse in the Illinois Elder Abuse System. *The Gerontologist, 36,* 694–700.

Idler, E. L., & George, L. K. (1998). What sociology can help us understand about religion and mental health. In H. Koenig (Ed.), *Handbook of religion and mental health* (pp. 52–64). San Diego, CA: Academic Press.

Idler, E. L., & Kasl, S. V. (1991). Health perceptions and survival: Do global evaluations of health status really predict mortality? *Journal of Gerontology: Social Sciences, 46,* S55–S65.

Idler, E. L., & Kasl, S. V. (1992). Religion, disability, depression, and the timing of death. *American Journal of Sociology, 97,* 1052–1079.

Ikels, L. (1980). The coming of age in Chinese society. In C. L. Fry (Ed.), *Aging in culture and society.* New York: J. F. Bergin.

Iris, M. A. (1988). Guardianship and the elderly: A multi-perspective view of the decision-making process. *The Gerontologist, 28,* 39–45.

Jackson, J. J. (1985). Race, national origin, ethnicity, and aging. In R. H. Binstock & E. Shanas (Eds.), *Handbook of aging and the social sciences* (pp. 264–303). New York: Van Nostrand Reinhold.

Jagger, C., Priers, N. A., & Clarke, M. (1993). Factors associated with decline in function, institutionalization, and mortality of elderly people. *Age and Aging, 22,* 190–197.

Janson, P., & Ryder, L. K. (1983). Crime and the elderly: The relationship between risk and fear. *The Gerontologist, 23,* 207–212.

Johansson, B., Zarit, S. H., & Berg, S. (1992). Changes in cognitive functioning of the oldest old. *Journal of Gerontology: Psychological Sciences, 47,* P75–P80.

Johnson, C. B., & Slaninka, S. C. (1999). Barriers to accessing hospice services before a late terminal stage. *Death Studies, 23,* 225–238.

Johnson, C. L., & Troll, L. (1992). Family functioning in late late life. *Journal of Gerontology: Social Sciences, 47,* S66–S72.

Kaasalainen, S., Middleton, J., Knezacek, S., Hartley, T., Stewart, N., Ife, C., & Robinson, L. (1998). Pain and cognitive status among the institutionalized elderly. *Journal of Gerontological Nursing, 24*(3), 24–29.

Kane, R. A. (1995). Expanding the home care concept: Blurring distinctions among home care, institutional care, and other long-term care services. *The Milbank Quarterly, 73,* 161–186.

Kaper, J. D., & Riley, G. (1992). Satisfaction with medical care among elderly people in fee-for-service care and an HMO. *Journal of Aging & Health, 4,* 282–302.

Kaplan, G. A., Strawbridge, W. J., Camacho, T., & Cohen, R. D. (1993). Factors associated with change in physical functioning in the elderly: A six-year prospective study. *Journal of Aging & Health, 5,* 140–153.

Karlin, N. J., & Bell, P. A. (1992). Self-efficacy, affect, and seeking support between caregivers of dementia and non-dementia patients. *Journal of Women & Aging, 4*(3), 59–77.

Kart, C. S. (1990). The realities of aging. Boston: Allyn and Bacon.

Kastenbaum, R. (1991). Racism and the older voter? Arizona's rejection of a paid holiday to honor Martin Luther King. *International Journal of Aging & Human Development, 32,* 199–209.

Kastenbaum, R. S., & Candy, S. (1973). The four percent fallacy: A methodological and empirical critique of extended care facility program statistics. *International Journal of Aging & Human Development, 4,* 15–21.

Katon, W. (1992). Epidemiology of depression in primary care. *General Hospital Psychiatry, 14,* 237–247.

Katz, P. R., & Seidel, G. (1990). Nursing home autopsies: Survey of physician attitudes and practice patterns. *Archives of Pathology and Laboratory Medicine, 114,* 145–147.

Katzman, R. (1993). Education and the prevalence of dementia and Alzheimer's disease. *Neurology, 43,* 13–20.

Kaufman, S. R. (1986). *The ageless self: Sources of meaning in late life.* Madison, WI: University of Wisconsin Press.

Kaufman, S. R. (1998). Intensive care, old age, and the problem of death in America. *The Gerontologist, 38,* 715–725.

Kavesh, W. (1996–1997). The practice of geriatric medicine: How geriatricians think. *Generations, 20*(4), 54–59.

Kehoe, M. (1986). Lesbians over 65: A triply invisible minority. *Journal of Homosexuality, 12,* 139–152.

Kelly, J. (1977). The aging male homosexual. *The Gerontologist, 17,* 328–332.

Kempen, G. I. J. M., van Sonderen, E., & Ormel, J. (1999). The impact of psychological attributes on changes in disability among low-functioning older persons. *Journal of Gerontology: Psychological Sciences, 54B,* P23–P29.

Kemper, P., & Murtaugh, C. M. (1991). Lifetime use of nursing home care. *New England Journal of Medicine, 324,* 595–600.

Kemper, P., Spillman, B. C., & Murtaugh, C. M. (1991). A lifetime perspective on proposals for financing nursing home care. *Inquiry, 28,* 333–344.

Kendig, H. L., Coles, R., Pittelkow, Y., & Wilson, S. (1988). Confidants and family structure in old age. *Journal of Gerontology: Social Sciences, 43,* S31–S40.

Kermis, M. D. (1986). *Mental health in late life.* Monterey, CA: Jones and Bartlett.

Kilata, G. (1996, February 27). New era of robust elderly belies the fears of scientists. *New York Times,* p. B1.

Kim, P. H. (1990). Asian-American families and the elderly. In M. S. Harper (Ed.), *Minority aging* (DHHS Publication No. HRS P-DV-90-4, pp. 349–363). Washington, DC: U. S. Government Printing Office.

Kirwin, P. M., & Kaye, L. W. (1991). Service consumption patterns over time among adult day care program participants. *Home Health Care Services Quarterly, 12*(4), 45–58.

Kish, G. R., & Moody, D. R. (1990). Psychopathology and life purpose. *International Journal for Logotherapy, 12,* 40–45.

Kitano, H. H. L. (1990). Values, beliefs, and practices of the Asian-American elderly: Implications for geriatric education. In M. S. Harper (Ed.), *Minority aging* (DHHS Publication No. HRS P-DV-90-4, pp. 341–348). Washington, DC: U. S. Government Printing Office.

Koenig, H. G. (1998). *Handbook of religion and mental health.* San Diego: Academic Press.

Koenig, H. G., George, L. K., Blazer, D. G., Pritchett, J. T., et al. (1993). The relationship between religion and anxiety in a sample of community-dwelling older adults. *Journal of Geriatric Psychiatry, 26,* 65–93.

Koff, T. H., & Park, R. W. (1993). *Aging public policy: Bonding the generations.* Amityville, NY: Baywood.

Kosberg, J. I. (Ed.). (1983). *Abuse and maltreatment of the elderly: Causes and interventions.* Boston: John Right.

Kosberg, J. I. (1988). Preventing elder abuse: Identification of high risk factors prior to placement decisions. *The Gerontologist, 28,* 43–50.

Kosloski, K., & Montgomery, R. J. V. (1994). Investigating patterns of service use by families providing care for dependent elders. *Journal of Aging and Health, 6,* 17–37.

Kramer, B., Gibson, J., & Teri, L. (1992). Interpersonal family stress in Alzheimer's disease: Perceptions of patients and caregivers. *Clinical Gerontologist, 12,* 57–75.

Kramer, B. J. (1991). Urban American Indian aging. *Journal of Cross-Cultural Gerontology, 6,* 205–217.

Kranczer, S. (1998, October–December). Banner year for U.S. longevity. *MetLife Statistical Bulletin, 79*(4), 8–14.

Krout, J. A. (1983a). Knowledge and use of services by the elderly: A critical review of the literature. *International Journal of Aging & Human Development, 17,* 153–167.

Krout, J. A. (1983b). Seasonal migration of the elderly. *The Gerontologist, 23,* 295–299.

Krout, J. A. (1991). Senior center participation: Findings from a multidimensional analysis. *Journal of Applied Gerontology, 10,* 244–257.

Kubler-Ross, E. (1969). *On death and dying.* New York: Macmillan.

Kuhn, D. R. (1998). Is home care always the best care? *Generations, 22*(3), 99–101.

Kunik, M. E., Mulsant, B. H., Rifai, A. H., Sweet, R., et al. (1993). Personality disorders in elderly inpatients with major depression. *American Journal of Geriatric Psychiatry, 1*(1), 38–45.

Kuo, J., & Porter, K. (1998, August 7). Health status of Asian-Americans. *Advance data from vital and health statistics* (No. 298). Hyattsville, MD: National Center for Health Statistics.

Lachs, M. S., Williams, C., O'Brien, S., Hurst, L., & Horowitz, R. (1997). Risk factors for reported elder abuse and neglect: A nine-year observational cohort study. *The Gerontologist, 37,* 469–474.

LaCroix, A. Z., Guralnik, J. M., Berkman, L. F., Wallace, R. B., & Satterfield, S. (1993). Maintaining mobility in late life: II. Smoking, alcohol consumption, physical activity, and body mass index. *American Journal of Epidemiology, 137,* 858–869.

Laitman, L. B., & Davis, K. L. (1994). Paraphrenia and other psychoses. In W. R. Hazzard (Ed.), *Principles of geriatric medicine and gerontology* (3rd ed., pp. 1111–1117). New York: McGraw-Hill.

Lakin, K. C., Hill, B. K., White, C. C., Wright, E. D., & Bruininks, R. H. (1989). Longitudinal patterns in ICF-MR utilization, 1977–1986. *Mental Retardation, 27,* 149–158.

Landreville, P., & Vezina, J. (1992). A comparison between daily hassles and major life events as correlates of well-being in older adults. *Canadian Journal on Aging, 11,* 137–149.

Lanksa, D. J. (1993). Decline in autopsies for deaths attributed to cerebrovascular disease. *Stroke, 24,* 71–75.

Lawton, M. P. (1990). Knowledge resources and gaps in housing for the aged. In D. Tilson (Ed.), *Aging in place: Supporting the frail elderly in residential environments.* Glenview, IL: Scott, Foresman.

Lawton, M.P., Moss, M., & Glicksman, A. (1990). The quality of the last year of life of older persons. *Milbank Quarterly, 68,* 1–28.

Lawton, M. P., & Yaffe, S. (1980). Victimization and fear of crime in elderly public housing tenants. *Journal of Gerontology, 35,* 768–779.

Leaf, A. (1975). *Youth in old age*. New York: McGraw-Hill.

Lefcourt, H. M. (1992). Durability and impact of the locus of control construct. *Psychological Bulletin, 112,* 411–414.

Lemke, S., & Moos, R.H. (1986). Quality of residential settings for elderly adults. *Journal of Gerontology, 41,* 268–276.

Lemke, S., & Moos, R. H. (1989). Ownership and quality of care in residential facilities for the elderly. *The Gerontologist, 29,* 209–215.

Lemon, B. W., Bengtson, V. L., & Peterson, J. A. (1972). An exploration of the activity theory of aging: Activity types and life satisfaction among in-movers to a retirement community. *Journal of Gerontology, 27,* 511–523.

Lesy, M. (1973). *Wisconsin death trip*. New York: Pantheon.

Levin, J. A., & Chatters, L. (1998). Research on religion and mental health. In H. Koenig (Ed.), *Handbook of religion and mental health* (pp. 65–75). San Diego, CA: Academic Press.

Levin, J. S., Markides, K. S., & Ray, L. A. (1996). Religious attendance and psychological well-being in Mexican Americans: A panel analysis of three-generations data. *The Gerontologist, 36,* 454–463.

Levin, J. S., Taylor, R. J., & Chatters, L. M. (1994). Race and gender differences in religiosity among older adults: Findings from four national surveys. *Journal of Gerontology: Social Sciences, 49,* S137–S145.

Lewis, M. A., Cretin, S., & Kane, R. L. (1985). The natural history of nursing home patients. *The Gerontologist, 25,* 382–388.

Lewis, M. L. (1993, July). Helping patients cope with change. *Nursing '93, 14,* 75.

The Lighthouse Center for Vision and Aging. (1998). *Aging and Vision News, 10*(1), 2.

Lindberg, G. L., Lurie, N., Bannick-Mohrland, S., Sherman, R. E., et al. (1989). Health care cost containment measures and mortality in Hennepin County's Medicaid elderly and all elderly. *American Journal of Public Health, 79,* 1481–1485.

Linn, M. W., Hunter, K. I., & Perry, P. R. (1979). Differences by sex and ethnicity in the psychosocial adjustment of the elderly. *Journal of Health and Social Behavior, 20,* 273–281.

Linsk, N. L., Keigher, S. M., & Osterbusch, S. E. (1988). States' policies regarding paid caregiving. *The Gerontologist, 28,* 204–212.

Litwak, E., & Longino, C. F. (1987). Migration patterns among the elderly: A developmental perspective. *The Gerontologist, 27,* 266–272.

Liu, K., & Manton, K. (1991). Nursing home length of stay and send down in Connecticut, 1977-1986. *The Gerontologist, 31,* 165–173.

Ljungquist, B., Berg, S., Lanke, J., McClearn, G. E., & Pedersen, N. L. (1998). The effect of genetic factors for longevity: A comparison of identical and fraternal twins in the Swedish Twin Registry. *Journal of Gerontology: Medical Sciences, 53A,* M441–M446.

Lo, B. (1995, November 22/29). Improving care near the end of life: Why is it so hard? *Journal of the American Medical Association, 274*(20), 1634–1636.

Loescher, L. (1995). The dynamics of skin aging. *Progressions: Developments in Ostomy, Wound, and Continence Management, 7*(2), 11.

Longino, C. F. (1995). *Retirement migration in America*. Houston: Vacation Publications.

Longino, C. F., & Serow, W. J. (1992). Regional differences in the characteristics of elderly return migrants. *Journal of Gerontology: Social Sciences, 47,* S38–S43.

Lopata, H. Z. (1988). Support systems of American urban widowhood. *The Journal of Social Issues, 44,* 113–128.

Lopata, H. Z., & Brehm, H. P. (1986). *Widows and dependent wives: From social problem to federal program.* New York: Prager.

Lord, S. R., Clark, R. D., & Webster, I. W. (1991). Physiological factors associated with falls in an elderly population. *Journal of the American Geriatrics Society, 39,* 1194–1200.

Lord, T. R., & Garner, J. E. (1993). Effects of music on Alzheimer patients. *Perceptual and Motor Skills, 76,* 451–455.

Lowenthal, M. F. (1964). Social isolation and mental illness in old age. *American Sociological Review, 29,* 54–70.

Lowenthal, M. F., & Haven, C. (1968). Interaction and adaptation: Intimacy as a critical variable. *American Sociological Review, 33,* 93–110.

Lubomudrov, S. (1987). Congressional perceptions of the elderly: The use of stereotypes in the legislative process. *The Gerontologist, 27,* 77–81.

Luchins, A. S. (1988). The rise and decline of the American asylum movement in the 19th century. *The Journal of Psychology, 122,* 471–486.

Luchins, A. S. (1989). Moral treatment in asylums and general hospitals in 19th-century America. *The Journal of Psychology, 123,* 585–607.

Lund, D. A., Caserta, M. S., & Dimond, M. F. (1986). Gender differences through two years of bereavement among the elderly. *The Gerontologist, 26,* 314–320.

Lynott, R. J., & Lynott, P. P. (1996). Tracing the course of theoretical development in the sociology of aging. *The Gerontologist, 36,* 749–760.

Maddox, G. L. (1964). Disengagement theory: A critical evaluation. *The Gerontologist, 4,* 80–82.

Maier, H., & Smith, J. (1999). Psychological predictors of mortality in old age. *Journal of Gerontology: Psychological Sciences, 54B,* P44–P54.

Making sense of Social Security. (1992). New York: Teachers Insurance and Annuity Association College Retirement Equities Fund.

Malone, D. M. (1990). Aging persons with mental retardation: Identification of the needs of a special population. *Gerontology Review, 3*(1), 1–14.

MaloneBeach, E. E., Zarit, S. H., & Spore, D. L. (1992). Caregivers' perceptions of case management and community-based services: Barriers to service use. *Journal of Applied Gerontology, 11,* 146–159.

Man charged in killing of his mother, 98. (1999, March 7). *Omaha World-Herald,* p. 16.

Man left at racetrack dies in Kentucky. (1992, November 10). *Omaha World-Herald,* p. 28.

Manton, K. G., Stallard, E., & Corder, L. (1995). Changes in morbidity and chronic disability in the U. S. elderly population: Evidence from the 1982, 1984, and 1989 National Long Term Care surveys. *Journal of Gerontology: Social Sciences, 50B,* S194–S204.

Markides, K. S. (1987). The changing economy and the future of minority aged. *The Gerontologist, 27,* 273–274.

Marshall, J. A., Hamman, R. F., Baxter, J., Mayer, E. J., Fulton, D. L., Orleans, M. (1993). Ethnic differences in risk factors associated with the prevalence of non-insulin-dependent diabetes mellitus. *American Journal of Epidemiology, 137,* 706–718.

Martikainen, P., & Valkonen, T. (1996). Mortality after the death of a spouse: Rates and causes of death in a large Finnish cohort. *American Journal of Public Health, 86,* 1087–1093.

Masoro, E. J. (1988). Minireview: Food restriction in rodents: An evaluation of its role in the study of aging. *Journal of Gerontology: Biological Sciences, 43*, B59–B64.

Masoro, E. J., Katz, M. S., & McMahan, C. A. (1989). Evidence for the glaciation hypothesis of aging from the food-restricted model. *Journal of Gerontology: Biological Sciences, 44*, B20–B22.

Masters, C. L., & Beyreuther, K. (1998). Science, medicine, and the future: Alzheimer's disease. *British Medical Journal, 316*, 446–448.

Matthews, S. H. (1995). Gender and the division of filial responsibility between lone sisters and their brothers. *Journal of Gerontology: Social Sciences, 50B*, S312–S320.

Mazess, R. B., & Forman, S. H. (1979). Longevity and age exaggeration in Vilcabamba, Ecuador. *Journal of Gerontology, 34*, 94–98.

McCarthy, M. J. (1992, December 3). Older people will do anything to avoid life in nursing home. *Wall Street Journal*, A1–A4.

McCay, C., Crowell, M., & Maynard, L. (1935). The effect of retarded growth upon the length of life and upon ultimate size. *Journal of Nutrition, 10*, 63–79.

McClain, J. W., Leibowitz, J. M., Plumer, S. B., & Lunt, K. S. (1993). The senior center as a community focal point. In C. N. Bull (Ed.), *Aging in rural America* (pp. 59–70). Newbury Park, CA: Sage.

McClusky, H. (1976). Education for aging: The scope of the field and perspectives for the future. In S. Grabowski & W. D. Mason (Eds.), *Learning for aging*. Washington, DC: Adult Education Association of the USA.

McCoy, H. V., Kipp, C. W., & Aheern, M. (1992). Reducing older patients' reliance on the emergency department. *Social Work in Health Care, 17*, 23–37.

McCrea, J. M., & Smith, T. B. (1997). Program profiles. In S. Newman (Ed.), *Intergenerational programs* (pp. 95–114). Philadelphia: Taylor & Francis.

McCrae, R. R., & Costa, P. T. (1984). Aging, the life course, and models of personality. In N. Shock (Ed.), *Normal human aging: The Baltimore Longitudinal Study of Aging* (pp. 292–310). Washington, DC: U.S. Government Printing Office.

McFall, S., & Miller, B. H. (1992). Caregiver burden and nursing home admission of frail elderly persons. *Journal of Gerontology: Social Sciences, 47*, S73–S79.

McIntosh, J. L. (1992). Epidemiology of suicide in the elderly. *Suicide & Life Threatening Behavior, 22*, 15–35.

McLaughlin, D. K., & Jensen, L. (1993). Poverty among older Americans: The plight of nonmetropolitan elders. *Journal of Gerontology: Social Sciences, 48*, S44–S54.

McShane, T. M., Wilson, M. F., & Wise, P. M. (1999). Effects of lifelong moderate restriction. *Journal of Gerontology: Biological Sciences, 54A*, B14–B21.

Medvedev, Z. A. (1974). Caucasus and Altay longevity: A biological or social problem? *The Gerontologist, 14*, 381–387.

Meek, S. S. (1993). Effects of slow stroke back massage on relaxation in hospice clients. *Image: Journal of Nursing Scholarship, 25*, 17–21.

Menec, V. H., Chipperfield, J. G., & Perry, R. P. (1999). Self-perceptions of health: A prospective analysis of mortality, control, and health. *Journal of Gerontology: Psychological Sciences, 54B*, P85–P93.

Metropolitan Life Insurance Company. (1988, April–June). *Statistical Bulletin, 69*(2). Baltimore, MD: Metropolitan Life Insurance Co.

Metropolitan Life Insurance Company. (1990, January–March). *Statistical Bulletin, 71*(1), 1–4. Baltimore, MD: Metropolitan Life Insurance Co.

Metropolitan Life Insurance Company. (1993, April–June). *Statistical Bulletin, 74*(2), 18. Baltimore, MD: Metropolitan Life Insurance Company.

Metropolitan Life Insurance Company. (1996, July–September). *Statistical Bulletin,* p. 18. Baltimore, MD: Metropolitan Life Insurance Company.

Metropolitan Life Insurance Company. (1997, July–September). *Statistical Bulletin, 78*(3), 6–9. Baltimore: Metropolitan Life Insurance Company.

Metropolitan Life Insurance Company. (1998, April–June). *Statistical Bulletin, 79*(2), 4; 10–15. Baltimore: Metropolitan Life Insurance Company.

Metropolitan Life Insurance Company. (1998, October–December). *Statistical Bulletin, 79*(4), 8–14. Baltimore: Metropolitan Life Insurance Company.

Meyer, J., & Speare, A. (1985). Distinctively elderly mobility: Types and determinants. *Economic Geography, 61,* 79–88.

Mikhail, M. L. (1992). Psychological responses to relocation to a nursing home. *Journal of Gerontological Nursing, 18,* 35–39.

Miles, S. H., & Irvine, P. (1992). Deaths caused by physical restraints. *The Gerontologist, 32,* 762–766.

Miller, B. L., Lesser, I. M., Boone, K. B., Hill, E., et al. (1991). Brain lesions and cognitive function in late-life psychosis. *British Journal of Psychiatry, 158,* 76–82.

Miller, M. (1978). Geriatric suicide: The Arizona study. *The Gerontologist, 18,* 488–495.

Miller, M. B., & Schumacher, F. J. (2000). The aged, the Judeo-Christian ethic, and misuse of illness for dependency needs. In J. A. Thorson (Ed.), *Perspectives on spiritual well-being and aging* (pp. 170–180). Springfield, IL: Charles C Thomas.

Minkler, M., & Robertson, A. (1991). The ideology of "age/race wars": Deconstructing a social problem. *Ageing and Society, 11,* 1–22.

Minkler, M., & Roe, K. M. (1996). Grandparents as surrogate parents. *Generations, 20*(1), 34–38.

Mishra, S. (1992). Leisure activities and life satisfaction in old age. *Activities, Adaptation, & Aging, 16,* 7–26.

Missinne, L. E. (1980). Aging in a Bakongo culture. *International Journal of Aging & Human Development, 11,* 283–295.

Mitchell, C. (1992, September). Gang of three. *The Washington Monthly, 24*(9), A10–A11.

Mittelman, M. S., Ferris, S. H., Steinberg, G., Shulman, E., et al. (1993). An intervention that delays institutionalization of Alzheimer's disease patients: Treatment of spouse-caregivers. *The Gerontologist, 33,* 730–740.

Molgaard, C., Poikolainen, K., Elder, J. P., Nissinen, A., et al. (1991). Depression late after combat: A follow-up of Finnish World War Two veterans from the seven countries East-West Cohort. *Military Medicine, 156,* 219–222.

Molinari, V. A. (1991). Mental health issues in the elderly. *Physical and Occupational Therapy in Geriatrics, 9*(3–4), 23–30.

Montgomery, R. J. V., & Kosloski, K. (1994). A longitudinal analysis of nursing home placement for dependent elders cared for by spouses vs. adult children. *Journal of Gerontology: Social Sciences, 49,* S62–S74.

Morrison, B. J., & Gresson, A. D. (1990). Curriculum content pertaining to the black elderly for selected health care professionals. In M. S. Harper (Ed.), *Minority aging* (DDHS Publication No. HRS P-DV-90-4, pp. 223–268). Washington, DC: U.S. Government Printing Office.

Morrow-Howell, N. (1992). Clinical case management: The hallmark of gerontological social work. *Journal of Gerontological Social Work, 18,* 119–131.

Mosher-Ashley, P. M., & Allard, J. J. (1993). Problems facing chronically mentally ill elders receiving community-based psychiatric services: Need for residential services. *Adult Residential Care Journal, 7*(1), 23–30.

Mosher-Ashley, P. M., Turner, B. F., & O'Neill, D. (1991). Attitudes of nursing and rest home administrators toward deinstitutionalized elders with psychiatric disorders. *Community Mental Health Journal, 27,* 241–253.

Moss, M. S., Lawton, M. P., & Glicksman, A. (1991). The role of pain in the last year of life of older persons. *Journal of Gerontology: Psychological Sciences, 46,* P51–P57.

Muram, D. (1992). Sexual assault of the elderly victim. *Journal of Interpersonal Violence, 7,* 70–76.

Murray, A. M., Levkoff, S. E., Wetle, T. T., Beckett, L., et al. (1993). Acute delirium and functional decline in the hospitalized elderly patient. *Journal of Gerontology: Medical Sciences, 48,* M181–M186.

Murray, H. A. (1938). *Explorations in personality.* New York: Oxford University Press.

Murray, J. (1992). Prevention and the identification of high risk groups. *International Review of Psychiatry, 4,* 281–286.

Mutchler, J. E., & Burr, J. A. (1991). Racial differences in health & health care service utilization in later life: The effect of socioeconomic status. *Journal of Health and Social Behavior, 32,* 342–356.

Nambudiri, D. E., & Young, R. C. (1991). A case of late-onset crack dependence and subsequent psychosis in the elderly. *Journal of Substance Abuse Treatment, 8,* 253–255.

National Center for Health Statistics. (1991). *Vital and Health Statistics, 10*(179), 32–33.

National Center for Health Statistics. (1998, October 7). *National Vital Statistics Report, 47*(4).

National Center for Health Statistics. (1998, November 10). *National Vital Statistics Report, 47*(9), 74.

National Institutes of Health. (1987, July 6–8). Differential diagnosis of dementing diseases. *Consensus Development Conference Statement, 6*(11), 2.

Netting, F. E., Paton, R. N., & Huber, R. (1992). The long-term care ombudsman program: What does the complaint reporting system tell us? *The Gerontologist, 32,* 843–848.

Neugarten, B. L. (1973). Personality change in late life: A developmental perspective. In C. Eisdorfer & M. M. P. Lawton (Eds.), *The psychology of adult development and aging* (pp. 311–335). Washington, DC: American Psychological Association.

Neugarten, B. L., Havighurst, R. J., & Tobin, S. S. (1961). The measurement of life satisfaction. *Journal of Gerontology, 16,* 134–143.

Neugarten, B. L., Havighurst, R. J., & Tobin, S. S. (1968). Personality and patterns of aging. In B. L. Neugarten (Ed.), *Middle age and aging.* Chicago: University of Chicago Press.

Newman, S., & Ward, C. (1993). An observational study of intergenerational activities and behavior change in dementing elders at adult day care centers. *International Journal of Aging & Human Development, 36,* 321–333.

Nicholson, N., & Goodge, P. (1976). The influence of social, organizational, and biographical factors on female absence. *Journal of Management Studies, 13,* 234–354.

Novack, J. (1991, November 25). Strength from its gray roots: American Association of Retired Persons pushes for higher government spending and higher taxes. *Forbes, 148,* 89–90.

Offen, C. (1972, December). Profile of a gray panther. *Retirement Living, 32*–37.

Older Americans Report (1998, April 24). Kaiser Commission report shows state-by-state medicaid statistics, 22(17), 142.

O'Loughlin, J. L., Robitalle, Y., Boivin, J-F., & Suissa, S. (1993). Incidence of and risk factors for falls and injurious falls among the community-dwelling elderly. *American Journal of Epidemiology, 137*, 342–354.

O'Toole, B. I., & Stankov, L. (1992). Ultimate validity of psychological tests. *Personality and Individual Differences, 13*, 699–716.

Palmore, E. (1975). *The honorable elders.* Durham, NC: Duke University Press.

Palmore, E., & Luikart, C. (1972, March). Health and social factors related to life satisfaction. *Journal of Health & Social Behavior, 13*, 68–80.

Palmore, E. B. (1982). Predictors of the longevity difference: A 25-year follow-up. *The Gerontologist, 22*, 513–518.

Palmore, E. B., Fillenbaum, G. G., & George, L. K. (1984). Consequences of retirement. *Journal of Gerontology, 39*, 109–116.

Palmore, E. B., & Manton, K. (1974). Modernization and status of the aged: International correlations. *Journal of Gerontology, 29*, 205–210.

Pamuk, E., Makuc, D., Heck, K., Reuben, C., & Lochner, K. (1998). *Health, United States, 1998.* Hyattsville, MD: National Center for Health Statistics.

Parker, M. G., Thorslund, M., & Nordstrom, M-L. (1992). Predictors of mortality for the oldest old: A 4-year follow-up of community-based elderly in Sweden. *Archives of Gerontology & Geriatrics, 14*, 227–237.

Parkinson, M. A. (1992). Maximizing personal efficacy in older adults: The empowerment of volunteers in a multipurpose senior center. *Physical & Occupational Therapy in Geriatrics, 10*(3), 57–72.

Parmelee, P. A. (1992a). Incidence of depression in long-term care settings. *Journal of Gerontology: Medical Sciences, 47*, M189–M196.

Parmelee, P. A. (1992b). Depression and mortality among institutionalized aged. *Journal of Gerontology: Psychological Sciences, 47*, P3–P10.

Passuth, P. M., & Bengtson, V. L. (1988). Sociological theories of aging: Current perspectives and future directions. In J. E. Birren & V. L. Bengtson (Eds.), *Emergent theories of aging* (pp. 333–355`). New York: Springer.

Patterson, O. (1982). *Slavery and social death: A comparative study.* Cambridge, MA: Harvard University Press.

Paveza, G. J., Cohen, D., Eisdorfer, C., Freels, S., Selma, T., Ashford, J. W., Gorelick, P. G., Hirschman, R., Luchins, D., & Levy, P. (1992). Severe family violence and Alzheimer's disease: Prevalence and risk factors. *The Gerontologist, 32*, 493–497.

Pechters, M. K., & Milligan, S. E. (1988). Access to health care in a black urban elderly population. *The Gerontologist, 28*, 213–217.

Pellman, J. (1992). Widowhood in elderly women: Exploring its relationship to community integration, hassles, stress, social support, and social support seeking. *International Journal of Aging & Human Development, 35*, 253–264.

Perlmutter, M., & Hall, E. (1985). *Adult development and aging.* New York: Wiley.

Peters, K. D., Kochanek, K. D., & Murphy, S. L. (1998, November 10). Deaths: Final data for 1996. *National vital statistics reports, 47*(9). Hyattsville, MD: National Center for Health Statistics.

Pillemer, K. A., & Finkelhor, D. (1988). The prevalence of elder abuse: A random sample survey. *The Gerontologist, 28*, 51–57.

Pillemer, K. A., & Moore, D. M. (1990). Highlights from a study of abuse of patients in nursing homes. *Journal of Elder Abuse and Neglect, 2*, 1–2, 5–29.

Pillemer, K. A., & Suitor, J. J. (1992). Violence and violent feelings: What causes them among family caregivers. *Journal of Gerontology: Social Sciences, 47*, S165–S172.

Pillemer, K. A., & Wolf, R. S. (Eds.). (1986). *Elder abuse: Conflict in the family.* Dover, MA: Auburn House.

Podgursky, M., & Swain, P. (1987). Job displacement and earnings loss: Evidence from the Displaced Worker Survey. *Industrial and Labor Relations Review, 41,* 17–29.

Poon, L. W., Messner, S. Martin, P., Noble, C. A., Clayton, G. M., & Johnson, M. A. (1992). The influences of cognitive resources on adaptation and old age. *International Journal of Aging and Human Development, 24,* 31–46.

Porterfield, J. D., & St. Pierre, R. (1992). *Healthful aging.* Guilford, CT: Dushkin Publishing Group.

Post, J. A. (1996). Internet resources on aging: Parts of the Internet. *The Gerontologist, 36,* 137–140.

Powell, F. C., & Thorson, J. A. (1990). Political behavior: Voting participation of inner-city elderly Blacks compared to other populations in a medium-sized city. *Psychological Reports, 67,* 64–66.

Powell, F. C., & Thorson, J. A. (1994). *Social conditions of Nebraska's elderly.* Omaha, NE: Department of Gerontology, University of Nebraska at Omaha.

Preston, S.H. (1984). Children and the elderly: Divergent paths for America's dependents. *Demography, 21,* 435–457.

Progress Report on Alzheimer's Disease. (1992). Washington, DC: U.S. Government Printing Offices.

Purohit, D. P., Davidson, M., Perl, D. P., Powchik, P., et al. (1993). Severe cognitive impairment in elderly schizophrenic patients: A clinicopathological study. *Biological Psychiatry, 33,* 255–260.

Puryear, D. A., Lovitt, R., & Miller, D. A. (1991). Characteristics of elderly persons seen in an urban psychiatric emergency room. *Hospital & Community Psychiatry, 42,* 802–807.

Quadagno, J. (1990). Generational equity and the politics of the welfare state. *International Journal of Health Services, 20,* 631–649.

Qualls, S.H. (1991). Resistance of older families to therapeutic intervention. *Clinical Gerontologist, 11,* 59–68.

Quam, J. K., & Whitford, G. S. (1992). Adaptation and age-related expectations of older gay and lesbian adults. *The Gerontologist, 32,* 367–374.

Raia, P.A. (1992). What are we trying to restore? A case for habilitation. *Generations, 16*(1), 37–39.

Rains, V. S., & Ditzler, T. F. (1993). Alcohol use disorders in cognitively impaired patients referred for geriatric assessment. *Journal of Addictive Diseases, 12,* 55–64.

Rajput, A. H., Rozdilksy, B., & Rajput, A. (1990). Alzheimer's disease and idiopathic Parkinson's disease coexistence. *Journal of Geriatric Psychiatry & Neurology, 6*(3), 170–176.

Rakowski, W., & Hickey, T. (1992). Mortality and the attribution of health problems to aging among older adults. *American Journal of Public Health, 82,* 1139–1141.

Ralston, P.A. (1991). Determinants of senior center attendance and participation. *Journal of Applied Gerontology, 10,* 258–273.

Rand, M. (1998, December). Criminal victimization 1997. *National Crime Victimization Survey,* p. 4. Washington, DC: Bureau of Justice Statistics.

Ranhoff, A. H., & Laake, K. (1993). The Barthel ADL Index: Scoring by the physician from patient interview is not reliable. *Age and Aging, 22,* 171–174.

Rapp, S. R., Parisi, S. A., & Wallace, C. E. (1991). Comorbid psychiatric disorders in elderly medical patients: A one-year prospective study. *Journal of the American Geriatrics Society, 39*, 124–131.

Raykov, T. (1995). Multivariate structural modeling of plasticity in fluid intelligence of aged adults. *Multivariate Behavioral Research, 30*, 255–287.

Raymondo, J. C. (1987). Who's on first? *American Demographics, 9*(11), 38–41.

Redjali, S. M., & Radick, J. R. (1988). ICF/General: An alternative for older ICF/MR residents with geriatric care needs. *Mental Retardation, 26*, 213–217.

Reifler, B. V., Henry, R. S., Sherrill, K. A., Asbury, C. H., et al. (1992, Fall). A national demonstration program on dementia day centers and respite services: An interim report. *Behavior, Health, & Aging, 2*(3), 199–206.

Reis, M., & Gold, D. P. (1993). Retirement, personality, and life satisfaction: A review and two models. *Journal of Applied Gerontology, 12*, 261–282.

Reisberg, B., Ferris, S. H., Leon, J. J., & Crook, T. (1982). The Global Deterioration Scale for the assessment of primary degenerative Dementia. *American Journal of Psychiatry, 139*, 1136–1139.

Remsen, M. F. (1993). The role of the nursing home social worker in terminal care. *Journal of Gerontological Social Work, 19*, 193–205.

Rhoads, E. C. (1984). Re-evaluation of the aging and modernization theory: The Samoan evidence. *The Gerontologist, 24*, 243–250.

Rhodes, E. R. (1990). Profile of American Indians and Alaska natives. In M. S. Harper (Ed.), *Minority aging* (DHHS Publication No. HRS P-DV-90-4, pp. 45–62). Washington, DC: U. S. Government Printing Office.

Rhodebeck, L. A. (1993). The politics of greed? Political preferences among the elderly. *The Journal of Politics, 55*, 342–346.

Rigdon, J. E. (1995, October 29). Older drivers pose growing risk on roads as their numbers rise. *The Wall Street Journal*, p. 1.

Ries, P. (1991). Educational differences in health status and health care. *Vital Health Stat 10*(179, p. 32). Hyattsville, MD: National Center for Health Statistics.

Ries, P., & Brown, S. (1991). Disability and health: Characteristics of persons by limitation of activity and assessed health status. *Advance data from vital and health statistics* (No. 197). Hyattsville, MD: National Center for Health Statistics.

Riley, M. W., Johnson, J., & Foner, A. (1972). *Aging and society: A sociology of age stratification*. New York: Russell Sage Foundation.

Rimer, S. (1998, March 23). Elderly ranks grow larger. *New York Times*, p. 67.

Roberto, K. A., & Scott, J. P. (1986). Equity considerations in the friendships of older adults. *Journal of Gerontology, 41*, 241–247.

Rohrer, J. (1992, June). Scudder's pampered seniors: Designing a family of mutual funds for the American Association of Retired Persons. *Institutional Investor, 26*, 115–119.

Rolvaag, O. E. (1971). *The third life of Per Smevik*. Minneapolis, MN: Dillon Press.

Romano, M. (1994, January). Home care. *Contemporary Long Term Care, 17*(1), 62–64.

Romanoski, A. J., Folstein, M. F., Nestadt, G., Chahal, R., et al. (1992). The epidemiology of psychiatrist-ascertained depression and DSM-III depressive disorders: Results from the Eastern Baltimore Mental Health Survey clinical reappraisal. *Psychological Medicine, 22*, 629–655.

Rose, A. M. (1965). The subculture of aging: A framework for research in social gerontology. In A. M. Rose & W. A. Peterson (Eds.), *Older people and their social world* (pp. 3–16). Philadelphia: Davis.

Rosenbloom, C. A., & Whittington, F. J. (1993). The effects of bereavement on eating behaviors and nutrient intakes in elderly widowed persons. *Journal of Gerontology: Social Sciences, 48,* S223–S229.

Rosow, I. (1974). *Socialization to old age.* Berkeley, CA: University of California Press.

Rowland, M. (1993, September 26). When working isn't worth it. *New York Times—Money,* 1–2.

Rozzini, R., Bianchetti, A., Franzoni, S., & Zanetti, O. (1991). Social, functional and health status influences on mortality: Consideration of a multidimensional inquiry in a large elderly population. *Journal of Cross-Cultural Gerontology, 6,* 83–90.

Ruhm, C. J. (1990). Career jobs, bridge employment, and retirement. In P. B. Doeringer (Ed.), *Bridges to retirement: Older workers in a changing labor market.* Ithaca, NY: ILR Press.

Ryan, E. B. (1992). Beliefs about memory changes across the adult life span. *Journal of Gerontology: Psychological Sciences, 47,* P41–P46.

Ryff, C. D., & Essex, M. J. (1992). The interpretation of life experience and well-being: The sample case of relocation. *Psychology & Aging, 7,* 507–517.

Sable, P. (1991). Attachment, loss of spouse, and grief in elderly adults. *Omega, 23,* 129–142.

Sager, M. A., Easterling, D. V., & Leventhal, E. A. (1988). An evaluation of increased mortality rates in Wisconsin nursing homes. *Journal of the American Geriatric Society, 36,* 739–746.

Sakauye, K. (1990). Differential diagnosis, medication, treatment, and outcomes: Asian-American elderly. In M. S. Harper (Ed.), *Minority aging* (DHHS Publication No. HRS P-DV-90-4, pp. 331–339). Washington, DC: U.S. Government Printing Office.

Sanders, A. J., & Long, L. (1987). New Sunbelt migration patterns. *American Demographics, 9*(1), 38–41.

Sands, L. P., & Meredith, W. (1992). Blood pressure and intellectual functioning in late midlife. *Journal of Gerontology: Psychological Sciences, 47,* P81–P84.

Sarode, V. R., Datta, B. N., Banerjee, A. K., Banerjee, C., et al. (1993). Autopsy findings and clinical diagnoses: A review of 1000 cases. *Human Pathology, 24,* 194–198.

Schaie, K. W., & Willis, S. L. (1993). Age difference patterns of psychometric intelligence in adulthood: Generalizability within and across ability domains. *Psychology and Aging, 8,* 44–55.

Scharlach, A. E. (1987). Role strain in mother-daughter relationships in later life. *The Gerontologist, 27,* 627–631.

Schulz, R., O'Brien, A. T., Bookwala, J., & Fleissner, K. (1995). Psychiatric and physical morbidity effects of dementia caregiving: Prevalence, correlates, and causes. *The Gerontologist, 35,* 771–791.

Schurenberg, E., & Luciano, L. (1988, October) The empire called AARP. *Money, 17*(10), 128–146.

Schwab, D., & Heneman, H. (1977). Effects of age and experience on productivity. *Industrial Gerontology, 4,* 113–117.

Seccombe, K., & Ishii-Kuntz, M. (1991). Perceptions of problems associated with aging: Comparisons among four older age cohorts. *The Gerontologist, 31,* 527–533.

Seeman, T. E., Kaplan, G. A., Knudsen, L., Cohen, R., & Guralnik, J. (1987). Social network ties and mortality among the elderly in the Alameda County study. *American Journal of Epidemiology, 126,* 714–723.

Selkoe, D. J. (1993). Amyloid protein and the mechanism of Alzheimer's disease. In D. J. Selkoe (Ed.), *A town forum on Alzheimer's disease* (pp. 11–13). Washington, DC: Institute for Advanced Studies in Immunology & Aging.

Seltzer, M. M. (1992). Training families to be case managers for elders with developmental disabilities. *Generations, 16*(1), 65–70.

Shah, A., Phongsathorn, V., George, C., Bielawska, C., et al. (1993). Does psychiatric morbidity predict mortality in continuing care geriatric inpatients? *International Journal of Geriatric Psychiatry, 8*, 255–259.

Shanas, E. (1979). The family as a social support system in old age. *The Gerontologist, 19*, 169–174.

Shanas, E., & Maddox, G. L. (1985). Health, health resources, and the utilization of care. In R. H. Binstock & E. Shanas (Eds.), *Handbook of aging and the social sciences* (pp. 697–726). New York: Van Nostrand Reinhold.

Shanas, E., Townsend, P., Wedderburn, D., Friis, H., Milhoj, P., & Stehouwer, J. (1968). *Old people in three industrial societies*. New York: Atherton.

Shapiro, J. P. (1992, January 13). The elderly are not children. *U.S. News & World Report*, pp. 26–28.

Shaughnessy, P. W. (1989, Winter). Quality of nursing home care. *Generations, 13*(1), 17–20.

Shellenbarger, S. (1994, February 16). The aging of America is making "elder care" a big workplace issue. *The Wall Street Journal*, p. 1.

Shenk, D. (1991). Older rural women as recipients and providers of social support. *Journal of Aging Studies, 5*, 347–358.

Shiferaw, B., Mittelmark, M. B., Wofford, J. L., Anderson, R. T., Walls, P., & Rohrer, B. (1994). The investigation and outcome of reported cases of elder abuse: The Forsyth County Aging Study. *The Gerontologist, 34*, 123–125.

Shock, N. (1976). The physiology of aging. In A.J. Vander (Ed.), *Human physiology and the environment in health and disease* (pp. 242–251). San Francisco: Freeman.

Shock, N. W. (1980). Current publications in gerontology and geriatrics. *The Journal of Gerontology, 35*, 961–986.

Shope, J. T., Holmes, S. B., Sharpe, P. A., Goodman, C., et al. (1993). Services for persons with dementia and their families: A survey of information and referral agencies in Michigan. *The Gerontologist, 33*, 529–533.

Siegler, I. C. (1980). The psychology of adult development and aging. In E. Busse & D. Blazer (Eds.), *Handbook of geriatric psychiatry* (pp. 169–211). New York: Van Nostrand Reinhold.

Silber, T. (1991, November). AARP inks $750 million printing deal. *Folio, 20*, 48.

Silverstein, M., & Angelelli, J. J. (1998). Older parents' expectations of moving closer to their children. *Journal of Gerontology: Social Sciences, 53B*, S153–S163.

Silverstone, B. M., & Horowitz, A. (1992). Aging in place: The role of families. *Generations, 16*(2), 27–30.

Simonsick, E. M. (1993). Relationship between husband's health status and the mental health of older women. *Journal of Aging and Health, 5*, 319–337.

Sinex, F. M. (1977). The molecular genetics of aging. In C. Finch & L. Hayflick (Eds.), *Handbook of the biology of aging* (pp. 37–62). New York: Van Nostrand Reinhold.

Singleton, J. R., & Keddy, B. A. (1991). Planning for retirement. *Activities, Adaptation & Aging, 16*, 49–55.

Skoog, I., Nilsson, L., Palmertz, B., Andreasson, L-A., et al. (1993). A population-based study of dementia in 85 year-olds. *New England Journal of Medicine, 328*(3), 153–158.

Smith, K. R., & Zick, C. D. (1996). Risk of mortality following widowhood: Age and sex differences by mode of death. *Social Biology, 43,* 59–71.

Smith, L. (1988, February 29). The world according to AARP. *Fortune, 117*(5), 96–98.

Smith, R. A. P., Woodward, N. J., Wallston, B. S., Wallston, K. A., et al. (1988). Health care implications of desire and expectancy for control in elderly adults. *Journal of Gerontology: Psychological Sciences, 43,* P1–P7.

Smyer, M. A. (1993, Winter). Aging and decision-making capacity. *Generations, 17*(1), 51–56.

Soloman, S. A., & Adams, K. H. R. (1993). Attitudes of relatives to autopsies of elderly patients. *Age and Aging, 22,* 205–208.

Sorenson, J. M., & Thorson, J. A. (1998). *Geriatric respiratory care.* Albany, NY: Delmar.

Speare, A., & Avery, R. (1993). Who helps whom in older parent-child families. *Journal of Gerontology: Social Sciences, 48,* S64–S73.

Spencer, D., & Steers, R. (1980). The influence of personal factors and perceived work experiences on employee turnover and absenteeism. *Academy of Management Journal, 23,* 567–572.

Spitze, G., Logan, J. R., Joseph, G., & Lee, E. (1994). Middle generation roles and the well-being of men and women. *Journal of Gerontology: Social Sciences, 49,* S107–S116.

Stansberry, R. (1988, January 17). A time of change. *Omaha World-Herald,* p. 34.

Starrett, R. A., Todd, A. M., & DeLeon, L. (1989). A comparison of the social service utilization behavior of the Cuban and Puerto Rican elderly. *Hispanic Journal of Behavioral Sciences, 11,* 341–353.

Stein, L. W., & Thienhaus, O. J. (1993). Hearing impairment and psychosis. *International Pschogeriatrics, 5,* 49–56.

Stein, S., Linn, M. W., & Stein, E. (1986). Patients' perceptions of nursing home stress related to quality of care. *The Gerontologist, 26,* 424–430.

Steinbach, U. (1992). Social networks, institutionalization, and mortality among elderly people in the United States. *Journal of Gerontology: Social Sciences, 47,* S183–S190.

Stephenson-Cino, P., Steiner, M., Krames, L., Ryan, E. B., et al. (1992). Depression in elderly persons and its correlates in family practice: A Canadian study. *Psychological Reports, 70,* 359–368.

Stinnett, N., & DeFrain, J. D. (1985). *Secrets of strong families.* Boston: Little, Brown.

Strahan, G. W. (1997, January 23). An overview of nursing homes and their current residents. *Advance data from vital and health statistics,* (No. 280). Hyattsville, MD; National Center for Health Statistics.

Strain, L. A. (1993). Good health: What does it mean in later life? *Journal of Aging and Health, 5,* 338–364.

Strate, J. M., Parrish, C. J., Elder, C. D., & Ford, C. (1989). Life span civic development and voting participation. *American Political Science Review, 83,* 443–464.

Suitor, J. J., & Pillemer, K. (1993). Support and interpersonal stress in the social networks of married daughters caring for parents with dementia. *Journal of Gerontology: Social Sciences, 48,* S1–S8.

Sundeen, R. A., & Mathieu, J. T. (1976). The fear of crime and its consequences among elderly in three urban communities. *The Gerontologist, 16,* 211–219.

SUPPORT Principal Investigators. (1995). A controlled trial to improve care for seriously ill hospitalized patients. *Journal of the American Medical Association, 274*(20), 1591–1598.

Sweeting, H. N., & Gilhooly, M. L. (1992). Doctor, am I dead? A review of social death in modern societies. *Omega, 24,* 251–269.

Swift, J. (1971). *Gulliver's travels.* London: Oxford University Press.

Szinovacz, M. E. (1998). Grandparents today: A demographic profile. *The Gerontologist, 38,* 37–52.

Takeida, K., Mishi, M., & Miyake, H. (1997). Mental depression and death in elderly persons. *Journal of Epidemiology, 7*(4), 210–213.

Tanjasiri, S. P., Wallace, S. P., & Shibata, K. (1995). Picture imperfect: Hidden problems among Asian Pacific Islander elderly. *The Gerontologist, 35,* 753–760.

Taylor, M. A. (1995). Benefits of dehydration in terminally ill patients. *Geriatric Nursing, 16*(6), 271–272.

Taylor, R. J. (1993). Religion and religious observances. In J. S. Jackson, L. M. Chatters, & R. J. Taylor (Eds.), *Aging in Black America* (pp. 101–123). Newbury Park, CA: Sage.

Taylor, R. J., & Chatters, L. M. (1986). Patterns of informal support to elderly black adults: Family, friends, and church members. *Social Work, 31,* 432–438.

Taylor, R. J., & Chatters, L. M. (1988). Correlates of education, income, and poverty among aged blacks. *The Gerontologist, 28,* 435–441.

Taylor, R. J., & Chatters, L. M. (1991). Non-organizational religious participation among elderly black adults. *Journal of Gerontology: Social Sciences, 46,* S103–S111.

Tellis-Nayak, V., & Tellis-Nayak, M. (1989). Quality of care and the burden of two cultures: When the world of the nurse's aide enters the world of the nursing home. *The Gerontologist, 29,* 307–313.

Tennstedt. S. L., Crawford, S., & McKinlay, J. B. (1993). Determining the pattern of community care: Is co-residence more important than caregiver relationship? *Journal of Gerontology: Social Sciences, 48,* S74–S83.

Teresi, J. A., Holmes, D., Bloom, H. G., Monaco, C., & Rosen, S. (1991). Factors differentiating hospital transfers from long-term care facilities with high and low transfer rates. *The Gerontologist, 31,* 795–806.

Thibaut, J. W., & Kelley, H. H. (1959). *The social psychology of groups.* New York: Wiley.

Thornburg, L. (1993, January). Day care for kids and elders is a natural. *HR Magazine,* 48–50.

Thorson, J. A. (1975). Attitudes toward the aged as a function of race and social class. *The Gerontologist, 15,* 343–344.

Thorson, J. A. (1981). An examination of personality and demographic factors on attitudes toward old people. *International Journal of Aging and Human Development, 12,* 187–195.

Thorson, J. A. (1984). The First Peoples' Social Welfare Institution for the Aged: A Chinese nursing home. *American Health Care Association Journal, 10*(3), 88–91.

Thorson, J. A. (1988). Relocation of the elderly: Some implications from the research. *Gerontology Review, 1,* 28–36.

Thorson, J. A. (1989a). She ain't heavy, she's my mother: On caring for older parents. *Adult Learning, 1*(3), 18–20.

Thorson, J. A. (1989b). *Tough guys don't dice.* New York: William Morrow & Co.

Thorson, J.A. (1990). The brave new world of educational gerontology. *Educational Gerontology, 16,* 327–337.

Thorson, J. A. (1998). Religion and anxiety: Which anxiety? Which religion? In H. G. Koenig (Ed.), *Handbook of religion and mental health* (pp. 147–160). San Diego, CA: Academic Press.

Thorson, J. A., & Cook, T. (1980). *Spiritual well-being of the elderly.* Springfield, IL: Charles C Thomas.

Thorson, J. A., & Horacek, B. J. (1986). Aging and long-term care in Nebraska. In V. Webb & J. Luke (Eds.), *Nebraska policy choices, Vol. 1.* (pp. 106–136). Omaha: University of Nebraska at Omaha Center on Applied Urban Research.

Thorson, J. A., & Horacek, B. J. (1987). Self-esteem, value, and identity: Who are the elderly, really. *Journal of Religion & Aging, 3,* 5–15.

Thorson, J. A., & Kasworm, C. E. (1985). Sunshine and suicide: Possible influences of climate on behavior. *Death Education, 8,* 125–136.

Thorson, J. A., & Perkins, M. (1981). An examination of personality and demographic factors on attitudes toward old people. *International Journal of Aging & Human Development, 12,* 187–195.

Thorson, J. A., & Powell, F. C. (1988). Elements of death anxiety and meanings of death. *Journal of Clinical Psychology, 44,* 691–701.

Thorson, J.A., & Powell, F.C. (1990). Meanings of death and intrinsic religiosity. *Journal of Clinical Psychology, 46,* 379–391.

Thorson, J. A., & Powell, F. C. (1991). Medical students' attitudes toward ageing and death: A cross-sequential study. *Medical Education, 25,* 32–37.

Thorson, J. A., & Powell, F. C. (1992a, April). *Health care perceptions of Nebraska's urban & rural aged.* Omah, NE: University of Nebraska at Omaha Center for Public Affairs Research.

Thorson, J. A., & Powell, F. C. (1992b). Rural and urban elderly construe health differently. *The Journal of Psychology, 126,* 251–260.

Thorson, J. A., & Powell, F. C. (1992c). *Report to the Eastern Nebraska Office on Aging: Aging persons with developmental disabilities.* Omaha, NE: Department of Gerontology, University of Nebraska at Omaha.

Thorson, J. A., & Powell, F. C. (1993a). Relationships of death anxiety and sense of humor. *Psychological Reports, 72,* 1364–1366.

Thorson, J. A., & Powell, F. C. (1993b). The rural aged, social value, and health care. In C. N. Bull (Ed.), *Aging in rural America.* Beverly Hills, CA: Sage.

Thorson, J. A., & Powell, F. C. (1994). A revised death anxiety scale. In R. A. Neimeyer (Ed.), *Death anxiety handbook* (pp. 31–43). Washington, DC: Taylor & Francis.

Thorson, J. A., & Powell, F. C. (1998). *Assessment and conditions study: Eastern Nebraska Office on Aging, 1998.* Omaha, NE: Department of Gerontology, University of Nebraska at Omaha.

Thorson, J. A., Powell, F. C., & Samuel, V. T. (1998a). African and Euro-American samples differ little in scores on death anxiety. *Psychological Reports, 83,* 623–626.

Thorson, J. A., Powell, F. C., & Samuel, V. T. (1998b). Age differences in death anxiety among African-American women. *Psychological Reports, 83,* 1173–1174.

Tough choices for American families: A Health/Gallup poll. (October, 1993). *Health,* 44–45.

Trinkle, D. (1992, Summer). Delusions and paranoia in the elderly. *Center on Aging, 8*(2), 5–6.

Turner, M. J. (1992, November 20). *Ethnic differences in the predictors of health care utilization among Mississippi elderly*. Paper presented at: the 45th Annual Scientific Meeting of the Gerontological Society of America, Washington, DC.

Uhlenberg, P. (1996). Mortality decline in the twentieth century and supply of kin over the life course. *The Gerontologist, 36,* 681–685.

Umberson, D., Wortman, C. B., & Kessler, R. C. (1992). Widowhood and depression: Explaining long-term gender differences in vulnerability. *Journal of Health & Social Behavior, 33,* 10–24.

Uncapher, H., Gallagher-Thompson, D., Osgood, N. J., & Bongar, B. (1998). Hopelessness and suicidal ideation in older adults. *The Gerontologist, 38,* 62–70.

Ungvari, G. S., & Hantz, P. M. (1991). Social breakdown in the elderly: I. Case studies and management. *Comprehensive Psychiatry, 32,* 440–444.

U.S. Bureau of the Census. (1997). *Statistical abstract of the United States: 1997* (117th ed.). Washington, DC: U.S. Government Printing Office.

U.S. Bureau of the Census. (1998a). *Population projections of the United States, 1998.* Washington, DC: U.S. Government Printing Office.

U.S. Bureau of the Census. (1998b). *Statistical abstract of the Unites States: 1998* (118th ed.). Washington, DC: U.S. Government Printing Office.

U.S. Bureau of the Census. (1998c). *Current population reports,* P20–463. P20–466. Washington, DC: U.S. Government Printing Office.

U.S. Bureau of the Census. (1999). *Current population reports,* P60–198. Washington, DC: U.S. Government Printing Office.

U.S. House of Representatives, Select Committee on Aging. (1992, August 6). *Insurmountable barriers: Lack of bilingual services at Social Security Offices.* Committee Publication No. 102–869, p. 21.

U.S. Senate Special Committee on Aging. (1985). *Health and extended worklife—An information paper* (p. 64). Washington, DC: U.S. Government Printing Office.

U.S. Social Security Administration. (1992). *Income of the Aged Chartbook, 1990.* SSA Publication No. 13-11727. Washington, DC: U. S. Government Printing Office.

Useem, M. (1993). The impact of American business restructuring on older workers. *Perspective on Aging, 22*(4), 12–14.

Vaillant, G. E. (1977). Adaptation to life. Boston: Little, Brown.

Vaillant, G. E., Bond, M., & Vaillant, C. O. (1986). An empirically validated hierarchy of defense mechanisms. *Archives of General Psychiatry, 43,* 786–794.

Vaillant, G. E., & Vaillant, C. O. (1990). Natural history of male psychological health, XII: A 45-year study of predictors of successful aging at age 65. *American Journal of Psychiatry, 147,* 31–37.

Van Atta, D. (1998). Trust betrayed: Inside the AARP. Washington, DC: Regnery.

van Dijk, P. T., Meulenberg, O. G. R. M., van de Sande, H. J., & Habbema, J. D. F. (1993). Falls in dementia patients. *The Gerontologist, 33,* 200–204.

Van Haitsma, K. (1986). Intrinsic religious orientation: Implications in the study of religiosity and personal adjustment in the aged. *Journal of Social Psychology, 126,* 685–687.

Van Hook, J., & Bean, F. D. (1999). The growth in noncitizen SSI caseloads 1979–1996: Aging versus new immigrant effects. *Journal of Gerontology: Social Sciences, 54B,* S16–S23.

Van Tilburg, T. (1992). Support networks before and after retirement. *Journal of Social & Personal Relationships, 9,* 433–445.

Ventura, S. J., Anderson, R. N., Martin, J. A., & Smith, B. L. (1998, October 7). Births and deaths: *Preliminary data for 1997. National vital statistics reports* (Vol 47, no. 4). Hyattsville, MD: National Center for Health Statistics.

Verdery, R. B. (1997). Failure to thrive in old age. *Journal of Gerontology: Medical Sciences, 52,* M333–M336.

Verhovek, S. H. (1999, February 18). Oregon reports 15 legal suicide in law's first year. *The New York Times Web Page.* http://www.nytimes.com

Versen, G. R. (1981). Native American elderly: Formal and informal support systems. *Journal of Sociology and Social Welfare, 8,* 513–528.

Vinton, L. (1992). Battered women's shelters and older women: The Florida experience. *Journal of Family Violence, 7*(1), 63–72.

Walford, R. (1982). Studies in immunogerontology. *Journal of the American Geriatrics Society, 30,* 617.

Wallace, S. P. (1990). Race versus class in the health care of African-American elderly. *Social Problems, 37,* 517–534.

Walz, T., Harper, D., & Wilson, J. (1986). The aging developmentally disabled person: A review. *The Gerontologist, 26,* 622–629.

Warshaw, G. (1997). Medicare HMOs pledge to train physicians in geriatric care. *Aging Research & Training News, 20*(14), 118.

Waterreus, A. (1992). Community psychiatric nursing in primary care. *International Review of Psychiatry, 4,* 317–322.

Webb, V. J., & Marshall, I. H. (1989). Response to criminal victimization by older Americans. *Criminal Justice and Behavior, 16,* 239–259.

Webster's ninth new collegiate dictionary. (1988). Springfield, MA: Merriam-Webster.

Weibel-Orlando, J. (1989). Elders and elderlies: Well-being in Indian old age. *American Indian Culture and Research Journal, 13,* 3–4, 149–170.

Weinberger, M., Gold, D. T., Divie, G. W., Cowper, P. A., et al. (1993). Expenditures in caring for patients with dementia who live at home. *American Journal of Public Health, 83,* 338–341.

Welin, L., Larsson, B., Svardsudd, K., & Tibblin, G. (1992). Social network and activities in relation to mortality from cardiovascular diseases, cancer, and other causes: A 12-year follow-up of the study of men born in 1913 and 1923. *Journal of Epidemiology & Community Health, 46,* 127–132.

Wendt, P. F., Peterson, D. A., & Douglass, E. B. (1993). *Core principles and outcomes of gerontology, geriatrics, and aging studies instruction.* Washington, DC: Association for Gerontology in Higher Education.

Wershow, H. J. (1976). The four percent fallacy: Some further evidence and policy implications. *The Gerontologist, 16,* 52–55.

Wershow, H.J. (1981). *Controversial issues in gerontology.* New York: Springer.

Whipple, B., & Scura, K. W. (1996). The overlooked epidemic: HIV in older adults. *American Journal of Nursing, 96*(2), 23–29.

Whittier, J. R., & Williams, D. (1956). The coincidence and constancy of mortality figures for aged psychotic patients admitted to state hospitals. *Journal of Nervous and Mental Diseases, 124,* 618–620.

Wiener, C. L., & Kayser-Jones, J. (1989). Defensive work in nursing homes: Accountability gone amok. *Social Science in Medicine, 28,* 37–44.

Wilber, K. H. (1990). Material abuse of the elderly: When is guardianship a solution? *Journal of Elder Abuse and Neglect, 2*(3–4), 89–104.

Wilcox, J. A., & Taber, M. A. (1991). Informal helpers of elderly home care clients. *Health & Social Work, 16,* 258–265.

Williams, B. C., Fries, B. E., & Mehr, D. R. (1993). Length of stay in VA nursing homes. *Journal of Aging and Health, 5,* 208–228.

Wilmoth, J. R., & Lundstrom, H. (1996). Extreme longevity in five countries: Presentation of trends with special attention to issues of data quality. *European Journal of Population, 12,* 63–93.

Wilmoth, J. R., Skytthe, A., Frious, D., & Jeune, B. (1996). The oldest man ever? A case study of exceptional longevity. *The Gerontologist, 36,* 783–788.

Wojciechowski, C. (1998). Issues in caring for older lesbians. *Journal of Gerontological Nursing, 24*(7), 28–33.

Wolf, R. S., & Li, D. (1999). Factors affecting the rate of elder abuse reporting to a state protective services program. *The Gerontologist, 39,* 212–228.

Wolfe, S. (1998, November). When is it time to die? *RN, 61*(11), 50–56.

Woman, 84, dies after being locked out of house. (1999, January 10). *Omaha World-Herald,* p. 14.

Woman faces trial for abandoning father. (1992, November 16). *Omaha World-Herald,* 44.

Wood, J. B., & Estes, C. L. (1990). The impact of DRGs on community-based service providers: Implications for the elderly. *American Journal of Public Health, 80,* 840–843.

Wurzbach, M.E. (1990). The dilemma of withholding or withdrawing nutrition. *Image: Journal of Nursing Scholarship, 22,* 226–230.

Wykle, M., & Kaskel, B. (1994). Increasing the longevity of minority older adults through improved health status. In J. S. Jackson (Ed.), *Minority elders: Five goals toward building a public policy base* (pp. 32–39). Washington, DC: The Gerontological Society of America.

Yee, B. W. K. (1992). Elders in Southeast Asian refugee families. *Generations, 17*(3), 24–27.

Yin, P., & Shine, M. (1985). Misinterpretations of increases in life expectancy in gerontology textbooks. *The Gerontologist, 25,* 78–82.

Youmans, E. G. (1969). Some perspectives on disengagement theory. *The Gerontologist, 9,* 254–258.

Young, M., Benjamin, B., & Wallis, C. (1963). Mortality of widowers. *Lancet, 2,* 454.

Zaptochny, J. (1999). *Scott's Canadian sourcebook.* Don Mills, Ontario, Canada: Scutham Information Products.

Zarit, S. H., Johansson, B., & Berg, S. (1993). Functional impairment and co-disability in the oldest old: A multidimensional approach. *Journal of Aging & Health, 5,* 291–305.

Zhao, Z. (1997). Long-term mortality patterns in Chinese history: Evidence from a recorded clan population. *Population Studies, 51,* 117–127.

Zika, S., & Chamberlain, K. (1992). On the relation between meaning in life and psychological well-being. *British Journal of Psychology, 83,* 133–145.

Zubenko, G. S., Mulsant, B. H., Sweet, R. A., Pasternak, R. E., & Tu, X. M. (1997). Mortality of elderly patients with psychiatric disorders. *American Journal of Psychiatry, 154,* 1360–1368.

Author Index

Berkman, L. S., 76
Berman, P. L., xv, 166, 168
Besant, W., 32–3
Beyreuther, K., 231
Bhat, P. V., 134
Bianchetti, A., 193
Bielawska, C., 216
Biggar, J. C., 326–7
Binstock, R. H., 384
Bishop, J. M., 340
Blau, Z., 62, 55–6, 148
Blazer, D. G., 209–10, 215, 221, 245, 272
Bloom, B., 193–4
Blumberg, M., 316
Boatwright, F., 389
Bodkin, N. L., 134
Boivin, J-F., 188
Bond, M., 162
Bongar, B., 289, 291
Bookwala, J., 81
Borgatta, E. F., 371
Boswell, J., 280
Botwinick, J., 313
Bourne, B., 316
Bower, B., 342
Branch, L. G., 60
Braun, J. V., 239, 284
Bray, G. A., 134
Brayne, C., 211–2, 231
Brehm, H. P., 51, 94
Breuss, T., 60
Brief, A., 314
Brodaty, H., 377
Brody, S., 173–4
Brody, E. M., 71, 87, 248
Brook, O. H., 394
Brostoff, S., 359
Brown, S., 100–1, 192
Bruininks, R. H., 240
Buhaug, H., 265
Bulcroft, K., 371
Bullard, D. M., 238
Bung, F. R., 136
Burgener, S. C., 247
Burgess, E. W., 53
Burke, P., 71
Burns, B. J., 394
Burr, J. A., 101
Burrough, G., 315
Burrows, M. T., 135

Burton, L., 103
Burwell, B. O., 265
Butler, R. N., 158–60, 278
Byrd, M., 60

Caine, E. D., 215
Calment, J., 25
Camacho, T., 165, 193
Camden, P., 299
Campbell, A., 355–6
Campbell, J. C., 355–6
Candy, S., 266
Carlin, L., 210
Carlson, E., 343
Carmago, O., 267
Caro, F. G., 86
Carpio, M., 27
Carrel, A., 135
Carrier, J., 332–3
Carson, D. K., 342
Carson, J., 340
Caserta, M. S., 288
Cash, T., 279, 285, 337, 342
Cassel, C. K., 192
Castro, F., 104
Cavan, R., 53, 59
Cavanaugh, J. C., 146, 154
Cerami, A., 140
Chamberlain, K., 158
Chan, C. G., 320
Chang, R. W., 195
Chapleski, E. E., 111
Chatters, L. M., 99–100, 102–3, 392
Cherrington, D., 314
Chichin, E. R., 376
Chipperfield, J. G., 194, 196, 374
Christensen, K., 320
Cicero, M. T., 165
Cippera, J., 374
Clark, A. N. G., 223
Clark, R. D., 189
Clarke, M., 194
Cleaver, V. A., 307
Clinton, W. J., 360
Coberly, S., 374
Cohen, C. A., 319
Cohen, C. I., 210, 238, 245, 248, 323, 394
Cohen, C., 394
Cohen, D., 248
Cohen, E. S., 373

Riley, G., 393
Riley, M. W., 56, 357
Rimer, S., 20
Roberto, K. A., 57
Roberts, M. D., 87, 371
Roberts, R. E. L., 60
Robertson, A., 363
Robitalle, Y., 188
Roe, K. M., 86
Rolvaag, O. E., 98
Romano, M., 393
Romanoski, A. J., 209, 217
Romanoski, A. J., 217
Roosevelt, F. D., xiii, 355, 377
Rose, A. M., 91
Rosenberg, H. M., 131, 179
Rosenbloom, C. A., 288
Rosow, I., 58
Roth, E., 323
Roth, G. S., 134
Rothberg, S. T., 151
Rowland, M., 319
Rozdilsky, B., 233
Rozzini, R., 193
Rudberg, M. A., 192
Ruhm, C. J., 320
Ryan, E. B., 150
Ryan, N., 123
Ryder, L. K., 346–7
Ryff, C. D., 158

Sable, P., 287
Sager, M. A., 269
Sakauye, K., 113
Samuel, V. T., 280
Sanders, A. J., 326
Sands, L. P., 203, 233
Santmyer, H. H., 255
Sarode, V. R., 177
Satterfield, S., 186
Sayers, G., 123
Sayers, R., 332
Schaie, K. W., 168
Scharlach, A. E., 370
Schlipp, P. A., 331
Schmitt, N., 236
Schoonover, C. B., 71
Schulz, R., 81, 87
Schumacher, F. J., 155
Schurenberg, E., 357

Schuster, M., 314, 315
Schwab, D., 315
Scott, J. P., 57
Scura, K. W., 227
Seccombe, K., 149–50
Seelbach, W. C., 97
Seeman, T. E., 76, 79, 87, 286
Seidel, G., 177
Selkoe, D. J., 232
Seltzer, M. M., 243
Serow, W. J., 356
Shah, A., 216
Shanas, E., 78, 100, 190, 261
Shapiro, J. P., 336
Sharot, S., 99
Shaughnessy, P. W., 273
Shellenbarger, S.374
Shenk, D., 395
Shi, I., 61
Shibata, K., 112
Shiferaw, B., 335, 344
Shine, M., 28
Shinkle, R. R., 273
Shock, N., xiv, 127, 147
Shope, J. T., 389
Siegler, I. C., 161
Silber, T., 357
Silverstein, E., 71, 80
Silverstein, M., 80
Silverstone, B. M., 80
Simonsick, E. M., 247
Simpson, A., 324
Sinex, F. M., 139
Singer, R. H., 195
Singleton, J. R., 320
Sisson, G., 243
Skaff, D., 374
Skinkle, R. R., 80
Skoog, I., 211
Skytthe, A., 28
Slaninka, S. C., 301
Smaha, B., 79
Smith, B. L., 178
Smith, C., 24–6
Smith, J., 167
Smith, K. R., 286
Smith, L., 356–7
Smith, R. A. P., 374–5
Smith, S. K., 356
Smith, T. B., 391

Subject Index

Community mental health, 393–4
Confabulation, 231
Confidant, 74–6, 216, 245, 285, 289
Continuing care retirement community (CCRC), 263–5, 325–6, 346
Continuum of care, 325, 386, 427
Continuity theory, 49, 54, 147, 152
Control, 45, 83, 164–5, 196, 291, 373–4
Coping, coping mechanisms, 161–3, 193, 214, 282
CPR (cardiopulmonary resuscitation), 297–9
Crime, 103, 345–7
Cross-sectional research design, 127
Cuban elderly, 105, 110
Customs, 45

Death, 196, 217, 227, 277–303
Death anxiety, 277, 280–3
Death rates, 173–80, 279
Defense mechanisms, 162–6
Deinstitutionalization movement, 240–1
Delirium, 213, 225–9
Dementia, 183, 202, 229–35
Demography, 8
Depression, 76, 102–3, 106, 202, 210, 214–19, 287, 291
Developmental disabilities, 202, 224, 233–7
Developmental Disabilities, U.S. Administration on, 240
Developmental-genetic theories of aging, 133–4
Developmental tasks, 155–60
Diabetes, 112, 172, 187
Diagnostic-related groups (DRGs), 269–70, 376
DiMaggio, Joe, 195
Diogenes syndrome, 221–2
Disability, 190–5
Discrimination, 312
Disengagement theory, 33–4, 155
Down's syndrome, 231, 235–7, 244
Drug abuse, 103, 226, 229, 250, 315, 342
DSM-IV (*Diagnostic and Statistical Manual of the American Psychiatric Association*, Fourth Edition), 213, 218, 219, 225
Duke Longitudinal Study of Aging, 54, 194
Durable power of attorney, 246, 295–7
Durkheim, Emile, 291
Dysthymia, 214

Economics, 307–30
Ego integrity, 152, 155, 157
Elder abuse, 247–8, 331–349

Elderhostel, 169, 392
Epilepsy, 234
Error theory, 132–3
Established Populations for Epidemiological Studies of the Elderly, 193–4
Exchange theory, 56–7, 82
Existentialism, 157
Extended family, 77–8

Failure to thrive, 238–9
Families, 63–88
FICA (Federal Insurance Contributions Act), 378
Filial obligation, 57–8
Filipino aged, 113–9
Fixx, Jim, 195
Folkways, 45
Food restriction, 133
Fractures, 189
Framingham Study, 211
Free radicals, 133, 140
Fries, James, 195
Functional ability, 190–5, 285

Gay aged, 6, 71–3
Gender issues, 93–7
Generational conflict, 361–3
Gerontological Society of America, 359
Gerontologist, The (journal), 26
Gray Panthers, 340, 361
Great Depression (1929-1940), 6, 7, 14, 48, 67
Grief, 86, 226
Guardian, guardianship, 338, 391

Harris, Louis & Associates, 149–50
Hasid, 98
Havighurst, Robert J., 157
Hayflick, Leonard, 135, 137
Health and illness, 171–99
Health care system, 255, 275
Heart disease, 184
Helplessness, 164, 284, 291
Hip fracture, 189
Hispanic elderly, 86, 95, 106–11
Historical life-course perspective, 65–7
History-normative, 48
HIV 73, 179, 210, 227
Hoarding, 219
Holmes, Oliver Wendell, 159
Holocaust, 157
Homelessness, 238, 245, 323, 394